P9-AQR-493

Encyclopedia of
AGING

EDITORIAL BOARD

Encyclopedia of
AGING

David J. Ekerdt, Editor in Chief

VOLUME 4

Qualitative Research – Yeast

Index

**MACMILLAN
REFERENCE
USA™**

THOMSON

GALE

New York • Detroit • San Diego • San Francisco • Cleveland • New Haven, Conn. • Waterville, Maine • London • Munich

Encyclopedia of Aging

David J. Ekerdt, Editor in Chief

Copyright © by Macmillan Reference USA, an imprint of The Gale Group, Inc., a division of Thomson Learning.

Macmillan Reference USA™ and Thomson Learning™ are trademarks used herein under license.

For more information, contact
Macmillan Reference USA
An imprint of the Gale Group
300 Park Avenue South, 9th Floor
New York, NY 10010

Macmillan Reference USA
The Gale Group, Inc.
27500 Drake Rd.
Farmington Hills, MI 48331-3535

For permission to use material from this product, submit your request via Web at http://www.gale-edit.com/permissions, or you may download our Permissions Request form and submit your request by fax or mail to:

Permissions Department
The Gale Group, Inc.
27500 Drake Rd.
Farmington Hills, MI 48331-3535
Permissions hotline:
248-699-8006 or 800-877-4253, ext. 8006
Fax: 248-699-8074 or 800-762-4058

LIBRARY OF CONGRESS CATALOG-IN-PUBLICATION DATA

Encyclopedia of aging / David J. Ekerdt, editor.— 1st ed.
    p. cm.
       Includes bibliographical references and index.
       ISBN 0-02-865472-2 (set : hardcover : alk. paper)
       1. Gerontology—Encyclopedias. 2. Aged—Encyclopedias. 3.
       Aging—Encyclopedias. I. Ekerdt, David J. (David Joseph), 1949-

   HQ1061 .E534 2002
   305.26'03—dc21
     2002002596

ISBNs
Volume 1: 0-02-865468-4
Volume 2: 0-02-865469-2
Volume 3: 0-02-865470-6
Volume 4: 0-02-865471-4

Printed in the United States of America
10 9 8 7 6 5 4 3 2 1

Q

QUALITATIVE RESEARCH

Qualitative research aims to understand the richness and complexity of social experience by attending closely to the actions, interactions, and social contexts of everyday life. It involves systematically "watching people in their own territory" (Kirk and Miller, p. 9) or speaking with them in depth about their thoughts and feelings. In some instances, this will lead to descriptions of multilayered and intricate worlds of experience. In other cases, the researcher may show how everyday experience is meaningfully constructed in social interaction. In still others, the results are reports of experience from the perspectives of the research subjects. Throughout, qualitative research strives to be rigorously empirical, even while its subject matter requires flexible methodologies and hands-on involvement in the lives of the persons being studied.

Qualitative research focuses on the "qualities" of social life. The goal is to describe the dynamics and texture of everyday life that quantitative research methods typically overlook in their formal operationalizations and numerical representations. Rather than simply designating and enumerating categories of experience, qualitative researchers provide detailed descriptions of the social organization and interpersonal processes in question. Quantitative researchers who seek predictive or explanatory models of social behavior often diminish the importance of qualitative studies by calling them "preliminary," "exploratory," or "merely descriptive." Qualitative researchers staunchly resist this, insisting that we must have clear understandings of the qualities of the social world before we can attempt to explain or predict it.

Common threads of qualitative inquiry

Qualitative research is methodological and theoretically diverse (see Denzin and Lincoln; Silverman, 1993, 2000), so any portrait done in broad strokes will blur crucial differences. At the same time, there are common threads that run throughout qualitative inquiry (see Gubrium and Holstein, 1997). The first is a *working skepticism* with respect to what everyone ostensibly "knows." This derives from a distrust of surface descriptions and facile explanations. Commonsense wisdom and even fixed-variable analysis in the social sciences often fail to appreciate the often hidden nuances of social life. Qualitative research explores the complexities. This results in the development of strategies of critical inquiry, from debunking what is commonly thought to be true and thereby exposing the shortcomings of everyday understandings, to empathizing as completely as possible with those being studied and appreciating the surprising richness of their lives. Across the board, the researcher implicitly challenges what is conventionally known. Arlie Hochschild's book *The Unexpected Community* (1973) is exemplary in this regard; as the title suggests, this qualitative study found "community" to thrive in a residential setting for older people where commonsense (and some academic theories of aging) predicted just the opposite. David Unruh's *Invisible Lives* brings similar sensibilities to the study of the social worlds of the aged.

The skepticism that galvanizes qualitative inquiry prompts qualitative researchers to scrutinize social life at close range, to place themselves in direct contact with, or in the immediate proximity of, the lived world of those being studied.

A second common thread is an abiding *commitment to close scrutiny*. Qualitative researchers study things "up close" in order to understand and document the organization of social life as it is practiced. The goal has been to look carefully at social phenomena to view in detail what other forms of observation may have "missed." The tendency is also to begin "where people are" and work upwards toward generalizations from there rather than to start with large-scale structures and work down to the level of everyday life.

While methods of close scrutiny vary, the goals are basically the same: to see the commonplace as important in its own right, to represent the previously unknown in fine detail and rich texture. Qualitative researchers typically emphasize the subtle aspects of experience, deferring if not eschewing broad generalizations in favor of describing the particulars. Sweeping claims about the influence of social forces that often characterize nonqualitative research are likely to be softened, qualified, set aside, or replaced by more painstaking accounts of the complex ins and outs of experience. The detail is far from trivial, as qualitative researchers point out, because only close scrutiny can give voice to the significance and eloquence of the ordinary.

A third commonality is that qualitative research is committed to *investigating social life in process,* as it unfolds in practice. Qualitative researchers typically conceive of the social world as fluid, contingent, and always-emerging. Correspondingly, they see people as active agents of their affairs, engaged in constructing the worlds they live in. There is an enduring appreciation for the working subject who actively injects life into, and shapes, his or her experience.

Fourth, because the active subject and his or her point of view are central to qualitative research, it has an abiding *appreciation for subjectivity.* For qualitative researchers, the conception of the subject and the realm of subjective experience are integral features of social life. Qualitative researchers acknowledge that the researcher is a subject in his or her own right; he or she is present in the same world as those studied, and actively participates in the formulation of what comes to be regarded as data.

Qualitative researchers have long resisted the view that the investigation of the subjective side of experience is imprecise or unsystematic, and have now assembled a massive technical literature attesting to this (see Denzin and Lin-

coln). The growing technical sophistication and rigor does not, however, necessitate an estrangement from subjectivity, inasmuch as rigorous and careful analysis must be applied to the subjective world as much as to any domain of inquiry. Reluctance to standardize data collection and an unwillingness to sacrifice depth for generality are matters of analytic necessity, not technical inadequacies. A world comprised of meanings, interpretations, feelings, talk, and interaction must be scrutinized on its own terms.

Fifth, qualitative research honors *perspective.* This often means documenting diverse, even competing, versions of experience, such as describing how something looks or feels from various subjects' viewpoints. Indeed, portraying the world from alternate viewpoints has been a goal of qualitative research from its inception, and continues to this day in the work of contemporary, even postmodern, researchers. As different as qualitative researchers' descriptions might be, the common thread here is the recognition that subjectivity is perspectival.

Finally, a sixth commonality is that qualitative researchers maintain a steadfast *tolerance for complexity.* While this is sometimes mistaken for analytic fuzziness or a reluctance to generalize, it more accurately reflects the researcher's orientation to the lived intricacies of everyday interaction. A skeptical orientation to the commonplace, a commitment to the close scrutiny of social action, the recognition of variety and detail, the focus on process, and the appreciation of subjectivity all, in one form or another, suggest that everyday life is not readily described in a simple, straightforward manner. This can hardly be captured by the operational designation of variables, social forces, and the like, which is typical of quantitative inquiry. A tolerance for complexity militates against the impulse to gloss over troublesome uncertainties, anomalies, irregularities, and inconsistencies in the interest of comprehensive, totalizing explanation. As a matter of principle, qualitative inquiry accommodates and pursues the problematic finding or the unanticipated occurrence.

These common threads intertwine into an abiding concern for meaning. Qualitative research typically regards social life as a vast interpretive process in which people guide themselves by defining the objects, events, and situations which they encounter. With respect to the aging experience, qualitative research focuses on the ordinary ways persons experience time in relation to their age. This comprises a field of meanings centered on how people themselves interpret and discern what it is like to grow older, face the challenges of aging, deal with those who are aging, and simply experience aging in today's world. A leading distinction is the difference between subjective aging or how old one feels, and chronological age or how many years one has lived.

Qualitative research methods

Qualitative research on the aging experience draws upon a variety of techniques and procedures (see Gubrium and Sankar). One of these is observational fieldwork. This may range from the unobtrusive observation of persons interacting in informal settings such as friendship groups, to participant observation in which the researcher is actively involved in the setting which he or she is studying, such as a retirement community. Hochschild, for example, conducted her study of what she eventually called "a community of grandmothers" while serving as an assistant recreation director of the senior citizen housing project. Similarly, Jaber F. Gubrium conducted participant observation in an American nursing home, focusing on the everyday "bed-and-body" work of the frontline staff as it related to other worlds of meaning in the home, including the administrative staff's idealized perspective and the residents' daily routines of passing time.

In-depth interviewing is another commonly employed qualitative technique (see Gubrium and Holstein, 2002). In contrast to survey research or other forms of "forced choice" questioning, qualitative interviewing is more "open-ended," allowing the interviewer and the interviewee to participate in the development of responses (see Holstein and Gubrium). Such interviews encourage participants to explore the complexity of the lives and experiences under consideration. For example, Kathy Charmaz's in-depth study of the experience of chronic illness among older adults documented the surprising daily alterations of the meaning of being ill. Frequently, researchers combine interviewing with observation in what might be called "ethnographic interviewing." Hochschild's fieldwork, for example, also called upon both open-ended interviewing and careful observation to reveal highly variegated relationships and statuses in the community being studied.

Interviewing may elicit many forms of data. Ethnographic interviews typically supply native accounts and understandings of what is going on in a particular setting. In-depth interviews strive for detailed, richly textured accounts and descriptions of the experiences of individuals. Sometimes interview responses come in the form of life stories (see Gubrium, 1993). Life story interviews themselves may be treated as different sorts of data. They may be viewed as a means of discovering the objective facts of an individual's life, but increasingly they have been utilized to document how the course of life is socially constructed (Holstein and Gubrium, 2000). Life story interviews reveal the perceptions, values, goals, and understandings of persons through time.

Lately, narrative analysis (see Riessman) is being applied to life stories in order to understand how narratives of the past, present, and future are assembled to provide a sense of meaningful coherence to the lives under discussion. For example, Gubrium's (1993) life story interview study of nursing home residents used narrative analysis to show how the ways in which the quality of life and of care in the home, as understood by the residents, related to lives as a whole.

Narrative analysis is but one aspect of the recent "linguistic turn" in qualitative research. Talk and interaction have long been the stock-in-trade of qualitative researchers, and the attention has been amplified in rapidly developing methods of discourse analysis and other approaches to studying the fine-grained detail of conversation. All of these approaches focus on what people "do with words" as they construct the meaningful parameters of their everyday lives. Audio and video taped recordings and highly detailed transcripts of interactions are analyzed to discern how participants conduct their lives through conversation and communication. James Holstein, for example, in a careful analysis of court proceedings, illustrated how age is negotiated and altered in meaning in practice, rather than being a fixed category of time.

Finally, modes of literary analysis and other forms of representation from the humanities are being imported to the study of aging-in-progress. Anne Wyatt-Brown and Janice Rossen's important collection of studies of creativity in the later years shows how individual writing careers, among others, change with the passing years. Ruth E. Ray's research on life-story writing among older adults directs us to the ways that writing one's life story, as Ray puts it, "initiates change and personal growth among older people." These are but two instances from the growing body of research in which qualitative research is being fertilized by the humanities.

JAMES A. HOLSTEIN
JABER F. GUBRIUM

See also NARRATIVE; SURVEYS.

BIBLIOGRAPHY

CHARMAZ, K. *Good Days, Bad Days: The Self in Chronic Illness and Time.* New Brunswick, N.J.: Rutgers University Press, 1991.

DENZIN, N. K., and LINCOLN, Y. S., eds. *Handbook of Qualitative Research,* 1st ed. Thousand Oaks, Calif.: Sage, 1994. 2d ed., 2000.

GUBRIUM, J. F. *Living and Dying at Murray Manor.* Charlottsville, Va.: University Press of Virginia, 1975. Reprint, 1997.

GUBRIUM, J. F. *Speaking of Life.* Hawthorne, N.Y.: Aldine de Gruyter, 1993.

GUBRIUM, J. F., and HOLSTEIN, J. A. *Handbook of Interviewing.* Thousand Oaks, Calif.: Sage, 2002.

GUBRIUM, J. F., and HOLSTEIN, J. A. *The New Language of Qualitative Method.* New York: Oxford University Press, 1997.

GUBRIUM, J. F., and SANKAR, A., eds. *Qualitative Methods in Aging Research.* Thousand Oaks, Calif.: Sage, 1994.

HOCHSCHILD, A. R. *The Unexpected Community.* Berkeley: University of California Press, 1973.

HOLSTEIN, J. A. "The Discourse of Age in Involuntary Commitment Proceedings." *Journal of Aging Studies* 4 (1990): 111–130.

HOLSTEIN, J. A., and GUBRIUM, J. F. *The Active Interview.* Newbury Park, Calif.: Sage, 1995.

HOLSTEIN, J. A., and GUBRIUM, J. F. *Constructing the Life Course.* Dix Hills, N.Y.: General Hall, 2000.

KIRK, J., and MILLER, M. L. *Reliability and Validity in Qualitative Research.* Thousand Oaks, Calif.: Sage, 1986.

RAY, R. E. *Beyond Nostalgia: Aging and Life-Story Writing.* Charlottesville, Va.: University Press of Virginia, 2000.

RIESSMAN, C. K. *Narrative Analysis.* Newbury Park, Calif.: Sage, 1993.

SILVERMAN, D. *Doing Qualitative Research.* London: Sage, 2000.

SILVERMAN, D. *Interpreting Qualitative Data.* London: Sage, 1993.

UNRUH, D. R. *Invisible Lives: Social Worlds of the Aged.* Beverly Hills: Sage, 1983.

WYATT-BROWN, A. M., and ROSSEN, J., eds. *Aging and Gender in Literature: Studies in Creativity.* Charlottesville, Va.: University Press of Virginia, 1993.

QUALITY OF LIFE, DEFINITION AND MEASUREMENT

"Quality of life" (QOL) subsumes two distinct domains in gerontological research. One is health-related quality of life (HRQOL); the other, nonhealth or environment-based quality of life (Spilker and Revicki). HRQOL encompasses domains of life directly affected by changes in health. Jaschke and colleagues provide a good thumbnail test of whether a domain falls within the category of health-related QOL. In their view, HRQOL domains are aspects of life that improve when a physician successfully treats a patient. A clinically significant change in HRQOL is indicated by a decline in a domain that leads a physician or health care provider to alter a medication or medical treatment. HRQOL domains minimally include functional status (e.g., whether a patient is able to manage a household, use the telephone, or dress independently), mental health or emotional well-being (e.g., depressive symptoms, positive affect), social engagement (e.g. involvement with others, engagement in activities), and symptom states (e.g., pain, shortness of breath, fatigue). These domains represent typical outcomes in medical and social science research.

Non-health-related QOL domains include features of both the natural and the created environment (i.e., economic resources, housing, air and water quality, community stability, access to the arts and entertainment) and personal resources (i.e., the capacity to form friendships, appreciate nature, or find satisfaction in spiritual or religious life). These factors affect health-related QOL but, unlike health-related QOL domains, are less likely to improve with appropriate medical care.

The two components of QOL need to be kept separate. First, non-health-related QOL can be viewed as causally prior to or as a determinant of HRQOL. Components of non-health related QOL (i.e., social support, economic resources, religion, and housing) may affect HRQOL outcomes, such as social integration and functional and emotional well being. Second, non-health-related QOL is more heterogeneous, with less consensus about the range of domains that should be included in the measure. For example, no one would suggest that severe abdominal pain is preferable to a runny nose; most would agree that the runny nose is associated with a better health-related QOL state. Consensus of this sort is harder to establish for spirituality, friendship, or access to the arts.

It is valuable to obtain information on both kinds of QOL because economic and social status affect HRQOL, and both are necessary to understand health-related outcomes. However, more emphasis has been placed on the study of HRQOL for several reasons. First, older people are at risk for chronic conditions, and effective disease management in large part consists of finding treatments that minimize the QOL impact of disease. Second, HRQOL measurement is further advanced than measurement of non-health-related QOL. Finally, while housing, air quality, and other components of the environment are clearly important features of QOL, they are important mainly because of their effect on health and health-related QOL (Albert). On the other hand, Lawton states that the two are sometimes hard to separate; for example, successful treatment by a physician may improve one's capacity to make friends.

Health-related QOL emerged from research on health status. Early measures, such as the Sickness Impact Profile (SIP) (Bergner, et al.), sought to identify common domains affected by disease that would allow clinicians to gauge the impact of a clinical condition. The SIP identified twelve health-related QOL domains, which include ambulation, mobility, body care and movement, communication, alertness behavior, emotional behavior, social interaction, sleep and rest, eating, work, home management, and recreation. A key element of the SIP, and of almost all QOL measures since, has been that patients themselves rate their level of impairment. This subjective element is the essential feature of health-related QOL, for who can better report on the QOL impact of a medical condition than the patient (Gill and Feinstein)? Indeed, health-related QOL is sometimes called "patient-reported outcomes" to stress this subjective focus. Of course, the focus on self-reported status is problematic for people with cognitive disorders, such as Alzheimer's disease, who may be unable to comprehend questions about their status. QOL measurement for such populations may require simplified questionnaires, use of proxy reports, or observational measures (Albert and Logsdon).

A second source for the current interest in health-related QOL is its potential significance for economic evaluation of medical therapeutics and technologies. The goal of economic studies of HRQOL has been to assign values to health states. To return to an earlier example, an economic approach to HRQOL asks how much worse "severe abdominal pain" is than "runny nose." Suppose two numeric anchors are established: 1.0 for the state of no symptoms/no daily limitations and 0.0 for death (recognizing, however, that some people consider certain health states, such as coma or intractable pain, as states worse than death). Kaplan's Quality of Well-Being/General Health Policy Model subtracts 0.17 for the state of "runny nose"; thus, someone with a runny nose is at about 83 percent of optimal health. "Sick or upset stomach, vomiting" is associated with a score of -0.29; someone with the condition would be at 71 percent of optimal health. These numerical ratings, derived from respondents who rated descriptions of a wide variety of health states, confirm people's intuitions and offer one way to establish how much worse one clinical state is relative to another in terms of HRQOL.

An alternative tradition in QOL measurement avoids the assignment of numeric values to health states. This tradition relies on naturally occurring indicators of impairment or disability. Thus, Sullivan developed an early index based on living arrangement (nursing home or community), mobility impairment, ability to perform major age-appropriate roles (school, work, home maintenance, personal self-maintenance), and limitation in usual, daily activities. From this classification emerged five QOL states, ranging from institutional residence to community residence without disability or limitation in daily activities. Similarly, the Behavioral Risk Factors Surveillance System used by the Centers for Disease Control relies on reports of "not good health days," days when a component of health is adversely affected (Hennessey, et al.). Respondents are asked, "Thinking of the past 30 days, how many days were there when your physical health was not good?" Other questions ask about mental health, sleep, energy, anxiety, and related domains.

Introduction of a QOL focus in research on aging was pioneered by Katz and colleagues, and by Lawton and Brody, with a focus on functional status and behavior, which is now universal in gerontology and geriatrics. Lawton and Brody summarized a QOL emphasis for care of older people, thus: "Function and behavior, rather than diagnosis, should determine the service to be prescribed." The common, final pathway of different diseases is their impact on functional ability and other domains of QOL; thus, the focus in later life should be development of strategies, both clinical and environmental, to minimize these effects and to work with the strengths older people continue to retain.

However it may be measured, health-related QOL declines with age. This is a central, inescapable consequence of the increased life span and consequent increased prevalence of chronic disease and the effects of senescent changes in many physiologic systems. Senescence, apart from disease, is evident in declines in working memory, psychomotor speed, touch sensibility, vision, and hearing; loss of skeletal muscle and strength; and reduction in joint range of motion. These changes affect HRQOL; for example, pain in arthritic joints leads to circumscription of choice in daily activities; lower-extremity weakness means difficulty climbing stairs or standing up long enough to prepare a meal; and slowing of psychomotor skills may mean inability to drive safely. Older people adjust their daily lives to accommodate these decrements and in this way preserve HRQOL. Still, cross-sectional studies show major declines in health-related QOL with increasing age. For example, mean health-related QOL scores for the U.S. population (with 1.0 optimal health and 0.0 death) ranged from 0.90 to 0.94 for people under age thirty, 0.81–0.90 for people age thirty-five–sixty, 0.70–0.79 for people aged sixty–eighty, and 0.51–0.63 for people over age eighty (Erickson, et al.). By this formulation, a medical intervention that improved health-related QOL from 0.74 to 0.81 would therefore be equivalent to a reduction in age, in this case from seventy–seventy-five to fifty-five–sixty. Thus, clinical trials for medical interventions and therapeutics have increasingly turned to health-related QOL as an outcome to capture the broad effects of treatment.

In contrast to health-related QOL, environmental or non-health-related QOL may remain high throughout life or even improve with greater age. With retirement, for example, older people have more leisure time; and with children gone, houses paid for, and successful investments, they may have more disposable income. As a result, older people have more opportunities to develop interests and create satisfying environments. Better health care and effective disease management also play a major role in fostering QOL in late life. These factors counterbalance declines in health-related QOL and may be responsible for the great resiliency older people show in the face of declining health and death.

In short, health-related and environment-based quality of life must be distinguished. The former is linked to age and shows clear decline across the life span, due in large part to senescent processes and to increased susceptibility to chronic disease. The latter is not as strongly related to age, and older people can build environments that promote QOL. The two come together in older people's ability to modify environments in ways that limit the QOL impact of poor health.

STEVEN M. ALBERT
JEANNE A. TERESI

See also FUNCTIONAL ABILITY; LONG-TERM CARE; QUALITY OF LIFE, PHILOSOPHICAL AND ETHICAL DIMENSIONS.

BIBLIOGRAPHY

Albert, S. M. "Assessing Health-Related Quality of Life Chronic Care Populations. In *Measurement in Elderly Chronic Care Populations*. Edited by J.A. Teresi, M. P. Lawton, D. Holmes, and M. Ory. New York: Springer Publishing Company, 1997. Pages 210–227.

Albert, S. M., and Logsdon, R. G. eds. *Assessing Quality of Life In Alzheimer's Disease*. New York: Springer Publishing Company, 2000.

Bergner, M.; Bobbit, R. A.; Pollard, W. E.; Martin, D. P.; and Gilson, B. S. "The Sickness Impact Profile: Validation of a Health Status Measure." *Medical Care* 14 (1976): 57–67.

Erickson, P.; Wilson, R.; and Shannon. I. *Years of Healthy Life*. Healthy People 2000, Statistical Notes. Washington, D.C.: U,S, Department of Health and Human Services, National Center for Health Statistics, (1995).

Gill, T., and Feinstein, A. R. "A Critical Appraisal of the Quality of Quality of Life Measurements." *Journal of the American Medical Association* 272 (1994): 619–626.

Hennessey, C. H.; Moriarty, D. G.; Zack, M. M.; Scherr, P. A.; and Brackbill, R. "Measuring Health-Related Quality of Life for Public

Health Surveillance." *Public Health Reports* 109 (1994): 665–672.

Jaschke, R.; Singer, J.; and Guyatt, G. H. "Measurement of Health Status: Ascertaining the Minimal Clinically Important Difference." *Controlled Clinical Trials* 10 (1989): 407–415.

Kaplan, R. M., and Anderson, J. P. "The General Health Policy Model: An Integrated Approach." In *Quality of Life and Pharmacoeconomics in Clinical Trials.* Edited by B. Spilker. Philadelphia: Lippincott-Raven, 1999. Pages 309–322.

Katz, S.; Ford, A.; Moskowitz, R. W.; Jackson, B. A.; and Jaffe, M. W. "Studies of Illness in the Aged. The index of ADL: A Standardized Measure of Biological and Psychosocial Function." *Journal of the American Medical Association* 185 (1963): 914–919.

Lawton, M. P. "A Multidimensional View of Quality of Life in Frail Elders." In *The Concept and Measurement of Quality of Life in the Frail Elderly.* Edited by J. E. Birren, J. E. Lubben, J. C. Rowe, and D. D. Deutchman. San Diego: Academic Press, 1991. Pages. 3–27.

Lawton, M. P., and Brody, E. M. (1969) "Assessment of Older People: Self-Maintaining and Instrumental Activities of Daily Living." *The Gerontologist* 9 (1969): 179–186.

Spilker, B., and Revicki, D. A. (1999) "Taxonomy of Quality of Life." In *Quality of life and Pharmacoeconomics in Clinical Trials.* Edited by D. Spilker. Philadelphia: Lippincott-Raven, 1999. Pages 25–32.

Sullivan, D. F. (1966) "Conceptual Problems in Developing an Index of Health." *Vital and Health Statistics, Data Evaluation and Methods Research* series 2, no. 17. (1966).

QUALITY OF LIFE, PHILOSOPHICAL AND ETHICAL DIMENSIONS

The phrase "quality of life" is almost always controversial. The basic idea behind the concept of quality of life is that some characteristics of the person and his or her surrounding environment are better than others from the point of view of the human good or human flourishing. Nearly all the major thinkers of the Western tradition, from Plato and Aristotle through Jeremy Bentham, Immanuel Kant, John Stuart Mill, Karl Marx, Friedrich Nietzsche, and John Dewey have given their preferred accounts of the good or the best human life, as have the world's great playwrights, poets, and novelists. In recent years the Nobel Prize–winning economist Amartya Sen has made important contributions to the topic. Nonetheless, no single account has ever won universal agreement. Many of these accounts overlap, however, and the outlines of at least three general orientations can be discerned. These are: hedonic theories, rational preference theories, and theories of human flourishing. Despite its difficulty and frequent lack of clarity, the concept of quality of life seems to be an indispensable one, particularly in the domain of health care and social services.

Sources of controversy

One school of thought in philosophy and ethics holds that the concept of quality of life should not be used because it undermines the intrinsic dignity and worth of human life. Something (human life) is being evaluated that should not be evaluated. Human life is valuable for its own sake and not merely as a means for something else. The term *quality of life* seems to imply that life is not intrinsically worthy of respect, but can have greater or lesser value according to its circumstances.

In addition to those who regard all talk about the quality of life as an affront to the inherent dignity of the human person, objections to the term also come from the disability rights community. From this perspective, the notion of quality of life is part of a broader normalizing ideology in the mainstream culture and works to the detriment of persons with disabilities by perpetuating stigmatization and discrimination against them.

To what does quality of life refer?

If we pay close attention to the different ways in which the concept of quality of life is used in health care, it is possible to make one's way successfully through this semantic minefield. In order to do so it is important to distinguish four different senses of the notion of quality of life.

Quality of life as a property of the individual. First, the notion of quality of life is used to refer to some characteristic or state of being of the individual person. A quality of life (whether good or poor) is something one has or possesses, much as one has a physical characteristic or an occupation. Understood in this way, one's quality of life is not essential to one's identity or self-esteem. As such it has no straightforward moral significance. A poor quality of life (due to ill health, loss of a job, breakdown of personal relationships, or the like) is not necessarily a sign of a person's moral failing, and it says nothing about the intrinsic value of life as such, or even about the moral value of that particular life at that particular time.

Quality of life as a goal of care. A second common meaning of quality of life defines it as a goal of care. The moral point of our dealings with another (whether the situation be health care or some other form of relationship) is to sustain and improve the quality of life. In this sense, quality of life becomes a benchmark to guide human activity and a concept of assessment and evaluation. But notice that the evaluation here is directed primarily at the caregiver and the caregiving process, not at the recipient of care, who partakes of the quality of life achieved but is not judged by it. Moreover, quality of life can be thought of as an interaction between the person and his or her surrounding circumstances, including other people. Thus understood as a goal or outcome of care, an improved quality of life may be a change (for the better) in the person's symptoms or perceptions; or it may be a change in the person's relationship with his or her environment. Medical cure, symptom relief, psychological happiness, or social empowerment may all be goals of care as comprehended by the concept of quality of life.

Quality of life as a social situation. Next, quality of life may refer to a state of interaction between an individual and his or her social and physical environment. Here a certain quality of life is not a property of the individual per se, but a function of that individual's form of life. So understood a low quality of life assessment does not necessarily suggest a negative evaluation of the person or his worth; it can equally well imply a critical evaluation of the person's environment and indicate ways in which that environment could be changed so as to enhance the quality of life according to some scale of norms such as justice, freedom, health, happiness, and the like.

Quality of life as the moral worth of a life. Finally, it must be acknowledged that the term *quality of life* is sometimes used to refer to the moral worth or value of a person and his or her life. Pushed to its logical extreme, this understanding of the quality of life takes us to the infamous Nazi concept of "life unworthy of life," (*lebensunwertes Leben*), which was used to rationalize everything from active euthanasia of those

with disabilities to the genocidal death camps. To say that a person has no quality of life or a very low quality of life is to say that prolonging this person's life has no moral significance, either to the person himself or to society.

In this author's view, it is a mistake to use quality of life as a measure of the moral worth of human beings. The notion of the moral worth of a life is logically quite distinct from the notion of quality of life. An account of moral worth is based on an underlying account of humanness or the human person; an account, that is, of what it is to be human. The concept of quality of life, on the other hand, is based on an account of a person's inherent capacities and external circumstances. Quality of life may tell us what is required in order to become (more fully) human, but never about the value of being human.

Philosophical theories of quality of life

Philosophical theories are systematic accounts that can be used to provide a foundation for our beliefs and to sort out those ideas that should be held with rational conviction from those that should be discarded. Thus a philosophical theory of quality of life is an account of what makes human life worth living and an attempt to single out those fundamental elements of human experience or the human condition that provide the content for such an account. In the history of philosophy there are, of course, innumerable such accounts, presented as each philosopher explicates his or her preferred account of the human good. Most of these theories fall into the following three categories:

Hedonic theories. Hedonic theories identify quality of life with states of awareness, consciousness, or experience of the individual. Happiness or pleasure, however those terms are precisely to be defined, are the sine qua non of quality of life. This allows for considerable individual variation in assessing good quality of life because different things make different people happy, but it also allows for some kind of common metric (at least on the negative side) because there are seemingly universal negative states of pain or suffering or unhappiness that all (normal) persons avoid.

An interesting question is whether it is necessary for the person to realize he is happy in order to be happy. In other words, is the kind of happiness (or pleasure) that makes for a good quality of life a direct, unmediated sensation, or is it a psychic state that results from some act of self-interpretation? If it is the former, then it would seem to follow that a person locked in a cell with an electrode implanted in a pleasure center of the brain would be experiencing the highest quality of life. That conclusion must be mistaken and counts against the theory. On the other hand, if the pleasure or happiness the theory requires involves some form of cognitive mediation and secondary interpretation, then persons who have serious cognitive deficits will be automatically judged to have a poor quality of life by definition, and that view seems unduly biased against nonintellectual goods in life.

Rational preference theories. The second type, rational preference theories, define quality of life in terms of the actual satisfaction or realization of a person's rational desires or preferences. This is a much more objective theory than the hedonic account in that a person need not be aware that his or her preferences are being fulfilled (or need not take pleasure in that knowledge) in order for the quality of his life to be good; it just must be the case that they are being fulfilled in fact. The underlying appeal of theories of this type is the notion that individuals have a good life when the objective state of the world conforms to what they rationally desire.

Theories of human flourishing. Theories of human flourishing attempt to base our understanding of the good life on an account of those functions, capacities, and excellences that are most fully and constitutively human. To the extent that we attain and master those capacities, and to the extent that we avoid those conditions that would stunt or undermine those capacities, we flourish as human beings. Theories of this type also usually have a developmental component built into them, for those most fully human capacities are ones that are not mastered at birth or automatically expressed by instinct, but must be developed and nurtured by education, interaction with others, and practice over the course of a lifetime. To the extent, then, that the individual continues to grow and develop throughout his or her life, the quality of life is enhanced thereby.

Accounts of these most fully human capacities differ among philosophers working in this tradition of theorizing, but as a generalization we can say that philosophical accounts of this type usually emphasize the human capacity to express and to experience meaning in social relationships of intimacy, friendship, and cooperation; the capacity to use reason and to develop and follow a life plan of self-fulfillment and self-realization; the capacity for independence and self-reliance; and the human need for an appropriate social and cultural environment that provides the individual with various types of resources—material, symbolic, spiritual—necessary to live a developmentally human life and to meet both basic and secondary needs.

Future work on quality of life

Reviewing each of these three philosophical approaches to quality of life, one can argue that the concept of quality of life should not be construed as a floor below which no significant societal expenditure of resources is required, and below which personal caregiving efforts may be reduced to the decent minimum. A much better way to think about quality of life is to see it as a ceiling, a potential level of functional capacity and capacity for relationship, toward which caregiving efforts should be designed to strive. The height of this ceiling will not be the same for everyone, and quality of life is not a test that you fail if you do not reach a certain height. But the important point is that quality of life should be used as a teleological concept—setting a goal to reach and a process to reach it, rather than as a prioritizing concept—setting a rank ordering for the allocation of scarce resources.

In conclusion, it is important to note that no one of these philosophical theories has completely carried the day among philosophers, and each of the three is still under development in the philosophical literature on quality of life. None of them offers a complete account; elements of all three are essential to cover the broad range of circumstances and individual needs pertinent to the issue of quality of life in an aging society.

BRUCE JENNINGS

See also DEATH AND DYING; DEFINITION AND MEASUREMENT; EUTHANSIA AND SENICIDE; QUALITY OF LIFE; REFUSING AND WITHDRAWING MEDICAL TREATMENT; SUBJECTIVE WELL-BEING.

BIBLIOGRAPHY

ALBERT, S. M., and LOGSDON, R. G., eds. *Assessing Quality of Life in Alzheimer's Disease.* New York: Springer, 2000.
BROCK, D. "Quality of Life Measures in Health Care and Medical Ethics." In *The Quality of*

Life. Edited by M. C. Nussbaum and A. Sen. New York: Cambridge University Press, 1993. Pages 95–139.

COHEN, C. "'Quality of Life' and the Analogy with the Nazis." *Journal of Medicine and Philosophy* 8 (1983): 113–135.

DRESSER, R. S. "Life, Death and Incompetent Patients: Conceptual Infirmities and Hidden Values in the Law." *Arizona Law Review* 28 (1986): 373–405.

DRESSER, R. S., and ROBERTSON, J. A. "Quality of Life and Non-Treatment Decisions for Incompetent Patients: A Critique of the Orthodox Approach." *Law, Medicine, and Health Care* 17 (1989): 234–244.

DWORKIN, R. *Life's Dominion.* New York: Knopf, 1993.

GOODE, D., ed. *Quality of Life for Persons with Disabilities: International Perspectives and Issues.* Cambridge, Mass.: Brookline Books, 1994.

Hastings Center. *Guidelines on the Termination of Life-sustaining Treatment and the Care of the Dying.* Bloomington: Indiana University Press, 1987.

JENNINGS, B. "A Life Greater than the Sum of Its Sensations: Ethics, Dementia, and the Quality of Life," In *Assessing Quality of Life in Alzheimer's Disease.* Edited by S. M. Albert and R. G. Logsdon. New York: Springer, 2000. Pages 165–178.

LAWTON, M. P. "A Multidimensional View of Quality of Life in Frail Elders." In *The Concept and Measurement of Quality of Life in the Frail Elderly.* Edited by J. E. Birren, et al. New York: Academic Press, 1991. Pages 3–27.

LIFTON, R.J. *Nazi Doctors.* New York: Basic Books, 1986.

McCORMICK, R. "The Quality of Life, the Sanctity of Life." *Hastings Center Report* (February 1978): 30–36.

MOSS, S. "Quality of Life and Aging." In *Quality of Life for Persons with Disabilities: International Perspectives and Issues.* Edited by D. Goode. Cambridge, Mass.: Brookline Books, 1994. Pages 218–234.

NUSSBAUM, M. C., and SEN, AMARTYA, eds. *The Quality of Life.* New York: Cambridge University Press, 1993.

POST, S. *The Moral Challenge of Alzheimer's Disease.* Baltimore: Johns Hopkins University Press, 1995.

SCANLON, T. "Value, Desire, and Quality of Life." In *The Quality of Life.* Edited by M. C. Nussbaum and A. Sen. New York: Cambridge University Press, 1993. Pages 185–200.

SOLOMON, M. Z., and JENNINGS, B. "Palliative Care for Alzheimer Patients: Implications for Institutions, Caregivers, and Families." In *Hospice Care for Patients with Advanced Progressive Dementia.* Edited by L. Volicer and A. Hurley. New York: Springer, 1998. Pages 132–154.

TAYLOR, S. J. "In Support of Research on Quality of Life, but Against QOL." In *Quality of Life for Persons with Disabilities: International Perspectives and Issues.* Edited by D. Goode. Cambridge, Mass.: Brookline Books, 1994. Pages 260–265.

WOLFENSBERGER, W. "Let's Hang Up 'Quality of Life' as a Hopeless Term." In *Quality of Life for Persons with Disabilities: International Perspectives and Issues.* Edited by D. Goode. Cambridge, Mass.: Brookline Books, 1994. Pages 285–321.

R

REACTION TIME

In cognitive psychology, reaction time (RT) is used to measure the amount of time that it takes an individual to process information (Luce). It is the duration of the interval between presentation of a stimulus (e.g., a word on a computer monitor) and the participant's response to the stimulus. RT is considered to be a dependent variable because it "depends" on the manipulation of an independent variable (such as the exposure duration of a stimulus). RT is related to response accuracy (the other primary dependent variable in cognitive psychology), because participants can often trade off speed for increased accuracy, or conversely, trade off accuracy for increased speed (Pachella). It is important to note, though, that accuracy and RT are often used for different purposes. Accuracy tells us whether a series of perceptual and mental processes is completed correctly. RT is used to infer process duration.

Stages of information processing

Overall task RT data can certainly be interesting; older adults have consistently been shown to be slower than younger adults, for example. But it is the decomposition of RT into times for individual stages in mental processing that is of most scientific interest. Figure 1 illustrates attentional resources and the basic stages of human information processing: perceptual encoding, memory activation, decision-making, response selection, and response execution (Wickens). Attentional resources provide the processing "energy" to the information processing system. Encoding involves the initial processing of sensory and perceptual information. For example, while driving we must convert the physical energy of the light waves hitting our eyes into neural impulses that the rest of the cognitive system can understand before we can begin to identify a circular yellow approaching object. After encoding has occurred, we compare the perceived stimulus to information stored in long-term memory. This comparison process is likely based upon the similarity of the input stimulus code to codes stored in long-term memory. Pattern recognition has occurred when the system identifies the yellow stimulus as a "yellow traffic signal." The decision[M1]-making stage of processing then begins. Based on vehicle speed and distance from the intersection, we must decide whether to slow down or to continue to accelerate. Response selection then occurs—we decide to press either the brake or the accelerator pedal. And finally, response execution involves carrying out the decision made during response selection (actually moving one's foot to the brake pedal).

It is seldom possible to get exact processing times for each stage of mental processing. As a result, psychologists frequently study peripheral or sensorimotor processing by combining input (encoding) and output (response execution) times. The central processing stages of memory retrieval, decision-making, and response selection are also combined. Processing times for peripheral and central processing can be empirically separated with experimental manipulations that affect one stage (say, central), but not the other (peripheral). Consider an experiment using a lexical decision task (does a letter string form a real word or not) with three levels of word frequency. Since a word's frequency,

Figure 1
Attentional Resources

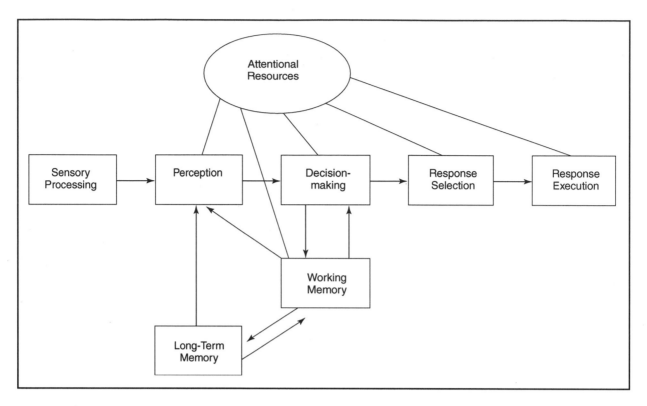

SOURCE: Author

how common it is, should affect neither initial registration of the light waves nor speed of response execution, we can reasonably assume that differences in RT that are dependent on word frequency must be due to central processes. In Figure 2, separate functions are plotted for younger and older adults across word frequency. Older adults have a higher y-intercept than younger adults, but both age groups show the same slope. Our logic, supported by past research, suggests that the level of the function is primarily a measure of peripheral processing, but that the slope of the function is a measure of central processing (Allen, Smith, Jerge, and Vires-Collins; Sternberg). Since slopes are the same, there is no evidence of age-related slowing of the central processes affected by word frequency. In this case, overall age differences in RT are due to peripheral processes and possibly some central processes that are not affected by word frequency (Allen, Madden, Weber, and Groth).

Age differences in reaction time

More generally, how does adult age affect RT? Information processing takes longer (Cerella; Salthouse) and its duration becomes more variable (Allen, Kaufman, Smith, and Propper) with increasing age. This has led many people to believe that aging is invariably associated with slowing and decline. However, increased adult age does not affect all processing stages equivalently.

For example, the lexical decision data in Figure 2 show that while older adults show a peripheral-process decrement, they show no drop in speed compared to younger adults in lexical access speed (a central process involving memory retrieval). Using a word-naming task, similar results were observed by Balota and Ferraro (1993). Reviews of the literature on lexical processing conclude that there are no appreciable age differences in central processes, but that older adults do show longer overall RTs due to slower peripheral processing (Allen, Madden, and Slane; Lima, Hale, and Myerson; Madden,

Figure 2
Word Frequency

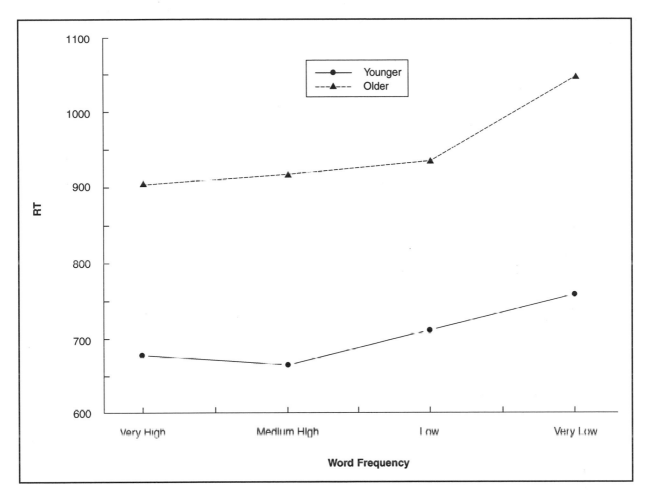

SOURCE: Author

Pierce, and Allen). Lexical tasks involve semantic memory or knowledge, including vocabulary (Tulving, E., 1985). Semantic memory tasks all tend to show a similar pattern of age differences: peripheral-, but no central-process decrements.

Other types of information processing, though, do show both central- and peripheral-process age differences. Episodic memory tasks ask individuals to remember personally experienced events and their temporal relations (e.g., what you had for breakfast this morning; see Tulving, E., 1985). Large age differences are found in episodic memory (Burke and Light, 1981; Light, 1991), and as can be observed in Figure 3 (from Allen et al., 1998, Experiment 1), these appear in both slope and intercept. The steeper slope shown by older adults across *trans-position distance*—i.e., how far probe items are shifted relative to where they occurred as targets—provides specific evidence for slowing of central processes in this episodic task (smaller distances require more central processing). Central slowing is a hallmark of episodic memory tasks, as well as many other information-processing tasks (Cerella).

Conclusion

While it is true that older adults do show longer overall processing time than younger adults (Birren), this RT slowing is not constant across all processing stages and tasks. For semantic memory tasks such as a lexical decision (Allen et al., 1993) or a naming (Balota and Ferraro), older adults show slower peripheral processing (en-

Figure 3
Transposition Distance

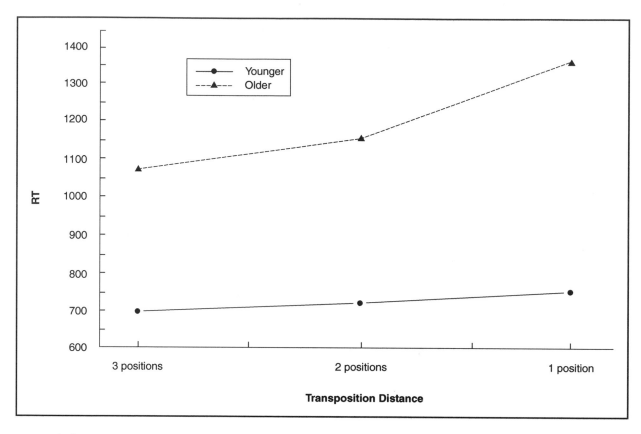

SOURCE: Author

coding and response execution), but there are no appreciable age differences in central processing (particularly for memory retrieval). However, for many episodic memory tasks, there are actually larger central-process than peripheral-process age differences (Cerella). Research using RT, especially when it can be decomposed to shed light on specific stages of mental processing, will ultimately move us toward a deeper understanding of the changes in thinking that accompany aging.

PHIL ALLEN

BIBLIOGRAPHY

ALLEN, P. A.; KAUFMAN, M.; SMITH, A. F.; and PROPPER, R. (1998). "A Molar Entropy Model of Age Differences in Spatial Memory." *Psychology and Aging* 13 (1998): 501–518.

ALLEN, P. A.; MADDEN, D. J.; and SLANE, S. "Visual Word Encoding and the Effect of Adult Age and Word Frequency." In *Age Differences in Word and Language Processing.* Edited by P. A. Allen and T. R. Bashore. New York: North-Holland., 1995.

ALLEN, P. A.; MADDEN, D. J.; WEBER, T. A.; and GROTH, K. E. "Influence of Age and Processing Stage on Visual Word Recognition." *Psychology and Aging* 8 (1993): 274–282.

ALLEN, P. A.; SMITH, A. F.; JERGE, K. A.; and VIRES-COLLINS, H. "Age Differences in Mental Multiplication: Evidence for Peripheral But Not Central Decrements." *Journal of Gerontology: Psychological Sciences* 52B (1997): P81–P90.

BALOTA, D. A., and FERRARO, F. R. "A Dissociation of Frequency and Regularity Effects in Pronunciation Performance Across Young Adults, Older Adults, and Individuals with Senile Dementia of the Alzheimer's Type." *Journal of Memory and Language* 32 (1993): 573–592.

BIRREN, J. E. "Age Changes in the Speed of Behavior: Its Central Nature and Physiological Correlates." In *Behavior, Aging, and the Nervous System.* Edited by A. T. Welford and J. E. Birren. Springfield, Ill.: Charles C. Thomas, 1965.

BURKE, D. M., and LIGHT, L. L. "Memory and Aging: The Role of Retrieval Processes." *Psychological Bulletin* 90 (1981): 513–546.

CERELLA, J. "Information Processing Rates in the Elderly." *Psychological Bulletin* 98 (1985): 67–83.

LIGHT, L. L. "Memory and Aging: Four Hypotheses in Search of Data." *Annual Review of Psychology* 42 (1991): 333–376.

LIMA, S. D.; HALE, S.; and MYERSON, J. "How General Is General Slowing? Evidence from the Lexical Domain." *Psychology and Aging* 6 (1991): 416–425.

LUCE, R. D. *Response Times*. New York: Oxford University Press, 1991.

MADDEN, D. J.; PIERCE, T. W.; and ALLEN, P. A. "Age-Related Slowing and the Time Course of Semantic Priming in Visual Word Identification." *Psychology and Aging* 8 (1993): 490–507.

PACHELLA, R. "The Use of Reaction Time Measures in Information Processing Research." In *Human Information Processing*. Edited by B. H. Kantowicz. Hillsdale, N.J.: Erlbaum, 1974.

SALTHOUSE, T. A. "The Processing-Speed Theory of Adult Age Differences in Cognition." *Psychological Review* 103 (1996): 403–428.

STERNBERG, S. "Two Operations in Character Recognition: Some Evidence from Reaction Time Measurements." *Perception & Psychophysics* 2 (1967): 45–53.

WICKENS, C. D. *Engineering Psychology and Human Performance*. New York: Harper Collins, 1992.

REALITY ORIENTATION

Reality Orientation (RO) is a general philosophy of inpatient treatment for reducing confusion in geriatric patients. According to its philosophy, confusion results from (a) understimulation of the patient, (b) care providers' lack of insistence or expectation that the patient perform normal behaviors, and (c) care providers' nonreinforcement of desired behaviors when they are performed (Taulbee and Folsom; Folsom, 1968). It follows, therefore, that confusion can be reduced through mental stimulation, social interaction, and adjustment of behavioral contingencies.

Treatment approach

The primary goal of RO is to reduce confusion. In its initial conceptualization RO was believed to accomplish this goal through three components. The first component was staff maintenance of a specific attitude toward the patient, usually one of "active" or "passive" friendliness (Folsom, 1968). This component has been referred to as attitude therapy. The second component involved staff's (a) presentation of basic orienting information during interactions with confused patients (e.g., reminding patients of who and where they are) and (b) involvement of patients in their environment, by commenting on what was happening in the environment at that time and by reinforcing individuals' awareness of and interest in their environment. The third component entailed the use of basic and advanced classes in orientation as an adjunct to the second component. The use of props or environmental cues was encouraged, including signs, clocks, calendars, reality orientation boards (information about location, date, day, weather, holidays, etc.), newspapers, television, pictures, and personal belongings. Classes were small groups with an optimal size of three to six individuals meeting with one or two staff members (Woods, 1992). The second and third components make up, respectively, what is now known as twenty-four-hour reality orientation and classroom reality orientation.

Since RO's conception, therapeutic goals have been elaborated, techniques have been more clearly defined (e.g., Drummond et al.) and manuals have been developed (e.g., Holden and Woods). Certain aspects of the philosophy have proliferated—for example, calendars and other orienting materials can be found in almost all long-term care facilities. The evolution of RO programs also has resulted, often, in the use of classroom RO without twenty-four-hour RO, despite the assertion by Folsom and colleagues that classroom RO will not be effective on its own. This modification deemphasizes the focus on social interaction with others in the environment that, increasingly, appears to be the most beneficial aspect of RO.

Use with individuals with dementia

RO was developed for reducing confusion in institutionalized individuals. The source of confusion could be any of various conditions (e.g., stroke, dementia, psychiatric disorder). However, little consideration has been given to whether there should be differences in RO according to the reason for confusion. In practice, RO is used most commonly with patients with dementia, but few attempts have been made to explain the way in which dementia might affect the individual's ability to benefit from RO.

Some have suggested that RO permits the demented individual to build competency (e.g., relearning information), thereby reducing feelings of helplessness engendered by repeatedly failing to accomplish simple tasks because of progressive impairment. However, feelings of competence are contingent on the use of activities that are appropriate to the ability level and needs of the demented individual (Woods, 1979). Targets also must be carefully considered; for example, rote learning of the day, date, and time does no good the following day. These issues have led some professionals to recommend that care providers implement only techniques that will impact quality of life (Woods, 1992). For example, it has been argued that it may be better to teach a general mnemonic strategy such as use of a diary (e.g., Hanley and Lusty), or to implement ward orientation procedures (e.g., Williams et al.) rather than to directly teach orienting information that either is not very important or could be obtained from external sources (Woods, 1992).

In addition, when working with individuals with dementia, staff need to be aware of the effects of their body language, tone of voice, and facial expressions on patients. They also should be sensitive to the patients' nonverbal communication because as verbal expression becomes more difficult, nonverbal gestures give cues about what individuals are trying to communicate (Woods, 1992).

Empirical evidence

It is beyond the scope of this entry to examine individual studies of RO. However, a number of reviews (see Kasl-Godley and Gatz; Spector et al.) cover empirical investigations of RO with both demented and nondemented older adults. Investigations tend to focus almost exclusively on the evaluation of classroom RO. In general, these investigations find that RO has circumscribed cognitive effects, largely on orientation, and little to no effect on behavioral functioning. When improvement is observed, it is usually in mildly impaired individuals. Continuation of gains after the discontinuation of treatment is uncommon. Conclusions, however, must be considered in light of a number of design issues. These issues include use of small sample sizes, use of mixed di-

agnostic groups, nonrandom assignment or lack of a comparison group, lack of standardized assessment, use of training material in the evaluation of the technique, and variability in the administration of intervention techniques. Interventions vary in duration of treatment, frequency and length of individual sessions, and use of additional potentially therapeutic components, such as increasing the number of activities available to residents. Nonspecific treatment effects (e.g., increased communication with staff, involvement in social activity, attention to appropriate behavior) apparently do help to explain treatment outcomes (see Woods, 1979; Gerber et al.). These results suggest that improvement in orientation may be facilitated through social activity and raise questions as to whether social activity (ongoing interactions with care providers that focus on maintaining communication and contact) is the more useful component of reality orientation.

JULIA KASL-GODLEY

See also ALZHEIMER'S DISEASE; DEMENTIA.

BIBLIOGRAPHY

DRUMMOND, L.; KIRCHHOFF, L.; and SCARBROUGH, D. R. "A Practical Guide to Reality Orientation: A Treatment Approach for Confusion and Disorientation." *The Gerontologist* 18 (1978): 568–573.

FOLSOM, J. C. "Intensive Hospital Therapy of Geriatric Patients." *Current and Psychiatric Therapies* 7 (1967): 209–215.

FOLSOM, J. C. "Reality Orientation for the Elderly Mental Patient." *Journal of Geriatric Psychiatry* 1 (1968): 291–307.

GERBER, G. J.; PRINCE, P. N.; SNIDER, H. G.; ATCHISON, K.; DUBOIS, L.; and KILGOUR, J. A. "Group Activity with Cognitive Improvement among Patients with Alzheimer's Disease." *Hospital and Community Psychiatry* 42 (1991): 843–845.

HANLEY, I. G. "The Use of Signposts and Active Training to Modify Ward Disorientation in Elderly Patients." *Journal of Behavior Therapy and Experimental Psychiatry* 12 (1981): 241–247.

HANLEY, I. G. *Manual of the Modifications of Confused Behavior*. Edinburgh: Lothian Regional Council, Department of Social Work, 1982.

HANLEY, I. G., and LUSTY, K. "Memory Aids in Reality Orientation: A Single-Case Study." *Behavior Research and Therapy* 22 (1984): 709–712.

HOLDEN, U. P., and WOODS, R. T. *Reality Orientation: Psychological Approaches to the Confused Elderly,* 2d ed. Edinburgh: Churchill Livingstone, 1988.

KASL-GODLEY, J., and GATZ, M. "Psychosocial Interventions for Individuals with Dementia: An Integration of Theory, Therapy, and a Clinical Understanding of Dementia." *Clinical Psychology Review* 20, no. 6 (2000): 755–782.

POWELL-PROCTOR, L. and MILLER, E. "Reality Orientation: A Critical Appraisal." *British Journal of Psychiatry* 140 (1982): 457–463.

SPECTOR, A.; DAVIES, S.; WOODS, B.; and ORRELL, M. "Reality Orientation for Dementia: A Systematic Review of the Evidence of Effectiveness from Randomized Controlled Trials." *The Gerontologist* 40 (2000): 206–212.

TAULBEE, L. R., and FOLSOM, J. C. "Reality Orientation for Geriatric Patients." *Hospital and Community Psychiatry* 17, no. 5 (1966): 133–135.

WILLIAMS, F. M. "Reality Orientation Groups." In *Working with Older Adults: Group Process and Techniques.* Edited by I. Burnside and M. G. Schmidt. Boston: Jones and Bartlett Publishers, 1994. Pages 139–152.

WILLIAMS, R.; REEVE, W.; IVISON, D.; and KAVANAGH, D. "Use of Environmental Manipulation and Modified Informal Reality Orientation with Institutionalized, Confused Elderly Subjects: A Replication." *Age and Aging* 16 (1987): 315–318.

WOODS, B. "Reality Orientation and Staff Attention: A Controlled Study." *British Journal of Psychiatry* 134 (1979): 502–507.

WOODS, B. "What Can Be Learned from Studies on Reality Orientation?" In *Care-Giving in Dementia: Research and Applications.* Edited by G. M. M. Jones and B. M. L. Miesen. New York: Tavistock/Routledge, 1992. Pages 121–136.

REFUSING AND WITHDRAWING MEDICAL TREATMENT

Decisions to withhold or withdraw medical treatment are now commonplace, and both legal and ethical support for such decisions is well established. Even in the case of medical interventions necessary to sustain a patient's life, it is generally acknowledged that ethical and legal backing exists for decisions to forgo treatment and allow a patient to die. At the same time that law and ethics have sought to protect the patient's or surrogate's refusal of medically beneficial interventions, patient and family requests for nonbeneficial treatments have generally not been recognized by ethical standards of the professions, health care institutions, or the courts.

Historical background

For most of its long history, medicine was guided by the Hippocratic ideal, which places emphasis on the health professional's special knowledge, training, and experience that is used to direct the course of patient care. The doctor gave the orders and the good patient followed these orders, knowing that a person with superior knowledge and skills was working to promote his or her interests. With the advent of new medical technologies during the latter half of the twentieth century, it was becoming clear that the new interventions medicine had to offer, such as intensive care units, assisted ventilation, kidney dialysis, and organ transplantation, did not always have happy outcomes. Patients and families were no longer comfortable with physicians maintaining authority over patient care decisions. Increasingly patients challenged the foundations of Hippocratic ethics in important respects. In particular, the autonomy of the medical profession to determine what constitutes harm and benefit to the patient was called into question.

The social and cultural milieu of the 1960s, a time of rebellion against formal authority in many areas, encouraged such questioning. During this time the civil rights movement, the anti-Vietnam War movement, the national debate about abortion, and the beginnings of the feminist movement of the 1970s and 1980s caused large numbers of people to question paternalism in many spheres of life. It was against this historical backdrop that the 1970s and 1980s witnessed a series of highly publicized legal and ethical cases in which patients or families challenged the treatment recommendations of physicians and hospitals. In these cases the patient or family sought to withdraw treatments required to keep a patient alive over the objections of the hospital or health care team. The health care team or institution either felt it was ethically improper to withhold or withdraw treatment, or wanted legal immunity before doing so. In the 1976 case *In re Quinlan,* the family of Karen Ann Quinlan, a twenty-one-year-old patient in a persistent vegetative state, requested that she be taken off the respirator, and that all extraordinary procedures used to keep her alive be discontinued. Over the objections and misgivings of the institution where Ms. Quinlan was treated this finally occurred following a 1976 decision of the New Jersey Supreme Court. Ms. Quinlan survived in a persistent vegetative state for 10 years, dying on June 11, 1985. The court ruled that Karen Quinlan's father could assert a right of privacy on Karen's behalf. It also held that the institutions and providers caring for Karen were immune from criminal liability even if the removal of medical treatment resulted in her death.

Like the family in *Quinlan,* families and/or patients in a series of later cases sought legal backing for withholding and withdrawing treatment. These challenges to medical authority established that the patient, or the family speaking on the patient's behalf, had the authority to stop medical treatments over the objections of the health care team or the institution caring for the patient. The courts developed specific rules for legally justifying withholding or withdrawing treatments during this time. In 1977 the Supreme Judicial Court of Massachusetts held in the *Saikewicz* case that decisions to withhold or withdraw life-prolonging treatment from terminally ill, incompetent patients must be made according to the test of "substituted judgment." Substituted judgment requires that surrogate decision makers act in accordance with the patient's wishes as they were expressed when the patient was competent.

Further legal backing for the standard of substituted judgment came in *Brophy* v. *New England Sinai Hospital, Inc.* In *Brophy,* the Supreme Judicial Court of Massachusetts authorized removal of the artificial feeding tube from an incompetent patient in a persistent vegetative state. It held that the "substituted judgment" of an incompetent person in a persistent vegetative state to refuse artificially administered sustenance must be honored.

Like the "right to die" cases that preceded it, the case of Nancy Cruzan lent support to patients' and families' wishes to discontinue medical treatment. In *Cruzan* the family of a twenty-five-year-old Missouri woman who never regained consciousness following an automobile accident asked the doctors caring for her to remove the feeding tube so that she could die in peace. Ms. Cruzan's father asserted that his daughter would never have wanted to live in her present state. Despite the family's wishes, doctors and the hospital caring for the patient refused to withdraw the feeding tube without a court order. Although the Missouri Supreme Court declared that the state had an "unqualified" interest in life, the court also ruled that it would have allowed withdrawal of Nancy Cruzan's feeding tube if she had provided others with "clear and convincing evidence" that she would not have wanted to be kept alive in a persistent vegetative state. The U.S. Supreme Court upheld Missouri's right to apply a "clear and convincing" standard for evidence of Nancy Cruzan's wishes.

Whereas during the 1970s and 1980s patients and families typically sought to withdraw or withhold medical treatments, during the 1990s patients and families more often wished to "do everything possible" for a loved one in situations where health care professionals or institutions judged that such treatments were nonbeneficial or "futile." This trend is evident, for example, in the 1990 case of Helga Wanglie. Mrs. Wanglie was eighty-five years old when she tripped on a rug and fell, breaking her hip. During hospitalization, she developed respiratory failure requiring her placement on a mechanical respirator. Subsequently she suffered cardiac arrest and received emergency resuscitation. Although she survived the arrest, she never regained consciousness, and eventually was diagnosed as being in a permanent vegetative state. When asked to consider withdrawing life-support measures, including the mechanical respirator, Mrs. Wanglie's family refused. Physicians recommended withdrawing life-sustaining treatment because it was not benefiting Helga Wanglie. Yet the family believed that life should be maintained as long as possible, no matter what the circumstances, and asserted that the patient shared this belief.

A series of subsequent cases demonstrated patient or family requests for nonbeneficial or futile treatment. Such cases represent heightened expectations among patients and the public at large about what medicine can accomplish. Widespread concern arose among health professionals about the ethically inappropriate use of medical technologies. Professional organizations and health care institutions responded by establishing standards and policies limiting physicians' obligations to offer or continue interventions that are contrary to standards of the health care professions.

Although courts have consistently upheld a right to refuse life-sustaining treatments, they generally distinguish between the patient's or surrogate's right to refuse treatment, on the one hand, and the patient's right to demand specific treatments from physicians and hospitals, on the other hand. The patient's right to privacy encompasses the right to be left alone, but does not provide legal backing for patients or families to obtain specific treatments against the recommendations of the health care team, or of the professional or institutional standards for care.

The ethics of refusing and withdrawing treatment

Just as the aforementioned cases facilitated development of professional, institutional, and legal standards for withholding and withdrawing care, so they also sparked continued debate over the ethical basis for forgoing treatment. Ethical reasons for withholding and withdrawing medical treatments can be usefully grouped under three general headings. First, the ethical principle of autonomy implies respecting the wishes of a competent patient who refuses medical interventions. Patients express autonomous wishes in a variety of ways. At the time treatment is offered, a competent patient may refuse it. Or at some prior time, a now incapacitated patient may have made a reasoned decision that certain interventions should not be provided. Often, patients express such a preference through a directive to physicians (living will) that provides both ethical and legal support for respecting the patient's competent choices. Alternatively, a decision may be made by others who claim to represent the wishes of the now incompetent patient. Here the ethical mandate to respect patient autonomy corresponds to the legal requirements of substituted judgement established in *Brophy* v. *New England Sinai Hospital.*

A second ethical basis for forgoing medical treatment is the ethical obligation to promote the patient's good and avoid harm to the patient. There are at least two ways in which principles of beneficence and nonmaleficence give ethical underpinning to withholding or withdrawing treatment. On the one hand, a surrogate decision maker may decide to forgo medical interventions because this is considered to be in the patient's best interest. On the other hand, benefit is also at stake when treatment is forgone because the health care team judges that treatment is futile and provides no medical benefit to the patient.

A third ethical basis for forgoing medical treatment appeals to the ethical standard of justice. Justice arises in situations where medical resources are scarce or the dollars to pay for them are limited. In such cases justice furnishes an ethical reason for rationing beneficial care to particular patients; health care dollars or resources can be put to better (more just) use elsewhere in the health care system. Unlike arguments that find their source in ethical principles of autonomy, beneficence, or nonmaleficence, arguments appealing to justice generally spring from health care policies that seek to provide the best care to a population of patients. Support for applying particular justice rules in the clinical setting depends upon establishing that particular instances of health care rationing are part of a larger system of rules for distributing health care that itself meets ethical standards of justice.

Summary

Decisions to withhold or withdraw medical treatment will continue to attract widespread attention in scholarly and public policy discussions. Legal and ethical cases provide the basis for developing standards for settling disputes between patients and families, on the one hand, and the health care team or institution, on the other hand. Increasingly, legal and ethical guidelines support the patient's right to be left alone while limiting the patient's right to request specific treatments that run contrary to standards of the health care professions. In law and ethics, patient privacy and autonomy protect the patient's right to refuse or withdraw treatment. At the same time, legal and ethical support for patients' requesting futile interventions has generally not been forthcoming.

NANCY S. JECKER

See also ADVANCE DIRECTIVES FOR HEALTH CARE; AGE-BASED RATIONING OF HEALTH CARE; AUTONOMY; COMPETENCY; DEATH AND DYING; EUTHANSIA AND SENICIDE; SUICIDE AND ASSISTED SUICIDE, ETHICAL ASPECTS.

BIBLIOGRAPHY

American College of Chest Surgeons/Society of Critical Care Medicine Consensus Panel. "Ethical and Moral Guidelines for the Initiation, Continuation and Withdrawal of Intensive Care." *Chest* 97 (1990): 949.
American Medical Association, Council on Ethical and Judicial Affairs. "Guidelines for the

Appropriate Use of Do-Not-Resuscitate Oders." *Journal of the American Medical Association* 265 (1991): 1868–1871.

American Medical Association, Council on Ethical and Judicial Affairs, Medical Futility in End of Life Care. Located at http://www.ama-assn.org/meetings/public/i96/summary/

American Thoracic Society. "Withholding and Withdrawing Life-Sustaining Therapy." *Annals of Internal Medicine* 115 (1991): 478.

ANNAS, G. L. "Reconciling Quinlan and Saikewicz: Decision Making for the Terminally Ill Incompetent." *American Journal of Law and Medicine* 4, no. 4 (Winter 1979): 367–396.

CAPRON, A. M. "Baby Ryan and Virtual Futility." *Hastings Center Report* (March–April 1995).

GREENHOUSE, L. "Court Order to Treat Baby Prompts a Debate on Ethics." *New York Times*, 19 February 1994.

In the Matter of Karen Quinlan: The Complete Legal Briefs, Court Proceedings, and Decisions. Arlington, Va.: University Publications of America, 1975.

JOHNSON, S. H.; GIBBONS, V.; GOLDNER, J. A.; WIENER, R. L.; and ETON, D. "Legal and Institutional Policy Responses to Medical Futility." *Journal of Health and Hospital Law* 30, no. 1 (1997).

MILES, S. H. "Informed Demand for 'Nonbeneficial' Medical Treatment." *New England Journal of Medicine* 325 (1991): 512–515.

QUINLAN, J., and QUINLAN, J., with BATELLE, P. *Karen Ann Quinlan.* New York: Doubleday, 1977.

SCHNEIDERMAN, L. J., and JECKER, N. S. *Wrong Medicine: Doctors, Patients, and Futile Treatment.* Baltimore: John Hopkins University Press, 1995.

SCHNEIDERMAN, L. J.; JECKER, N. S.; and JONSEN, A. R. "Medical Futility: Its Meaning and Ethical Implications." *Annals of Internal Medicine* 112 (1990): 949–954.

Society for the Right to Die. "*Brophy* v. *New England Sinai Hospital Inc.* Brief Amicus Curiae, Society for the Right to Die, Inc. on Behalf of Appellant." *Journal of the American Geriatrics Society* 35, no. 7 (July 1987): 669–678.

SOLOMON, M.; O'DONNELL, L.; JENNINGS, B.; GUILFOY, V.; WOLF, S.; NOLAN, K.; JACKSON, R.; KOCH-WESER, D.; and DONNELLEY, S. "Decisions Near the End of Life: Professional Views on Life-Sustaining Treatment." *American Journal of Public Health* 83, no. 1 (1993): 14–23.

CASES

Bryan v. *Rectors and Visitors of the University of Virginia*, 95 F. 3d 349 (4th Circuit, 1996).

Cruzan v. *Director, Missouri Department of Health*, 110 S. Ct. 2841 (1990).

Gilgunn v. *Massachusetts General Hospital*, no. 92-4820 (Mass. Super. Ct., Suffolk County, 21 April 1995). Reported in Gina Kolata, "Withholding Care from Patients: Boston Case Asks, Who Decides?" *New York Times*, 3 April 1995, p. A1.

In re Baby K, 832 F. Supp. 1022 (E.D. Va. 1993), aff'd, 16 F.3d 590 (4th Cir. 1994).

REHABILITATION

Rehabilitation is one of the basic elements of comprehensive geriatric care. Rehabilitation is indicated when someone is not functioning at their full potential. It involves an assessment of the underlying causes of activity limitation, treatment of the primary impairment to the extent possible, prevention of further disability, and interventions to promote adaptation of the person to their disability. The goal of geriatric rehabilitation is to maximize functional independence.

Rehabilitation in general, and geriatric rehabilitation in particular, is provided by an interdisciplinary team. The basic team consists of one (or more) occupational therapist, physiotherapist, physician, rehabilitation nurse, and social worker. Other disciplines that can be involved either as part of the core team, or on a consultation basis, include dietetics, pharmacy, psychology, recreational therapy, or speech-language pathology. A team that works well together, and whose members have an understanding of and respect for each other's contributions and strengths, is integral to a successful rehabilitation program.

Assessment

Assessment begins with establishing the patient's suitability for a rehabilitation program. In order to benefit from a geriatric rehabilitation program, the patient must be medically stable and have a minimum of endurance to undergo at least an hour per day of therapy. Patients must be motivated to participate actively in the program, and must have sufficient cognitive function to be able to learn simple tasks with repetition. They must require the expertise of at least two different rehabilitation disciplines.

The World Health Organization has defined several terms to facilitate communication. These include *impairments*, which are problems in body function or structure (e.g., an arthritic joint or a stroke). *Activity limitations* are difficulties an individual has in performance of activities (e.g., being unable to walk safely on stairs). *Participation restrictions* are problems an individual may have concerning involvement in life situations (e.g., being housebound because the only access requires using stairs, and there is no ramp or elevator in place). The rehabilitation team addresses activity limitations and participation restrictions associated with specific impairments.

It is important to get a good picture of the patient's weaknesses and strengths in the spheres of mobility, self-care (bathing, dressing), continence, cognition, mood, and social situation. There are many different outcome measurements that are used to record and follow level of function. It is important to be aware of the patient's previous level of function in order to set appropriate goals. Priority is given to the goals of the patient and family members.

Intervention

Intervention begins with prevention of further injury. This means preventing the complications that can arise from bedrest following the initial problem (stroke, hip fracture, medical illness). If older people are left convalescing too long, they become at risk for infections, pressure ulcers, and muscle atrophy. Early mobilization is essential. Risk factors for future falls, fractures, or strokes are identified and addressed, if possible, to try to prevent any further impairment.

The physiotherapist (PT) can design an exercise program to increase flexibility, strength, balance, and endurance. PT's evaluate and train the patient in getting up from sitting, walking, stepping over curbs and going up stairs, using walking aids as necessary. The occupational therapist's (OT) emphasis is on self-care skills, including bathing, dressing, and eating. They also focus on instrumental activities of daily living, such as cooking, housekeeping, using the telephone, and money management. The OT assists with education, training, compensatory skills, and adaptive equipment. The social worker plays a crucial role in discharge planning and as the primary communicator between the rehabilitation team and the family. Rehabilitation nurses encourage independence by providing physical or verbal assistance. They monitor skin care, bowel and bladder management, and provide guidance about medications.

Discharge planning begins as soon as the patient's condition stabilizes and the likely functional outcome becomes clear. A home visit by a PT or OT may be useful to determine accessibility of the home environment and appropriate home modifications. Important considerations are the amount of support available (which can be a problem when the spouse is also frail and elderly) and the extent of care needs. Family meetings with representatives from the rehabilitation team, as well as community care providers, are often necessary to set up needed home help prior to discharge.

Stroke rehabilitation

Rehabilitation following a stroke should begin as soon as possible, to avoid the complications of immobility and to allow for maximal functional gains. Most functional recovery occurs within the first two to six months following a stroke, and early prediction of outcome is useful to set appropriate goals, facilitate discharge planning, and anticipate the need for home adjustments and supports. Muscle strengthening and general conditioning can reduce impairment and disability. Task-oriented exercise may be more meaningful to elderly patients and can contribute to motor recovery and gait retraining. Many stroke survivors have persistent activity limitation of the affected arm. Immobilization of the unaffected arm combined with intensive training of the affected one is occasionally used to improve arm function. Another approach involves facilitation of appropriate movement patterns in the affected arm. Depression is common after stroke and, unless treated, can interfere with recovery. Swallowing dysfunction should be looked for by an OT or speech-language pathologist.

Hip fracture rehabilitation

Falls and hip fractures are unfortunately common in frail elderly patients, and hip fracture rehabilitation is an important concern. Breaking a hip can result in nursing home placement or even death. An important predictor of being able to return home is pre-fracture mobility. Ongoing communication with the orthopedic surgeon is important to establish hip precautions, to avoid dislocation of an artificial joint, and for guidance on when the patient can begin to bear his full weight on the operated leg. Older patients may be unable to cooperate with partial weight-bearing restrictions, because of poor balance, weakness, or cognitive impairment. Although pain must be adequately treated, it is important to avoid overmedication and delirium in frail older adults. Fear of falling can become a limiting factor, and confidence must be addressed. Strengthening exercises (sometimes including treadmill gait retraining), balance training, and walking aids are standard components of hip fracture rehabilitation. Therapy can continue on an outpatient basis.

Inpatient rehabilitation can take place on the acute care unit (medical or surgical) or on specialized geriatric rehabilitation wards. If the patient is well enough to go home, outpatient rehabilitation can be facility-based or home-based. In some areas, geriatric day hospitals offer an intermediate solution to frail patients who have returned to the community. The types of geriatric services available vary depending on local preference, economics, and cultural attitudes toward the elderly. Particularly as the population ages, resources may not keep pace with needs. Outcome in geriatric rehabilitation very often depends upon the type and degree of social support available to the patient.

SUSAN FRETER

See also BALANCE AND MOBILITY; GERIATRIC MEDICINE; HIP FRACTURE; OCCUPATIONAL THERAPY; PHYSICAL THERAPY; STROKE; WALKING AIDS; WHEELCHAIRS.

BIBLIOGRAPHY

BARER, D. "Rehabilitation." In *Geriatric Medicine and Gerontology*, 5th ed. Edited by J. C. Brocklehurst. London: Harcourt Brace, 1998. Pages 1521–1550.

BRUMMEL-SMITH, K. *Clinics in Geriatric Medicine: Geriatric Rehabilitation.* Philadelphia, Pa.: W. B. Saunders Co., 1993.

LÖKK, J. "Geriatric Rehabilitation Revisited." *Aging Clinical and Experimental Research* 11 (1999): 353–361.

STEINBERG, F. U., and DEAN, B. Z. "Physiatric Therapeutics: Geriatric Rehabilitation." *Archives of Physical Medicine and Rehabilitation* 71 (1990): S278–S280.

TAUB, E.; USWATTE, G.; and PIDIKITI, R. "Constraint-Induced Movement Therapy: A New Family of Techniques with Broad Application to Physical Rehabilitation—A Clinical Review." *Journal of Rehabilitation Research and Development* 36 (1999): 237–251.

WEBER, D. C.; FLEMING, K. C.; and EVANS, J. M. "Rehabilitation of Geriatric Patients." *Mayo Clinic Proceedings* 70 (1995): 1198–1204.

World Health Organization. *ICIDH-2: International Classification of Functioning and Disability.* Beta-2 draft. Geneva: World Health Organization, 1999. www.who.int/icidh

ZUCKERMAN, J. D.; FABIAN, D. R.; AHARANOFF, G.; KOVAL, K. J.; and FRANKEL, V. H. "Enhancing Independence in the Older Hip Fracture Patient." *Geriatrics* 48 (1993): 76–81.

RELIGION

The United States is a nation of religious believers. National surveys consistently find that nine in ten Americans affiliate with a religion or religious denomination. This is true regardless of age. Older adults, however, participate on average in certain religious activities more frequently than younger individuals. Religion also appears to represent a more salient influence in the lives of older adults. A possible explanation for this may be found in the differing life experiences and developmental trajectories of today's older Americans, unique features characteristic of their period of religious socialization, and anticipation of forthcoming challenges associated with aging. Both personal and social resources provided by religious belief and participation, and by religious institutions, can prove valuable as adults age through the life course and face the physical and interpersonal changes that often accompany old age.

This entry will explore these and other issues, particularly as they relate to the consequences of religious involvement in the lives of older adults. After describing the field of religious gerontology, the area of study devoted to the relationship between religion and aging, existing research that characterizes the role of religion in older adulthood will be summarized. This includes scientific findings documenting (a) patterns of religious participation; (b) determinants of religious participation; (c) the role of religion in preventing illness and promoting health, longevity, and psychological well-being; and (d) the social and psychological functions and benefits of both formal participation in organized religious activities and private religious involvement.

Religious gerontology

The field dedicated to the study of religion among older adults and across the life course is known as religious gerontology. This large field of study encompasses basic and applied research and writing on a wide range of topics, including human services delivery, pastoral counseling, theology, ministry, congregational programming, community intervention, health services research, behavioral and psychiatric epidemiology, and social and health indicators related to quality of life.

Systematic empirical research in religious gerontology dates to the early 1950s, when the sociologist David O. Moberg began a series of investigations into the impact of religious participation on the general well-being of older adults. He found that indicators of personal adjustment to aging were higher among people who were involved in organized religious activities. These included active church membership, attending worship services, and serving in church leadership roles. Small-scale studies on similar topics continued to appear throughout the next two decades.

Beginning in the middle 1980s, religious gerontology experienced a period of dramatic growth that has continued to this day. Both qualitative and quantitative research has flourished, with an emphasis on the identification of factors that are associated with positive life circumstances in older adulthood. Qualitative research using a variety of historical, literary, and phenomenological methods has been instrumental in fashioning a deeper understanding of the critical significance of meaning and context as adults move through the stages of the life course, from youth to senescence and death. Much of this research is cross-cultural and takes a comparative approach. The best of this work is in *Aging and the Religious Dimension* and *Religion, Belief, and Spirituality in Late Life* (Thomas and Eisenhandler, 1994, 1999).

Another key development has been recognition of the importance of religion in the lives of older adults by public and private institutions that fund research studies. Foremost among these is the National Institute on Aging (NIA) of the National Institutes of Health. Throughout the 1990s the NIA funded several large studies of religion, aging, and health by leading scientists, including the psychiatrist Harold G. Koenig, the sociologist Neal Krause, the epidemiologist Jeff Levin, and the team of the sociologist Robert Joseph Taylor, and the psychologist Linda M. Chatters. Findings from these studies

provide considerable support for the idea that active religious involvement is both an epidemiologically and a therapeutically significant factor in the lives of older adults, regardless of gender, social class, race or ethnicity, or religious affiliation.

Many other signs point to the institutionalization of religious gerontology as a defined field of study. These include establishment of the Forum on Religion, Spirituality, and Aging within the American Society on Aging, and a Religion and Aging special interest group within the Gerontological Society of America; publication of the large edited volume *Aging, Spirituality, and Religion: A Handbook* (Kimble et al.), and of a scholarly journal, *Journal of Religious Gerontology*; and funded academic centers for education and research, notably the Center for Aging, Religion, and Spirituality at Luther Seminary, in St. Paul, Minnesota, and the Center for the Study of Religion/Spirituality and Health at Duke University Medical Center, in Durham, North Carolina.

Patterns of religious participation

Many studies in religious gerontology have sought to document how often older adults engage in various kinds of religious expression. Through this research gerontologists typically differentiate among several discrete dimensions of religious participation. These include formal or organizational religiousness, informal or nonorganizational religiousness, and what is termed subjective religiousness.

Gerontologists define organizational religiousness as public participation in organized activities of churches, synagogues, and other religious institutions. Indicators of organizational religiousness include affiliating with a denomination or congregation, regularly attending worship services, taking a leadership role in one's congregation, and volunteering at one's place of worship. According to data from the 1990 General Social Survey of the National Opinion Research Center at the University of Chicago, attendance at religious services at least once per week is increasingly common among successively older age groups. Among adults age sixty-five and older, at least weekly attendance exceeds 46 percent. This represents a rise of nearly 10 percent over data collected in the 1970s.

Gerontologists define nonorganizational religiousness as participation in private religious activities, most typically at home or with one's family. Nonorganizational religious indicators include regular prayer, participation in study of the Bible or other scriptures, watching religious television or listening to religious radio, and saying grace at meals. Findings from the 1988 General Social Survey paint a picture for many of these activities that is similar to that for organizational religiousness. Daily prayer, for example, is considerably more common in older than in younger adults. Nearly three-quarters of adults age seventy-five and over pray at least every day—almost twice the frequency of adults age eighteen to twenty-four.

Besides organizational and nonorganizational religiousness, both of which have to do with religious behavior, religious gerontologists are interested in self-assessments of personal religious attitudes, beliefs, and motivations. These are sometimes classified under the heading of subjective religiousness. Indicators of subjective religiousness include self-ratings of overall religiousness, reports of the importance of religion, intense feelings of religiousness, and professions of belief in God or a higher power. National survey data are less consistent for this type of religiousness than for public or private religious behavior, but still show markedly higher ratings among older adults.

An important issue that arises in interpreting data on age patterns in religious participation is the need to address aging, period, and cohort effects. The disentanglement of these possible effects is an issue that arises frequently in gerontological research. It concerns identifying the underlying explanation for age differences observed in a particular phenomenon, such as the age differences that exist in patterns of religious participation. Only through multiwave longitudinal studies lasting many decades can these three types of effects begin to be separated. Until such studies are conducted in religious gerontology, the best that scientists can do is to rely on reasoned speculation.

The presence of a cohort effect in religious participation is suggested by generational differences in religious socialization experienced by older age cohorts. Examples include religious formation before Vatican II among Catholics, during the flourishing of Classical Reform Judaism, and prior to the decline of mainline Protestantism in the face of evangelical inroads. Not all of these trends, however, imply greater religious

training in prior generations. Further, as Moberg noted, if a cohort effect were present, then we would expect to observe less religious participation among each successive generation of older adults. There is little evidence for this; as trends toward greater religiousness in older age have persisted for decades.

This might be explained by the presence of a period effect—that is, an influence of a past epoch or event of religious or societal history that significantly impacted all people living at a certain period of time, but exerted a differential or diffused impact across subsequent periods. Examples, both secular and religious, include the Great Depression, World War II, and the charismatic movement. Evidence of a period effect in religious participation, however, is weak. Not only have trends toward greater religiousness in older age persisted, but absolute levels of religiousness have persisted as well. For example, in the United States national survey data on the frequency of weekly attendance at religious services, across all groups, has hovered just above 40 percent for decades.

Cohort and period effects on religious participation may still be present to a limited extent in certain subgroups of the population, but the most acceptable explanation for greater levels of religiousness observed among older adults is the presence of an actual aging effect. This means a trend toward greater religiousness throughout the life course, signifying increasing reflection on matters of ultimate concern as people age. The psychologist Sheldon S. Tobin, writing from psychoanalytic and developmental perspectives, explains that religion offers continuity across the life course through emphasizing the enduring meaning of life, engendering a sense of being blessed, and providing personal and community resources that enhance coping with age-related losses.

Determinants of religious participation

In contrast to the many national probability-sample studies of patterns of religious participation, research on the determinants or predictors of religiousness in older adults has drawn mostly on small, nonrandom samples of patients, community-center attendees, church members, or students. Since the advent of research funding by the NIA in the 1990s, this has begun to change. Reliable national findings pointing to differences in religious participation by age, gender, race or ethnicity, social class, and other sociodemographic variables are starting to accumulate.

Taylor and Chatters have presented quite a bit of evidence for significant sociodemographic differences in religious participation among older adults, especially older African-Americans. Older age, more education, greater income, being married, female gender, and living in the southern United States each has been found in multiple studies to predict greater levels of organizational, nonorganizational, and subjective religiousness. These important findings firmly contradict commonly held assumptions that religious people, especially religious older people and older African-Americans, tend to be poorer and less educated.

In one NIA-funded study, Levin, Taylor, and Chatters analyzed data from four separate national probability-sample surveys of older adults conducted from the early 1970s to the late 1980s. Collectively these surveys examined twenty religious indicators of all three types (organizational, nonorganizational, and subjective) of religiousness in a total of over six thousand respondents. Significant racial differences were found for sixteen of these variables; significant gender differences were found for twelve variables. In every instance greater levels of religiousness were found among African-Americans and females. Gerontological research among older Hispanics, Jews, and Asian-Americans has focused less on religion, but sociodemographic correlates of religious participation have been identified in these groups.

Religious participation and health

Since the middle 1980s research findings have begun to accumulate on the salutary effects of active religious involvement on objective and subjective indicators of quality of life among older adults. Foremost among these are studies of the impact of organizational and nonorganizational religious participation on a host of psychosocial and health-related outcomes. Scientific investigations by medical sociologists, social epidemiologists, health psychologists, and physicians have confirmed a generally positive effect of religion in relation to physical health and to measures of mental health and psychological well-being. Much of this research has been funded by the NIH and has been conducted by prominent scientists at leading universities and academic medical centers.

Various dimensions of religious participation have been found to be positively associated with a wide range of health indicators in older adults. These include global self-ratings of health, functional disability, physical symptomatology, prevalence of hypertension, prevalence of cancer, and even rates of death. Many studies, for example, have found that active participation in organized religion seems to be associated with greater longevity. In epidemiologic terms both public and private religious behavior seems to be a protective factor against morbidity and mortality.

Likewise, religious dimensions have been shown to have protective effects in relation to a wide variety of measures of mental health and psychological well-being in older adults. These include self-esteem, self-efficacy or mastery, coping, life satisfaction, happiness, addictive behaviors, anxiety, and depressive symptoms. Longitudinal research by Koenig and colleagues at Duke University suggests that religious participation not only exerts a protective or preventive effect, but also may be therapeutic, hastening recovery from clinical depression in hospitalized medically ill patients.

An important issue in social, psychiatric, and epidemiologic research on religion, aging, and health has been the differential saliences of organizational, nonorganizational, and subjective religiousness as sources of protection. Reviews of existing research findings have reached the following consensus: (a) organizational religious involvement is fairly stable throughout the life course, and then declines on average among the very old or disabled; (b) nonorganizational and subjective religiousness also remain stable throughout the life course, then increase slightly on average, perhaps to offset existing declines in organizational religiousness; (c) organizational religiousness is positively associated with greater physical and mental health and well-being; and (d) nonorganizational religiousness seems to be inversely related to health and well-being.

This latter observation is surprising and seems contrary to expectations, yet it has been observed, off and on, for many years. Only with the advent of good longitudinal studies has this anomalous finding been interpretable as a methodological artifact of the cross-sectional nature of most gerontological research on religion. In short, among very old or disabled respondents, nonorganizational religiousness may increase in response to health-necessitated declines in public worship. This would show up in analyses of study data as an inverse or negative effect of nonorganizational religious behavior on health. It does not mean, of course, that private religious practices cause illness; rather, illness or disability leads to an increase in certain types of religious expression as compensation for the inability to practice others. The complexity of this issue exemplifies the importance of longitudinal research for religious gerontology.

Functions of religion among older adults

Research findings such as those summarized above provide the who, what, where, and when of religion's influence in the lives of older adults. With few exceptions religion has consistently been found to be an important source of meaning, coping, and adjustment with positive consequences for health and well-being. Understanding the how and why of this seemingly beneficial impact of religion is another matter altogether. The question that needs to be asked is what are the functions, characteristics, expressions, or manifestations of being religious or practicing religion that account for its being a protective factor? Or, in simpler terms, just what is it about religion that explains its impact on health and other outcomes?

Gerontologists have pursued efforts to answer this "why" question. A variety of sophisticated theoretical perspectives, frameworks, and models have been advanced to explain why religious participation is so vital for the well-being of older adults. For example, the sociologist Christopher G. Ellison discusses how religious participation benefits older adults by (a) reducing the risk of acute and chronic stressors, such as marital problems or deviant behavior; (b) offering institutional or cognitive frameworks, such as a sense of order, meaning, or coherence, that serve to buffer the harmful effects of stress and lead to successful coping; (c) providing tangible social resources, such as religious fellowship and congregational networks; and (d) enhancing personal psychological resources, such as feelings of worthiness. In addition, Koenig outlines ways that religious faith helps older adults who are suffering physical challenges by emphasizing interpersonal relations, stressing the seeking of forgiveness, providing hope for change, emphasizing the forgiveness of oneself and others, providing hope for healing, providing a context and

role models for suffering, engendering a sense of control and self-determination, promising life after death and ready accessibility to God, and providing a supportive community.

Another approach to understanding the salutary functions of religion comes from a more epidemiologic perspective. Levin and the sociologist Ellen L. Idler, among others, have described those biobehavioral and psychosocial functions of religion that could account for its positive effects on rates of morbidity and mortality. The key here is to identify the factors that mediate a religion-health relationship—factors that, independently of religion, are known to prevent illness and promote health. These include healthy behaviors and lifestyles (promoted by active religious affiliation and membership); socially supportive resources (offered by regular religious fellowship); physiological effects of positive emotions (engendered by participation in worship and prayer); health-promoting beliefs and personality styles (consonant with certain religious and theological beliefs); and cognitions such as hope, optimism, and positive expectation (fostered by faith in God or a higher power).

In summary, religion is a key feature and salient force for good in the lives of older adults. Both public and private religious activity is common throughout the life course, and increasingly engaged in by older people. Attendance at worship services and the practice of prayer are especially representative expressions of religiousness. Research has identified age, gender, race or ethnicity, and other sociodemographic factors as important sources of variation in religious expression. Other research points to both organized religion and private or informal religious involvement as epidemiologically significant sources of protection against physical and mental illness and mortality. These findings can be explained by the salutary functions of religious participation, including the provision of personal and interpersonal resources and of a context and meaning for age-related changes in life circumstances such as health.

JEFF LEVIN

See also SOCIAL SUPPORT.

BIBLIOGRAPHY

ATCHLEY, R. C. "Religion and Spirituality." In *Social Forces and Aging: An Introduction to Social*

Gerontology, 8th ed. Belmont, Calif.: Wadsworth, 1997. Pages 294–315.

CLEMENTS, W. M., ed. *Religion, Aging and Health: A Global Perspective.* Compiled by the World Health Organization. New York: Haworth Press, 1989.

ELLISON, C. G. "Religion, the Life Stress Paradigm, and the Study of Depression." In *Religion in Aging and Health: Theoretical Foundations and Methodological Frontiers.* Edited by Jeffrey S. Levin. Thousand Oaks, Calif.: Sage, 1994. Pages 78–121.

FECHER, V. J. *Religion & Aging: An Annotated Bibliography.* San Antonio, Texas: Trinity University Press, 1982.

IDLER, E. L. "Religious Involvement and the Health of the Elderly: Some Hypotheses and an Initial Test." *Social Forces* 66 (1987): 226–238.

KIMBLE, M. A.; MCFADDEN, S. H.; ELLOR, J. W.; and SEEBER, J. J., eds. *Aging, Spirituality, and Religion: A Handbook.* Minneapolis, Minn.: Fortress Press, 1995.

KOENIG, H. G. *Aging and God: Spiritual Pathways to Mental Health in Midlife and Later Years.* New York: Haworth Press, 1994.

KOENIG, H. G. *Research on Religion and Aging: An Annotated Bibliography.* Westport, Conn.: Greenwood Press, 1995.

KOENIG, H. G.; SMILEY, M.; and GONZALES, J. A. P. *Religion, Health, and Aging: A Review and Theoretical Integration.* New York: Greenwood Press, 1988.

KRAUSE, N. "Religion, Aging, and Health: Current Status and Future Prospects." *Journal of Gerontology: Social Sciences* 52B (1997): S291–S293.

LEVIN, J. S. "Religion." In *The Encyclopedia of Aging,* 2d ed. Edited by George L. Maddox. New York: Springer, 1995. Pages 799–802.

LEVIN, J. S., ed. *Religion in Aging and Health: Theoretical Foundations and Methodological Frontiers.* Thousand Oaks, Calif.: Sage, 1994.

LEVIN, J. S.; TAYLOR, R. J.; and CHATTERS, L. M. "Race and Gender Differences in Religiosity among Older Adults: Findings from Four National Surveys." *Journal of Gerontology: Social Sciences* 49 (1994): S137–S145.

MAVES, P. B. "Aging, Religion, and the Church." In *Handbook of Social Gerontology: Societal Aspects of Aging.* Edited by Clark Tibbitts. Chicago: University of Chicago Press, 1960. Pages 698–749.

MCFADDEN, S. H. "Religion and Spirituality." In *Encyclopedia of Gerontology,* vol. 2. Edited by James E. Birren. San Diego: Academic Press, 1996. Pages 387–397.

MCFADDEN, S. H. "Religion, Spirituality, and Aging." In *Handbook of the Psychology of Aging,* 4th ed. Edited by James E. Birren and K. Warner Schaie. San Diego: Academic Press, 1996. Pages 162–177.

MOBERG, D. O. "Religion and Aging." In *Gerontology: Perspectives and Issues.* Edited by Kenneth F. Ferraro. New York: Springer, 1997. Pages 179–205.

TAYLOR, R. J., and CHATTERS, L. M. "Religious Involvement among Older African-Americans." In *Religion in Aging and Health: Theoretical Foundations and Methodological Frontiers.* Edited by Jeffrey S. Levin. Thousand Oaks, Calif.: Sage, 1994. Pages 196–230.

THOMAS, L. E., and EISENHANDLER, S. A., eds. *Aging and the Religious Dimension.* Westport, Conn.: Auburn House, 1994.

THOMAS, L. E., and EISENHANDLER, S. A., eds. *Religion, Belief, and Spirituality in Late Life.* New York: Springer, 1999.

TOBIN, S. S. "Preserving the Self Through Religion." In *Personhood in Advanced Old Age: Implications for Practice.* New York: Springer, 1991. Pages 119–133.

RESEARCH

See AGE; AGE-PERIOD-COHORT MODEL; BIOMARKERS OF AGING; COHORT CHANGE; EPIDEMIOLOGY; EVIDENCE-BASED MEDICINE; DEVELOPMENTAL PSYCHOLOGY; FRUIT FLIES; GERONTOLOGY; LIFE CYCLE THEORIES OF AGING AND CONSUMPTION; LIFE EVENTS AND STRESS; NARRATIVE; NATIONAL INSTITUTE ON AGING; NEUROSPSYCHOLOGY; PANEL STUDIES; PERSONALITY; PHYSIOLOGICAL CHANGES; PRIMATES; PSYCHOLOGICAL ASSESSMENT; PSYCHOSOCIAL-BEHAVIORAL INTERVENTIONS; REACTION TIME; RODENTS; ROUNDWORMS; QUALITATIVE RESEARCH; SURVEYS; VETERANS CARE; YEAST

RETAILING AND OLDER ADULTS

Older adults have become an attractive market for retailers and marketers. People over the age of fifty-five, a fast-increasing part of the population, have a growing amount of spending potential. They are rather affluent in terms of discretionary income, and many have both time and resources to devote to shopping. In the past, older adults' spending habits were more conservative than their younger cohorts. However, in the last twenty years older adults have begun to spend at about the same rate as younger people.

The older population's expenditures cover a variety of goods and services: health care products, travel, recreational vehicles, sporting equipment, secondary homes (apartments, condos, cabins, summer homes), luxury cars, electronic equipment, home improvement, clothing, gifts, and philanthropy. Nevertheless, in many product and service areas, such as the movie and television industries, marketers and retailers still insist on targeting younger consumers.

Yet many retailers and marketers have begun to target a wider variety of products to older consumers beyond those traditionally associated with older adults. Retailers and marketers face an increasingly competitive market, and find that one way to improve their competitive position and profitability is to target an underserved and growing part of the population. Some of this interest in the older population is due to significant social and demographic shifts that result from the growth of the population of older adults. In 1996, 13 percent of the population was over sixty-five years old. This will increase to 20 percent by 2030. Also of interest to retailers and marketers is that older people are living longer with more active lifestyles, and life expectancies are expected to continue to increase (Henderson). As people age, they continue to shop, and the majority of older adults do their own shopping for goods and services.

Obviously, older people are not a homogeneous group. Their behavior regarding the purchasing and consuming of products and services varies depending on age, income, and other demographic, sociological, and health factors. Purchasing and consuming decisions will be quite different for an individual who is fifty-five years old and in good health and one who is eighty-five years old and in poor health.

Direct marketing and retailing to older adults

In addition to traditional advertising and store shopping, retailers and marketers have also promoted products and services to older adults through nonstore ventures including catalog, direct mail, and electronic shopping on cable television and the Internet. These methods of promoting and selling are often called "direct marketing" or "direct retailing." Both catalog and electronic shopping can be convenient for older adults. Although most products could be sold through catalogs or the Internet, some more readily lend themselves to this form of retailing. Insurance, credit cards, magazines, books, clothing, audiocassette tapes and CDs, toys, and gardening supplies are frequently sold to older adults through direct marketing (McDonald).

The products most likely to be sold to older adults through direct marketing are not widely distributed. In other words, a product such as paper towels would seldom be sold by direct marketing because it is readily available in outlets ranging from grocery stores to discount and drug stores. Obviously, most consumers would not want to wait for this type of product to be shipped when they could easily purchase it at a local store. On the other hand, supplements designed to help keep older adults' bodies more flexible or tools to assist with a hobby such as musical instrument tuning and repair can be more effectively sold through direct marketing. To reduce the risk to consumers who are purchasing goods they cannot see or touch, unconditional guarantees are a standard business practice in the direct marketing industry (Katzenstein and Sachs).

Convenient shopping and special promotions

Older adults tend to be quality-conscious, preferring a few high-quality items rather than a larger number of lower-quality ones. In addition, they look for added comfort. For most, the ski jacket that costs an extra fifty dollars but keeps them dry and warm is worth the higher price. Like most other consumers, they want hassle-free shopping and do not like long checkout lines. Safe and convenient shopping locations are especially important to older consumers. In fact, housing that attracts older adults is often located close to grocery stores and shopping malls.

Some retailers have special promotions designed to attract older people into their stores. Some may offer special delivery services, and others may offer senior citizen days or open houses just for them and their caregivers. Others offer senior citizen discounts and special services such as free giftwrapping. However, some older adults reject these discounts as stigmatizing and damaging to their self-image. Retailers and marketers cannot assume that senior discounts will appeal to all older adults.

Health care, cosmetics, and personal care products and services

Older adults are targeted for health products and services that are less likely to be marketed to younger consumers and that may be designed to assist them in retaining a youthful appearance. These include products such as pharmaceuticals, and services such as eye and ear surgery as well as cosmetic surgery. The "fountain of youth" is often stressed in personal care products. Hairpieces and hair dyes, creams designed to make the skin look younger, and even outpatient cosmetic surgery are available for both men and women who want to "look as young as they feel."

Retailers and marketers promote health products specifically designed to treat illnesses that most often affect older adults. These promotions and products offer treatments, remedies, and therapies for afflictions such as arthritis, fibromyalgia, eye and ear afflictions, Parkinson's disease, Alzheimer's disease, diabetes, and osteoporosis. Those suffering from these and other functional disorders may require special diets and adaptive equipment. Adaptive devices such as wheelchairs, walkers, and beds, as well as monitors of blood pressure and sugar levels, are promoted to older adults. Other products targeted to older adults include vitamins and nutritional supplements, such as high protein drinks and prescription and over-the-counter drugs. Older adults are also targeted for specific types of insurance focused on health issues such as long-term care insurance and insurance for specific illnesses such as cancer.

Caregiver and grandparent roles

Older adults often find themselves in the role of caregiver—caring for a spouse, a friend, or a parent. Caregivers are targeted by marketers and retailers for products designed to make this role easier. Included are adaptive devices such as a ramp or stair lift that takes the place of steps or stairs. Also promoted to the caregiver are home security systems and emergency response systems that automatically notify authorities in case of a medical or fire emergency. Smaller items include tape to secure carpets and rugs, and throw rugs designed not to slip on floor surfaces.

Products and services are also targeted to older people as the grandparents/caregivers of young people. These include toys—often expensive ones—designed for the doting grandparent to give to a grandchild, as well as investments such as a college education for the grandchild. Some prospective grandmothers are even given baby showers. Cribs, strollers, books and videotapes, computer games and videogames, safety gates for stairs, and children's apparel are often marketed and sold to older adults to be given as gifts. Some retailers estimate that 30 percent of all sales of children's products are to grandparents (Jeffrey and Collins). In addition, many older adults provide childcare for grandchildren and other young people—thus, another reason to purchase such products.

Entertainment and educational activities

Older adults are the targets of travel promotions such as special tour packages and transportation offers, which often include plane, train, and bus discounts. Even cruises are designed to accommodate older adults' needs. Hobbies that older adults are likely to engage in, such as woodworking, gardening, cooking, and handicrafts, are promoted (Schofield-Tomschin and Littrell). Entertainment centers, such as the one located in Branson, Missouri, provide celebrity entertainment specifically marketed to older adults. However, the movie and television industries do not target older adults. The movie industry targets individuals between the ages of eighteen and forty-nine. Some observers consider older adults a missed market.

In addition to entertainment activities, some older adults seek educational opportunities. They often combine travel, entertainment, and educational activities. To meet these needs, a nonprofit organization called Elderhostel was founded in 1975. Elderhostel organizes learning activities for older people and offers programs throughout the world. These are often held on college and university campuses during the summer or vacation times. Courses focus on a large variety of subject matter from astronomy to English literature.

In addition to the Elderhostel movement, colleges and universities target older adults as consumers of special learning opportunities. Learning is promoted as a lifelong activity, with workshops and courses targeted to older adults. For example, in May of 2000, the governor of Wisconsin signed a bill allowing free college attendance to those sixty and older. Thus, older adults can attend classes at schools in the University of Wisconsin system and in the Wisconsin

Technical College system, provided there is space available.

Older adults as investors

The financial industry often targets older adults as consumers of mutual funds, annuities, estate planning, and long-term care insurance. Many older adults have benefited from the appreciated value of stocks and mutual funds as the world's stock markets have prospered throughout the 1990s, and are looking for ways to invest their money. Thus, the older adult population has become the perfect market for retailers of financial products.

Housing and home modifications

With the majority of older adults staying in their single-family home for at least ten years after retirement, home modifications are promoted to them. These include sit-to-work areas in the kitchen, adjustable-height work surfaces, single-lever faucet control, bathroom grab bars, movable shower heads, beds that can easily be adjusted at the touch of a button, and door knobs and light switches that require little hand dexterity.

Communities, often with residential living arrangements such as retirement apartments, have been designed and marketed specifically to older adults. The retail housing industry offers many alternatives to older adults, including independent living, assisted living, and nursing homes. Services such as housekeeping, meal preparation, transportation, and home maintenance may be included. These facilities are promoted in magazines, newspapers, and radio and television advertisements as well as Internet sites. Most of these advertisements invite the older consumer to live luxuriously by using promotional phrases such as "spectacular community center," "stimulating activities and outings" and "spacious one- and two-bedroom apartment-homes."

Ethical issues

Although most retailers and marketers are honest, a few unethical ones target older adults. Schemes such as free gift and get-rich-quick offers, fraudulent travel awards, and sweepstakes can plague older adults. Other problems come from deceptive advertisers, telemarketers, and door-to-door sellers who prey on older people whom they may believe to be isolated and lonely. Although any product or service can be sold in an unethical manner, those most often associated with unethical promotions to older adults, including hearing aids, insurance, home improvements and repairs, investments, medical devices and cures, and recreational property such as time-shares or membership camping.

Shopping by mail can also be a problem for older adults. In fact, the number one consumer complaint in the United States is mail order problems. Although there are many reputable firms, there are some that overprice and misrepresent their products and services. In addition, telemarketing fraud aimed at older adults has been a growing problem in both the United States and Canada. The U.S. Justice Department estimates telemarketing fraud is costing victims $40 billion a year (Wisconsin Department of Agriculture, Trade, and Consumer Protection).

Some unethical retailers and marketers specifically target older adults because, compared to younger adults, they are less likely to report unethical practices for fear they will be viewed as incompetent to handle their own affairs. However, federal and state rules and laws help to protect consumers. At the federal level, the Federal Trade Commission has rules obligating retailers to be ethical in advertising and to have adequate quantities of sale items in stock. At the state level, states such as Wisconsin have enacted legislation that stipulates additional fines and penalties for those who specifically take advantage of older persons. Wisconsin law (sec.100.264, Stats) allows courts to impose additional fines of up to ten thousand dollars for violations of consumer laws. This law includes violations related to a number of different consumer problems targeted at older adults, such as false advertising, home improvement schemes, mail order and telecommunications fraud, and prizes that require purchases (Wisconsin Department of Agriculture, Trade, and Consumer Protection).

Retailers as employers of older persons

Retailers often employ older people who wish to work part-time or full-time in positions ranging from cashier to management. The discount firm Wal-Mart employs older adults as greeters to welcome customers into its stores. Other retailers actively recruit older workers, who often bring experience, maturity, and a good work ethic to the retail establishment.

Conclusion

Overall, older adults make up a dynamic market that will be increasingly targeted by retailers and marketers as their population keeps growing. The roles of older adults within the retail marketplace will continue to change as the ways in which older people are perceived change. Stereotypical views of older adults as incapable of change, ill, and controlled by routine are giving way to the perception that older adults seek new experiences and personal challenges. Retailers and marketers will need to develop new marketing and retailing techniques to meet the needs of this market. The older market will probably be divided in different ways, and new categories of goods and services will likely be developed to meet the needs of older adults. This market will probably be segmented in more specific ways based on lifestyle, value orientations, and demographic factors such as income and educational level. These efforts to further segment the older market will help retailers to sell, and marketers to create and promote, new products and services to meet the needs of older adults.

CYNTHIA R. JASPER

See also CONSUMER PROTECTION; CONSUMPTION AND AGE.

BIBLIOGRAPHY

BIVENS, J. "Retailers Slow to Target Older Consumers: Failure to Understand 50+ Customers Hampers Marketing Efforts." *Chain Store Age Executive* 64, no. 8 (1988): 79–82.

BONVISSUTO, K. "Net Latest Snare for Senior Scams." *Crain's Cleveland Business* 22, no. 31 (2001): 17.

BRANDT, J. "Housing and Community Preferences: Will They Change in Retirement?" *Family Economics Review* 2, no. 2 (1989): 7–11.

BROWN, D. "Home Design for the Golden Years." *The Saturday Evening Post* May/June (2000): 18.

HARRISON, B. "Spending Patterns of Older Persons Revealed in Expenditure Survey." *Monthly Labor Review* 109, issue 10 (October 1986): 15–17.

HENDERSON, C. "Today's Affluent Oldsters: Marketers See Gold in Gray." *The Futurist* 32, issue 8 (November 1998): 19–23.

JEFFREY, N., and COLLINS, S. "The Grandparent Industry: Special Camps. How-to Videos. Whoever Thought Grandparenting Could Get So Complicated?" *Wall Street Journal* November 2, 2001, pp. W1–W14.

KATZENSTEIN, H., and SACHS, W. *Direct Marketing* 2d ed. New York: Macmillan, 1992.

LEE, J., and SOBERON-FERRER, H. "An Empirical Analysis of Elderly Consumers' Complaining Behavior." *Family and Consumer Sciences Research Journal* 91 (March 1999): 341–371.

LEVANTHAL, R. "Aging Consumers and Their Effects on the Marketplace." *Journal of Consumer Marketing* 14, no. 4–5 (1997): 276–282.

LEVY, M., and WEITZ, B. A. *Retailing Management* 3d ed. Boston: Irwin/McGraw-Hill, 1998.

LUMPKIN, J., and HITE, R. "Retailers' Offerings and Elderly Consumers' Needs: Do Retailers Understand the Elderly?" *Journal of Business Research* 16 (1988): 313–326.

McCONNEL, C., and DELJAVAN, F. "Consumption Patterns of the Retired Household." *Journal of Gerontology* 38, no. 4 (1983): 480–490.

McDONALD, W. *Direct Marketing—An Integrated Approach.* Boston: Irwin McGraw-Hill, 1998.

McMELLON, C., and SCHIFFMAN, L. "Cybersenior Research: A Practical Approach to Data Collection." *Journal of Interactive Marketing* 15, no. 4 (2001): 47–55.

MILLER, N., and KIN, S. "The Importance of Older Consumers to Small Business Survival: Evidence from Rural Iowa." *Journal of Small Business Management* 37, no. 4 (1999): 1–15.

MOEHRLE, T. "Expenditure Patterns of the Elderly: Workers and Nonworkers." *Monthly Labor Review* 113 (May 1990): 34–41.

"Over 50 and Misunderstood." *Sales and Marketing Management* 140 July (1988): 19.

RUBIN, R. M., and NIESWIADOMY, M. L. "Expenditure Patterns of Retired and Nonretired Persons." *Monthly Labor Review* 117 (April 1994): 10–21.

RUBIN, R. M., and NIESWIADOMY, M. L. *Expenditures of Older Americans* Westport, Conn.: Praeger, 1997.

SCHIFFMAN, L., and SHERMAN, E. "Value Orientations of New-Age Elderly: The Coming of an Ageless Market." *Journal of Business Research* 22 (1991): 187–194.

SCHOFIELD-TOMSCHIN, S., and LITTRELL, M. A. "Textile Handcraft Guild Participation: A Conduit to Successful Aging." *Clothing and Textile Research Journal* 19, no. 2 (2001): 41–51.

SWARTZ, L. "Marketing to Maturity." *Franchising World* 31, no. 6 (1999): 47–50.

TEPPER, K. "The Role of Labeling Processes in Elderly Consumer's Responses to Age Segmentation Cues." *Journal of Consumer Research* 20, no. 4 March (1994): 503–519.

Wisconsin Department of Agriculture, Trade and Consumer Protection. *Preventing Senior Citizens Ripoffs*. Madison, Wisc.: Bureau of Consumer Protection, Department of Agriculture, Trade and Consumer Protection, 2000.

RETIREE HEALTH INSURANCE

See RETIREMENT, EARLY RETIREMENT INCENTIVES

RETIREMENT AGE

See PENSIONS, HISTORY; RETIREMENT, EARLY RETIREMENT INCENTIVES

RETIREMENT COMMUNITIES

Retirement communities are age-homogeneous living environments for older persons, almost all of whom are retired. The communities usually have defined boundaries, and often have age restrictions. Retirement communities come in many varieties and sizes, and no one type fits all older adults. The variety occurs because older Americans are a heterogeneous population, and those who choose living in retirement communities represent a broad spectrum of older Americans. How can one classify the variety of communities? One major axis is a planning criterion: Was the community planned or unplanned?

Planned retirement communities include: Leisure Oriented Retirement Communities (LORCs); Continuing Care Retirement Communities (CCRCs) and various kinds of Public Housing (PH). Unplanned retirement communities are Naturally Occurring Retirement Communities (NORCs).

Within these types of retirement communities there are other major defining characteristics. A prime characteristic is the cost of buying or renting a dwelling unit. Some retirement communities such as public housing have residents of low or moderate income, while at the other end of the income and asset scale are half-million-dollar homes for affluent elderly persons. The economic level of a retirement community will determine the kind of housing, the quality of the building and facilities, and the services and amenities that may be available to the residents. Thus retirement communities vary from a modest mo-

bile home to a luxurious five-bedroom house with a three-car garage and a view of a golf course. Obviously one must be specific when one generalizes about retirement communities in contemporary America.

There are some extremely large retirement communities in the Sun Belt that have upwards of forty thousand residents. These large communities are broken down into neighborhoods to give more of a small-town experience. The large communities contain almost all the facilities needed by most residents—shopping, banking, medical facilities, recreational areas, and more so that one's needs can be met in the immediate community. It is a safe and protected lifestyle. Other retirement communities are smaller in size and are adjacent to towns or cities, or are in rural areas where residents must leave their campuses for many of their needs. However, retirees in such settings may have the advantage of a feeling of "closeness" to their fellow residents.

Planned retirement communities

Leisure-oriented Retirement Communities (LORCs) emphasize the provision of the opportunities, services, and facilities to pursue a wide variety of leisure activities. A great deal of personal support may be found in the LORCs, but supportive activities tend to be informal. Gerontologists have been studying these kinds of communities for over a half century. The early communities were often affiliated with fraternal or religious organizations and unions, and usually provided low-cost housing and activities for the residents, who were often members of the sponsoring organization. Around 1960 there was a sudden spurt in the development of LORCs as a result of changing attitudes toward retirement and an increase in the number of healthy older persons with adequate income to pursue an active lifestyle.

Entrepreneurial developers began to establish LORCs in the Sun Belt states in the 1960s. More luxurious, "club-like" environments had facilities that were designed to encourage and enhance leisure pursuits. Gradually there was a shift from modest-priced housing for retirees to luxury homes. This has resulted in the creation of two broad types of LORCs: those for lower income levels that provide low cost housing and a limited range of activities, and those for affluent residents that have a rich program of activities, services, and programs. Some of the more afflu-

RETIREMENT COMMUNITIES   1187

ent communities may have multiple golf courses, a large auditorium to attract celebrity entertainers, and so forth.

As residents have aged in all kinds of communities, there has been an increasing awareness among both residents and developers that attention must be paid to the health and physical needs of residents who are aging in place.

Another important trend among the planned retirement communities are the development of "life-care retirement communities" and "continuing care retirement communities" (CCRCs). Both the for-profit and nonprofit segments of the industry have moved into development of this kind of retirement community. The early forms of life care communities were denominational in origin and were planned to care for specific groups of individuals. The life care aspect usually required that the resident give a large percentage of his or her assets to the community for housing and life care.

As CCRCs developed and spread, more flexible arrangements have developed. Residents pay a specified entrance fee and a monthly fee, with a variety of arrangements as to whether some of the entrance fee is recovered when the person dies. The idea governing CCRCs was a self-insured health care component. The CCRC receives revenues in advance of the services required, and the resident is assured housing and life care in a variety of settings and the availability of assisted living and nursing home care. Applicants for residency in CCRCs are required to provide a medical history, have a pre-entrance physical examination, and furnish detailed financial information about assets, liabilities, and income.

CCRCs are a form of long-term care insurance, with some states assigning regulatory authority to the State Department of Insurance. The CCRC business has become more sophisticated and tries to predict long-term costs accurately. Thus there is a need to have a rather stringent health and economic criteria to avoid financial and service delivery problems. Acturial predictions must be carefully utilized in order to assure both solvency and the guarantee of housing and long-term care if it is required.

"Unplanned" communities

An overlooked type of retirement communities is the most prevalent: Naturally Occurring Retirement Communities (NORCS). Hunt and others (1994) offer three reasons why such communities tend to be neglected: they are not planned or designed; there are no age restrictions; and they are not advertised as retirement communities by the residents, owners, or managers. NORCS may be in a city, a small town, or a rural area. They can be apartment complexes, a changing neighborhood, or a vacation area. A pressing problem facing NORCs and other communities without some form of assisted living is how to accommodate the changing needs of the residents as they age in place.

Migration patterns

Retirement communities, particularly those in the Sun Belt states, have a considerable number of residents who are called "snowbirds": residents who come to a warmer climate during the winter and then move back to a cooler climate in spring and summer, or become traveling retirees. The snowbird phenomenon includes as many as half of the residents in some communities. Generally the higher the income level of a community the larger the number of snowbirds. Another trend that has been observed is that as persons become older they are less likely to migrate seasonally. Some residents find the annual treks south and north too difficult and they tend to age in place in a warmer climate. Snowbirds also find that as they become older their roots become deeper in a retirement community, and the annual migration home to the cold is less attractive.

Statistics on retirement communities

Statistics about all the various kinds of retirement communities are not precise because of the diversity of sponsorship, geographical spread, and the types of housing provided. However, the following are some statistics that are approximate and provide benchmarks for the retirement community market at the beginning of the twenty-first century.

The Department of Housing and Urban Development (HUD) is the only federal agency that gathers statistics on retirement communities that are part of the public housing programs. The HUD retirement communities are subsidized, rental communities that are organized under eight different federal programs. In 1998 there were approximately five million housing units that were HUD sponsored and approximately eleven million persons lived in all these projects. Approximately one-third of the households had elderly residents and thus about four million persons lived in this type of retirement community.

The American Association of Homes and Services for the Aging estimated that at the end of 1999 there were approximately 2100 CCRCs in the United States. If one assumes that each CCRC has about 350 residents, the number of older persons who lived in this kind of retirement community numbered about 735,000.

Assisted Living Facilities, a type of retirement community, vary considerably in size, services, and costs. In September 1999 the Assisted Living Federation of America offered a broad estimate that there were twenty to thirty thousand facilities in the United States. If one assumes the midpoint of the estimate and makes the additional assumption that there are about forty residents in each assisted living facility, then this kind of retirement community would house about one million residents.

The number of LORCs and the number of residents living in them are difficult to estimate because they are not licensed like CCRCs or Assisted Living Facilities. Thus there is no central statistical gathering organization—federal, state, or private—to provide estimates. A considerable proportion of LORCs are in unincorporated areas of the states, thus many residents of this kind of retirement community would be counted as rural dwellers, but have a somewhat urban lifestyle.

In November 1999 HUD published a detailed report on the housing conditions and needs of older Americans. The report to Congress was a special supplement to the American Housing Survey of 1995. The survey reported that approximately 6 percent of the elderly persons (sixty-two and older) lived in manufactured homes, mostly in rural areas. A considerable number of these elderly residents lived in retirement communities, and it is estimated they may constitute about one million persons.

Retirement communities in other countries

The United States has more retirement communities per capita than other countries. The reasons for this situation include availability of undeveloped land for communities, Sun Belt areas that are attractive, the wide acceptance of physical mobility, and a standard of living for many people that enables mobility and in some cases permits a second home in a retirement community.

Other countries have adapted to the demographic trends of an increased life expectancy, and to pension plans that enable older persons to retire and have an adequate income. Canada has some retirement communities in British Columbia, a province that includes areas with a milder climate than most of Canada. There is also a large seasonal migration of Canadians to retirement communities in warmer climates in the United States. Australia has a thriving retirement community industry in which retirees move to small communities located on the outskirts of the large cities. Retired Europeans who live in northern countries are often seasonal migrants who live in enclaves of fellow countrymen during the winter: e.g., Germans come to Spain, British to Portugal and so forth.

The political economy and retirement communities

Retirement communities are integrated in the governmental and economic systems and they shape the environment in which the communities are embedded. On the local level, the linkage between a retirement community and the adjacent city or surrounding country varies considerably. How are land use law and zoning regulations enforced? Does the retirement community have its own water and sewer system or does it use the services provided by a municipality or water/sewer district? Uncertainty and risk are involved in the development and operation of retirement communities. They do serve a broad spectrum of income levels, and retirement communities are also congruent with basic American values: thrift, self-reliance, independence, material comfort, and a mixture of freedom and conformity.

In both LORCs and CCRCs the residents expect the delivery of programs, services, activities, and the security that was promised. They may register complaints about the services and programs, and they do so. In CCRCs it is very difficult for residents to take their business elsewhere for they would lose some or all of their initial deposit. This lack of a genuine market force for the residents is one reason some states have created social control mechanisms to ensure the delivery of services, and to avoid the exploitation of older people. The residents lack of market "freedom" does not mean that the managers operate in social and economic environment devoid of risk and uncertainty. Looking to the future of retirement communities raises the important issue of how the baby boomer generation will be involved in retirement communities. The first cohort is now ten or fifteen years from traditional retirement. Baby boomers are not homogeneous and one must consider the variations in economic, political and social characteristics. However, when the baby boom generation retires, the small percentage that chooses to relocate will have a wide choice of retirement communities. New environments will probably be initiated and there will be a competitive situation in which particular communities will compete. A changing economic and political situation adds uncertainty to the level and stability of pension incomes. The behavior of the housing and equity markets also adds additional uncertainty to the housing choices and the future of retirement communities for the boomers.

The pros and cons of retirement communities

Although millions of older persons live in retirement communities of the various kinds described here, some people regard the lifestyle negatively. The development of the retirement community industry is controversial. Proponents and opponents of retirement communities point up the positive strengths and weaknesses of retirement communities. One of the most cogent analyses of both sides of the argument is found in Golant. Some of the positive aspects are that age-dense communities provide older residents with opportunities for friendship with persons of similar interests and backgrounds. Residents can create their own social worlds, and can offer help and companionship to each other. The residents approve overwhelmingly of the ordered and predictable setting and lifestyle, and the "village atmosphere." The many clubs and recreational facilities are the deciding factor for some. Other persons value the security of living in a "protected" environment. Older people who can no longer drive find the transportation facilities a crucial consideration.

Other seniors move to a location near their children but do not want to be a burden to their families. They value the services available in many retirement communities. Their families, in turn, have the assurance that there is immediate help for the older person in case of an emergency. Pressure from children is often the deciding factor in the decision to move to a retirement community.

Most persons, however, do not want to move to a retirement community. Some cannot bear the thought of moving away from their friends and familiar pattern of life. Others cannot face the disruption of moving from their home and downsizing. They cannot adapt to new circumstances but wait until the death of a spouse or a medical condition forces them to consider alternatives to their housing situation. Some older persons feel there is a stigma in living with other people of their age group. They consider it to be "healthier" to live in an age-heterogeneous community. Perhaps one explanation might be that they seek to deny their own aging.

On the negative side the critics argue that some persons object to the planned nature of the structure and the activities of the communities. Others view the communities as "geriatric ghettos," and think it is undesirable to live in a community without a mixture of ages. Persons who dislike retirement communities are suspicious of management and the idea that cliques or factions develop among the residents and influence the programs. Members of some ethnic and racial minorities may find living in a retirement community unacceptable because of the small representation of their population in these communities.

Streib has stated that the various forms of retirement communities are an expression of the pluralism in American society. Although many persons—both old and young—would not choose to live in age-homogeneous communities, other persons currently prefer them. And for the foreseeable future, many thousands will choose the kind of lifestyle and housing arrangements that the variety of retirement communities provides their residents.

GORDON F. STREIB

See also CONTINUING CARE RETIREMENT COMMUNITIES; HOUSING; LIVING ARRANGEMENTS; MIGRATION, GEOGRAPHIC MOBILITY, AND DISTRIBUTION.

BIBLIOGRAPHY

The Directory of Retirement Facilities, 1993. Baltimore: HIA, Inc., 1992.

FOLTS, W. E., and STEIB, G. F. "Leisure-oriented Retirement Communities." In *Housing and the Aging Population: Options for the New Century.* Edited by W. E. Folts and D. E. Yeatts. New York: Garland, 1994. Pages 121–144.

HUNT, M. E.; FELDT, A. G.; MARANS, R. W.; PASTALAN, L. A.; and VAKALO, K. L. *Retirement Communities: An American Original.* New York: Hawthorne Press, 1984.

HUNT, M. E.; MERRILL, J. L.; and GILKER, C. M. "Naturally Occurring Retirement Communities in Urban and Rural Settings." In *Housing and the Aging Population: Options for the New Century.* Edited by W. E. Folts and D. E. Yeatts. New York: Garland, 1994. Pages 107–120.

GOLANT, S. M. *Housing America's Elderly: Many Possibilities/Few Choices.* Newbury Park, Calif.: Sage, 1992. See chaps. 3, 4, and 11.

MANGUM, W. P. "Planned Housing for the Elderly Since 1950: History, Policies, and Practices." In *Housing and the Aging Population: Options for the New Century.* Edited by W. E. Folts and D. E. Yeatts. New York: Garland 1994. Pages 25–58.

NENNO, M. K. "Public Housing: A Pioneer in Housing Low Income Older Adults." In *Housing and the Aging Population: Options for the New Century.* Edited by W. E. Folts and D. E. Yeatts. New York: Garland, 1994. Pages 61–81.

OSGOOD, N. J. *Senior Settlers: Social Integration in Retirement Communities.* New York: Praeger, 1982.

PEARCE, B. W. *Senior Living Communities.* Baltimore: Johns Hopkins University Press, 1998.

SHERWOOD, S.; RUCHLIN, H. S.; SHERWOOD, C. C.; and MORRIS, S. A. *Continuing Care Retirement Communities.* Baltimore: Johns Hopkins University Press, 1997.

STREIB, G. F. "Retirement Communities: Linkages to the Locality, State, and Nation." *Journal of Applied Gerontology* 9 (1990): 405–419.

U.S. Department of Housing and Urban Development. *Housing Our Elders: A Report Card in the Housing Conditions and Needs of Elder Americans.* Washington, D.C.: Office of Policy and Development, 1999.

RETIREMENT, DECISION MAKING

Early literature on retirement focused almost exclusively on men. More recently, researchers have recognized that women may make the decision to retire somewhat differently from men due to differences in caregiving responsibilities, employment opportunities and cultural expectations. In addition to the economic and health factors, recognition of these differences reminded researchers that, in addition to economic and health factors, caregiving responsibilities and the desire to retire at the same time as a spouse can influence both men and women's decisions. Significant differences in the economic resources and care-giving responsibilities of older men and women can lead to differences in the timing of retirement and also to the adequacy of income in retirement.

Since World War II men have been retiring at earlier ages, while the trend in older women's work force participation has been upward. Between 1950 and 1999, the labor force participation of men fell from about 86 to 68 percent while women's participation increased from 25 to 50 percent. At ages 65 and over, men's participation declined even more, from 47 to 16 percent compared with a marginal decline from 10 to 9 percent for women. Most of the decline for men occurred before 1985 with fairly stable rates since then, while older women's work force participation has continued to increase.

Retirement trends have important implications for public policy. The age at which workers retire has an important impact on labor supply, affecting job prospects for younger workers as well as employers' access to experienced workers. The financial solvency of government retirement programs such as Social Security and Medicare are directly affected by retirement trends. Public policies and tax law regulating employer-based pensions, individual retirement accounts, and other savings vehicles are also impacted by trends in retirement. Thus, there is a public interest in the retirement decision-making process.

Defining retirement

To fully understand older men's and women's experience of retirement, it is necessary to define what the term *retirement* means. A commonly used definition is that retirement is an "age-related withdrawal from active working life." Of course, defining what constitutes an "active working life" is not so simple. Does it mean paid employment only? Should leaving employment because of job loss, disability, or caring for a sick family member constitute retirement? At what age does leaving an active work life constitute retirement?

Some researchers have tried to bypass these questions by simply allowing survey respondents to define themselves as either retired or not retired. The disadvantage of this approach is that the definition of *retired* will not be the same for everyone. Some people who are still working may consider themselves retired if they are receiving a pension from a previous job. Others who have been out of the labor force for many years to care for children and elderly relatives, or because they themselves are disabled, may not consider themselves retired even though they are well past the age when many people retire.

Different definitions of retirement lead to different conclusions about the retirement patterns of women and men. Defining retirement as "not working or looking for work" at specific ages always counts more women than men as retired at each age. However, if one looks at self-reported retirement, women are often less likely to be retired than men. The major source of difference is the nonmarket work of women, including caregiving responsibilities for children, parents, spouses, and other relatives, as well as housekeeping tasks culturally expected of women. For example, one study found that over 20 percent of women in their fifties and early sixties were not in the labor force due to reasons other than retirement, compared with only 8 percent of men. At the same time, more men than women considered themselves to be retired.

As there is no single best definition of retirement, it is appropriate to tailor the definition of retirement to whatever question is being asked. If one is interested in when workers decide to collect pensions and/or Social Security benefits, it is appropriate to treat retirement as an event. Another kind of research focuses on the economic and social well-being of retired people. In this case, retirement is considered to be a stage of life rather than an event. Most such research considers everyone who has reached a stated age, usually sixty-five, as retired, regardless of whether they continue to work. Less commonly, two or more criteria are combined. For example, only people over sixty-five who are not in the paid work force may be included in the retired population. Multiple definitions of retirement are useful in addressing specific questions about differences in men's and women's decisions about leaving the paid work force, and about

their economic well-being after the age when people's active working lives usually end.

What influences the decision to retire?

For an understanding of why workers retire when they do, it is necessary to follow people's work experiences as they approach and enter retirement. This is possible only with longitudinal surveys, in which the same people are interviewed over time. One commonly used source of this kind of information is the Health and Retirement Study (HRS), conducted by the University of Michigan, in which a sample of men and women between fifty-one and sixty-one years of age were interviewed in 1992 and then reinterviewed at two-year intervals. Much of the recent research on retirement relies on these data (information on the HRS is available on line at www.umich.edu/~hrswww/).

Longitudinal surveys have found that many workers do not go from full-time employment to not working at all, but rather to what some researchers have called *partial retirement* or *bridge jobs* which are part-time or short-term jobs. Part-time employment is particularly common among workers age sixty-five and older. Among workers age fifty-five to sixty-four, 83 percent work full-time; among workers age sixty-five and older, only 49 percent work full-time. An increase in workers aged sixty-five or older who have been at their current jobs less than one year is further evidence of the prevalence of bridge jobs. From 1987 to 1998, the proportion of workers age sixty-five and older who had been at their jobs less than one year increased from 10 percent to 16 percent. While some of these workers may be continuing their careers, albeit with different employers, it is likely that many are employed in bridge jobs.

There is evidence that women are more likely to go through this intermediate bridge stage of retirement. One study estimated that 40 percent of women (compared with 25 percent of men) hold a bridge job before retiring completely (see Quinn and Kosy, 1996). Defining partial retirement is again an issue. Because women are more likely to work part-time at any stage of life, they are more likely than men to be considered partially retired, even though they may not have reduced their work hours. However, when asked in surveys, more men than women described themselves as partially retired.

An added complication is that some people who are considered retired at one point in time may later return to work. Over 10 percent of women and 12 percent of men who were not working and considered themselves retired at the first HRS interview were employed two years later; an additional 1 to 2 percent were looking for work. An earlier study using a sample of workers who began receiving Social Security benefits in 1980 found that about 20 percent of both women and men were working when interviewed about two years later (see Iams 1986). Some of these workers may have been partially retired when they began receiving Social Security benefits, but others may have stopped working entirely and started working again when they found a good opportunity or felt they needed more income after they had stopped working.

A great deal of research on the factors that influence workers' decisions to retire has focused on the incentive effects of Social Security and employer-provided pensions. Economic theory posits that workers will decide whether an additional year of work adds enough to their retirement income to balance the loss of a year of retirement leisure. When a worker becomes eligible for a pension or Social Security, the added earnings from another year of work may seem less rewarding. Evidence on retirement timing shows that the peak age of retirement for both men and women is sixty-two, when workers first become eligible for a retired worker's benefit from Social Security. A second cluster forms at age sixty-five, when full benefits for many pensions, as well as Social Security, become available. Women are slightly less likely than men to retire at these peak ages. These results hold up whether using labor-force participation or self-definition as the measure of retirement.

Some workers can gain substantially higher Social Security or other pension benefits by continuing to work past these peak retirement ages. For women especially, determining whether continuing to work is advantageous can be complicated under Social Security rules. Women can only gain from additional work if Social Security benefits based on their own work records will exceed those from their status as wives or widows. Women who are married are entitled to either a benefit based on their own work record, or to a spouse benefit, which is equal to 50 percent of their husband's benefit. If their own benefit is at or above the level of the spouse benefit, they usually gain from additional work, especially if they have been employed for less than the thirty-five years used to calculate benefits.

Based on the Health and Retirement Study, researchers estimate that about two-thirds of women will receive a benefit based on their own work record. However, a widow or widower may receive 100 percent of the deceased spouse's benefit or a benefit based on their own work record, whichever is higher. Only 15 percent of these women had an earnings record equal to or higher than their husbands' earning record, and thus 85 percent of women will receive a widow's benefit based on their husband's earning record if they outlive their spouse. The situation of divorced women is more complicated. Women must have been married for at least ten consecutive years to the same husband to be eligible for dependent benefits. If eligible, they are entitled to benefits under the same rules as wives when their former husbands are still living, and as widows after their husbands have died.

For employer-sponsored pensions, there is considerable variation in the incentives to retire. Many pension plans depend on years of service and earnings averaged over a stated period of years. These *defined benefit* plans are commonly offered by government, unions, and large private employers. These plans can encourage early retirement by failing to adjust benefits upward if they are taken at older ages, or by not counting years worked beyond some maximum number in calculating benefits. One study estimated that one-quarter of the decline in men's labor-force participation between 1950 and 1985 could be explained by the extension of pension coverage (Samwick, 1998, cited in Quinn, 1999). Women are less likely than men to face such limits. In fact, because women often take time out of the labor force, many women need to work into their sixties and seventies to qualify for a pension.

However, employers are increasingly offering *defined contribution* pension plans, in which benefits are based on contributions made by employers and/or workers to an individual account. When the employee retires, benefits are calculated as the sum of all contributions plus interest, dividends, and capital gains (or losses). Between 1975 and 1997, the share of pension plan participants in defined contribution plans rose from 13 percent to 42 percent. Defined contribution plans do not appear to have the same disincentive effects as defined benefit plans. To the extent that defined contribution pensions continue to grow in popularity (relative to defined benefit plans), eligibility for private pensions will diminish as a factor affecting retirement decisions.

Health is another influence on the decision to retire for both women and men, but there is considerable dispute about its relative importance. Some health conditions clearly prevent work entirely, but many conditions, while making work more difficult, do not completely preclude it. For example, common aliments like arthritis may make older workers less employable long before they qualify for private or public disability benefits. In these cases, health status and the availability of retirement income may interact, decreasing the monetary gains from continuing employment while making work itself more burdensome and leisure more appealing. It has often been thought that health and disability problems at older ages primarily affect men in blue-collar jobs. However, some pink-collar jobs held by women, such as waitressing, practical nursing, and childcare, are also difficult for older people with even minor health problems.

The state of the economy has been shown to have an impact on men's retirement decisions, and it probably influences women as well. Much of the research on retirement decision-making was undertaken in the 1970s and 1980s, which saw periods of relatively high unemployment. Older workers who lose their jobs tend to remain unemployed longer than younger workers, and they are also much more likely than others their age to retire. Employers who are downsizing their workforces often offer special retirement incentives to their older and (generally most costly) workers. In periods of rapid growth, of course, new jobs are much easier to find for those who lose their jobs. When employers find it difficult to fill vacancies, they may actively recruit older workers who would not previously have been considered. Probably part of the reason that labor-force participation of workers over age fifty-five was increasing in the 1990s was due to economic growth and an increasing demand for workers of all ages.

Marital status and the retirement decisions of a spouse can also influence the timing of retirement. Some of the earliest research on women's retirement focused on unmarried women and tended to find few differences between these women and men. When researchers first began studying married women, they had to confront the possibility that couples might try to coordinate their retirement in order to enjoy leisure time together. Assuming that the husband was the primary earner, researchers expected the wife's retirement to be influenced by that of her husband. Considerable research has, in fact, shown such an effect. However, women who stayed at home to raise children and then began to work later are less likely to retire when their husbands do, and married women who will become entitled to their own pensions if they continue to work are also less likely to retire when their husbands do. Some research has shown that a wife's retirement affects when her husband retires.

Since women continue to be perceived as caregivers, the effect of the husband's health on the wife's retirement has also been investigated. Results on this issue have been mixed. Many researchers have found such an effect, but some have not. This kind of decision is probably more complex than it might first appear. There are two possibilities if a husband becomes ill or disabled: (1) the wife might quit work to care for her husband, or (2) she might continue to work and hire someone else to help with his care (as many men would do in case of a wife's poor health). The ages of the spouses when the health problem occurs, as well as the earnings potential of the healthy spouse, would be important considerations. An additional consideration would be the source of the family's health insurance—and whether the continued employment of the working spouse is necessary for continued insurance coverage. Workers who will not continue to be covered by health insurance if they should retire may be more likely to continue working.

Research on the effects of the poor health of parents and other family members is much less developed, partly due to data limitations. One recent study showed that women in their fifties who had a parent needing help with activities of daily living were more likely than others to leave the labor force. No such relationship was found for men who had a parent needing care.

Some parents have dependent children when they reach retirement age; with the trend toward later childbearing, this situation may become more common in the future. Few women have preschool children after they are in their fifties, but having school-age children is more common for these women. Parents must consider the cost of continuing to provide for these children into adulthood while still preparing for their own retirement. Having college-age dependent children has been shown to lead to delayed retirement for both women and men.

The most important influences on retirement vary considerably by race. Older African-

American and Hispanic men are more likely to be unemployed or out of the labor force than white men. Older African-American women have rates of labor-force participation similar to white women, but Hispanic women are more likely to be unemployed or out of the labor market than are white or African-American women. Both African-American and Hispanic men and women are more likely to be influenced by *push factors* such as involuntary loss of a job or poor health. African-American and Hispanic workers are also more likely to be concentrated in low-wage occupations that are physically demanding and/or lack pension coverage.

There are a number of trends that suggest that the age of retirement may rise in the future. Americans are healthier and living longer. The shift in the proportion of the population working in manufacturing (rather than in service occupations) makes working with minor health problems feasible for more workers. The growth of defined contribution pension plans that reward employees for working longer is also an important trend. The extension of the age of eligibility for full Social Security benefits to sixty-seven, as well as the elimination of retirement incentives (including changes in the earnings test and the delayed retirement credit), may be expected to increase the average age of retirement, but the effects are expected to be small.

The state of the labor market is likely to have the most important impact on retirement. It is widely anticipated that labor shortages will develop as the large baby-boom generation reaches retirement age. In that case, some companies may offer incentives to older workers to delay retirement. Others may create attractive part-time positions for which they will recruit older adults. This scenario might not materialize, however, either due to a prolonged recession or to more rapid immigration due to increased recruitment of foreign workers by companies.

Polls indicate that well over 60 percent of workers intend to continue working past normal retirement age, with well over half citing "quality of life" rather than economic necessity as their reason. It is unlikely that labor force participation will increase as dramatically as these responses imply. Health, inability to find work, or other personal reasons will probably intervene in many cases. Workers citing quality-of-life reasons for delaying retirement will probably not continue to work unless they find a job they will enjoy.

An increase in Americans' wealth is often cited as an important factor affecting the trend toward earlier retirement during the post—World War II period. Poverty among the elderly, though still high for some groups of women (and men), decreased markedly between 1959 and 2000. In 1959 the overall poverty rate for the elderly population was 35 percent, considerably higher than the rate for the whole population. In 1999 the poverty rate among the elderly was 9.7 percent, compared with an overall poverty rate of 13.3 percent. Most of the improvement in elderly poverty came in the first fifteen years of this period. By 1979, poverty among the older population had fallen to about 15 percent (17 percent for women). Since then, the decline has been much slower. Much of the improvement can be attributed to the increase in coverage and benefits made available through improvements in Social Security.

The economic status of women and men during retirement

There are important differences in the economic circumstances of women and men as well as in the retirement decision-making process. Women enter retirement with fewer resources than men. In 1998, the median income for an unmarried woman age sixty-five or older was $11,382, compared with $14,496 for an unmarried man and $30,176 for a household headed by a person age sixty-five or older. To a large extent, lower incomes among older women and minorities reflect disparities in pensions and other assets, with Social Security benefits partially narrowing the gap. Postretirement earnings are a significant source of income for some younger retirees, who will tend to lose this source of income as they grow older. Although retirement at a younger or older age can influence income in retirement, marital history, work history, health, and savings during younger years are the primary factors affecting retirement income.

Differences by race and gender in pension coverage and assets are particularly striking. In 1998, nearly half (49 percent) of white men age sixty-five and over had income from employer-sponsored pensions from either private sector or government jobs, while only 34 percent of African-American men and 26 percent of Hispanic men had pension income. Older women were even less likely to have pension income. Only 28 percent of white women, 21 percent of African-

American women, and 10 percent of Hispanic women had such income.

The size of pensions also varies markedly by race and gender. Among older women who do receive income from pensions, benefits are approximately half the size of men's pension benefits. There are also significant differences in the size of pensions by race and ethnicity.

Marital status is important not only because of the large gap between the income of couples and unmarried persons, but also because older women are much less likely to be married than older men. In 1998, 75 percent of men age sixty-five and older were married, compared with 43 percent of women. Because of their longer life expectancy and because men tend to be older than their wives, women are more likely than men to outlive their spouses and less likely to remarry as the pool of eligible partners shrinks.

The lower-paid jobs that women frequently hold are less likely to carry pensions and health insurance. While there has been some improvement in the number of women receiving pensions based on their own work records, women's access and participation in workplace pensions continue to lag behind men's. In the 1990s, women who were working full-time were enrolled in employer-provided pension plans at about the same rate as men, but many more women than men work at part-time jobs that do not provide pensions. Overall, more than 44 percent of women age forty-five to sixty-four were not participating in a pension plan from any employer (including former employers), compared with 36 percent of men. Because women have shorter and less lucrative careers, they will also continue to have smaller pensions than men. Furthermore, small accumulations in pension plans are typically cashed out either before or after retirement.

Women's shorter working lives and lower earnings contribute to a reduced ability to save for retirement. Women who spend time as unpaid family caregivers are at least partially dependent on the earnings of their husbands, and on how these earnings are translated into retirement income. Pensions that provide no survivor benefits or that give the survivor only a small portion of the worker's pension can lead to greatly reduced income for widows in retirement. If a couple is divorced, or if the husband dies before reaching retirement age, the wife is unlikely to be able to make up entirely for the loss of income and savings that follows divorce or widowhood.

Health problems can occur at any age for both women and men and may reduce savings, especially if health insurance has been inadequate. Problems of health, low-paying jobs, and periods of unemployment also contribute to the lower likelihood of pensions and savings for minorities, both women and men.

To what extent will retired women be better off in the future? The Social Security Administration's Modeling Income in the Near Term (MINT) model projects that poverty among older women will be as big a problem in 2020 as it was in 1991 when 12 percent of older women were living in poverty. This is partly due to the persistence of the wage gap and women's greater propensity to work part-time. It also reflects a prediction that more women will enter retirement divorced or never married. Poverty among older divorced women will remain high (22 percent) and poverty among never-married mothers will increase from 29 percent to 35 percent. Poverty rates among older people of color are also expected to remain high.

Public policy issues

At the beginning of the twenty-first century, issues related to retirement were receiving increased political attention. The number of people reaching the peak retirement years will increase rapidly early in the century as members of the baby boom generation reach their sixties. The number of very old people is also likely to grow due to expected longevity increases for both women and men. The changes that will be needed in the Social Security and Medicare systems to insure benefits for such a large retired population is the subject of heated public debate.

Feminist economists have pointed out that many proposed changes fail to consider that the majority of Social Security and Medicare beneficiaries are women, and that women are more dependent on these forms of social insurance than men. In 1998, for example, unmarried women age sixty-five and over received about half of their retirement income from Social Security. For 25 percent of unmarried retired women, Social Security was the only source of income. It is important for the system to give careful consideration to the importance of Social Security for this group.

Many proposed changes are likely to be especially harmful for women with modest incomes. Privatization schemes usually involve large reductions in regular Social Security benefits in the hope that private accounts will make up the difference; this is risky, however, especially for small accounts with high administrative costs. Plans that maintain the current benefit structure, while making smaller cuts, sometimes favor policies such as scaling back cost-of-living increases, which would be most harmful for the oldest of the old (predominately women). Other policies that are less harmful for women and other low earners include increasing the amount of earnings subject to the payroll tax or taxing Social Security benefits like other pensions. Even a small percentage cut in all benefits would be less harmful to women than many of the other proposals being discussed.

Women are more likely than men to time retirement based on family caregiving responsibilities. Although some older men perform unpaid caregiving for family members, older women are much more likely to "work" in retirement as caregivers to spouses, parents, or other relatives. Advocates for women contend that policies intended to raise the ages at which most people retire from paid employment should take the needs of unpaid caregivers into account.

Women and men experience retirement differently. These differences may lessen, but are not likely to disappear, in the future. Gains in women's retirement income resulting from longer careers are also expected to be offset by the number of women entering retirement as either divorced or never married. For the foreseeable future, therefore, issues of gender are likely to remain important for studying retirement timing and the economic status of retired persons.

LOIS SHAW
CATHERINE HILL

See also ECONOMIC WELL-BEING; EMPLOYMENT OF OLDER WORKERS; PENSIONS, PUBLIC PENSIONS; PENSIONS, HISTORY; PENSIONS, PLAN TYPES AND POLICY APPROACHES; RETIREMENT PLANNING; RETIREMENT, EARLY RETIREMENT INCENTIVES; RETIREMENT, PATTERNS; SAVINGS; SOCIAL SECURITY ADMINISTRATION; SOCIAL SECURITY, HISTORY AND OPERATIONS; SOCIAL SECURITY, LONG-TERM FINANCING AND REFORM; TAXATION.

BIBLIOGRAPHY

AARON, H. J., and REISCHAUER, R. D. *Countdown to Reform: The Great Social Security Debate.* New York: Century Foundation Press, 1998.

ARNOLD, R. D.; GRAETZ, M. J.; and MUNNEL, A. H., eds. *Framing the Social Security Debate: Values Politics and Economics.* Washington, D.C.: National Academy of Social Insurance, 1998.

BURTLESS, G., and QUINN, J. *Retirement Trends and Policies to Encourage Work Among Older Americans.* Boston, Mass.: Center for Retirement Research at Boston College, 2000.

FLIPPEN, C., and TIENDA, M. "Pathways to Retirement: Patterns of Labor Force Participation and Labor Market Exit Among the Pre-Retirement Population by Race, Hispanic Origin, and Sex." *Journal of Gerontology* 55B (2000): 14–27.

GUSTMAN, A. L.; MITCHELL, O. S.; and STEINMEIER, T. L. "Retirement Measure in the Health and Retirement Study." *The Journal of Human Resources* 30 (1995): 57–83.

HENRETTA, J. C.; O'RAND, A. M.; and CHAN, C. G. "Joint Role Investments and Synchronization of Retirement: A Sequential Approach to Couples' Retirement Timing." *Social Forces* 71 (1993): 981–1000.

IAMS, H. M. "Employment of Retired-Worker Women." *Social Security Bulletin* 49 (1986): 5–13.

JOHNSON, R. *The Gender Gap in Pension Wealth: Is Women's Progress in the Labor Market Equalizing Retirement Benefits?* Washington, D.C.: Urban Institute, 2000.

MISHEL, L.; BERNSTEIN, J.; and SCHMITT, J. *The State of Working America.* Ithaca, N.Y.: Cornell University Press, 2000.

MITCHELL, O. S.; LEVINE, P. B.; and PHILLIPS, J. W. *The Impact of Pay Inequality, Occupational Segregation, and Lifetime Work Experience on the Retirement Income of Women and Minorities.* Washington D.C.: AARP, 1999.

PARNES, H. S. "The Retirement Decision." In *The Older Worker.* Edited by Michael Borus, Herbert Parnes, Steven Sandell and Bert Seidman. Madison, Wisc.: Industrial Relations Research Association, 1988.

QUINN, J. F. *Retirement Patterns and Bridge Jobs in the 1990s.* Employee Benefit Research Institute, 1999.

QUINN, J. F., and KOZY, M. "The Role of Bridge Jobs in the Retirement Transition: Gender, Race, and Ethnicity." *The Gerontologist* 36 (1996): 363–372.

RIX, S. *Update on the Older Worker: 1998—Employment Gains Continue.* Washington, D.C.: AARP, 1999.

SHAW, L., and HILL, C. *The Gender Gap in Pension Coverage: What Does the Future Hold?* Washington, D.C.: Institute for Women's Policy Research 2001.

SMEEDING, T.; ESTES, C.; and GLASSE, L. *Social Security in the 21st Century: More than Deficits,*

Strengthening Security For Women. Washington, D.C.: Gerontological Society of America, 1999.

Social Security Administration. *Income of the Population 55 or Older: 1998*. Washington D.C.: Social Security Administration, 2000.

WEAVER, D. A. "The Work and Retirement Decisions of Older Women: A Literature Review." *Social Security Bulletin* 57 (1994): 3–24.

WIATROWSKI, W. "Changing Retirement Age: Ups and Downs." *Monthly Labor Review*. April 2001.

RETIREMENT: EARLY RETIREMENT INCENTIVES

Early retirement incentives (ERIs) are programs or characteristics of benefit plans that encourage older workers to retire before the normal retirement age. This statement raises a series of questions: What is the normal retirement age? What is retirement? Are these incentives permanent components of human resource policies or temporary windows of opportunity? Why do firms seek to encourage early retirement? This entry examines each of these questions and also considers the ERIs in public programs and government regulation of private policies that encourage early retirement.

Employer-provided pension plans

Pension plans are an integral component of human resource policies in many firms. Approximately half of the labor force is covered by a retirement plan on their job (Employee Benefit Research Institute). There are two basic types of pension plans: defined benefit plans and defined contribution plans (McGill et al.). In a defined benefit plan, the retirement benefit is based on a formula that typically specifies benefits based on retirement at a certain age as a function of final average earnings, years of service, and a generosity parameter. Reduced benefits are usually available at a younger age. The employer has the responsibility for paying the promised benefits. Therefore, the plan sponsor makes annual contributions to the pension fund, invests the plans' assets, and is required to purchase benefit insurance from the Pension Benefit Guaranty Corporation.

In defined contribution plans, the employer, the employee, or both contribute to individual accounts for each participant. The employee manages the account and makes all investment choices. The benefit is determined by the size of the account at retirement. Defined contribution plans include 401(k) plans, money purchase plans, and profit-sharing plans. Traditionally, defined benefit plans have been the dominant type of pension plan in the United States; however, since the mid-1970s there has been a major shift away from these plans and toward the increased utilization of defined contribution plans (Pension Benefit Guaranty Corporation).

Pension plans usually specify a "normal retirement age." In defined benefit plans, this is the age at which a worker can begin to receive pension benefits under the plan's benefit formula. If benefits are paid before this age, they typically are reduced by a factor that is a function of age and service. The normal retirement age is not the age at which a normal or average person retires, nor is it the age at which most people retire. Instead, the normal retirement age is the age at which a person qualifies for full or unreduced retirement benefits. In this discussion, "retirement" refers to workers leaving a particular company and does not mean that they completely leave the labor force, nor does it imply that the individual necessarily has substantially reduced his or her hours of work. For example, a person can retire from one job, start receiving a pension, and begin working full- or part-time for another employer (Quinn). Transition to a postcareer or bridge job is encouraged by ERIs because they provide an incentive for a person to leave a career job but not necessarily to leave the labor force.

Defined benefit plans. Defined benefit plans specify a retirement benefit that a worker will receive if he or she starts to draw a pension at the normal retirement age. While the most frequently used normal retirement age is sixty-five, many plan sponsors have a normal retirement age of sixty-two or sixty, and in some plans, workers can receive unreduced benefits after a specified length of service regardless of age—for example, thirty years of employment with the firm. Virtually all defined benefit plans also include early retirement ages, often as young as fifty or fifty-five. Individuals who start to receive retirement benefits before the normal retirement age have their annual benefits permanently reduced relative to the benefit they would receive at the normal retirement age.

The U.S. Bureau of Labor Statistics (1998, 1999) provides detailed information concerning important provisions of pension plans, including normal retirement ages, early retirement ages, and reduction factors for those who start to receive benefits prior to the normal retirement age. In most plans, the magnitude of the reduction in annual benefits for taking early retirement is less than the reduction required to set the actuarial present value of benefits beginning at the earlier age equal to the value of actuarial present benefits if they were started at the normal retirement age. This means that the present value (or discounted value) of benefits beginning at early retirement would exceed the present value of benefits beginning at normal retirement. This characteristic provides a subsidy to individuals who decide to take early retirement, and thus encourages retirement from the firm prior to the normal retirement age.

Another way of illustrating the early retirement incentive is to consider the annual gain in the value of actuarial present pension benefits (often called pension wealth) from working an additional year. In most defined benefit plans, the wealth value of pension benefits increases rapidly as a worker approaches the age of early retirement. The change in the wealth (or present) value of benefits is called the pension accrual. The pension accrual increases in absolute size and relative to annual earnings up until the age of early retirement. It rises with additional years of service and increases in annual earnings, and because the worker is getting closer to the time that he or she can begin to receive the pension benefit. The size of the pension accrual also depends on the firm's choice of pension characteristics.

After the worker reaches the age of eligibility for early retirement, the pension accrual stops increasing and actually begins to decline. This is because the worker can now retire and start receiving pension benefits, and because the penalties for early retirement are less than the actuarially fair reduction. Thus, an employee who keeps working will forgo a year of benefits. The decline in pension accruals represents a reduction in total compensation, that is, it is equivalent to taking a pay cut. The reduction in compensation, combined with access to retirement benefits, provides a clear incentive to employees to leave the firm prior to the normal retirement age (Kotlikoff and Wise, 1985). This is the basic early retirement incentive that is embedded in virtually all final-pay-defined benefit plans.

The economics of employer pensions shows that firms can influence retirement decisions through choice of a pension plan, setting the normal and early retirement ages, and selecting the magnitude of reductions in the early retirement benefit. The change in pension accruals as the worker approaches and passes the ages for early and normal retirement can be very large. For example, Kotlikoff and Wise (1989a) found a pension accrual in one plan of 150 percent of salary for a person working from age fifty-four to age fifty-five, the latter being the age of early retirement. After passing the age of early retirement, the accrual dropped sharply, and by age sixty the pension accrual was only 10 percent of salary. Thus, the total compensation from working (salary plus pension accrual) dropped from 2.5 times annual salary at age fifty-four to 1.1 times annual salary at age sixty. In other words, the value of working an additional year after age sixty was only half that of working an additional year after age fifty-four.

Empirical research shows that individuals respond to these incentives by retiring in greater numbers when they qualify for early retirement benefits (Quinn et al.; Kotlikoff and Wise, 1989b). These types of early retirement incentives are inherent in most traditional defined benefit plans. They provide strong encouragement for workers to leave the company at these ages, and workers respond to the retirement incentives. Companies seeking to provide ongoing incentives for workers to retire at specified ages prior to sixty-five can effectively achieve their objective by adopting a defined benefit plan with subsidized early retirement provisions.

Defined contribution plans. Pension accruals based on employer contributions to defined contribution plans are less variable with age and service. Most plans specify an employer contribution that is a fixed percentage of salary. However, in many 401(k) plans, employee contributions are voluntary and thus depend on the worker's decision to make annual contributions. Pension accounts in defined contribution plans grow because of these annual contributions and in response to returns on invested assets. There are no magic dates in which pension accruals spike up or drop sharply. In general, these plans provide actuarial equivalent benefits regardless of the age at which the benefits start or a lump sum is taken. Thus, defined contribution plans tend to be more age neutral in their retirement incentives and do not have ERIs. The dramatic growth in defined contribution plans means that fewer pension participants are covered by the ERIs that are part of most defined benefit plans.

Hybrid pension plans. During the 1990s an increasing number of large employers converted traditional defined benefit plans to cash balance plans and pension equity plans. These plans are technically defined benefit plans because the firm remains responsible for pension contributions and the management of the pension fund; however, they have many of the characteristics of defined contribution plans. The retirement benefit is specified as an account balance that grows with annual credits based on salary and returns to the pension account balance. Workers can leave the firm at any age and take the account balance with them. These hybrid plans do not contain the ERIs that are inherent in the traditional defined benefit plans (Clark and Schieber). In addition, managers at many of the firms that have converted their pensions from a traditional defined benefit plan to a hybrid plan give as one of the primary reasons for the change the desire to eliminate early retirement incentives (Clark and Munzenmaier; Brown et al., 2000). The trend toward increased use of these hybrid plans also means that fewer pension participants will be eligible for ERIs in the future.

Special window plans

Early retirement programs that are available to workers for a specified period of time are often called window plans. Such plans offer special terms for retirement, but the worker must accept the offer and retire by a certain date; the retirement window opens and then closes. These plans have taken many forms but are often linked with an existing defined benefit plan. For example, the plan might state that if the worker retires within the window, pension benefits will be calculated by adding three or five years to the worker's actual age, or by adding three or five years to the worker's years of service, or both. Obviously, retirement benefits will be higher under the terms of the window plan, thus providing the worker with an incentive to retire now rather than waiting. Window plans were widely used by large corporations in the 1980s and early 1990s in efforts to downsize their workforces. Switkes provides a detailed assessment of the effectiveness of window plans offered by the University of California.

Workers respond to these special retirement incentives by moving up their retirement date and leaving the firm sooner than they had planned. Firms typically introduce window plans when they are attempting to reduce the size of the labor force. By downsizing, firms reduce the cost of active workers; however, pension costs are increased. This may not be considered a problem if the pension is overfunded, so that new contributions are not required to support the cost of the window program. These plans are less cost effective if the company is trying to address imbalances in the age or skill mix of its workforce at the same time higher payments to retirees are coupled with additional wage payments to persons hired to replace the departing workers.

Companies that adopt early retirement window plans are usually large firms seeking to reduce the size of their labor force and, thus, their labor costs. These offers have to be generous enough to alter the retirement decisions of workers. One problem often associated with these plans is that high-quality workers (the ones the company would like to keep) are often the first to leave because they can take the ERI from their current firm and find employment with another company. Workers with fewer employment opportunities (lower-quality workers) may be less likely to accept the ERI. Because of this incentive, some organizations have attempted to target their window plans to certain divisions or workers with below-average pay.

Employer-provided retiree health insurance

A major factor influencing the retirement decision of many workers is the ability to purchase health insurance and the cost of this coverage. Medicare provides almost universal coverage to persons age sixty-five and over; however, individuals considering early retirement must be concerned with how to pay for their health care from retirement until age sixty-five. Workers who are covered by employer-provided health insurance while employed must include the cost of buying individual health insurance coverage if they retire. Comprehensive health coverage for a retiree and spouse is very expensive. The prospect of paying for health insurance until age sixty-five reduces the probability that older workers will take early retirement.

Beginning in the 1960s, many large companies adopted retiree health plans that allowed workers to remain in their former employer's health plan until age sixty-five, or, in many instances, for life. Employer-provided retiree health insurance should be considered an important ERI program. Limited evidence indicates that persons covered by retiree health plans are more likely to retire than other older workers (Currie and Madrian). These plans are often used in conjunction with pension plans to facilitate retirement (Clark et al.). The incidence of coverage by retiree health plans declined substantially during the 1990s in response to increases in medical costs, changes in accounting rules, and reductions in Medicare payments (U.S. Bureau of Labor Statistics, 1998).

Impact of ERIs

Early retirement incentives can be either permanent or temporary, part of an ongoing pension plan or a special offer to workers. In general, ERIs are adopted by firms seeking to reduce their labor forces by increasing retirements rather than resorting to layoffs. ERIs provide workers with monetary incentives to leave the firm. Evidence indicates that older employees respond to these incentives and retire earlier than they would without the ERI. The impact of ERIs on labor costs depends on the generosity of the incentive plan, whether all retiring workers are replaced or the workforce is actually reduced, and whether the organization is able to use monies in overfunded pensions to finance the ERI. Typically, wage and salary costs will decline; however, pension costs including the ERI will increase. The impact on the quality of remaining workers is less certain, and depends on which workers accept the ERI. Given the economic incentives, firms risk losing their best older workers. As a result, companies may attempt to target their ERIs.

ROBERT L. CLARK

See also PENSIONS, FINANCING AND REGULATIONS; PENSIONS, PLAN TYPES AND POLICY APPROACHES; RETIREMENT, DECISION MAKING; RETIREMENT PLANNING; RETIREMENT PLANNING PROGRAMS.

BIBLIOGRAPHY

BROWN, K.; GOODFELLOW, G.; HILL, T.; JOSS, R.; LUSS, R.; MILLER, L.; and SCHIEBER, S. *The Unfolding of a Predictable Surprise: A Comprehensive Analysis of the Shift from Traditional Pensions to Hybrid Plans.* Bethesda, Md.: Watson Wyatt Worldwide, 2000.

CLARK, R.; GHENT, L.; and HEADEN, A. "Retiree Health Insurance and Pension Coverage." *Journal of Gerontology* 49 (1994): S53–S62.

CLARK, R., and MUNZENMAIER, F. "Impact of Replacing a Defined Benefit Plan with a Defined Contribution or Cash Balance Plan." *North American Actuarial Journal* 5, no. 1 (January 2001): 32–56.

CLARK, R., and SCHIEBER, S. "Taking the Subsidy Out of Early Retirement: The Story Behind the Conversion to Hybrid Pensions." In *Innovations in Managing the Financial Risks of Retirement.* Edited by Olivia Mitchell, Zvi Bodie, Brett Hammond, and Steve Zeldes. Philadelphia: University of Pennsylvania Press, 2001.

CURRIE, J., and MADRIAN, B. "Health, Health Insurance and the Labor Market." In *Handbook of Labor Economics.* Edited by David Card and Orley Ashenfelter. Amsterdam: Elsevier Science, 1998.

Employee Benefit Research Institute. *EBRI Databook on Employee Benefits,* 4th ed. Washington, D.C.: EBRI, 1997.

KOTLIKOFF, L., and WISE, D. "Labor Compensation and the Structure of Private Pension Plans: Evidence for Contractual vs. Spot Labor Markets." In *Pensions, Labor, and Individual Choice.* Edited by D. Wise. Chicago: University of Chicago Press, 1985. Pages 55–85.

KOTLIKOFF, L., and WISE, D. "Employee Retirement and a Firm's Pension Plan." In *The Economics of Aging.* Edited by D. Wise. Chicago: University of Chicago Press, 1989. Pages 279–330.

KOTLIKOFF, L., and WISE, D. *The Wage Carrot and the Pension Stick.* Kalamazoo, Mich.: W. E. Upjohn Institute for Employment Research, 1989.

McGILL, D.; BROWN, K.; HALEY, J.; and SCHIEBER, S. *Fundamentals of Private Pensions,* 7th ed. Philadelphia: University of Pennsylvania Press, 1996.

Pension Benefit Guaranty Corporation. *Pension Insurance Data Book 1998.* Washington, D.C.: U.S. Government Printing Office, 1999.

QUINN, J. *Retirement Patterns and Bridge Jobs in the 1990s.* Employee Benefit Research Institute Issue Brief no. 206. Washington, D.C.: EBRI, 1999.

QUINN, J.; BURKHAUSER, R.; and MYERS, D. *Passing the Torch: The Influence of Economic Incentives on Work and Retirement.* Kalamazoo, Mich.: W. E. Upjohn Institute for Employment Research, 1990.

SWITKES, E. "The University of California Voluntary Early Retirement Incentive Programs." In *To Retire or Not? Faculty Retirement Policy in*

Higher Education. Edited by Robert Clark and Brett Hammond. Philadelphia: University of Pennsylvania Press, 2000.

U.S. Bureau of Labor Statistics. *Employee Benefits in Medium and Large Establishments, 1995.* Washington, D.C.: U.S. Government Printing Office, 1998.

U.S. Bureau of Labor Statistics. *Employee Benefits in Small Private Establishments, 1996.* Washington, D.C.: U.S. Government Printing Office, 1999.

RETIREMENT, PATTERNS

The pattern of retirement at the end of the work career is shaped less by aging per se than by institutional mechanisms that provide incentives and support structures for workers' exits from the labor force. The origins of retirement institutions across industrial societies have been traced to emergent economic and governmental conditions in the late nineteenth century. These institutions developed gradually until the mid-twentieth century, then rapidly over the next quarter-century, and are undergoing critical review and reorganization in the early twenty-first century. Factors driving these developments changed over time, and ranged from the politics of veterans' pensions to class politics in the context of economic downturns and globalization. The twenty-first-century reorganization of retirement and other welfare institutions is being motivated by population aging, the growing insecurity of financial and labor markets stemming from global economic restructuring, and the changing nature of the family. These changes raise questions regarding the future of retirement as a standardized and permanent age-related transition from an income status based on employment to one based on transfers and assets at the end of the work career.

The institutionalization of retirement

The earliest pensions in U.S. history emerged in both public and private contexts. In the public sector, Union Army veterans' pensions began benefiting northern white males in particular before 1900 (Skocpol). By 1900, thirty-five percent of white males age fifty-five to fifty-nine were receiving Civil War pensions (Costa). And while ill health and unemployment were factors in these retirement rates (Graebner), the availability of these pensions probably motivated their recipients' exits from the labor force. Other early pension schemes are traceable to the private sector, where they were developed by employers to control the age composition of their workforces and to ensure labor stability. The American Express Company initiated a pension plan in 1875 for incapacitated workers who had been with the firm for twenty years or more. And in 1884 the Baltimore and Ohio Railroad instituted a pension plan that, in many respects, anticipated the major structure of twentieth century pensions. It called for mandatory retirement at age sixty-five after a minimum of ten years' service. Age, years of service, and salary level were the elements of the benefit calculation.

The first three decades of the twentieth century brought a slow development of retirement plans although the number of workers covered by pensions, health insurance, profit-sharing, and other employee benefits grew steadily (Jacoby). Industrialization consisted of more than production lines; it included the development of personnel management and the growth of unionization, both of which would shape the boundaries of the regular work career with negotiated rule structures regulating hiring, promotion, wages, and income maintenance (including health insurance and retirement). Over time, these workplace regimes created age-structured work careers (Henretta).

The passage of the Social Security Act in 1935 stimulated the more rapid growth of pension plans by establishing minimum standards. Its setting of sixty-five as the age of eligibility eventually made that age the most common age for retiring (Costa). And, somewhat paradoxically, wage control policies during World War II further stimulated the development of more elaborate employee benefit packages (termed "the hidden payroll" by the U.S. Chambers of Commerce in 1947) to permit employers to compensate their most valued workers without violating wage limits. These highly valued workers constituted internal labor markets whose long-term commitments to their employers were shaped, in part, by back-loaded pension plans. Such plans encouraged long tenure but also presented strong incentives to retire by a specific age. Unions also negotiated or provided for these plans for their workers. Referred to as *defined benefit plans,* they were, in effect, earnings predictably derived from formulas linking age, years of service, and peak salary levels.

The institutionalization of retirement is best characterized as the regularized exit from the workforce when income changes from wages and salaries based on employment to public transfers like Social Security and private assets including employee pensions. In industrialized societies, retirement has become a universal transition among workers and their families. However, it has changed as economic fortunes have varied, the political climate has shifted, and the structural and demographic compositions of the workplace have been transformed. These changes are addressed below.

From early retirement to variable retirement

Economic prosperity followed by economic turndown in the post–World War II period led to changes in retirement patterns. By the end of the 1960s a trend toward early retirement emerged, especially among workers covered by private pensions in major manufacturing and related sectors. *Early retirement* meant that more and more workers began to voluntarily and permanently exit the labor force prior to Social Security eligibility, in large part because of eligibility for private pension benefits. Economic downturn and restructuring between the early 1970s and the early 1990s further accelerated early retirement, but in this period it was also motivated by incentive packages used by employers to trim their liabilities via plant closings and workforce downsizing (Hardy et al.). Two streams of early retirees developed by the 1980s, one representing the most privileged category of "pension elites" from professional, managerial, and skilled sectors and the other representing workers in declining industries whose early retirements were accelerated by employers' efforts to downsize and reorganize their production and distribution systems.

These economic cycles coincided with the growth in government regulation of pension plans beginning with the Employee Retirement Income Security Act (ERISA) in 1974 and extending through the Retirement Equity Act of 1984, and the Pension Protection Act and later amendments of ERISA in the 1990s. These legislative actions extended minimum standards of reporting, disclosure, vesting, and benefit management, and sought to regulate plan termination policies by holding employers liable for their "pension promises." These rising pension liabilities, coupled with growing market uncertainties, provoked employers to abandon the long-term

contracts implicit in back-loaded, defined benefit plans and to adopt new pension instruments. The rapid spread of these new instruments, called defined contribution plans, redesigned the pension landscape at the end of the twentieth century. *Defined contribution plans* are retirement accounts invested by workers in a mix of equity, bond, or money market funds that do not promise a specific benefit level. Workers are primarily responsible for contributions and the financial risks associated with different investment mixes. Employers have limited responsibility and do not always contribute on behalf of employees. The accounts are portable across jobs and can usually be borrowed against, under strict rules of repayment and penalty. Thus they are highly individualized and reflect a departure from the defined benefit plans, born in the nineteenth century, that standardized the work career and the exit from it.

The effect on retirement patterns of these more widely adopted plans is not well established. However, the trend toward early retirement has reversed (Quinn; O'Rand and Henretta). Four patterns appear to have emerged more strongly than at earlier times. Workers are leaving their major jobs later, although still before normal Social Security ages. More workers, especially in the public sector, are reducing their work hours rather than leaving the labor force completely, following what has come to be called "phased retirement." They are moving to post career jobs, sometimes referred to as "bridge jobs." And they are returning to work after retirement. Accordingly, retirement is increasingly less "crisp" as a life transition. Jan Mutchler and her colleagues report that as early as the mid-1980s a significant minority of men age fifty-five to seventy-four who were observed over twenty-eight months followed patterns characterized by repeated exits and entrances and spells of unemployment. These patterns appear to have increased over the 1990s (Herz).

The volatility of labor and financial markets in the 1990s and its direct bearing on the performance of defined contribution accounts and on workers' perceptions of economic security, are potentially important sources of the variability in retirement behaviors. Employers and employees are renegotiating the employment contract. The implicit "lifetime employment" model associated with industrialization and personnel policies over most of the twentieth century is being replaced with a more "contingent" model. Higher rates of job mobility, job displacement, and "retirements" follow. However, these retirements are increasingly less likely to be crisp and permanent. The growing responsibility of workers to manage their own retirements with less institutional support increases expectations of more diversity and heterogeneity in retirement behavior.

However, factors besides labor and financial markets probably also play important roles in these complex patterns (Kim and Moen). The first is that the workforce has become steadily more heterogeneous in its composition: more women and more minority groups participate in the labor market than during the peak period of voluntary early retirement. Women and ethnic minority workers are more likely to have less stable wage/salary histories, more job shifts, multiple spells of unemployment, and higher rates of contingent work. These workers are less likely to be covered by pensions, and when they are covered, they are more likely to be covered by defined contribution plans. There is evidence that these lower wage groups contribute proportionately less to their pensions and are more risk-averse in their choice of investment mix (Bajtelsmit and VanDerhei). In addition, these workers are less likely to be covered by retiree health insurance, another employee benefit that has influenced retirement patterns. Workers with this coverage tend to retire at higher rates. Trends beginning in the 1990s suggest that access to retiree health insurance is declining rapidly for all workers (U.S. Department of Labor) and may disappear for all but the most privileged labor sectors.

The changed demographic composition of the U.S. labor force has had implications for retirement patterns above and beyond the effects of differential access to employee benefits. Disparities in health over the life course allocate workers down different paths to retirement. Racial health disparities account significantly for pre-retirement labor force patterns. Black men and women are more likely to enter retirement via a disability pathway (as disability insurance recipients) or as previously unemployed (Flippen and Tienda). The concentration of Hispanic and African-American males in manual and blue-collar jobs with greater exposure to environmental hazards and occupational injury systematically selects them into disability categories prior to retirement eligibility (Hayward and Grady).

Finally, the recent trend toward increased active life expectancy, especially among white aging cohorts, may become a stronger force to further differentiate retirement behaviors. Active life expectancy is the average number of years of impairment-free life estimated for a population, based on the distribution of aged-based prevalence of functional impairment. Active life expectancy has increased across recent cohorts of those age sixty-five and older, meaning that the prevalence of functional impairments is occurring at later and later ages (Manton and Land), with a notable disparity in this trend between whites and Hispanics and African Americans (Hayward and Heron).

The improved health of current and future aging cohorts may have significant implications for retirement, especially in the context of an aging society. *Population aging* results from increased life expectancy and declining fertility, with fertility decline the more important factor. It is reflected in the increased ratio of older to younger population groups (e.g. in the ratio of those aged sixty-five and over to those younger or to those of working ages eighteen to sixty-four). Aging societies are confronted by the fiscal implications of these changing ratios. How can fewer workers support more retirees? The trend toward increased active life expectancy may in fact provide a solution to this problem. Healthier, older workers may choose to remain at work, and employers may choose to retain these workers in one fashion or another (e.g., through later retirement, phased retirement, or even post retirement contingent reemployment). The coincidence of increased active life expectancy with public policies that delay eligibility for Social Security to later ages and that eliminate earnings limits while collecting Social Security, and with private policies that place more savings responsibilities on workers, has the potential impact of diversifying retirement even more, with major subgroups of early permanent retirees, intermittent retirees, later retirees, and so on. Consequently, a dominant pattern such as early retirement may be supplanted by multiple patterns.

Gender and retirement

Gender has differentiated retirement behavior over the twentieth century, although women's and men's work histories have become more similar. The household division of labor and women's limited opportunities for pension acquisition based on their own employment resulted in the past in the prevalent tendencies of women to retire (1) earlier than men or jointly with their husbands; (2) as spouses, survivors (widows), divorced dependents, or welfare recipients (Supplemental Security Income recipients) whose employment histories do not qualify them for worker Social Security benefits; (3) with greater and increasing dependence on Social Security as income over retirement; and (4) at higher risk for poverty after retirement, especially following the death of a spouse and when reaching the oldest age categories.

Employer pensions and Social Security account for 80 percent of median incomes of retirement households (Clark and Quinn). However, the significant majority of retiree households with any employer pension income fall above the median total income of all households. Moreover, less than one-third of women over age sixty-five receive employer pensions, whereas nearly half of men over sixty-five receive pensions; women's pension benefit levels average about 60 percent of men's, mirroring preretirement wage ratios (O'Rand and Henretta). One consequence of this distribution of pension income across households and gender groups is women's greater dependence on social retirement benefits (i.e. Social Security). When husbands with pensions die, their pensions may not continue to support their survivors over the remainder of retirement. About one-third of husbands still do not elect joint-survivor options, which offer them the opportunity to reduce their initial benefits and spread them longer into the future to support their survivors (Smeeding). Accordingly, as widows age, their incomes from private pensions held by their deceased spouses (if they had them) decline.

Extensions of the Social Security Act since 1935 have slowly progressed to meet the needs of older women, beginning with widows in the 1939 extension and finally reaching divorced spouses in marriages that lasted ten years or more in the 1983 amendment. However, the system still places women at risk for poverty with its survivor benefit policies. Women tend to outlive men and survive an average of fifteen years as widows. Social Security benefit rules result in a significant reduction in benefits following the spouse's death, with women who have retired as workers rather than as dependent spouses often penalized more as widows. While this bias toward

traditional male breadwinner couples can be criticized as unfair, the benefit reductions to both groups of widows are nevertheless at odds with women's well-being, especially as out-of-pocket medical costs increase over the remainder of life and as other sources of income diminish (Smeeding).

Joint retirement.   One source of variability in women's retirement patterns now, and increasingly in the future, is their retirement to their own pensions and Social Security based on longer work careers over the life course. More than half of women between the ages of fifty-five and fifty-nine and nearly 40 percent of women in their early sixties were participating in the labor force by the late 1990s. Projections of future cohort participation patterns at these ages foretell significant increases in these rates (Bianchi). And, currently, women and men are about equally likely to participate in pension plans; approximately half of each group participates. Finally, approximately two-thirds of women currently retire as workers rather than as dependent spouses under Social Security (U.S. Social Security Administration). Accordingly, women's retirement as dependent spouses is decreasing, although the continuing gender-based wage and pension gaps will slow their retirement income parity with men.

These changes in the economic roles of women suggest that the dynamics of decision-making in retirement may be shifting in a direction that will produce even more heterogeneity in couples' retirement behaviors. Joint retirement may change from a process in which wives retire ahead of or with their husbands, based on their dependent statuses, to a more complex decision based on balancing independent opportunity sets and common preferences, especially within the context of the changing pension environment described earlier. Research on retirement of worker couples finds strong patterns of synchronization or joint exit among couples retiring between the 1970s and the 1990s (e.g., Henretta et al.; Gustman and Steinmeier; Blau). The studies also show that wives are more responsive to their spouses' exits. Yet, the most recent patterns reveal that wives' labor exits are also highly influenced by their own market characteristics, specifically their own earnings, health insurance coverage, and pension eligibility (Honig). The extent to which these characteristics will become more important in the retirement decisions of future cohorts is a matter of conjecture.

Solitary retirement. One final pattern of retirement with gender-related implications is solitary retirement. The growing proportions of never-married and divorced and unremarried persons entering retirement are changing the composition of the retired population. Historically, widowhood has been the predominant solitary status among retirees. However, the Social Security Administration has projected that by 2020 the widowhood rate will decline to 31 percent from 42 percent in 1991; less than half of women over age sixty-two (46 percent) will be married; and nearly one-fifth (19 percent) will be divorced, up from 6 percent in 1991. The likelihood of remarriage among women is lower than among men, and this disparity increases with age. Thus, among women, solitary retirement will include women without spouses and with fewer benefits from marriage, including disposable shared assets and social support. Eligibility for divorced spouse Social Security benefits does not provide adequate support against poverty, and poverty rates in the older population are highest among widowed, divorced, and never-married women (Smeeding).

The future of retirement

Population aging has proceeded faster in other advanced societies than in the United States, although the aging of the post–World War II baby boom cohorts is increasing the U.S. rate dramatically at the turn of the twenty-first century. Early retirement in Europe was a response primarily to public institutions erected to control the age composition of the labor force, making room for younger workers (Kohli et al.). Since the 1980s, however, the fiscal burden of these regimes has motivated even the most advanced welfare states (e.g., Sweden, Germany, the Netherlands) to develop flexible extensions of disability and unemployment compensation policies to manage high unemployment among younger age groups and to introduce more privatized pension schemes, including defined contribution accounts following the U.S. model, in order to ameliorate the crisis of public pension financing (Esping-Andersen).

Some scholars anchor the crisis of the welfare state primarily in the changing family and economic stagnation following global restructuring. Esping-Andersen argues that the welfare state was constructed on three institutional foundations: family reciprocity, market distribution, and state redistribution. Family reciprocity refers to the nonmonetary exchange of goods and services in families on which welfare programs have been predicated. The existence of unpaid domestic work by family members, especially wives and children, has always been a presumption of welfare policies. Social Security policies in the United States, described earlier, exemplify this taken-for-granted aspect of welfare policies. Except in the most socially democratic states like Sweden, the breadwinner (single wage earner) model has linked the labor market and the family directly to welfare programs on the basis of the industrial nuclear family with a gendered division of labor (Ginn et al.).

However, the market has changed: the decline in wages or jobs for men's and women's increased labor force participation has changed economic roles in the family; structural forces have increased the demand for female labor and decreased the demand for male labor. The family, in turn, also has changed: declines in fertility, delays in marriage, the increase in divorce, childbearing out of wedlock, and geographic mobility away from families of origin have transformed the "family reciprocity" system. In the absence of the family's capacity to absorb social risks related to the welfare of its members and of the labor market's capacity to sustain full employment, the three-legged stool of the welfare state is collapsing and impelling changes in family and labor policies, including retirement policies.

Alan Walker has argued further, and cogently, that the future of retirement institutions is integrally connected with the health status of aging populations: "If the health of workers is maintained then they will be willing and able to extend their working lives" (p. 14). Recent trends in increased active life expectancy in the United States and other countries raise hopes along these lines. However, health status over the life course is also supported by the three-legged stool of the welfare state. Health disparities begin early in the life course and become accentuated with differential exposures to life course hazards and health maintenance systems. In the United States, where health and economic disparities are among the highest among advanced countries, the market dominates health care over the life course and is available primarily through employment. Those outside the insured employment system are disadvantaged and at risk of ill health (Landerman et al.). The price of formal care over the life course—from premature births through nursing home care at the end of life—is rapidly increasing. In a world of diminishing informal support, the future of health maintenance and productive aging is less hopeful.

Health insurance systems are confronting crises of financing similar to those facing pension systems. Responses to these crises are familiar: increased privatization and healthcare rationing. Privatization shifts the system to the market, where efficiency criteria operate against universal health delivery and equal opportunity.

In short, interdependent demographic, market, and state forces have produced highly diverse life courses in advanced societies, including variable retirement patterns. The United States perhaps has the most variable retirement patterns because of stronger market and weaker state policies. However, all countries face the challenges of population aging, global markets, increased inequality, and family transformation that will require new views of the life course and new institutions to reconstruct it.

ANGELA M. O'RAND

See also EMPLOYEE RETIREMENT INCOME SECURITY ACT; EMPLOYMENT OF OLDER WORKERS; PENSIONS; POPULATION AGING; SOCIAL SECURITY; WELFARE STATE.

BIBLIOGRAPHY

BAJTELSMIT, V. L., and VANDERHEI, J. L. "Risk Aversion and Pension Investment Choices." In *Positioning Pensions for the Twenty First Century*. Edited by M. S. Gordon, O. S. Mitchell, and M. M. Twinney. Philadelphia: Pension Research Council, University of Pennsylvania, 1997. Pages 45–66.

BIANCHI, S. M. "Changing Economic Roles of Women and Men." In *State of the Union: America in the 1990s*. Vol. 1: *Economic Trends*. Edited by R. Farley. New York: Russell Sage Foundation, 1995.

BLAU, D. M. "The Labor Force Dynamics of Older Married Couples." *Journal of Labor Economics* 16 (1998): 595–629.

CLARK, R., and QUINN, J. F. *The Economic Status of the Elderly*. Medicare Brief no. 4. Washington, D.C.: National Academy of Social Insurance, 1999.

COSTA, D. *The Evolution of Retirement: An American Economic History, 1880–1990*. Chicago: University of Chicago Press, 1998.

ESPING-ANDERSEN, G. *Social Foundation of Postindustrial Economies*. New York: Oxford University Press, 1999.

FLIPPEN, C., and TIENDA, M. "Pathways to Retirement: Patterns of Labor Force Participation and Labor Market Exit Among the Pre-Retirement Population by Race, Hispanic Origin and Sex." *Journal of Gerontology-Social Sciences* 55B (2000): S14–S27.

GINN, J.; STREET, D.; and ARBER, S., eds. *Women, Work and Pensions: International Issues and Prospects*. Buckingham, U.K.: Open University Press, 2001.

GRAEBNER, W. *A History of Retirement: The Meaning and Function of an American Institution, 1885–1978*. New Haven, Conn.: Yale University Press, 1980.

GUSTMAN, A., and STEINMEIER, T. *Retirement in a Family Context: A Structural Model for Husbands and Wives*. National Bureau of Economic Research Working Paper no. 4629. Cambridge Mass.: NBER, 1994.

HARDY, M.; HAZELRIGG, L.; and QUADAGNO, J. *Ending a Career in the Auto Industry*. New York: Plenum, 1996.

HAYWARD, M. D., and GRADY, W. R. "Work and Retirement among a Cohort of Older Men in the United States, 1966–1983." *Demography* 27 (1990): 337–356.

HAYWARD, M. D., and HERON, M. "Racial Inequality in Active Life Expectancy Among Adult Americans." *Demography* 36 (1999): 77–91.

HENRETTA, J. C. "Uniformity and Diversity: Life Course Institutionalization and Late Life Work Exit." *Sociological Quarterly* 33 (1992): 265–279.

HENRETTA, J. C.; O'RAND, A. M.; and CHAN, C. "Joint Role Investments and Synchronization of Retirement: A Sequential Approach to Couples' Retirement Timing." *Social Forces* 71 (1993): 981–1000.

HERZ, D. "Work after Early Retirement: An Increasing Trend among Men." *Monthly Labor Review* 118 (1995): 3–9.

HONIG, M. "Married Women's Retirement Expectations: Do Pensions and Social Security Matter?" *American Economic Review Papers and Proceedings* 88 (1998): 202–206.

JACOBY, S. *Employing Bureaucracy: Managers, Unions and the Transformation of Work, 1900–1945*. New York: Columbia University Press, 1985.

KIM, J. E., and MOEN, P. "Moving into Retirement: Preparation and Transitions in Late Midlife." In *Handbook of Midlife Development*.

Edited by M. E. Lachman. New York: John Wiley and Sons, 2001. Pages 487–526.

KOHLI, M.; REIN, M.; GUILLEMARD, A. M.; and VAN GUSTEREN, H., eds. *Time for Retirement.* Cambridge, U.K.: Cambridge University Press, 1991.

LANDERMAN, L. R., et al. "Private Health Insurance Coverage and Disability Among Older Americans." *Journal of Gerontology-Social Sciences* 53B (1998): S258–S266.

MANTON, K. G., and LAND, K. C. "Active Life Expectancy Estimates for U.S. Elderly Population: Multidimensional Continuous Mixture Model of Functional Change Applied to Completed Cohorts, 1982 to 1996." *Demography* 37 (2000): 1–13.

MUTCHLER, J. E.; BURR, J. A.; PIENTA, A. M.; and MASSAGLI, M. P. "Pathways to Labor Force Exit: Work Transitions and Work Instability." *Journal of Gerontology-Social Sciences* 52B (1997): S4–S12.

O'RAND, A. M., and HENRETTA, J. C. *Age and Inequality: Diverse Pathways Through Later Life.* Boulder, Colo.: Westview Press, 1999.

QUINN, J. F. "Retirement Trends and Patterns in the 1990s: The End of an Era?" *Public Policy and Aging Report* 8 (1997): 10–15.

SKOCPOL, T. *Protecting Soldiers and Mothers: The Political Origins of Social Policy in the United States.* Cambridge Mass.: Belknap, 1992.

SMEEDING, T. M. "Social Security Reform: Improving Benefit Adequacy and Economic Security for Women." *Aging Studies Program Policy Brief no. 16.* Syracuse, N.Y.: Maxwell School of Citizenship and Public Affairs/Center for Policy Research, Syracuse University, 1999.

U.S. Department of Labor. *Retirement Benefits of American Workers: New Findings From the September 1994 Current Population Survey.* Washington, D.C.: U.S. Government Printing Office, 1995.

U.S. Social Security Administration. *Annual Statistical Supplement to the Social Security Bulletin.* Washington, D.C.: U.S. Government Printing Office, 2000.

WALKER, A. "The Future of Pensions and Retirement in Europe: Towards Productive Ageing." *Hallym International Journal of Aging* 1 (1999): 3–15.

RETIREMENT PLANNING

The vast majority of individuals and couples in the United States can look forward to their retirement—that period later in life when they are no longer working full-time and are supported by financial resources accumulated during their working years. The average retirement age in the United States, based on data from the 1998 Survey of Consumer Finances, is 62.7 years. At this age, in 1998, life expectancy in retirement for an unmarried male was 16.4 years; while for an unmarried female life expectancy at this age was 19.8 years; and for a married couple it was 23.9 years. This means that the typical American needs to be able to fund spending needs for about twenty years of retirement living. Since life expectancies are increasing with advances in medicine, younger generations will have even longer retirements to contemplate. The main implication of this is that longer life expectancies can represent an increase in the risk of a shortfall in financial resources, or in the risk of outliving one's resources. The risk of shortfall can be greatly reduced with proper financial planning.

The idea that it is never too early to begin planning for retirement is a reasonable one. For example, one should identify employer-provided retirement plans as part of the job selection process. Starting to plan while younger allows one to plan a long-term strategy that can be maintained and adjusted over time. In a world that is uncertain and volatile, retirement planning must be an ongoing process, with decisions made and reviewed as conditions and life circumstances change.

Retirement planning, broadly conceived, means preparing for one's retirement years, which could extend for two or more decades of later life. This includes consideration of issues such as long-term care and the provision of an estate to one's heirs. Planning for retirement comes down to a comparison of needs and resources. The main goal is to ensure that one is able to meet annual spending requirements as well as any one-time expenses that may arise. This is done by not only considering resources such as Social Security and defined benefit pension plans, but also considering personal savings. Defined benefit pensions, also known as formula-based pensions, are typically fixed annual payments based on years of service and salary level. Personal savings may include an individual retirement account (IRA) and 401(k), 403(b), or Keogh plans. Due to high administrative costs and maintenance, many companies have opted for, or converted to, defined contributions plans such as a 401(k). These plans allow an employee to make tax-deferred contributions through a payroll deduction. In some of these types of employer-provided plans, the employer may match some level of the employee's contributions, which provides a guaranteed return. However the investment assets selected or asset allocation must be decided, at least in part, by the employee. This places the responsibility on the employee to not only elect how to fund the account, but also to determine how the account will be invested—which may or may not be advantageous, depending on the individual level of investment knowledge.

Timing retirement

One factor that distinguishes retirement planning from other aspects of financial planning (such as risk management) is that the timing can be, in most cases, anticipated. While some individuals experience early retirements due to health reasons, the majority of Americans have some measure of control over retirement age. This provides an advantage for planning purposes, since a specific horizon is known for asset allocation. Further, it allows one to anticipate what other resources may be available. In fact, the timing of retirement is often related to the timing or availability of Social Security or any defined benefit pensions.

Social Security retirement benefits have gone through some changes, one of which is that the age of eligibility for full retirement benefits is scheduled to increase for most recent birth cohorts. As of 2001, an individual can elect to take a reduced benefit as early as age sixty-two. Thus, it is no surprise that the average retirement age is just over sixty-two. For anyone that retires prior to age sixty-two, there will be some period during which there is no Social Security benefit. This is certainly an issue that should be considered when choosing a retirement age.

Eligibility benefits from other defined benefit pensions adds an additional element to the timing issue, since these plans may lessen the financial impact of retiring prior to age sixty-two. Since eligibility is (as well as benefits from) typically based on years of service, an individual who was first covered by this type of plan in his or her twenties could be eligible for benefits at some point after age fifty. Some people might retire earlier as a result, while others might retire from their current careers but still work elsewhere.

Retirement adequacy

One's desired annual spending in retirement is a more ideal choice for determining annual needs in retirement. Some methods argue for use of an income replacement rate, but this assumes that a single percentage would work for a large number of households and individuals. Instead, a planner can help a client think through this situation. There are several ways this is done. One such approach, from economic theory, assumes that households seek to smooth consumption across changes in the life cycle and that ideal annual spending is equal to average annual income—taking into account issues such as taxes and interest rates. Another approach is more introspective. This method begins with an existing and comprehensive income and expenditure statement. This process involves examining each expense and determining how it might change in retirement. Examples might include a mortgage being paid off, children who become independent, or increasing health care costs. Additional considerations for retirement spending needs include ties to family, obligations to children and parents, whether to continue some type of employment, creative use of leisure time, and community service. What a person will do once retired is at least partly a question about identity and meaning, but financial implications will affect such decisions.

One should also try to anticipate the impact of taxes. Even though there are some tax advantages for retirement savings and Social Security benefits, taxes will still be owed on all tax-deferred assets as distributions are taken. This is important because spending estimates show how much after-tax income is required for a household. However, distributions from most retirement plans will face taxation when withdrawn and as such, one should consider what pretax amount should be withdrawn to provide the after-tax spending requirement.

Resources expected to continue in retirement, such as defined benefit pension plans and Social Security, are used to help meet desired annual spending needs. For many households, this would still mean that there is an annual spending gap, which represents the amount of one's desired annual spending not covered by continuing resources such as Social Security. The annual spending gap represents the amount of annual spending needs that is to be provided by investment proceeds and distributions from retirement savings. This gap is likely to be considerably higher for those who have enjoyed higher incomes throughout their working years. This is because higher income tends to indicate higher spending, and the income replacement rate of Social Security retirement benefits diminishes with higher levels of income. However regardless of a person's pre-retirement level of living, Social Security is not likely to be sufficient as a sole resource for retirement spending needs. This makes investing for retirement essential for all households.

The annual spending gap estimation can be complicated by several issues. Since the starting age for benefits such as pensions and Social Security may differ, there may be different stages of retirement where different resources are available. For example, a husband and wife may retire in different calendar years, resulting in more than one annual spending gap. Other situations where there might be multiple planning periods include retiring before Social Security benefits are available and working during the early retirement years. Each of these stages should be considered and accounted for by discounting the annual spending gap for each year, up to the day of retirement.

The determination of retirement planning adequacy can then be thought of as comparing the annual spending gap with income from investments accumulated during the pre-retirement years. This comparison can be done by comparing the total value of the annual spending gap for all retirement years, adjusting them downward to reflect the future compounding they would have during retirement. The appropriate discount rate would be the expected portfolio rate of return for investments during retirement, based on asset allocation. The expected value of investments should be based on historical returns for the asset types. Calculations should consider that the asset allocation is likely to change over time. While average returns are most appropriate, some planners may also include an estimate based on a more pessimistic return for those who would like to be prepared for the worst case. If expected investment levels are equal to or greater than the discounted annual spending gaps, then the current investment strategy is adequate.

In the event of inadequacy, there are two potential courses of action that can be taken to improve the situation. The first possibility is to increase investment contributions to the required levels. However, this is only possible if the investor has additional investment capital and is not currently maximizing tax-advantaged contributions to retirement savings. If tax-advantaged contributions are already at the maximum allowed levels, then the investor may also use non-tax-advantaged accounts. The second option would be to increase the aggressiveness of the portfolio, if prudent to do so. This could be accomplished by placing a higher percentage of the portfolio into equity investments. However, it is possible that a more aggressive portfolio might conflict with one's risk tolerance. It is prudent for most investors to consider enlisting the advice of a professional to explain the risks and make recommendations regarding portfolio strategy. Others may simply have a planner perform a retirement adequacy assessment to ensure that the retirement plan is on target.

A second approach to determining adequacy uses advances in simulation methods and is known as a *Monte Carlo* approach. Often, individuals perceive risk as the likelihood of goal achievement or failure. The Monte Carlo simulation determines the odds of success of a specific financial plan. Most simulations will use several inputs, including asset allocation, bequest motives, pension plans, and desired annual spending. One advantage of this program is an estimation of odds of success, which has direct meaning to an individual. Further, if the odds of success are too low for an individual to accept, changing different inputs can show how the odds can be improved. One such change may include changes in asset allocation. However, while the programs will generate asset allocations, it is still up to an investor to select appropriate assets that conform to the recommendations. Many individuals may choose to use a professional for this.

Both of these approaches to determining asset adequacy require information about expected retirement benefits. Fortunately, this information tends to be readily available. Individuals age twenty-five and older who participate in Social Security will periodically receive a Personal Earnings and Benefit Estimate Statement (PEBES). This statement provides the taxpayer with information about his or her retirement benefits based on retiring at the age of full benefit eligibility, about the maximum delayed benefit, and about the reduced benefit obtainable at age sixty-two. The Social Security website (www.ssa.gov) provides online estimators for retirement benefits. Similar types of statements or calculators are available for most defined benefit pensions. This allows an individual or household to consider expected benefits when making planning decisions.

Asset allocation

While several factors need to be considered for asset allocation, including risk tolerance, the investment horizon is a key factor. This is because of the *law of large numbers*. As it relates to investing, the law of large numbers states that the longer an asset is held, the more the average annualized return can be expected to behave like the historical average for that asset type. This means that, while in any given year the return may be positive or negative, on average it should earn a return close to the historical average. This is important since, in the long run, stocks outperform all other asset types and small stocks tend to have the highest average return. One caveat is that this concept assumes that one holds a portfolio that is representative of the data. That is to say that owning one stock is not necessarily sufficient to assume that it should perform the same as the overall market. The idea is that one has a well-diversified portfolio that mitigates or eliminates any company-specific risks. This can be easily accomplished through the use of mutual funds, especially funds that are broadly based. One example of such a portfolio might be an index mutual fund that is based on the Standard and Poor 500.

The risk tolerance of an individual is the amount of risk that one is willing to assume in investment choices. This may be thought of as being related to the proportion of wealth that one would be willing to place in riskier assets such as stocks. Many financial planners will use some subjective measure of risk tolerance based on hypothetical scenarios. Using results from these measures, the planner formulates investment recommendations. However, a good planner will not only consider the client's risk tolerance, but also more objective measures such as investment horizon (time until retirement).

A person's asset allocation choice will determine the composition of the investment portfolio, that is the allocation of portfolio shares to stocks, corporate and government bonds, and money market instruments. Since stocks outperform all other investments in the long run, younger investors saving for retirement can take advantage of the time that they have before retirement and invest more aggressively. Some would say that individuals with at least twelve years or more to retirement should consider a portfolio heavily weighted with equities. However, as retirement looms closer and the horizon grows shorter, an all-stock portfolio is no longer an optimal choice because the confidence that stocks will have a higher return in the shorter-term decreases. At that time, it becomes prudent to shift some of the equity to fixed-income securities such as bonds or bond mutual funds. This uses the fixed return on the bonds to offset the increased volatility of the equity holdings. Therefore, in early working years, investors should be more aggressive when saving for retirement, and as investors approach retirement (within ten years or so) they should become more conservative.

At retirement, investors can spend accumulated asset to purchase a life annuity. This insurance contract promises an annual or monthly payment for the rest of one's life in exchange for a lump sum payment. This eliminates the risk of outliving one's assets, since the payments would be assured for one's remaining life expectancy. There may be survivorship provisions as well in these contracts that provide income for surviving spouses or others. However, there is minimal control over the investment management of the annuity. Another potential disadvantage is that the annuity would not allow for advance payments which might be needed should any large one-time costs arise.

Other methods provide more control over assets. An alternative, the perpetuity approach, involves holding accumulated investments and using their proceeds for spending purposes. This gives the individual more control over distributions and investment management. However, without proper guidance, this approach increases the risk of outliving one's assets. Some combination of both approaches may be more ideal, but is not necessarily feasible for households without significant wealth. A choice between the two approaches must therefore often be made. This choice can be made by comparing the perceived risk of asset shortfalls with the perceived risk of having any need for large distributions. One other consideration is the perceived opportunity cost of reduced management control. While annuities greatly reduce the shortfall risk, and the perpetuity approach allows the distribution amount to be determined by the investor. Another factor influencing this choice may be the desire to leave a bequest to heirs. While annuities may provide for survivorship, the ability to leave assets to heirs is much simpler when assets remain in the estate.

During retirement, assuming one does not annuitize all wealth, asset allocation becomes essential. Assets must maintain a level of return that will be sufficient to avoid shortfall and, potentially, provide for a desired bequest. The retirement asset allocation needs to include some highly liquid investments, as well as ones that will provide a reasonable rate of return. The use of money market transaction accounts might be advantageous, rather than a checking account, since money market accounts usually provide a real rate of return slightly higher than a regular savings account. Use of laddered Certificates of Deposit (CDs) can be useful as well. The laddered approach is to purchase CDs of varying maturities so that they mature as they are needed. Since there are other assets available in an emergency, these CDs should typically be able to be held until maturity. The remaining portfolio should be well diversified to minimize risk. Again, mutual funds may be ideal for this situation, as they bring inherent diversification.

Using a professional

Having access to some level of retirement advice has become easier than it once was. The Certified Financial Planner (CFP) designation has become the symbol for a financial advisor; a CFP practitioner has passed a comprehensive exam covering all major financial planning topics and is bound by a code of ethics that is strongly enforced by the CFP Board of Standards. Some of the known benefits of using a professional include improved asset allocation and asset choice. Planners can more efficiently evaluate adequacy of current financial plans than can most individuals, and they can provide advice on how to improve the likelihood of success by finding ways to improve the current plan. CFP practitioners can be found at most large financial institutions, including brokerage houses and investment companies.

Not every individual is comfortable with, or needs, formalized planning when other alternatives might be useful. Individuals with Internet access can find a wide variety of information and strategies online, for example. However, the majority of these strategies will come down to asset allocation based on investment risk tolerance and horizon. Common themes will include stocks for the long run and some level of liquidity in retirement. Some websites even have information for contacting representatives who are qualified to answer questions. Benefit counselors can typically answer basic questions and provide simple interpretations of information. Employer-provided counselors can also clarify issues related to any employer-provided benefits that exist, including pension plans and health benefits.

Special considerations

One important issue in retirement planning is the gender and marital status of an individual. Women tend to have a higher life expectancy than men, and married couples should consider the increased likelihood of shortfall for women—due not only to increased life expectancy but also because one or more of a couple's retirement resources will be lost with the passing of a spouse, which may place an even greater importance on investments after this point.

Another source of concern is that women may have lower risk tolerance than men. While this difference is still under dispute, it has important implications for women preparing for retirement. Women may tend to be too conservative in their investing, and they therefore are less likely to be invested in stocks. Financial planners should be certain to spend time explaining the ideas behind the strategy of investing in stocks for the long run.

Historically married women have been able to rely on a husband's savings, even when their own employers have offered defined contribution plans. However, given the increased likelihood of divorce today, women should be certain that they are contributing to assets in their own name and are part of the decision-making process. Then, should they find themselves on their own, they will not only have begun accumulation of their own resources, but will know why those decisions were made and will be able to participate in future investment choices.

Another important issue is the consideration of health concerns. While one may accumulate a significant amount of wealth prior to retirement, this wealth could easily be diminished because of illness. Medicare is generally not available until one is sixty-five years of age, and anyone retiring prior to this age should therefore make arrangements for some protection. However, Medicare is not all-inclusive and currently does not provide for nonhospital prescriptions or long-term care needs beyond 120 days. Therefore any long-term illness could quickly use up any personal savings. The financial effect of such an illness can be mitigated through the use of private insurance plans. This may include continued participation in private health insurance plans through a previous employer. However, a more common trend has been for households to acquire long-term care insurance. These plans can typically be purchased for five different levels of coverage, including skilled nursing care, intermediate nursing care, custodial care, home care, and adult day care. These policies can be quite costly, but lower rates may be attainable for those who elect to enroll at younger ages, such as in their mid-fifties. Despite their cost, these plans may prevent the diminishing of an otherwise sufficient investment portfolio.

Overall the key elements to a retirement plan include choosing a retirement age and level of living, making investment choices, and assuring proper health care coverage. Taking advantage of time and investing principles can lead to higher levels of accumulated savings by retirement, and thus a higher level of living in retirement.

MICHAEL S. GUTTER

See also RETIREMENT, DECISION-MAKING; RETIREMENT, EARLY RETIREMENT INCENTIVES; RETIREMENT PATTERNS; RETIREMENT PLANNING PROGRAMS; RETIREMENT, TRANSITION

BIBLIOGRAPHY

GARNER, R. J.; YOUNG, E.; ARNONE, W. J.; and BAKER, N. A. *Ernst and Young's Retirement Planning Guide: Take Care of Your Finances Now . . . And They'll Take Care of You Later.* New York: John Wiley and Sons, 1997.

MSN Money. Available on the World Wide Web at http://moneycentral.msn.com

American Association of Retired Persons (AARP). AARP Webplace. Available on the World Wide Web at www.aarp.org

mPowerCafe. Available on the World Wide Web at www.mpowercafe.com

KIYOSAKI, R. T., and LECHTER, S. L. *Retire Young, Retire Rich.* New York: Warner Books Inc., 2001.

SIEGEL, ALAN M.; MORRIS, V. B.; and MORRIS, K. M. *The Wall Street Journal Guide to Planning Your Financial Future: The Easy-To-Read Guide to Planning for Retirement.* New York: Fireside, 1998.

STANLEY, T. J., and DANKO, W. D. *The Millionaire Next Door: The Surprising Secrets of America's Wealthy.* New York: Simon and Schuster, 1998.

RETIREMENT PLANNING PROGRAMS

For many people, a cornerstone of retirement planning is participation in an employer-sponsored savings program. Ideally, this should start early in one's career to maximize the effects of compound interest. Additional retirement programs are available to self-employed persons as well as individual retirement accounts (IRAs) for all workers with earned income.

Most employer retirement programs are qualified plans, meaning they qualify for special tax benefits. For example, a plan must be in writing and cannot discriminate among employees at different salary levels. In return, employers receive a tax deduction for their contributions and employees need not include these employer contributions in their taxable income. In certain situations (e.g., to attract highly paid executives), companies may offer nonqualified savings programs.

Types of employer retirement programs

There are four major types of qualified employer-sponsored retirement programs: pensions, profit-sharing and stock ownership plans, salary reduction, and thrift plans.

Pensions. *Defined-benefit pensions* provide benefits according to a formula based on income and/or years of service (e.g., two percent for each year of employment multiplied by a worker's highest three or five year's average pay). Benefits are unaffected by investment gains and losses and employers shoulder the risk of accumulating sufficient funds. Employer contributions are calculated according to actuarial tables.

Defined-contribution pensions provide benefits based on the performance of workers' individual retirement savings accounts. Employers make contributions based on a fixed or variable percentage of pay, and workers receive the amount contributed plus plan earnings. Thus, employees shoulder the investment risk.

Cash-balance pensions became increasingly popular during the 1990s. Benefits accrue at an even rate throughout workers' careers, in contrast to the higher benefits toward the end of a career offered by defined-benefit pensions. Employers contribute a percentage of workers' salaries and credit a return that is generally tied to a market index. Cash-balance plans are controversial because workers with long service often earn less than they would have if their employer retained a defined-benefit plan. Some workers have responded with charges of age discrimination.

Profit-sharing and stock ownership plans. *Profit-sharing plans* allow employers to make flexible contributions contingent upon company profits. There is no requirement that contributions be made annually. Instead, they are decided by a corporation's board of directors and can be lean or generous, depending on company earnings. Because of the uncertainty of payment, profit-sharing plans often supplement a pension. The maximum allowable contribution is $40,000 or 100 percent of compensation; if less, beginning in 2002.

Stock bonus plans are similar to profit-sharing plans, except that contributions do not depend upon profitability and are made in the form of company stock. *Employee stock ownership plans* (ESOPs) provide shares of company stock as an employer's retirement fund contribution. They provide a ready market for corporate stock, a feeling of participation in company management, and an incentive for employees to work hard.

Incentive stock options are sometimes provided to nonmanagerial employees, especially in start-up companies. They allow the holder to receive cash or stock after a specified vesting period, generally three to five years. Many people use this money for retirement.

Salary reduction plans. These plans allow workers to save a portion of their income, tax-deferred. These plans are named for specific sections of the tax code.

401(k) plans allow employees of for-profit corporations to save up to $11,000 (year 2002 limit) annually for retirement. The contribution and earnings are tax-deferred until withdrawal. Many employers also match employee contributions by a certain percentage and allow participants to borrow up to half of their account balance. The deferral limit will increase to $12,000 in 2003, $13,000 in 2004, $14,000 in 2005, and $15,000 in 2006.

403(b) plans are available to employees of non-profit organizations, such as public schools, hospitals, and public and private universities. The 2002 contribution limit is also $11,000 and gradually rises to $15,000 like 401(k)s. Fewer employers match contributions because many participants are public employees. Plans include catch-up provisions for workers who did not contribute fully in the past.

457 plans are available to state and local government workers and tax-exempt organizations. The maximum 2002 contribution is $11,000 and employer matching is rarely available.

For all of the above plans, participants age 50 and older who have made the maximum deferral can contribute an additional "catch up" amount: $1,000 in 2002, $2,000 in 2003, $3,000 in 2004, $4,000 in 2005, and $5,000 in 2006 and later.

Thrift plans. These are after-tax, employer-sponsored savings programs. In other words, workers cannot deduct their contributions from gross income, as is possible with salary-reduction plans. Employers generally match thrift plan contributions at a certain rate. For example, with a 50 percent match, an employer would contribute fifty cents for every dollar saved by employees.

Plans for the self-employed

Simplified employee pension plans (SEPs) allow business owners to contribute to special IRAs for themselves and their employees. The contribution limits are 15 percent of earned income for employees and 13.04 percent for the owner. SEP contributions are a business tax deduction and can be forgone in low earning years. Required paperwork is minimal. Salaried workers with outside self-employment income can also use SEPs.

Keogh plans allow self-employed persons to contribute the lesser of 100 percent of net self-employment income, or $40,000, starting in 2002. Contributions must also be made for all eligible employees. Several types of Keoghs are available. A major disadvantage is an annual disclosure form that must be filed with the IRS.

The *Savings Incentive Match Plan for Employees* (SIMPLE) is available to businesses with no more than one hundred employees. Employees can contribute up to $7,000 annually in 2002 and employers can match up to 3 percent of workers' compensation. Like SEPs, SIMPLEs have low administrative responsibility, compared to Keoghs. Contribution limits will be increasing to $8,000 in 2003, $9,000 in 2004, and $10,000 in 2005.

Individual retirement accounts (IRAs)

An IRA is a personal tax-deferred savings plan that can be set up at a variety of financial institutions. The maximum annual contribution is $3,000 in 2002–2004, $4,000 in 2005–2007, and $5,000 in 2008 and later, and earned income from a job or self-employment is required. IRAs are not an investment, per se, but, rather, an account for which a variety of investment products (e.g., stock, CDs, mutual funds) can be selected.

Traditional deductible IRAs offer a double tax benefit: tax-deferred growth and a federal tax deduction for the contribution amount. Income limits ($44,000 of adjusted gross income for singles and $64,000 for joint filers in 2002) and availability of a qualified employer plan determine eligibility for a tax deduction.

Roth IRAs provide no up-front tax deduction. However, earnings grow tax-deferred and withdrawals are tax-free if made more than five years after a Roth IRA is established and after age 59 1/2. Unlike traditional IRAs, Roth IRAs don't require minimum distributions after age 70 1/2, and contributions can continue after this age if a person has earned income. Roth IRAs are available to single taxpayers with up to $110,000 of adjusted gross income ($160,000 for married couples).

Traditional nondeductible IRAs offer neither an up-front tax deduction nor tax-free earnings. Still, they provide tax-deferred growth and are generally better than taxable accounts for taxpayers that don't qualify for other IRA options.

Starting in 2002, persons aged 50 and older may make additional "catch-up" contributions to either a traditional or Roth IRA. An additional $500 can be saved in 2002–2005 and an extra $1,000 in 2006 and later.

To determine which IRA is best, based on personal factors such as age and household income, individuals can check one of the IRA calculator links on the website www.rothira.com. It should be noted that withdrawals before age 59 1/2 from IRAs, salary reduction plans, and plans for the self-employed are considered premature distributions. A 10 percent penalty will be levied, except in specific instances like disability, in addition to ordinary income tax at an investor's marginal tax rate (e.g., 28 percent).

Getting help: hiring professional advisors

Some people seek professional assistance with retirement planning, often because they lack the time or expertise to do investment research, or because they are faced with an immediate decision, such as handling a lump-sum pension distribution or evaluating an early retirement buyout offer. There are many types of financial advisors, including bankers, accountants, insurance agents, employee benefit counselors, and stock brokers. In addition, over 250,000 professionals call themselves financial planners. Many have earned the certified financial planner (CFP) or chartered financial consultant (ChFC) credential or are certified public accountants with a personal financial specialist (CPA/PFS) designation. To select a financial professional, consider the "three Cs": credentials, competence, and cost.

Credentials. Certified financial planners are licensed by the Certified Financial Planner Board of Standards (CFP Board) to use the CFP marks upon successful completion of a ten-hour examination, three years of financial planning experience, and a biennial continuing education requirement. The names of local CFPs can be obtained at the CFP Board's website, www.cfp-board.org.

Chartered financial consultants receive the ChFC designation from The American College, located in Bryn Mawr, Pennsylvania. ChFCs must also have three years of professional experience, pass exams, and complete continuing education courses. Information is available on the Society of Financial Service Professionals' website, www.financialpro.org.

CPA/PFS designees are certified public accountants who have passed a financial planning exam and a rigorous tax exam, and who have met continuing education requirements. Additional information is available on the website at www.cpapfs.org.

Competence. Financial advisors with more than $25 million of assets under management are required to register with the U.S. Securities and Exchange Commission, while smaller firms must register with state securities regulators. Investors can call the North American Securities

Administrators Association (NASAA) at 1-888-84-NASAA, or their state securities agency, to obtain information about specific financial professionals. These agencies can access the Central Registration Depository (CRD), which contains licensing and disciplinary information about financial advisors nationwide.

Cost. Financial planners are generally compensated in one of four ways: through salary, fees, commissions, or a combination of fees and commissions. Fee-only planners are compensated entirely by their clients. The fee can be an hourly rate, a fee per plan, or a percentage of assets under management. Commission-only planners receive commissions from the sale of products such as mutual funds. Some advisors charge both fees and commissions or use commission income to offset all or part of the fees charged for financial advice.

Those wanting to hire a financial advisor should follow this six step process:

1. Obtain referrals from other people or professional organizations
2. Call several planners for information about their services
3. Check planners' references and CRD registration information
4. Interview several planners and ask questions such as: What services do you provide? How are you compensated? What is your investment philosophy? How often will my financial plan be reviewed? May I see a sample financial plan?
5. Assess your comfort level with each financial planner
6. Hire a financial planner upon receipt of a written agreement

Getting help: retirement planning tools

Software programs, worksheets, and online financial calculators are available to assist with retirement decisions. These tools are only as good as their underlying assumptions about key variables, however. One of the simplest retirement planning tools is the American Savings Education Council's *Ballpark Estimate* (see www.asec.org). This one-page form consists of just six steps but makes certain assumptions about longevity and investment return. Another popular website is www.financialengines.com, which predicts an investor's probability of reaching his or her retirement goal. Other sources of

retirement planning tools include investment companies and county Cooperative Extension offices.

According to the 2000 Retirement Confidence Survey (RCS) conducted by the Employee Benefit Research Institute, 53 percent of American workers have calculated how much money they need to save for retirement, up from 35 percent in 1993. The 1999 RCS also found that those who have done a retirement-savings need calculation have saved considerably more than those who have not. The study found that the median amount accumulated by households that have tried to figure out how much money they will need is $66,532, compared with a median of $14,054 accumulated by those who have not done a calculation.

Getting help: formal retirement planning education

With so many retirement savings programs available at worksites, formal retirement-planning education is often provided by employers. Benefits to program sponsors include workers who more fully appreciate their employee benefits package, improved morale and productivity, and increased participation in tax-deferred retirement plans. Employers also offer educational seminars to comply with section 404(c) of ERISA (the Employee Retirement Income Security Act) and to head off future lawsuits by employees who inadequately prepare for retirement.

The U.S. Department of Labor (DOL) encourages employers to provide "sufficient information" so employees can make informed investment decisions. Section 404(c) permits employers to provide certain information to employees without increasing their fiduciary liability. A 1996 interpretation of section 404(c) identified four categories of financial education that do not constitute the rendering of investment advice:

- Information about an employer's specific retirement plan
- General financial and investment information
- Information about asset allocation models (e.g., the historical performance of combinations of stocks, bonds, and cash)
- Interactive materials (e.g., worksheets and computer analyses)

Implementing a financial education program with any or all of these four categories can assure employers that they will not lose their exemption from fiduciary status as set forth in ERISA 404(c). In addition, employers must provide plan participants with at least three different investment choices and independent control over their accounts.

There are also benefits to workers who participate in formal retirement-education programs. Several studies have found that workers who attend retirement-planning seminars save more money and make wiser asset allocation decisions. Asset allocation is the placement of a certain percentage of investment capital within different asset classes (e.g., 50 percent of an investor's portfolio in stock, 30 percent in bonds, and 20 percent in cash).

The 1998 Retirement Confidence Survey found that, among workers who received educational material or attended employer seminars about retirement planning during the previous year, 43 percent reported that the information led them to both change the amount that they contribute and reallocate the way their money was invested. In addition, 41 percent said employer-provided information led them to begin contributing to a retirement savings plan. Similar results were found from a survey of almost 700 plan sponsors by Buck Consultants, a worldwide human resources consulting firm. This study found that, of companies providing financial education programs, 60 percent reported that their employees were making larger plan contributions and 58 percent reported that employees were becoming less conservative in their investment choices.

Some employers go beyond retirement planning and provide seminars on credit and cash management. Others provide individual financial counseling. Especially difficult to reach are low-wage workers. Employers can help employees increase their take-home pay through the IRS earned income credit tax program and by providing services (e.g., child care) that would otherwise consume scarce take-home pay. Savings campaigns, such as saving one percent or more of pay, may also be effective, particularly when employer matching is provided.

Unfortunately, some employers focus their educational efforts on older workers that are within ten years of retirement. This is unfortunate because the earlier one gets started, the less one needs to save. Compound interest is not retroactive. For every decade a worker postpones saving, he or she needs to save about three times more to accumulate a specific sum. For example, a 20 year old needs to invest only $67 per month to accumulate $1 million by age 65. By waiting until ages 30, 40, and 50, the monthly savings amount needed increases to $202, $629, and $2,180, respectively, assuming an 11 percent average annual return.

Summary

A number of tax-deferred retirement plans are available to employees and self-employed persons. Thanks to the Economic Growth and Tax Relief Reconciliation Act of 2001, contribution limits have been increased and catch-up provisions established. Some retirement savings programs (e.g., 401(k)s) allow an up-front tax deduction of the amount contributed, in addition to tax-deferred growth of the principal. Additional information is available through professional financial advisors, retirement-planning software and worksheets, websites, and employer educational programs. The sooner one starts to save, the longer compound interest will work its magic. Even small dollar amounts add up. A $20 weekly deposit earning a 10 percent average return over forty years will grow to $506,300.

BARBARA O'NEILL

See also ANNUITIES; ASSETS AND WEALTH; CONSUMER PRICE INDEX AND COLAS; ESTATE PLANNING; INDIVIDUAL RETIREMENT ACCOUNTS; RETIREMENT PLANNING; SAVINGS.

BIBLIOGRAPHY

American Savings Education Council. *Choose to Save Forum on Retirement Security and Personal Savings: Agenda Background Materials.* Washington D.C.: ASEC, 2000.

BABICH, A. C. "Cash Balance Plans: The New Trend in Retirement." *Journal of Financial Planning,* (April 2000): 92–99.

CARLSON, C. B. *Eight Steps to Seven Figures.* New York: Doubleday, 2000.

Certified Financial Planner Board of Standards. *Ten Questions to Ask When Choosing a Financial Planner.* Denver, Colo.: CFPBoS, 1998.

Employee Benefit Research Institute. *The 2000 Retirement Confidence Survey Summary of Findings.* Washington D.C.: EBRI, 2000.

MCREYNOLDS, R. "How's Your Pension?" *Mutual Funds,* May, 2000, p. 107–108.

O'Brian, B. "Calculating Retirement? It's No Simple Equation." *The Wall Street Journal*, 7 February 2000, p. R1, R5.

O'Neill, B. *Investing On A Shoestring*. Chicago: Dearborn Financial Publishing, 1999.

Opiela, N. "401(k) Education: Planners Responding to Plan Participants' Calls For Help." *Journal of Financial Planning*, June, 1999, p. 58–64.

Ostuw, P.; Pierron, B.; and Yakoboski, P. "The Evolution of Retirement: Results of the 1999 Retirement Confidence Survey." In *EBRI Issue Brief* 216. Washington D.C.: Employee Benefit Research Institute, 1999.

Personal Tax Planning After the 2001 Tax Law. Albany, N.Y.: Newkirk Publishing, 2001.

Roha, R. "Stock Options Aren't Just for Bigshots Anymore." *Kiplinger's Personal Finance Magazine*, April, 1999, p. 99–101.

Rutgers Cooperative Extension. *Investing For Your Future: A Cooperative Extension System Basic Investing Home Study Course*. New Brunswick, N.J.: RCE, 2000.

Storms, R. "Financial Education: Employer Trends, Benefits, and Considerations." *Personal Finances and Worker Productivity* 3, no. 2 (1999): 25–28.

2001 Tax Law Summary. Albany, N.Y.: Newkirk Publishing, 2001.

U.S. Department of Labor. *Simplified Employee Pensions: What Small Businesses Need to Know*. Washington D.C.: DOL, 1997.

Whelehan, B. M. "The 123s of 401(k), 403(b), and 457 Plans." *Mutual Funds*, July, 1998, p. 31–32.

Yakoboski, P.; Ostuw, P.; and Hicks, J. "What Is Your Savings Personality? The 1998 Retirement Confidence Survey." *EBRI Issue Brief* 200. Washington, D.C.: Employee Benefit Research Institute, 1998.

RETIREMENT, TRANSITION

This article addresses retirement as a stage of life as well as the long-term processes through which people anticipate, enter, and adapt to that stage. The word "retirement" derives from the French *retirer* (to withdraw), and although retirement is a withdrawal from paid employment, what it is progress toward or into is not always well defined.

The modern norm of retirement

Workers through the ages have sought relief from labor and responsibility toward the end of their lives. Western literature's most famous retiree, King Lear, using the royal "we," set Shakespeare's (1606) play in motion with this opening speech:

Know that we have divided In three our kingdom. And 'tis our fast intent To shake all cares and business from our age, Conferring them on younger strengths while we Unburdened crawl toward death. (act 1, Scene 1)

A fortunate king or proprietor could contemplate retirement, trading land and property for the promise of material support until life's end. Yet unless one had sufficient wealth with which to finance withdrawal from work, retirement as we know it today—leaving the labor force in advance of disability—was possible only for a privileged minority. A predictable period of retirement, available to most workers, awaited the development of public and private pension schemes in the twentieth century. These in turn needed the rise of strong governments and welfare states, productive economies, and large numbers of workers surviving into later life.

A retirement stage has now become a normative feature of the life course: people expect, and are expected, to retire. This is true in advanced economies and is becoming so in the developing world. The necessary condition for a retirement stage is people's reliable access to income that replaces the wages and salaries earned from employment. Governments, employers, and unions pursue various objectives in developing pension arrangements (including public pensions such as Social Security in the United States) and in promoting devices for retirement saving. These objectives include the regulation of labor markets, reduction of unemployment, career stability, and the orderly turnover and replacement of personnel. The general goal is to create a structure of financial incentives, typically tied to age, that eventually draws older people out of the labor force.

Succeeding cohorts of older workers by and large have welcomed these developments; average age of retirement has dropped and the cultural acceptance of retirement has increased. Although retirement was once primarily a male transition, female workers followed the retirement pattern after they had entered the labor force in large numbers. By the 1990s, in the United States the majority of Social Security retirement beneficiaries were taking their first benefit prior to the traditional age of sixty-five. Studies in the 1960s traced growing positive attitudes toward retirement as a time of leisure and not just as a refuge for those unable to work. Marketers of real estate, financial services, and leisure goods have steadily promoted an active, "golden years" image of retirement.

Despite all this organizational, political, economic, and cultural encouragement of retirement, some 5 to 10 percent of workers in U.S. surveys say they will never retire, and even at ages seventy to seventy-four, 17 percent of men and 9 percent of women still participate in the paid labor force (U.S. Department of Labor). Some who are still working past age seventy do so out of economic necessity, but most of this employment is voluntary. Resolute nonretirees have in common a continuing demand for their skills, good health, a disapproval of retirement, and occupations that allow them to control their conditions of work.

Anticipation and preparation

With a retirement stage solidly lodged on the mental map of life, there is a gathering, informal involvement in the topic that begins years prior to the event. In thinking about their retirement timing and lifestyle, current workers can now draw on the experience of a generation of older role models who have already retired in an era of reasonable income security.

Thoughts of retirement have many prompts. Nearly half of U.S. workers participate in a pension plan at their place of employment. All of these plans have eligibility ages with which employees are familiar, and some plan participants direct their accounts. In the media, adults of all ages have been targeted with ubiquitous advertising of products and services for retirement saving. In politics, the solvency of Social Security has become a prominent theme of each national election cycle.

Workplaces in particular shape an awareness of retirement. For workers with steady employment, promotional timetables and seniority principles draw the arc of an organizational career. Seniority principles grant long-tenure workers better positions and pay in return for the acknowledgment that they will someday surrender their jobs to younger workers. Pension plans can have incentives that encourage retirement within a certain age window, which then becomes a firm's customary time for retirement. Employers and coworkers can communicate subtle biases against older workers. Despite legal prohibition of age discrimination in matters of promotion and hiring, and despite evidence that amply demonstrates the skills, loyalty, and trainability of older workers, the idea remains firmly entrenched that creativity and energy are qualities found in younger workers. Job uncertainty, undesirable work assignments, promotion disappointments, supervision by younger managers, or a perception that "this isn't the place it used to be" are all cues that raise the attractiveness of retirement and hasten emotional disengagement from work roles. However, it is pension availability that permits workers to covet the greener grass of retirement.

With advancing age, retirement becomes topical not just among coworkers and friends, but also at home. Marriage and other family responsibilities influence retirement preparations. Spouses, particularly those in dual-earner households, have an obvious stake in one another's plans, and they may coordinate their exits if each one's respective pension eligibility schedule allows it. Families that still include dependent children are likely to delay the consideration of retirement while educational expenses compete with retirement saving needs.

These are external cues to an awareness of retirement. Health problems and diminished work capacity are a well-established prompt to retirement. Some authors have identified a subjective switch that takes place in the minds of people in their fifties. Having previously assumed an unbounded future, adults come to focus on the finiteness of life. Mindful of their mortality and now starting to experience the deaths of age peers, workers grow to view retirement as a means to conserve their health and pursue valued personal goals.

The top piece of advice that current retirees offer to those who are still working is "Plan ahead." Most formal programs and aids for planning one's retirement center on financial topics, but finances always presume many other questions about lifestyle preferences. Whether with the advice of experts, family members, coworkers, or friends, the immediate preretirement period is a good time to take stock of numerous issues. These include residential options, family ties and obligations, preservation of health, legal matters, and use of time once re-

RETIREMENT, TRANSITION   1219

tired. Couples should also make contingency plans for widowhood.

Passage to retirement

Retirement was once assumed to be a one-way exit from a one-job work career of some twenty-five or thirty years' duration upon eligibility for pension or Social Security benefits. Closer study of work and retirement patterns in the 1980s and 1990s revealed the growing variety of paths and job sequences by which workers can retire. One can stop altogether, or switch to part-time work, or start a new full-time job while drawing pension income. These transitions can begin earlier or later than the conventional retirement age window of sixty-two to sixty-five. The earlier they begin, the greater is the likelihood of a complex, multistep path to retirement. Workers differ considerably in their ability to control the form and timing of these transitions, however, and the choices may be limited in practice.

Being retired is also a matter of self-definition. Workers who are disabled or displaced can convert their nonemployment to "retirement" once they qualify for pension income. There are also former workers who, meeting all apparent criteria as retired, will deny that they are retired because they dislike that identity. Despite the variety of forms, most people understand retirement to mean full or partial reduction in work hours along with the initiation of pension income from public or private sources. By their own understanding, most older people can readily identify themselves as completely, partially, or not retired.

The temporal event of leaving a long-term job or career can be marked with a ceremony organized at the workplace or among friends. Employers' ceremonies and parting gifts—the emblematic watch or other token—can strike honorees as impersonal if large numbers of people are involved. Ceremonies organized among coworkers or friends can be an emotionally satisfying way to recognize the transition, commemorate the career, and greet the future. That so many retirements are soon followed by long-deferred trips and travel suggests the need for symbolic and concrete ways to celebrate the break.

Table 1
Retirement attitudes of persons age 62 to 65 who say that they are completely retired.

	525 Men	577 Women
Would you say that your retirement has turned out to be:		
Very satisfying	64%	59%
Moderately satisfying	29%	34%
Not at all satisfying	7%	7%
Thinking about your retirement years compared to the years just before you retired, would you say the retirement years have been:		
Better	50%	50%
About the same	32%	31%
Not as good	14%	15%
Retired less than a year ago	4%	4%

SOURCE: Adapted from: Juster, F. T., and Suzman, R. "An Overview of the Health and Retirement Study." *Journal of Human Resources* 30, supp. (1995): S7–S56.

Adaptation

Once retired, whatever form retirement may take, the majority of people say that they are satisfied with their decision, and many say that they should have retired sooner. These sentiments are shared by men and women alike, as shown by responses to a national survey of U.S. retirees aged sixty-two to sixty-five (Table 1). A good experience with retirement is more likely among people in good health, with adequate finances, positive attitudes, and supportive relationships—the same factors that contribute to well-being at any age.

What retirees say they value most about their new status is a feeling of emancipation that they express with the words "time" (to do what I want to do) and "freedom" (from daily schedules, for personal pursuits). Yet liberation from work structures is also separation from arenas for status, stimulation, mastery, and social commerce. Free but marginal, retirees can feel ambivalent about their status. "It doesn't matter what I do" can be a joyous or a bittersweet expression.

As befits a withdrawal that is prized for its freedom, retirement is a do-it-yourself role with few specific expectations for its performance. Retirees should try to live independently, and they should not interfere at the former place of work. Retirees and those around them tend to emphasize a "busy ethic" that prizes activity and engagement, thereby justifying a life of pensioned leisure. While affirming the importance of activity, one can fill time in many fashions. People's orientation toward time can differ. Martin Kohli (1986) points out that some people approach time as a task or resource that must be used sensibly, whereas others view time as something to be gotten through as pleasurably as possible. Whatever the level or nature of activity, the absence of rigid expectations is certainly beneficial to those retirees whose health limitations do not allow them to perform at a high level.

Before experience with retirement was widespread and before reliable pension income raised the cultural appreciation of retirement leisure, there was a belief that the transition to retirement would put workers at risk of health decline. Men especially might be undone by the loss of a central life role. Epidemiological studies have discounted the idea that retirement characteristically harms physical or emotional health, or contributes to premature mortality. Indeed, retirees cite the benefits of retirement for preserving health and reducing stress. At the same time, studies have shown that about 30 percent of retirees say that their transition to or life in retirement has at times been stressful (Bossé et al.). This may occur because long-standing personal problems continue into retirement, because retirement was unwanted or unanticipated, or because of the coincidence of other negative life events, such as health or financial difficulties.

Popular lore also warns about the marital problems that can follow retirement as spouses find themselves in unaccustomed daily proximity. Colorful as these anecdotes are, strains are manageable and most couples make the adaptation over time. When still working, couples tend to look forward to the time together as a resource for their relationship, hitherto occupied with work and parenting routines. However, the best-laid plans for a joint retirement can be spoiled by health problems of the spouses or by crises that arise among family members. What's more, retirement is not likely to transform an unhappy marriage.

Retirement entails a reduction in income, but there are also reductions in the expenses associated with employment, for example, the costs of commuting. Experts say that if households can replace 65 percent to 80 percent of their prior earnings with income from pension sources, sav-ings, or part-time work, they can have a comparable standard of living. An income that seems sufficient or comfortable in the initial postretirement period is nevertheless vulnerable to erosion over the longer term. Unlike the retirement benefit of Social Security, few other pension distributions protect recipients against a rising cost of living. Besides inflation, overconsumption, health expenses, and widowhood also threaten income security. A man in the United States reaching age sixty-five in 2000 has a life expectancy of sixteen more years; a woman at age sixty-five can expect to live twenty more years, but these are averages. Uncertainty about longevity and future expenses means that personal finances and their management will continue to be a concern well after withdrawal from work.

Opinion surveys of working adults consistently find that a large proportion—approximately 70 percent—want to work after retirement. Many such plans go unfulfilled, whether through eventual lack of interest, opportunity, or ability. Perhaps one-third of "retired" persons participate in the labor force, mainly in part-time work and for limited periods. Pension rules tend to bar phased retirement at the original workplace, so new jobs are usually found elsewhere and at lower rates of pay. Nevertheless, income and stimulus from paid work can sustain a satisfying retirement and give one a feeling of control.

Retirees gravitate to quite a variety of lifestyles, no single one of which is the only formula for a successful retirement. Recreation, tourism, and travel certainly do preoccupy some people, and others use retirement as the opportunity to take up pursuits that they have long deferred, such as further education or skill development, a time-consuming hobby, or even a new line of work. Permanent or seasonal migration to retirement havens or resort communities is undertaken by a relatively small percentage of people, even though this mobile style of retirement dominates popular culture. Such leisure consumption notwithstanding, some observers point out the considerable productivity of retired workers as they assist their children and grandchildren in various ways, undertake care and support of other relatives, and volunteer their time and skills in their churches and communities. Whatever the mix of leisure and productive activities, a lot of retirement time becomes absorbed by mundane tasks of household maintenance and by tending relationships with friends and family members.

Unless one re-enters the labor force, the pensioned leisure of retirement extends to the end of life. The retirement stage, however, ends informally when disability curtails the pursuit of accustomed leisure and productive activities. Popular ideas of retirement suppress this darker side—the eventuality of dependency and death—in favor of images of free, secure, healthy, and mobile individuals. At its most desirable, retirement appears as a hard-earned suspension of time between work and frailty. In reality, retirement is integrated with the rest of life, woven through with ongoing family, social, religious, and geographical ties that can ground the self across the later years.

What should retirement be?

The retirement stage that workers anticipate, enter, and occupy is widely available only because of larger political and economic arrangements that created pension supports for retirement. These supports developed across the twentieth century in order to manage the size and composition of the labor force. As a creation of institutional policy, the evolving practice of retirement continues to be a policy focus for the future.

After a decades-long trend toward earlier exits—now halted—powerful interests are pulling the timing of retirement in more than one direction as the twenty-first century begins. Concerned about population aging and the solvency of public pension schemes, the nations of the industrialized West have begun to favor policies that extend work life. For example, the U.S. Social Security program is gradually raising its eligibility age for full benefits from sixty-five to sixty-seven. At the same time, advertisers are strenuously pushing a positive image of retirement to middle-aged and older adults who are a prime market for financial, health, and recreational products. Such promotions raise expectations for a life stage promising release, self-development, and active lifestyles. Finally, employers want flexibility above all in the management of personnel flow. Prevailing conditions in different industries and occupations will shape demand for older workers, and with it the shifting of incentives to remain, retire, or work part-time.

Some have argued that the time has come to rethink retirement, what with increased longevity, health, and wealth among the new cohorts of retirees, as well as pointed political challenges to their age entitlements. A "third age" devoted primarily to leisure washes meaning from people's later years and wastes human resources that could be applied to pressing social problems. New organizational forms could channel the energies and talents of elders toward civic contributions and build a legacy for their communities.

The retirement stage will continue to serve both social and personal purposes. Organizational, societal, and economic objectives will further fashion the arrangements that make retirement feasible, even as individuals use the opportunity to seek security and novelty, self and service.

DAVID J. EKERDT

See also LEISURE; LIFE COURSE; PENSIONS, PUBLIC; RETIREMENT, DECISION-MAKING; RETIREMENT, PATTERNS; SOCIAL SECURITY, LONG-TERM FINANCING AND REFORM.

BIBLIOGRAPHY

ATCHLEY, R. C. "Critical Perspectives on Retirement." In *Voices and Visions of Aging: Toward a Critical Gerontology.* Edited by Thomas R. Cole, W. Andrew Achenbaum, Patricia L. Jakobi, and Robert Kasterbaum. New York: Springer, 1993. Pages 3–19.

BLAIKIE, A. *Ageing and Popular Culture.* New York: Cambridge University Press, 1999.

BOSSÉ, R.; SPIRO, A.; and KRESSIN, N. R. "The Psychology of Retirement." In *Handbook of the Clinical Psychology of Ageing.* Edited by R. T. Woods. Chichester, U.K.: John Wiley, 1996. Pages 141–157.

EKERDT, D. J. "The Busy Ethic: Moral Continuity Between Work and Retirement." *The Gerontologist* 26 (1986): 239–244.

EKERDT, D. J.; KOSLOSKI, K.; and DEVINEY, S. "The Normative Anticipation of Retirement Among Older Workers." *Research on Aging* 22 (2000): 3–22.

FREEDMAN, M. *Prime Time: How Baby Boomers Will Revolutionize Retirement and Transform America.* New York: PublicAffairs, 1999.

GRUBER, J., and WISE, D. A. *Social Security and Retirement Around the World.* Chicago: University of Chicago Press, 1999.

HABER, C., and GRATTON, B. *Old Age and the Search for Security: An American Social History.* Bloomington: Indiana University Press, 1994.

HANSSON, R. O.; DEKOEKKOEK, P. D.; NEECE, W. M.; and PATTERSON, D. W. "Successful Aging at Work: Annual Review, 1992–1996. The Older Worker and Transitions to Retirement." *Journal of Vocational Behavior* 51 (1997): 202–233.

JUSTER, F. T., and SUZMAN, R. "An Overview of the Health and Retirement Study." *Journal of Human Resources* 30, supp. (1995): S7–S56.

KARP, D. A. "The Social Construction of Retirement Among Professionals 50–60 Years Old." *The Gerontologist* 36 (1989): 750–760.

KOHLI, M. "Social Organization and Subjective Construction of the Life Course." In *Human Development and the Life Course: Multidisciplinary Perspective*. Edited by Aage B. Sørensen, Franz E. Weinert, and Lonnie R. Sherrod, Hillsdale, N.J.: Lawrence Erlbaum, 1986. Pages 271–292.

MONK, A., ed. *The Columbia Retirement Handbook*. New York: Columbia University Press, 1994.

MUTCHLER, J. E.; BURR, J. A.; PIENTA, A. M.; and MASSAGLI, M. P. "Pathways to Labor Force Exit: Work Transitions and Work Instability." *Journal of Gerontology: Social Science* 52B (1997): S4–S12.

PARNES, H. S., and SOMMERS, D. G. "Shunning Retirement: Work Experience of Men in Their Seventies and Early Eighties." *Journal of Gerontology: Social Sciences* 49 (1994): S117–S124.

QUADAGNO, J., and HARDY, M. "Work and Retirement." In *Handbook of Aging and the Social Sciences*, 4th ed. Edited by Robert H. Binstock and Linda K. George. San Diego: Academic Press, 1996. Pages 326–345.

QUINN, J. F., and BURKHAUSER, R. V. "Retirement and the Labor Force Behavior of the Elderly." In *Demography of Aging*. Edited by Linda G. Martin and Samuel H. Preston, Washington, D.C.: National Academy Press, 1994. Pages 50–101.

SAVISHINSKY, J. *The Broken Watch: Retirement and Meaning in America*. Ithaca, N.Y.: Cornell University Press, 2000.

SCHULZ, J. H. *The Economics of Aging*, 7th ed. Westport, Conn.: Auburn House, 2001.

SZINOVACZ, M., and EKERDT, D. J. "Families and Retirement." In *Handbook of Aging and the Family*. Edited by Rosemary Blieszner and Victoria H. Bedford. Westport, Conn.: Greenwood Press, 1995. Pages 375–400.

U.S. Department of Labor, Bureau of Labor Statistics. *Employment and Earnings* 45, no. 1 (January 2000): Table 3.

VINICK, B. H., and EKERDT, D. J. "The Transition to Retirement: Responses of Husbands and Wives." In *Growing Old in America*, 4th ed. Edited by Beth B. Hess and Elizabeth W

Markson. New Brunswick, N.J.: Transaction Books, 1991. Pages 305–317.

WEISS, R. S. "Processes of Retirement." In *Meanings of Work: Considerations for the Twenty-first Century*. Edited by Fred C. Gamst. Albany: State University of New York Press, 1995. Pages 233–250.

WISE, D. A. "Retirement Against the Demographic Trend: More Older People Living Longer, Working Less, and Saving Less." *Demography* 34 (1997): 83–95.

RETROGENESIS

Retrogenesis is the reversal of normal developmental biologic processes during the course of disease. The retrogenic process has been described clearly for the brain diseases known as the dementias. The most common form of dementia is Alzheimer's disease (AD), and retrogenesis has been demonstrated in striking detail in this common disorder of the elderly.

It is well established that normal human growth and development is marked by a series of landmarks. The most evident landmarks of human development are known as *functional landmarks*, representing the time course of acquisition of normal abilities. These functional landmarks are illustrated in Table 1. They begin with the ability of infants to hold up their heads independently, and proceed to the acquisition of the capacity to smile, to sit up, to walk, to speak, to toilet independently, to bathe, to dress, to manage money, and to hold a job. Studies have shown that the loss of these abilities in AD progresses in precisely the reverse order.

When the course of Alzheimer's disease differs markedly from the retrogenic functional pattern, the differences are often the result of other illnesses or conditions, which add to the disability of an AD patient. For example, arthritis or a hip fracture can cause an elderly person with AD to prematurely lose the ability to walk. This *excess disability* may add to the AD patient's functional downhill course.

Interestingly, not only does the order of functional losses in AD mirror that of normal human development, but, to some extent, the course of functional losses in AD mirrors the course of the acquisition of the same functions until the final, seventh stage of AD, which corresponds to infancy. For example, the average Alzheimer's patient regresses from the loss of

Table 1
Retrogenesis: functional landmarks in normal human development and Alzheimer's disease.

Retrogenesis

Functional Landmarks in Normal Human Development and Normal Human Development and Alsheimer's Disease (AD)

Approximate Age		Approximate Duration in Development	Aquired Abilities	Lost Abilities	Alzheimer Stage	Approximate Duration in AD	Development Age of AD
Adolscense years	13–19	7 years	Hold a Job	Hold a Incipient	3–	7 years Adolescence	19–13 years:
Late Childhood	8–12 years	5 years	Handle Simple Finances	Handle Simple Finances	4–Mile	2 years	12–8 years: Late Childhood
Middle Childhood	5–7 years	2 1/2 years	Select Proper Clothing	Select Proper Clothing	5– Moderate	1 1/2 years	7–5 years: Middle Childhood
Early Childhood	5 years		Put on Clothes unaided	Put on Clothes unaided	6a– Moderately Severe	2 1/2 years	5–2 years: Early Childhood
		4 years					
	4 years		Shower unaided	Shower unaided	b		
	4 years		Toilet undaided	Toilet unaided	c		
	3–4 1/2 years		Control urine	Control urine	d		
	2–3 years		Control bowels	Control bowels	e		
Infancy	15 months		Speak 5–6 words	Speak 5–6 words	7a- Severe	7 years or longer	15 months to birth: Infancy
		1 1/2 years					
	1 year		Speak 1 word	Speak 1 word	b		
	1 year		Walk	Walk	c		
	6–10 months		Sit up	Sit up	d		
	2–4 months		Smile	Smile	e		
	1–3 months		Hold up head	Hold up head	f		

Normal Development Approximate Total Duration: 20 Years

Alzheimer's Degeneration Approximate Total Duration: 20 Years ability to select clothing properly (in the beginning of functional stage 5) to double incontinence (in functional stage 6e) over approximately the same three to four year interval as a child develops from the acquisition of fecal continence at about two to three years of age to the acquisition of the ability to pick out clothing independently at about five to seven years of age. Similarly, just as the ability to dress and bathe independently are acquired at about the same time in normal child development, these abilities are lost at almost the same time in the degenerative course of AD.

The time course similarities do not hold for the final, seventh stage of AD, however. During this stage, functions that are acquired in infancy over only about a year-and-a-half are lost over many years in the course of progressive AD. Despite these differences, the overall temporal similarities between development and Alzheimer's degeneration are remarkable. The total developmental time from birth to young adulthood is approximately twenty years, approximately the same as the total degenerative course of AD, from the earliest clinically manifest symptoms of AD at the beginning of stage 3, to the final 7f stage, when patients can no longer hold up their head independently.

In Alzheimer's disease, not only do functional losses follow a retrogenic pattern of loss of capacity, losses of language abilities and general thinking abilities also follow a retrogenic pattern of loss. For example, studies have shown approximately the same relationship between a general mental-status measure of Alzheimer's degeneration and the retrogenic progression of functional losses in Alzheimer's disease as is seen between the mental age of children and scores on the same mental-status examination.

Because of the strong retrogenic relationships, in terms of both thinking ability and functioning, it is useful to translate the stages of Alzheimer's into corresponding developmental ages. The developmental age of the Alzheimer's patient provides very useful information about the patient. For example, certain involuntary motor responses that are present in infants, the so-called infantile neurologic reflexes, emerge in the Alzheimer's patient at the developmental age-appropriate point. These infantile reflexes include the so-called sucking reflex and grasping reflex. Furthermore, the developmental age of the Alzheimer' patient provides an accurate and

useful index of the overall care and management needs of an Alzheimer's patient. For example, an Alzheimer's patient in stage 5, which corresponds to a developmental age of five to seven years, requires about the same amount of care as a five to seven year old. Similarly, an Alzheimer's patient in stage 7, corresponding to an infantile developmental age, requires about the same amount of care as an infant.

Despite the general care and management implications of the developmental age model of the stages of Alzheimer's, important differences between Alzheimer's patients at each stage and their developmental age "peers" must be noted. For example, Alzheimer's patients do not undergo a physical regression. Consequently, a stage 7 Alzheimer's patient is much larger and stronger than an infant. Therefore, the stage 7 Alzheimer's patient's grasp reflex is stronger than an infant's, and an Alzheimer's patient can be much more difficult to care for and keep clean and hygienic than an infant. Also, Alzheimer's patients have a history of learned skills and behaviors that infants lack. Consequently, Alzheimer's patients late in stage 7 may on occasions utter seemingly forgotten words. It is also important to note that, like children, dignity is important for the Alzheimer's patient, and neither the child nor the Alzheimer's patient wishes to be humiliated or "infantilized." A ten-year-old child would be infuriated and humiliated if treated like a four year old, and a stage 4 Alzheimer's patient would be similarly infuriated and/or humiliated if treated like a stage 6 Alzheimer's patient. Because of appropriate concerns regarding dignity, Alzheimer's patients should be treated at all stages as adults with the mental and functional capacity of their corresponding developmental age. This melding in terms of treatment is termed the *science of Alzheimer's management*.

The developmental age of the Alzheimer's patient can be useful in assisting in understanding other aspects of the disease. For example, the developmental age also indicates the nature of some of the emotional changes seen in the Alzheimer's patient. Wrong beliefs (so-called delusions) frequently occur in stage 5 and 6 Alzheimer's patient's. These wrong beliefs are similar to the fantasies seen in children at a corresponding developmental age (two to seven years).

Interestingly, the remarkable retrogenic relationships noted in Alzheimer's patients are sometimes observed, to a greater or a lesser extent, in non-Alzheimer's forms of dementia. For example, the order of loss of function in some patients with non-Alzheimer's dementias is sometimes the same as in Alzheimer's disease. In these cases, the reflex changes and emotional changes noted may be the same as those at the corresponding stage of Alzheimer's disease, and, consequently, mirror the changes at the corresponding developmental age. However, the time-course retrogenic similarities generally do not apply in non-Alzheimer's dementias.

Why do these retrogenic relationships occur in dementing disorders? One possible explanation is that the white matter covering the axonal processes extending out from the nerve cells is injured in retrogenic dementias such as Alzheimer's. This white matter, known as *myelin*, is continuously produced throughout life and appears to protect the axon. A functional pathway is dependent upon this myelination process. The functional pathway may become stronger as myelin is produced over the years. The newer functional/axonal myelin pathways are the thinnest, and are probably also the most vulnerable to degenerative processes such as Alzheimer's. Myelin vulnerability—based upon the thickness (age) of this protective sheath—may also be a factor in traumatic processes that produce other retrogenic dementias, such as lack of oxygen from a stroke.

BARRY REISBERG
GUARAV GANDOTRA
SUNNIE KENNEDY
EMILE FRANSSEN

See also ALZHEIMER'S DISEASE; BRAIN; LANGUAGE DISORDERS.

BIBLIOGRAPHY

REISBERG, B. "Dementia: A Systematic Approach to Identifying Reversible Causes." *Geriatrics* 41, no. 4 (1986): 30–46.
REISBERG, B. "Functional Assessment Staging (FAST)." *Psychopharmacology Bulletin* 24 (1988): 653–659.
REISBERG, B.; KENOWSKY, S.; FRANSSEN, E. H.; AUER, S. R.; and SOUREN, L. E. M. "President's Report: Towards a Science of Alzheimer's Disease Management: A Model Based upon Current Knowledge of Retrogenesis." *International Psychogeriatrics* 11 (1999): 7–23.
REISBERG, B.; FRANSSEN, E. H.; HASAN, S. M.; MONTEIRO, I. BOKSAY, I.; SOUREN, L. E. M.; KENOWSKY, S. AUER, S. R.; ELAHI, S.; and KLUGER, A. "Retrogenesis: Clinical, Physiologic and Pathologic Mechanisms in Brain Aging, Alzheimer's, and Other Dementing Processes." *European Archives of Psychiatry and Clinical Neuroscience* 249, supp. 3 (1999): 28–36.

REVASCULARIZATION: BYPASS SURGERY AND ANGIOPLASTY

Ischemic heart disease is the commonest form of heart illness. It increases in frequency with increasing age, and outcomes are much worse in elderly patients. Ischemia is caused by narrowings or blockages in the coronary arteries, resulting in an inadequate blood supply to the heart. The disease spectrum ranges from subclinical disease (no symptoms) to angina, and, finally, to a heart attack (myocardial infarction, or MI). Typical angina is marked by exertional chest pain and shortness of breath that settles with rest. With stable angina, people may limit their activities to avoid symptoms, but it is generally well-tolerated and can be controlled with medication.

With acute ischemic syndromes, which include both unstable angina and myocardial infarctions, the risks are much greater. Unstable angina is marked by an increase in the severity or duration of pain or symptoms—and having them occur with lower levels of activity or at rest. If unstable angina progresses in a crescendo pattern, it may lead to a myocardial infarction. With a myocardial infarction, the ischemia to the heart is so severe that permanent damage occurs to the muscle. Major complications from heart attacks include life-threatening arrhythmias, congestive heart failure, and death.

Mortality rates from myocardial infarction for patients younger than sixty-five are generally less than 5 percent, while mortality rates for those over the age of seventy-five are greater than 20 percent.

There are six medications used to treat ischemic heart disease. Aspirin, cholesterol-lowering medications, and ACE inhibitors all reduce the risk of future heart attacks and strokes but have no other effect on the symptoms of angina. Beta blockers help reduce the symptoms of angina and the risk of heart attacks and strokes. Calcium channel blockers and nitroglycerin also help con-

Figure 1
The Heart: Coronary Arteries with Bypass

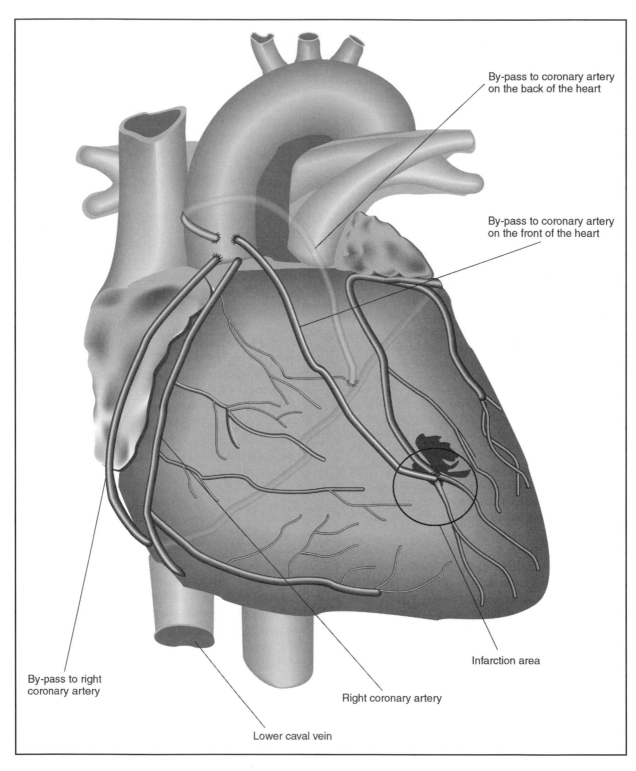

By-pass to coronary artery on the back of the heart

By-pass to coronary artery on the front of the heart

Infarction area

By-pass to right coronary artery

Right coronary artery

Lower caval vein

SOURCE: Suggested by brochure issued by Pfizer Canada Inc. (1996) and created by Symphony Medical Communications of Oslo, Norway (1996).

trol symptoms of angina. As patients get older, especially diabetics and women, they are more likely not to have typical chest pain and angina, which can lead to misdiagnosis.

Coronary artery bypass grafting

If angina cannot be controlled adequately with medications, or if patients have severe side effects such as asthma or depression with beta blockers or severe headaches with nitroglycerin, then revascularization may need to be considered. This consists of opening clogged arteries or replacing blocked arteries with a patient's own veins or arteries to bypass the blockage. Coronary artery bypass grafting (CABG) is open-heart surgery, and it has been available since the early 1970s. In the mid 1980s, nonsurgical revascularization was developed using balloons guided to the coronary arteries through X-ray equipment. This is known as percutaneous transluminal coronary angioplasty (PTCA).

Patients with unstable angina, or those who are felt to be at high risk, are referred for coronary angiography. This is a specialized X ray used to determine exactly where the blockages to the coronary arteries exist. An intravenous catheter is inserted into the femoral artery in the groin or into the brachial artery at the elbow. Through this sheath long catheters are guided using X-ray equipment through the major arteries to the heart. Dye is injected into the coronary arteries and X rays measure the extent of blockages.

Cardiac catheterization does carry a small but real risk, including allergic reactions (one in one thousand patients), MI (one in one thousand), stroke (one in two thousand), or death (one in one thousand). Other complications include renal failure. Risk factors that predispose to heart disease and that increase with age (e.g., diabetes, hypertension) also increase the risk for renal disease.

Patients are required to lie on their back for five to six hours after the catheter has been removed to prevent significant bleeding. Even with precautions, large bruising may occasionally result. This will resolve spontaneously, but may take days or even weeks.

Following angiography, the type or extent of blockage and the number of coronary arteries involved determines the best treatment. Studies comparing surgery to medical therapy have determined what degree of blockage most benefits

from surgery. Unfortunately, patients over the age of sixty-seven were excluded from these trials. Because older patients have an increased risk of dying from surgery, as well as other complications such as stroke, renal failure, postoperative infection, and prolonged hospitalization, it is difficult to be certain that this same benefit is present. By benefit we understand a reduction in mortality. The original trials showing the benefit of surgery also tended to exclude women, who make up more than 50 percent of the elderly population. In addition, these trials were conducted in the 1970s, and since then there have been considerable improvements in both medical therapy and surgical therapy.

The rationale for surgical intervention is that risks taken at the time of surgery will pay off with long-term benefits. A review by Yusuf, Zucker, Peduzzi, et al. of the trials comparing bypass surgery and medical therapy show that the peak benefit of surgery over medical therapy occurs at five years after surgery. At this point, mortality rates are 10.2 percent for surgical patients vs. 15.8 percent for those having medical therapy in the under sixty-five age group.

Expected mortality for patients under the age of sixty-five who undergo bypass surgery and have no other major medical problems is less than 1 percent. Over the age of seventy, operative mortality may increase to 2 to 5 percent; and over the age of eighty this increases to 5 to 10 percent. Depending on operative risk factors, which are certainly increased in older patients, mortality may climb to 20 percent, and emergency surgery has a ten-fold increase in risk to 35 percent. The major risk factors include an ejection fraction (fraction of blood pumped out of the heart with each beat) less than 20 percent, repeat surgery, emergency surgery, female sex, diabetes, age greater than seventy, left main disease (two of the three arteries to the heart branch of the short left main artery; if it is blocked fifty percent, this is considered a significant risk), recent MI, and/or three-vessel coronary artery disease. The incidence of coronary artery disease also increases with age, and the greatest growth in the use of bypass surgery has been in the elderly. Older age also predisposes to other risk factors for heart disease, such as underlying lung disease, kidney problems, cerebrovascular disease, diabetes, and problems with infection and healing postoperatively.

Stroke is another possible operative complication. The risk of stroke is less than 2 percent for

Figure 2
The Heart: Frontal View

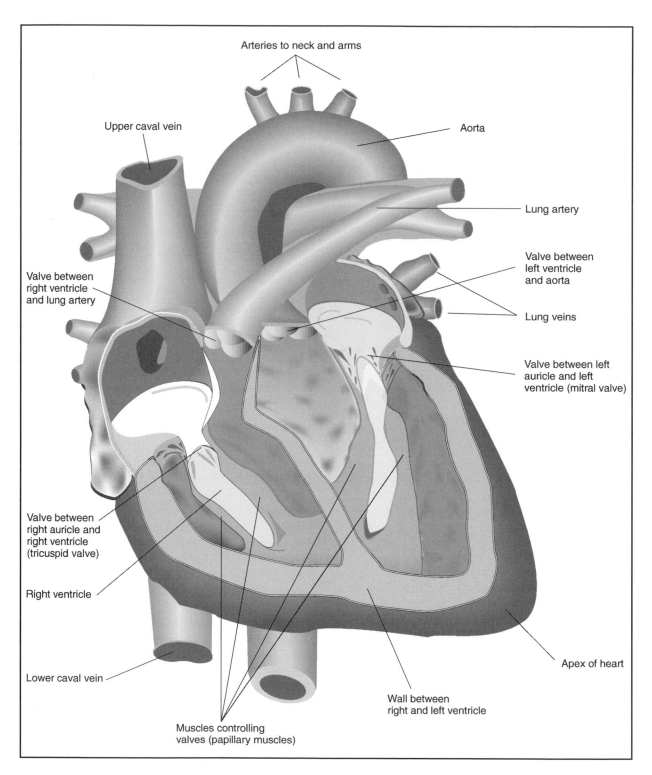

SOURCE: Suggested by brochure issued by Pfizer Canada Inc. (1996) and created by Symphony Medical Communications of Oslo, Norway (1996).

Figure 3
The Heart: Pacemaker

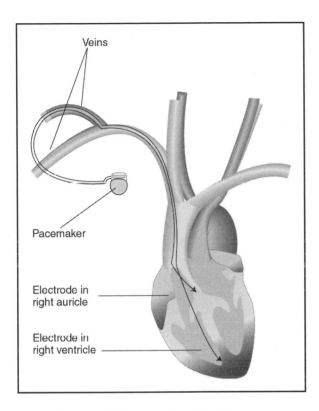

Veins

Pacemaker

Electrode in
right auricle

Electrode in
right ventricle

SOURCE: Suggested by brochure issued by Pfizer
Canada Inc. (1996) and created by Symphony
Medical Communications of Oslo, Norway (1996).

survival. The reasons to undertake any intervention, whether it be medication or surgery, are either to prolong life or to improve symptoms. While the evidence for bypass surgery prolonging life in patients over the age of sixty-five remains unclear, there certainly is improvement in symptoms of angina and quality of life in older patients, provided major complications are avoided.

Bypass surgery is done under general anesthesia, usually lasting three to four hours. The chest or sternum is split, while a specialized pump maintains circulation to the vital organs. The heart is then stopped and arteries or veins are attached to the aorta. The other ends are reattached to the native arteries beyond the blockages. Veins are generally harvested from the leg; arteries from the forearm or chest. Although there are three major arteries supplying the heart, these all have multiple branches, and patients may have up to five or six bypasses done during surgery. During the first twenty-four to forty-eight hours after surgery, the patient is placed in the intensive care unit. Following this, the patient is transferred to a regular hospital ward for mobilization and monitoring of complications. The great majority of patients do very well with this surgery and return to a full and active life.

Angioplasty

Revascularization can also be accomplished using percutaneous transluminal coronary angioplasty (PTCA), which is much less invasive. This is done using catheters, which are passed through the femoral or brachial arteries to the heart, as with coronary angiography. Wires are then passed through the catheter and down the coronary arteries past the narrowings. A balloon, which is deflated, is passed over the wire to the point of greatest narrowing. The balloon is then inflated, compressing the plaque or obstruction. When the balloon is deflated, the artery usually remains open. Blood thinners are used to prevent immediate clotting while the area heals over, and oral antiplatelet agents also prevent blood clots from forming on the torn or damaged artery. Twenty to 30 percent of arteries reocclude following the procedure, with up to one-half of these occurring in the first twenty-four hours. While many of these can be reopened with a balloon and kept open using a coil or stent, occasionally a dissection or acute closure results in

those under age seventy and greater than 6 percent for those over age seventy. A less well-documented area of concern is that of cognitive change or decline following bypass surgery. While more difficult to measure, this may have great significance for patients' independent living and quality of life postoperatively.

Renal failure also increases with increasing age after bypass surgery. It occurs in less than 1 percent of patients under the age of seventy, but is present in almost 2 percent of patients over the age of eighty. Predisposing factors would be renal failure preoperatively, diabetes, and hypertension. Older patients tend to have longer hospital stays postoperatively.

The long-term mortality rates are three to four times greater for older patients at five to ten years after surgery. It is, therefore, somewhat difficult to extrapolate older data on younger patients to older patients, who clearly have greater risks but may not have as much benefit regarding

Figure 4
The Heart: Lysis of Clot

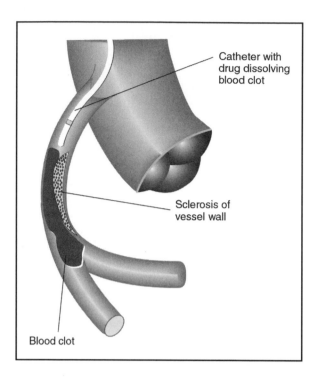

SOURCE: Suggested by brochure issued by Pfizer Canada Inc. (1996) and created by Symphony Medical Communications of Oslo, Norway (1996).

Figure 5
The Heart: Percutaneous Transluminal Coronary Angioplasty (PTCA)

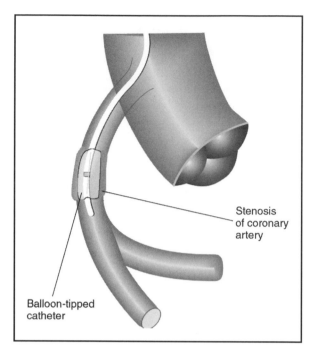

SOURCE: Suggested by brochure issued by Pfizer Canada Inc. (1996) and created by Symphony Medical Communications of Oslo, Norway (1996).

the need for emergency surgery. These complications are more common in the elderly. Gregorio, Kobayashi, Albiero, et al. found that 3.7 percent of angioplasty patients over the age of seventy-five required emergency CABG, compared with 1.4 percent for those under the age of seventy-five. They also found that mortality was markedly increased, at 2.2 percent for the older patients, compared with 0.1 percent for the younger group. This procedure is very operator-dependent, and experience certainly results in better outcomes. While complication rates are lower than for bypass surgery, they are more significant with increasing age. Bypass surgery results in more complete revascularization and better reduction of symptoms than PTCA, but it has not been shown to prolong survival. Diabetics, the BARI (Bypass Angioplasty Revascularization Investigation) trial showed, have had improved five-year mortality with bypass surgery compared to angioplasty (5.8 percent vs. 20.6 percent).

The most striking difference between the two procedures is the need for repeat revascular-

ization procedures. Less than 10 percent of bypass surgery patients require another procedure in five years, compared to 50 percent of angioplasty patients. Further, not all blockages are amenable to angioplasty. Experience of the physician performing the angioplasty (interventionalist) is critical with more difficult lesions.

Following angioplasty or coronary artery bypass grafting, risk management is important to maintain artery patency. This includes the use of aspirin and antiplatelet agents, aggressive lipid lowering, smoking cessation, and managing blood pressure and diabetes. Revascularization may reduce the need for antianginal medication. These treatments should not be considered curative; patients must still be aware of the possibility of recurrence of angina and ischemic heart disease.

The utilization of coronary angiography and subsequent revascularization varies considerably within different jurisdictions and health care systems. An interesting study compared patients over the age of sixty-five having a heart attack from a United States Medicare database and an Ontario, Canada database. Catheterization rates in the United States approached 40 percent, compared to 10 percent in Ontario, and revascularization rates were 28.5 percent versus 6.3 percent, respectively. Despite this marked increase in revascularization in the United States, mortality rates at one year were identical. Symptom control was not assessed, however.

In summary, while ischemic heart disease and associated risks increase with increasing age, there is also increased risk with revascularization procedures. In addition, comorbidities such as diabetes, hypertension, renal failure, prior strokes, lung disease, heart failure, and deconditioning may also be increased with increasing age. If medical therapy cannot adequately control symptoms of ischemic heart disease, then revascularization procedures must be considered. While angioplasty carries less risk, it is not always technically possible, and the need for repeat procedures is greater than with bypass surgery. Bypass surgery carries far greater risk but may provide the greatest benefit. Further, there seems to be an increasing physiological variability with aging. Multiple organ systems are at risk during bypass surgery and complications may be more devastating if coping skills and general health are reduced. There is no substitution for an open and frank discussion with physicians and family before embarking on revascularization. Technical expertise of surgeons, physicians, and the entire health care team are crucial to achieve optimal outcomes.

PAUL MacDONALD

See also ANESTHESIA; HEART DISEASE; SURGERY IN ELDERLY PEOPLE; QUALITY OF LIFE.

BIBLIOGRAPHY

ACC/AHA Task Force Report. "Guidelines for Percutaneous Transluminal Coronary Angioplasty." *Journal of the American College of Cardiology* 22 (1993): 2033–2054.

BARI Investigators. "Influence of Diabetes on 5-Year Mortality and Morbidity in a Randomized Trial Comparing CABG and PTCA in Patients With Multivessel Disease." *Circulation* 96, no. 6 (1997): 1761–1769.

CHERTOW, G. M.; LAZARUS, J. M.; CHRISTIANSEN, C. L.; et al. "Preoperative Renal Risk Stratification." *Circulation* 95, no. 4 (1997): 878–884.

EAGLE, K. A.; GUYTON, R. A.; DAVIDOFF, R.; et al. "ACC/AHA Guidelines for Coronary Artery Bypass Graft Surgery: A Report of the American College of Cardiology/American Heart Association Task Force on Practice Guidelines (Committee to Revise the 1991 Guidelines for Coronary Artery Bypass Graft Surgery)." *Journal of the American College of Cardiology* 34 (1999): 1262–1346.

EDWARDS, F. H.; CLARK, R. E.; and SCHWARTZ, M. "Coronary Artery Bypass Grafting: The Society of Thoracic Surgeons National Database Experience." *Annual of Thoracic Surgery* 57 (1994): 12–26.

GERSH, B. J.; KRONMAL, R. A.; SCHAFF, H. V.; et al. "Long-Term (5 year) Results of Coronary Bypass Surgery in Patients 65 Years Old or Older: A Report From the Coronary Artery Surgery Study." *Circulation* 68, suppl. II (1983): 190–199.

GREGORIO, J. D. E.; KOBAYASHI, Y. ; ALBIERO, R.; et al. "Coronary Artery Stenting in the Elderly: Short-Term Outcome and Long-Term Angiographic and Clinical Follow-Up." *Journal of the American College of Cardiology* 32 (1998): 577–583.

PETERSON, E. D.; COWPER, P. A.; JOLLIS, J. G.; et al. "Outcomes of Coronary Artery Bypass Graft Surgery in 24,461 Patients Aged 80 Years or Older." *Circulation* 92, no. 9, suppl. II, 85–91.

RITA Trial Participants. "Coronary Angioplasty versus Coronary Artery Bypass Surgery: The Randomised Intervention Treatment of Angina (RITA) Trial." *Lancet* 341 (1993): 573–580.

RITA-2 Trial Participants. "Coronary Angioplasty Versus Medical Therapy for Angina: The Second Randomised Intervention Treatment of Angina (RITA-2) Trial." *Lancet* 350 (1997): 461–468.

ROACH, G. W.; KANCHUGER, M.; MANGANO, C. M.; et al. "Adverse Cerebral Outcomes After Coronary Bypass Surgery." *The New England Journal of Medicine* 335, no. 25 (1996): 1857–1863.

SCHLANT, R. C., and ALEXANDER, R. W. *The Heart, Arteries, and Veins,* 8th ed. New York: McGraw-Hill, 1994.

TU, J. V.; PASHOS, C. L.; NAYLOR, C. D.; et al. "Use of Cardiac Procedures and Outcomes in Elderly Patients with Myocardial Infarction in the United States and Canada." *The New England Journal of Medicine* 336, no. 21 (1997): 1500–1505.

YUSUF, S.; ZUCKER, D., PEDUZZI, P.; et al. "Effect of Coronary Artery Bypass Graft Surgery on Survival: Overview of 10-Year Results From Randomised Trials by the Coronary Artery Bypass Graft Surgery Trialists Collaboration." *Lancet* 334 (1994): 563–570.

YUSUS, S. *Evidence Based Cardiology.* London: British Medical Journal Publications, 1998.

RISK MANAGEMENT AND INSURANCE

As people age, the chances increase that some conditions (e.g., disability) or events (e.g., retirement, loss of spouse) may alter their financial status. Risk management is a field that seeks to reduce the economic costs that would otherwise be associated with those conditions and events. These costs may be reduced both by reducing the probability or severity of the event (e.g., adding safety railings) and by reducing the economic losses should the event occur (e.g., through insurance). For some events there are good insurance products on the market, and for others there are not. Several components of the total retirement package (pensions, retiree health plans, long-term care policies, and personal care provided for those who need special assistance) may help in the management of post-retirement risks. Individual risks are discussed in more detail in other entries in this encyclopedia; in this section general risks and insurance considerations that are important for the management of these risks will be examined.

Post-retirement risks

It may seem surprising that the term *risk* heard so frequently in casual conversations and in discussions with financial professionals, has no single, widely accepted definition. However, all definitions share the concept of uncertainty. From the perspective of the individual, uncertainty arises for two reasons. First, even though the probability of occurrence can be predicted for a group (e.g., the risk of death at a specific age), its timing cannot be predicted for an individual. Second, even though the average loss from an event's occurrence may be estimated, variations in actual losses across individuals will occur. Thus, the risk of retired-life events can be considered in two parts; (1) the probability of occurrence, and (2) the loss associated with an event's occurrence.

A review of the pattern and economic costs of post-retirement risks suggests that retirement income distributions may not be well matched to the risks faced in the post-retirement years. Social Security benefits are paid to couples as a fam-

ily, and reflect the work history of both members of the couple. In addition, benefits are continued to the surviving spouse. These benefits are indexed to provide increases linked to increases in living costs. Private pension benefits may be distributed in one of several forms: as a lump sum, as a level income, as an indexed income, and as an income with continued payment to a survivor after one of the annuitants dies. None of these forms has any component linked to changing consumption needs. Insurance can help provide security and help protect against some changing needs, but it does not offer a perfect solution.

Events of the post-retirement period

There are a number of events, some of which are described below, that can change the economic circumstances of the individual retiree after retirement. The example in Table 1 illustrates one of these hypothetical individuals.

In this example, Joan's family members are critical in her support from age seventy-seven until her death. But since no suitable family household was available for her to join, she has lived in special housing since age seventy-five. Starting at age seventy-eight, she has needed daily support, and starting at age eighty, support throughout the day.

The higher out-of-pocket costs of accommodating her functional limitations places Joan at risk of outliving the resources that she and Robert may have thought sufficient for their lifetimes. For low-income persons, Medicaid is available to pay for nursing home care, but not for help until the individual is severely disabled. If Joan had purchased long-term care insurance, exactly when benefits would be payable would vary depending on the provisions of the specific insurance policy, but benefits would have probably started around age eighty. Joan's medications are about $250 per month, which are paid for by her private insurance, but not by Medicare. Many private insurance programs, however, limit what can be paid for drugs, and some policies offer no coverage for prescription drugs. If Joan has limited assets and income, she may become eligible for Medicaid at some point between ages eighty and eighty-two.

This example is presented to illustrate some of the economic issues involved with the gradual change of functional status, including the use of the telephone, ability to drive, ability to pay bills

Table 1
Timeline of a hypothetical person (Joan) as she ages beyond 70.

Joan's Age	Joan's Situation	Help Needed and Cost in Year 2000 Dollars
70	Joan and her husband, Robert, both age 70 have been retired for several years. They are happy, active, walk almost every day, but are phasing down their activity level. Robert has heart disease, controlled by medication. They live in their own home with a yard in a suburb of a major northern city.	
73	Joan and Robert find it difficult to care for the house and yard and feel trapped in the winter. It's hard to get help with snow removal, and they don't like to drive in snow. They're exploring other options for living and they've slowed down activities further. Joan is in good health but concerned about meeting the demands placed on her.	
75	Robert dies. Joan relocates to an independent-living apartment complex. She keeps her car. She has dinner provided, has access to activities, transportation, etc. Her apartment is cleaned weekly.	Cost of apartment and services is about $2,500 per month.
76	Joan is diagnosed with Parkinson's disease. With medication, she can handle most of her needs. She needs five separate medications taken in different combinations four times a day to help control the Parkinson's and high blood pressure. Joan stops driving, and no longer keeps the car.	Same cost for apartment. Her health care costs are paid by a combination of Medicare and insurance provided by Robert's former employer.
77	Joan needs help paying her bills and managing her finances, plus help with shopping and errands. A family member is helping her about twice a week for a minimum of six hours per week with bill paying, errands, and doctor's appointments. She can answer the phone and make calls only to preprogrammed numbers. She can get messages on her answering machine. She is able to take a short walk on her own.	Same as age 76.
78	Joan can no longer manage her own medication and can't use the answering machine. A paid helper comes in for about three hours a day, in addition to twice-a-week help from a family member.	$2,500 per month for the apartment plus $1,200 per month for the helper.
80	Joan can no longer manage without help in bathing, dressing, and administering medication. She moves to an assisted-living facility. She can feed herself if meals have been prepared and served, but she is no longer able to fix a cup of coffee or to pour coffee from a coffee pot. A family member helps her two to three times a week with errands, bill-paying, and doctor's appointments.	$4,000 per month, including all meals, administering medication, and assistance in bathing and dressing.
82	Joan has extreme difficulty walking and trouble feeding herself. She has a great deal of difficulty speaking or hearing and often gets confused. She moves to a nursing home. She continues to get help from a family member three times a week.	$6,000 per month for the nursing home.
84	Joan dies.	

SOURCE: Author

and manage personal affairs, management of medication, and going out independently. It intends to illustrate the key issue in risk management: how to assure coverage of increases in living costs when neither the timing nor the size of those increases can be precisely predicted for any individual.

Increasing life expectancies, even for retirees, increase the risk of a person outliving their resources. One can protect against this risk by annuitizing assets; for example, choosing a payment form that will continue income payments regardless of the number of years the annuitant (and surviving spouse) lives. However, other post-retirement risks interact with length of life in ways that make this an imperfect strategy for complete insurance of levels of economic well-being. For example, inflation over a longer lifetime will further erode the purchasing power of an annuity that is not indexed for inflation. In addition, while lengthening lifetimes may extend the period of joint survival for a couple, it also extends the number of years of widowhood when one's spouse dies. Likewise, lengthening life expectancies increases the chances that at least one parent may still be alive when an individual retires, raising the possibility that a parent's health care needs may place demands on a retiree's resources.

Changed consumption needs. A variety of unexpected post-retirement changes in family, work, and health status can lead to changes in consumption needs. The death of a spouse diminishes the food and clothing consumption needs of a now smaller household, but may increase the costs of leisure and household repairs that were formerly provided by the deceased spouse. It may also mean there is no longer someone available to help other household members. Loss of functional status by any household member increases health care costs and may increase transportation and home maintenance costs when that person is no longer mobile or requires facility adaptations. If someone's retirement planning did not incorporate the chances of these post-retirement risks, then the selected pattern of resource distribution may not be well matched to subsequent needs.

Death of a spouse. A spouse's death can cause a major change in both the personal and financial situation for the survivor. While group probabilities of losing a spouse can be calculated, an individual's death may be unexpected, leaving a spouse bereaved and impoverished. The survivor is most often female, but there are also differences in what typically happens after the loss of a spouse. Men are much more likely to remarry. Women often experience a substantial decline in economic status and discover that they and their spouse had not planned adequately for widowhood. Women's longer life expectancies and marriages to younger men means that survival as a widow is expected to be much longer than it is for widowers.

A financial retirement plan for a couple is not adequate unless it also provides for what happens when one of them dies. There are a variety of different financial strategies available to help in planning for widowhood. Assets are generally left to the survivor, but depending on other resources of the survivor, they may not be adequate to meet lifetime needs. Life insurance provides lump-sum funds for widowhood. Survivor options in pensions and annuities provide for continued income, and a fully owned home can be an important asset.

Other family changes. Retirees increasingly find themselves responsible for the physical and financial care of parents and children. Unexpected events in the lives of these individuals and their families can lead to immediate changes in the financial demands placed on retirees. This can be addressed by reviewing the financial strategies of these individuals, but for parents of retirees there may be few options at their time of life (see discussion of uninsurable risks below).

Inflation. Price increases erode the purchasing power of savings, with a relatively low rate of 2 percent reducing purchasing power by one-third over a twenty year period, and a rate of 5 percent reducing it by two-thirds. Asset, annuity income, and life insurance amounts need to be planned with the expectation of future inflation, the exact path of which can only be imperfectly estimated. Social Security benefits rise annually with the consumer price index, but, in general, employer-provided pension benefits do not. Investment strategies in which the growth in personal assets counteract the effect of inflation on the purchasing power of a retiree's portfolio can be used.

Unexpected health care needs. Post-employment medical coverage is important for retired individuals and spouses, particularly for retirees below the age of eligibility for Medicare coverage. While persons age sixty-five and over are covered by Medicare, this program covers only a portion of medical costs and does not provide coverage for prescription medications.

Changes in functional status. A decline in the ability to perform designated activities of daily living may require special help. These are tasks required on a daily basis, such as eating, toileting, and dressing. They are important because the ability to perform such tasks is the way most long-term insurance policies determine eligibility for receipt of benefits. Organized retirement systems do not adjust to increasing income needs as functional status declines, though medical coverage may reimburse for some care, and long-term care insurance can help pay for part of the cost of special disability help. However, as described below, the gradual nature of functional declines may not be well accommodated by insurance. Some declines can be addressed initially by redesigning housing space to make it more user-friendly to those with the anticipated problems, or so it can accommodate assistants.

It is important to be aware well ahead of time of the possible need for these services, and what is covered and what is not covered by available insurance. The alternative is financing extra costs through savings or income.

How insurance fits in

Insurance allows a large number of people who share a similar risk to pool their risks. For insurance to be viable, there needs to be a large group with similar risks, and it must be impossible or very difficult for them to determine in advance which particular individuals will have losses and when they might occur. Legally, insurance can be provided only when there is insurable interest and a legitimate purpose for the insurance. For example, it is reasonable to sell life insurance to people who have an economic loss if the person insured dies, but not reasonable to allow a person to purchase life insurance on strangers. That would be gambling, and there is no insurable interest. In addition to needing a large pool of people, there must be an insurance organization willing to provide and market the product, and a large enough marketplace so that the product is financially viable. Insurance is regulated in every state, and insurance arrangements must comply with the regulations.

Life insurance.   There are a wide variety of different types of life insurance policies available. These policies can be used to provide death benefits upon the loss of a spouse, and many of them can also be used to help accumulate retirement assets and to address other risks. Some policies have provisions that allow the benefits to be paid out early in the event of severe disablement, so that they can be used to help pay for long-term care. Inflation should be considered in determining the amount of life insurance needed.

Health (medical) insurance.   Health insurance covers both expected and unexpected health care costs. Depending on policy design, all costs may not be covered, and premiums and benefits caps may or may not increase with inflation. Medicare pays for about half of the total health care needs of the elderly. Some employers offer supplemental coverage for retirees, but others do not. A premium may be required for employer-sponsored coverage. If there is no employer coverage, then there are two different strategies for buying insurance to add to what Medicare covers. Medicare supplements work in partnership with traditional Medicare and cover some of what Medicare does not cover. Many do not cover prescription drugs, and those that do offer only limited coverage. Federal law specifies eight different benefit designs that can be offered as Medicare supplements.

Another alternative for Medicare-eligible persons is a Medicare+Choice plan. Under these plans, the federal government pays a flat amount per covered person to the plan, and a total benefit package is offered by the plan. The plan is chosen instead of traditional care. These plans differ in whether they charge premiums in addition to the payment by Medicare, and in what benefits are offered. Different plans are available by geographic area, and enrollees are limited to the use of contracted physicians and hospitals. Some of these plans offer prescription drug coverage, but others do not. There are generally limits on what is offered, so plans need to be analyzed carefully. Depending on the geographic area, what is available will vary, and it may be quite expensive. Purchasing coverage can be difficult for those in poor health, and many states have high-risk pools available for covering people who have difficulty purchasing coverage as an individual.

Long-term care insurance.   Long-term care insurance provides for part of the cost of extra care resulting from frailty. It does not provide coverage for the less severely disabled, and it pays up to a specific limit, which may be less than the total cost of care. Some people may seem to be quite disabled and still not qualify for benefits. Inflation of these costs may be covered, depending on the policy design. Long-term care insurance can be purchased to cover an individual and spouse, and also parents, if they are living and insurable.

Annuities.   Annuities provide insurance against the risk of outliving assets. They also provide coverage of investment risks, as the insurance company handles investments. They can be inflation adjusted, but most are not. A reverse mortgage is a special type of annuity that enables a person to borrow against the equity value in a home, receiving periodic payments which are repaid upon the death of the person or sale of the home.

What risks are not insurable

Inflation.   It is not possible to insure against inflation directly, but various strategies can be used to offer a better hedge against inflation. For example, if annuities are purchased, either inflation-adjusted annuities with a fixed, built-in escalator, such as 3 percent or 5 percent can be used. An investment strategy for financial assets should take into account expectations with regard to inflation, and should also reflect the individual's view as to the best investments considering the expected economic environment. Many people feel that investing part of their assets in common stocks is a good hedge against inflation. Whether this is sensible depends on the total portfolio, and on all sources of retirement income.

Other family changes. The death of a spouse is a very common change for elderly Americans, and the economic loss associated with the death of a spouse can be insured. Many older Americans also provide assistance to parents, children, or grandparents. This assistance can be in the form of care during frailty, it can be financial assistance, or it can be other support. In some cases, older Americans are asked to care for a parent after the spouse of that person is disabled or deceased. Generally, these are a challenge to plan for and are not insurable, but they are a reason for having more savings. Some of them can be partly insured. For example, long-term care insurance can be purchased on parents. [Life insurance can be purchased on a parent if the child expects to become responsible for the surviving parent after the death of one parent.]

Changes in functional status.   Services to the frail elderly can be provided at home, in nursing homes, or in a variety of housing settings. In general, there is no insurance against moderate changes in functional status and the extra needs that result; long-term care insurance is activated upon evidence of need of assistance in several activities of daily living. An individual experiencing and needing help as functioning status declines may need to draw on savings. An individual can also plan housing that is flexible. Developments of the past several decades in public- and private-sector approaches to housing for older adults have been motivated in part by the need for housing that adjusts to these gradual, noninsurable, declines. For example, many elderly housing developments accommodate wheelchairs easily and have handrails in corridors for those with balance problems.

Another way to plan for moderate changes in functional status is to live near children or other family members who can provide some help if it is needed. Some retirement communities provide help. A continuing care retirement community (CCRC) integrates housing, medical care, assistance with daily living, and a variety of social and other activities. This type of community is of particular interest to actuaries, in that it often provides a form of medical and/or long-term care

insurance. CCRCs typically require a down payment at entry and a monthly fee. They also have health requirements at entry and provide a range of services, some of which may require additional fees.

Changed housing needs. Owning a home with a good resale value offers a good chance that one will have the resources to move into different housing as needs change. The CCRC is a way of insuring that housing will be available that fits one's needs as one becomes more frail. However, it does not guarantee that one will be near children, or fit new interests. There is no other direct financial vehicle to protect one in the event of changing housing needs.

Buying insurance

There are some general things to be aware of in buying insurance. In addition, there are details specific to each type of plan (these are not covered here). General things to watch for include:

- Is the company licensed in my state?
- What is the financial rating and reputation of the company? (Best's is one service that rates insurance companies.)
- How does the insurance policy match one's specific needs? In all of these areas, there are a number of areas in which policies differ. Be sure that the details of the policy fit your needs.
- Is the policy a good value? What sales charges are included?
- What provisions does the policy include in the event one's needs change or in the event one changes his or her mind later about this coverage?
- Does the company have a good reputation for paying claims promptly and fairly? How committed is the company to the particular type of business? This is particularly important in areas like annuities and long-term care, where it is expected that the policy will be ongoing for the rest of one's life.

ANNA M. RAPPAPORT
KAREN HOLDEN

See also ANNUITIES; CONTINUING CARE RETIREMENT COMMUNITIES; EMPLOYEE HEALTH INSURANCE; FUNCTIONAL ABILITY; HEALTH INSURANCE, NATIONAL APPROACHES; LONG-TERM CARE INSURANCE; MEDICAID; MEDICARE: WIDOWHOOD, ECONOMIC ISSUES.

BIBLIOGRAPHY

ESCHTRUTH, A. D., and LONG, C. "A Primer on Reverse Mortgages." *Just the Facts on Retirement Issues,* Number 3. Chestnut Hill, Mass.: Center for Retirement Research at Boston College, 2001.

RAPPAPORT, A. "Retirement Needs Framework." *Retirement Needs Framework Monograph.* SOA Monograph M-RSOO-1. Schaumburg, Ill..: Society of Actuaries, 2000.

REJDA, G. E. *Principles of Risk Management and Insurance,* 7th ed. Boston: Addison Wesley Longman, 2000.

VAUGHAN, E. J., and VAUGHAN, T. M. *Fundamentals of Risk and Insurance,* 8th ed. New York: John Riley and Sons, 1999.

RODENTS

Rodents are members of the order Rodentia, a large group of biologically similar animals that includes rats, mice, and beavers. Two of these species, rats and mice, are the most commonly used animal models for aging research.

Many types of aging research cannot be conducted with human subjects. In situations where the research requires a living organism, and humans are not suitable, investigators must search for a suitable animal model. Humans may not be suitable because they choose their mates, and thus genetic control is not possible; because they live freely, rather than in controlled environments; because the research may result in unacceptable risks of pain, emotional distress, or illness; or because the research requires observing the subjects for a lifetime and humans live too long.

The range of animal models used in aging research is very wide and includes very small nematode worms (*Caenorhabditis elegans*), fruit flies (Drosophila melanogaster), rats, mice, dogs, monkeys, and chimpanzees. Of all of these models, rats and mice are the most commonly used because they have reasonable lifespans (two to four years), they are mammals and therefore share a great many genes with humans, and because a very great deal is known about their physiology, behavior, and genetic makeup. Thousands of mice and rats are specially bred each year throughout the world for biological, biomedical, and behavioral research. Much of what is learned is published in the scientific literature and available to scientists virtually anywhere on earth. The publication of research results in this way allows the sharing of information, reducing the amount of duplication of research. Information sharing also makes each piece of research more meaningful than it might otherwise be, since each investigator can place his or her research in the context of what else is known about that species.

While rats and mice are not as similar to humans as are nonhuman primates (monkeys and chimps), they have the advantages of small size and relatively easy husbandry, and they share many genes with all mammals including humans. Nonhuman primates are very much like humans, sharing perhaps 95 percent of their genes with humans. They are therefore the model of choice for some sorts of research, especially research that requires large brains, complex behavior, and long life spans. Chimps, for example, live up to seventy-five years, are capable of very complex behaviors and emotions, and probably develop late life diseases like Alzheimer's disease that seem to require years to develop. Because they are large, complex animals with long life spans they are very expensive to maintain. They also cannot be used in many of the same types of research where humans cannot be used.

The use of animal models for research is controversial. Special attention is paid to nonhuman primate research. Use of all animals is carefully monitored, housing requirements are justifiably strict, and social needs are regulated. The large size and complex behavior of nonhuman primates makes these animals especially expensive to maintain and study.

Since rats and mice are relatively easy to maintain, relatively economical, and large numbers can be bred and maintained in relatively small vivaria, they have been the models of choice for decades. Many of the mouse strains currently used for research are descendants of mice bred by European zoologists in the nineteenth century. These zoologists bred their mice for specific characteristics, such as coat color, and began analysis of the genetic control of such characteristics. In the early part of the twentieth century biologists began to breed mice, and to a lesser extent rats, for susceptibility to diseases, especially cancer. Rats were used where a larger body size or blood volume were needed for research, mice where small body size and smaller fluid volumes were acceptable. Mice, being smaller, were cheaper, and somehow seemed more attractive—or less objectionable—as well. In research programs throughout the twentieth century, rats have been most used for physiological research because of their large size, and mice in genetic research because of their small size. Use of mice and rats continues to follow this general pattern although micro-methods have made mice more available for physiological research and the collection of more genetic information about rats has made them more available to geneticists.

Genotype

Among the tremendous advantages that recommend rodents for research, the ability to control genetic and environmental variables are the most significant. By rearing the animals in controlled environments, it is possible to almost completely eliminate the risks of infectious diseases. This is accomplished by placing the animals in facilities called barrier facilities. These facilities have no windows, which allows control of the exposure to light; the animal rooms are sealed and air entering the rooms is filtered to exclude airborne sources of infection or irritation; food bedding cages and water are sterilized; and caretakers take complete showers before entering these rooms. These precautions reduce the possibility that changes observed with advancing age are due to disease. This makes it more likely that changes are the result of "normal aging." The development of such barrier facilities led to a doubling of the observed life span of rats and mice over the twenty years from 1970 to 1990. Much of what was once thought to be the inevitable consequence of aging appears to be the consequence of disease. This evolution in health and life span of laboratory animals with improvements in husbandry is reminiscent of the similar changes in human health and life span with the development of improved public health and the advent of antibiotics during the twentieth century.

Environment

Environmental control has another very important function. By producing controlled environments that differ in some single variable (e.g., temperature) it is possible to isolate that variable and determine its effects upon the health, behavior, or longevity of the animals being studied. Variables that can be tested in this way range from simple aspects of the environment such as day length, temperature, and humidity to more complex variables such as feeding regimen and nutrition, drug dose or route of administration, or social interaction with cage mates.

The power of environmental control in these rodent models (and in some lower species such as fruit flies as well) is greatly increased by the genetic control that can be applied at the same time. By a process of inbreeding (mating to close relatives) mice and rats can be made to share all or most of their genes. Inbred strains are the most commonly used examples of such control. Inbred strains are the result of at least twenty generations of brother-sister mating. After twenty generations new mutations are adding genetic diversity, in the form of new genes at the same rate that gene differences are being eliminated by the inbreeding process. However, at this point the differences between the animals within the inbred strain are very slight. The animals are as genetically identical as are identical twins. Thus, it is possible to produce large numbers of genetically identical mice or rats, all the same age and at the same time.

Gene environment interaction

By studying genetically controlled rodents in controlled environments, it is possible to discover whether a phenomenon is determined by genes, the environment, or both. For example, assume an investigator wanted to discover whether genetic differences or exposure to some environmental factor causes cataracts in mice. In this example, the investigator suspects that the cause is bright light, but he has also noticed that not all of his animals get cataracts. To further complicate matters, the animals that do get cataracts get them at different ages. To test whether environmental factors affect cataract formation, this investigator can place genetically identical mice in different parts of the animal room, near to lights and further away from lights. Differences in number of cataracts formed and the age at which they are formed must be due to environmental differences, since the animals are genetically identical. In this case, he will find that animals on the top of the cage rack will develop more cataracts sooner than animals further from the ceiling lights in the room. To determine whether genes affect cataract formation the investigator can place mice of different strains in the same environment. By putting mice of more than one strain close to the lights he will find that mice of some strains are more susceptible to cataract formation than are others. Thus, he will have shown that both the environment and genes are important in the development of cataracts.

While many, perhaps most, variables are affected by gene-environment interaction, the relative contributions of genes and environment differs from one variable to another. Eye color is largely determined by genes. Skin wrinkling is largely determined by exposure to sunlight (U.V. light). One of the objectives of research is to find the genetic and environmental factors that underlie age changes and age-related diseases in order to be able to improve the health of individuals and allow them to reach their maximum potential life span.

The *genotype* of the individual (or inbred strain) is the total set of genes that animal carries. The *phenotype* of the individual is the set of characteristics that the animal manifests, and is the result of the genotype and its interaction with the environment in which it is expressed. Most such interactions are complex and not as simple as hair color or eye color. Genes interact with one another and with environmental variables. Single traits, such as height or body weight, may be the result of several genes and their interaction with nutritional variables, activity level, and room temperature. Very complex traits, such as depression, anxiety, emotionality, intelligence, and longevity, are undoubtedly the result of the interactions of many, many genes and many environmental factors as well.

Special populations

A variety of special genetic populations of rodents have been developed in order to try to conduct analyses of these complex interactions. These include hybrid populations that carry genes from more than one parental type in predictable proportions, congenic lines that are genetically identical except for differences in a single gene of interest, and genetically selected lines that have been selected for a single trait such as long life, absence of cancer, or high activity rate. Selected populations offer a chance to find sets of genes that influence a trait such as longevity. In the selection process, mice (or rats or nematodes or fruit flies) are mated and then the life spans of the offspring are observed. The longest-lived are mated to one another and so on for many generations. The result is a population of mice with increased longevity. The genetic dif-

ferences between these animals and their shorter-lived progenitors can then be studied for clues to fundamental aging processes. These genetic factors are likely to be complex and multifactorial. Some genes may be parts of large arrays of genes all of which contribute a small amount to the final expression of a trait. Traits of this type are referred to as quantitative traits. New methods of analysis, such as quantitative trait locus (QTL) analysis, are being developed to cope with this complexity.

Molecular genetics

A major area of rodent model development that has resulted from the revolution brought to biology by molecular genetics is the creation of mice that are lacking a specific gene (called *knock outs*) or that have extra copies of such a gene (called *knock ins*). By deleting or adding genes it is possible to observe the effects of that gene very specifically. While the results of these manipulations have not always been as clear-cut as expected, this research approach offers a significant increase in the precision of genetic manipulation. These and other genetic manipulations result in what are commonly called designer mice and rats and as such represent the cutting edge of current animal model development.

RICHARD L. SPROTT

See also GENETICS; LONGEVITY: SELECTION; NUTRITION; PATHOLOGY OF AGING, ANIMAL MODELS.

BIBLIOGRAPHY

GREEN, E. L., ed. *Biology of the Laboratory Mouse.* New York: McGraw-Hill, 1966.

GREEN, M. C., ed. *Genetic Variants and Strains of Laboratory Mouse.* Stuttgart: Gustav Fischer Verlag, 1981.

SPROTT, R. L. "Development of Animal Models of Aging at the National Institute on Aging." *Neurobiology of Aging* 12 (1991): 635–638.

SPROTT, R. L. "Mouse and Rat Genotype Choices." *Aging Clinical Experimental Research* 5 (1993): 249–252.

ROUNDWORMS: *CAENORHABDITIS ELEGANS*

Aging is a complex deteriorative process affecting the survival of both living and nonliving things. To understand the underlying molecular and physiological processes of human aging, it is necessary to study a system that is less complex than humans—one where experiments can be easily performed. In response to these needs, a number of invertebrate models have been identified. Such models invariably are quite short-lived; in fact, the species described here, the nematode *Caenorhabditis elegans,* (see Figure 1) lives for only three weeks under normal conditions.

Overview of *C. elegans.*

During the first three days of life, the worm grows from an egg into an immature larval form that molts four times before finally becoming an adult. Most adults are hermaphrodites, producing both sperm and eggs, and producing about three hundred offspring over the next five days of life. By ten days of age, this species is finished with reproduction, but goes on to live for another ten days.

A great deal of research has been carried out since Dr. Sydney Brenner began his studies of the humble worm around 1965. Most research has concentrated on the development of the animal, but an increasing amount of interest into the aging process in *C. elegans* is apparent, with a dozen or more high-profile articles on genes that slow the aging process appearing around the turn of the century.

Gerontogenes.   Genes are DNA-based entities that code for proteins (and RNA), which function to carry out all of the biological needs of the organism. Geneticists discovered many years ago that disruption of these genes (called mutations) are inherited by offspring of all living things. Moreover, by careful comparisons of mutant and normal genes, geneticists can infer the normal function of the protein encoded by the disrupted gene. One can think of this process by analogy with a mechanic who knows nothing about how a car functions, but pulls one part at a time to see what function is changed as a result. Thus, removing the battery stops electrical function while removing the radiator makes the car overheat.

Nematode geneticists began looking for mutations in genes that affected aging (so-called gerontogenes) around 1980. In particular, the doctors Tom Johnson and Mike Klass genetically manipulated worms so as to lengthen their life

span. They reasoned that by increasing longevity they could be assured that the basic aging process is affected. (Most short-lived mutants would probably be merely dysfunctional in some key process, rather than aging rapidly.) Indeed, these searches for longevity mutants have turned out to be quite productive, and many gerontogenes (close to sixty) have been identified. At first glance, it is counterintuitive that altering a gene can lead to increased longevity—this implies that the normal gene is somehow shortening the life span. It must be remembered that evolution does not care about postreproductive longevity and that only the individual, not the species, benefits from increased longevity. All longevity mutants found so far decrease evolutionary fitness by decreasing reproductive capacity or slowing development.

The first gerontogene identified was age-1. A combined effort of both the Johnson and Klass labs resulted in identifying this gene in 1988, which was ultimately cloned in 1996 by Gary Ruvkun. (When a gene is cloned, it is isolated from all other genes so that its DNA sequence can be ascertained and the proposed molecular function of the protein encoded by that gene can be predicted.) In the case of age-1 (and other gerontogenes in the same molecular pathway), the sequence suggested that the gene was a signaling element and should function to regulate another gene, daf-16, which encodes a protein that has a sequence similar to a type of transcription factor in humans. (Transcription factors regulate the amount and types of RNA synthesized.) In fact, this nematode pathway has a very strong relationship to that encoding the mammalian insulin-response pathway and has revealed previously unknown mammalian genes involved in insulin signaling. Clearly, function can be highly conserved between species that have been separated by over a billion years of evolution.

More than sixty gerontogenes have been identified. These fall into multiple different classes, including age-1 (about fifteen mutants), "clock" slow development (about ten mutants), decreased fertility (two mutants), and reduced food intake (five mutants), among others.

By 2001, the entire worm sequence had become known. Some large labs, and even entire companies, have been formed to harvest the results of this sequence, and hopes are high that the nematode can be used to find proteins in humans that can be targeted by drugs with the goal

Figure 1
C. elegans

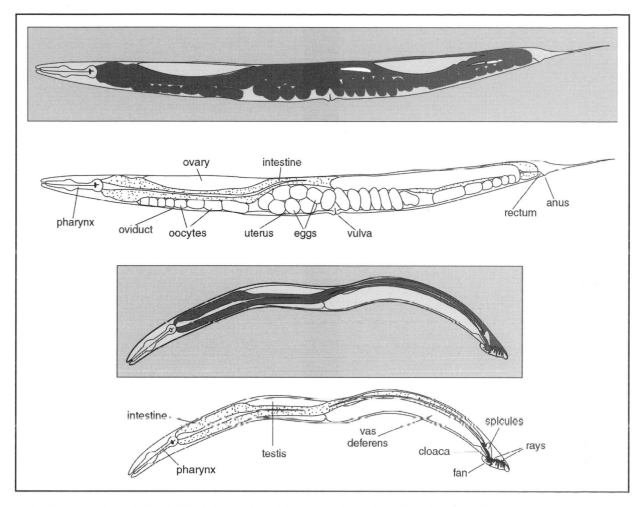

SOURCE:Wood, W. B. and the Community of C. Elegans Researchers, eds. *The Nematode Caenorhabditis Elegans*. Woodbury, NY: Cold Spring Harbor Laboratory Press, 1988.

of retarding and even eliminating aging. The first study on this possibility by doctors Simon Melov and Gordon Lithgow appeared in September 2000. They showed that a drug could increase the life span of the worm by 60 percent. The drug has not yet been tested in humans (see Figure 2).

Stress, Biomarkers, and Molecular Changes

Nematodes show many of the same signs of aging that are seen in humans. They accumulate a fluorescent pigment in their cells that is called lipofuscin. They move slower and slower and finally stop moving altogether a few days before they die. They eat less and less (and defecate less and less too), as they near death. They get wrinkled. They show a lot of other pathological changes associated with aging. However, all tissues do not change at the same rate. The gonad changes quite rapidly but neurological tissue seems to remain quite intact.

Among the most consistent changes associated with increased longevity of the mutants is the increased resistance to many forms of environmental stress (see Figure 3). Johnson's lab has found that heat, UV, reactive oxidants, etc. are all less toxic to the long-lived mutants. Although not all agree, it seems likely that the increased stress resistance plays a key role in the life prolongation of these mutants. Indeed, the

Figure 2
Effect of age-1 on survival

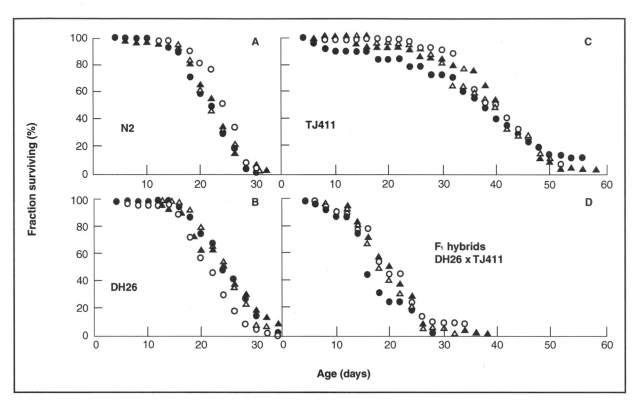

SOURCE: Adapted from: Melov, S., et al. "Extension of Life-Span with Superoxide Dismutase/Catalase Mimetics." *Science* 289: (2000): 1567–1569.

drug that prolonged life in the worms was an antioxidant designed to mimic the effect of a normal protein found at higher levels in age-1 mutants. This is a very exciting and extremely competitive area of research but may well yield secrets that will result in doubling the human life span within the life times of our children, if not ourselves.

THOMAS E. JOHNSON

BIBLIOGRAPHY

Brenner, S. "The Genetics of *Caenorhabditis Elegans*." *Genetics* 77 (1974): 71–94.

Friedman, D. B., and Johnson, T. E. "A Mutation in the *Age-1* Gene in *Caenorhabditis Elegans* Lengthens Life and Reduces Hermaphrodite Fertility." *Genetics* 118 (1988): 75–86.

Johnson, F. B.; Sinclair, D. A.; and Guarante, L. "Molecular Biology of Aging." *Cell* 96 (1999): 291–302.

Johnson, T. E. "The Increased Life Span of *Age-1* Mutants in *Caenorhabditis Elegans* Results from Lowering the Gompertz Rate of Aging." *Science* 249 (1990): 908–912.

Johnson, T. E., and Wood, W. B. "Genetic Analysis of the Life-Span of *Caenorhabditis Elegans*." *Proceedings of the National Academy of Sciences USA* 79 (1982): 6603–6607.

Klass, M. R. "A Method for the Isolation of Longevity Mutants in the Nematode *Caenorhabditis Elegans* and Initial Results." *Mechanisms of Ageing and Development* 22 (1983): 279–286.

Martin, G. M.; Austad, S. N.; and Johnson, T. E. "Genetic Analysis of Aging: Role of Oxidative Damage and Environmental Stresses." *Nature Genetics* 13 (1996): 25–34.

Riddle, D. L.; Blumenthal, T.; Meyer, B. J.; and Priess, J. R. *C. elegans II.* Cold Spring Harbor, N.Y.: Cold Spring Harbor Press, 1997.

Wood, W. B., ed. *The Biology of* Caenorhabditis elegans. Cold Spring Harbor, N.Y.: Cold Spring Harbor Press, 1988.

Figure 3

Survival curves of two wild-type age strains, an age mutant strain, and a heterozygous strain of C. elegans.

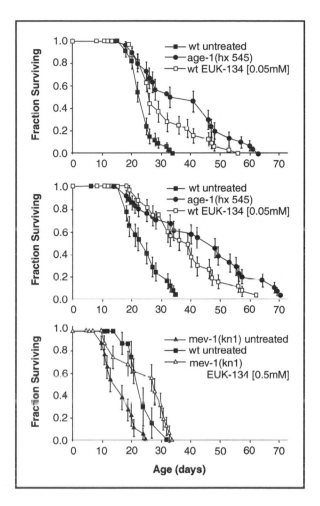

SOURCE: Adapted from: Johnson, T. E. "Increased Life-Span of Age-1 Mutants in *Caernobditis elegans* and Lower Gompertz Rate of Aging.". *Science* 249 (1990): 908–913.

RURAL ELDERLY

Description of the life circumstances of older people living in remote or rural areas is complicated by different definitions of rural residence and by the lack of variability within residential categories. The U.S. Bureau of the Census, for example, classifies residence based solely on the size of the population living in a predetermined geographical area. An "urbanized area" refers to one or more places plus the surrounding territory or fringe that include at least fifty thousand people. Urban residents are people living in either an urbanized area or outside an urbanized area in a place (e.g., township) with at least twenty-five hundred total residents. All other residents are considered rural. Rural residents are subdivided further into "farm" and "nonfarm" designations. According to the Census Bureau, about 24 percent of people aged sixty-five and over lived in rural areas in 1990, approximately the same proportion as the general population living in rural areas. About 16 percent of people aged sixty-five and over were rural farm residents in 1990, compared to only 1.5 percent of the total population (McLaughlin and Jensen).

Because the definition of rural residence used by the U.S. Office of Management and Budget (OMB) includes other criteria, such as commuting patterns and business activity, the Census and OMB sometimes classify residence differently. Different definitions and simplistic dichotomous categories frustrate efforts to learn more about the lives of rural elderly persons because researchers often rely upon data gathered by government agencies. Indeed, the terms "rural" and "nonmetropolitan" will be used here interchangeably, depending upon the data source cited. Rural elderly residents include those living in a remote county on a Wyoming ranch forty-five miles from the nearest small town, as well as those living on the outskirts of a large city. Similarly, the nonmetropolitan category includes remote counties as well as those with populations over 100,000 people. These definitions also matter because they influence national and state funding allocations. Further, the tax base contained within the geographic boundaries of these areas affects local millage rates and the potential to provide needed health and human services. Whether counties are nonmetropolitan or communities have fewer than 2,500 people would also make little difference if these counties or communities were alike. It is known, however, that counties differ according to indicators such as premature mortality (Mansfield, Wilson, Kobrinski, and Mitchell) and small communities differ according to poverty (Weinberg) and health services delivery and availability. Such differences affect the lives of elders with regard to availability and access to needed health and other services, opportunities for paid employment, or involvement in volunteer or leisure activities.

A farmer drives his tractor past the Danish Windmill in May 2001 in the town of Elk Horn, Iowa, where figures from the 2000 census show that more than 42 percent of the town's population is 65 and older. (AP photo by Charlie Neibergall.)

The changing rural older adult population

With the exception of the Northeast, nonmetropolitan residents are older than their metropolitan counterparts. Although there are signs that this distinction is beginning to reverse (e.g., Beale), the Census Bureau estimates that the nonmetropolitan population over age sixty-five grew by over 7 percent and the population aged eighty-five and older increased by about 21 percent from 1990 to 1996 (Ricketts et al.) Change in the percentage of older persons who live in rural areas is influenced by both immigration and a phenomenon called *aging in place,* accompanied by the outmigration of younger people. Comparing census data from 1970 to 1990 (McLaughlin and Jensen), states associated with retirement immigration, including Florida and Arizona, and states with elderly populations that are small to begin with, such as Alaska, have the fastest growing elderly populations. In primarily southern and western states impacted by retirement migration out of northern states, however, growth in the number of elders is not uniform across rural areas. Elderly people who are generally more affluent tend to move to areas within

states or from one state to another with features such as bodies of water and a strong tourism base (Johnson). The short- to medium-term impact of this movement on receiving rural communities is generally economically positive (Glasgow and Reeder, 1990; Serow, 1990). Elderly migrants purchase property, increasing the tax base, and they create service sector employment (Reeder and Glasgow). Over the long run, however, Longino and Smith speculate that the demand for social and medical supportive services will gradually increase as elderly migrants age in place and experience associated illness and disability.

States with large numbers of older adults who are aging in place (e.g., Kansas and Iowa) are also experiencing outmigration of younger people from rural areas in search of employment. When this happens, the proportion of the population that is older becomes relatively large and stable. The situation of rural older adults who are aging in place is better understood by considering their lifelong work and economic histories. Census data from 1990 show that rural workers hold lower paying and lower occupational status jobs. This explains why younger people are moving to areas with better jobs, leaving older family members behind to age in place. Compared to urban elders, rural elders have likely held jobs throughout their working lives in seasonal farming, forestry, fishing, or in lower paying occupations. This explains why older persons in rural regions characterized by aging in place are economically vulnerable. They have lower incomes and are more likely to be poor, and they are less educated then their urban counterparts (Coward, McLaughlin, Duncan, and Bull). Thus, increases in the proportion of rural older persons can have negative or positive economic precursors. In either case, however, the long-term effect will likely be increasing demand for services and assistance.

Characteristics of rural older adults

As stated previously, nonmetropolitan older adults are more likely than their metropolitan counterparts to have low incomes (below 200 percent of poverty) and lower lifetime earnings that negatively impact social security benefits (Krout, 1994). At the same time, they derive a higher proportion of their incomes from social security (Coburn and Bolda). The rural elderly are more likely than older urban residents to rely on Medicaid, because of lower lifetime earnings, or Medicare as their sole health insurance provider. Although rural older persons are more likely than urban older adults to own their homes outright, their homes tend to be of lower value and in need of repair compared to the homes of urban elderly people (Coburn and Bolda). Coburn and Bolda also describe rural or nonmetropolitan elderly people as significantly more likely than their urban or metropolitan counterparts to rate their health as fair or poor and to have problems doing activities of daily living, increasing their risk of premature mortality and diminished life satisfaction.

In contrast to popular notions about rural life, there is little evidence that older adults living in rural areas have more extensive kin networks from which to draw informal support than their urban counterparts (Coward and Cutler). Although rural elders are more likely than urban residents to be married, providing a source of assistance when needed, Stoller points out that the rural-urban difference in marital rates disappears by age eighty-five, when older people are more likely to need assistance. Stoller also points out that about one-third of rural elders are wid-

owed. By age eighty-five, over 80 percent of rural women are widows, compared to 40 percent of men. Given more traditional views of marital roles among older rural couples, particularly among husbands who often assume responsibility for transportation and finances, older rural widows are at high risk for financial vulnerability due to a lifetime of unpaid work and isolation. Remote locations and small community sizes that limit sources of assistance, combined with the outmigration of younger family members, places rural older adults in a vulnerable position concerning access to formal services and the availability of informal assistance from outside the home when needed.

On the positive side, older people living in rural areas are more likely than their urban counterparts to be married and less likely to be divorced until age eighty-five, when this rural advantage disappears (Stoller). Rural farm, but not necessarily nonfarm, elders are more likely than urban residents to live with or near at least one of their children. According to Lee et al., this child is often also engaged in the farm enterprise. Aside from the results of statistical comparisons, an obvious conclusion is that the majority of older persons living in rural areas are there because they prefer this environment: they have chosen to live in locations that are quieter and less populated, so their lives are less impacted than those of urban residents by the press of humanity. Fewer amenities and complex supportive services are not a problem as long as functional independence can be maintained.

Health and home- and community-based service use among rural older adults

National Health Interview Survey data point to a tendency for nonmetropolitan elders aged sixty-five to sixty-nine, adjacent to a metropolitan area, to visit physicians less frequently than same-aged people living in other locations. Rural elderly residents aged seventy-five and over, however, were as likely or more likely to visit a physician as their urban counterparts (Coburn and Bolda). It seems that rural elders who are financially able manage to get to physicians when there is a need, regardless of distance. In their study of health and community-based service use among rural southeastern community-dwelling older adults, Mitchell, Mathews, and Griffin (1997) found that rural and small town (under twenty-five hundred) residence had no effect on visits to primary care or specialty physicians when poverty status, transportation needs, and the availability of informal care were considered. This suggests that the poverty status, transportation problems, and lack of informal assistance coinciding with rural residence may be more important predictors of visits to primary care and specialty physicians than residence.

Services that help older persons stay in their homes as long as possible include those available through the Older Americans Act (OAA), the Social Services Block Grant (SSBG) program, Medicaid waivers, and largely for-profit in-home care. Initially assisting all older persons, OAA services now target socially impaired and economically disadvantaged people age sixty-five and over. OAA services include senior centers, transportation, in-home services, legal assistance, congregate meals, home delivered meals, and in-home services for the frail. Allocated to states through Title XX of the Social Security Act based upon the size of the needy population, SSBG assistance includes homemaker, chore service, home health care, protective services, and nutrition for older people. Medicaid funds home- and community-based long-term, skilled nursing care for eligible older adults as an alternative to institutional care. With Medicare restrictions in hospital care reimbursement in the 1980s, the private sector began to offer home health care following hospital discharge. Many agencies have expanded their services to include other types of in-home assistance, including chore service. This array of services is so complex that some have tried to categorize them in a more meaningful way. For example, Cox (1993) groups them as preventive for those less impaired, supportive for the moderately impaired, and protective for the severely impaired.

Assessment of the extent to which rural residence compromises access to home- and community-based services among older adults has been frustrated by inconsistent definitions of rural residence and because of different service designations across studies. Federal service delivery requirement (e.g., only volunteers can deliver meals), transportation costs, and the lack of larger numbers of service personnel found in urban areas, certainly limits innovation and the penetration of specialized services into rural communities (e.g., Salmon, Nelson, and Rouse). Consequently, Rowles concludes that relocation away from the rural community becomes the only option when rural elderly people lose capacity to accommodate declining physical capability, and when the support from kin, neighbors, or aging peers is no longer viable. Since the supply of nursing homes and nursing home beds is nearly 43 percent greater in nonmetropolitan than metropolitan areas (Coburn and Bolda) and complex in-home services that replace or delay institutionalization are generally less available in rural compared to urban areas (Nelson), this rural relocation is more likely to be to a skilled nursing facility than would be an urban relocation.

Regional studies with samples sufficiently large to uncover variability among older rural residents are needed to unmask findings of "little if any residential variability" resulting from simplistic dichotomous residential definitions. For example, virtually all of the contributors to Coward and Krout's (1998) edited volume called for research to better understand the implications of the variety of rural locations across America. The culture of rural Kansas is certainly different than the culture of rural Vermont, and such cultural difference impacts all aspects of rural aging, from the propensity towards self-care to the availability of residential alternatives.

JIM MITCHELL

See also LIVING ARRANGEMENTS; MIGRATION, GEOGRAPHIC MOBILITY, AND DISTRIBUTION.

BIBLIOGRAPHY

BEALE, C. "Nonmetro Population Growth Rebound of the 1990's Continues, but at a Slower Rate." *Rural Conditions and Trends* 8 (1997): 46–50.

COBURN, A. F., and BOLDA, E. J. "The Rural Elderly and Long-Term Care." In *Rural Health in the United States.* Edited by T. C. Ricketts, III. New York: Oxford University Press, 1999. Pages 179–189.

COWARD, R. T., and CUTLER, S. J. "Informal and Formal Health Care Systems for the Rural Elderly." *Health Services Research* 23 (1989): 785–806.

COWARD, R. T., and KROUT, J. A. *Aging in Rural Settings: Life Circumstances and Distinctive Features.* New York: Springer, 1998.

COWARD, R. T.; MCLAUGHLIN, D. K.; DUNCAN, R. P.; and BULL, C. N. "An Overview of Health and Aging in Rural America." In *Health Services for Rural Elders.* Edited by R. T. Coward, C. N. Bull, G. Kukulka, and J. M. Galliher.

New York: Springer Publishing Company, 1994. Pages 1–32.

COX, C. *The Frail Elderly: Needs and Community Responses*. Westport, Conn.: Auburn House, 1993.

GLASGOW, N. L., and REEDER, R. J. "Economic and Fiscal Implications of Nonmetropolitan Retirement Migration." *Journal of Applied Gerontology* 9 (1990): 433–451.

JOHNSON, K. M. "Demographic Change in Nonmetropolitan America." *Rural Sociology* 58 (1993): 347–365.

LEE, G. R.; DWYER, J. D.; and COWARD, R. D. "Residential Location and Proximity to Children among Impaired Elderly Parents." *Rural Sociology* 55 (1990): 579–589.

LONGINO, C. F., and SMITH, M. H. "The Impact of Elderly Migration on Rural Communities." In *Aging in Rural Settings*. Edited by R. T. Coward and J. A. Krout. New York: Springer Publishing Company, 1990. Pages 209–226.

MANSFIELD, C. J.; WILSON, J. L.; KOBRINSKI, E. J.; and MITCHELL, J. "Premature Mortality in the United States: The Roles of Geographic Areas, Socioeconomic Status, Household Type, and Availability of Medical Care." *American Journal of Public Health* 89 (1999): 893–898.

MITCHELL, J.; MATHEWS, H. F.; and GRIFFIN, L. W. "Health and Community-Based Service Use: Differences between Elderly African-Americans and Whites." *Research on Aging* 19 (1997): 199–222.

MCLAUGHLIN, D. K., and JENSEN, L. "The Rural Elderly: A Demographic Portrait." In *Aging in Rural Settings*. Edited by R. T. Coward and J.

A. Krout New York: Springer Publishing Company, 1998. Pages 15–43.

NELSON, G. M. "In-Home Care for Rural Elders." In *Health Services for Rural Elders*. Edited by R. T. Coward, C. Neil Bull, G. Kukalka, and J. M. Galliher. New York: Springer, 1994. Pages 65–83.

REEDER, R. J., and GLASGOW, N. L. "Nonmetro Retirement Counties: Strengths and Weaknesses." *Rural Development Perspectives* 6 (1990): 12–17.

RICKETTS, T. C.; JOHNSON-WEBB, K. D.; and RANDOLPH, R. K. "Populations and Places in Rural America." In *Rural Health in the United States*. Edited by T. C. Ricketts, III. New York: Oxford University Press, 1999. Pages 7–24.

ROWLES, G. D. "Community and the Local Environment." In *Aging in Rural Settings*. Edited by R. T. Coward and J. A. Krout. New York: Springer Publishing Company, 1998. Pages 105–125.

SALMON, M. A. P.; NELSON, G. M.; and ROUSE, S. G. "The Continuum of Care Revisited: A Rural Perspective." *The Gerontologist* 33 (1993): 658–666.

SEROW, W. J. "Economic Implications of Retirement Migration." *Journal of Applied Gerontology* 9 (1990): 452–462.

STOLLER, E. P. "Families of Elderly Rural Americans." In *Aging in Rural Settings*. Edited by R. T. Coward and J. A. Krout. New York: Springer Publishing Company, 1998. Pages 127–146.

WEINBERG, D. H. "Rural Pockets of Poverty." *Rural Sociology* 52 (1987): 398–408.

S

SARCOPENIA

Sarcopenia, from a Greek word meaning "poverty of flesh," is the loss of muscle mass and strength caused by normal aging. It is distinct from muscle loss caused by inflammatory disease (cachexia), and from the weight loss and attendant muscle wasting caused by starvation or advanced disease. Compared to young, healthy, physically active young adults, reduced muscle mass and strength are evident in all elderly persons. If the sarcopenia progresses beyond a threshold of functional requirements, it leads to disability and frailty, and this can occur independently of any disease-induced frailty. Of course, a superimposed illness will accelerate the loss of muscle mass, and thus increase the risk of disability, frailty, and death.

There is no absolute level of lean mass, body cell mass, or muscle mass at which one can definitely say that sarcopenia is present. However, it is important to consider two important and generally agreed-upon concepts in relation to lean body mass. First, there is a direct structure-function link between muscle mass and strength—more muscle generally equals greater strength, and vice versa. Second, there is reasonable evidence that there is a limit on how much lean body mass can be lost before death supervenes. The available data, based on patients suffering from starvation, AIDS, and critical illnesses, suggest that loss of more than about 40 percent of baseline lean mass is fatal. Kehayias, et al. (1997) defined baseline lean mass as the mean for adults between twenty and thirty years of age; no healthy elderly adults were found below approximately 70 percent of that standard, and there was a steady decline in body cell mass for both men and women across age groups between the ages of thirty and one hundred.

This decline in body cell mass with age raises the issue of the importance of sarcopenia as an indicator of reduced protein stores for times of stress. During illness, protein is burned for energy in excess of the levels seen in starvation adaptation. Given the anorexia caused by acute illness, endogenous protein stores are crucial in determining the availability of metabolic substrate needed to cope with the illness, and thus the ability to survive it. It is no wonder, then, that elderly, sarcopenic patients fare worse than young, healthy adults for almost all diseases. For this reason, the metabolic significance of sarcopenia in illness should be considered independently of its functional impact during times of better health, as both are important to the survival and well-being of elderly persons.

Prevalence

The prevalence of sarcopenia was studied in the New Mexico Elder Health Survey, which measured appendicular muscle mass by dual-energy X-ray absorptiometry (DXA) in 883 elderly Hispanic and non-Hispanic white men and women. Sarcopenia was defined as a muscle mass two or more standard deviations below the mean for young healthy participants. The prevalence of sarcopenia by this definition increased from between 13 percent and 24 percent of persons under age seventy to over 50 percent of those over eighty years of age. Sarcopenic women had 3.6 times higher rates of disability, and men 4.1 times higher rates, compared to study participants with normal muscle mass.

Kehayias, et al. (1997) found that the quality of the lean body mass, defined as the ratio of cell mass (the metabolically active portion of the body) to lean mass (cell mass plus extracellular water and connective tissue), declined with age. These data suggest that sarcopenia is universal, and indeed this would be consistent with an age-related phenomenon. It also complements the data of Baumgartner, et al., where a cutoff was used to define sarcopenia. Cross-sectional data also indicate that older persons have a lower amount of type II (fast-twitch, glycolytic) fibers in their muscles than young adults, but that type I (slow-twitch, oxidative) fibers are comparable in number.

Structural and functional relationships

As noted earlier, these data all define sarcopenia in terms of its compositional, rather than functional (strength) aspect. However, there are data suggesting that the decline in strength with age exceeds the decline in lean mass. Studies of change in muscle strength over time have shown declines, no change, or gains in strength over periods ranging from four to twenty-five years. A reduction in type II muscle fibers has been shown in some studies, but no change was found in others. In addition to the quantitative decline in muscle with age, there is a qualitative decline, with reduced force production by single fibers from elderly men compared to young men.

Etiology

The etiology of sarcopenia remains unclear, but there are many possible factors involved (see Roubenoff and Hughes, 2000, for a detailed review). These include: (1) loss of alpha motor neurons in the central nervous system with age; (2) change in hormonal milieu in favor of a more catabolic muscle profile, with reductions in growth hormone, testosterone, and estrogen; (3) increased production of catabolic cytokines, especially interleukin-6 and possibly interleukin-1 beta and tumor necrosis factor-alpha, which favor muscle protein breakdown; (4) reduced physical activity, which leads to increased fat accumulation and possibly to resistance to the anabolic effects of insulin, perhaps due to increased tumor necrosis factor production by fat cells; and (5) reduced dietary intake of protein and energy.

Treatment of sarcopenia

While both cardiopulmonary fitness and muscle strength are important determinants of functional capacity; in frail, elderly persons with advanced sarcopenia, muscle weakness may be more limiting than aerobic fitness. Weakness in turn leads to further disuse, as people avoid activities that are uncomfortable. Thus, reduced physical activity follows loss of muscle mass, and then accelerates it by removing the trophic stimulus of the activity. The improved survival and reduced disability of elderly athletes who remain physically active suggest that such a vicious cycle is avoidable under some circumstances. More importantly, perhaps, the ability to reverse these changes with progressive resistance training (PRT) suggests that they are modifiable effects of aging.

Many studies have now documented that exercise training can reverse sarcopenia, and that people who retain a high level of physical activity throughout their lives maintain a higher level of physical functioning and live longer. In addition, physical activity is one of the few factors that are within the control of nearly everyone, and it does not require pharmacological treatment. Moreover, Fiatarone, et al. have shown that it is never too late to begin strength training, and that even frail, elderly, nursing home patients in their nineties retain the plasticity of muscle in response to training. The effectiveness of strength training is clear, and the effect can be obtained in as little as eight weeks with training two to three times per week. Strength training can be done with low-tech, relatively low-cost equipment in the home, or in congregate settings such as gyms or senior centers. In addition, strength training can be used safely in people with arthritis, coronary artery disease, heart failure, and renal failure. The difficulty with strength training is translating it into an effective public health intervention on a large scale. This requires training an adequate number of exercise leaders who can, in turn, train others. This is a serious impediment to application of this therapy.

RONENN ROUBENOFF

See also ANDROPAUSE; DECONDITIONING; EXERCISE; FRAILTY.

BIBLIOGRAPHY

BAUMGARTNER, R. N.; KOEHLER, K. M.; GALLAGHER, D.; ROMERO, L.; HEYMSFIELD, S. B.;

Ross, R. R.; Garry, P. J.; and Lindeman, R. D. "Epidemiology of Sarcopenia among the Elderly in New Mexico." *American Journal of Epidemiology* 147 (1998): 755–763.

Fiatarone, M. A.; O'Neill, E. F.; Ryan, N. D.; Clements, K. M.; Solares, G. R.; Nelson, M. E.; Roberts, S. B.; Kehayias, J. J.; Lipsitz, L. A.; and Evans, W. J. "Exercise Training and Nutritional Supplementation for Physical Frailty in Very Elderly People." *New England Journal of Medicine* 330 (1994): 1769–1775.

Frontera, W. R.; Hughes, V. A.; Fielding, R. A.; Fiatarone, M. A.; Evans, W. J.; and Roubenoff, R. "Aging of Skeletal Muscle: A 12-Year Longitudinal Study." *Journal of Applied Physiology* 88 (2000): 1321–1326.

Kallman, D. A.; Plato, C. C.; and Tobin, J. D. "The Role of Muscle Loss in the Age-Related Decline of Grip Strength: Cross-Sectional and Longitudinal Perspectives." *Journal of Gerontology* 45 (1990): M82–M88.

Kehayias, J. J.; Fiatarone, M. F.; Zhuang, H.; and Roubenoff, R. "Total Body Potassium and Body Fat: Relevance to Aging." *American Journal of Clinical Nutrition* 66 (1997): 904–910.

Poehlman, E. T.; Toth, M. J.; and Gardner, A. W. "Changes in Energy Balance and Body Composition at Menopause: A Controlled Longitudinal Study." *Annual of Internal Medicine* 123 (1995): 673–675.

Roubenoff, R.; Harris, T. B.; Abad, L. W.; Wilson, P. W. F.; Dallal, G. E.; and Dinarello, C. A. "Monocyte Cytokine Production in an Elderly Population: Effect of Age and Inflammation." *Journal of Gerontology* 53A (1998): M20–M26.

Roubenoff, R., and Hughes, V. A. "Sarcopenia: Current Concepts." *Journal of Gerontology* 55A (2000): M716–M724.

SAVINGS

Savings, from the perspective of the individual, comprises money set aside for future use. Savings, from the perspective of the economy, includes all of the money set aside by all individuals, employers, governments, and other groups. Savings are important to the individual because they enable people to make purchases in the future and to be prepared for unforeseen financial needs. Savings are important to the economy because they allow investment to occur: one person or organization uses the savings of others to finance the making of a movie, to construct a home or building, or for other uses. If a person did not save, then he or she would not be able to borrow money to purchase a home.

For the individual, money to be saved may be placed in a piggy bank; put under a mattress; placed in a savings account or a certificate of deposit at a bank or savings and loan; or invested in a U.S. Savings Bond, a home, a stock or a bond, or some other asset that can later be sold or cashed in. When savings are put in a piggy bank or under a mattress the money is not available for others to use, and is therefore not helpful to the economy, even though it will be available for the individual to use. When savings are deposited in a bank account, the depositor is normally paid for use of the money in the form of interest. Generally, an individual can assume that he or she will get back the money deposited plus the interest income. This money is then loaned to someone else who is willing to pay even higher interest to the intermediary, such as a bank. When savings are invested, an individual generally hopes to earn more than would be provided by an interest payment from a savings account, but has the potential of earning nothing, or of actually losing the money that was invested. This is what happens if an individual invests in a share of stock valued at $100, and then has to sell it at $50. This can also happen with a home or any other investment.

When viewed from the individual perspective, savings are described as being at the *micro* level—that is, the primary impact is on the individual. Savings from the perspective of the economy, are described as being at the *macro* level—that is, the cumulative effect of what everyone does is considered. At the micro level, for example, those who have savings may feel secure; but if many individuals do not have savings, then there may be no macro savings in the economy.

The economy needs savings so that the money can be borrowed by others, allowing investment and growth. Individuals save so that they can spend in the future without having to borrow as much, or any, money from others. A child may save to purchase a bike; a young adult may save for a first car; and a newly married couple may save for a first home. All workers save so that they can someday stop working and still have money to live on.

How is savings measured?

Saving is measured in different ways, which frequently leads to confusion. One measure is the National Income and Product Accounts (NIPA), produced by the Bureau of Economic Analysis (BEA) of the U.S. Department of Commerce. Another is the Flow of Funds Accounts (FFA), produced by the board of governors of the Federal Reserve System. The news media typically cite the NIPA measure, and not the FFA measure. This can lead to a feeling among individuals that they have growing savings, even though the papers say that people are not doing well at saving.

NIPA. Under NIPA, personal savings is a residual. This means that personal savings is what is left over from personal income after subtracting payments for personal income taxes, individual payroll taxes (i.e., individual contributions for Social Security and Medicare), and all other personal outlays, such as food, housing, and clothing expenditures.

Personal income includes the following:

- Wages and salaries
- Other labor income (i.e., employer contributions to pensions and profit-sharing plans, group insurance, such as health, workers' compensation, and supplemental unemployment coverage)
- Rental income
- Personal dividend income
- Personal interest income
- Transfer payments (i.e., Social Security benefit payments, government unemployment and insurance payments, veterans benefits, government employees retirement benefits, and welfare payments)

Personal taxes include the following:

- Federal income tax payments
- State and local income tax payments
- Any penalties, fines, or interest payments made on income tax statements
- Contributions to social insurance programs (i.e., Social Security and Medicare payroll taxes)

Personal outlays include the following:

- Personal consumption expenditures (i.e., spending on food, housing, clothing, household operations such as utility bills, transportation, and medical care)
- Consumer interest payments (i.e., payments of credit card interest)

- Personal transfer payments to persons located outside the U.S. are treated as outlays, whereas transfers among persons within the U.S. are not

Disposable personal income equals personal income after deducting personal income taxes and payroll taxes, but before personal outlays are deducted. Personal savings is what is left over from disposable personal income after deducting personal outlays. Personal savings divided by disposable personal income is the personal saving rate. For the individual, this rate is the measure of how much was saved in a particular month.

FFA. Whereas NIPA measures personal savings as a residual, the FFA personal saving rate is a direct measure of the net acquisition of assets by households. FFA methodology differs from that used by NIPA in two ways: (1) in the treatment of consumer durables and (2) in the definition of personal income.

The FFA treats the net acquisition of consumer durable goods (i.e., automobiles, major household appliances, and other products that can be used for several years) as a form of saving, whereas the NIPA treats expenditures on consumer durables as a component of personal consumption. The FFA also makes some adjustments to the NIPA measure of personal income: The FFA includes certain credits from government insurance programs and *realized* capital gains distributions, whereas NIPA does not. (It is important to note that neither FFA nor NIPA includes unrealized capital gains.) For example, if an individual purchases ten shares of corporate stock at $10 a share, and the stock then increases to $30 a share, the increased value of the stock is not considered part of personal income under FFA until the individual sells the stock and realizes the capital gain. By contrast, under NIPA the increased value of the stock is never considered part of personal income.

For the individual this means that how much is saved is derived from a broader definition of income (wages or salary, plus interest income, plus gains from the sale of a house or stock), but with some of what one might have spent actually counted as saving (i.e., appliances, automobiles, etc.) even though one won't be able to sell what was bought for the amount paid.

Implications. Neither NIPA nor FFA calculate savings the way most individuals think of it on a day-to-day basis. The individual looks at what is being saved now (the $500 just put into a savings bond), as well as the growth of what was saved before (how much did my 401(k) account go up this quarter), and thinks about savings as accumulated wealth. The individual does not generally think about a credit-card balance or a home mortgage as negative savings, meaning that if they charged $1,000 and put $500 into a savings account, they are likely to still say they saved $500.

NIPA and FFA, using different methods, add transactions together to get net figures. This is what the mortgage applicant does when filling out a "net worth" statement so that the bank can see how much "net" savings a person actually has.

Individuals who owned equities during the 1990s generally experienced tremendous increases in the value of those financial assets (i.e., they became wealthier). According to data from the Federal Reserve's Survey of Consumer Finances (SCF), the net worth (the difference between a family's gross assets and liabilities) of the typical American family (i.e., median net worth) rose 17.6 percent between 1995 and 1998—from $60,900 to $71,600. This increase in net worth was driven by strong growth in the financial assets held by families, especially direct and indirect holdings of stocks. As of 1998, 92.9 percent of American families held some type of financial asset, and the median value of assets, among those with financial assets, was $22,400 (comparable figures for 1995 are 91.0 percent and $16,500, respectively) (median means midpoint or 50 percent above and 50 percent below). Almost one-half (48.8 percent) of families held stock (directly or indirectly) in 1998, compared with 40.4 percent in 1995, and 31.6 percent in 1989. The median value of stock among families with holdings increased from $10,800 in 1989 to $15,400 in 1995, and to $25,000 in 1998. Over the same period, stock holdings as a share of families' financial assets increased from 27.8 percent in 1989 to 40 percent in 1995, and to 53.9 percent in 1998.

One could argue that a more complete measure of saving would include increased wealth through capital gains (both realized and unrealized) as part of personal income. As mentioned above, FFA includes realized capital gains in its measure of saving, but not unrealized capital gains.

William Gale and John Sabelhaus (1999) identified other shortcomings, in addition to the exclusion of accrued and realized capital gains from income—and thus from savings—in the NIPA measure of saving. Among these shortcomings are:

- While net acquisition of owner-occupied housing is considered saving, net acquisition of other consumer durables is counted as current consumption, not saving
- Nominal (as opposed to just the real component of) interest receipts are counted as income, whereas nominal interest payments are counted as outlays
- NIPA does not factor in the implicit tax liability of saving in tax-qualified plans

Tax incentives for savings

Since 1926 the Internal Revenue Code has provided for deferral of taxes on retirement savings in plans that file with the government to be "qualified" for this special tax treatment. Contributions to such plans are not taxed as income when made, and interest and investment gains are not taxed when realized. Instead, both are taxed upon withdrawal from the plan. Many such incentives have been added to the law since 1926. Not all are for retirement savings, with incentives now offered for saving towards the purchase of a new home, saving for sending children to college, or saving for medical expenses.

The savings issue that arises when such incentives are discussed, is the impact of such incentives (in particular, IRAs and 401(k) plans) on personal saving rates. At the aggregate level, tax-qualified retirement plans represent a tremendous store of wealth in vehicles earmarked specifically for retirement—$10.5 trillion as of 1998, up from $3 trillion just one decade earlier. At the individual level, the latest data on 401(k) accumulations indicate the potential these vehicles have for generating retirement wealth. According to the EBRI/ICI Participant-Directed Retirement Plan Data Collection Project, the average 401(k) account balance was $55,000 at year-end 2000 (up 47 percent from the average account balance at year-end 1996). More significantly, the average balances of older workers with long tenure indicate that a mature 401(k) program will produce substantial account balances. For example, individuals in their 60s with at least 30 years of tenure have average account balances in excess of $185,000.

Some argue that the tax-preferred treatment and the implicit government subsidy of saving through such plans, along with the provision of a degree of self-discipline that results from automatic saving, results in higher levels of saving than would otherwise exist without such programs. Others maintain that such preferential tax treatment merely serves as an inducement to transfer existing savings into such vehicles or to use such vehicles for saving that would have occurred even without such programs.

Interest in this issue is spurred by the fact that individual tax deferrals for employer-based retirement plan contributions and earnings carry a high estimated cost to the federal government, relative to other programs. The U.S. Treasury Department estimates that in fiscal 2000, the net exclusion of pension contributions and earnings will result in a federal tax revenue loss of $99.8 billion, and for fiscal years 2000 through 2004, these provisions will result in a tax revenue loss of $527.2 billion over the five-year period (see Executive Office of the President 1999). One analysis (Salisbury 1993) found that about one-half of the retirement-tax preference was attributable to public-sector-defined benefit retirement plans, about one-third to private-sector-defined contribution plans, 15 percent to private-sector-defined benefit plans, and 2 percent to public-sector-defined contribution plans.

Impact on savings. James Poterba, Steve Venti, and David Wise (1996), based on a body of research that they conducted over time, concluded that contributions to tax-qualified personal-retirement savings plans (IRAs and 401(k) plans) represent largely new savings and thus such plans have a significant positive effect upon saving rates.

Steven Venti and David Wise (1995), utilizing the Survey of Income and Program Participation (SIPP), and based on a household longitudinal methodology, found no significant reduction in other saving when households begin contributing to IRAs.

What would households eligible for saving incentives have saved in the absence of these incentives? Eric Engen, William Gale, and Karl Scholz (1996) argue that empirical analysis of this question is difficult and subject to biases that generally lead to overestimation of the impact of saving incentives. They conclude, based on a body of empirical work, that controlling for these biases largely or completely eliminates estimated positive effects of saving incentives on saving. They do qualify this conclusion by stating that

such incentives may increase saving for some people and that they may eventually increase saving in the long run.

Are people saving enough to retire?

Another major policy issue is whether current workers are saving enough for their retirement, in particular the post-World War II baby boom generation (those born between 1946 and 1964). The Employee Benefit Research Institute (EBRI) hosted a policy forum on this topic in 1994 (see Salisbury 1994) and subsequently published an *issue brief* on retirement saving adequacy (see Yakoboski and Silverman, 1994). This section updates that material.

According to the 1999 EBRI Retirement Confidence Survey (RCS), 74 percent of workers say they have established an investment or savings program for their retirement, and 70 percent report they are personally saving money for retirement—an increase from the 63 percent who reported saving for retirement in 1998. However, the amounts accumulated are generally unimpressive. The median amount accumulated for retirement by all households was $29,514. While the median amount saved increased by age (ages 25–39, $20,588; ages 40–49, $45,238; ages 50–59, $71,250), working households of individuals age sixty and older accumulated less ($39,286)—perhaps because they are more likely to expect to rely on Social Security for a major portion of their retirement income. To put these accumulations in perspective, suppose a single male, age 65, purchased a life annuity in 2001. With $71,250, he could have purchased a nominal monthly annuity for life of $631; while with $39,286, he would have gotten a monthly annuity of only $348.

What is clear is that even though most workers and households are saving for retirement, relatively few have a good idea of how much they need to save. In 1999, 52 percent of all households reported in the RCS that they had tried to figure out how much money they will need to have saved by the time they retire so that they can live comfortably in retirement (among households that have saved for retirement the figure was 61 percent). So while most people may be saving for retirement, they appear to be simply assuming (or hoping) that they will accumulate enough. Given the upward trend in life expectancies of individuals once they reach age 65 (and projections of future growth in these life expectancies), hoping and assuming will likely not be good enough in light of retirements that could span decades.

On average, those who have done a needs calculation have saved considerably more than those who have not done the calculation. The 1999 RCS found that the median amount accumulated by households that have tried to figure out how much money they will need in retirement is $66,532, compared with a median of $14,054 accumulated by those who have not done the calculation. Planning, therefore, plays an important role in explaining the saving behavior of many households.

The 1999 Retirement Confidence Survey found that 57 percent of workers who are not currently saving for retirement say it is reasonably possible for them to save $20 per week for retirement. In addition, 69 percent of workers who are already saving report that it is possible for them to save an additional $20 per week (see Ostuw, Pierron, and Yakoboski 1999). Saving $20 per week amounts to more than $1,000 per year, which, over time, can add up to a significant sum of money. The power of compound interest allows a twenty-five-year-old saving $20 a week, assuming a 5 percent annual real rate of return over forty years, to accumulate a retirement nest egg worth nearly $132,000. With a 10 percent annual real rate of return, $20 a week saved over forty years can accumulate to more than $500,000.

Concerns about low levels of aggregate personal saving at the national level appear misplaced. Americans—in the aggregate—are saving. That saving, however, is partially the result of large capital gains that have been experienced in the financial markets over recent years. Since NIPA, the most commonly cited measure of personal saving, does not factor capital gains (neither realized nor unrealized) into income, the saving rate appears to have dropped dramatically over the past decade. Accounting for capital gains changes the picture dramatically, however. By one measure, aggregate personal saving is 33 percent of "income" and has increased dramatically over the past decade. However, while there may not be an aggregate "saving crisis" per se, a note of caution is warranted: To the degree that aggregate personal saving is driven by a bull market in equities, as in the 1990s, a sharp contraction in the equities market could have potentially drastic consequences.

Also, while the rate of aggregate personal saving may be healthy at the national level, this does not mean that fears about inadequate retirement preparations among current workers are misplaced. While sweeping generalizations are to be avoided, and while some workers are on track for adequate retirement savings, the evidence indicates that many groups of American workers appear unlikely to be able to afford a retirement that maintains their current lifestyle (at least not without working more years than currently planned). Consensus does not exist on how many workers are at risk, or on the typical magnitude of their retirement savings shortfall. There is a consensus, however, that a substantial number of individuals are at risk. This is not surprising—despite the fact that the 70 percent of workers are saving for retirement—since relatively few workers know how much it is that they need to accumulate to fund their retirement.

One question yet to be addressed is whether and how retirement assets will be affected by the ever-growing initiatives in Congress to expand tax-deferred savings accounts for nonretirement purposes (such as education, health care, job training, and other costs). As the options grow among tax-deferred savings accounts, or as Congress passes new laws relaxing the tax penalties for using retirement account assets for nonretirement purposes, the competition for retirement savings is certain to grow—and this growth is likely to occur just when the demographic wave of Americans reaching retirement age is starting to crest.

Issues regarding saving levels and the adequacy of retirement preparations will continue to capture the attention of policymakers, the news media, and the public as the baby boom generation moves toward its retirement years. This is most evident with Social Security, as changes needed to ensure the long-term financial viability of the system are debated. Many reform proposals involve elements designed to give workers their own individual retirement savings accounts through the Social Security system.

Education efforts related to saving and financial literacy now abound because the data says that those who get such education begin to save, to increase what they save, and to invest on a more diversified basis.

At one level, success has already been achieved: 70 percent of American workers report that they have begun to save for their retirement.

However, this still means that 30 percent (disproportionately younger and lower-earning individuals) are not in the retirement savings game at all. These individuals likely do not appreciate the difference that even seemingly small amounts of money saved on a regular periodic basis can make over time. For the nation, a higher bar to strive for is not merely to create savers, but rather to create *planners* who can develop a specific dollar goal for their retirement and then save accordingly. On this latter point, there remains plenty of room for improvement, and this goal would seem to be the next crucial step to ensuring individual retirement-income security for American workers.

DALLAS SALISBURY

See also ANNUITIES; ASSETS AND WEALTH; BEQUESTS AND INHERITANCES; FINANCIAL PLANNING FOR LONG-TERM CARE; INDIVIDUAL RETIREMENT ACCOUNTS; LIFE CYCLE THEORIES OF SAVINGS AND CONSUMPTION; PENSIONS, PLAN TYPES AND POLICY APPROACHES; RETIREMENT PLANNING; RETIREMENT PLANNING PROGRAMS.

ATTANASIO, O., and DE LEIRE, T. "IRAs and Household Saving Revisited: Some New Evidence." *NBER Working Paper 4900.* Cambridge, Mass.: National Bureau of Economic Research, 1994.

BERNHEIM, D. B. *Is the Baby Boom Generation Preparing Adequately for Retirement? Summary Report.* Merrill Lynch & Co., Inc. 1993.

BERNHEIM, D. B. *Is the Baby Boom Generation Preparing Adequately for Retirement? Technical Report.* Merrill Lynch & Co., Inc. 1992.

COPELAND, C., and VANDERHEI, J. "Personal Account Retirement Plans: An Analysis of the Survey of Consumer Finances." *EBRI Issue Brief* 223. Employee Benefit Research Institute, 2000.

DAVIS, J. "Pensions, Social Security, and Saving." *EBRI Issue Brief* 97. Employee Benefit Research Institute, 1989.

ENGEN, E. M.; GALE, W. G.; and SCHOLZ, J. K. "Do Saving Incentives Work?" *Brookings Papers on Economic Activity,* Vol. 1. 1994.

ENGEN, E. M.; GALE, W. G.; and SCHOLZ, J. K. "The Illusory Effects of Saving Incentives on Saving." *The Journal of Economic Perspectives* 10, no. 4 (Fall 1996).

Executive Office of the President, Office of Management and Budget. *Analytical Perspectives, Budget of the United States Government, Fiscal Year 2000.* Washington, D.C.: U.S. Government Printing Office, 1999.

GIST, J. R.; WU, K. B.; and FORD, C. *Do Baby Boomers Save and, If So, What For?* Washington, D.C.: AARP Public Policy Institute, 1999.

HUBBARD, R. G., and SKINNER, J. S. "Assessing the Effectiveness of Saving Incentives." *The Journal of Economic Perspectives* 10, no. 4 (Fall 1996).

IMROHOROGLU, A.; IMROHOROGLU, S.; and JOINES, D. H. "The Effect of Tax-Favored Retirement Accounts on Capital Accumulation." *The American Economic Review* 88, no. 4 (September 1998).

MITCHELL, O. S.; MOORE, J.; and PHILLIPS, J. "Explaining Retirement Saving Shortfalls." In *Forecasting Retirement Needs and Retirement Wealth.* Edited by Olivia Mitchell, Brett Hammond, and Anna Rappaport. Philadelphia: University of Pennsylvania Press, 2000.

MOORE, J. F., and MITCHELL, O. S. "Projected Retirement Wealth and Saving Adequacy." In *Forecasting Retirement Needs and Retirement Wealth.* Edited by Olivia Mitchell, Brett Hammond, and Anna Rappaport. Philadelphia: University of Pennsylvania Press, 2000.

MOULTON, B. R.; PARKER, R. P.; and SESKIN, E. P. "A Preview of the 1999 Comprehensive Revision of the National Income and Product Accounts." *Survey of Current Business* 79, no. 8 (August 1999).

OSTUW, P.; PIERRON, B.; and YAKOBOSKI, P. "The Evolution of Retirement: Results of the 1999 Retirement Confidence Survey." *EBRI Issue Brief* 216. Washington, D.C.: Employee Benefit Research Institute, 1999.

POTERBA, J. M.; VENTI, S. F.; and WISE, D. A. "Do 401(k) Contributions Crowd Out Other Personal Saving?" *Journal of Public Economics* 58 (September 1995).

POTERBA, J. M.; VENTI, S. F.; and WISE, D. A. "401(k) Plans and Tax-Deferred Saving." In *Studies in the Economics of Aging.* Edited by David Wise. Chicago: University of Chicago Press, 1994.

POTERBA, J. M.; VENTI, S. F.; and WISE, D. A. "How Retirement Saving Programs Increase Saving." *The Journal of Economic Perspectives* 10, no. 4 (Fall 1996).

SABELHAUS, J. "Projecting IRA Balances and Withdrawals." *EBRI Notes* 5. Washington, D.C.: Employee Benefit Research Institute, 1999.

SALISBURY, D. L. "Pension Tax Expenditures: Are They Worth the Cost?" *EBRI Issue Brief* 134. Washington, D.C.: Employee Benefit Research Institute, 1993.

SALISBURY, D. L., ed. *Retirement in the 21st Century. . . Ready or Not . . .* Washington, D.C.: Employee Benefit Research Institute, 1994.

SALISBURY, D. L., ed. *Retirement Income and the Economy: Policy Directions for the 80s.* Washington, D.C.: Employee Benefit Research Institute, 1981.

SESKIN, E. P. "Improved Estimates of the National Income and Product Accounts for 1959–98, Results of the Comprehensive Revision." *Survey of Current Business* 79, no. 12 (December 1999).

U.S. Department of Labor, Pension and Welfare Benefits Administration. *Private Pension Plan Bulletin, Abstract of 1995 Form 5500 Annual Report.* (Spring 1999).

VANDERHEI, J. "Pensions, Social Security, and Saving." *EBRI Issue Brief* 129. Washington, D.C.: Employee Benefit Research Institute, 1992.

VANDERHEI, J.; HOLDEN, S.; and QUICK, C. "401(k) Plan Asset Allocation, Account Balances and Loan Activity in 1998." *EBRI Issue Brief* 218. Washington, D.C.. Employee Benefit Research Institute, 2000.

VENTI, S. F., and WISE, D. A. "Individual Response to a Retirement Saving Program: Results from U.S. Panel Data." *Ricerche Economiche* 49 (1995).

VENTI, S. F., and WISE, D. A. "The Wealth of Cohorts: Retirement Saving and the Changing Assets of Older Americans." NBER Working Paper No. 5609. Cambridge, Mass.: National Bureau of Economic Research, 1996.

WARSHAWSKY, M. J., and AMERIKS, J. "How Prepared Are Americans for Retirement?" In *Forecasting Retirement Needs and Retirement Wealth.* Edited by Olivia Mitchell, Brett Hammond, and Anna Rappaport. Philadelphia: University of Pennsylvania Press, 2000.

YAKOBOSKI, P. "Large Plan Lump-Sums: Rollovers and Cashouts." *EBRI Issue Brief* 188. Washington, D.C.: Employee Benefit Research Institute, 1997.

YAKOBOSKI, P. "Lump-Sum Distributions Total $87.2 Billion in 1995." *EBRI Notes* 10. Washington, D.C.: Employee Benefit Research Institute, 1999.

YAKOBOSKI, P. "Retirement Plans, Personal Saving, and Saving Adequacy." *EBRI Issue Brief* 219. Washington, D.C.: Employee Benefit Research Institute, 2000.

YAKOBOSKI, P., and SILVERMAN, C. "Baby Boomers in Retirement: What Are Their Prospects." *EBRI Issue Brief* 151. Washington, D.C.: Employee Benefit Research Institute, 1994.

YUH, Y.; MONTALTO, C. P.; and HANNA, S. "Are Americans Prepared for Retirement?" *Financial Counseling and Planning* 9, no. 1 (1998).

SELECTION, OPTIMIZATION, AND COMPENSATION

The model of selection, optimization, and compensation (SOC) posits that these three fundamental processes of developmental regulation are essential for successful development and aging. Selection, optimization, and compensation are thought to advance the maximization of gains and minimization of losses associated with aging, thus promoting successful development and aging.

Basic assumptions underlying the SOC model

There are a number of basic assumptions underlying the use of the SOC model as a model of successful aging. Life-span psychology holds that *development* comprises developmental trajectories of growth (gains e.g., the acquisition of language) and decline (losses e.g., decline in health in old age). A person's internal and external resources are, at each point of life, finite. Very broadly, resources can be defined as personal or environmental characteristics that support a person's interaction with his or her environment.

There are age-related changes that occur in the availability and efficiency of resources. The ratio of gains to losses becomes less positive with age because resources are replenished less often and drawn upon more exhaustively with increasing age. This reduction in resources occurs because: (1) advantages of evolutionary selection decline across the life span; (2) the need for culture (i.e., in the Vygotskian tradition, a set of socially constructed behaviors, beliefs, and objects) increases across the life span; and (3) the efficacy of culture decreases across the life span—particularly in old age. Each of these points is discussed below.

Life expectancy has only fairly recently extended into old age. Because evolutionary selection benefits decrease with age, there is less effective genetic material, mechanisms, and expressions for developing or maintaining high levels of functioning. In addition, most modern cultures do not provide the same richness of opportunities to older persons as are provided to younger members of society. This is in spite of the fact that cultural opportunities are especially needed by older adults to compensate for biologically based decreases in functioning. Moreover, due to reduced resources, older adults can make lesser use of supportive environmental conditions. Because of these factors, the balance of growth and decline becomes less favorable with increasing age. Thus, in old age, individuals have to allocate more of their resources to the maintenance of functioning and providing resilience against losses, rather than into processes of growth.

The (pro)active role of the individual in successful aging. How do people efficiently use their resources to promote continued growth and the maintenance of functioning in the face of losses when approaching old age? People not only react to environmental demands, but they also shape their environment to fit their needs. One important way in which individuals play an active role in their development is by choosing, committing to, and pursuing a set of goals (e.g., wanting to stay healthy). What kinds of goals a person selects is in part determined by sociocultural, biological, and phylogenetic factors. The lesser the influence stemming from these factors, the more degrees of freedom a person has to develop and choose his or her goals (and ways of pursuing them). In old age, there are fewer normative age-related expectations about the goals a person ought to pursue. This relative greater social freedom in old age gives more weight to goal selection and goal pursuit as processes of developmental regulation. On the other hand, old age is also characterized by diminishing resources that might limit the degree to which a person is able to shape the environment according to his or her goals. Thus, in old age it seems particularly crucial to wisely select the goal domains on which to focus one's resources.

The model of selection, optimization, and compensation

In this light, then, it is not surprising that processes of goal selection and goal pursuit have a prominent place in models of successful aging. According to the SOC model, successful aging encompasses *selection* of functional domains on which to focus one's resources, *optimizing* developmental potential (maximization of gains) and *compensating* for losses—thus ensuring the maintenance of functioning and a minimization of losses.

The SOC model constitutes a general model of development that defines universal processes of developmental regulation. These processes vary pheno-typically, depending on sociohistorical and cultural context, domain of functioning (e.g., social relations, cognitive functioning), as well as on the level of analysis (e.g., societal, group, or individual level). Taking an action-theoretical perspective, selection, optimization, and compensation refer to processes of setting, pursuing, and maintaining personal goals.

Selection. Selection refers to developing, elaborating, and committing to personal goals. Throughout the life span, biological, social, and individual opportunities and constraints specify a range of alternative domains of functioning. The number of options, usually exceeding the amount of internal and external resources available to an individual, need to be reduced by selecting a subset of these domains on which to focus one's resources. This is particularly important in old age, a time in life when resources decline.

Selection directs development because personal goals guide and organize behavior. Successful goal selection requires individuals to develop and set goals in domains for which resources are available or can be attained, and that match a person's needs and environmental demands.

The SOC model distinguishes between two kinds of selection, *elective selection* and *loss-based selection*. Both aspects of selection differ in their function. Elective selection refers to the delineation of goals in order to match a person's needs and motives with the available or attainable resources. Elective selection aims at achieving higher levels of functioning. In contrast, loss-based selection is a response to the loss of previously available resources that are necessary to maintain functioning. Loss-based selection refers to changes in goals or the goal system, such as reconstructing one's goal hierarchy by focusing on the most important goals, adapting standards, or replacing goals that are no longer achievable. This allows the individual to focus or redirect his or her efforts when resources used for the maintenance of positive functioning or as a substitute for a functional loss (compensation) are either not available or would be invested at the expense of other, more promising goals.

Selection promotes successful aging in a number of ways. To feel committed to goals contributes to feeling that one's life has a purpose. Furthermore, goals help organize behavior over time and across situations and guide attention and behavior. One of the central functions of selection is to focus the limited amount of available resources. In old and very old age, when resources become more constrained, selection becomes even more important. Empirical evidence shows that selecting a few life domains on which to focus is particularly adaptive for those older people whose resources are highly constrained.

Optimization. For achieving desired outcomes in selected domains, goal-relevant means need to be acquired, applied, and refined. The means that are best suited for achieving one's goals vary according to the specific goal domain (e.g., family, sports), personal characteristics (e.g., age, gender), and the sociocultural context (e.g., institutional support systems). Prototypical instances of optimization are the investment of time and energy into the acquisition of goal-relevant means, modeling successful others, and the practice of goal-relevant skills.

In old age, optimization continues to be of great importance for successful development because engaging in growth-related goals has positive regulative functions. Trying to achieve growth-oriented goals is associated with a higher degree of self-efficacy and leads to positive emotions and enhanced well-being. In old age, when losses are prevalent, it might be of particular importance to sustain growth-related goals for promoting well-being, rather than focusing primarily on losses. The positive function of optimization in old age has also been empirically supported in the Berlin Aging Study. In this study, older people who reported to engage in optimization processes reported more positive emotions and higher satisfaction with aging.

Compensation. How do older people manage to maintain positive functioning in the face of health-related constraints and losses? The maintenance of positive functioning in the face of losses might be as important for successful aging as a sustained growth focus. One relevant strategy for the regulation of losses—loss-based selection—has already been discussed. Loss-based selection denotes the restructuring of one's goal system, for example, by giving up unattainable goals and developing new ones. Developing new goals and investing in their optimization, however, can also deplete resources. Moreover, important personal goals might be central to a person's

well-being and not easily abandoned in the face of loss. In this case, it might be more adaptive to maintain one's goal by acquiring new resources or activating unused internal or external resources for alternative means of pursuing goals. This process is referred to as *compensation*.

As previously discussed, the means that are best suited for maintaining a given level of functioning in the face of loss or decline depend on the domain of functioning. Compensation, in contrast to optimization, aims at counteracting or avoiding losses, rather than achieving positive states. Again, data from the Berlin Aging Study support the positive effect of compensation in old age—self-reported compensation was associated with subjective indicators of successful aging (i.e., emotional well-being, satisfaction with aging, and life satisfaction).

ALEXANDRA M. FREUND

See also DEVELOPMENTAL PSYCHOLOGY; DEVELOPMENTAL TASKS; FUNCTIONAL ABILITY; LIFE SPAN DEVELOPMENT; SUCCESSFUL AGING.

BIBLIOGRAPHY

BALTES, M. M., and CARSTENSEN, L. L. "The Process of Successful Aging." *Aging and Society* 16 (1996): 397–422.

BALTES, P. B. "On the Incomplete Architecture of Human Ontogeny: Selection, Optimization, and Compensation as a Foundation of Developmental Theory." *American Psychologist* 52 (1997): 366–380.

BALTES, P. B., and BALTES, M. M. "Psychological Perspectives on Successful Aging: The Model of Selective Optimization with Compensation." In *Successful Aging: Perspectives from the Behavioral Sciences*. Edited by P. B. Baltes and M. M. Baltes. Cambridge, U.K.: Cambridge University Press, 1990. Pages 1–34.

BRANDTSTÄDTER, J., and GREVE, W. "The Aging Self: Stabilizing and Protective Processes." *Developmental Review* 14 (1994): 52–80.

EMMONS, R. A. "Striving and Feeling: Personal Goals and Subjective Well-Being." In *The Psychology of Action: Linking Cognition and Motivation to Behavior*. Edited by P. M. Gollwitzer and J. A. Bargh. New York: Guilford Press, 1996. Pages 313–337.

FREUND, A. M., and BALTES, P. B. "Selection, Optimization, and Compensation as Strategies of Life-Management: Correlations with Subjective Indicators of Successful Aging." *Psychology and Aging* 13 (1998): 531–543.

FREUND, A. M.; LI, K. Z. H.; and BALTES, P. B. "Successful Development and Aging: The Role of Selection, Optimization, and Compensation." In *Action and Self Development: Theory and Research through the Life Span*. Edited by J. Brandtstädter and R. M. Lerner. Thousand Oaks, Calif.: Sage Publications, 1999. Pages 401–434.

FREUND, A. M., and RIEDIGER, M. "Successful Aging." In *Comprehensive Handbook of Psychology*, vol. 6: *Developmental Psychology*. Edited by R. M. Lerner, A. Easterbrooks, and J. Mistry. New York: Wiley, in press.

HECKHAUSEN, J., and SCHULZ, R. "A Life-Span Theory of Control." *Psychological Review* 102 (1995): 284–304.

KLINGER, E. *Meaning and Void: Inner Experience and the Incentives in People's Lives*. Minneapolis: University of Minnesota Press, 1977.

LAWTON, M. P. "Environmental Proactivity in Older People." In *The Course of Later Life: Research and Reflections*. Edited by V. L. Bengston and K. W. Schaie. New York: Springer, 1989. Pages 15–23.

STAUDINGER, U. M.; MARSISKE, M.; and BALTES, P. B. "Resilience and Reserve Capacity in Later Adulthood: Potentials and Limits of Development Across the Life Span." In *Developmental Psychopathology*, vol. 2: *Risk, Disorder, and Adaptation*. Edited by D. Cicchetti and D. Cohen. New York: Wiley, 1995. Pages 801–847.

SELF-EMPLOYMENT

Self-employment has greater importance among older workers. The self-employed in 1994, for example, numbered 1.5 million at ages 55 to 64 and 1 million at ages 65 and older (Bregger, Table 4). Although a tenth of workers in the labor force was self-employed in the 1979 to 1996 period, the self-employment rate at ages 55 to 64 was about two and one-half times that at ages 25 to 34 (Manser and Picot, p.4 and Table 2). The self-employment rate in the labor force was about 18 percent at ages 55 to 64 years and about 25 to 29 percent at age 65 years and older.

Increasing percentages of self-employed older workers result from either the self-employed retiring later than employed workers or from workers shifting from wage and salary work into self-employment after retirement from a long-term, career job. Bruce, Holtz-Eakin, and Quinn examined the job shifting between 1992 and 1996 among persons born from 1931 to 1941 using the Health and Retirement Survey data. A net increase in self-employment occurred because more wage and salary workers shifted to self-employment than self-employed workers shifted to wage and salary jobs. Further, the self-employed in 1992 were more likely than wage and salary workers to be employed in 1996. Finally, 30 percent of the re-entrants into the labor force between 1992 and 1996 entered self-employment. Analyzing who was more or less likely to make these changes, the investigators found that women and African Americans were less likely to make the transition from wage and salary work to self-employment. Interestingly enough, the portability of health benefits from wage and salary jobs appears unrelated to the decisions to continue working or to move into self-employment jobs.

Are older workers attracted to self-employment or "pushed out" of wage and salary jobs at older ages? The answer is conjectural but several influences affect older workers. Some are attracted to self-employment by the flexibility and control over hours of work and wages. While wage-and-salary workers commonly work in full-time, full-year jobs, the self-employed are more likely working in part-time and/or part-year jobs (Devine). Part-time work would be particularly attractive to older workers because of limits set by Social Security legislation over the taxable earnings allowable while collecting benefits. Social Security limits the taxable earnings of some working beneficiaries, reflecting its goal of replacing lost income from retirement. Social Security legislation allows working beneficiaries at ages 62 to 64 to keep full benefits with earnings up to a threshold ($10,680 in 2001) and then reduces benefits $1 for each $2 of earnings over the threshold. Legislation in March 2000 eliminated a similar restriction on working beneficiaries at ages 65 to 69. Consequently, workers in full-time, full-year jobs would be unable to receive full Social Security benefits, while those who flexibly control their work hours could receive full benefits working part-time.

Consistent with the importance of reducing hours, about 84 percent of men and 74 percent of women reported reduced hours between their preretirement jobs and their postretirement jobs shortly after starting Social Security benefits in mid-1980 to 1981 (Iams 1987). In the decade after starting Social Security benefits, about one-third of retired men and one-fourth of retired women worked, with a much higher percentage self-employed on their "retirement job" than on their longest job before retirement (Iams 1995; Social Security Administration).

Although self-employment attracts many older workers, some may be "pushed" toward self-employment. Influences such as health and job loss could push wage-and-salary workers toward self-employment, and a major push probably would be pension plans, which seldom permit beneficiaries to continue working on the pension-covered job (Bureau of Labor Statistics 1999). Defined contribution plans may require that a person leave employment in order to receive an annuity or a lump sum payment from the pension plan. Defined benefit plans commonly require job termination for benefit receipt, and penalize part-time work prior to retirement by indexing the pension to the highest few years of earnings. Years of prior full-time earnings would determine benefits, and inflation would erode the value of the highest earnings for pension calculation of those who reduced to part-time work prior to retirement.

Who are the self-employed? Unfortunately, information on jobs of the self-employed must come from information for the total labor force rather than from information on older workers alone (Manser and Picot; Bruegger; Devine). This reflects small sample sizes in data and an infrequent focus on older self-employed workers. In 1975 and 1990, self-employed jobs were more likely held by men, non-Hispanics, the married, and the more educated (Devine, Table 1). Although men were more likely than women to be self-employed, the rate of self-employment among women increased after 1975 while remaining relatively constant among men (Devine). There are substantial differences in the self-employment rate among sixty ethnic/racial groups using 1990 census data (Fairlie and Meyer). Ethnic groups with higher earnings than average seem more likely to enter self-employment.

What kind of jobs do the self-employed generally have? The self-employed were more likely among workers in agriculture, construction, retail and wholesale trades, financial, and other service industries (Manser and Picot, Table 2). The self-employed in 1996 also were more likely among managers, sales workers, precision production or craft workers, and farming or related occupations (Manser and Picot, Table 2). Looking at recent Social Security beneficiaries, the jobs of the self-employed varied by gender (Iams 1987). Beneficiary women most commonly were working in sales; as general managers, hairdressers, or cosmetologists; and as bookkeepers or accountants. About a quarter of the beneficiary men were working as managers and professional employees, primarily managers, lawyers, accountants and auditors, and clergy, while another quarter were in sales and about a quarter also worked as farmers and grounds keepers or gardeners. These self-employed beneficiaries averaged lower median hourly wages than the beneficiaries working in wage and salary jobs.

Self-employment may be an effective method for increased earnings over time. Holtz-Eakin, Weathers and Rosen (2000) found self-employment increased earnings from 1969 to 1990 when looking at five-year intervals with the Panel Study of Income Dynamics. They found that a higher percentage moved up from lower income levels in a five-year interval than wage and salary workers when they were self-employed or when they became self-employed. This occurred for both men and women and for African Americans and non-African Americans. However, the self-employed in upper income levels were more likely to experience downward mobility relative to wage and salary workers.

Income varies between two clusters of self-employed workers: those legally incorporated as a small business with an owner and those who are sole proprietors or in a partnership (the unincorporated self-employed). The unincorporated self-employed receive lower income than wage and salary workers (Devine, Table 9 and Table 10). For example, unincorporated, self-employed men receive 85 to 90 percent and women receive only 54 to 59 percent of the median hourly income relative to wage and salary workers. In contrast, the self-employed with incorporated businesses received 25 to 49 percent higher hourly income than wage and salary workers depending on gender and year. The self-employed owners of incorporated businesses are disproportionately men and full-time workers (Devine, Table 9 and Table 10). A gender differences remains even after considering full-time work and incorporated self-employment, because self-employed women had far lower median earnings than men in both incorporated and unincorporated jobs of part-time and of full-time workers. The advantages of incorporation may have increased over time as evidenced by an increasing percentage of incorporation among the self-employed—from 24 percent in 1975 to 31 percent in 1990 for men, and from 8 percent to 18 percent, respectively, for women.

One possible reason for the rapid increase in incorporation of the self-employed could be the legal advantages of business ownership, such as provision of health and pension benefits. While employers provide health and retirement benefits through costs partly supported by tax advantages, the self-employed have to pay these costs themselves if they are unincorporated. The self-employed were less likely to have health insurance coverage in 1990 than the wage and salary workers, taking into account gender and full-time/part-time hours of work (Devine, Table 11). Among the self-employed, the incorporated self-employed were more likely to have health insurance than the unincorporated self-employed. About 90 percent of incorporated self-employed had coverage although only a quarter of women and half of men had jobs that provided coverage rather than coverage from other family members. In contrast, the majority of unincorporated self-employed had health coverage but seldom from their own job—23 percent of men and 9 percent of women had insurance through a job. The majority of men and women wage and salary workers have pension coverage provided by an employer. The self-employed can have retirement coverage by saving tax advantaged funds in Individual Retirement Accounts or Keogh plan accounts. In 1993, about 16 percent of the self-employed ages 30 to 54 had any pension or Keogh account coverage compared with 60 percent of wage and salary workers (Iams 1995, Table 1).

Given the marked economic advantages displayed by the incorporated self-employed, it is no surprise that those with assets in businesses are concentrated among the upper ten percent of the wealth distribution in America (Kennikell and Sunden 1997, Table 4 and Table 5). Among those aged sixty-five and older, the upper wealth decile owns 82 percent of all business assets and the upper 0.5 percent own 44.5 percent of business assets.

See also AUTONOMY; EMPLOYEE HEALTH INSURANCE; EMPLOYMENT OF OLDER WORKERS; INDIVIDUAL RETIREMENT ACCOUNTS; JOB PERFORMANCE; PENSIONS, PLAN TYPES AND POLICY APPROACHES; RETIREMENT PLANNING; WORKFORCE CHALLENGES.

HOWARD M. IAMS

BIBLIOGRAPHY

BRUCE, D.; HOLTZ-EAKIN, D.; and QUINN, J. *Self-Employment and Labor Market Transitions at Older Ages.* Boston, Mass.: Boston College Center for Retirement Research, 2000.

BRUEGGER, J. E. "Measuring Self-Employment in the United States." *Monthly Labor Review* 119, no. 1–2 (January/February 1996): 3–9.

Bureau of Labor Statistics. "Employee Benefits in Medium and Large Private Establishments, 1997." Bulletin 2517 (September 1999).

DEVINE, T. J. "Characteristics of Self-Employed Women in the United States." *Monthly Labor Review* 117, no. 3 (1994): 20–34.

FAIRLIE, R. W., and MEYER, B. D.. "Ethnic and Racial Self-Employment Differences and Possible Explanations." *Journal of Human Resources* 31, no. 4 (1996): 757–794.

HOLTZ-EAKIN, D.; ROSEN, H. S.; and WEATHERS, R. "Horatio Alger Meets the Mobility Tables." *Small Business Economics* 14, no. 4 (2000): 243–274.

IAMS, H. M. "Jobs of Persons Working After Receiving Retired-Worker Benefits." *Social Security Bulletin.* 50, no. 11 (1987): 4–15.

IAMS, H. M. "The 1993 SIPP and CPS Pension Surveys." *Social Security Bulletin.* 58, no. 4 (1995): 125–130.

KENNICKELL, A. B., and SUNDEN, A. E. "Pensions, Social Security, and the Distribution of Wealth." Washington, D.C.: Board of Governors of the Federal Reserve, 1997.

MANSER, M. E., and PICOTT, G. "The Role of Self-Employment in U.S. and Canadian Job Growth." *Monthly Labor Review* 122, no. 4 (1999): 10–25.

Social Security Administration. "Statistical Notes from the New Beneficiary Data System." *Social Security Bulletin.* 57, no. 1 (1994): 60–71.

SENIOR CENTERS

The modern-day senior center traces its roots back to the early 1940s when one of the earliest centers (the Hodson Center in New York City) focused on meeting the needs of lower income older people (Gelfand). The number of senior centers has grown to between twelve thousand and fourteen thousand depending on what one considers a senior center to be (Krout, 1989b; Wagner). Three White House Conferences on Aging, the passage of the Older Americans Act in 1965 and its subsequent amendments, and the activities of the National Council on the Aging have played important roles in this growth and expansion. According to the National Council on the Aging's National Institute of Senior Centers, "A senior center is a community focal point on aging where older adults come together for services and activities that reflect their experience and skills, respond to their diverse needs and interests, enhance their dignity, support their independence, and encourage involvement in and with the community" (p. 5).

Most senior centers are multipurpose in that they provide a range of activities and services and are multifaceted in terms of the functions they fulfill for older participants as well as the roles they play in local social and health service networks. Throughout their history, senior centers have responded to the needs of at-risk and well older persons, with some centers developing a greater emphasis on one group or the other. Thus, perhaps more than any other word, *variation* defines senior centers today. Depending on the senior center and the geographic area in which it is located, considerable diversity is found in who attends a center, the number of programs it offers, and the size of its facility, staff, and resources.

Senior centers find themselves facing fundamental questions about what they do, who they serve, and how they can best respond to recent and projected demographic and social changes in the United States. Some of the most important questions are: How successfully do senior centers respond to the economic, cultural, and social diversity among older adults, and how should/can they best meet the needs of an increasingly diverse older population? What roles can senior centers best play in the menu of community-based services and what must centers do to ensure their viability in the future? Will the programming that people in their sixties found appealing twenty years ago attract baby boomers when they begin to reach retirement age beginning in the year 2010?

Focal points

Senior centers have played an important and highly visible role in the aging services network since its creation by the Older Americans Act (OAA) in the 1970s. This network is made up of State Units on Aging (SUAs), Area Agencies on Aging (AAAs), and community-based service providers such as senior centers. The 1978 amendments to the OAA explicitly outlined the role that local senior centers should play as "focal points" to bring older adults in contact with the myriad of programs and agencies designed to meet their needs. Researchers have found that most multipurpose senior centers do play focal point roles providing information and linkages to other programs and collocation of services with other agencies (Krout, 1989a). Thus, senior centers generally have a considerable degree of visibility and support in these communities and often serve as a major "entry point" into the service system.

Awareness and utilization

Although only a handful of studies have been carried out on the awareness of senior centers (as opposed to services in general), it would appear that the large majority of older adults are aware of these organizations (Krout, 1984). As for center utilization, it is difficult to say with certainty just what percentage of older adults actually use senior centers, how frequent and intense this use is, and what activities and services older adults participate in when they do attend. Data from a 1984 national study focusing on health and social situations of older adults reveal that 13.7 percent of those persons sixty or over had attended a senior center in the preceding year (Krout et al.). Studies from the 1980s and 1990s have reported a wide range of utilization rates from 8 percent to 21 percent (Calsyn and Winter; Krout, 1983, 1996a). Thus, it would appear reasonable to state that between 10 to 20 percent of elderly adults in this country currently attend senior centers at least once a year. This figure translates into three and a half to seven million people age sixty-five and over. This figure should probably be increased by around one to one and a half million to include an additional 10 or more percent of the almost twelve million persons age sixty to sixty-four. The total number then might be as high as seven million and could even be higher if one considers that at least some nonusers might want to participate but do not for one reason or another.

What about change in the numbers or rates of senior center participation? Data collected as part of a longitudinal study of a national sample of senior centers conducted in the 1980s indicate that one-quarter of the centers experienced a decline in the number of participants or did not change while one-half had an increase. It is likely that the rates of center use among the older population did not change significantly in the 1990s, but the numbers have increased nationwide because the number of senior centers and seniors continued to grow in the 1980s and 1990s. However, senior center utilization patterns no doubt vary widely. For example, the majority of the more than one hundred rural AAA directors interviewed in the late 1980s reported significant declines in senior center attendance in their planning and service areas (Krout, 1989b). More recent anecdotal accounts indicate that many suburban senior centers, as well as those in big cities experiencing growth in their older population, have seen increases in participation.

Programs and activities

It is clear that the breadth and depth of senior center programming has expanded considerably in the past fifty years. As senior centers enlarged their resource and user base and provisions of the Older Americans Act evolved to more clearly specify the types of services fundable at the local level, a progressive increase in service offerings followed. Data from a national longitudinal study of senior centers found a mean of eleven activities and sixteen services for 1989 (Krout, 1994a). Approximately 90 percent of the centers were reported to offer information and referral, transportation, and congregate meals, and 70 percent home-delivered meals. Over three-quarters of the centers offered health screening and maintenance, health education, and nutrition education. Telephone reassurance, friendly visiting, and information and assistance services —for consumers, housing, crime prevention, financial and taxes and legal aid, and social security—were offered by around two-thirds of the centers. Similar figures were found in a 1995 survey of over four hundred upstate New York congregate programs (Krout, 1996b).

A smaller percentage of the centers reported in-home services with one-third offering homemaker, home health, and home repair/winterization. Special services, income supplement, and personal counseling and mental health services were reported by an even smaller percentage of centers (between 20 and 40 percent,) and adult day care by 15 percent. Not surprisingly, centers with larger budgets, more staff, and affiliations with multiservice organizations, as well as with a greater percentage of users with higher incomes and over age seventy-five, reported a greater number of programs. Longitu-

dinal research found that during the 1980s, 60 percent of centers were reported to have experienced an increase in the number of activities they offered and only one in eight noted a decrease (Krout, 1994a).

Characteristics of senior center participants

An extremely important question is simple: Who participates in senior centers? The answer of who uses and benefits from senior centers has considerable policy and funding implications. As usual, generalizations are risky because most senior centers draw their users from a fairly limited geographic area and have user populations that reflect those areas. Centers located in minority communities will have largely minority users, while those in largely white suburbs will have mostly white, middle-income users. Krout's longitudinal study found the following averages for participant characteristics in 1989: 11 percent under sixty-five; 41 percent between the ages of sixty-five and seventy-four; 37 percent aged seventy-five to eighty-four; and 10 percent age eighty-five and over. Three-quarters were female and 71 percent unmarried, and 85 percent were reported to be white. Slightly more than one-quarter reported incomes of less than $5,000, 36 percent from $5,000 to $9,999 and 37 percent more than $10,000 (Krout, 1994b).

Several studies conducted in New York in the 1990s report some similar findings, but also illustrate the great diversity among senior center users. While similar in terms of age and gender, senior centers in upstate New York surveyed in 1995 reported higher percentages of whites and higher incomes (Krout, 1996b) than reported for a 1999 sample of New York City participants (Berman).

Krout's national research also provides some insight into changes experienced by senior centers in the 1980s that likely continued in the 1990s. Fifty six percent of center directors surveyed said the age of participants had gotten older on average and only 14 percent said it had gotten younger, suggesting the aging "cohort" of current senior center users is not being replaced by the "young-old." Respondents were about equally split when it came to changes in the health of participants. Three out of ten indicated the health had decreased while 27 percent said it had increased. Almost 60 percent reported an increase in the number of participants categorized as frail while only 12 percent indicated a decrease in that number. Almost three-quarters noted no change in the percentage of participants that were non-white.

Programming for the frail

An important question related to participant characteristics and a key to senior center identity and the roles they play in the community-based service network is the degree to which senior centers serve older adults with cognitive and/or physical limitations. A number of researchers looking at senior center participation and participants have observed that frail older persons are underserved by such places, and that older individuals who are frail physically and mentally or are members of minority groups make up a very small percentage of senior center users. On the other hand, research also suggests that relative to other organizations, senior centers are significantly involved with programming for frail people. For example, Cox and Monk (1989, 1990) report that 90 percent of the New York State center directors they surveyed said frail older adults were integrated into center programming and 16 percent said their centers had developed separate programs for this populations. Conrad and others found that senior centers were the most prevalent co-location site for nonfreestanding adult day care programs in the United States.

Krout conducted an exhaustive review of the research on this topic in the early 1990s (Krout, 1995) and concluded that the lack of data and definitional inconsistencies made it difficult to assess the exact degree to which senior centers serve frail older adults. Many of the services that centers routinely offer can be of value to individuals who need assistance with daily activities (e.g., adult day care, transportation, in-home meals and other in-home services, telephone reassurance). A much smaller but still significant number of centers develop programs to meet the needs of older adults with particular functional limitations. Planning, financial resources and time, appropriate space, and staff training are often cited as critical to successful senior programming for frail older adults. Again, considerable variation is found between senior centers in the numbers of elders with significant physical or cognitive limitations served. As senior center user populations "age-in-place," these organizations are facing increasing numbers of physically and mentally frail participants in need of supportive programming. Thus, there is a demographic as well as a social imperative for more information on and support of center activities for at-risk older populations.

Future challenges

It is clear that senior centers face many challenges as they mature from their beginnings as recreational and congregate meal programs to multipurpose, multiservice organizations serving a variety of communities and older persons. Some senior centers function more as service agencies serving economically disadvantaged, socially isolated, or functionally impaired older adults, while others provide a rich menu of educational health promotion and volunteer opportunities to financially secure, well educated, and physically active seniors. But regardless of their resources and foci, all senior centers face a myriad of challenges as the older population itself grows in numbers and diversity. Perhaps the biggest challenge facing senior centers is how they will respond to the baby boomers as they enter older age.

Senior centers face four challenges if they are to remain a vital part of their communities and attract the coming generations of older adults. The first challenge is for senior centers to examine and articulate their goals and identity. What role(s) will they play and what programs will they offer in the future? It is clear that newly retired older adults today want more than group dining, recreation, and socialization opportunities. Many, but not all, centers today offer a wide range of wellness and educational activities. Some centers will keep or find an important niche in their communities offering traditional programs or serving lower-income and less healthy older adults. The majority will have to continue to respond to the changes in the "senior marketplace" and develop new program options. Second, senior centers will have to develop more effective marketing strategies that can compete with all the other organizations that hope to get the attention and participation of middle-aged adults as they become older. A clear, positive, and well-articulated message of what senior centers can do to keep older adults vibrant and involved with the larger community will be key to this marketing effort.

Third, as center staff plan for new programming, they must remember that the older population is not monolithic, but rather made up of individuals with different interests. The baby boom includes two "generations," those who experienced the 1960s and 1970s as teenagers and very young adults, and those who reached those ages a decade later. Add education, ethnicity, and income, and the diversity becomes very apparent. Thus, choices and flexibility will be important to attracting boomers as they reach retirement age as will an understanding of the differences based on these sociodemographic characteristics. Finally, senior center advocates must step back and consider the strengths of centers within the context of the larger public policy issues that face America as it prepares for the baby boom to age. The issues include: retirement and financial security; housing and long-term care; spiritual and individual well-being; and how society can continue to provide opportunities for older adults to remain productive, contributing members of their communities and the nation as a whole.

Conclusions

It is clear that senior enters have grown and diversified over the years. Shifts in federal and state spending and priorities in health and social services for older adults to a great focus on cost containment and targeting the at-risk, and changing demographics and retirement patterns have had considerable impacts on senior center programming. Senior center professionals in the 1980s worked to identify and refine the roles of centers in relation to focal point functions and the (not always compatible) needs and interests of the newly retired, long-time center users, and frail, at risk older persons. They expanded center linkages with other agencies.

One of the biggest strengths of senior centers is their diversity and their ability to serve different segments of the older population in many different ways. Senior centers do many things well with relatively few resources and certainly are capable of improving and expanding existing functions given the appropriate resources and mission. They have been challenged by the growth of a larger and more diverse older population during times of fiscal constraints; challenges that will increase many fold with the aging of the baby boom. Although clearly a part of the community-based services system, they still carry an image for some (older persons, policymakers, and academics) of places largely for recreation and socialization. Much of the future success of senior centers will depend on the ability of center professionals to articulate and realize new visions of center roles and programming that respond to the interests and capabilities of both current and coming generations of older adults.

JOHN A. KROUT

See also CONGREGATE AND HOME-DELIVERED MEALS; OLDER AMERICANS ACT.

BIBLIOGRAPHY

BERMAN, J. *Senior Center Utilization Study.* Report prepared for The New York City. New York: New York City Department for the Aging, 1999.

CALSYN, R., and WINTER, J. "Who Attends Senior Centers?" *Journal of Social Service Research* 26 (1999): 53–69.

CONRAD, K. J.; HUGHES, S. L.; COMPIONE, P. F.; and GOLDBERG, R. S. "Shedding New Light on Adult Day Care." *Perspective on Aging* (November/December 1987): 18–21.

COX, C., and MONK, A. "Measuring the Effectiveness of a Health Education Program for Older Adults." *Educational Gerontology* 15 (1989): 9–23.

COX, C., and MONK, A. "Integrating the Frail and Well Elderly: The Experience of Senior Centers." *Journal of Gerontological Social Work* 15 (1990): 131–147.

GELFAND, D. *The Aging Network: Programs and Services,* 2d ed. New York: Springer Publishing Company, 1990.

KROUT, J. "Correlate of Service Utilization Among the Rural Elderly." *The Gerontologist* 23 (1983): 500–504.

KROUT, J. "Senior Center Linkages and the Provision of Services to the Elderly." Final Report To the AARP Andrus Foundation, Fredonia, NY, 1989a.

KROUT, J. "Community Size Differences in Senior Center Programs and Participation: A Longitudinal Analysis." *Research on Aging* 16 (1994a): 440–462.

KROUT, J. "Changes in Senior Center Participant Characteristics During the 1980s." *Journal of Gerontological Social Work* 22 (1994b): 41–60.

KROUT, J. "Senior Centers and Services for the Frail Elderly." *Journal of Aging and Social Policy* 7 (1995): 59–76.

KROUT, J. "Senior Center Programming and Frailty Among Older Persons." *Journal of Gerontological Social Work* 26 (1996a): 19–34.

KROUT, J. "Congregate Programs and Participants in New York State." Paper presented at the Annual Meeting of the State Society on Aging of New York, Albany, NY, 1996b.

KROUT, J.; CUTLER, S.; and COWARD, R. "Correlates of Senior Center Participation: A National Analysis." *The Gerontologist* 30 (1990): 72–79.

MONK, A. "The Integration of Frail Elderly into Senior Centers." Final Report to the AARP Andrus Foundation, New York: Columbia University, 1988.

National Council on the Aging. *Senior Center Standards: Guidelines for Practice*. Washington D.C.: The National Council on the Aging, Inc., 1991.

WAGNER, D. "Senior Center Research in America: An Overview of What We Know." In *Senior Centers in America; A Blueprint for the Future*. Edited by Debra Shollenberger. Washington, D.C.: The National Council of the Aging, 1995. Pages 3–10.

SEXUALITY

Despite the many changes in sexual attitudes and behavior in Western societies over the last few decades, myths and misinformation abound when it comes to the sexuality of older adults. Aging individuals who express interest in or enjoy sex are portrayed frequently with humor or disdain in the media, and often younger persons find it difficult to conceive of or accept sexuality as normal behavior spanning the entire life course. Yet sex can play an important part in the lives of older adults, and many individuals remain sexually active into their eighties and nineties (Schiavi and Rehman).

Sex and aging

By itself, the biological process of aging does not reduce the need or desire for sex. A significant number of older adults enjoy sexual activity and believe that it plays an important role in maintaining physical and psychological health (Meston). For many older adults, the concept of sexuality includes nongenital practices such as kissing, hugging, and fondling. Such activity may replace actual intercourse and becomes increasingly important for those who no longer desire or are capable of coitus (Hodson and Skeen).

Two large surveys of midlife and older adults provide basic information on their sexual attitudes and behavior. The National Council on the Aging (NCOA), found that 61 percent of men and 37 percent of women over age sixty reported being sexually active. Differences in frequency of sexual activity by gender result, in part, from the greater longevity of women that makes them more likely than men to be widowed and without a partner. Also, while age norms permit and even encourage men to seek younger women, such social sanctioning does not hold true for older women and younger men.

Of those NCOA respondents who reported being sexually active at least once a month, well over half perceived maintaining an active sex life as an important aspect of their relationship with their partner. About three-quarters said they were at least as satisfied or more satisfied sexually than they were in their forties. In general, the survey revealed that the lack of a partner and having a disabling medical condition, and not a diminution of desire, were the two main factors limiting sexual behavior.

A survey commissioned by the AARP (formerly American Association of Retired Persons) produced similar findings about older persons and sex (Jacoby). About two-thirds of the study's respondents who reported being sexually active rated their sexual relationships as being very to extremely satisfying. Although frequency of intercourse decreased with age, over 70 percent of those who were sexually active reported engaging in sex at least once a month. About half between the ages of forty-five and fifty-nine had sex at least once a week, a proportion that decreased to 30 percent for men and 24 percent for women among those age sixty to seventy-four. Being ill or on medication appeared to lessen sexual desire, a circumstance that may explain why those age sixty and over believe that better health would improve their sex lives. Nonetheless, more than half of men and 85 percent of women (including those age seventy-five and older) reported that illness did not adversely affect their sexuality. Both men and women between the ages of forty-five and fifty-nine were more likely than those age sixty and over to approve of sex between unmarried partners and to engage in oral sex and masturbation. They also were less likely to believe that "sex is only for younger people."

Normal physiological changes in older adults

While older adults experience many of the same sexual problems and concerns as younger people, a number of biological, psychological, and social factors influence sexual behavior as people age. In general, physiological changes that accompany the aging process occur gradually among men and women, and vary individually.

Among men, normal physiological changes associated with the aging process include a slower, less firm erection that recedes quickly after orgasm. The force of ejaculation decreases, producing a lower volume of semen and an increase in the duration of the refractory phase (the time needed before it is possible to be sexually stimulated) after orgasm. "Seepage" (semen leaking out rather than being ejaculated) or retrograde ejaculation (ejaculation back into the bladder rather than out through the penis) may occur. Men also may experience a decrease in size and firmness of the testes, a change in testicle elevation, an absence of the sex flush (a rash that appears on the stomach and chest areas in some sexually responsive men), and a decrease in testosterone level (Schiavi and Rehman; Shell and Smith). No clinical consensus exists as to the physiological occurrence of "male menopause" (Morley and Perry), but gradually lowering testosterone levels in men as they age are associated with increased rates of sexual, mood, and cognitive disorders (Gould and Petty).

Normal physiological changes that affect sexual function in women as they age primarily are due to reduction in circulating estrogen after menopause. The rate and amount of vaginal lubrication decreases and a general atrophy of vaginal tissue occurs. In addition, the clitoral, vulvar, and labial tissues shrink, the size of the cervix, uterus, and ovaries decreases, and some loss of elasticity and thinning of the vaginal wall occurs. Intercourse may become painful if thinning of the vaginal walls is significant (Shell and Smith). Hormone replacement therapy can ameliorate this condition, but not without some concerns about possible side effects (Lock).

Sexual dysfunction

A number of factors influence mature people's interest in and capacity for sex as they age. Common medical conditions of older adults—hypertension, heart disease, osteoporosis, arthritis, rheumatism, urinary incontinence, diabetes, prostate enlargement, and emphysema—can reduce their sexual interest and functioning. Furthermore, medications that are prescribed to treat these and other problems can adversely affect erectile function and libido (Hernandez-

Lopez). Other clinical factors that impact older persons' sexuality include surgical procedures such as mastectomy, hysterectomy, colostomy, prostatectomy (removal of all or part of the prostate gland), angioplasty, and heart surgery.

Social factors such as excessive alcohol use, depression, and poor self-esteem also can exert a toll. Fear and lack of understanding about normal genital changes can impact sexual expression. Attitudes, both individual and social, can negatively affect sexual activity. Among men, retirement can lead to a loss of self-esteem, depression, and subsequent loss of interest in sex. Women's negative early experience with sexual activity, in some cases sexual abuse, can affect sexual interest and behavior in later years. Also, religious sanctions that restrict sex for any purposes other than reproduction strongly influence sexual behavior in later life.

Although it is not the only means for treating sexual dysfunction in men, the prescription drug Viagra has received much professional and popular attention (Lamberg; Morgentaler). The majority of those in the AARP study who were taking Viagra reported that the drug improved their sex lives. Among women, estrogen has been used to increase desire and arousal, and testosterone has been prescribed to address more generalized sexual dysfunction. Meanwhile, alprostadil (Caverject, Muse) is used to treat erectile dysfunction in men, and some amphetamines, such as methylphenidate (Ritalin), have been used to increase sexual responsiveness in women. In addition to prescription medications, many older adults turn to alternative herbal remedies such as gingko biloba, ginseng, and ma huang to address sexual dysfunction, although no controlled studies have been published on these supplements and they are not approved by the U.S. Food and Drug Administration (Knowlton).

While research continues to find new medications and remedies for treating sexual dysfunction, many sex therapists believe that the problem often is psychological, and should be treated using behavioral strategies. Considerable evidence, however, suggests that organic causes underlie erectile dysfunction in 80 percent of the men who experience the condition for longer than a year (Morgentaler). Moreover, psychogenic responses that inhibit sexual arousal may result from an inability to perform with a partner rather than cause it. The best predictor of sexual behavior in later years is the pattern of sexuality in younger years, barring any physical limitations (Tichy and Talaschek). Attitudes that predispose an individual to enjoy sexual activity in youth and young adulthood typically continue across the larger stages of the life course.

Nursing homes

Entrance into a nursing home can represent the end of any sexual life for older people. Due to a lack of privacy, segregation of men from women, and lack of accommodations for married couples, limited opportunities exist for men and women to engage in sexual activity if they so wish. Sexual history is rarely included in screening information for new residents. In addition, general negative attitudes and lack of knowledge among nursing home staff members regarding sex and older people contribute to an atmosphere that is not conducive to healthy sexuality. Patients who exhibit any form of sexuality are often treated as a joke or with derision. Residents who express interest in sex may be considered "difficult" by staff members, and it is not uncommon for some form of sedation to be administered to them (Hodson and Skeen).

HIV/AIDS and other sexually transmitted diseases

Adults age fifty and over represent more than 10 percent of the annual AIDS caseload in the United States. In the early days of the epidemic, HIV infection occurred disproportionately among older persons through the receipt of contaminated blood or blood products during transfusions. Because of implementation of voluntary donor deferral and routine screening of blood donations implemented in 1985, the number and proportion of AIDS cases associated at any age with this risk factor is minute.

For persons age fifty and over, HIV has most often been transmitted through male-to-male sexual contact. The number of cases reported among homosexual and bisexual men, however, has been steadily declining. Despite this decrease, findings indicate that a sizable number of older men who have sex with men continue to engage in practices that put them at risk for HIV (Anderson). Meanwhile, the number of AIDS cases among men attributable to heterosexual contact increased by 94 percent between 1991 and 1996. Among women age fifty and over,

cases attributed to heterosexual contact increased 106 percent. Injection drug use, either directly through using contaminated drug paraphernalia or indirectly through sexual partnering with a drug injector, accounts for a rising number of cases among older adults each year (Levy).

The behaviors that put older adults at risk for HIV also place them at risk for other sexually transmitted diseases (STDs): primary and secondary syphilis, gonorrhea, and herpes simplex. In 1997, 4 percent of the cases of primary and secondary syphilis and 1 percent of the cases of gonorrhea were reported in persons fifty-five and over (CDC, 1998). Actual incidence rates, however, may be higher than reported due to underdiagnosis and underreporting.

Despite such risks, older high-risk persons are much less likely to have adopted prevention strategies than their younger counterparts who engage in similar sexual practices. In a survey of over two thousand adults age fifty and over, Stall and Catania (1994) found that only a small percentage with a known behavioral risk for HIV infection use condoms during sex or have undergone HIV testing. More than 63 percent report having multiple sex partners. A study conducted by Durex on condom use found that older adults are more resistant to using condoms and modifying sexual behavior than are younger adults. In general, older men are less likely than their younger counterparts to use condoms because their partners, in general, are past childbearing age. Postmenopausal women may not recognize their risk for HIV or other STDs because they equate STD risk with risk of pregnancy. With the current extent of sexual activity in older age groups and the possibility of an increased activity due to medications for erectile dysfunction, safer sexual practices are important for STD and HIV prevention. Educational strategies and interventions targeting adults over age fifty can aid in these efforts (Strombeck and Levy).

Education

Many older adults were raised during an era of sexual repression and may have a high level of internalized negative attitudes and misinformation about sex. Although such attitudes could be addressed through education (Hillman and Stricker), older adults often have few opportunities to receive education about sexual issues.

While health care providers are in a good position to inform older individuals about sexual issues and dispel myths and misunderstandings, this education seldom occurs. The idea that sexuality is a lifelong process contradicts the beliefs of many health care providers, and all too often they fail to take into account sexual issues when treating older patients (Kennedy et al.). The AARP survey found that most older adults receive information about sex from books or magazines. A widespread need exists to educate all health care providers, including nursing home caregivers, about sex and older adults to help promote a more natural integration of sexual activity into the lives of those who desire it.

JUDITH LEVY
RITA STROMBECK

See also ANDROPAUSE; MENOPAUSE; URINARY INCONTINENCE.

BIBLIOGRAPHY

ANDERSON, G. "The Older Gay Man." In *HIV/ AIDS and the Older Adult.* Edited by Kathleen M. Nokes. Washington, D.C.: Taylor and Francis, 1996. Pages 63–76.

Centers for Disease Control. *Sexually Transmitted Disease Surveillance.* Atlanta: Centers for Disease Control, 1997.

Durex. *Americans' Concern About HIV/AIDS Not Translating to Safer Sex Behavior.* London: Durex Consumer Products, 1997.

GOULD, D. C., and PETTY, R. "The Male Menopause—Does It Exist?" *British Medical Journal* 320, no. 7238 (2000): 858–861.

HERNANDEZ-LOPEZ, C. "Drugs Do Not Only Relieve Male Menopause." *British Medical Journal* 321, no. 7258 (2000): 451.

HILLMAN, J., and STRICKER, G. "A Linkage of Knowledge and Attitudes Toward Elderly Sexuality: Not Necessarily a Uniform Relationship." *The Gerontologist* 34 (1994): 256–260.

HODSON, D. S., and SKEEN, P. "Sexuality and Aging: The Hammerlock of Myths." *Journal of Applied Gerontology* 13 (1994): 219–235.

JACOBY, SUSAN. "Great Sex—What's Age Got to Do with It?" *Modern Maturity* (September–October 1999): 41–45+.

KENNEDY, G. J.; HAQUE, M.; and ZARANKOW, B. "Human Sexuality in Late Life." *International Journal of Mental Health* 26 (1997): 35–46.

KNOWLTON, L. "Sexuality and Aging." *Psychiatric Times* 17 (2000): 1.

LAMBERG, L. "New Drug for Erectile Dysfunction Boon for Many, 'Viagravation' for Some." *Journal of the American Medical Association* 280, no. 10 (1998): 867–869.

LEVY, J. A. "AIDS and Injecting Drug-Use in Later Life." *Research on Aging* 20, no. 6 (1998): 776–797.

LOCK, M. "Accounting for Disease and Distress: Morals of the Normal and Abnormal." In *Social Studies in Health and Medicine.* Edited by Gary L. Albrecht, Ray Fitzpatrick, and Susan C. Scrimshaw. London: Sage, 2000. Pages 259–276.

MESTON, C. M. "Aging and Sexuality." *West Journal of Medicine* 167, no. 4 (1997): 285–290.

MORGENTALER, A. "Male Impotence." *The Lancet* 354, no. 9191 (1999): 1713–1718.

MORLEY, J. E., and PERRY, H. M. "Androgen Deficiency in Aging Men: Role of Testosterone Replacement Therapy." *Journal of Laboratory and Clinical Medicine* 135 (2000): 370–378.

National Council on the Aging. *Healthy Sexuality and Vital Aging.* Washington, D.C.: NCOA, 1998.

SCHIAVI, R. C., and REHMAN, J. "Sexuality and Aging." *Urologic Clinics of North America* 22 (1995): 711–726.

SHELL, J., and SMITH, C. K. "Sexuality and the Older Person with Cancer." *Oncology Nursing Forum* 21 (1994): 553–558.

STALL, R., and CATANIA, J. "AIDS Risk Behaviors Among Late Middle-Aged and Elderly Americans." *Archives of Internal Medicine* 154 (1994): 57–63.

STROMBECK, R., and LEVY, J. A. "Educational Strategies and Interventions Targeting Adults Aged 50 and Over for HIV/AIDS Prevention." *Research on Aging* 20, no. 6 (1998): 776–798.

TICHY, A. M., and TALASCHEK, M. L. "Sexually Transmitted Diseases and Acquired Immunodeficiency Syndrome." *Nursing Clinics of North America* 27 (1992): 937–949.

SIBLING RELATIONSHIPS

Siblings are family members who are ascribed by birth (full siblings), by law (adopted siblings) or by marriage (half-siblings, step-siblings, and siblings-in-law). Full siblings have two biological parents in common, whereas half-siblings have one biological parent in common. Legal siblings and step-siblings have no biological parents in common, but their parents are married. A sibling-in-law is related to one's spouse rather than one's parent, in any of the previous ways mentioned. A sibling-in-law can also be the spouse of one's siblings. Social siblings are friends or nonsibling relatives who are transformed into siblings informally, or, in some cultures, through a formal ceremony.

Research on siblings in old age has been limited primarily to full siblings. Important exceptions are the General Social Survey (GSS), which uses nationally representative samples, and the National Survey of Families and Households (NSFH), based on data collected in 1987 and 1988. Both studies include data on step-siblings. Only the NSFH includes data on siblings-in-law (siblings of one's spouse and spouses of one's siblings). Neither study has data on social siblings.

Many questions arise when considering siblings among older adults, including: (1) Do older adults usually have living siblings? (2) How many living siblings do they typically have? (3) Can future older adults expect to have living siblings? (4) How important are siblings to older adults? (5) What do siblings do for one another in later years? (6) What factors influence what siblings do for each other and how they feel about each other?

Prevalence of siblings in later life

Most older adults have at least one living sibling. According to the General Social Survey's data from the mid-1980s, the majority of community-dwelling older adults are likely to have a sister until age eighty-five and a brother until age eighty. This sex difference is likely due to the gender mortality gap, whereby men predecease women by seven to nine years, on average. In general, however, a high proportion of older adults has at least one sibling until the mid-eighties, when a precipitous drop occurs. This pattern is shown in Table 1.

According to General Social Survey data, the number of living siblings an elderly person has depends on the age of the older adult and the sex of his or her siblings. The majority of respondents who had any sisters had two or more until their early eighties while the majority of respondents who had brothers had multiple brothers until their mid-seventies. Whether future older adults can expect to have at least one sibling until advanced old age depends upon two factors. One is the fertility pattern for the birth cohorts in question; that is, the number of babies born to the parents of the older adults. In large families, one would expect a larger pool of potential siblings to survive into old age. The second factor is life expectancy for the cohorts in question—a

Table 1

Percent of older adults who have any living siblings.

Age	One or more living sisters	One or more living brothers	One or more living siblings
60–69 (N=192)	75.0	65.6	91.1
70–74 (N=79)	75.9	62.0	84.8
75–79 (N=57)	68.4	59.6	84.2
80–84 (N=36)	61.2	50.0	63.9
85 90 (N=15)	33.3	6.7	33.3
Total (N=379)	71.2 (270)	60.2 (228)	83.9 (318)

SOURCE: General Social Survey, 1986.

longer life expectancy is related to the survival of a greater number of siblings. Assuming the dramatic increases in life expectancy of the twentieth century will be sustained, if not increased, in the twenty-first century, then fertility rates will be the determining factor.

Fertility rates declined in Western societies during the nineteenth and twentieth centuries; meaning that families have been producing fewer numbers of offspring. Amidst this general decline, however, a baby boom occurred immediately following World War II (between 1946 and 1964, approximately), thereby increasing the potential pool of siblings who might survive into the baby boomers' old age. The fertility of baby boomers' children on the other hand, appears to be substantially lower than that of their parents, thereby returning to the overall general decline in family size. Predictions tend to support a drastic reduction in siblings after the baby boom. However, these predictions do not seem to take into account the higher life expectancy and the increase in blended and reconstituted families.

Table 2 shows cohort trends in the number of siblings (dead or alive) for people born between 1911 and 1980. One-child families (respondents with no siblings) were most common during the Great Depression and the decade preceding it; but, for all cohorts, one-child families were the exception rather than the rule. Comparing current older adults with baby boomers, greater proportions of boomers have

Table 2

Distribution of people born at different historical periods by number of siblings (half- or step-siblings, adopted, biological), whether dead or alive.

Cohort	Number of Siblings				
	0	1	2	3	4+
1965–1980	5.8%	23.9%	24.7%	15.2%	30.4%
Late Boomers (1951–1964)	2.6%	14.7%	20.2%	20.5%	42.0%
Early Boomers (1946–1950)	4.8%	14.5%	17.7%	19.0%	44.0%
World War II Babies (1941–1945)	6.2%	16.9%	17.5%	18.8%	40.6%
Great Depression (1931–1940)	7.4%	17.3%	17.0%	11.8%	46.5%
1921–1930	8.6%	13.6%	12.2%	15.4%	50.2%
World War I Babies (1911–1920)	6.0%	18.7%	15.7%	11.2%	48.5%

SOURCE: General Social Survey, 2000.

ever had two, three, four or more siblings than war babies. The post-boomer cohorts show a reduction in the number of siblings, so that a larger proportion have one and two siblings, but 30 percent of post-boomers still have four or more siblings. Because these siblings are more likely to survive into old age than those of earlier cohorts, predictions of greatly decreased availability of siblings in later years may be exaggerated, especially when all varieties of siblings are considered.

How important are siblings for older adults?

As seen above, until very old age, adults are likely to have at least one sister and/or brother. There is little doubt that siblings are highly valued in later life. This value is based on: (1) physical proximity and the amount of contact siblings have with one another, (2) the functions they serve one another related to contact, and (3) the functions they serve one another independent of contact. As will be seen, the third, symbolic function tends to best capture the importance of siblings for older people.

Sibling proximity and contact. Based on a representative sample of black and non-Hispanic white Americans age fifty-five and older (Minor and Uhlenberg, 1997), about 30 percent live between two and twenty-five miles from their nearest sibling. Just over 20 percent live at least 300 miles apart. As for the remaining 50 percent, most blacks (41 percent) have a sibling neighbor (within two miles) while whites are nearly evenly split between having a sibling neighbor (22 percent) and having a sibling between 26 and 299 miles away (25 percent).

Sibling contact (visits, phone calls, and letters) decreases in the course of adulthood, but in later life it increases somewhat. Adults generally maintain contact with their step- and half-siblings, but less than they do with full siblings. Whether this pattern is found for older adults as well is not known at this time. In general, sibling contact is meager. In an Indiana study (see Cicirelli, 1995), only 17 percent of the older respondents saw their most frequently contacted sibling weekly or more often, and one third saw their sibling monthly. The most typical frequency was several times per year.

What do siblings do for each other? Most studies confirm that siblings do not provide much instrumental support (e.g., performing household and other tasks) for each other in later years. Of those with a sibling within twenty-five miles, providing and receiving help with transportation is the most common form of instrumental support, yet such support is found only for 6 percent (providing transportation) and 5 percent (receiving transportation help) of older adults. Expressive support (e.g., advice, encouragement, moral or emotional support) can be transmitted and received from any distance and is more common, with 14 percent receiving and 16 percent providing expressive support. Some of these percentages vary by ethnic communities and by gender composition of the sibling pair, but, overall, sibling relationships in later life are not characterized primarily by the giving and receiving of social support, whether instrumental or expressive.

Symbolic functions of siblings.   Despite the relatively infrequent rates of sibling contact or social support, most older adults report feeling very close to their siblings. Feelings of closeness have a cognitive (symbolic) component based on a shared past. Siblings are likely to share values, goals, and knowledge domains based on generational commonalities, such as fads or sociopolitical and historical events. Unlike friends, however, they also share early memories, which allows them to know each other's personal references. As peers, siblings are unique family members throughout life, because they have the potential to share ideas and experiences more openly than parents and children who may be inhibited in some domains by generational barriers.

Siblings also serve as a special kind of attachment figure to one another in later life. Although their physical presence may not be sought frequently, most older adults sincerely believe that a sibling would come to their aid in a crisis, regardless of whether they get along well. In this way, siblings provide a safety net that, although rarely mobilized, provides a sense of security.

Factors affecting sibling relationships

The relationship between twins in late life is being studied for the first time. Such studies may reveal whether genes, environment, or both contribute to the quality of sibling relationships in late life. Because both identical and fraternal twins have more contact, provide more support, live closer, and feel emotionally closer than other siblings, it appears that the early environment has some kind of influence on the late-life relationship. By virtue of being born at the same time, both kinds of twins have more in common, such as more shared experiences early in life, than other siblings. But genes also play a role in the late-life relationship. For identical twins, satisfaction with the relationship and attachment security are completely independent of contact with the sibling, but this is not the case with fraternal twins, who have no more genes in common than any other siblings. (Neyer).

Race appears to have some influence on late-life sibling relationships. Compared to non-Hispanic whites, blacks tend to live nearer to their siblings, they tend to have more contact with siblings who live nearby, and they report that they provide more emotional support to their siblings. Race does not appear to influence instrumental support exchanges, however.

The general pattern of low social support from siblings in later life changes when a spouse, adult child, or other close relative is unavailable or nonexistent. For instance, feelings of closeness to a sibling and confiding in a sibling increase in the absence of other core family members. This substitution function of siblings becomes increasingly likely in very old age, particularly for women. While 53 percent of very old men (over age eighty-four, community-dwelling, and white) have a living spouse, only 9 percent of comparable women have a spouse. The increased divorce rate, the higher rate of childlessness, and the reduced fertility of younger cohorts are likely to result in a greater reliance on siblings for informal support in later years, compared to previous cohorts.

Gender also seems to influence sibling closeness. Sister dyads tend to be the most intimate, but there is less agreement on which combination of siblings is more intimate, sister-brother or brother dyads. Men are less likely than women to reveal their feelings toward siblings, but they may, nonetheless, hold sentiments of value and affection as deeply as women do.

VICTORIA HILKEUITCH BEDFORD

See also INTERGENERATIONAL SUPPORT; KIN; SOCIAL SUPPORT.

BIBLIOGRAPHY

BANK, S. P., and KAHN, M. D. *The Sibling Bond.* New York: Basic Books, 1997.

BEDFORD, V. H. "Sibling Relationships in Middle Adulthood and Old Age." In *Handbook on Aging and the Family.* Edited by R. Blieszner and V. H. Bedford. Westport, Conn.: Greenwood, Press, 1995. Pages 201–222.

BEDFORD, V. H. "Sibling Interdependence in Adulthood and Old Age." In *Vision 2010: Families and Aging*, vol. 3, no. 2. Edited by T. Brubaker. Minneapolis, Minn.: National Council on Family Relations, 1996. Pages 18–19.

BEDFORD, V. H., and AVIOLI, P. S. "Variations on Sibling Intimacy in Old Age." *Generations* 25 (2001): 34–40.

CICIRELLI, V. G. *Sibling Relationships Across the Life Span.* New York: Plenum Press, 1995.

CONNIDIS, I. A. *Family Ties and Aging.* Thousand Oaks, Calif.: Sage Publications, 2001.

CONNIDIS, I. A., and CAMPBELL, L. D. "Closeness, Confiding, and Contact Among Siblings in Middle and Late Adulthood." *Journal of Family Issues* 16 (1995): 722–747.

CONNIDIS I. A., and DAVIES, L. "Confidants and Companions in Later Life: The Place of Family and Friends." *Journal of Gerontology* 45 (1990): S141–S149.

General Social Survey. Cumulative datafile. Available online at http://sda.berkeley.edu.

GOLD, D. T. "Late-life Sibling Relationships: Does Race Affect Typological Distribution?" *The Gerontologist* 30 (1990): 741–748.

HOCHSCHILD, A. R. *The Unexpected Community.* Berkeley: University of California Press, 1973.

MINOR, S., and UHLENBERG, P. "Intragenerational Proximity and the Social Role of Sibling Neighbors After Midlife." *Family Relations* 46 (1997): 145–153.

NEYER, F. J. "Twin Relationships in Old Age." *Journal of Social and Personal Relationships* 7 (2001): 767–789.

WHITE, L. K., and RIEDMANN, A. "When the Brady Bunch Grows Up: Step/Half- and Full Sibling Relationships in Adulthood." *Journal of Marriage and the Family* 54 (1992b): 197–208.

SKIN

The existence of two different types of aging of the human skin has been recognized only since the mid-1980s. Normal internal (intrinsic) changes are differentiated from the effects of external influences (extrinsic). These differences have been made more apparent by a dramatic increase in life expectancy. The average life expectancy in ancient Rome was 22 years, compared with 78.6 years in Canada in 1996.

Intrinsic changes

The intrinsic changes are best seen in places where there has been minimum light exposure. The upper inner arm and covered buttocks are good examples. Here the top layer of the skin (epidermis) is thinned only slightly. Its cells do not adhere as well as in younger skin, and there is comparatively increased architectural irregularity. The number of pigmentary cells (melanocytes) is reduced, and the junction with the dermis (underlayer of the skin) shows some degree of flattening.

The dermis itself shows a thinning (atrophy) in which its major fibrous and cellular components are diminished. The number of sweat glands is reduced. Hair is grayer, and its individual diameters are narrower. In addition, the hair roots (follicles) on the scalp and face are fewer but the associated "grease" (sebaceous) glands are larger. Nails become fragile and develop longitudinal lines. The subcutaneous tissue under the dermis is thinner about the face, hands, shins, and feet but thicker on the waists of men and the thighs of women.

Coarse skin folds emphasize expression lines. They follow the contour of the larger muscles of the face.

The physiological activity of the various skin elements is generally reduced. This applies particularly to the immune response, the response to injury, cellular replacement, glandular activity, heat regulation, and sense of touch.

The effect on the individual can be summed up as the minor nuisances of old age and but mainly harmless. It is the external influence that is potentially harmful.

Extrinsic changes

The major extrinsic agent causing damage is sunlight. This damaging effect is termed photoaging. It is the result of prolonged and repeated damage caused by ultraviolet radiation, most frequently sunlight. The main damaging effect is caused by the shorter wavelength radiation (UVB), which has a limited penetration of the upper epidermal cells. The longer wavelength radiation (UVA) penetrates into the dermis and further increases the damage.

The main clinical change caused by sunlight is wrinkling. The elastic fibers present in the upper dermis swell initially. Later they become coarse and twisted, and finally lose their fibrous character. Under the microscope, the fibers are a diffuse, characterless mass that stains differently than the normal skin. The coarser, deeper, and more voluminous collagen fibers show similar degradation. This all leads to a loss of skin elasticity termed "elastotic degeneration." If this skin is pinched and pulled, it fails to rebound to its normal state over a short period of time. In contrast, youthful skin or skin that is usually covered in the older person rapidly springs back to its normal state.

Sunlight is essential to well-being, and in moderation it enhances immunity; it makes Vitamin D in the skin; it induces a normal pigmentary protective response; and it makes people feel and look "good." Episodic excessive exposure, or a cumulation over many years, can be damaging and is particularly related to the pigment character of the individual's skin.

How much any individual shows the changes in the skin due to a lifetime of chronic sun exposure and weathering depends on the amount of sun to which the person has been exposed and where, geographically, this occurred. Other modifying factors include genetic endowment, skin pigmentation (dark, fair or gingery), and lifestyle factors such as smoking.

A wrinkled, coarse skin is the most characteristic of these changes. Smokers particularly have enhanced facial aging. Their skin wrinkling and appearance are more aged than those of nonsmokers. The deeper folds of the expression lines may be more emphasized.

The wrinkling may give cosmetic concern; many active old people wish to retain a youthful appearance. "Cellulite" is a harmless form of deep dimpling which occurs on the outer thighs. Some of the concerns can be met by the many cosmetic applications on the market. In other situations, cosmetic surgery can bring much benefit.

Growth and changes in color

The exposed skin is thinner in older people than in younger people. Occasionally coarse comedones (blackheads) are present. Discrete white, firm lesions may appear on the forehead and cheeks. These are harmless milia made up of keratin, the horny, fibrous protein of the outermost layer of the skin.

Though the color of the face is generally more pallid with age, the overall appearance varies due to blood vessel changes and pigmentary abnormalities. A mottled, blotchy redness is due to dilatation of small surface vessels (telangiectasia). Sometimes the vessels are individually quite prominent. At other times, the surface capillaries may have leaked due to solar deterioration of the supporting tissue. This produces livid blotches termed ecchymoses which may be present for a long time before resorption occurs.

Coarse yellow markings may be present on the forehead and sometimes on the cheeks. The skin surface seems to be filled with rectangular patches of varying size between the folds. This elastotic degeneration is due to thickening and clumping of light-damaged fibrous tissue under the skin surface. It is finer about the lips, where it emphasizes the skin folds.

Although the pigmentary cells are reduced in number as a natural result of aging, irregular pigmentation appears on the light-exposed areas. This may be simple freckling (lentigines) seen particularly on fair or gingery skins. Larger patches of melanin pigmentation 0.5 to 1.5 centimeters in diameter, are common. These are known colloquially as "sunspots," "liver spots," or "age spots." Raindrop-size nonpigmented white areas appear on the outer arms and legs. Long forgotten scars are also revealed due to loss of obscuring pigment.

Apart from causing cosmetic concern in some, none of these changes is harmful in nature. However, irregular horny lesions can present. They are termed *actinic keratoses*. They may be flat and scaly on the ear tips or lips, or thicker and more craggy on the cheeks or sides of the neck. It is debatable whether they ever become malignant, but they can be a mechanical or cosmetic nuisance and do occur in skin more prone to malignant change.

Various other warty excrescences are found in the aging skin. They can be common warts, which are often present singly in unusual places and are of unusual form.

Seborrheic warts (keratoses) are more common. They are waxy, brown lesions varying in size from a few millimeters to two to three centimeters in diameter. There may be one or two lesions on the face. However, on the back the number may be much greater, and they tend to lie along the skin folds. They are harmless, but may be a cosmetic or mechanical nuisance.

The *Hutchinson's freckle* (now termed lentigo maligna) is a rare growth most commonly present on the face. It is an irregular, flat brown patch one to three centimeters in diameter. It is seen in those who have had much sun exposure throughout their lives, as witnessed by their weathered faces. Though it usually remains quiescent, it may ultimately develop into malignant melanoma.

Skin cancer

Malignant melanoma is a dangerous, life-threatening tumor that may be unnoticed in older age. Its nodular form may mimic a mole or seborrheic keratosis. It may be a flat, irregularly colored lesion on the palm or sole, or present under the nail in pigmented or unpigmented form. This condition has received much attention from cancer prevention authorities as an overlooked life-threatening lesion. Self inspection, or inspection by a family member, or a caregiver is promoted.

A mnemonic has been developed that suggests immediate skilled medical assessment if

A for **A**symmetry. . . one half being unlike the other half is present

B for a **B**order which is irregular, being either scalloped or poorly circumscribed

C for **C**olor, which varies from one area to another; there may be shades of tan or brown, black, or sometimes red or blue

D for a **D**iameter larger than six millimeters, the size of an average pencil eraser.

There are other cancerous conditions that are much less dangerous. *Basal cell carcinoma* is quite common. Its origin likely lies in light exposure during childhood and adolescent years, but it may present only in later life, as a small, pearly nodule barely visible to the naked eye. Enlarged surface blood vessels may be present about its edge. It grows slowly and asymptomatically, doubling its size each year. It can ulcerate, and in that form is known as a rodent ulcer. Less often it is flat, pigmented, or cystic. Though it rarely metastasizes, it can erode locally, and for that reason should be removed.

Squamous cell carcinoma is ten times less common than the basal cell carcinoma. It is an irregular, scaling, fairly well-defined lesion most commonly found on the face, lips, or back of the hand. Sometimes it is fairly flat, but at other times it is heaped up and craggy. It can metastasize, particularly when it is on mucous membrane, such as the lips. For that reason, early recognition and management are important.

Conditions of the normal aging skin

The challenge of the clinical look of the aging skin is to separate the normal changes of age. This must take into account external damage from sunlight and changes due to internal disorders.

Among common conditions that can confuse is chronic vitamin deficiency, found mainly in older persons living on their own. This may be a pellagra type of condition due to vitamin B deficiency. In this, the exposed skin, particularly of the arms, turns a dusky shade and is somewhat dry and scaly. Those prone to diet deficiency can also get scurvy due to vitamin C deficiency. Again, the skin is dry and scaly, but there are also horny spines at the openings of the hair follicles. Overall protein deficiency in the diet manifests as wasting which appears as enhanced aging.

Cachexia is the term used for progressive wasting due to an unrecognized malignancy. It is often misinterpreted as premature and undue aging. Generalized itching without apparent cause may signify an underlying malignancy. Since there are a number of other causes for this miserable affliction, skilled medical help is required for full investigation.

Dryness of the skin of older people (xerosis) can cause fissures and develop into a persistent, uncomfortable, and disabling eczema (dermatitis). A common cause is excessive showering or bathing in the winter months. Whereas younger persons can bathe daily throughout the year, this is too drying for most older skins. So-called winter eczema in the northern climates can occur. It is usually first seen on the shins, where the skin surface looks somewhat like cracked pavement. Scratch marks and pinpoint oozing are present. At that stage it can rapidly spread to the arms and over the trunk. Medical assistance is necessary.

Those who have a disposition to atopy may suddenly be troubled by extensive atopic eczema after not having had trouble for many years, or, indeed, ever. The term *atopy* is used for a hereditary hypersensitivity such as asthma, eczema, hay fever, or hives. Those who are subject may have had one, some, or all of these conditions earlier in their life, then experience it or them again in older age.

An altered immune response may allow the parasitic infection scabies, due to the scabies mite, to become very extensive in the skin. It is commonly called Norwegian scabies. This causes much scaling. Each scale contains numerous mites, and thus is highly infectious. If the affected person is in an institution, a very wide outbreak of the condition may result. It will cease only when the asymptomatic carrier is identified.

In all, the common complaints of older people about their skin are related to its normal anatomic and physiological changes. Pride and self-esteem depend so much on appearance that any concern of older people about their skin should be attended in a respectful and noncondescending manner.

J. B. ROSS

See also BREAST; HAIR; PRESSURE ULCERS.

BIBLIOGRAPHY

CLADERONE, D. C., and FENSKE, N. A. "The Clinical Spectrum of Actinic Elastosis." *Journal of the American Academy of Dermatology* 32 (1995): 1016–1024.
DRAKE, L., et al. "Guidelines of Care for Photo Aging/Photodamage." *Journal of the American Academy of Dermatology* 35 (1996): 462–464.
FENSKE, N. A., and LOBER, C. W. "Structural and Functional Changes of Normal Aging Skin." *Journal of the American Academy of Dermatology* 15 (1986): 571–585.
ROOK, A.; WILKINSON, D. S.; and EBLING, F. J. G. *Textbook of Dermatology*, 6th ed. Edited by R. H. Champion, J. L. Burton, D. A. Burns, and S. M. Breathnach. Blackwell Science, 1998. Pages 3277–3287.

SLEEP

Many aspects of sleep change gradually from infancy to old age. A variety of primary sleep disorders that are relatively uncommon in younger age groups become more common in old age, and many medical conditions that increase in prevalence with age also disrupt sleep. Even those sleep changes that are typical of healthy older people may be problematic for many. Thus, there is a high probability that older people will complain about the quality of their sleep. Addressing these problems requires an understanding of normal sleep patterns at different phases of the life span, of the pathologies of sleep that arise during aging, and of the treatment options available.

The structure of sleep

Sleep can be defined in many ways—behavioral, subjective, physiological—but the standard definitions of sleep and of its internal structure are derived from the patterns of electrical activity in the brain, which are recorded as an electroencephalogram (EEG) using surface electrodes on the head. EEG recordings during sleep reveal gradual, cyclic changes during the night in both the background frequencies and transient electrical events. These, in combination with recordings of muscular electrical activity, are used to define a number of standardized stages of sleep.

The five stages of sleep include the *rapid eye movement* (REM) stage and stages 1–4, which are the non-REM (NREM) stages. REM sleep dominates during the earliest stages of human development, but NREM increases during childhood, with the gradual emergence of the deepest NREM stages (3 and 4), characterized by the presence of slow EEG waves (delta waves). Newborn babies spend about 50 percent of their sleep time in REM sleep. REM sleep is typically stabilized by adolescence and accounts for 20 to 25 percent of sleep time. The precise age at which the deepest stage of NREM (stages 3 and 4) occurs has not been conclusively determined but evidence suggests a decline starting by age 20. Stages 3 and 4 are collectively called *delta-* or *slow-wave sleep* (SWS). In healthy, young adults, there is an orderly progression during sleep from the shallowest (stage 1) to deepest (stages 3 and 4) stages of NREM, followed by a period of REM sleep. The sleep pattern cycles back through stage 2 and then to REM regularly four to six times during the night, with a cycle length of about 90–120 min. NREM sleep, including SWS, dominates the first half of the night, while the second half includes more REM sleep and little or no SWS. In young adults, stage 2 occupies about 50 percent of the sleep period, and REM about 25 percent.

SWS is considered a deep-sleep stage because quite intense external stimuli are needed to arouse an individual from SWS, and reports of preceding mental activity after awakening from SWS are very limited. It is relatively easier to arouse people from REM sleep, and dream reports after arousal are vivid and often bizarre. NREM stages are characterized by reductions in physiological activity and more difficult arousal, while REM presents a picture of chaotic physiological activity and easier arousal. Typical REM features include rapid or unstable heart rate, respiration and temperature change; rapid horizontal eye movements; twitching of the extremities and facial muscles; and penile erection in males. The EEG pattern resembles that of an awake, aroused individual, despite continued sleep and a profound loss of muscle tone in the major postural muscles.

Sleep changes during aging

After middle age, there is a decline in the duration of SWS, especially in men, from 20 percent to 5 percent or less of total sleep time. There is some debate as to whether this change reflects a significant physiological process, or whether it reflects the inappropriateness of using the standard criteria to define SWS in older people. Amounts of stage 1 sleep increase at this age, perhaps reflecting more nighttime arousals and lighter sleep. REM duration remains relatively constant after early childhood, but its timing changes with age. After about fifty years of age, there is a shortening of the latency (delay from sleep onset) to the first REM episode of the night, perhaps associated with the reduction in SWS durations early in the night.

Although the total duration of sleep may not change dramatically, older people redistribute their sleep throughout the twenty-four-hour day-night cycle. Naps increase in frequency, and sleep during the night tends to become more fragmented and interrupted by longer periods of waking. In contrast to healthy young adults, healthy elderly people may spend only 80 percent of their bedtime at night asleep. Older people also show a preference for both earlier bedtimes and awakening times. It remains unclear to what degree increased napping reflects reduced social pressure to stay awake, compensation for disrupted sleep at night, or a spontaneous change in the daily rhythms of sleep.

An internal daily (circadian) clock regulates the expression of daily rhythms, including the rhythm of sleep and waking. Changes in clock function with aging, including reduced strength (amplitude) of the circadian signal and disrupted rhythm organization, may contribute to changes in sleep habits. These alterations may reflect anatomical changes in the hypothalamic mechanisms that are responsible for circadian rhythm generation.

Sleep disorders during aging

One of the most common sleep disorders is *sleep apnea*—the cessation of breathing during sleep for periods from seconds to minutes. Apnea may result from a loss of respiratory effort (central sleep apnea) or, more commonly, by an upper airway obstruction (obstructive sleep apnea), usually accompanied by loud snoring. An apneic episode usually ends with arousal to wakefulness and a gasping intake of breath. The resulting sleep disruptions lead to poor sleep and excessive daytime sleepiness (EDS). The incidence of apnea increases with age in both sexes, but it is more common in men, especially if they are overweight. Among people over age sixty-five, 24 percent have sleep apnea.

Sleep apnea and snoring have been implicated as secondary causes of morbidity and mortality in patients with cardiac and cerebrovascular disease, probably because of increased hypertension, lowered brain oxygen levels, and irregular heartbeats. EDS secondary to sleep apnea may be a serious and important risk factor for motor vehicle and other accidents. Use of sedative or hypnotic agents in undiagnosed apnea patients may exacerbate breathing problems and may even be fatal. Treatments for sleep apnea include continuous positive airway pressure (CPAP) to open up collapsed airways, weight loss, reduction of alcohol and sedative use, surgery, and dental devices.

Behavioral disorders associated with sleep are common, but increase further with age. A major concern is that these disorders disrupt sleep and lead to EDS, as well as decrements in daytime performance, social interactions, and physical and psychological health. *Restless legs syndrome* (RLS), is a disorder marked by a restless, "crawling" sensation in the legs that creates an irresistible urge to move them. Walking, massage, leg movements, or cold-water immersion may temporarily relieve the symptoms, but these are incompatible with sleep. Most RLS patients also have *periodic limb movement* (PLM) disorder, though this disorder can also occur independently. While PLM disorder is rare in those under thirty years of age, it occurs in approximately 45 percent of those over age sixty-five. PLM disorder involves repetitive movements of the feet and legs in bouts lasting several minutes. These occur frequently in stage 2 and often disrupt sleep. PLMs have been observed in patients with medical conditions such as uremia or diabetes, in patients with sleep apnea and narcolepsy, and in relation to the use or withdrawal of some drugs.

REM-sleep behavior disorder involves agitated movements during sleep in response to vivid dreams, resulting from a lack of the normal inhibition of muscle tone during REM. Trigger dreams often include themes of fleeing or fighting, resulting in the sleeper showing vigorous punching, kicking, and other movements, which may lead to injury to the sleeper or bed partner. While this condition is relatively rare, it increases in prevalence in males over age sixty. Pharmacological treatments may reduce but not eliminate these behavioral disorders of sleep.

Insomnia, or insufficient sleep, is characterized by self-reports of unsatisfactory sleep, daytime fatigue, and social or work impairment. Many factors (medical, psychological, environmental) contribute to insomnia, and it takes several different forms. Women complain more often of insomnia than men, especially during and after menopause. While younger adults typically show initial insomnia (difficulty falling asleep), older people tend to have difficulty with early awakening and sleep maintenance during the night. Among adults over sixty-five, 29 percent complain of problems maintaining sleep.

Medical conditions and sleep disruption

Medical and psychiatric conditions may disrupt sleep, and pharmacological treatments for these conditions are often unrecognized contributors to sleep disruption. Pain is a common symptom of many acute and chronic illnesses that increase in frequency with aging. Conditions such as arthritis, cancer, cardiovascular disease, and musculoskeletal degeneration or injury may be accompanied by pain. Pain can disturb sleep if it is not adequately controlled, and it may be exacerbated by the postures usually adopted during sleep.

Patients with heart disease may awaken out of REM sleep suffering from angina (chest pain) or chest tightness because of changes in heart rate and breathing that occur in this sleep stage. Symptoms of respiratory illnesses (asthma, emphysema) and gastrointestinal conditions (acid reflux) typically worsen during the night and contribute to sleep disruption. Stroke, a common condition in elderly people, may lead to insomnia or daytime drowsiness, depending on a variety of antecedent conditions and the location of the brain damage. In addition, infectious diseases may have a greater impact on older people and may affect sleep patterns.

Many of these serious medical conditions are accompanied by anxiety or depression, both of which can further disrupt normal sleep patterns. Independent of specific medical conditions, both anxiety and depression have important impacts on sleep quality and quantity. Anxiety, and accompanying muscle tension and pain, may make it difficult to initiate and to sustain sleep. Depression often leads to early morning awakening, awakenings during the night, reduced levels of SWS, and a shortened latency to the first nightly REM period.

Several progressive, dementing illnesses (e.g., Alzheimer's, Parkinson's, and Huntington's diseases) increase in both prevalence and severity with increasing age, and they can amplify sleep disruptions in older people. Alzheimer's disease is the most common of these conditions, and is characterized by disturbances in daily rhythms, including disrupted sleep, daytime napping, and periodic agitation, especially in its later stages. Some studies indicate that the amounts of both SWS and REM sleep decrease in patients with Alzheimer's, but other studies have not confirmed this observation. Disruption of sleep and daily rhythms in patients with dementia places a further burden on caregivers at home, who may consequently become sleep deprived. The occurrence of nocturnal activity and wandering is often a major consideration in the decision to institutionalize Alzheimer's patients.

Behavioral treatment of sleep disorders

A number of behavioral approaches should be considered first in treating sleep disturbances in any age group. These can be summarized as maintaining appropriate "sleep hygiene." Included in this concept are:

- avoidance of caffeine, alcohol, and nicotine (all of which disrupt sleep), especially in the second half of the day
- assessing the effects of prescription drugs on sleep and modifying these as appropriate
- maintaining a regular bedtime and wake time throughout the week
- avoiding daytime napping, except for a regularly scheduled, early nap, which may be beneficial for some in reducing daytime sleepiness
- maintaining a relaxing evening routine in preparation for bedtime, which may include reading, meditation, work on a quiet hobby, and a warm bath (except for those for whom warm baths are contraindicated)
- use of the bedroom only for sleep or sex

- regular, moderate exercise, but not within four hours of bedtime
- reduced fluid intake late in the day to avoid frequent awakening to urinate during the night
- reduced noise or light in the bedroom, if these disturb sleep, or separate bedrooms if a bed partner's snoring or movements disturb sleep
- an extra pillow to elevate the head in order to reduce symptoms of nocturnal acid reflux

If sleep has been chronically disrupted for whatever reason, people may develop conditioned responses to the bedroom environment that preclude sleeping. Worrying about whether one will be able to sleep is itself a common cause of poor sleep. A *deconditioning* approach can be used to learn to associate the bedroom with sleep rather than with anxiety about sleep. An individual undergoing deconditioning is instructed to go to bed only when sleepy and to get out of bed and go to a different room if sleep does not follow within a short, fixed interval, returning to the bed only when sleepy.

Pharmacological treatment of sleep disorders

When sleep disruptions are severe and unresponsive to behavioral and environmental strategies, a pharmacological approach may be warranted, but these must be acknowledged to be symptomatic and not a cure for the underlying causes of sleep disturbances. Because of the high incidence of insomnia among older people, they are frequent consumers of both prescription and nonprescription sedatives. However, since they typically have increased sensitivity and reduced ability to metabolize these same drugs, physicians must monitor these treatments carefully to avoid overdoses and increased risks of falls, accidents, and daytime confusion or cognitive problems.

Barbiturates are rarely used today to aid sleep because of high risks of toxicity, tolerance, dependence, and the potential for life-threatening interactions with other medications. Benzodiazepines are currently the most commonly prescribed medications for sleep problems. Relative to barbiturates, they have a wider safety margin between effective and toxic doses and less potential for development of tolerance (the need for a progressively larger dose to achieve equivalent effects). They can, however, pose serious health threats when used in conjunction with sedating medications or alcohol, especially in older people. Benzodiazepines increase stage 2 sleep but reduce amounts of SWS; thus, they may aid sleep onset and/or maintenance but alter its characteristics.

Different benzodiazepines may be short-, intermediate-, or long-acting. Short-acting benzodiazepines can reduce the time it takes to fall asleep, but may not aid sleep maintenance, and thus may exacerbate early-morning insomnia. Intermediate-acting drugs have effects that last throughout the night and into early morning. Long-acting benzodiazepines are also effective in both initiating and maintaining sleep, but may lead to daytime sedation and impaired cognitive and psychomotor performance. These residual or *hangover* effects may contribute to increased confusion, falls, and memory disturbances. Another serious problem associated with prolonged use of benzodiazepines is rebound insomnia—an increase in sleep disruption after withdrawal of the drug—which may be worse than the original sleep complaint. Thus, benzodiazepines are best used as a short-term sleep aid, rather than as a long-term maintenance strategy for sleep.

Benzodiazepines are not the sedative of choice in two situations. When insomnia arises from depression, an antidepressant with sedative properties may be a preferred treatment. The antidepressant effect is typically delayed for two weeks or more, but the sedative property can improve sleep shortly after initiating treatment. Patients with symptoms of sleep apnea should avoid sedating medications because these have respiratory depressant properties, which may worsen the symptoms of sleep apnea.

Nonbenzodiazepine sedatives, which have been marketed in some countries, act on similar brain mechanisms, but in a different way. These drugs (zopiclone and zolpidem) are short-acting and have been reported to have fewer unwanted effects than benzodiazepines. They cause less residual daytime anxiety than some short-acting benzodiazepines, fewer cognitive effects than longer-acting drugs, appear to have little abuse potential, and are reported not to generate rebound insomnia after discontinuation. Because of their short action, they are useful for sleep initiation, but they are less useful for treating early morning insomnia.

BENJAMIN RUSAK
PEGGY RUYAK

See also ALZHEIMER'S DISEASE; BRAIN; DEPRESSION.

BIBLIOGRAPHY

ASHTON, H. "The Effects of Drugs on Sleep." In *Sleep*. Edited by R. Cooper. London: Chapman and Hall, 1994. Pages 175–211.

BLIWISE, D. "Dementia." In *Principles and Practice of Sleep Medicine*, 3d ed. Edited by M. Kryger, T. Roth, and W. Dement. Philadelphia: W. B. Saunders, 2000. Pages 1058–1071.

BLIWISE, D. "Normal Aging." In *Principles and Practice of Sleep Medicine*, 3d ed. Edited by M. Kryger, T. Roth, and W. Dement. Philadelphia: W. B. Saunders, 2000. Pages 26–42.

CARSKADON, M. A., and DEMENT, W. C. "Normal Human Sleep: An Overview." In *Principles and Practice of Sleep Medicine*, 3d ed. Edited by M. Kryger, T. Roth, and W. Dement. Philadelphia: W. B. Saunders, 2000. Pages 15–25.

CHOKROVERTY, S. "Sleep Disorders in Elderly Persons." In *Sleep Disorders Medicine: Basic Science, Technical Considerations, and Clinical Aspects*. Edited by S. Chokroverty. Boston: Butterworth-Heinemann, 1994. Pages 401–415.

FOLEY, D. J.; MONJAN, A. A.; BROWN, L. S.; SIMONSICK, E. M.; WALLACE, R. B.; and BLAZER, D. G. "Sleep Complaints Among Elderly Persons: An Epidemiological Study of Three Communities." *Sleep* 18, no. 6 (1995): 425–432.

MORIN, C. M. *Insomnia: Psychological Assessment and Management*. New York: The Guilford Press, 1993.

OHAYON, M. M.; CAULET, M.; and PRIEST, R. G. "Violent Behavior during Sleep." *Journal of Clinical Psychiatry* 58 (1997): 369–376.

RECHTSCHAFFEN, A., and KALES, A., eds. *A Manual of Standardized Terminology, Techniques and Scoring System for Sleep Stages of Human Subjects*. Los Angeles: UCLA Brain Information Services/Brain Research Institute, 1968.

SMOKING

In some industrialized communities smoking prevalence in elderly people is as high as 30 percent, and smoking prevalence is highest in low socioeconomic groups so that those older people with smoking-related diseases may also have other poverty-related social and medical problems. In the United Kingdom the smoking-related disease epidemic has probably passed its peak in men but is reaching its peak in women—in whom the maximum smoking uptake began with those born in the 1920s and 1930s.

Almost all smoking-related diseases are more common in old age. Furthermore, the beneficial effects of quitting smoking are for the most part maintained into old age. The reduction in risk of myocardial infarction (heart attack) is certainly not affected by aging, so that an older smoker who quits reduces his or her heart attack risk almost to normal after about three years. Quitting smoking can reduce the complications of peripheral vascular disease (hardening of the arteries to the legs and feet) in both young and elderly sufferers. Quitting produces a reduced risk of lung cancer (and probably many other cancers) in old people as well as in the middle-aged. Though only about one-quarter of heavy smokers will develop smoking-related airways obstruction (chronic obstructive pulmonary disease) resulting in chronic respiratory disability, quitting smoking will stop the accelerated decline of lung function in sufferers from this condition independent of the age at which they quit, at least up to the age of eighty.

Recent research shows that stopping smoking in middle age may extend the life of men by over seven years and in particular reduces deaths from heart disease. Even in those with preexisting smoking related lung disease, quitting smoking may extend life by up to six years.

We thus know that quitting smoking gives health gains for elderly people, but are they able to quit? The simple answer is that they are probably overall just as likely to be able to stop as younger smokers, however the situation is complex. Nicotine is an extremely addictive substance and quitting is difficult. Simply being told to quit by a medical professional produces a quit rate of about two to three percent. The most important predictor of whether a smoker is able to quit is their motivation (often judged by previous failed attempts to quit). In motivated elderly people without drug help (nicotine replacement) quit rates can be as high as 15 percent—slightly higher perhaps than in the young. However, there has been little research work into the value and acceptability of nicotine replacement or other newer drug therapies in old people. Fur-

An elderly man smokes a cigar in the Poletown neighborhood of Detroit, which was later leveled for an auto plant. In 2000, the American Heart Society reported that cigar smoking was just as serious a public health risk as cigarette smoking. (Corbis photo by David Turnley.)

thermore, at least in the United States older smokers are, overall, probably less likely to want to quit than to accept advice that smoking is bad for them, however among those who do recognize the dangers there is greater motivation and urgency to quit and a higher success rate.

MARTIN J. CONNOLLY

See also HEART DISEASE; LUNG, AGING; VASCULAR DISEASE.

BIBLIOGRAPHY

BURCHFIEL, C. M.; MARCUS, E. B.; CURB, D.; et al. "Effects of Smoking and Smoking Cessation on Longitudinal Decline in Pulmonary Function." *American Journal of Respiratory and Critical Care Medicine* 151 (1995): 1778–1785.

RAW, M.; MCNEILL, A.; and WEST, R. "Smoking Cessation Guidelines for Health Professionals." *Thorax* 53, supp. 5 (1998): S1–S38.

ROSENBERG, L.; PALMER, J. R.; and SHAPIRO, S. "Decline in Risk of Myocardial Infarction Among Women Who Stopped Smoking." *New England Journal of Medicine* 332 (1990): 213–217.

RUCHLIN, H. S. "An Analysis of Smoking Patterns Among Older Adults." *Medical Care* 37 (1999): 615–619.

SOCIAL COGNITION

The basic goal of social cognition is to understand how people make sense of themselves, others, and events in everyday life. Research from the perspective of adult development and aging has focused on broadening the understanding of cognitive aging include how life experiences and changes in pragmatic knowledge, social expertise, and values influence age-related differences in how people think. In order to address these issues, one must consider both the basic cognitive architecture of the aging adult and the functional architecture of everyday cognition in a social context. Even if certain basic cognitive mechanisms decline (such as memory recall or how fast information is processed), older adults may still possess the social knowledge and skills that allow them to function effectively.

Social cognition and cognitive mechanisms

In the mainstream social cognition literature, researchers use an information-processing approach to examine social cognitive processes. In particular, they examine how the accuracy of social perceptions can be impaired by cognitive load (i.e., attending to too many cognitive activities at one time). A heavy cognitive load depletes the resources required to devote the time necessary to make an accurate judgment or assessment of a situation. A good illustration of impaired social perception accuracy is exemplified in how a person's behavior is explained. If a person is observed behaving in an anxious way, it may erroneously be inferred that he or she is, in general, an anxious person. However, the judgment would have been more accurate if the observer had considered the situational information. In this case the person was waiting to give an important speech to an audience of over a hundred individuals. This is an example of a "correspondence bias" where the cause of a person's behavior is attributed to a predisposed characteristic and the observer does not attend to compelling extenuating circumstances. Dan Gilbert and colleagues found that the propensity to commit a correspondence bias was exacerbated if individuals had to attend to another task at the same time (i.e., increased cognitive load). In other words, they lacked the cognitive resources to deliberate and adjust initial judgments about people and events because they were busy thinking about something else. What implication does this have for the aging adult? Because older adults typically exhibit lower levels of cognitive processing resources (e.g., they are slower at processing information), this may impact their social judgment processes.

The literature on aging supports this notion. Fredda Blanchard-Fields found in a number of studies that older adults consistently exhibit the correspondence bias. In this case individuals are presented with stories in which a main character is associated with a situation's negative outcome. For example, Doug insists that he continue to work long hours despite his wife's protests, which results in their divorce. Older adults blamed Doug more than young adults. Older adults relied more on dispositional information (personality characteristics, the character of the individual) to explain the behavior and ignored compelling situational information (such as the wife's pressure). Her studies have repeatedly shown that older adults tend to blame the main character in relationship conflicts with negative outcomes despite the existence of situational causal factors. In a number of studies Thomas Hess and colleagues have shown that older adults tend to rely on easily accessible knowledge as opposed to engaging in more elaborative processing. They have found that older adults do not modify their first impression of an individual when presented with new information, especially when positive information follows an initially negative portrayal of the individual. For example, when older adults are initially given a description of a person portrayed as dishonest and subsequently receive information about that person performing honest behaviors, they do not adjust their initial impression regarding honesty. Overall, it appears from these studies that limitations on processing resources could play an important role in understanding why older adults produce biased social judgments.

Social cognition and social knowledge

In contrast to the influence of limitations on processing resources on social judgment biases, social cognition research also suggests that when strong beliefs and knowledge are activated automatically, they can influence social judgments in general, and invite social judgment biases in particular. Walter Mischel suggests that there are individual differences in the strength of social representations of rules, beliefs, and attitudes that are associated with specific situations. Thus, when individuals encounter specific situations, their belief systems trigger emotional reactions and goals that are closely linked to those situations, which in turn drive social judgments.

Blanchard-Fields and colleagues suggest that the observed dispositional biases described above might occur when older adults' strongly held beliefs about how the particular character should have acted in the specific situation are violated. For example, in the case of Doug and his wife, older adults may have blamed Doug not because they did not have the cognitive capacity to do so, but because he violated the strongly held belief that marriage comes before career. Accordingly, the investigators examined the degree to which limitations on processing resources and/or strong social beliefs and social rules accounted for dispositional biases observed in older adults. They found that older adults produced more dispositional biases when placed under the cognitive constraint of a time limit to respond. However, they also found that older adults produced more social beliefs and rules pertaining to the main character than young adults did. This accounted for age differences in dispositional biases above and beyond the influence of time constraints. This provides evidence against a cognitive resource limitation explanation. It appears that the degree to which a social rule has been violated determines when a dispositional bias will be made. Such findings suggest that a social knowledge-based explanation of social judgments is a viable alternative to limitations on cognitive resources.

Social cognition and processing goals

Change in the relative importance of social goals as people grow older profoundly influences how individuals interpret and use social information. Laura Carstensen and colleagues suggest that emotional goals become increasingly important and salient across the adult life span. They have demonstrated that older adults pay more attention to emotional information in text, and thus remember it better than neutral information. Another motivational goal shown to influence social information processing is cognitive style or how one approaches problem solving. For example, an individual with a high need for closure, such as the need to come to quick and decisive answers without deliberation, is more likely to commit the correspondence bias. Hess and colleagues found that need for closure did not influence judgment biases in young and middle-aged adults, but did predict social judgment biases in older adults. Because of age-related changes in personal resources (both social and cognitive), motivational factors (such as need for closure) oriented toward conserving resources may become more important to the older adult.

Stereotypes and cognitive functioning

Finally, the literature suggests that there is a negative impact of age-related stereotypes on cognitive functioning in older adults. Such stereotypes represent a set of socially shared beliefs about personal attributes and behaviors of older adults. Studies examining age-related differences in the content and structure of stereotypes find that older and young adults hold similar age-related negative stereotypes, such as slow-thinking, senile, incompetent, and feeble. However, older adults display more complex representations of the category "older adults," including both positive (e.g., wise, dependable) and negative stereotypes.

Studies have examined under what conditions stereotypes are activated, and if they are, how they affect behavior and social judgments. Claude Steele and colleagues found that stigmatized groups such as African Americans and women are vulnerable to fears of being judged in accordance with negative stereotypes about the group to which they belong. This in turn impairs performance relevant to the stereotype associated with their group, such as academic ability. Similarly, Becca Levy found that automatically activated stereotypes about aging and memory adversely affect the cognitive performance of older adults. Although at this point there is a need for replication for this study, it does suggest that social factors such as negative stereotypes may have some effect on decline in cognitive performance although not account for all of it.

In conclusion, research on social cognition and aging underscores the importance of social factors as potential mechanisms contributing to age-related differences in cognitive functioning. In addition, it suggests that it is important not to limit explanations of changes in social cognition to cognitive processing variables alone. The social factors highlighted above influence social information processing in important ways including how, when, and why older adults attend to specific information and how this information will be used.

FREDDA BLANCHARD-FIELDS

See also IMAGES OF AGING; INTELLIGENCE; MEMORY; MOTIVATION.

BIBLIOGRAPHY

BLANCHARD-FIELDS, F. "Social Schematicity and Causal Attributions." In *Social Cognition and Aging*. Edited by T. M. Hess and F. Blanchard-Fields. San Diego: Academic Press, 1999. Pages 222–238.

CARSTENSEN, L. L., and TURK-CHARLES, S. "The Salience of Emotion across the Adult Life Span." *Psychology and Aging* 9 (1994): 259–264.

GILBERT, D., and MALONE, P. "The Correspondence Bias." *Psychological Bulletin* 117 (1995): 21–38.

HESS, T. M. "Cognitive and Knowledge-Based Influences on Social Representations." In *So-*

cial Cognition and Aging. Edited by T. M. Hess and F. Blanchard-Fields. San Diego: Academic Press, 1999. Pages 239–267.

LEVY, B. "Improving Memory in Old Age through Implicit Stereotyping." *Journal of Personality and Social Psychology* 71 (1996): 1092–1107.

MISCHEL, W., and SHODA, Y. "A Cognitive-Affective System Theory of Personality: Reconceptualizing Situations, Dispositions, Dynamics, and Invariance in Personality Structure." *Psychological Review* 102 (1995): 246–268.

STEELE, C. "A Threat in the Air: How Stereotypes Shape Intellectual Identity and Performance." *American Psychologist* 52 (1997): 613–629.

SOCIAL SECURITY ADMINISTRATION

The Great Depression of the 1930s exacerbated a growing need for income support in the United States that could not be met by the limited resources of states, local communities, or private charities. In response, President Franklin D. Roosevelt announced his intention to make recommendations for additional measures of protection against destitution and dependency during a message to Congress on 8 June 1934. A year later, the Social Security Act of 1935 was passed, symbolizing the essence of President Roosevelt's New Deal. Included in the Social Security Act was a social insurance program to pay benefits to retired workers age sixty-five or older. This federal Old-Age Benefit system formed the basis for the current Old Age, Survivors, and Disability Insurance (OASDI) programs now administered by the Social Security Administration (SSA).

Evolution of the OASDI programs

Development of the Social Security Act began with the Committee on Economic Security (CES), which President Roosevelt created by Executive Order on June 29, 1934. The CES's function was to study problems relating to economic security and make recommendations for legislation that would promote the economic well-being of individuals. The CES was composed of Secretary of Labor Frances Perkins; Secretary of the Treasury, Henry Morgenthau, Jr.; Secretary of Agriculture, Henry Wallace; Attorney General, Homer Cummings; and Federal Emergency Relief Administrator, Harry Hopkins. In January 1935, the committee sent its report to the president, who introduced the report to both houses of Congress on 17 January 1935. President Roosevelt signed the Social Security Act on 14 August 1935.

The Social Security Act of 1935 provided for several new programs. The one that would grow to affect the largest population was the Old-Age Benefit system, which is now commonly known as Social Security retirement benefits. Even before the Old-Age Insurance program was in full operation, lawmakers enacted significant changes. As originally enacted, Old-Age Insurance would pay benefits only to retired workers. The Social Security Amendments of 1939 broadened the program to include benefits for spouses, dependents, and survivors. The first monthly checks were issued in January 1940, even though they were not originally scheduled to begin until 1942.

The next major changes in benefits and coverage were made in the 1950s. The 1950 Social Security Amendments, signed by President Harry S. Truman, provided the first cost-of-living adjustment (COLA) in monthly benefits since they began in 1940—providing an (average) increase of 77 percent (the increase was more generous to low wage than to high wage workers). The 1950 amendments also extended coverage to several categories of workers, including regularly employed farm and domestic workers, federal civilian employees not covered under the Federal Civil Service Retirement System, some state and local government employees (at the election of employers) some not covered under another retirement program, and employees of nonprofit organizations. Even more categories of workers were added in subsequent years. On 1 August 1956, lawmakers amended the Social Security Act to provide monthly benefits to permanently and totally disabled workers age fifty to sixty-four, and to adult children who became disabled before age eighteen and whose parents were deceased or retired workers. Two years later, lawmakers eliminated the minimum age requirement for disabled workers. The 1956 amendments also made reduced, early retirement benefits available for women between sixty-two to sixty-four years of age. Amendments enacted in 1961 extended early retirement to men.

By the 1960s, the basics of the OASDI programs were in place, but further program changes created new categories of beneficiaries, increased benefits to maintain purchasing power, and adjusted tax rates to insure adequate financing. President Lyndon B. Johnson signed the 1965 amendments that created the Medicare program, to be administered by the Social Security Administration. The Medicare program originally provided health insurance to people age sixty-five and older, but was expanded in 1972 to include disabled persons who had received Social Security or Railroad Retirement benefits for twenty-four months. In 1969, the responsibilities of the Social Security Administration were further increased through the creation of Black Lung Benefits for miners and their dependents.

Two major changes in the 1970s were the automatic indexation of OASDI benefits and the creation of the Supplemental Security Income (SSI) program. In the time between the OASDI program's enactment and the 1972 amendments, Congress and the president provided benefit increases on an ad hoc basis. The 1972 amendments provided that, effective in 1975, increases in the cost of living, as measured by the Consumer Price Index, would determine annual benefit increases. These annual increases would help insure that inflation would not erode the value of benefits. The 1972 Amendments also created the SSI program, to be administered by the Social Security Administration. The SSI program replaced state programs that provided benefits for low-income aged, blind, and disabled persons. Payment of SSI benefits began in 1974.

In the late 1970s, the OADSI programs faced new challenges precipitated by economic and demographic conditions that were unfavorable to the program's finances. High inflation, coupled with low or negative real wage growth, caused benefit expenditures to increase rapidly while payroll taxes went up more slowly. This was exacerbated by high unemployment, which also reduced payroll tax revenue. Since the payroll tax is the primary source of funding for the OASDI programs, this meant that financing would become inadequate to pay benefits in the future. In addition, demographic projections showed declining birth rates and increased life expectancy. This meant there would be fewer workers paying payroll taxes per retiree, and that retirees would be receiving benefits longer.

In 1979, actuaries estimated the Old-Age and Survivors Insurance Trust Fund, through which retirement and survivors' benefits were paid, would not be able to fund benefits by some point in the 1980s. In December 1981, President Ronald Reagan formed the National Commission on Social Security Reform (NCSSR). Based on the NCSSR's recommendations, the Congress enacted a package of provisions in 1983 intended to resolve the financing crisis. This package moved to earlier years the tax rate increases already scheduled in law, taxation of Social Security benefits for certain higher-income beneficiaries, and gradual increases in the age of eligibility for unreduced retirement benefits. The 1980s also saw changes in the Disability Insurance program regarding periodic review of a worker's disability status.

From the mid-1980s through the 1990s, program changes centered on refinement of disability determinations, adjustments in taxation of Social Security benefits and the payroll tax, and expanded benefit coverage for certain groups of workers. One significant change was instituted with the Social Security Independence and Program Improvements Act of 1994, signed by President William J. Clinton. This act made the Social Security Administration an independent agency effective 31 March 1995.

A major change also occurred in the disability program on 17 December 1999, when President Clinton signed the Ticket to Work and Work Incentives Improvement Act of 1999. This law provides disability beneficiaries with a voucher to be used to purchase vocational rehabilitation services, employment services, and other support services from an employment network of their choice. The Ticket to Work initiative shifted the disability program's emphasis away from administration of monthly benefits and more toward rehabilitation and assistance in helping disabled beneficiaries return to work.

Programs the Social Security Administration currently administers

SSA's responsibilities have evolved as the OASDI programs expanded and lawmakers created additional programs to meet the needs of society. Today, SSA has complete responsibility for administering the Old-Age Insurance program, the Survivors Insurance program, the Disability Insurance program, and the Supplemental Security Income program. SSA also administers enrollment in the Medicare program; however, the Centers for Medicare and Medicaid Services (CMS) administers benefit payments and other aspects of the Medicare program. Finally, SSA provides administrative support to other programs, such as the Black Lung program, Medicaid, Food Stamps, and Railroad Retirement. The following descriptions provide a basic overview of the current programs for which the Social Security Administration has primary responsibility.

Old-Age Insurance. Retirement benefits are available to retired workers as early as age sixty-two, at a reduced rate. Unreduced benefits are available at age sixty-five if the worker was born before 1938. The age for full retirement benefits is scheduled to rise gradually from age sixty-five to sixty-seven, with the first increase affecting workers who reached sixty-two in the year 2000. To qualify for retirement benefits, a worker must have paid Social Security payroll taxes for at least ten years (or forty quarters) over the course of a lifetime.

Survivors' and Disability Insurance. If a worker who has paid Social Security taxes for a specific length of time dies, monthly survivor insurance benefits may be paid to the worker's widow or widower (including those from marriages ending in divorce) as well as to children, and dependent parents. If a worker becomes disabled and meets certain conditions related to his ability to work, he or she may qualify for disability insurance benefits. The disabled worker's dependent children and the other parent of his children may also qualify for benefits.

Supplemental Security Income. If a worker is not eligible for benefits under the OASDI programs, or only qualifies for a small payment, he may receive benefits under the SSI program. The SSI program is a means-tested program designed to help low-income aged, blind, or disabled individuals. Unlike OASDI benefits, SSI payments and related administrative expenses are financed from general tax revenues rather than a specific payroll tax.

Over the years, these programs have grown both in terms of beneficiaries served and dollars spent. The Old-Age Insurance program, as originally enacted, covered approximately 60 percent of jobs. Over time, the OASDI programs changed, and today they cover 98 percent of jobs. The Social Security programs are now an essential part of insurance coverage for today's society. Approximately one in six Americans receives a Social Security benefit.

SSA's current organization and operations

A commissioner, who serves for a term of six years and is appointed by the president and subject to Senate confirmation, heads the Social Security Administration (SSA). The Social Security Administration has a staff of over 65,000 employees, with a central office located in Baltimore, Maryland. SSA relies on its decentralized field structure, including 10 regional offices, 1,340 field offices (FOs), 138 hearings offices, 36 teleservice centers, and 6 program service centers, to provide services at the local level. All components within SSA's central office perform a supporting role to SSA FOs by providing uniform directions, guidance, and resources.

Regional offices oversee operations of the field offices within a specific geographic area and assist field offices with administrative tasks and operational issues. Field offices are located both in cities and rural areas across the nation and are the agency's main physical point of contact with beneficiaries and the public. Field office employees explain the various Social Security programs and Medicare, discuss and review whether an applicant qualifies for benefits, and process claims for benefits. Field office staff also provides assistance in applying for other programs, such as Medicaid and food stamps.

If an individual's initial request for benefits and first level of appeal for benefits are denied, the Office of Hearings and Appeals (OHA) is responsible for holding hearings and issuing decisions to determine whether or not an applicant may receive benefits. Most cases handled by OHA deal with Disability Insurance and SSI claims.

Teleservice centers answer calls to Social Security's 800 number and provide answers to public inquires over the phone and referrals to other appropriate sources of information. Program service centers act as application processing centers for OASDI benefits. The data operations center maintains records of individuals' earnings and prepares benefit computations.

How to access SSA resources

The public has four methods available to access information on the Social Security Administration and the programs it administers: (1) visit a field office; (2) call the Social Security 800 number; (3) submit a request by U.S. mail, fax, or e-mail; or (4) visit the Social Security Web site.

To find the most convenient field office location, one need only visit the Social Security Web site or call the agency. The public can obtain recorded information twenty-four hours a day, including weekends and holidays, by calling Social Security's toll-free number, 1-800-772-1213. Service representatives are available on business days. People who are hearing impaired may call SSA's toll-free TTY number, 1-800-325-0778, on business days.

Social Security Online, the SSA's Internet Web site, is located at www.ssa.gov and contains a variety of information and services, including downloadable publications on all aspects of Social Security programs and forms to request various services. Social Security *e-News,* an electronic newsletter received by e-mail, is also available to help people keep up with the latest changes in Social Security programs.

JANE L. ROSS
SOPHIA WRIGHT
LAURA HALTZEL

See also MEDICAID; MEDICARE; SOCIAL SECURITY, AND THE U.S. FEDERAL BUDGET; SOCIAL SECURITY, HISTORY AND OPERATIONS; SOCIAL SECURITY, LONG-TERM FINANCING AND REFORM; SUPPLEMENTAL SECURITY INCOME.

BIBLIOGRAPHY

KENNEDY, DAVID M. *Freedom From Fear.* New York: Oxford University Press, 1999.
KOLLMAN, GEOFFREY. *Summary of Major Changes in the Social Security Cash Benefits Program: 1935–1996.* Washington, D.C.: United States Congressional Research Service, 1996.
MCSTEEN, MARTHA. "Fifty Years of Social Security." *Social Security Bulletin* 8 (1985): 36–44.
United States Social Security Administration. *Annual Statistical Supplement 2000.* Washington, D.C.: 2000.
United States Social Security Administration. *A Brief History of Social Security.* Baltimore, Md.: August, 2000.
United States Social Security Administration. *The 2000 Annual Report of the Board of Trustees of the Federal Old-Age and Survivors Insurance and Disability Insurance Trust Funds.* Washington, D.C.: 2000.

SOCIAL SECURITY, HISTORY AND OPERATIONS

Enacted in the midst of the Great Depression of the 1930s, Social Security—the Old-Age, Survivors, and Disability Insurance program (OASDI)—protects virtually every American. The nation's central retirement income program is also its most important disability and life insurance program. After discussing the historical development of Social Security, this entry briefly describes the structure of the program, including revenue sources, benefits, and its importance to different groups of Americans. Contemporary Social Security policy issues are then identified.

History

In seeking to provide widespread and basic protection against what President Franklin D. Roosevelt called "the vicissitudes of life," the Social Security Act of 1935 initiated two social insurance programs, three public assistance programs (i.e., welfare), and several public health and social service programs. Until 1950, Social Security, which was initially a social insurance program providing protection against loss of income in retirement, was neither the largest nor the most popular of the act's programs. It was the state-run welfare programs included in the act, which provided aid to widows with dependent children, the old, and the blind, that gained swift public acceptance, mainly because they quickly sent funds to states to distribute to these needy groups. In contrast, and in keeping with social insurance principles in which the right to a benefit is based on the prior payroll tax contribution of employees and their employers, the Social Security program began collecting taxes during the late 1930s—though the program was not scheduled to pay its first benefits to retirees until the early 1940s. Where welfare programs seek to give immediate relief to those in extreme financial distress, the Social Security Act's social insurance programs—Social Security, Unemployment Insurance, and later, Medicare—seek to prevent financial distress.

The "genius" of Social Security and related social insurance programs is that they represent, and build upon, a compromise between sometimes conflicting political values; the concern that all Americans should have adequate protection against selected contingencies (e.g., retirement) and a commitment to the work ethic. Near universal coverage assures widespread protection. Social insurance provides a social and work-related means of pooling risks. In exchange for making modest work-related contributions over many years, the social insurance approach provides individuals and their families with an earned right to protection against predictable risks. Social Security, for example, is structured in a manner that seeks to provide benefits that are adequate to maintain basic living standards, especially for low and modest income persons. However, in keeping with the principle of individual equity, persons who have paid more in Social Security taxes generally receive larger monthly benefits.

Incremental expansion characterized the development of Social Security from 1939 through the mid-1970s. The 1935 Act provided for benefits to workers in manufacturing and commerce who retired at age sixty-five or later. Benefits were added in 1939 for the wives of retired workers and for the surviving wives and children of deceased workers. These benefits were made available to men in 1950. Importantly, the 1950 Amendments to the Social Security Act defined social insurance as the nation's dominant public policy approach to protecting older Americans against loss of income in retirement. These amendments expanded coverage to include regularly employed domestic and farm workers and increased benefits, assuring that Social Security benefits would generally be more available and more beneficial to receive than benefits provided through the federal/state Old Age Assistance program, also funded under the Social Security Act.

Disability insurance protections for permanently and severely disabled workers age fifty to sixty-four were added to the Social Security program in 1956, and extended to all workers under age sixty-five in 1960. The 1956 amendments also gave women the right to accept permanently reduced retired workers benefits between ages sixty-two and sixty-four, an option that was extended to men in 1961. The high rate of poverty and near-poverty among the old combined with a growing economy to provide political rationale for substantial benefits increases from 1965 through 1972, greatly improving the economic status of elderly Americans. In 1972, the automatic cost-of-living allowance (COLA) was incorporated into the law. Beginning in 1974, benefits were adjusted annually for changes in the cost of living. This new provision assured that, once received, benefits would maintain their purchasing power no matter how long a beneficiary lived. While critically important for helping to assure stable incomes for the old, disabled, and surviving family members, this provision is expensive and made financing the program more sensitive to economic change.

In the mid-1970s the focus shifted to program financing, followed a few years later by a political climate that challenged the support for the traditional Social Security program. Unanticipated economic changes (i.e., high inflation, lower than anticipated wage growth, a slowed economy) created short-term financing problems in the mid-1970s and again in the early 1980s. Demographic changes—including declining birth rates, increased life expectancies, and the anticipated aging of 76 million baby boomers born from 1946 through 1964—fueled long-term financing problems. Legislation was crafted in 1977 and 1983 involving modest benefit reductions and tax increases, spreading the pain of these changes across many constituencies, including working persons, employers, and current and future beneficiaries (especially those most well-off). By the mid-1980s, when the rest of the federal government began running large annual deficits, the Social Security program began accumulating large yearly surpluses, a trend expected to continue through about 2020. Even so, the impending retirement of the baby boomers, a declining ratio of workers to beneficiaries, and anticipated increases in longevity mean that financing reforms will be needed to assure the timely payment of benefits after 2038 or thereabouts.

Social Security is arguably the nation's most successful and popular public policy. A favorable climate incubated its expansion through the mid-1970s. Even during the financing problems of the late 1970s and the 1980s, little support existed for substantially reducing benefits or retreating from the social insurance principles that guided the program. Except for a few advocates on the extreme outskirts of American politics, the voices favoring means-testing Social Security (limiting benefit receipt to persons whose incomes and/or assets fell below certain levels) were silent until the early 1990s. Similarly, during the early 1980s virtually no one in the political mainstream was giving serious consideration to privatizing aspects of the program. For example, in 1982, a commission headed by Federal Reserve Chairman Alan Greenspan unanimously agreed that Congress "should not alter the fundamental principles of the Social Security Program" (National Commission on Social Security Reform, 1983). This commission also rejected "proposals to make the Social Security program a voluntary one, or to transform it into. . . a program under which benefits are conditioned on the showing of financial need." But persistent claims that Social Security is unfair to the young, false claims that the program is financially unsustainable, a soaring stock market, and growing skepticism (especially among the young) about whether the program will meet people's needs, combined with the deficit politics of the 1980s and 1990s to spawn an environment that legitimized calls to radically transform the program. Indeed, irrespective of their validity, by the year 2001 proposals to partially privatize Social Security were being given very serious consideration.

Today's Social Security program

Who benefits? Social Security has achieved its goal of providing widespread protection against financial risks associated with retirement, disability, and survivorship. Coverage is virtually universal, with 152 million workers (over 95 percent of the workforce) and their families included in the program. In February 2001, monthly benefits were paid to over 45 million persons, including almost 29 million retired workers; nearly 5 million surviving aged widows and widowers; 400,000 surviving mothers and fathers; 5 million disabled workers; and 3 million children under eighteen, mostly survivors or dependents of disabled workers.

Social Security's benefits bridge the generations. The main source of survivor and disability protection for America's families, for a "typical" twenty-seven year old couple with two children under age four, Social Security is the equivalent of a term life insurance policy in excess of $300,000 and a disability policy in excess of $200,000. The only pension protection available to six out of ten working persons in the private sector, it provides the equivalent of $12.1 trillion dollars in life insurance protection, more than the entire value ($10.8 trillion) of all the private life insurance protection in force (Ball, 1998). Even retirement benefits have clear cross-generational value. Assuming that one accepts the view that the United States government cannot renege on its commitment to provide benefits to future retirees, then, by making Social Security payroll tax contributions, younger workers earn the right to benefits when they retire. Also, by providing benefits to today's elderly persons, Social Security frees up resources that allow the adult children of retirees to invest more in the education of their own children (or their own retirements), rather than in the financial support of their aged parents.

Social Security has transformed old age in America. While government employee pensions and private pensions, annuities, assets, and earnings provide important sources of cash income for many elderly persons age sixty-five and older, Social Security remains the heart of the retirement income system. In part, because of the progressive nature of the benefit formula, more than 70 percent of the income going to aged households in the bottom 60 percent of the elderly income distribution comes from Social Security (see Table 1). Only for those in the highest 20 percent of the elderly income distribution do other sources of income, such as earnings and assets, eclipse Social Security in terms of their aggregate contribution to household income (U.S. Department of Health and Human Services, 2000). Occupational pensions make significant contributions to the aggregate incomes going to households in the three highest quintiles, but this source of income falls well short of Social Security for these households. While not unimportant, the aggregate contribution of cash welfare benefits (9.8 percent) to the 4.9 million aged units with less that $8,792 in annual income in 1998 was substantially less than that of Social Security (82.1 percent). Moreover, without Social Security, the poverty rate among Social Security beneficiaries age sixty-five and older would jump from 9 percent to 48 percent; for unmarried older beneficiaries, it would jump from 15 percent to 58 percent; and for older African-American beneficiaries the poverty rate would rise from 24 percent to 75 percent.

Financing and administering Social Security. Retirement, survivor, and disability protections are earned through the payment of payroll taxes by working persons and their employers. Today, most people know that their payroll taxes do not go into a special savings account earmarked for particular workers and their families. Current benefits are funded largely from the taxes paid by current workers, with the promise that the current workers will themselves receive benefits when they become eligible for them. Additional revenues come from treating a portion of Social Security benefits as taxable income and from the interest earned from investing the growing OASDI trust fund assets in government bonds. Social Security financing is held together primarily by the taxing power of the government

Table 1

Importance of various sources of income to elderly households (aged units), 1998* (all members over age 65)

	All Aged Units	Quintiles				
		Units Under $8,792 (Q1)	$8,792– $14,224 (Q2)	$14,224– $22,255 (Q3)	$22,255– $37,962 (Q4)	$37,962 and over (Q5)
Number of Units (in millions)	24.7	4.9	5.0	5.0	4.9	4.9
Percent of Total Income From:**						
Social Security (OASDI)	37.6	82.1	80.5	63.8	45.2	18.3
Railroad Retirement	0.5	0.5	0.6	0.6	1.1	0.3
Government employee pension	8.4	0.8	2.1	5.5	10.4	9.9
Private pension/annuity	9.9	2.0	3.9	8.8	12.9	10.3
Income from assets	19.9	2.4	6.1	10.5	13.7	27.9
Earnings	20.7	0.7	3.2	7.3	13.1	31.1
Public cash assistance (Welfare)	0.7	9.8	1.8	0.7	0.2	0.0
Other	2.4	1.8	1.8	2.8	3.3	2.1

* All members of households are 65 or over. Aged units are married couples living together—at least one of whom is 65—and nonmarried persons 65 or older.
**Details may not sum to totals due to rounding error.

SOURCE: U.S. Department of Health and Human Services, Social Security Administration, Office of Policy Office of Research, Evaluation and Statistics, Income of the Population 55 and Over

and the public's (and hence politicians') strong interest in maintaining the program

The Social Security Administration maintains a record of the earnings on which workers have paid payroll taxes. This record provides the basis for establishing eligibility to program benefits and determining the size of those benefits. Interestingly, each year less than 1 percent (0.9 percent) of trust fund revenues is spent on the administration of OASDI.

Employed persons contribute 6.2 percent of their earnings (with an equal employer match) up to a maximum taxable ceiling ($76,200 in 2000) into two trust funds—one for Old-Age and Survivors Insurance (OASI) and one for Disability Insurance (DI)—which are often referred to as the combined OASDI trust fund. Self-employed persons make contributions equivalent to those made by regularly employed persons and their employers. The maximum taxable ceiling is adjusted each year for changes in average wages. Another 1.45 percent payroll tax goes to Medicare's Hospital Insurance (HI) trust fund.

Social Security benefits. Elaborate rules link contributions to benefits. Four general rules are worth keeping in mind. First, persons who

have worked for ten years or more (that is, earned credit for forty quarters) in covered employment are almost always eligible to receive retirement benefits at age sixty-two or later and their survivorship protections are in force. One credit for a quarter is actually given (a maximum of four per year) for having $830 of earnings in covered employment. Second, for disability protections to be in force, workers generally need to have worked for five out of the previous ten years. Third, there are exceptions to these basic rules. Younger workers, for example, are subject to far less restrictive eligibility requirements for survivorship and disability protections.

The fourth basic rule is that, in keeping with the program's goal of providing widespread and adequate protection, the Social Security benefit formula works to assure that long-term, low-wage workers receive a proportionately larger benefit (relative to their contributions) than high-wage workers. The increased payroll tax contributions of high-wage workers is recognized by a larger monthly benefit, but such workers receive a proportionately smaller benefit. This is done through a benefit formula that replaces a smaller percentage of covered earnings as a worker's average covered earnings rise. For example, for workers retiring at age sixty-five in January 2001, Social Security replaces about 28 percent of earnings for those with earnings consistently at the maximum taxable ceiling, compared to about 58 percent for those whose earnings were consistently at 45 percent of median wages, and 42 percent for those with average earnings. The monthly retired workers benefit for this maximum earner would be $1,538 compared to $637 for the low earner and $1,051 for the average earner.

Nearly all covered workers are eligible to accept actuarially reduced early retirement benefits at age sixty-two or full benefits at the normal retirement age—in 2002, age sixty-five and scheduled to gradually increase to age sixty-seven by 2027. Workers electing to postpone benefits past the normal retirement age receive credits that permanently increase the value of their monthly benefits. The surviving spouses of retired workers may receive reduced survivor benefits at age sixty (or age fifty if severely disabled) or full benefits at age sixty-five or later. Severely disabled workers are also eligible to receive monthly benefits if their condition meets the disability eligibility criteria. Other dependents of retired, deceased, or disabled workers (even, in some cases, financially dependent grandchildren, divorced spouses caring for dependent children, or adult children who were disabled prior to age nineteen) may also be eligible for monthly benefits. (Note: additional benefit information can be found by accessing the Social Security Administration's Web site: www.ssa.gov.)

Contemporary issues

How to address the projected Social Security shortfall, while also maintaining (and even strengthening) the social protections the program offers is one of the most pressing domestic policy issues of the twenty-first century. Even though Social Security is running substantial yearly surpluses ($155 billion in 2000), the long-term financial stability must be addressed.

The most commonly accepted estimates of Social Security actuaries suggest that the program has sufficient funds to meet all its obligations through 2038. After that, its projected revenue stream will be sufficient to pay 72 cents of every dollar promised through 2075 (estimates made in 2000 extend only for seventy-five years). These estimates suggest that tax revenues (payroll tax receipts and receipts from taxation of benefits) will be exceeded by outlays in 2015, but that income from all sources, including interest on trust fund investments in U.S. government obligations, is expected to exceed expenditures through about 2025 (Board of Trustees). After that, timely payment of benefits would require drawing down the assets of the OASDI trust fund until its depletion in 2037. Of course, the size of the actual problem could be larger or smaller. The SSA's more pessimistic estimates project a shortfall beginning in 2026 that is roughly 150 percent larger than its most commonly accepted estimates. On the other hand, its more optimistic estimates project that the OASDI trust funds can meet all its obligations through 2074.

Theoretically, the long-term financing problem could be addressed by immediately raising the Social Security payroll tax on employers and employees from 6.2 to 7.2 percent, or by immediately reducing all future benefits by about 14 percent. While this provides a sense of the size of the problem, no one is seriously suggesting either approach.

Social Security's estimated shortfall is not highly disputed, but the perceived implications of the shortfall fuels a lively policy debate (see Aaron and Reischauer; Peterson). Conflicting approaches to reform reflect differing views of the extent to which individuals, rather than the national community, should be responsible for preparing for their retirement, disability, or survivorship. The traditional view emphasizes providing widespread and adequate protection as Social Security's fundamental purpose. Hence, stabilizing financing while assuring adequate benefits that are not subject to erosion by inflation, business cycles, and market fluctuations are central reform concerns. Strong commitment exists for the moderate redistribution inherent in the benefit structure as a means of assuring that those who have worked for many years at relatively low wages will have minimally adequate incomes. In contrast, those seeking to shift Social Security towards a more private savings model draw on their strong belief in individual responsibility, limited taxation, and freedom of choice. They tend to emphasize maximizing rates of return and shrinking the role of government. While safeguards may be built in for some of the most disadvantaged, these proposals tend to be most beneficial to persons with higher earnings. For instance, most women would not fare well under a privatized retirement income savings program because women tend to have more intermittent work histories and lower earnings, and they live longer.

As in the past, incremental changes in benefits and financing can effectively address the projected financing problem. The large annual surpluses projected through about 2020 provide an opportunity to buy down the federal debt, arguably strengthening the economy in preparation for the retirement of the baby boomers. If the savings from interest the government would otherwise have to pay on the federal debt were then transferred to the Social Security trust funds (essentially a general revenue transfer after 2036), the program would be able to meet its obligations through about 2050. Diversification of trust fund investments, allowing for a small portion of the trust fund assets to be invested by an independent board in a broad selection of private equities, could help address the program's financing while also improving rates of return. There are many other proposals which, if done in moderation, would not greatly compromise the fundamental purposes of the program. These include raising the ceiling on wages subject to the payroll tax, increasing the normal retirement age, bringing the rest of state and local government employees into the program, small payroll tax increases, a technical adjustment in the COLA, and other small benefit reductions. As in the recent past, such changes will not be pain-free. But, given the larger goal of assuring financial stability of this popular program, the public is likely to accept such changes, especially if the burdens of change are viewed as being distributed equitably.

Because OASDI provides widespread protection across all income classes, and because it is especially important to low- and moderate- income groups, it is especially important to carefully assess the distributive implications of various policy options. Certain changes, such as COLA reductions or retirement age increases, especially if done in the extreme, will have a more deleterious effect on low-income persons who rely more heavily on Social Security for their retirement income. Also, in the context of reforming Social Security's financing, it will be important to explore what can be done to improve the benefit for persons who continue to be at financial risk during their old age. For example, many women, especially divorced or very old widowed women, are very much at risk today, and, absent changes, this will also be the case for future cohorts of older women (Smeeding, Esters, and Glasse).

Too often, media, politicians, and analysts have reduced Social Security discussions to mere accounting exercises about the financial cost of the program, overlooking the benefits this program provides and the real consequences of possible changes to the well-being of individuals and families. Social Security is an institution that has strengthened the nation's families and communities. As Social Security continues to evolve, it will be important to not lose sight of the moral dimension of a program that gives expression to and reinforces the values that hold us together as a nation and a people.

ERIC R. KINGSON

See also DISABILITY, ECONOMIC COSTS AND INSURANCE PROTECTION; ECONOMIC WELL-BEING; GENERATIONAL EQUITY; SOCIAL SECURITY ADMINISTRATION; SOCIAL SECURITY, AND THE U.S. FEDERAL BUDGET; SOCIAL SECURITY, LONG-TERM FINANCING AND REFORM; WELFARE STATE; WIDOWHOOD: ECONOMIC ISSUES.

BIBLIOGRAPHY

AARON, H. J., and REISCHAUSER, R. D. *Countdown to Reform: The Great Social Security Debate.* New York: Twentieth Century Fund Press/Priority Press Publications, 1998.

BALL, R. M. *Straight Talk About Social Security: An Analysis of the Issues in the Current Debate.* New York: The Century Foundation Press, 1998.

BERKOWITZ, E. *America's Welfare State: From Roosevelt to Reagan.* Baltimore, Md.: Johns Hopkins University, 1991.

Board of Trustees. *2001 Annual Report of the Trustees of the Federal Old-Age and Survivors Insurance and Disability Insurance Trust Funds.* Washington, D.C.: U.S. Government Printing Office, 2001.

KINGSON, E. R., and SCULZ, J. H., eds. *Social Security in the 21st Century.* New York: Oxford University Press, 1997.

KINGSON, E. R., and WILLIAMSON, J. B. "Economic Security Policies." In *Handbook of Aging and the Social Sciences.* Edited by Robert H. Binstock and Linda K. George. New York: Academic Press, 2001.

National Commission on Social Security Reform. *Report of the National Commission on Social Security Reform.* Washington, D.C.: NCSSR, 1983.

PETERSON, P. G. "How Will America Pay for the Retirement of the Baby Boom Generation?"

In *The Generational Equity Debate*. Edited by J. B. Williamson, D. M. Watts-Roy, and E. R. Kingson. New York: Columbia University, 1999. Pages 41–57.

Schulz, J. H. *The Economics of Aging*, 7th ed. Westport, Conn.: Auburn House, 2000.

Smeeding, T. M.; Esters, C. L.; and Glasse, L. *Social Security Reform and Older Women: Improving the System*. Washington, D.C.: Gerontological Society of America, 1999.

Social Security Administration, Office of Policy, Office of Research, Evaluation and Statistics. *Income of the Population 55 and Over*. Washington, D.C.: SSA, 2000. Available at www.ssa.gov

Social Security Administration, Office of Policy, Office of Research, Evaluation and Statistics. *Fast Facts and Figures about Social Security*. Available on the World Wide Web at www.ssa.gov

Steuerle, C. E., and Bakija, J. M. *Retooling Social Security for the Twenty-First Century*. Washington, D.C.: Urban Institute Press, 1994.

SOCIAL SECURITY: LONG-TERM FINANCING AND REFORM

The Social Security Act and its transformation

The provisions of the Social Security Act (signed into law by President Franklin D. Roosevelt on 14 August 1935) were tailored to model a private insurance system and avoid any hint of socialism. Some degree of individual equity would be maintained, with those who paid in more receiving greater benefits upon retirement. OASI (Old Age and Survivors Insurance) would not be means-tested, reflecting American preferences against welfare. These provisions helped to make the Social Security Act the most successful and enduring of the New Deal programs—indeed, many analysts claim that Social Security is the most popular federal government program ever adopted. In truth, however, Social Security has never closely approximated a private insurance plan, and changes to the Social Security Act over the years have moved it ever farther from that model. Thus, while Americans still tend to think of Social Security as a system of "retirement insurance," in fact almost 28 percent of the beneficiaries of OASI (which excludes disability benefits covered under the full program of Old Age, Survivors and Disability Insurance, OASDI) in 1997 were spouses or survivors of covered workers. Though the discussion that follows will focus on the aspects of Social Security that relate most closely to issues surrounding aging and retirement, it must be kept in mind that Social Security is a much bigger program with broader coverage, and any reforms must take account of the large percent of beneficiaries without normal work histories.

U.S. workers began to pay payroll taxes for Social Security in 1937, and the first benefits were paid in 1940. Over the years tax rates were increased, the percent of the workforce covered grew, and benefits were expanded. A substantial change was made in 1972, when automatic cost-of-living adjustments were added to benefits. The next few years experienced high inflation and slower real economic growth—together these raised program benefit payments and lowered tax receipts, generating the first crisis for Social Security when it was feared that receipts might fall below expenditures. This led to the first significant cutbacks in the program's history, with inflation adjustments delayed, tax rates increased, and some benefit cuts for civil servants. By the early 1980s it was realized that these changes had not been sufficient. A commission was appointed (with future Federal Reserve Board Chairman Alan Greenspan at its head) to study the long-term financial situation of Social Security. One significant issue that had arisen was the aging of the U.S. population. This was compounded by the baby boom bulge created in the early postwar period when fertility rates (number of children per woman) rose and remained high until the baby boom bust of the 1970s, when fertility rates fell. Combined with rising longevity, this ensures that the baby boomers will create a relatively large number of elderly Social Security beneficiaries and relatively fewer workers to support them between 2015 and 2035. While the problems created by the baby boom receive most of the press, falling fertility rates and rising life expectancy are common experiences in all the major developed nations, leading to the social challenges that result from an aging population. Indeed, on current projections, Social Security will experience its greatest financial problems after all the baby boomers have died.

The Greenspan Commission published findings that resulted in the most significant changes made to Social Security since the addition of Medicare in 1965. These included higher tax rates, imposition of taxes on Social Security benefits, and phased increases in the normal retirement age. Most important, the 1983 revisions changed Social Security from pay-as-you-go to advance funding. In a pay-as-you-go (or paygo) system, current-year revenues are balanced against current-year expenditures. However, as the Greenspan Commission recognized, the aging of America created a special financing problem. During the late twentieth and early twenty-first centuries, OASDI was projected to run large annual surpluses, but sometime during the second decade of the twenty-first century, the program would begin to run annual deficits. Indeed, it was feared that the deficits would eventually become so large that it might be politically infeasible to raise taxes or cut benefits by the amount required to return the program to balance. For this reason, the paygo system was abandoned in favor of advance funding. In an advance funded system, near-term annual surpluses are accumulated in a trust fund that purchases special U.S. Treasury securities to earn interest. When program spending rises above tax revenues, interest earnings supplement revenues to maintain balance. At some point in the future, taxes plus interest earnings will fall below annual benefit payments; then the trust fund can sell its Treasury securities to make up the difference. In this way surpluses over the first three or four decades following the Greenspan Commission's changes could be used to offset projected annual deficits during the final decades, ensuring long-term financial solvency.

Long-term prospects

The changes made in 1983, including the move to an advance funded system, were believed at the time to have resolved the challenges created for Social Security by the aging of the population. Over subsequent years the board of trustees developed a rigorous method of financial accounting for the program that reported detailed projections for the next ten years (its short-range forecast) and a projection for the next seventy-five years (its long-range forecast) to capture the effects of demographic shifts, as well as alternative assumptions regarding economic factors, such as economic growth. By the end of the 1990s, they had settled on use of three alternative scenarios for the long-term forecasts: high-cost (pessimistic), intermediate-cost, and low-cost (optimistic). The long-term financial status of the program is summarized in a calculation of the actuarial balance for the seventy-five-year

period. This is the difference between the summarized income ratio (the ratio of the present value of payroll taxes to the present value of taxable payroll) and the summarized cost rate (the ratio of the present value of expenditures to the present value of the taxable payroll) over the valuation period. This is essentially similar to any comparison that discounts future revenues and costs to determine long-term net revenues. When the summarized income rate equals or exceeds the summarized cost rate, the program is said to be in actuarial balance. If the difference is negative, the program is in actuarial imbalance with an actuarial gap, measured as a percent of taxable payroll. For example, if discounted revenues fall short of discounted benefit payments by an amount equal to 1 percent of taxable payroll, this is said to represent an actuarial gap of 1 percent. An immediate increase of payroll taxes by a total of 1 percentage point (half on employers and half on employees) would close the gap.

OASDI began to show a large actuarial imbalance by the late 1990s, equal to more than 2 percent of taxable payroll. As an alternative to tax increases, the gap could be closed by cutting benefits or increasing the rate of return earned on trust fund assets. In fact, many proposals for reforming Social Security include provisions that would simultaneously pursue all three alternatives: tax increases, benefit cuts, and higher earnings. In addition, some proposals would move Social Security operations closer to a private insurance fund model—or, indeed, replace Social Security with a privately operated (and even purely voluntary) retirement system. Before turning to such proposals, the underlying causes of the gap will be examined.

According to the Social Security Administration's 1999 projections, on intermediate-cost assumptions the program achieved actuarial balance only for the first twenty-five years; over the fifty-year period the actuarial gap was −1.26; and it reached −2.07 for the entire seventy-five-year long-range forecast. However, on low-cost assumptions, the program maintained actuarial balance for the whole period, and on high-cost assumptions the program had an actuarial gap even for the first twenty-five-year period. This shows how critical the assumptions used in the forecasts are. Also, any crises are relatively far in the future; indeed, even on high-cost assumptions the actuarial imbalance is quite small for the first quarter of the twenty-first century. According to the 1999 projections, the Social Security trust funds would reach $2.3 trillion by 2008 on intermediate-cost assumptions, peak at more than $4.4 trillion in 2020, then decline to zero by 2035. Using low-cost assumptions, the trust fund would continue to grow over the entire seventy-five-year period, reaching more than $45 trillion by 2075. On the other hand, the trust fund would reach only $2.6 trillion in 2015 according to high-cost assumptions, and would then be depleted quickly, falling to zero by 2025. In other words, if Social Security is analyzed as if it were a private pension plan, it apparently will experience a crisis in 2025 or 2035, using high-cost or intermediate-cost assumptions. Most analysts focus on the intermediate-cost projections, according to which Social Security revenues would be sufficient to cover only three-fourths of expected expenditures after the mid-2030s.

The main demographic and economic assumptions that underlie the projections are fertility rates, immigration, labor force participation rates, longevity, growth of real wages, and taxable base. Together, fertility rates, immigration rates, longevity, and labor force participation rates determine the size of the pools of workers and retirees. The number of Social Security beneficiaries supported by workers will rise sharply in the early twenty-first century. For example, the number of OASDI beneficiaries per one hundred covered workers was thirty-one in 1975, but this will rise steadily between 2010 and 2075, when it will reach fifty-six, on intermediate-cost projections. To put it another way, while the United States had just over 3.3 workers per beneficiary in 2000, it may have fewer than 1.8 by 2075. Thus, the burden required of future workers to provide for OASDI beneficiaries could increase by almost a factor of two. On the other hand, workers in 2075 are projected to support fewer young people. If the population under age twenty is added to the population age sixty-five and over to obtain a dependent population (most of whom would not be expected to be working), the dependency ratio (the ratio of dependents to workers) actually peaked at 0.95 in 1965, fell to 0.71 by 1995, and will rise only slightly to 0.83 by 2075. In other words, the parents of the baby boomers supported more dependents in the mid-1960s than any generation is likely to support in the future.

In any case, as the number of beneficiaries rises relative to the number of workers paying Social Security taxes, the actuarial balance is negatively impacted. This results in part from a fall-ing fertility rate, which reduces the size of the younger population from which workers can be drawn. The fertility rate (children born per woman) stood at just over 2 at the end of the 1990s and was projected to fall to 1.9 under the intermediate assumptions. If the fertility rate were to rise back to 3.7 (where it stood in 1957 during the baby boom), over 90 percent of the actuarial gap would be eliminated. On the other hand, a falling fertility rate can be offset by rising net immigration (since immigrants can add to the worker pool, paying payroll taxes) and by rising labor force participation rates (the number working or seeking work per one hundred population). In the late 1990s net (legal and illegal) immigration reached about 960,000 per year. In their projections, however, the trustees assumed that annual net immigration would fall to 900,000 and remain there throughout the seventy-five-year period. Each additional 100,000 net immigrants above that level would reduce the actuarial gap by about 0.07 percent of taxable payroll. The trustees also project that labor force participation rates for men will fall (from 75.5 percent in 1997 to 74 percent by 2075). In contrast, since World War II, labor force participation rates for women have risen sharply (reaching 60 percent in 1997). The trustees project that this will nearly level off (reaching only 60.6 percent by 2075). If male labor force participation rates did not fall, and if female rates continued to rise, some of the actuarial gap would be eliminated. Finally, the trustees project that death rates will fall by 34 percent over the seventy-five-year period, and each ten percentage point decrease in the death rate increases the long-range actuarial gap by about 0.34 percent of taxable payroll.

While most of the debate over the Social Security program's solvency focuses on these unfavorable demographic trends, they were mostly known to the Greenspan Commission and the 1983 adjustments should have taken care of them. In fact, the reason for the looming Social Security crisis lies not in the demographics but in the increasingly pessimistic economic assumptions adopted by the trustees in their reports in the 1980s and 1990s. The main economic assumptions that lead to the financing gap are low growth of real wages and a falling taxable base. In 1999 the trustees projected that real wages would grow at only 0.9 percent per year. Real wage growth, in turn, is related to productivity gains. The trustees assume that productivity will grow at just 1.3 percent annually over the long-range period—well below long-term U.S. averages. If real wages were to grow at 2 percent per year, more than half of the actuarial gap would be eliminated. Finally, the trustees have projected that the taxable base will fall from 41 percent of GDP in 1999 to only 35 percent in 2075. This is for two reasons. First, Social Security taxes wages and certain kinds of self-employment income. Other types of income, such as interest income, are exempt. If these rise as a share of national income, the percent of income subject to the Social Security tax will fall. Second, payroll taxes are levied on only a portion of one's wage income—determined by the contribution and benefit base. In 1999 OASDI taxes were applied only to the first $72,600 of employment income (the contribution and benefit base for that year; this base is increased each year with rising nominal average wages). The trustees have assumed that the taxable base will fall both because a smaller portion of income will be received in the form of wages and because a higher percent of wages will accrue to those with earnings above the contribution and benefit base. Therefore, by 2075, a little over a third of national income will be taxed to support OASDI beneficiaries.

Some analysts have questioned the usefulness of calculating actuarial balance over a seventy-five-year period. Projections of demographic trends and, more important, economic variables over such long periods is inherently difficult, and relatively small changes in assumptions can change the projections significantly. Some analysts have argued that projections are based on rather pessimistic economic assumptions. For example, according to intermediate-cost projections, real GDP and labor productivity will grow at only 1.3 percent per year. In fact, labor productivity has grown at a rate of approximately 2 percent per year since 1870, and at 2.7 percent per year between World War II and 1973, while real GDP grew at an annual rate of 3.7 percent from 1870 to 1973. Even if productivity and GDP grew at only two-thirds of long-term trends, Social Security's financial problems would be eliminated. A counterargument is that U.S. economic performance since 1973 has generally been worse than long-term averages, and it is more prudent to project weak performance into the future than to presume that high growth might return. On the other hand, it has been noted that these pessimistic assumptions were incongruously adopted in the trustee forecasts during the "Goldilocks" 1990s expansion, when U.S. economic performance did return toward historical averages. Furthermore, the assumptions adopted may not be internally consistent. For example, if labor force growth rates are as low as the trustees have assumed, one might expect that real wage growth should be higher than the assumed 0.9 percent as excess demand for labor pushes up its relative return, and labor productivity growth should be higher as firms substitute capital for scarce labor.

More important, it is not clear that a national, public retirement system ought to operate as if it were a private pension fund, building reserves today that earn interest and can be depleted in future years. In, say, 2035 when the trust fund needs to sell securities to the Treasury, the Treasury will have to raise taxes, cut other spending, or sell securities to cover retirement of debt held by Social Security. Surprisingly, this is exactly what the government would have to do even if Social Security had no trust fund at all! Suppose Social Security were operated as a paygo system, with each year's receipts equal to spending. When revenues began to fall below benefit expenditures, the government would have to increase taxes, reduce other spending, or issue securities to cover the difference. Some, including Milton Friedman, have concluded that the trust fund is nothing more than an "accounting gimmick," because when Social Security begins to run deficits, existence of a trust fund cannot really provide for financing of its spending. Further, unlike a private firm, the U.S. government's revenues are not market-determined. If necessary, the government can raise tax rates or can deficit-spend to ensure that it meets its Social Security obligations—things that private firms cannot do. Hence, while government cannot really build up a trust fund, it also does not need to do so.

What really matters is whether the economy will be able to produce a sufficient quantity of real goods and services to provide for both workers and dependents in, say, the year 2035. If it cannot, then regardless of Social Security's finances, the real living standards of Americans in 2035 will have to be lower than they are today. Those who take this approach argue that any reforms to Social Security made today should focus on increasing the economy's capacity to produce real goods and services, rather than on ensuring positive actuarial balances. For example, policies that might encourage public and private infrastructure investment will ease the future burden of providing for growing numbers of retirees. In a sense, this would be a real reform rather than a financial reform, although it is possible that financial reforms might encourage greater investment. Indeed, some advocates of privatization argue this will encourage more investment by entrepreneurs. However, even with the trustees' rather pessimistic economic and demographic assumptions, real living standards are projected to rise substantially for both workers and retirees throughout the seventy-five-year, long-range period. Accordingly, Social Security does not face a real crisis even though it may face a financial crisis. Still, this may not be sufficiently comforting to future workers, because although they will enjoy a growing real economic pie, the share of the pie going to retirees will grow. In fact, the share of GDP going to OASDI will grow from about 5 percent in 2000 to 7 percent for the period between 2030 and 2075. On the one hand, this is a significant increase, but on the other hand, similar shifts have occurred in the past without generating an economic crisis.

Reform proposals

Of the most important reform proposals, perhaps the most extreme would be to abolish Social Security altogether, leaving it up to individuals to decide how to provide for their retirement. (However, it should be recalled that Social Security is not simply an old age security program; privatization could leave widows, dependents, and disabled persons to their own devices.) Some reformers recognize that individuals generally underestimate the future costs of retirement, so some sort of mandatory minimum contribution levels should be maintained even if the program is privatized. Another variation would maintain basic coverage in a mandatory, government-run program, but would allow individual control over supplemental investments in privately run pension funds. Finally, some proposals would retain most features of the current system but would direct the trustees to invest a specified portion of the trust funds in private equities.

Some reformers advocate privatization simply as a matter of principle—for example, Milton Friedman has long argued that there is no justification for mandatory participation in a public system. Others emphasize that, as currently designed, Social Security has a strong redistribu-

tional element—both within and across generations. They typically use a money's worth estimate to calculate a return on one's contributions. Those with high earnings, and thus high contributions, receive low returns when they eventually collect benefits, while those with low earnings receive higher returns. Many beneficiaries never actually contribute; thus, contributions of others are redistributed to them. Returns also vary greatly by generation—early participants in Social Security received very good returns on their contributions, but returns for later generations are much lower. Thus, some reformers emphasize that reform should be geared toward ensuring better money's worth outcomes for contributors, both within and across generations. It should be noted, however, that while some attention was paid to such equity concerns in the original Social Security Act, money's worth was not a high priority in the beginning and most amendments since then have moved the program ever farther from this consideration.

Nevertheless, most reformers in recent years have pushed privatization to resolve the long-range financial imbalance of Social Security, with money's worth calculations playing a smaller role. It is argued that under current arrangements, the trustees can hold only government bonds with relatively low interest rates. Allowing investments in the stock market and other private assets could increase returns on the trust fund. Such arguments were given a tremendous boost by the spectacular performance of U.S. stock markets from the mid-1980s through 2000. Many proponents argue that equity markets should earn real returns of about 7.5 percent per year—as they have averaged since the 1920s—probably more than double the real return on government debt. Over the long-range, seventy-five-year period, these higher returns could resolve Social Security's financial problems.

However, opponents have raised several objections. First, there will be a costly transition period as the system becomes privatized, during which current workers must finance the cost of the existing Social Security system (paying taxes to finance the benefits going to current retirees), plus the costs of building up their own retirement funds. Thus, a fairly large, immediate tax increase will be required, and must remain in place for several decades until all those covered under the old system have died. Second, it is probably inconsistent to argue that real GDP growth will slow (to 1.3 percent per year, little over one-third its long-term average) without affecting growth of equity prices. Critics have shown that this implies either that the share of distribution of national income going to profits must grow to implausibly high levels (indeed, Dean Baker has calculated that wages must be negative by 2070), or that price-earnings ratios (already at all-time highs in 2000) must rise to truly astronomical levels (on Baker's calculation, to 485-to-1 by 2070). On the other hand, privatizers believe that the influx of money into stocks would generate more investment, and thus higher economic growth. Third, privatization might place unacceptable levels of risk on workers. Even if the stock market were to grow at an average rate of over 7 percent per year, there could be relatively long periods of below-normal growth. In the past, equity prices have been fairly flat for decades at a time. Unlucky workers whose retirement happened to come after such a period could face deprivation during retirement. Furthermore, if workers are given individual control over their retirement accounts, they might do poorly even if the markets as a whole are doing well.

Fourth, numerous small retirement accounts can be very costly to administer and supervise. Current costs of administering Social Security are exceedingly small—well under 1 percent of revenues. Privatizers often point to the Chilean example as evidence that a private system can produce high returns for contributors; however, overhead costs in Chile are above 10 percent. While private fund managers were initially supportive of the move to privatize, they have become less enthusiastic as they have come to realize the logistics of managing many small accounts for lower income workers. Fifth, some critics have argued that because women typically have lower incomes, spend more time out of the labor force, and more often work part-time, most privatization reforms would adversely affect benefits paid to women. Others have noted that because African Americans and Hispanics typically have lower income and lower life expectancies, privatization reforms as well as raising the normal retirement age would have a disproportionately negative impact on those groups. Finally, critics note that privatization schemes do not, and probably cannot, offer the same kinds of coverage currently offered by Social Security. For example, private pension plans do not offer inflation indexing, as Social Security does. As discussed, Social Security also offers coverage for many individuals without significant work histories. If the program is privatized, a new social safety net would have to be created to cover individuals who could not purchase private insurance.

With the large turnaround of the U.S. federal government budget in the late 1990s (from chronic deficits to record surpluses), President Bill Clinton and many others proposed that budget surpluses could be set aside to resolve Social Security's financial problems. Essentially, President Clinton would have increased the size of the trust fund by an amount equal to just under two-thirds of annual budget surpluses. The larger trust fund would then earn more interest and would have more Treasury securities to sell when program revenues fall below expenditures. However, as noted above, when the trust fund sells securities, the Treasury will have to cut other spending, raise taxes, or sell securities to the general public to cover the payments made to the trust fund. Furthermore, like most financial fixes, this reform will not necessarily increase future productive capacity. Indeed, it is not necessary for the federal government to run surpluses for it to credit the trust fund with more securities—the Treasury can add securities worth any amount to the trust fund at any time (in principle, it can add an amount equal to the entire Social Security shortfall today, thereby resolving any financial difficulties). Alternatively, the Treasury could simply agree to pay a higher interest rate on trust fund assets—paying whatever interest rate would eliminate the actuarial gap. Though somewhat ludicrous, these alternatives emphasize that accumulating a trust fund of Treasury securities really cannot resolve future annual deficits in the Social Security program.

Furthermore, as emphasized above, what really matters is the economy's capacity to produce real goods and services in the future. Hence, if the amount that can be produced will not be sufficient to provide the level of consumption desired by all generations in the future, it will be necessary to either to boost production or to ration consumption. Extending the normal retirement age (which is essentially a benefit cut) will keep workers in the labor force longer, and will reduce the number of years they must be supported during retirement. Increasing taxes on future workers will leave them with lower purchasing power, ensuring that more of the nation's output can go to retirees. Cutting future OASDI benefits will do the opposite—allocating more output toward workers and others with incomes that are not dependent on Social Security. Fortunately, given increases in worker productivity that reasonably can be expected to occur, plus increases in production facilities that are likely to take place as a result of public and private investment, it appears quite likely that future workers and future retirees will enjoy higher living standards than do their counterparts today—in spite of the aging of America.

L. RANDALL WRAY

See also BABY BOOMERS; POPULATION AGING; SOCIAL SECURITY, AND THE U.S. FEDERAL BUDGET; SOCIAL SECURITY, HISTORY AND OPERATIONS.

BIBLIOGRAPHY

Advisory Council on Social Security. *Report of the 1994–1996 Advisory Council. Vol. I: Findings and Recommendations.* Washington, D.C.: Government Printing Office, 1997a.

Advisory Council on Social Security. *Report of the 1994–1996 Advisory Council. Vol. II: Report of the Technical Panel on Trends and Issues in Retirement Savings, Technical Panel on Assumptions and Methods and Presentations to the Council.* Washington, D.C.: Government Printing Office, 1997b.

BAKER, D. "Saving Social Security with Stocks, Introduction, Policy in Perspective." The Century Foundation. www.tcf.org

BAKER, D. "Saving Social Security in Three Steps." Briefing Paper. Washington, D.C.: Economic Policy Institute, 1998.

BALL, ROBERT M.; FIERST, EDITH U.; JOHNSON, GLORIA T.; JONES, THOMAS W.; KOURPIAS, GEORGE; and SHEA, GERALD M. "Social Security for the 21st Century: A Strategy to Maintain Benefits and Strengthen America's Family Protection Plan." In *Advisory Council on Social Security, Report of the 1994–1996 Advisory Council. Vol. 1: Findings and Recommendations.* Washington, D.C.: Government Printing Office, 1997.

CLINTON, W. J. State of the Union Address, January 19, 1999. Transcript. CNN Interactive, January 20. www.cnn.com

Congressional Budget Office. *Social Security Privatization: Experiences Abroad.* Washington, D.C.: Government Printing Office, 1999.

FRIEDMAN, M. "Social Security Chimeras." *New York Times,* January 11, 1999.

LANGER, D. "Social Security Finances are in Fine Shape." Remarks at the Congressional Conference to Fight Social Security Privatization. Washington, D.C.: January 21, 1999.

LANGER, D. "Social Security vs. Stock." Op-ed. *Christian Science Monitor,* June 19, 2000. Page 19.

PAPADIMITRIOU, D. B., and WRAY, L. R. "Does Social Security Need Saving?" *Public Policy Brief* no. 55. Annandale-on-Hudson, N.Y.: The Jerome Levy Economics Institute, 1999a.

PAPADIMITRIOU, D. B., and WRAY, L. R. "How Can We Provide for the Baby Boomers in Their Old Age?" *Policy Note* 1999/5. Annandale-on-Hudson, N.Y.: The Levy Economics Institute, 1999b.

PAPADIMITRIOU, D. B., and WRAY, L. R. "More Pain, No Gain: Breaux Plan Slashes Social Security Benefits Unnecessarily." *Policy Note* 1999/8. Annandale-on-Hudson, N.Y.: The Levy Economics Institute, 1999c.

SKIDMORE, M. J. *Social Security and its Enemies: The Case for America's Most Efficient Insurance Program.* Boulder, Colo.: Westview Press, 1999.

Social Security Administration. *Annual Report of the Board of Trustees of the Federal Old-Age and Survivors Insurance and Disability Insurance Trust Funds.* Washington, D.C.: Government Printing Office, 1998.

Social Security Administration. *Annual Report of the Board of Trustees of the Federal Old-Age and Survivors Insurance and Disability Insurance Trust Funds.* Washington, D.C.: Government Printing Office, 1999.

STEIN, H. "How to Solve Almost Everything." *New York Times,* February 3, 1999.

WRAY, L. R. "Can the Social Security Trust Fund Contribute to Savings?" *Journal of Post Keynesian Economics* 13, no. 2 (1990–1991).

WRAY, L. R. "The Emperor Has No Clothes: President Clinton's Proposed Social Security Reform." *Policy Note* 1999/2. Annandale-on-Hudson, N.Y.: The Levy Economics Institute, 1999a.

WRAY, L. R. "Surplus Mania: A Reality Check." *Policy Note* 1999/3. Annandale-on-Hudson, N.Y.: The Levy Economics Institute, 1999b.

SOCIAL SECURITY, AND THE U.S. FEDERAL BUDGET

The Social Security Old-Age, Survivors and Disability Insurance (OASDI) programs play an important role on both the individual level and in the overall United States economy. The most visible influence of the programs is as a source of income when workers retire, or in instances of death or disability. Less visible, but equally important, are its effects on the national economy. Social Security affects economic output primarily through its influence on individuals' decisions on how much to work, when to retire, and how much to save. As the largest function in government, based on expenditures, Social Security also contributes to government saving and spending.

This entry first describes how the OASDI programs are financed and how they relate to the federal budget. Next, the entry examines determinants of economic output and the influence Social Security exerts on two of those determinants: labor supply and national saving. Finally, it discusses the role of economic growth in meeting the needs of society and two options economists and policymakers have considered for using Social Security to increase national saving, and thereby increase economic output.

Social Security's financing

Nearly 90 percent of the funding for the OASDI programs' benefits and administration comes from a dedicated tax on earnings, called the Federal Insurance Contributions Act (FICA) tax. Employers and employees each contribute 6.2 percent of their gross wages up to a certain annual limit that is increased yearly to reflect wage growth ($84,900 in the year 2002). Self-employed persons pay both the employer and employee portions of the FICA tax. The remainder of program funding comes from taxation of Social Security benefits and interest from the investment of surplus revenues.

The government operates Social Security on a "pay-as-you-go" basis, meaning Social Security uses most of its annual revenues to pay current beneficiaries. Aside from benefit payments, the programs use approximately 1 percent of FICA taxes to pay for operational expenses. Since the mid-1980s, Social Security's revenues have exceeded its expenditures. The Treasury Department credits this excess revenue to the OASDI Trust Funds.

In 1999, Social Security revenues exceeded expenditures by approximately $134 billion (Trustees Report, Table II.F12). The Trust Funds invest excess revenues in special-issue Treasury bonds, which earn interest. The interest rate paid on the special-issue Treasury bonds equals the average yield on marketable Treasury bonds and other interest-bearing obligations of the United States that are not expected to be re-

deemed in the near future. In 1999, the Trust Funds earned approximately $56 billion in interest from their investments, which is equal to an effective interest rate of about 7 percent.

The federal government's use of Social Security's excess revenues is similar to how a bank uses money that is deposited into a bank account. The bank records the deposit on an account statement and pays the account holder interest for the bank's right to "borrow" those dollars, much like the Treasury records the surplus FICA taxes to the Social Security trust funds and pays interest on the borrowed funds. Treasury then uses the excess Social Security revenue to fund or reduce other cash needs. The Treasury bonds issued to the Social Security Trust Funds represent an obligation of the government to pay Social Security the amount invested, plus interest.

Social Security's treatment within the federal budget

Social Security's receipts and expenditures are part of government activities; therefore, they are viewed as part of the entire federal budget. Social Security receipts equal approximately 26 percent of all federal receipts and about 23 percent of all federal expenditures.

Even though Social Security is part of the overall (also known as *unified*) federal budget, it receives special treatment within the federal budgeting process because of its size, its importance, and its funding source (the dedicated payroll tax). Special rules apply when Congress considers and acts on changes to Social Security financing and benefits. Social Security is generally exempt from budget process rules. This special treatment means Social Security is considered *off-budget*.

In addition to off-budget treatment, Social Security is part of a special class of programs for which Congress does not make a decision on the annual funding level for benefit payments. The number of people entitled to a benefit and the size of those benefits determines the funding level. However, Congress makes annual decisions on how much the Social Security Administration may spend on running the programs. Also, Congress may change the program rules, thereby altering the number of people entitled or the size of benefits.

Although Social Security is officially off-budget, documents from the Congressional Budget Office (CBO) and the Office of Management and Budget (OMB) continue to show the unified budget (which contains all federal receipts and expenditures, including Social Security), as well as budget totals excluding Social Security. These entities emphasize unified budget totals, because persons interested in the impact of government on the economy need to know the total income, expenditures, and borrowing of the government.

Social Security's effect on the national economy

In fiscal year 1999, Social Security received payroll taxes and taxes on Social Security benefits equal to roughly 5 percent of the gross domestic product (GDP) and paid out benefits equal to approximately 4 percent of the GDP. Social Security influences economic output through these transactions.

Economic output is commonly measured using the GDP. The GDP is the market value of final goods and services annually produced within a nation over a certain period of time. Labor supply, capital investment, natural resources, and technology all determine economic output. Social Security is thought to primarily influence the first two categories: labor supply and capital investment.

The effect of Social Security on labor supply. Both Social Security taxes and benefits can influence an individual's decisions on whether to work and how much to work. The effect of the Social Security payroll tax is complex; it may either increase or decrease the incentive to work, depending on how much an individual wants to spend and save and how the individual views the payroll tax. Economic theories indicate Social Security taxes create two opposing effects, known as the *income effect* and the *substitution effect*. Social Security benefits, on the other hand, are believed to reduce the incentive to work based on their income effect.

The income effect describes how changes in real wages (the purchasing power of wages) or wealth influence how much a person may consume. Leisure time is something that individuals can consume, like clothing, cars, and other goods. Decreases in real wages or wealth decrease the amount of things, including leisure, that a person may consume. Likewise, increases in wages or wealth increase the amount of goods, including leisure, that a person may consume.

The substitution effect describes how changes in the price of something a person con-

sumes influences the composition of the entire collection of things that person may consume. Changes in real wages influence the opportunity cost of leisure. The opportunity cost of leisure is essentially equal to wages lost by not working during leisure time. When leisure becomes less expensive (i.e., wages decrease), individuals will substitute less work for more leisure and will reduce the amount of labor they supply to the economy.

If workers view the Social Security tax as only a tax, and not as a contribution toward retirement, then the income effect indicates workers would increase the amount they work in response to the perceived reduction in real wages. If workers view the tax as a retirement contribution that provides wealth in the form of earned Social Security benefits, then the income effect indicates workers may decrease the amount of labor they supply. The Social Security tax could also decrease labor supply through the substitution effect, because the reduced real wage reduces the opportunity cost of leisure.

The strength of the effect of Social Security benefits on labor supply depends on both the availability of benefits and the size of benefits. The availability of early retirement Social Security benefits at age sixty-two and regular retirement benefits at age sixty-five may reduce the supply of labor as a result of the income effect. Social Security retirement benefits provide a nonwork source of income, reducing the amount of work needed to achieve a desired level of income.

There is evidence indicating that labor force participation rates of persons around retirement age dropped when retirement benefits became available at age sixty-two in 1956 for women and in 1961 for men. Approximately half of all workers currently apply for Social Security benefits when they attain age sixty-two. Evidence also suggests that availability of benefits at the normal retirement age, which is gradually increasing from age sixty-five to age sixty-seven, induces workers to leave the workforce. Currently, age sixty-five is the second most common age for retirement, after age sixty-two.

Several Social Security program provisions affect the size of an individual's monthly benefit. The worker's earnings history is the primary determinant of the size of retirement benefits. However, the program reduces a person's monthly retirement benefits when he or she retires before the normal retirement age, which is age sixty-five for workers who attained age sixty-two before the year 2000. The program increases a person's monthly retirement benefits when he or she retires after the normal retirement age. Also, the program reduces a person's current monthly benefits if he or she retired early and has earnings exceeding a certain threshold ($11,280 in 2002) that is raised annually in line with national wage increases. These adjustments are designed to be neutral over an average lifetime, but some persons may alter their labor supply because of them.

There are two programmatic changes underway that may alter labor force participation among older Americans. First, the normal retirement age is increasing from sixty-five, beginning with people born in 1938, until it reaches sixty-seven for people born after 1959. As a result, persons taking early retirement benefits will receive an even greater decrease in annual benefits, compared to persons who retire at the normal retirement age. This may encourage work among persons between the earliest retirement age and the normal retirement age. Second, the delayed retirement credit is increasing from 6 percent per year of delay (for persons age sixty-two in years 1997–1998) to 8 percent (for persons age sixty-two in years 2005 and later).

Most economists agree that Social Security benefits have decreased the labor supply of older workers. Hurd and Boskin show that increases in real Social Security benefits in the early 1970s explain the majority of reduced labor force participation among married men aged fifty-eight to sixty-seven in 1969 through 1973. Hausman and Wise found a smaller effect—that the increase in Social Security benefits accounted for possibly one-third of the decrease in labor force participation of men age sixty and older between 1969 and 1975. Others have argued that factors unrelated to Social Security, such as health status, receipt of a private pension, availability of health insurance, and the retirement status of a spouse have a greater influence on the labor supply of older workers.

Social Security did not initiate the decline in labor force participation rates for older workers. According to a study by Dora Costa, 70 percent of the decline in the labor force participation rates of U.S. men age sixty-five or older occurred before 1960, when benefits were lower and fewer types of employment were covered under Social Security.

The effect of Social Security on national saving.   Social Security taxes and benefits influence capital investment, as well as labor supply. Social Security influences capital investment through its effects on private (includes personal and business) saving and government saving. Together, private and government saving are known as national saving.

The ability of a country to invest in capital is linked to the amount of national saving. National saving is the difference between what the U.S. economy produces and what it consumes and represents funds that are available for capital investment. Capital comprises items like buildings, computers, and machines. To the extent saved funds are invested in capital, they can increase economic output.

Social Security taxes and benefits have a direct effect on government saving. Government saving equals revenues (tax receipts) minus the purchase of goods and services, transfer payments, and interest payments to the public on government debt. To the extent that Social Security receipts equal the sum of benefits paid and administrative costs, it has no net effect on government saving.

However, the Social Security Trust Funds are currently building up reserves. To the extent Social Security tax receipts exceed benefits and administrative costs, they can increase government saving or reduce government dissaving. In times when the non-Social Security portion of the federal budget runs deficits, Social Security surpluses reduce the government's need to borrow, thereby reducing government dis-saving. In times of unified budget surpluses, the government uses the funds to buy back publicly held debt, making additional funds available for private saving and investment.

As Table 1 shows, Social Security has decreased government dis-saving or increased government saving since the mid-1980s. However, in the mid-1970s and early 1980s, the Social Security Trust Funds paid out more in benefits than they received in income, increasing government dis-saving. It is important to remember that the government does not make spending and taxing decisions regarding Social Security and the rest of the federal budget independently of each other, and these decisions influence each other. For example, if the existence of the Social Security tax kept the government from increasing other taxes, then Social Security's contribu-

Table 1

Sector as a percentage of gross domestic product

Year	Social Security	Other Federal	State/ Local	Private	National
1985	0.2%	-3.3%	1.6%	19.8%	18.3%
1986	0.3%	-3.4%	1.5%	18.1%	16.5%
1987	0.4%	-2.3%	1.3%	17.7%	17.1%
1988	0.7%	-2.2%	1.4%	18.5%	18.3%
1989	0.8%	-2.0%	1.4%	17.4%	17.6%
1990	0.9%	-2.7%	1.1%	17.5%	16.8%
1991	0.6%	-3.0%	1.0%	18.4%	17.0%
1992	0.5%	-4.0%	1.0%	18.4%	15.9%
1993	0.3%	-3.3%	1.1%	17.5%	15.6%
1994	0.4%	-2.3%	1.2%	17.0%	16.4%
1995	0.4%	-1.9%	1.3%	17.1%	17.0%
1996	0.5%	-1.1%	1.4%	16.5%	17.3%
1997	0.6%	-0.1%	1.5%	16.4%	18.3%
1998	0.7%	0.8%	1.6%	15.7%	18.8%

SOURCE: Author's calculations using data from Table B-8 and B-30 of the *Economic Report of the President*, February 2000, and the 2000 *Trustees Report*.

tion to government saving is larger and the rest of the budget's contribution is smaller than it would be otherwise.

The Social Security Trust Funds are not expected to maintain a surplus indefinitely. By the year 2015, benefits will exceed Social Security payroll tax revenues according to current law actuarial estimates. At that point, Social Security will decrease government saving. This does not mean that the government will be unable to pay Social Security benefits in 2015. However, the Trust Funds will use interest on its investments to help pay benefits. After 2025, actuarial estimates indicate the Trust Funds will begin to redeem their investments. Redeeming the Trust Fund investments will reduce budget surpluses or increase any deficits.

The effect of Social Security on personal saving is less clear. Many factors contribute to a person's consumption and saving decisions: income levels, the desire to bequeath assets to future generations, concern about unplanned events (disability, unemployment, health crises, etc.), the timing of retirement, and awareness of the amount of savings needed to generate a given level of income at retirement.

Various theoretical arguments support the belief that Social Security decreases personal sav-

ing. Social Security could reduce the need for personal saving, since it reduces the amount of spendable wealth needed to produce a specific level of income. Alternatively, Social Security may raise awareness of the need to plan for retirement or encourage workers to retire early, encouraging people to save more than they would otherwise. Finally, some theoretical arguments indicate Social Security has a roughly neutral effect on personal saving. Some persons may increase bequests to their children, knowing that the payroll tax paid by their working children funds their Social Security benefits in retirement. It may also have no effect if workers choose to increase nonpension saving by an amount roughly equal to any reduced saving for retirement.

Economists have not completely modeled all the factors that contribute to decision-making; therefore, they rely on a combination of theory and empirical evidence to try to determine Social Security's effect on personal saving. Most current research shows Social Security reduces personal saving to some degree. For example, Feldstein and Diamond and Hausman found that Social Security has a negative effect on saving. However, a few studies show Social Security may not decrease overall personal saving. For example, Gullason, Kolluri, and Panik found that Social Security has no significant effect on overall personal wealth, but decreases pension wealth.

We do not know the exact degree to which Social Security influences national saving (combined government, personal, and business saving). If Social Security decreases national saving, then economic output/national income is less than it could be in the absence of Social Security. If the less likely scenario is true—if Social Security increases national saving—then economic output/national income is higher than it would be in the absence of Social Security.

Social Security as a tool in promoting economic growth

Economic growth is critical to a nation's ability to improve standards of living over time, because citizens are able to purchase more goods and services. The desirability of increasing available goods and services will be more important as the baby boom generation starts retiring in about 2010. For example, expenditures for OASDI programs are estimated to increase from approximately 4 percent of GDP in 1999 to nearly 7 percent of GDP by 2075 (U.S. Social Security Administration). Economic growth will not entirely resolve questions about how large the Social Security programs or other federal programs ought to be in relation to the federal budget and the economy. However, economic growth can help future generations by providing a larger income base to use in meeting society's needs.

Some economists and policymakers believe the Social Security programs could be used to increase national saving and capital investment, and consequently promote economic growth. Some propose greater prefunding of Old-Age benefits (the program is currently a "pay-as-you-go" system), either through individual retirement accounts or larger Trust Fund reserves. Others propose reducing the amount of publicly held debt (meaning government bonds held by individuals or nongovernmental institutions) by running overall federal budget surpluses.

Prefunding Old-Age benefits does not automatically lead to increased national saving. Prefunding would only increase national saving to the extent that saving in one form is not offset by reductions in other types of saving. For example, if individuals offset other types of saving in direct relation to increases in their individual accounts, the net effect may be neutral. Also, if the government borrows from the public in order to fund the accounts, national saving will not change. In other words, decreases in government saving would offset increases in private saving. Likewise, increasing reserves held by the Trust Funds will not automatically lead to increased national saving if the government reduces taxes or increases spending in direct relation to resources held by the Trust Funds.

Reducing publicly held debt could potentially increase economic output by increasing national saving. Persons and institutions selling their Treasury bonds back to the government would potentially seek other ways to use their money. To the extent the private sector is more likely to use the funds for capital investment than the government, the funds would increase productivity and economic output.

Reducing publicly held debt would also reduce the government's expenditures on interest payments. In fiscal year 1999, the government spent approximately fourteen cents of every federal dollar on interest payments. To the extent the government's income increases by taxing the larger income base and the government's expenditures on interest payments decrease, government saving could increase (assuming no changes in tax rates or expenditures). These changes would help create room in the federal budget for the increased Social Security costs of baby-boomers and the generations that follow.

Summary

Social Security is an important part of the federal budget and influences the national economy. Although Social Security is considered separately during the budget process, the program contributes to the government's overall effect on the economy.

Social Security programs influence economic growth through their effects on labor supply and national saving. The exact degree of their effects is unclear. Economists generally agree that Social Security benefits reduce the labor supply of older workers. The effect of Social Security taxes on overall labor supply is more ambiguous and depends upon the consumption preferences of individual workers and whether workers perceive the tax merely as a reduction in income or as an increase in wealth. Likewise, the effect of Social Security on national saving is not perfectly understood, although most economists agree it reduces private saving to some extent.

Although there is uncertainty about the exact effect of Social Security on national saving, some economists and policymakers believe it may be possible to use Social Security financing to improve economic growth, particularly if Social Security could be used to increase national saving. However, prefunding retirement benefits does not guarantee that increased saving in one sector of the economy will not be offset by decreased saving in another sector. Many economists and policymakers agree that paying down publicly held debt will help the economy and the government prepare for anticipated increases in expenditures resulting from the aging of the baby boom generation.

JANE L. ROSS
SOPHIA WRIGHT
LAURA HALTZEL

See also SOCIAL SECURITY, ADMINISTRATION; SOCIAL SECURITY, HISTORY AND OPERATIONS; SOCIAL SECURITY, LONG-TERM FINANCING AND REFORM.

BIBLIOGRAPHY

BURKHAUSER, R. V., and TURNER, J. A. "A Time-Series Analysis on Social Security and Its Effect on Market Work of Men at Younger Ages." *Journal of Political Economy* 4 (1978): 701–714.
COSTA, D. "Pensions and Retirement: Evidence from Union Army Veterans." *Quarterly Journal of Economics* 4 (1995): 297–319.
DIAMOND, P. A., and HAUSMAN, J. A. "Individual Retirement and Savings Behavior." *Journal of Public Economics* 1/2 (1984): 81–114.
FELDSTEIN, M. S. "Social Security and Private Saving: Reply." *Journal of Political Economy* 3 (1982): 630–642.
GULLASON, E. T.; KOLLURI, B. R.; and PANIK, M. J. "Social Security and Household Wealth Accumulation: Refined Microeconomic Evidence." *Review of Economics and Statistics* 3 (1993): 548–551.
HAUSMAN, J. A., and WISE, D. A. "Social Security, Health Status, and Retirement." In *Pensions, Labor, and Individual Choice.* Edited by David Wise. Chicago, Ill.: The University of Chicago Press, 1985. Pages 159–191.
HURD, M. D., and BOSKIN, M. J. "The Effect of Social Security Retirement in the Early 1970s." *Quarterly Journal of Economics* 4 (1984): 767–790.
IPPOLITO, R. A. "Toward Explaining Early Retirement After 1970." *Industrial and Labor Relations Review* 5 (1990): 556–569.
President of the United States. *Economic Report of the President.* Washington, D.C.: Government Printing Office, 2000.
U.S. Social Security Administration. *The 2000 Annual Report of the Board of Trustees of the Federal Old-Age and Survivors Insurance and Disability Insurance Trust Funds.* Washington, D.C.: 2000.

SOCIAL SERVICES

Funded through an array of federal, state, and local sources, social services are designed to enhance the independence and quality of life for elderly people in America. The use of public funds to support services exclusively for the elderly has become controversial as the nation's elderly have become more financially secure, and public resources have become more scarce.

Following a brief review of early approaches to serving the nation's elderly, this entry considers the use of social services to prevent nursing home placement and describes the range of social services available. A brief discussion of strategies for accessing public social services is followed by a review of the relationship between family care and social services. The entry closes with brief consideration of the challenges of providing services for emerging cohorts of older Americans.

Early approaches to serving the elderly

The eligibility requirements of major programs for the elderly influence our understanding of what it means to be "old" in America today. At sixty-two years of age an American is eligible to begin collecting Social Security benefits. Eligibility for most programs funded under the Older Americans Act begins at age sixty. Medicare eligibility begins at age sixty-five. So, for twenty-first-century Americans, "old age" might begin in the early- to mid-sixties.

Lacking programs and policies to define them as "old," elderly people prior to the twentieth century were judged by their individual attributes. Infirmity, more than chronology, was the hallmark of old age. Services for the elderly were based not on their age but on their needs. Consequently, destitute elderly people might have been found in early nineteenth century almshouses along with children and young adults.

Beginning in the 1830s, this notion of a homogeneous class of needy Americans was challenged. Reformers who served the urban poor became interested in more efficient use of their resources and decided to focus on those most capable of reform, "the redeemable poor." The elderly were not included in this category. In 1855, for example, the New York Association for Improving the Condition of the Poor resolved, "to give no aid to persons who, from infirmity, imbecility, *old age,* or any other cause are likely to continue unable to earn their own support and consequently to be permanently dependent" (italics added). Urban Charity Organization Societies (COSs) took the same position. In 1892, Amos Warner expounded on the hopelessness of work with the aged, "In work with the aged one is conscious that for the individuals dealt with there is no possibility of success" (Haber, p. 40).

So, while COS and other philanthropies were providing rehabilitative and educational services to the young, elderly people were confined to public almshouses. Over time they made up a growing proportion of the almshouse population and so (particularly among charity professionals) age came to be associated with destitution.

In 1902 Homer Folks, New York City's Commissioner of Charities, announced a new name for the city almshouse, the Home for the Aged and Infirm. Folks intended to send the message that the residents of this facility were not the lazy able-bodied, but simply too old or sick to earn a living. In time, institutions like the home came to be seen as the most appropriate setting for needy elders.

As "homes" or "asylums" were populated by the elderly and infirm, they took on a more medical focus. The line between hospital and almshouse blurred and "old age homes" began to employ physicians and nurses, setting the stage for the expansion of facilities we now call nursing homes.

African Americans were generally denied access to these and other public sources of assistance. Using a "self-help" model, "benevolent societies" were organized to provide assistance to needy African Americans. In the antebellum era, African American elders often lived in abject poverty. Benevolent societies were formed, primarily in northern urban communities, to help them in times of need. Society members paid annual dues and in return were given sickness and death benefits. The number of these societies quickly mushroomed. Philadelphia alone had over one hundred societies serving over seven thousand members. During the latter part of the nineteenth century the resources of benevolent societies were strained by the aging of their members. Ultimately they were replaced by insurance firms with greater financial reserves. Nonetheless, the benevolent societies represented a significant resource to meet the needs of elderly African Americans (Pollard).

In sum, the nineteenth century saw an evolution in the treatment of indigent elders. They were initially grouped with other groups of "worthy poor," but over time the elderly came to be distinguished from other indigents. Agencies that focused on the "redeemable poor" gave up on elderly people, reserving their energy and resources for young people with some hope of employment. Needy elderly people increasingly found themselves "warehoused" in institutional settings—precursors of twenty-first-century nursing homes.

Formal services for the elderly consisted primarily of institutional care. Informal arrangements, such as those provided by the benevolent societies, and through churches and families, constituted the primary source of services for needy elders who lived in the community. The twentieth century saw two significant social trends that were to permanently alter patterns of elder care in the United States: the widespread entry of women into paid employment, and the dramatic increase in life expectancy.

Social services to prevent nursing home placement

The twentieth century brought tremendous growth in elderly populations, not only in the United States, but throughout the world. With this growth, the cost of institutional care became a significant burden on public resources in the United States. By mid-century, the idea that social services might prevent nursing home placement contributed to the expansion of public services for older adults.

The most significant and enduring manifestation of this expansion was the Older Americans Act (OAA), signed into law by President Johnson on 14 July 1965. In his remarks upon signing the bill the president suggested the legislation would provide "a coordinated program of services and opportunities for our older citizens." Through partnerships between federal, state, and local authorities, the act established a network of 57 State Offices on Aging and 670 Area Agencies on Aging that today effectively blanket the United States.

Less enduring that the OAA, but equally influential, was the Channeling Demonstration, funded through the Health Care Financing Administration in 1980. The demonstration was implemented in ten states throughout the country to test the notion that services delivered to the frail elderly in the community would reduce nursing home admissions and improve wellbeing. Channeling programs varied somewhat between sites, but case management was a central feature of each. Case management involves the use of a single professional, usually either a social worker or a nurse, to coordinate service delivery for an older adult. Case managers typically conduct detailed need assessments, develop a service plan designed to meet identified needs, then select providers to deliver services and monitor the process.

Programs funded through the Channeling Demonstration did meet the needs of frail elders, and they enhanced the quality of life enjoyed by their clients. But they failed to demonstrate cost-effectiveness by reducing nursing home admissions. The primary reason for this failure was what Kane and Kane referred to as "the problem of shifting targets." Far more frail elderly people live in the community than in nursing homes. Approximately 5 percent of Americans over the age of sixty-five live in nursing homes. Even fewer of the nation's elderly enter a nursing home in any given year. So, while it is possible to identify frail elderly people in need of support, it is difficult to determine who, within this pool, is most likely to enter a nursing home. As a result, services for the frail elderly serve many who would never have entered a nursing home. Thus, social services seldom reduce nursing home admissions. Nonetheless, in testimony to their positive effects on quality of life, the popularity of social services for frail elderly people continues unabated and a wide range of these services are available today.

The range of social services available today

Today professional services are offered under a variety of auspices and for a variety of purposes. Funding sources and eligibility requirements, even within a single organization, can vary tremendously. For example, an agency might provide assistance with several different funding streams, such as the Older Americans Act, the Social Services Block Grant, the Community Development Block Grant, Medicaid, and Medicare. Each of these streams might impose different eligibility requirements and require different program procedures.

The information and outreach program provided through an Area Agency on Aging (AAA) is an excellent starting point in the search for supportive services for an older adult. Under the OAA, all AAAs must provide information and outreach. Every jurisdiction in the United States provides this means of accessing needed services. Area Agencies on Aging may be housed in different types of organizations, such as local or county government, state government, or even nonprofit organizations. AAAs usually contract for services, hiring private or other governmental organizations to deliver assistance to older adults. If no other organization is available, an agency might provide the service directly. AAAs can be located by calling the national hotline (1-800-677-1166) or through the Web site maintained by the U.S. Administration on Aging (www.aoa.dhhs.gov). Eligibility for assistance is based on age. Anyone over sixty years old may access services through the AAA. Some services are restricted to individuals with limited financial resources (Gelfand).

Several of the AAA services are "mandated," in that the agencies are required to spend an adequate proportion of their yearly allocation for them. These include access services, which help people reach the services they need; in-home services; and community services.

Access services include outreach or information and referral programs, as well as transportation programs. The information and referral phone number for the AAA is usually listed in the government section of the phone book. By calling this number, an individual can receive information about both public and private services available in his or her community. Most AAAs provide transportation only for specific purposes, usually medical need. This might involve doctors' appointments or visiting a family member in a nursing home. Some also provide transportation to senior citizen centers and other services such as grocery runs and trips to entertainment.

In-home services consist of homemaker services, home health aides, visiting or telephone reassurance, and chore services. Homemaker services help with light housekeeping tasks, such as vacuuming, dusting, and dishwashing. Home health aides provide personal care and limited health-related care. An aide may help with bathing or dressing, or might check blood pressure. Aides do not perform health-related tasks, such as changing a catheter. Many AAAs provide telephone and personal contacts for elderly persons by using volunteers. These individuals contact older homebound people periodically to see how they are doing and identify pressing needs. In-home services are typically restricted to individuals with limited financial resources, though some agencies offer the services to those with higher incomes using a sliding scale fee system. Chore services help with home maintenance, performing tasks such as clearing rain gutters, minor home repairs, and shoveling snow. Usually eligibility for in-home services is restricted to the financially needy.

Community services include the long-term care ombudsman program, and legal services. Each state employs a professional long-term care ombudsman. Many states also train volunteer ombudsmen. These individuals are charged with advocating on behalf of residents of long-term care facilities. They receive and investigate complaints, and maintain a record of facility compliance. These records, often called "report cards," are usually available for public inspection. Legal services are usually available to people with limited incomes. Through legal services programs lawyers assist with wills and guardianships, but usually not with civil suits or criminal matters.

AAAs may also provide other services, including nutrition programs, socialization programs, protective programs, employment programs, and case management.

Nutrition programs may provide congregate meals in senior centers, and/or home-delivered meals known as Meals on Wheels. Congregate meals usually consist of a lunch, followed by a brief program of education or entertainment. These meals are available to anyone over the age of sixty. Sometimes a small donation is requested. The meals usually provide a menu that is familiar to the majority community, which may not be attractive to cultural and ethnic minorities. Home-delivered meals usually have more restrictive eligibility requirements. In most areas a physician must certify that a person is unable to prepare meals. Generally demand for home-delivered meals exceeds supply. Sometimes a nominal donation is requested. The people who deliver meals can be wonderful resources for older adults. Usually the same driver delivers the meals each day, so he or she can check on a person and secure attention for medical emergencies.

Socialization programs include the Senior Companion program, senior center activities, Foster Grandparents, and Retired Senior Volunteer Program (RSVP). The Senior Companion program provides employment for low-income seniors and help for the homebound elderly. Companions are trained and receive a small stipend for their services. They visit frail, community-living elderly people, providing company for them and respite for their caregivers. Senior centers provide a wide range of activities, including arts and crafts, discussion of current events, dancing, health promotion, and other social activities. These are available for anyone over the age of sixty. They typically reflect the cultural and social interests of the majority population in a community, so members of cultural and ethnic minorities are often under-represented in senior centers. The Foster Grandparent program was established to provide meaningful activities for elderly individuals and assistance to children. Foster grandparents work with children in a variety of settings, including schools, nurseries, Head Start programs, hospitals, and treatment centers. The RSVP program offers additional opportunities for meaningful activities. These volunteers provide services in diverse settings such as hospitals and libraries. The program offers recognition and covers volunteers' expenses.

Protective services investigate reports of elder abuse and neglect and intervene on behalf of the victim. In most states professionals are required by law to report cases of suspected elder abuse, neglect, or exploitation to the protective services agency. Intervention may take the form of family counseling or guardianship proceedings. In some cases the AAA may become a guardian.

Employment services provide training and subsidies for older adults who are seeking employment. Most of these programs are federally funded, and some also have job-development components, with staff who work with corporations and organizations to identify jobs for seniors. The Senior Community Service Employment Program (SCSEP) provides part-time employment to low-income individuals age fifty-five and over. Typically the SCSEP program offers both training and employment in nonprofit and government agencies. Age discrimination in employment is a continuing concern. Individuals who suspect that they have been victims of age discrimination should seek assistance through their AAAs.

Caregiver services were introduced as part of the National Family Caregiver Support Program established under the 2000 amendments to the Older Americans Act. Under the auspices of the U.S. Administration on Aging, this program offers funding for a wide range of services that support family members who provide care to frail elderly people.

In addition to services available through the Area Agencies on Aging, mental health services and housing assistance often prove valuable to older adults.

Housing assistance. Federal housing assistance dates to the New Deal, when public housing was developed for low-income working families. Through incremental changes, the structure of the federal program of low-income housing has evolved. The elderly have been the greatest beneficiaries of that evolution, making up a significant proportion of those served by low-income housing facilities and rent subsidies.

Three major housing programs provide assistance to low-income elderly people; Section 202 of the Housing Act of 1959; Section 8 of the Housing and Community Development Act of 1974, and public housing. Section 202 provides low-interest construction loans to nonprofit sponsors (such as churches and civic organizations) for up to forty years. Once constructed, the Section 202 development is operated by the nonprofit sponsor, with federal oversight. Section 8 offers rent subsidies for low-income families. While some senior households do receive rent subsidies through this program, the vast majority of those in need do not, because need for housing assistance greatly exceeds the supply of rent vouchers. Public housing was developed as part of the New Deal, to house working families with children. Since then the eligible population has changed considerably. The elderly and people with disabilities are frequent residents of public housing, often sharing the same facility.

Housing developments exclusively for the elderly offer a modicum of safety, and a convenient site for the delivery of other kinds of social services. Many communities offer health promotion and other services on site at senior housing facilities.

Mental health services. Mental health services often include counseling and support groups to assist people coping with age-related changes. Growing numbers of older adults have participated in the "self-help" movement by joining support groups. These groups, designed for everyone from the physically ill, to the bereaved, to people suffering from addictions, often provide a sense of comradery and a source of information and advice. Support groups may be operated by a wide range of organizations or agencies, from churches to senior centers. Some are led by a professional, and others by a volunteer.

Older men are usually more reluctant than older women to participate in support groups. Participating in a support group does not match popular notions of masculinity. So, while older women may be comfortable admitting weakness and sharing emotions, older men may resist these activities and deprive themselves of the benefits of a support group. Recruiting and management strategies that are sensitive to the needs and relationship styles of older men can enhance the effectiveness of a support group for this vulnerable population (Kosberg and Kaye).

Accessing social services

Older adults who want to use public social services often encounter a hostile and demanding environment. Many public social services are underfunded, and staffed with professionals who deny services more often than they provide assistance. Older adults can find the regulations and paperwork intimidating and frustrating. Getting satisfactory service from a provider can require persistence and assertiveness. Indeed, older adults frequently benefit from having a family member or friend serve as their advocate as they seek assistance.

Before contacting an agency, it helps to spend some time thinking about the problem and what might be done to address it. In addition to a written description of the problem, older adults may want to collect the following information before contacting a potential service provider: Their latest tax return, or other information about income and assets; the potential client's age, medical diagnoses, and functional abilities; a list of family members and friends who can provide assistance; and times and dates when they are available for an appointment.

It is rare to find the right service provider upon first contact, so it is best to begin the search for service by phone rather than in person. The caller is advised to keep a log of contacts, as the first person or agency contacted may not be the right one. The log should include the name and title of each person contacted, the date of the contact, and what the person said. This will prevent the famous "runaround," in which providers focus more on referring an older adult to other providers than on what their own organizations might be able to do to help.

Most of the publicly funded services available through AAAs can be purchased in the private market. The classified sections of newspapers in any major city will reveal individuals who offer their services to care for elderly people. The dilemma, for families who have the means to purchase assistance on their own, is how to select a qualified provider. Here, too, the AAA can be of assistance. Many information and referral programs maintain files of private providers who have been screened by agency staff. Other agencies, such as visiting nurse services and hospice organizations, might also be able to provide a list of providers who have been screened. Regardless of the source of the referral, individuals purchasing care through private sources must be vigilant to prevent the abuse or exploitation of their elderly loved ones.

The relationship between social services and family care

The family is widely seen as an elderly person's first line of defense against the risks associated with advanced age. Family members provide a tremendous amount of care for older Americans, a situation that both the elderly and their families generally prefer over professional care. Given the importance of family care, and the high cost of professional services, policymakers and researchers in the field have been concerned about the possibility that public social services might replace family care.

Numerous studies have demonstrated that social services do not replace family care. Indeed, professional assistance may even enhance a family's ability to provide care. Respite care is probably the best example of this. When family caregivers have access to respite care they often report being able to give more and better care to their loved ones. Similar results have been obtained with case management, personal care, and homemaker services. Despite the lack of evidence that services displace family care, this concern arises frequently when funding for social services is up for debate.

The future of social services for the elderly

Targeting of public social services has become a source of tension in recent decades. The Older Americans Act requires that services be made available to all older Americans, regardless of their income or assets. Yet today's elderly are, on average, considerably more affluent than the aged were in 1965 when the act passed. As a result, OAA services often benefit elders who are middle-class members of the cultural majority. The recipients of programs funded under the act may not be those most in need of assistance (Barusch).

Congregate meals programs have been criticized as failing to serve cultural minorities and frail elders. The climate in most senior centers reflects the majority culture in the area. While not overtly hostile to cultural minorities, the activities, food, and atmosphere are often not familiar or welcoming. As a result, those most likely to use senior centers are typically of the majority culture. Similarly frail elders, those most in need of assistance to maintain their independence, are unable to participate in congregate meals. Yet congregate meals programs are popular, and have consistently been one of the AAA's biggest budget items.

In response to this tension, the 1987 amendments to the Older Americans Act added Section 305 of Title III to require that states, "E) Provide assurances that preference will be given to providing services to older individuals with the *greatest economic or social need, with particular attention to low-income minority individuals. . .*" (italics added). Subsequent appropriations have revealed an increased emphasis on cultural minorities and vulnerable individuals. So, for example, funding for home-delivered meals constituted a much greater proportion of OAA spending in the late 1990s than it had prior to the amendment. Similarly, allocations for Native American tribes increased dramatically. Programs serving frail and vulnerable elders were also initiated, including in-home and protective services and caregiver support.

As the population of America's elderly citizens grows, it becomes more diverse. There are more women, more cultural minorities, and more extremely old, frail people. The challenge for publicly funded social services will be to maintain a strong constituency that will support their continuation, even as they target services toward the very needy—those least likely to have a voice in the political arena.

This illustrates a fundamental tension inherent in the delivery of publicly financed social services. When public resources are scarce, there is a compelling argument in favor of targeting these services toward the most needy. Yet those most in need are least likely to provide political support when funding is up for debate. A program that benefits only low-income, homebound elders is likely to have few supporters at its budget review. Social services for the elderly must demonstrate their effectiveness—not only at reducing suffering of the vulnerable—but at enhancing the quality of life for the politically active.

AMANDA SMITH BARUSCH

See also ADULT DAY CARE; CASE MANAGEMENT; CONGREGATE AND HOME-DELIVERED MEALS; HOUSING; MENTAL HEALTH SERVICES; OLDER AMERICANS ACT; PERSONAL CARE; SOCIAL WORK.

BIBLIOGRAPHY

BARUSCH, A. S. "The Elderly." In *Foundations of Social Policy: Social Justice, Public Programs, and the Social Work Profession.* Chicago: F. E. Peacock, 2002. Pages 266–300.

GELFAND, D. E. *The Aging Network: Programs and Services,* 5th ed. New York: Springer, 1998.

HABER, C. *Beyond Sixty-Five: The Dilemma of Old Age in America's Past.* Cambridge, U.K.: Cambridge University Press, 1983.

KANE, R., and KANE, R. A. "Alternatives to Institutional Care of the Elderly: Beyond the Dichotomy." *The Gerontologist* 20, (1980): 249–259.

KOSBERG, J. I., and KAYE, L. W., eds. *Elderly Men: Special Problems and Professional Challenges.* New York: Springer, 1997.

POLLARD, L. J. "Black Beneficial Societies and the Home for Aged and Infirm Colored Persons: A Research Note." *Phylon* 41, no. 3 (Sept. 1980): 230–234.

SOCIAL SUPPORT

Research on social support and social relationships among older adults—and their correlates and consequences—is voluminous and growing. The beneficial effect of social support on individual well-being is one of the most consistent findings in this literature. In summarizing the importance of social relations to successful aging, John W. Rowe and Robert L. Kahn (1998) drew four conclusions:

- A lack of social ties is a risk factor for poor health
- Social support in various forms can have direct positive effects on health
- Receipt of social support can buffer some of the negative effects of health declines associated with aging
- The type of social support found to be effective varies by individual needs and situations

Conceptualizing social support and social integration

Although sometimes used interchangeably with terms such as *social integration, social networks,* or *social relationships,* a narrower definition of *social support* is also common. In that narrower usage, *social support* refers to social interaction in which the actions of one party are intended to benefit another party. Thus, though social support may be seen as one aspect of other, broader terms, it is differentiated in part by its focus on the provider's intentions and the potential benefits to the recipient.

No clear consensus exists regarding definitions of the other descriptors of social interaction, but, in general, the following distinctions are made. *Social integration* denotes the existence, quantity, and/or breadth of social ties. Synonyms are *social connectedness* and *social embeddedness*. A lack of social integration has been labeled *social isolation. Social network* refers to the entire structure of an individual's social relationships and the connections among them. A network may be described in multiple ways, such as its homogeneity (similarity among members) or density (ties among all members). *Social relationships* and *social ties* are broad, general terms that refer to an individual's connections to others.

While social integration, social isolation, and social networks primarily refer to the structure of an individual's relationships, the concept of social support is used to denote possible functions of those relationships. Much of the research examining the association of social relationships to well-being has been limited to measures of social integration or isolation. In interpreting the usually positive effects of integration on well-being, some researchers have suggested that integration is, in part, a proxy for social support. Thus, it is necessary to discuss social integration and social isolation in conjunction with social support. Although social support specifically focuses on the positive side of social interaction, the other terms (integration, networks, and relationships) include consideration of the negative side of interaction (e.g., conflict or excessive demands). Research on the potential costs of social relationships is more limited and is not addressed here.

Measures of social integration capture information about the quantity and variety of social ties maintained by an individual. To assess quantity of ties, seniors may be asked how many people they interact with on a regular basis or how many people to whom they feel close ties. Variety of ties addresses how many different social roles an individual occupies, including spouse, parent, grandparent, sibling, friend, neighbor, employee, volunteer, church member, organization member, and others.

Possible functions of relationships are also identified in measures of social support. As noted, the provision of social support in a relationship refers to actions taken by one party to assist or benefit another party. Several aspects of the interaction may be of interest, including:

- The type of support provided
- The quantity, timing, and/or frequency of support provided
- Whether the support was actually received or simply is perceived as available
- The recipient's satisfaction with the level of support provided or available
- The relationship between the parties involved
- Whether or not the support has been or will be reciprocated

The types of social support fall into five general categories. *Instrumental support* refers to tangible items, such as financial assistance, goods, or services. For example, a disabled older person may receive meals or help with housework. To quantify instrumental support, studies have collected data on the dollar value of money or goods transferred and on hours of time given in services during a given time period. A simpler approach is to ask whether or not the amount transferred within the time period exceeded a specific level (e.g., $200 in the past twelve months). *Emotional support* includes provision of love, caring, sympathy, and other positive feelings. *Appraisal support* includes feedback given to individuals to assist them in self-evaluation or in appraising a situation. *Informational support* refers to helpful advice, information, and suggestions. For example, a senior may ask a friend's opinion regarding which doctor to see. *Companionship support* refers to the presence of others with whom to participate in meaningful or enjoyable activities. Companionship is considered to provide the individual with a sense of belonging to a group. Differentiating among the intangible types of support (emotional, appraisal, informational, and companionship) can be difficult, as can quantifying the level of support provided. Collection of information typically is limited to whether or not the specific type of support was provided during the specified time period and, perhaps, the frequency with which the support was provided.

Some researchers have suggested that the quantity of support received is less important to well-being than the individual's perception that support is available if needed. This distinction between received and perceived support has proven valuable in clarifying how social relations influence well-being. Received support appears to be more important in the face of specific problems or stressors, whereas perceived support seems to be of ongoing benefit. Measures of perceived support include questions regarding whether or not the senior has someone in whom to confide, someone to provide emotional support, or someone to provide caregiving should the need arise.

The relationship between the support provider and recipient is also relevant, as suggested by some popular gerontological models. In 1979, Marjorie Cantor proposed the *hierarchical compensatory model*, in which older individuals exhibit a hierarchy of preferences regarding who should provide support. A spouse typically is the first choice, followed by adult children; other kin, friends, and neighbors; and, finally, formal service providers. Who actually provides support to an older person needing assistance depends upon the availability, proximity, and emotional closeness of individuals in the person's network, as well as on cultural norms.

Another important determinant is the older person's level and types of needs; the more disabled an older person is, the more likely he or she is to rely on formal providers, particularly for instrumental support. The *task-specific model*, developed by Eugene Litwak (1985), takes account of both the older individual's specific needs and the characteristics of the potential helpers. The model posits that the group or person most likely to be preferred as a support provider will be the one best suited to manage the necessary tasks. The model matches tasks to providers according to the following structural dimensions: proximity, length of commitment, commonality of lifestyle, group size, sources of motivation, division of labor, and level of technical knowledge. Litwak and colleagues have argued that the hierarchical-compensatory model is simply a special case of the task-specific model.

The hierarchical-compensatory model and the task-specific model primarily focus on provision of instrumental support and emphasize the distinction between informal and formal care. Informal care is defined as unpaid assistance provided to needy seniors. Family, friends, and neighbors represent informal sources of care and often provide aid with such tasks as light housekeeping, food shopping, meal preparation, and transportation. Formal sources of care include a range of services, from Meals-on-Wheels to home health care visitors, from adult day care to nursing home care. The more disabled an older person becomes, the more likely he or she is to rely on formal care providers.

The *convoy model of social relations,* proposed by Robert L. Kahn and Toni C. Antonucci, offers a broader view of social ties in old age. This model also incorporates the notion of a hierarchy of relationships in personal networks, but it bases this hierarchy on emotional closeness. The convoy model uses a life-span perspective; thus the focus on convoys as opposed to networks. The concept of the convoy captures the dynamic aspects of social ties, taking account of qualitative changes at the level of the individual, the dyad, and the network, as well as changes in network membership. Cause-and-effect relations are also an important part of the model. Because relationships unfold over time, past interactions influence future interactions. For example, past receipt of emotional support from a friend will predispose an individual to assist that friend in the future. Reciprocity in relations is viewed as the ideal and is positively related to well-being.

Benefits of social support and social integration

Rowe and Kahn identify active engagement with life as one of the key components of successful aging, along with avoiding disease and maintaining high cognitive and physical function. They view these three components as intertwined, with high performance in any one area enabling higher performance in the others. Research on the benefits of social support and social integration suggests that social relationships can contribute to all three components.

John Cassel and Sidney Cobb have been credited with stimulating the flood of research on social support and health that began in the 1970s. In separate review articles, both men argued that social relationships appeared to be protective of health. The early evidence, however, primarily was cross-sectional, and thus unable to establish causation. It was unclear whether strong social ties protect health (social causation hypothesis), or whether individuals in poor health are unable to maintain strong social ties (social selection hypothesis).

In the late 1970s and early 1980s, prospective mortality studies from several community epidemiologic surveys were published and provided evidence for the social causation hypothesis. James House and colleagues reviewed this evidence in a 1988 *Science* magazine article. They concluded that low levels of social integration represented a "cause or risk factor of mortality, and probably morbidity, from a wide range of diseases."

Subsequent research has replicated and expanded on these findings by examining a variety of health outcomes in different populations. Further, researchers have attempted to elucidate the mechanisms linking social ties and health by developing more sophisticated measures of social relationships and testing more elaborate models.

The vast amount of research conducted on the relationship between social relationships and health in middle and old age has produced some mixed results, but it is possible to draw some generalizations.

Mortality. Low levels of social integration place individuals at higher mortality risk. Researchers have considered whether this relationship represents a threshold or gradient effect. In other words, is there a minimum number of social ties necessary to receive the health benefit (threshold effect)? Or, does the risk of mortality lessen with each increase in the number of ties (gradient effect)? Some evidence supports the threshold model, but the issue is not resolved. Fewer mortality studies have examined specific measures of social support, but there is limited evidence of an association between support and mortality.

Onset of physical disease. Few studies have produced evidence of an influence of social integration or social support on the development of physical disease.

Progression of and recovery from physical disease. Receipt of emotional support (and perhaps other forms of intangible support) contributes to physical health by slowing the progression of chronic disease and aiding in recovery from other physical ailments. Studies have examined conditions such as post–myocardial infarction, stroke, arthritis, different cancers, hip fractures, and extremity injuries from falls.

Emotional or mental health. Both social integration and social support are important for the maintenance of emotional health. Low levels of integration and support place seniors at heightened risk for depression, anxiety, and psychological distress. Social isolation and lack of emotional support are particularly strong predictors of emotional health problems. Perceived quality of life and positive affect are enhanced by social integration and reciprocal support networks.

Functional health Various aspects of social integration reduce the risks of developing physical disabilities (difficulty performing activities of daily living) and experiencing cognitive declines.

Why do social integration and social support promote health? Despite the vast number of studies, there is no clear answer to this question. The diversity of findings suggest, however, that there are several different mechanisms. The operative mechanism likely depends on the characteristics of the individual, his or her social situation, and the health condition of interest. Proposed mechanisms include the following:

- Provision of health-enhancing material resources and services
- Reduction of the perceived severity of stressors
- Reduction in the occurrence of stressors
- Improved coping skills and assistance with coping

- Promotion of positive health behaviors (social control or social influence model)
- Increased social bonding and attachment
- Stronger sense of coherence and self-esteem

Differentials in social support and social integration

One stereotype of old age says that it is a time of loneliness and isolation, a time characterized by the loss of social ties when adult children leave home, seniors retire, and peers and spouses die. Although this portrait is certainly true for some older people, the majority of seniors appear to keep active social ties. Rowe and Kahn invoke the concept of *convoys of social support* to describe the way in which individuals maintain supportive networks into old age. Whereas seniors do experience losses to their networks over time, they replace many losses with new ties. In fact, network size appears to be fairly stable across the life course, with, on average, eight to eleven members in personal networks. Compared to the networks of younger adults, seniors' networks tend to include more kin and, perhaps, be less proximate. Thus, the number of close social ties declines only modestly with age, while the types of ties change.

This picture of the typical senior, however, can mask important variations in social support and integration. The structure and function of social ties appears to vary by gender, marital status, race and ethnicity, socioeconomic status, and residence in rural, urban, or suburban areas.

Gender differences in social support and social integration have been one of the most consistent research findings. In general, women have markedly higher levels of social interaction than do men. Women provide and receive more social support, exchange a greater variety of types of support, and have larger numbers of social ties. Men, however, may benefit more than women from the support they receive. In other words, the health benefits of social ties appear to be greater for older men than for older women. Support provided through the marital relationship seems to be an important part of this gender difference. Older women are more likely to be widowed, and thus without the emotional support of a spouse. Further, however, men receive more health benefits from marital support than do women.

Evidence regarding racial and ethnic group differentials in social ties is mixed. Seniors from all groups tend to maintain active networks, both giving and receiving support. Most seniors also benefit from frequent involvement with church and family. The composition of social networks, however, differs across groups. Compared to white seniors, African Americans and Mexican Americans include more extended family members in their personal networks. Minority seniors are also more likely to rely exclusively on family members and close friends for instrumental assistance, whereas older whites use more formal support providers.

Knowledge about social network differences across socioeconomic status (SES) groups is limited. In general, evidence suggests that higher-SES individuals have more support available, provide more support, and include more friends in their networks. Providing emotional support to others has been associated with higher self-esteem—with the association being strongest for upper-SES seniors. Group differences in involvement with family are minimal. It is not clear to what extent SES differences in social ties are confounded with racial and ethnic group differences.

Place of residence also has some influence on social ties. Elderly urban-dwellers are more likely to use formal care providers and have more diverse personal networks than rural seniors. In contrast, older rural residents report a higher proportion of family members in their networks. Older residents of poor and deteriorating urban neighborhoods have smaller networks and less emotional support. Differences in availability of contacts and support may explain some of these differences.

LAURA RUDKIN
IVONNE-MARIE INDRIKOVS

See also CAREGIVING, INFORMAL; FAMILY; FRIENDSHIP; HEALTH, SOCIAL FACTORS; RELIGION; SIBLING RELATIONSHIPS.

BIBLIOGRAPHY

ANGEL, R. J., and ANGEL, J. L. *Who Will Care for Us? Aging and Long-Term Care in Multicultural America.* New York: New York University Press, 1997.

ANTONUCCI, T. C., and AKIYAMA, H. "Social Support and the Maintenance of Competence." In *Societal Mechanisms for Maintaining Competence in Old Age.* Edited by S. L. Willis, K. W. Schaie, and M. Hayward. New York: Springer Publishing, 1997. Pages 182–206.

BERKMAN, L. F. "The Role of Social Relations in Health Promotion." *Psychosomatic Medicine* 57(1995): 245–254.

BERKMAN, L. F., and GLASS, T. "Social Integration, Social Networks, Social Support, and Health." In *Social Epidemiology.* Edited by L. F. Berkman and I. Kawachi. New York: Oxford University Press, 2000. Pages 137–173.

BERKMAN, L. F.; GLASS, T.; BRISSETTE, I.; and SEEMAN, T. E. "From Social Integration to Health: Durkheim in the New Millenium." *Social Science & Medicine* 51 (2000): 843–857.

BOWLING, A. *Measuring Health: A Review of Quality of Life Measurement Scales,* 2d ed. Philadelphia: Open University Press, 1997.

CANTOR, M. H. "Neighbors and Friends: An Overlooked Resource in the Informal Support System." *Research on Aging* 1 (1979): 434–463.

COHEN, S.; UNDERWOOD, L. G.; and GOTTLIEB, B. *Social Support Measurement and Intervention: A Guide for Health and Social Scientists.* New York: Oxford University Press, 2000.

COHEN, S., and WILLS, T. A. "Stress, Social Support, and the Buffering Hypothesis." *Psychological Bulletin* 98 (1985): 310–357.

HEANEY, C. A., and ISRAEL, B. A. "Social Networks and Social Support." In *Health Behavior and Health Education: Theory, Research, and Practice,* 2d ed. Edited by K. Glanz, F. M. Lewis, and B. K. Rimer. San Francisco: Jossey-Bass Publishers, 1997. Pages 179–205.

HOUSE, J. S.; LANDIS, K. R.; and UMBERSON, D. "Social Relationships and Health." *Science* 241 (1988): 540–545.

HOUSE, J. S.; UMBERSON, D.; and LANDIS, K. R. "Structures and Processes of Social Support." *Annual Review of Sociology* 14 (1988): 293–318.

KRAUSE, N. "Issues of Measurement and Analysis in Studies of Social Support, Aging and Health." In *Aging, Stress, and Health.* Edited by K. S. Markides and C. L. Cooper. New York: John Wiley & Sons, 1989. Pages 43–66.

LITWAK, E. *Helping the Elderly: The Complementary Roles of Informal Networks and Formal Systems.* New York: The Guilford Press, 1985.

McDOWELL, I., and NEWELL, C. *Measuring Health: A Guide to Ratings Scales and Questionnaires,* 2nd ed. New York: Oxford University Press, 1996.

MESSERI, P.; SILVERSTEIN, M.; and LITWAK, E. "Choosing Optimal Support Groups: A Review and Reformulation." *Journal of Health and Social Behavior* 34 (1993): 122–137.

PILLEMER, K.; MOEN, P.; WETHINGTON, E.; and GLASGOW, N. *Social Integration in the Second Half of Life.* Baltimore: Johns Hopkins University Press, 2000.

Rowe, J. W., and Kahn, R.L. *Successful Aging*. New York: Pantheon Books, 1998.

Seeman, T. E. "How Do Others Get under Our Skin? Social Relationships and Health." In *Emotion, Social Relationships, and Health*. Edited by C. D. Ryff and Burton H. Singer. New York: Oxford University Press, 2001. Pages 189–210.

Seeman, T. E. "Social Ties and Health: The Benefits of Social Integration." *Annals of Epidemiology* 6 (1996): 442–451.

Wills, T. A., and Fegan, M. F. "Social Networks and Social Support." In *Health Psychology*. Edited by A. Baum, T. A. Revenson, and J. E. Singer. Mahwah, N.J.: Lawrence Erlbaum Associates, 2001. Pages 209–234.

SOCIAL WORK

While many medical and social advances have resulted in longer lives, older adults often find themselves coping with multiple health problems that affect their quality of life. It is in this context that the role of the social worker becomes paramount. The main focus of a gerontological social worker is to maintain and enhance the quality of life of older adults and their families. Gerontological social workers often find themselves members of an interdisciplinary team composed of several health care professionals who must collaborate and communicate with each other in order to achieve the best possible outcome for the older adult (Linderman and Mellor).

Role of social work

Though the role of the social worker can vary from one team to another, several key tasks are essential for the gerontological social worker who is a member of an interdisciplinary team. The first is that of diagnosis and assessment. Here the social worker determines how the older adult and his or her family are functioning in physical, psychological, social, cultural, environmental, and spiritual areas. This will provide a holistic view of the persons involved. The second task is individual and group counseling, a very broad and diverse domain, the main focus of which is to help the older adult and his or her family adjust to major stressors and changes in their lives as a result of illness or various losses. The third task is advocacy. Older adults often find themselves having to deal with a variety of overwhelming systems. The social worker can help by acting on their behalf or teaching them ways to navigate these systems. The fourth task is acting as a liaison. This is vital when there is an interdisciplinary team involved. It can become confusing for the older adult and his or her family when several professionals are trying to obtain information. Having the social worker as a liaison with the various professionals is vital.

The fifth task is to serve as a community resource expert. The knowledge of community resources and how to access them is one of the most valuable skills of any social worker, but even more so for those who work with older adults. When there are multiple problems, there generally are multiple systems to deal with. Therefore having an individual who is familiar with these systems is indeed an asset. The final task is the coordination of care, which is both particularly important and very time-consuming. Many aspects of care are being communicated by various team members, and many agencies have actual or potential roles in the provision of care. Thus things can become very confusing unless someone takes on the role of coordinator.

The caregiver

Families often play an essential role in providing care to older adults. It is estimated that between 70 and 80 percent of the help received by older adults in the community is provided by family members (Cox et al.). This figure undermines the myth of family abandonment that arises from stories of families who leave an elderly member at the emergency department and then refuse to take that person home. With the financial restraints that the U.S. health care system is facing at the beginning of the twenty-first century, the number of older adults requiring families to provide their care is expected to grow. Social workers are concerned not only with the older adult but also with the family or caregiver, because it is essential that the family be included in all aspects of care planning.

Support for the caregiver

As with most roles in life, there are both positive and negative aspects to being a caregiver to an older adult. Caregivers struggle to balance the personal, physical, and emotional aspects of caregiving, as well as their other roles and responsibilities. It is not surprising that many feel overwhelmed and stressed. This phenomenon is generally referred to as caregiver burden. Social workers play a key role in monitoring for signs of caregiver burden and helping families learn to cope with and prevent increased stress levels. It is important for social workers to maintain regular contact with the caregiver in order to assess for increased stress levels. Administrating surveys or questionnaires that are designed to measure caregiver burden can be helpful in this regard. Though assessment skills are clearly important, another necessary skill is being a good listener. Being able to discuss concerns with someone who is genuinely concerned and willing to listen can be therapeutic in and of itself. Caregivers report that talking to others who are going through similar experiences can also be helpful. Therefore, social workers often connect caregivers with support groups. Work with caregivers and review of the literature on caregiving, make it evident that one of the most important ways to support caregivers is to ensure that they have adequate time away from their caregiving roles. This supplemental care is often referred to as respite care. Social workers work with the caregivers to ensure that adequate respite care is in place through either formal or informal systems.

DOROTHY WAMBOLT

See also ASSESSMENT; CAREGIVING, INFORMAL; CASE MANAGEMENT; FRAILTY; FUNCTIONAL ABILITY; HOME CARE AND HOME SERVICES; MULTIDISCIPLINARY TEAM; SOCIAL SERVICES.

BIBLIOGRAPHY

COX, E.; PARSONS, R.; and KIMBOKO, P. "Social Services and Intergenerational Caregivers: Issues for Social Work." *Social Work* (September–October 1988).
LINDERMAN, D., and MELLOR, J. "The Distinctive Role of Gerontological Social Work." *Continuum* 19, no. 1 (1999): 1–3.
MCCALLION, P.; TOSELAND, R.; and DIEHI, M. "Social Work Practice with Caregivers of Frail Older Adults." *Research on Social Work Practice* 4, no. 1 (1994): 64–88.
WALKER, A.; MARTIN, S.; and JONES, L. "The Benefits and Costs of Caregiving and Care Receiving for Daughters and Mothers." *Journal of Gerontology* 47, no. 3 (1992): S130—S139.
Work Interest Group of the Hartford Geriatric Interdisciplinary Team Training Program. "The Role of the Social Worker in Interdisciplinary Geriatric Teams. *Continuum* 19, no. 1 (1999): 4–6

A elderly Muslim vendor sells shoes at an outdoor marketplace in Pakistan. (Photo by Mr. Cory Langley.)

SOUTH ASIA

South Asia is the region approximately encompassed in the Indian subcontinent. It includes the modern nations of Bangladesh, India, Nepal, Pakistan, and Sri Lanka. Though these countries are very diverse in religion, language, customs, food, dress, political systems, and other details, they share broad historical and cultural similarities.

Trends in population aging

Until recently most South Asian populations were marked by high fertility and mortality, and therefore a younger age structure. In the 1950s fertility across South Asia was uniformly high (see Table 1). By 2000 Sri Lanka, India, and Bangladesh had markedly lower fertility. By 2050 all countries are projected to reach replacement level fertility. The decrease in mortality is reflected in increasing life expectancy at birth, with Sri Lanka in the lead. In the 1950s the South Asian countries under consideration had shorter life spans for women than for men (contrary to global mortality norms), for a variety of reasons ranging from discrimination against girl children to

Table 1

Fertility and Mortality Indicators for Asian Countries 1950–2050

Total Fertility Rate

		1950–1955	2000–2005	2045–2050
Bangladesh		6.7	2.9	2.1
India		6.0	2.7	2.1
Pakistan		6.5	4.5	2.1
Sri Lanka		5.7	2.1	2.1

Expectation of Life at Birth (years)

Bangladesh	Male	38.3	60.6	73.2
	Female	34.9	60.8	73.6
India	Male	39.4	63.4	73.1
	Female	38.0	64.8	76.9
Pakistan	Male	40.1	64.9	74.8
	Female	37.6	67.4	78.8
Sri Lanka	Male	57.6	70.9	77.6
	Female	55.5	75.4	82.5

SOURCE: United Nations, 1998

Table 2

Number and Proportion of the Elderly in South Asian Countries 1950–2050

Elderly Population (in millions)

	1950	2000	2025	2050
Bangladesh	1.50	4.23	10.43	29.26
India	11.79	50.33	111.73	232.97
Pakistan	2.09	4.84	14.30	36.81
Sri Lanka	0.29	1.13	2.85	5.24

% of Elderly 65 Years and Above in Total Population

Bangladesh	3.6	3.3	5.8	13.4
India	3.3	5.0	8.4	15.2
Pakistan	5.3	3.1	5.3	10.3
Sri Lanka	3.9	6.0	11.9	19.4

SOURCE: United Nations, 1998

high maternal mortality rates. By 2000 female life expectancy at birth equaled or exceeded that of males in the countries being studied, except Nepal, reflecting amelioration of the female mortality disadvantage.

Concerns regarding the aging population are therefore coming to the forefront in South Asia, though they have been less documented and explored there than in other parts of the world where population aging has advanced further.

South Asian aging in regional perspective. Asia currently accounts for approximately 6 percent of the global elderly population (those age sixty-five and above). However, the proportion of old varies across its regions. In 2000 in East Asia, almost 8 percent of the population was age sixty-five and over. South Asia, Southeast Asia, and West Asia each had approximately 5 percent. In 2050 the figures are expected to be one in five in East Asia, one in seven in South Asia and Southeast Asia, and one in eight in West Asia (United Nations, 1998).

From 2000 on, India is expected to have the greatest absolute number of elderly persons, and in South Asia the highest proportion of seniors is projected to be in Sri Lanka (see Table 2).

Measures of population aging. The median age (the age that divides the population into equal halves) also illustrates the changing age structure of a population. The median age in the countries being considered will rise into the thirties by 2050 (see Table 3).

Living arrangements

Familial coresidence remains the norm for most seniors in South Asia. The availability of extrafamilial facilities for elderly persons is minimal, and social norms strongly favor familial coresidence and care. Variations in family and kinship structures in South Asia thus illustrate living arrangements and support for seniors.

Broadly speaking, South Asian kinship systems range from exogamous, patrilineal, and patrilocal systems in the northern half of the subcontinent, to endogamous, matrilineal, and matrilocal systems in many groups in southern India and Sri Lanka. These diverse systems all imply coresidence in joint family groups, but have different implications for elderly men and women. For example, under patrilineal/patrilocal systems, elderly men, as the senior male in the household, can expect lifelong residential support and care, usually from married sons. However, such support is not universal, varying by socioeconomic status, landholding, presence of spouse, and number of surviving sons. Elderly women, particularly widows with no son, are more vulnerable under patrilineal/patrilocal systems. While women have varying inheritance and property rights, in practice these are dependent upon the goodwill of male kin

Table 3

Median Ages in South Asian Countries, 2000 and 2050

	Median Age	
	2000	**2050**
Bangladesh	20.4	36.9
India	24.0	38.3
Pakistan	19.0	34.3
Sri Lanka	27.4	39.3

SOURCE: United Nations, 1998

(Agarwal). The desire to bear several sons, in order to ensure that at least one will survive to adulthood and provide old-age care, underpins the persistent high fertility in South Asia.

Elderly women in groups that practiced matrilineal inheritance/matrilocal residence usually enjoyed considerable old-age security, because they resided with their married daughters and property was inherited in the female line. However, social and legal changes in the twentieth century dismantled these arrangements and introduced patrilineal inheritance and nuclear residence patterns. This has manifested in the hitherto unheard-of phenomenon of destitute elderly women in the state of Kerala in southwestern India, a region usually noted for the high status of women.

Before longevity increased, there was comparatively less chance that a husband and wife would survive to see all their grandchildren. Now people live longer on average, which implies a prolonged period of multigenerational family life. Declining fertility means fewer descendants to provide support. Other important changes influencing the living conditions of seniors include geographical mobility of the working-age population, increasing numbers of women working outside the household, and a greater move toward the nuclear family with emphasis on providing for children's nurture, education, and careers. Working-age adults with young children and elderly parents thus encounter increasing difficulties. They face economic hardship when allocating resources between support of their elderly relatives and financing of their own advancement and the education of their children, and all generations face psychological stress. Where the working-age generation has migrated for employment, financial hard-

ships may decrease, but at the cost of loneliness or isolation of the seniors.

One study in southern India (Irudaya Rajan et al.) suggests that only 46 percent of elders (and only 25 percent of female elders) who stated a preference to stay with their children during old age were actually able to do so. Indian National Sample Survey data for 1991 show that elderly persons express an increasing preference over time to stay in old age homes. The number of old age homes in India increased from 29 before 1901 to 329 after 1976; 57 percent of them were located in southern India. These facilities are far fewer than the number needed to meet the potential demand.

Widowhood. South Asian women are more at risk of widowhood than men, partly because of early and nearly universal marriage of younger women to older men. Though until recently the life expectancy at birth was lower for most South Asian women than for men, the risk of widowhood still remains substantially higher for women, and life expectancy is projected to increase more for women. This means that many more women than men will be widowed, for several years, in these populations. There are region-, religion-, and caste-based restrictions on widow remarriage, ranging from enforced leviratic unions to bans on remarriage. Widowed men usually do not face these restrictions.

There appear to be broad similarities in the socioeconomic situation of widows in Pakistan, northern India, and Bangladesh. Widows in northern India suffer from economic deprivation, social isolation, and higher morbidity and mortality rates, compared with married women in the same age groups (Chen and Dreze).

Increasing age brings the growing risk of widowhood and of female household headship, though the proportion of female-headed households in South Asia is much lower than elsewhere in Asia. Forty-seven percent of the widows in one study resided in households headed by themselves (Chen and Dreze). Evidence for Bangladesh suggests that 12 percent of widows lived alone (Chen and Dreze). Members of female-headed households are more at risk of poverty because of the absence of a male earner. Men usually hold the titles to productive assets, command higher wages than women, and are more likely to be economically active. Female-headed households tend to be smaller but have a higher proportion of dependents than households

Table 4
Work Participation Rate Among the Elderly

	1995	2000
Bangladesh	48.7	46.6
India	33.5	32.1
Pakistan	31.6	30.1
Sri Lanka	17.2	15.6

SOURCE: International Labor Office, 2000

Table 5
Males Per 100 Females in Populations Age 65-Plus in South Asia, 2000 and 2025

	2000	2025
Bangladesh	117.5	102.9
India	103.4	94.4
Pakistan	97.2	84.1
Sri Lanka	92.9	72.2

SOURCE: U.S. Bureau of the Census, International Database

headed by males. Members of such households are less likely to be beneficiaries of government programs designed to help the poor (United Nations, 1994).

Economic status and retirement patterns

In most South Asian countries only the very small proportion of the population that belongs to the salaried class (overwhelmingly urban and male) has access to pensions and social security after retirement. In many cases widows can draw a deceased husband's pension. Rural women in particular are often not aware of their entitlements or are not easily able to keep track of the rules and regulations that govern their receipt. The bulk of the population depends on familial support or personal savings, or simply keeps working as long as possible. The formal age of retirement for the salaried class in most South Asian countries ranges from fifty-five to sixty years. Nevertheless, work participation among those age sixty-five and above for the South Asian countries being studied (except Sri Lanka) is high, ranging from almost one-third to almost one-half, and is projected to decline very little by 2050 (see Table 4).

Pension and social security programs in South Asia. Old age pensions and other forms of social security are less developed programs in most of South Asia. As the population ages, the issue of financing social security will grow more pressing. In 1989 social security expenditures accounted, on average, for approximately 0.9 percent of gross domestic product in Bangladesh, India, Pakistan, and Sri Lanka; by 1992 the average had increased to 1.6 percent. For instance, the percentage was 1.8 for India and 4.7 percent for Sri Lanka (International Labour Office).

Sex ratios in the elderly population

The male-dominant sex ratios in the age group above sixty-five in some South Asian countries are counter to the global norm of female-dominant sex ratios among older age groups. Male-dominant sex ratios were observed in 2000 for those age sixty-five and above in Bangladesh and India (see Table 5). This indicates a cumulative female mortality disadvantage over the life course, though age-specific death rates are higher for men than for women in India after about age thirty-five. Nepal, Pakistan and Sri Lanka exhibit "normal" female-dominant sex ratios among the elderly age group. By 2025 only Bangladesh is projected to have a male-dominant ratio. Other countries' ratios are expected to decline steeply (plunging to 72.2 in Sri Lanka), reflecting amelioration of the female mortality disadvantage.

Emerging health concerns

Increasing longevity implies a rising burden of degenerative disease that characterizes an elderly population, but health care systems across most of South Asia are designed to cope with infectious disease control and maternal/child health issues that face a younger population. Preventive or palliative care for chronic conditions among elders is lacking. The concept of "healthy aging" has yet to be widely accepted. Individuals expect to "suffer various aches and pains" as they grow older, and may not seek treatment for even quite serious conditions. Health practitioners also tend to view chronic conditions as a natural consequence of aging rather than as diseases to be prevented or treated.

Above age thirty-five, Indian men have significantly shorter life expectancies than women, and the age-specific death rates are about twice those for women above thirty-five (review in Basu). High levels of adult male mortality may be partly attributed to tuberculosis and to aggravating lifestyle factors, such as tobacco and alcohol consumption. Increasing rates of cardiovascular disease can also be attributed to lifestyle factors. For women, increasing rates of cervical and breast cancer are noted. Indian women develop osteoporosis (and consequent hip fractures, therefore experiencing premature death) ten to fifteen years earlier than their counterparts elsewhere. Indian men also have a higher risk of hip fracture than do other men (Gupta).

Conclusion

South Asian countries need to document and face the challenges posed by the increasingly elderly populations. Timely collection and release of high-quality data should be prioritized to facilitate the planning process. Social security schemes need to be expanded to cover vulnerable segments of the population. Familial support systems also should be strengthened by various means. Private and nonprofit sector efforts must be developed to supplement those of the overburdened public sector. At the same time elements of Asian culture that respect elders and view old age as a time of wisdom should not be lost. That is, making adequate provision for seniors should not be accompanied by approaches or assumptions that view old age as a looming problem or the proportion of elders in society as a burden. A social construction of the aging process as inherently problematic serves to legitimize a transfer of responsibility for elders from the state to individual older persons (Estes et al.). For each country or subgroup in South Asia, an appropriate balance needs to be developed between individual and public provision for the growing elderly population.

S. SUDHA
S. IRUDAYA RAJAN

See also CHINA; JAPAN; POPULATION AGING.

BIBLIOGRAPHY

AGARWAL, B. *A Field of One's Own: Gender and Land Rights in South Asia.* Cambridge: Cambridge University Press, 1994.

BASU, A. M. "Women's Roles and the Gender Gap in Health and Survival." In *Women's Health in India: Risk and Vulnerability.* Edited by Monica Das Gupta, L. C. Chen, and T. N. Krishnan. Bombay: Oxford University Press, 1995. Pages 153–174.

CHEN, M. A., and DREZE, J. "Widowhood and Well Being in Rural North India." In *Womens Health in India: Risk and Vulnerability.* Edited by M. Das Gupta, L. C. Chen, and T. N. Krishnan. Bombay: Oxford University Press, 1995. Pages 245–288.

ESTES, C. L.; LINKINS, K. W.; and BINNEY, E. A. "The Political Economy of Aging." In *Handbook of Aging and the Social Sciences*, 4th ed. Edited by Robert H. Binstock and Linda K. George. San Diego, Calif.: Academic Press, 1996. Pages 346–361.

GUPTA, A. "Osteoporosis in India: the Nutritional Hypothesis." *National Medicine Journal of India* 9, no. 6 (1996): 268–274.

International Labour Office. *World Labour Report 2000.* Geneva: United Nations, 2000.

IRUDAYA RAJAN, S.; MISHRA, U. S.; and SARMA, P. S. "Living Arrangements among the Indian Elderly." In *Hong Kong Journal of Gerontology* 9, no. 2 (1995): 20–28.

MURRAY, C. J. L., and LOPEZ, A. D. *Global Health Statistics: A Compendium of Incidence, Prevalence, and Mortality Estimates for over 200 Conditions.* Cambridge, Mass.: Harvard University Press, 1996.

RAMA RAO, S., and TOWNSEND, J. "Health Needs of Elderly Women: An Emerging Issue." In *Gender, Population and Development.* Edited by Maithreyi Krishnaraj, Ratna M. Sudarshan, and Abusaleh Shariff. Delhi: Oxford University Press, 1998.

United Nations. *Demographic Yearbook Special Issue: Population Ageing and the Situation of Elderly Persons.* New York: United Nations, 1991. Special Topic Table 4. Page 394.

United Nations. *Women in Asia and the Pacific: 1985–1993.* New York: United Nations, 1994.

United Nations. *World Population Prospects.* New York: Population Division, Department of Economic and Social Affairs, 1998.

U.S. Census Bureau. "International Data Base Summary Demographic Data." Available on the World Wide Web at www.census.gov

SPEECH

Speech consists of the sounds that humans produce, most often for the purpose of expressing language orally. Speech is just one mode of expressive language; other modes are writing and the production of manual signs. Very generally, language is a system of symbols that humans use to communicate. (See "Language Disorders" entry in this volume.)

Although most of the time speech sounds are produced in various combinations that convey meaning (and thus are being used to express language), their combinations can be meaningless (e.g., "bababa"). The meaningfulness aspect is the purview of language. The physical production aspect is the purview of speech.

The production of speech sounds requires that head, neck, and trunk muscles work in a coordinated fashion. Speech is often described in terms of the following component processes: respiration, phonation (voicing), resonance, and articulation. The respiratory system is the power source for our ability to produce sound. In the context of speech production, the air in our lungs is exhaled via active and passive thoracic and abdominal muscle activity, until it is halted at the larynx (in the case of voiced sounds).

The larynx sits at the top of the trachea and is comprised of muscle, cartilage, and membrane. In the context of speech production, the larynx is involved in voicing. Most speech sounds are voiced, but some are not (e.g., /s/). Without voicing, speech would be whispered. Airflow from the lungs is halted by the vocal folds (cords) of the larynx because they are closely approximated at midline. Eventually, air pressure builds up below the folds and forces them apart. The air flowing through the vocal folds sets into motion their vibration and also their cyclic opening and closing. Muscles are not the only laryngeal structures involved in voicing; the arytenoid cartilages also play an important role (their rocking motion toward midline helps to achieve complete closure of the vocal folds). The voice can change in pitch and loudness, and these too are functions of the larynx.

The vast majority of speech sounds are nonnasal (e.g., /b/, /d/), but a few are nasal (e.g., /m/, /n/). During the production of nasal sounds, the airflow above the vocal folds passes through the nasal and oral cavities. The airflow passes through the oral cavity alone during the production of nonnasal sounds. Thus, speech sounds have either a nasal or an oral resonance. Nonnasal sounds are produced when the soft palate (a muscle) moves upward and backward to make contact with the pharyngeal walls to block air from escaping through the nasal port. The soft palate is relaxed and the nasal port is open during the production of nasal sounds.

The speech sound is altered further by changing the position of the following structures of the oral cavity in relation to one another: lips, tongue, teeth, and jaw. These structures are known as the articulators, and their movement is known as articulation. In the articulation of some speech sounds, the flow of air is constricted but not stopped (e.g., /f/, /z/), whereas other speech sounds are produced by stopping the air in the oral cavity (e.g., /b/, /k/).

The central nervous system (e.g., motor cortex, upper motor neurons (UMNs), basal ganglia, cerebellum) and the peripheral nervous system (e.g., cranial and spinal nerves) are involved in speech production. UMNs originate in the primary motor cortex and project to cells in the brainstem or spinal cord. Lower motor neurons (LMNs) begin in the brainstem (cranial nerves) or spinal cord (spinal nerves) and project to the muscles on the same side of the body. For the most part, cranial nerves (which innervate head and neck muscles) receive input from left and right UMNs; this bilateral innervation offers superb protection. In the event of unilateral cortical/UMN damage, speech is affected minimally. However, unilateral cranial nerve damage has more devastating consequences for speech.

Older and younger adults can guess fairly accurately the chronological age of elderly individuals by listening to them speak (Caruso, Mueller, and Xue). However, physiological age rather than chronological age may be a better predictor of who is perceived as having an "aging voice" (Ramig and Ringel). Respiration and phonation are most affected by the aging process. Older people may have a restricted loudness range due to reduced vital capacity. The voice of older individuals is often perceived as hoarse. The physiological correlate of hoarseness is aperiodicity of vocal fold movement, which in the older adult may be caused by physical changes in the vocal folds (e.g., atrophy, bowing) or dehydration of the vocal folds because of decreased laryngeal gland secretions. The older voice is sometimes perceived as breathy and reduced in loudness, either of which may be due to reduced vital capacity and/or incomplete valving at the level of the larynx because of tissue changes in the vocal folds (atrophy, bowing) and/or because of changes to the laryngeal cartilages (ossification and calcification). There is not much change in the pitch of the female voice with age, except with extreme old age (higher pitch). As males age, pitch rises. A higher pitch may be the result of thinning vocal folds.

Several disease processes associated with aging can negatively affect speech production. Stroke and Parkinson's disease (PD) can result in dysarthria, a motor speech disorder characterized by weakness, slowness, reduced range of motion, or dyscoordination of any or all of the muscles of speech. Poststroke speech impairments can include imprecise consonant articulation, a breathy voice, strained-strangled phonation, and/or hypernasality. The underlying pathophysiology of the dysarthria associated with PD is muscle rigidity, with resulting speech characteristics of monopitch, monoloudness, and reduced stress. Another motor speech disorder is apraxia of speech (AOS), a deficit in the ability to program or plan the motor movements of speech. Stroke is the most common cause of AOS.

Speech-language pathologists diagnose and treat motor speech disorders in older adults. Contact the American Speech-Language-Hearing Association for more information about speech disorders (www.asha.org).

SUSAN JACKSON

See also BRAIN; HEARING; LANGUAGE DISORDERS; PARINSONISM; STROKE.

BIBLIOGRAPHY

CARUSO, A. J.; MUELLER, P. B.; and XUE, A. "The Relative Contributions of Voice and Articulation to Listener Judgements of Age and Gender: Preliminary Data and Implications." *Voice* 3 (1994): 3–11.

DUFFY, J. R. *Motor Speech Disorders*. St. Louis: Mosby, 1995.

RAMIG, L. O., and RINGEL, R. L. "Effects of Physiological Aging on Selected Acoustic Characteristics of Voice." *Journal of Speech and Hearing Research* 26 (1983): 22–30.

YORKSTON, K. M.; BEUKELMAN, D. R.; STRAND, E. A.; and BELL, K. R. *Management of Motor Speech Disorders in Children and Adults*, 2d ed. Austin: PRO-ED, 1999.

SPIRITUALITY

Spiritual concerns, experience, and development become increasingly important for many people in middle and later life. Beginning around age thirty-five or forty, as age increases, so does the proportion of people who are consciously involved in an inner exploration of the meaning of their existence and their relation to the universe. Such people are often engage in practices that heighten the possibility of spiritual experiences. In addition, those who experience spiritual levels of consciousness often feel called to serve, and spiritually rooted service takes many forms.

Important concepts

As used here, "spirituality" refers to an inner, experiential aspect of being. Spirituality is a region of awareness within which people experience, not just think about, a higher power, the absolute, God, Allah, Nirvana, Yahweh, Cosmic Consciousness, Christ Consciousness, the Void, or whatever label is used for that which is not an object but which instead forms the undivided ground of all being (Huxley). Spirituality can also refer to actions arising from spiritual experiences.

Spiritual experience can occur at several levels: physical, emotional, cognitive, and transcendent. Spirituality is a quality that can infuse experience in a wide variety of settings. Spiritual experience can be both transcendent and immanent: it can be both an experience of transcending worldly concerns and an intense present-moment perception that the ground of all being permeates all things. The essence of spirituality is an intense aliveness and deep sense of understanding that one intuitively comprehends as having come from a direct, internal link with that mysterious principle which connects all aspects of the universe.

There are many spiritual traditions, each of which has its own unique language and concepts concerning the nature of the ultimate, the path that must be followed to experience the ultimate, how spiritual realizations are confirmed, the nature of spiritual enlightenment, and the implications of spiritual understanding for ordinary human life.

In most spiritual traditions, mysticism lies at the heart of spirituality. "Mysticism" refers to transcendent, contemplative experiences that enhance spiritual understanding. Mystical experiences can occur during intentional practices designed to create openings for transcendent experiences, such as Christian contemplative prayer, Zen meditation, or Sufi dance; or they can occur in the process of living a lifestyle that is conducive to transcendent experiences, as in contemplative gardening. In either case, contemplative or transcendent knowing is associated with spiritual experience.

"Transcendence" refers to contemplative knowing that occurs outside the boundaries of verbal thought (Wilber). Although transcendence can refer to increasingly abstract thought, contemplative transcendence involves transcending thought itself. Mystical experiences of transcendence can be brought into thought, but they do not originate in thought or sensory perception.

Organized religions are social groups or social institutions that have theological and behavioral doctrines, ministerial or clerical authority, and ritualized social worship. Of course, individual members can and do internalize both the theological beliefs and the behavioral prescriptions and proscriptions associated with their organized religion. But individuals often have their own unique interpretations of the tenets of their religion as well.

The relation of religion and spirituality is in the eye of the beholder. Many people use the two words as synonyms and see no difference between them. Others use "religion" to refer to a sociocultural program for developing spiritually and for bringing spiritual realizations into everyday life, and they use "spirituality" to refer to the inner experiences that arise from trying to put such programs into practice. Most people see spirituality as a broader term that includes a greater variety of experiences than they would include under religion. Some people attach little or no importance to organized religion but at the same time see themselves as very spiritual persons.

Spiritual development

In the view of spirituality presented here, enlightenment is a result of spiritual development. However, it would be a mistake to assume that progress toward enlightenment is linear or predictable, or that enlightenment is always total. Many people describe their spiritual journeys in terms of alternating periods of crystal-clear enlightenment and periods of struggle. But a person who has experienced absolute enlightenment, however briefly, knows that enlightenment is a real possibility in a way that those who only think about or aspire to enlightenment cannot. Enlightenment has two important aspects: a

capacity to be intensely present without preconceptions or judgments, and constant awareness of oneself as being permeated by the ground of all being.

In 1944 Aldous Huxley published "The Perennial Philosophy," in which he offered persuasive evidence that basic views about the nature of human spirituality espoused by the mystical strains of each major faith group, Eastern or Western, could be traced to a common underlying set of understandings about the human spirit that originated in India thousands of years ago. According to this view, personal realities are always incomplete pictures of spirituality; intuitive, mystical connection with the ground of being is superior to merely thinking about the ground of being; the human spirit has a divine nature and a person can come to identify with that universal Self rather than with the personal ego; and the ultimate purpose of spiritual development is to experience no separation from the ground of being.

Thus, spiritual development can be defined in terms of movement toward ultimate possibilities, and the highest regions of spiritual development occur in the development of a capacity that allows consciousness to transcend the boundaries of body, language, reason, and culture. Movement toward ultimate possibilities means movement from simple imitative and dependent spiritual thought and behavior; toward a personal mental picture of spiritual issues that integrates both inner and outer life experiences of spirituality; toward subtle, contemplative, and transcendent understanding of the common ground of both inner and outer life experiences; toward being fully united with the ultimate ground of all being. Spiritual development is a process of transcendence that could be seen as a continuing spiral of increasingly broad understanding and experience of oneself and the universe.

Some who write about spiritual development emphasize the continuing nature of spiritual development. For example, Zen master Joko Beck sees spiritual development as something that grows out of the daily practice of sitting meditation and bringing present-moment consciousness to everyday life. "Enlightenment is not something you achieve. It is the absence of something. All your life you have been going forward for something, pursuing some goal. Enlightenment is dropping all that. But to talk about it is of little use. The practice has to be done by each individual. There is no substitute. We can read about it until we are a thousand years old and it won't do a thing for us" (Beck, p. 5). Also, "Attention is the cutting, burning sword, and our practice is to use that sword as much as we can" (Beck, p. 32). In this view the process, not progress or achieving levels of spiritual understanding, is the focus.

Others view spiritual development as having identifiable stages. For example, Fowler conceived of adult spiritual development as having the following developmental stages: an individual-reflective stage in which the self begins to turn from external sources of spiritual authority, and toward the development of an internal moral and spiritual orientation that has personal meaning for the individual; a conjunctive stage characterized by greater acceptance of paradox and ambiguity, a deepening sense of understanding, disillusionment with the overreliance on logic and rational thought that typifies the individual-reflective stage, and a more open attitude toward religions or views of spirituality other than one's own; and a universalizing stage involving a rare willingness to give up oneself and one's life to make spiritual values a reality in the social world. Fowler felt that there was a link between life stage and spiritual development, with the individual-reflective stage being likely in young adulthood and the conjunctive stage developing in midlife and later. He did not think that many people reached the universalizing stage.

Wilber saw spiritual development as progressing from an emphasis on sensory knowing in childhood, through various levels of rational knowing in early adulthood, to contemplative knowing, beginning in midlife. For example, children often have their first mystical experiences through sensory sources, such as communing with nature or listening to sacred music or seeing an awesome sunset. Later on, adults can experience tremendous inspiration through their minds, from written and spoken words, scarcely aware that the silence between and around those words may be crucial to their feeling of spiritual connection. As people continue on their spiritual journey, most develop some sort of discipline, a repetitive activity that allows them to transcend their self-consciousness to experience a serenity of inner being.

Moody and Carroll described five stages of spiritual development: the call, the search, the struggle, the breakthrough, and the return. The call occurs when one experiences an inner yearning for connection, or deeper connection, with the spiritual Self. The call may initially be a feeling that there is an empty part of oneself; later it may be a feeling that the spiritual aspect of oneself is not yet fully developed. The search involves finding and exploring a spiritual path. The search may occur in the context of a traditional religion, or it may involve an exploration and sampling of many sacred traditions. The struggle often involves overcoming the ego's resistance to meditative or contemplative practices aimed at transcendence. Beginning meditators often experience profound discomfort from the countless objections and obstacles the mind creates to prevent the experience of quiet mind. Breakthroughs occur when the obstacles or objections to transcendence have been overcome, even if the overcoming is temporary. However, once people experience pure mindfulness and transcendent consciousness, they are likely to remain motivated in their intention to be open to experiencing these qualities as part of their awareness.

When people develop transcendent awareness, they do not typically drop out of the world. Instead, they continue their customary lives, but their perspective on those lives is transformed. The return involves bringing the spiritual insights gained through transcendence into the world. The form such service takes depends in large part on the spiritual path chosen. A path of devotion can lead back to being an exemplar of devotion. A path of insight and understanding may come back in the form of being a teacher or a leader. One characteristic that all who have broken through share is the capacity to see the world from a nonpersonal perspective that is open, unselfish, honest, trustworthy, compassionate, and clear-minded, among many other qualities. Quietly bringing these qualities to all that one does in life can be a powerful effect of the return.

Moody and Carroll's progression is not meant to imply that there is just one course to complete, and then one is enlightened. Rather, it is a cyclic process through which one becomes more and more enlightened by going through the entire process they describe whenever one experiences a call for deeper development.

But how does one know that one's spiritual experiences are authentic? After all, the human mind is quite skillful in leading one to misperceive all manner of phenomena. First, millions of men and women over thousands of years and in a wide variety of historical eras and cultures have reported having experienced a universal presence as a part of themselves. This inner experience is reported as a direct connection that bypasses the verbal mind and therefore is less susceptible to personal or cultural bias. Second, spiritual communities serve an important function by collectively reflecting on individual spiritual experiences. Sharing of spiritual experiences and insights within a spiritual community is an important protection against mistaking a subtle ego agenda for spiritual realization.

Age and life stage in spiritual development

Aging does not inevitably bring spiritual development, but aging and the cultural concepts of what is appropriate or expected in later life stages do alter the conditions of life in ways that can heighten awareness of spiritual needs and can stimulate interest in a spiritual journey. Of course, physical aging and mental aging are not unitary phenomena. Different individuals can experience quite different age patterns in terms of what changes occur, at what age, and at what rate. Differences in genes, environment, society, and culture combine to produce a staggering variety of individual experiences of physical and mental aging.

Popular stereotypes of aging portray it as a process of decline, but for most people, at least prior to age eighty, aging is a relatively neutral balance of gains and losses that is experienced as a gentle slowing down that allows them to maintain their preferred lifestyle.

What does change significantly is interest in an inner journey. Numerous scholars have observed that middle and later life involve an experience of increasingly transcendent aspects of inner life (Alexander et al.; Erikson et al.; Thomas). Achenbaum and Orwoll tied the development of wisdom to an increasingly transcendent attitude toward oneself, toward relationships with others, and toward worldly aims. As age increases, many people perceive themselves as having increasingly transcendent attitudes. They take more delight in their inner world, are less fearful of death, and feel a greater connection to the entire universe (Tornstam; Atchley).

A study of active spiritual seekers among a representative sample of people born during the baby boom found that 62 percent of active seekers were middle-aged or older, and most felt that "People have God within them, so churches aren't really necessary" (Moody and Carroll, pp. 133–134). These findings affirm the ancient wisdom among groups as diverse as the Navajo and the Jewish cabalists that a person must be age forty to begin serious spiritual study. Many spiritual traditions assign special significance to age or life stage in terms of increased receptivity to spiritual development.

Social aging is mainly an experience of release from the heavy responsibilities of midlife. Launching one's children into adulthood and retirement are seldom experienced as life crises; instead, they are experienced as newfound freedom, and many elders use this freedom as an opportunity for increased spiritual reflection. As age increases, many individuals live an increasingly quiet lifestyle conducive to contemplation.

By late middle age, most adults have long since discovered that the modern prescriptions for life meaning—materialism and social achievement—do not meet the needs of the soul. In later adulthood, many people find that their attention shifts from competition toward affiliation and from self-centeredness toward generativity— care and concern for younger generations. By late middle age most adults have struggled with the challenge to life meaning that can come with the death of people with whom they had close personal relationships. If materialism, social achievement, and social relationships are not predictable sources of meaning in life, what is? This type of meaning question is more common and becomes more salient as people move into the last half of life (Moody and Cole). The lack of reliable social answers to meaning questions can be a powerful impetus for an inner, experiential quest for meaning—for a spiritual journey.

Although a large proportion of aging adults report being on a spiritual journey, by no means do all aging people follow this pattern. Some have a philosophy of life based on everyday humanistic principles, and see little need for spiritual or religious validation. They feel no call toward a spiritual journey but are nevertheless vital and involved. Others are so stuck in their habits of thinking and behaving that there is little chance for the kind of openness that is a prerequisite for a spiritual journey.

Evidence that spiritual growth is common in later life includes gradual increases with age in the prevalence of self-acceptance and perceptions of one's life as having integrity; service to others, especially community service and providing long-term care to family and friends; and interest in the young. This information comes from studies of earlier cohorts who have passed through the stages of later life. With their exposure to the recent heightened cultural interest in spirituality, upcoming cohorts of elders may be even more interested in spiritual journeys as a focal point of later life.

Increased perceptions of life meaning and integrity, service to others, and generativity all require an attitude of transcendence and a measure of selflessness. They suggest that growing older can represent a return home to the silence from which one came, and that on the way home, a nonpersonal state of consciousness may be gradually uncovered by conditions common in later life: a quiet mind, a simplified daily life, and a let-be attitude toward the world. The deepening spirituality of later life is often subtle and nondeliberate; it may occur naturally and spontaneously as a result of the physical, mental, and social processes of aging. Thibault described the conditions under which many people experience aging as a "natural monastery."

ROBERT C. ATCHLEY

See also RELIGION; WISDOM.

BIBLIOGRAPHY

ACHENBAUM, A. W., and ORWOLL, L. "Becoming Wise." *International Journal of Aging and Human Development* 32 (1991): 21–39.
ALEXANDER, C. N.; DAVIES, J. L.; DIXON, C. A.; DILLBECK, M. C.; DRUKER, S. M.; OETZEL, R. M.; MUEHLMAN, J. M.; and ORME-JOHNSON, D. W. (1990). "Growth of Higher Stages of Consciousness: Maharishi's Vedic Psychology of Human Development." In *Higher Stages of Consciousness*. Edited by C. N. Alexander and E. J. Langer. New York: Oxford University Press, 1990. Pages 286–341.
ATCHLEY, R. C. *Continuity and Adaptation in Aging.* Baltimore: Johns Hopkins University Press, 1999.
BECK, C. J. *Everyday Zen: Love and Work.* New York: HarperCollins, 1989.
ERIKSON, E. H.; ERIKSON, J. S.; and KIVNICK, H. Q. *Vital Involvement in Old Age.* New York: Norton, 1986.
FOWLER, J. W. *Weaving the New Creation: Stages of Faith and the Public Church.* San Francisco: Harper & Row, 1991.
HUXLEY, A. "The Perennial Philosophy." In *The Song of God: Bhagavad-Gita.* Edited by S. Prabhavananda and C. Isherwood. New York: Penguin Books, 1944. Pages 11–22.
MOODY, H. R., and CARROLL, D. *The Five Stages of the Soul.* New York: Anchor Books, 1997.
MOODY, H. R., and COLE, T. R. (1986). "Aging and Meaning: A Bibliographic Essay." In *What Does It Mean to Grow Old?* Edited by T. R. Cole and S. Gadow. Durham, N.C.: Duke University Press, 1986. Pages 247–253.
THIBAULT, J. M. "Aging as a Natural Monastery." *Aging and Spirituality* 8 (1996): 3, 8.
THOMAS, L. E. "The Way of the Religious Renouncer: Power Through Nothingness." In *Aging and the Religious Dimension.* Edited by L. E. Thomas and S. A. Eisenhandler. Westport, Conn.: Auburn House, 1994. Pages 51–64.
TORNSTAM, L. "Gero-Transcendence: A Theoretical and Empirical Exploration." In *Aging and the Religious Dimension.* Edited by L. E. Thomas and S. A. Eisenhanlder. Westport, Conn.: Auburn House, 1994. Pages 203–229.
WILBER, K. *Eye to Eye,* 3d ed. Boston: Shambhala, 1996.

STATUS OF OLDER PEOPLE: THE ANCIENT AND BIBLICAL WORLDS

Realities of aging

Many people today assume that individuals in the distant past grew old at a very young age, or that they tended to die at a young age. Yet there is abundant evidence that throughout history, at least some individuals lived to a ripe old age. In fact, if ancient testimony were to be believed, people lived a lot longer then than they do today. Whole races of people, mostly far distant if not mythical, were routinely credited with fantastic life spans, just as were various species of animals who were synonymous with long life (e.g., the crow, crab, stag, raven, and, of course, the phoenix). Ages of three hundred or five hundred years are cited for pseudo-historical individuals in classical literature, while mythical characters, such as Tithonus, Teiresias, and the Sibyls, were attributed with lives of several centuries, if not of eternity.

From Homer comes the epitome of old age throughout classical times, the pagan equivalent of Methuselah: Nestor, king of Pylos, who outlived three generations, or, as it came to be commonly understood, three lifetimes or centuries. The Old Testament attributes ages of up to a thousand years to individuals from the past. Saint Augustine (*City of God* 15–16, utilising Pliny the Elder's *Natural History* book 7) argues that the fabulous ages attributed to figures from the Old Testament are to be believed, despite the incredulity of many. He notes that in the days of *Genesis* people lived such a long time that they did not think a man of one hundred years was old.

From at least the time of Homer's Nestor, old age was conventionally associated with wisdom. Thus, for example, the Seven Sages of Greece were credited with extended life spans. Likewise, the somewhat nebulous figure of Pythagoras in the sixth century is usually credited with living eighty or ninety years, though one ancient source records that he lived to his 117th year in fine fettle, thanks to a special potion made of vinegar of squill (sea onion). This confusion concerning ages at death is a common one, and it is clear that the longevity of someone long dead, especially of someone notable, might become exaggerated as time passed and as circumstances suited.

Nevertheless, there is ample evidence from more "historical" times, of people surviving into their nineties and beyond, and often there is little obvious reason to doubt the figures quoted. It is important to realize that, despite the demographic transition following the Industrial Revolution and the advances in medicine in the twentieth century, people do not live significantly longer today than they did in the historical past. In classical times, dying in one's sixties or beyond was regarded as natural; to die younger was usually seen as a harsh and unnatural fate. The biblical "three score years and ten" (seventy years) was held to be a general figure for a good age, not a remarkably extended one. Very high levels of infant mortality meant that life expectancy at birth was indeed low in the worlds of ancient Greece and Rome and of the Bible. But those that survived their first years of life had a good chance of living to be at least sixty years of age.

Old age, in purely chronological terms, was regarded by people in antiquity not so differently from the way contemporary people view it. While some ancient poets might have expressed horror at the emergence of grey hairs on their head at the age of forty, most ancient writers seem to have assumed that people were old once they were in their sixties. No more specific age limit need be expected, especially as there were no general institutionalised schemes of retirement or pensions in ancient times. The tombstone of one fifty-year old male from Roman Algeria in the third century C.E. recorded that he died "in the flower of his youth," while a young lad in Egypt in the fourth century C.E. complains that his grandfather's sister is "really incredibly old: She's actually lived to be over sixty years old!" While we do not have comprehensive statistical evidence from ancient times, it may be estimated, for example, that around 6 to 8 percent of the population of the Roman Empire in the first century C.E. was over the age of sixty. A very select few would have even survived to be centenarians. The human life span has not increased dramatically over the past two or three millennia, it is just that a greater proportion of people now survive into old age.

It is also often alleged that older people in the classical past enjoyed something of a "golden age," during which time they were treated with great respect and held primary authority over political, religious, and social spheres. It is certainly true that in societies with a strong oral tradition, older members of society may have acted as important repositories of lore and wisdom. For some, old age was not an unhappy or unaccomplished time. We know of many individuals in the ancient world—politicians, writers, priests, prophets, and philosophers—who were admired for their active old age. Literature provides a host of both positive and negative images of old age. Philosophers attributed the perceived negative features of old age to people's dissipated youth (note *Proverbs* 10.27: "The fear of the Lord prolongeth days: But the years of the wicked shall be shortened") and they stressed the boons of aging, not least in the political sphere. Best known is perhaps Cicero's dialogue *Cato the Elder on Old Age*, written around the time of the assassination of Julius Caesar, when Cicero was sixty-two years old. But this work cannot be read in isolation, and dozens of other works are equally important to the overall picture. Not surprisingly, images of, and opinions about, older people cover a wide range, from cheerfully positive to bitterly negative.

This range of views is revealing. Old age did not automatically confer the respect and authority that some felt it deserved. Literary perceptions and artistic depictions alone do not provide a reliable picture of the realities of life. Most power, and indeed most wealth, in the ancient world usually lay with younger generations. From the aristocracy down to lower-class families and slaves, the realities of life for older people hinged predominantly on one factor: the individual's ability to remain a functioning member of society, be it as a leading politician or as a child minder. In the absence of any form of welfare state or effective medical care, the support of older individuals rested with their immediate kin. Even for the wealthy elite, about whom most of our surviving evidence is concerned, old age was viewed typically as a time to be endured rather than enjoyed.

In democratic Athens, seniority did not bring automatic political power. In Rome most authority—emperors (young or old) excepted—tended to lie with senators in their forties and fifties. Sparta alone operated along gerontocratic lines: members of its senate, the *gerousia,* had to be at least sixty years old. But even there, effective rule lay with younger elected officials called *ephors,* and Aristotle noted the risks in giving power to men subject to the potential liabilities of old age.

Theories on aging

While the afflictions old age may bring were well appreciated by the ancient writers, the literature is less pragmatic regarding the causes of such afflictions. Medical writers also attributed aspects of old age to bad habits in one's youth, but they realized that aging is inevitable. The most common theory to be found in the extant ancient literature, both medical and philosophical, on the cause of aging is that in time the body loses its innate heat and fluid—its life force, or *pneuma* (like a lamp running out of oil). Hence, the infant is warm and moist while the older person—like a corpse—is cold and dry. In other words, aging is a cooling and drying process, and the desiccation of the heart and liver leads to death. Just as during an illness, in old age the balance of the four humors has been lost: blood and yellow bile are lacking, phlegm and black bile [melancholy] are abundant. As heat dissipates, the body takes longer to recover from illness and injury, but for the same reason symptoms such as fever become less acute in older people, as does activity in general.

Twice in the Hippocratic corpus there appears another theory, namely that the elderly person is cold, but humidor moist (rather than dry). This countertheory is soundly and insistently refuted by the later medical writer Galen (129–199 C.E.): The mistake is due, he remarks, to the external appearance of moisture about the old person—coughing, runny nose, and the like—but these are merely an abundance of external, phlegmatic secretions, or the residue of humidity, and are not to be taken as an indication of the innate condition of the elderly individual.

This idea that old age is cold often recurs in general literature as well. As for its dryness, old age is regularly described as having been drained of the moist (and hot) humor of blood (note, for example, the image of the dry and shrunken Sibyl). What blood the aging body does have is thin and icy cold, an image Virgil evokes in the person of Entellus: "My blood is chilled and dulled by sluggish old age," (*Aeneid* 5: 395–396). Galen noted that the coldness of old age affects not only the body but also the mind: "So why do many people become demented when they reach extreme old age, a period which has been shown to be dry? This is not a result of dryness, but of coldness. For this clearly damages all the activities of the soul" (*Kühn* 4: 786–787) Old age, it was concluded, destroys everything.

Furthermore, because aging was conventionally seen as a process of desiccation, those who were by nature very humid were held to have the greatest chance of a long life. With similar logic it was stated that men, being warmer, age more slowly than women and hence live longer (the latter observation may well often have been accurate in the ancient world, though for other reasons). At any rate, physical exertion dries one out, and so hard-working people age more quickly. For the same reason it was believed that excessive indulgence in sexual intercourse is deleterious to the aging frame.

It was a literary commonplace, adopted by the Pythagoreans in a system of four ages (which mirror the four humors), that old age is like winter, at least in its coldness. Part of the theory was that one felt best in the season appropriate (that is, complementary, or opposite) to one's age. So it was observed that summer and early autumn were the seasons in which older people might thrive, and winter was the season to avoid as best one could.

To counter the dryness and coldness of old age, it was thought to be necessary to restore the balance of the humors, by giving warmth and humidity to the body. Finding a means to warm and moisten the body was the chief aim of what geriatric medicine there was in the ancient world. It was common in antiquity to state that old age was itself a disease; in fact, Seneca the Younger (*Epistles* 108: 28) stated that old age is an incurable disease. In the second century C.E., Galen, for one, disagreed vigorously: while diseases are contrary to nature, he claimed, old age is a natural process, just as to die of old age is natural. Therefore, Galen insisted, old age, is not a disease; though it is also not complete health either. Rather, old age has a state of health peculiar to itself, and this may be maintained through a moderate lifestyle. It was apparently a common practice for physicians to recommend a particular regimen or "diet" that older individuals should follow. Dietetics was one of the main traditional divisions of ancient medical therapy, the others being pharmacology and surgery.

In the fifth book of his work *On the Preservation of Health,* Galen provided abundant material on the subject, considerably more detailed than anything that preceded it and of considerable influence on treatments of the subject over the following centuries. Galen's concern was with lifestyle, not just diet: his recommendations incorporated massage and gentle exercise—not too much and not too little, depending upon the constitution of the patient. If strong enough, the elderly patient was advised to engage in horse riding and ball throwing, or travel on a ship or in a litter; if bedridden, reading aloud could be highly beneficial. Galen recommended for the older patient the right amount of sleep (good for moistening and warming the body), and tepid baths (two or three times a month, but never if bedridden). Blood-letting, according to Galen, is good for stronger patients up to the age of seventy years, though it was not recommended for the very elderly, who, Galen added, need every drop of blood that they have. As to diet, he believed older people need little food, which was perhaps just as well since many food items were not recommended or permitted. Some foods he considered to be beneficial (plums are good as laxatives for the older patient, according to Galen), but he thought many others to be dangerous (such as cheese, hard-boiled eggs, snails, lentils, mushrooms, and many vegetables). Also recommended were fish, some types of soft bread, and lean meat—especially young goat's flesh—but not pork.

Regarding beverages, water was not recommended, nor was milk, which was believed to rot aged teeth and gums. For older individuals, however, Galen did specifically recommend human breast milk and warm donkey's milk, or milk mixed with honey. One farmer is mentioned who survived beyond the century mark thanks to goat's milk mixed with honey and wine. Wine, the gift of Dionysus, was particularly commended, and in the name of science Galen devoted much study to the question of which wines were best for medicinal purposes. Wine was thought to have positively rejuvenating effects. Indeed, it was proverbial in antiquity that wine makes an old man dance, even against his will. Wine makes the body warm, and, Galen added, it also serves to counter the sadness and anxieties that long life may bring.

Images of aging

Certainly old age's negative repercussions were noted in general literature as well, most clinically by Aristotle (*Rhetoric* 2: 13) and most memorably by Juvenal (*Satires* 10: 188–288). (note also *Ecclesiastes* 12: 1–8, as well as, from ancient Egypt, Ptah-hotep's *Maxims* 4.2–5.2, probably the earliest extant text [ca. 2450 B.C.E.] to deal with old age). Literature focused on upperclass males. Elderly females tended to get stereotyped as sex-crazed witches or alcoholics. Besides being unpleasant, this points to marginalisation. Past reproducing, older women might be dismissed as nonfunctioning members of society.

For the poorer classes, old age must have been singularly unenviable: it was a common proverb that "old age and poverty are both burdensome, but in combination they are impossible to bear." Children were expected to look after parents in old age, though "honour thy father and thy mother" is only part of it. Indeed, security in old age was allegedly one motivation for having children. If you had no willing children, then a destitute and lonely old age may have ensued. And the obligation, enforced by law in some societies (such as classical Athens), may not always have extended to the female side of the family. "Hearken unto thy father that begat thee, and despise not thy mother when she is old" (*Proverbs* 23: 22) perhaps reveals something of the extent of the gender difference in terms of expectations.

In the case of the vast majority of the individuals we know of from ancient times, however, poverty was not a problem, and wealth, as well as the existence of slaves, must have helped to ease the problems for them. But if a person's failing health led to an inability to be self-supporting, then, in the absence of effective medication, dependence may have been short-lived anyway. The key was not how old, but how active or useful a person was. Cicero's words are timeless: "Old age will only be respected if it fights for itself, maintains its rights, avoids dependence on anyone, and asserts control over its own to the last breath" (*On Old Age*).

On the other hand, in antiquity, old age was less of a "problem," at least for men, than it appears to be today. Old age was not formally seen as a distinctive stage of the life cycle. In the absence of wage-labor and retirement, most people were expected to go on doing whatever they had always done until their last breath. Old age, with all the negative features it might entail, was still regarded as part of the natural course of adult life.

TIM G. PARKIN

See also GERONTOCRACY; PROLONGEVITY.

BIBLIOGRAPHY

BERTMAN, S., ed. *The Conflict of Generations in Greece and Rome*. Amsterdam: B. R. Gruner, 1976.

DAVID, E. *Old Age in Sparta*. Amsterdam: Adolf M. Hakkert, 1991.

DE LUCE, J. "Ancient Images of Aging: Did Ageism Exist in Greco-Roman Antiquity?" In *Changing Perceptions of Aging and the Aged*. Edited by D. Shenk and W. A. Achenbaum. New York: Springer, 1994. Pages 65–74.

DE LUCE, J.; HENDRICKS, J.; RODEHEAVER, D.; and SELTZER, M. M. "Continuity and Change: Four Disciplinary Perspectives on Reading Cicero's de Senectute." *Journal on Aging Studies* 7 (1993): 335–381.

EYBEN, E. "Roman Notes on the Course of Life." *Ancient Society* 4 (1973): 213–238.

FALKNER, T. M. *The Poetics of Old Age in Greek Epic, Lyric, and Tragedy*. Norman and London: University of Oklahoma Press, 1995.

FALKNER, T. M., and DE LUCE, J., eds. *Old Age in Greek and Latin Literature*. Albany: State University of New York Press, 1989.

FINLEY, M. I. "The Elderly in Classical Antiquity." *Greece and Rome* 28 (1981): 156–71. Reprinted in *Ageing and Society* 4 (1984): 391–408, and in Falkner and de Luce (1989): 1–20.

GARLAND, R. *The Greek Way of Life from Conception to Old Age*. London: Duckworth, 1991.

GNILKA, C. "Greisenalter." *Reallexikon fur Antike und Christentum* 12 (1983): 995–1094.

GRUMAN, G. J., ed. *Roots of Modern Gerontology and Geriatrics*. New York: Arno Press, 1979.

PARKIN, T. G. "Ageing in Antiquity: Status and Participation." In *Old Age from Antiquity to Post-Modernity*. Edited by P. Johnson and P. Thane. London: Roultledge, 1998. Pages 19–42.

PARKIN, T. G. "Out of Sight, Out of Mind: Elderly Members of the Roman Family." In *The Roman Family in Italy: Status, Sentiment, Space*. Edited by B. Rawson and P. Weaver. Canberra and Oxford: Oxford University Press, 1997. Pages 123–148.

PHILIBERT, M. "Le statut de la personne âgée dans les sociétés antiques et préindustrielles." *Sociologie et societes* 16.2 (1984): 15–27.

POWELL, J. G. F., ed. *Cicero: Cato Maior de Senectute*. Cambridge, U.K.: Cambridge University Press, 1988.

RICHARDSON, B. E. *Old Age Among the Ancient Greeks*. Baltimore, Md.: The John Hopkins University Press, 1933.

SCHARBERT, J. "Das Alter und die Alten in der Bibel." *Saeculum: Jahrbuch für Universalgeschichte* 30 (1979): 338–354.

STAHMER, H. M. "The Aged in Two Ancient Oral Cultures: The Ancient Hebrews and Homeric Greece." In *Aging and the Elderly: Humanistic Perspectives in Gerontology*. Edited by S. F. Spicker, K. M. Woodward, and D. D. van Tassel. Atlantic Highlands, N.J.: Humanities Press, 1978. Pages 23–36.

SUDER, W., ed. *Geras. Old Age in Greco-Roman Antiquity: A Classified Bibliography*. Wroclaw, Poland: Profil, 1991.

STATUS OF OLDER PEOPLE: MODERNIZATION

The nineteenth and twentieth centuries were marked by sweeping technological advances and rapid social transformations, particularly in Western Europe and North America. The proportion of older people in national populations grew, slowly at first, and then more rapidly as fertility behavior changed and public health measures contributed to increases in longevity. These socioeconomic and demographic changes created the context for the formal study of aging and old age, as historians and social scientists undertook systematic research in social gerontology after World War II.

One way researchers have sought to understand the effects of widespread social change on older people has been by researching aging and old age in the context of modernization. As a conceptual framework, *modernization* embraces the notion that large-scale social processes, like technological advances and changes in modes of production, create new roles and statuses for people (including older people) and their families. As a theoretical model, *modernization theory* involves a series of formal statements that can be tested with evidence and that specify how specific social or technological changes create particular socioeconomic effects for older people (and others) as societies modernize over time.

The modernization story

The term *modernization* came into popular use after World War II. It was used to describe the set of interrelated processes that occurred as Western societies were transformed from the agrarian, rural societies of the seventeenth century to the modern industrialized nations of the twentieth. Although the social changes wrought by the Industrial Revolution caused temporary social displacement as social institutions and individuals adapted to massive change, most modernization theorists believed such displacements were temporary and tolerable, given the progressive nature of modernization. Once a society had modernized its institutions, it was believed, it could fully embrace new scientific knowledge that would resolve remaining social and technological problems, creating a progressively wealthier and more stable society. This romanticized notion of the transformation of Western societies became a foundation for much social research in western Europe and North America.

In the postwar years, many argued that nonindustrial societies would proceed toward development along approximately the same lines as the advanced industrial Western countries. The expectation was that the developed countries would encourage development in nonindustrial societies through the export and diffusion of investment, education, technology, and values. Modernizing nonindustrial countries would replace their traditional institutions, practices, and beliefs (which were viewed as impediments to modernization) with Western practices and values. This perspective viewed Western practices and values as liberating, and the potential modernization of traditional societies was viewed, op-

timistically, as a progressive step likely to enrich the lives of all members of modernizing societies. There was a belief that transforming traditional, agricultural societies into modern industrial societies would replicate the path to wealth and stability experienced by modern Western countries.

Modernization theory and the study of aging

Modernization theory was formalized in social gerontology mainly through the work of sociologists. In 1972, Donald Cowgill and Lowell Holmes developed a theory of modernization as it related to aging and old age. Their position was that as societies *modernized*—undertaking the shift from farm and craft production within families to a dominantly industrial mode of production—repercussions of modernization would diminish the status of older people. Cowgill's later theoretical refinements (1974) identified four key aspects of modernization that undermined the status of older people: health technology, economic and industrial technology, urbanization, and education.

According to Cowgill's theory, improved health technology, including advances in both medical practice and public health, has positive effects of improving health and increasing longevity, but it also has negative effects for older people. When people live longer, there is more competition in the labor market. Employers in industrializing societies prefer younger workers with new occupational skills to older workers, forcing older workers out of the labor market into retirement. Once retired, according to modernization theory, loss of income, prestige, and honor arising from labor market participation lead to a decline in the status of older people.

Modernizing advances in economic and industrial technology create new occupations in factories located near transportation and services. Younger people acquire the skills for new occupational slots and join the industrial work force, relegating older people to less prestigious and increasingly obsolete jobs. This often leads to retirement, reversing the roles of old and young. In traditional societies, older family members control family production, and younger ones are dependent on the old. When older people are excluded from the industrial labor market, they become dependent on the young, losing social status.

Factory locations in urban areas are a magnet to young workers. The process of urbanization leaves older family members behind in rural areas, undermining the traditional extended family and the prominent position of older members within them. The new family form in modernizing societies is the nuclear family, and both social and spatial distance are increased between the young and the old, changing intergenerational relations. Modernization theorists viewed upward mobility of the young as being accompanied by downward mobility among the elders in their families.

Increased literacy, emphasis on the superiority of scientific over traditional forms of knowledge, and education targeted toward children can all create inequalities in the knowledge base among family members of different generations, making the generation gaps between young and old even wider. Developments in science and technology render much of the traditional knowledge and many of the skills of older people that previously contributed to their high social status obsolete, since direct contribution to an industrialized economy becomes impossible.

This general model of the relationship between modernization and aging predicts a linear relationship between the status of older people and the degree of modernization experienced in a given society. According to this theory, the more modernized a society becomes, the more the status of older people declines. Modernization thus inevitably affects the entire social structure of newly modernized societies, including the position customarily held by its elderly community, regardless of when or where it occurred.

The institutionalization of modernization theory as one of the foundational theoretical approaches to the study of aging gave impetus to further study. Not long after Cowgill and Holmes's original work, Erdman Palmore and Kenneth Manton used data from thirty-one countries to test modernization theory. Their findings suggested a refinement to modernization theory that involved taking the phase of modernization into account when exploring status changes among older people. Palmore and Manton's results showed that in the early stages of modernization, older people's social status was relatively lower, but that the decline in status leveled off and even rose somewhat after a period of modernization.

In both its original and more elaborate variants, modernization theory provided a springboard to theorizing and research into the relationship between aging and social change. Some researchers sought to improve modernization theory by refining it. Others contended that modernization theory was too flawed to be a useful general theory explaining the relationship between social change and aging.

Critiques of modernization theory

Critics of modernization theory have observed that the theory was based on faulty assumptions about the historical status of older people—that it represented an oversimplification of the effects of modernization and ignored important variations arising from cultural variations, family forms, and social statuses other than age. According to sociologist Jill Quadagno, historical evidence demonstrates that significant variation occurred in the treatment of older people across and within different societies and over time, that older people have not always been universally revered, and that modernization has both positive and negative affects on older people.

Researchers have refuted modernization theory on a number of fronts. They have challenged the inevitability and uniformity of the effects of modernization by providing an historical view of the roles of aged family members and their political and economic power, of elder health and longevity, and of cultural attitudes toward older people. Historians and sociologists have used historical evidence from Western countries to challenge assumptions built into the modernization model, while anthropologists have provided evidence from crosscultural studies to demonstrate that there is no uniform, linear outcome determining aged people's status in modernizing societies.

In 1976, British historian Peter Laslett challenged the universalist portrayal of "the aged" embodied by modernization theory, contending that theorists perpetuated a mythical "world we have lost" syndrome. He identified four aspects of the "golden age" myth: (1) before and after processes connecting the social outcomes of aging to modernization (i.e., that after modernization, older people's social status inevitably declined); (2) traditional societies regarded and bestowed on older people universal respect; (3) specified and valued economic roles existed for older people in traditional societies; and (4) the assumption that older persons were cared for by their relatives living in multigenerational households. He contended that modernization theorists mistakenly incorporated these myths into a formal theory of aging.

American historian David Hackett Fischer (1977) agreed with modernization theorists that the status of older people had declined over time, but argued that, in the United States, this status decline began long before modernization and industrialization could have been the cause. Fischer identified a the period of decline during the years preceding American industrialization. He argued that the cultural transformation in the status of older people occurred as Americans picked up on the ideals of liberty and equality in the late eighteenth and early nineteenth centuries influenced by their own experiences as founders of a new nation and by the ideals of the French Revolution. New cultural beliefs about equality destroyed the hierarchical conception of the world on which the authority of age had rested, while the ideal of liberty dissolved their communal base of power. Consequently, older Americans were displaced from their previously high status positions.

W. Andrew Achenbaum (1978) differed with Fischer in terms of the timing of negative cultural perceptions of older people in the United States. Achenbaum identified the post–Civil War era as the period during which negative views of older people became prominent. Elders were still called on for advice and were seen as moral exemplars of health and longevity until the 1860s, according to Achenbaum. Despite disagreements about timing, these two historians identified cultural factors, not the socioeconomic changes emphasized in modernization theory, as most influential in determining the social position of older people in U.S. society.

Other critiques of the modernization model examined its foundational assumptions. For example, modernization theorists assumed that the extended family form represented the typical family in pre-twentieth-century, nonindustrial societies, and that its displacement by the nuclear family contributed to the decline in the status of older people. Yet studies by John Demos (1978) and Peter Laslett (1976) have shown that extended multigenerational families were less common than other family forms, and that elder Americans and English people preferred living in primary residences rather than with their children. More recent work by Emily Abel (1992) also questioned modernization theory assumptions

about family life. Abel found that rural elders living in the 1800s did not necessarily enjoy high social status and that intergenerational living arrangements often caused problems for the children and their parents.

In 1994, Tamara Hareven critiqued the linear modernization approach to understanding social change, emphasizing the importance of an historical and life-course approach to studying old age. Her review of historical changes in generational relations in American society demonstrated that individual and familial experiences and specific historical circumstances were of utmost importance in understanding generational relations. She emphasized the importance of taking race and ethnicity, class, and family form into account when studying intergenerational family relationships.

Peter Stearns (1977) and Jon Hendricks and C. Davis Hendricks (1978) provided evidence that challenged the view that pre-industrial Western European societies valued old age and were tolerant of old people. Thomas Cole's (1992) cultural history of old age in the United States and Georges Minois's (1987) history of old age in Western culture both demonstrated ambivalent and evolving perceptions toward, and varied statuses experienced by, older people.

Researchers have also challenged the assumption in modernization studies that non-western societies would mirror changes Western countries experienced as they industrialized. Ellen Rhoads (1984) argued that culture was a more important factor than modernization in explaining the status of older people. From her work in Samoa, a modernizing society, she found little evidence to support the idea that individuals lose status as they age. If a society has a tradition of revering its elders, she argued, this tradition would likely persist even as the society becomes more modern.

In 1984, Ann Foner warned against assuming that the status of all older people deteriorates when nonindustrial societies begin to change. According to Monica Wilson (1977), under British colonial rule, the status of elderly African men actually increased. African elders in Nyakyusa remained chiefs and held offices much longer than they would have in precolonial times. More recently, York Bradshaw and Michael Wallace (1996) found that elder Africans are still deeply respected and never without the company of family members. Africans see Westerners as too quick to dispose of an older and wiser generation.

The historical status of older people varies according to race, gender, social class, and culture. Modernization theory overlooked the diverse positions of older people across different societies and the diversity of elders across gender, racial and ethnic groups, and economic classes within societies. For example, in 1990, Susan De Vos examined the extended-family household situations of elderly people in six Latin American countries. She found a larger number of elderly people living in extended households compared to Western nations, however, this was usually because they needed special support. Women were especially likely to live in extended families because they traditionally had been more economically dependent and emotionally closer to their kin than their male counterparts. De Vos found little difference between urban and rural residents in the likelihood of living in an extended family, undermining the modernization proposition of rural extended families and urban nuclear families. Among others, James Thorson (1995) identified economic status as an important variable in understanding the status of older people, since status is often gauged by relative income. The relative status of older people has improved in modernized societies as their relative economic position has improved.

Clearly, modernization theory created a growth industry of refinement and critique among social gerontologists. Modernization theory has been challenged in the decades since its original formulation for offering an oversimplified, linear explanation of inevitable decline in the status of older people in industrializing societies. Critiques of modernization theory have developed threads in social gerontological research that are attentive to issues of timing and pace of change, the evolution in family forms, cultural values about aging and old age, and the multiple statuses that people enjoy—and that endure—as they age in a modern world.

Modernization theory and social gerontology

The social processes involved in societal modernization have profound effects on all people living in modernizing societies, including people of advanced age. Industrialization changed the way goods and services were produced and where production occurred. The rise of mass education expanded literacy and exposed people to new ideas and practices in science and technology. Family forms, cultural values, and other social institutions were not immune from changes resulting from modernization processes. Despite its shortcomings, modernization, as a conceptual framework, provides a useful way to understand some of the processes and effects of the social transformations of the nineteenth and twentieth centuries. By considering the interrelationships between various types and paces of change, important insights about the potential effects of broad social transformations on societies and the people living in them have been gained.

Formal modernization theory provided a platform upon which historians and social scientists could ask research questions designed to better understand how older people fared under rapidly changing social circumstances. While it is a valid critique that modernization theory alone oversimplifies the complex processes and interactions that condition the status of older people in their social worlds, it is also true that modernization theory spurred thoughtful and sustained research designed to prove or disprove its assumptions. This research, building on the pioneering work of modernization theorists, has provided key findings that have clarified our understanding of the myriad and evolving roles of elderly persons in modern and modernizing societies. It has helped us to understand the complex interactions between changes in a society's social structure and people's racial, ethnic, gender, and cultural positions, and the outcomes that these complex social relationships generate.

DEBRA STREET
LORI PARHAM

See also GERONTOCRACY; POPULATION AGING; THEORIES, SOCIAL.

BIBLIOGRAPHY

ABEL, E. K. "Parental Dependence and Filial Responsibility in the Nineteenth Century: Hial Hawley and Emily Hawley Gillespie, 1884–1885." *The Gerontologist* 32 (1992): 519–526.

ACHENBAUM, A. W. *Old Age in the New Land.* Baltimore, Md.: Johns Hopkins University Press, 1978.

BRADSHAW, Y., and WALLACE, M. *Global Inequalities.* Thousand Oaks, Calif.: Pine Forge Press, 1996.

COLE, T. *The Journey of Life: A Cultural History of Aging in America*. Cambridge, U.K.: Cambridge University Press, 1992.

COWGILL, D. O. "Aging and Modernization: A Revision of the Theory." In *Communities and Environmental Policy*. Edited by Jaber F. Gubrium *Communities and Environmental Policy*. Springfield, Ill.: Charles Thomas, 1993. Pages 124–146.

COWGILL, D. O., and HOLMES, L. D., eds. *Aging and Modernization*. New York: Appleton-Century-Crofts, 1972.

DEMOS, J. "Old Age in Early New England." In *Turning Points: Historical and Sociological Essays on the Family*. Edited by J. Demos and S. Boocock. Chicago: University of Chicago Press, 1978.

DE VOS, S. "Extended Family Living Among Older People in Six Latin American Countries." *Journal of Gerontology* 45, no. 3 (1991): S87–94.

FISCHER, D. H. *Growing Old in America*. New York: Oxford University Press, 1977.

FONER, N. "Age and Social Change." In *Age and Anthropological Theory*. Edited by David I. Kertzer and Jennie Keith Ithaca, N.Y.: Cornell University Press, 1984. Pages 195–216.

HAREVEN, T. "Aging and Generational Relations: A Historical and Lifecourse Perspective." *Annual Review of Sociology* 20 (1994): 437–461.

HENDRICKS, J., and DAVIS, H. C. "The Age Old Question of Old-Age: Was It Really So Much Better Back When?" *International Journal of Aging and Human Development* 8 (1978): 139–154.

LASLETT, P. "Societal Development and Aging." In *Handbook of Aging and Social Sciences*. Edited by Robert H. Binstock and Ethel Shanas. New York: Van Nostrand Reinhold, 1976. Pages 57–116.

MINOIS, G. *History of Old Age*. Chicago, Ill.: University of Chicago Press, 1987.

PALMORE, E. B., and MANTON, K. "Modernization and Status of the Aged: International Correlations." *Journal of Gerontology* 29 (1974): 205–210.

QUADAGNO, J. *Aging in Early Industrial Society: Work, Family and Social Policy in Nineteenth Century England*. New York: Academic Press, 1982.

RHOADS, E. "Reevaulation of the Aging and Modernization Theory: The Samoan Evidence." *Gerontologist* 24 (1984): 243–250.

STEARNS, P. N. *Old Age in European Society*. New York: Holmes and Meier, 1977.

THORSON, J. A. *Aging in a Changing Society*. New York: Wadsworth Publishing, 1995.

WILSON, M. *For Men and Elders*. London: International African Institute, 1977.

STATUS OF OLDER PEOPLE: PREINDUSTRIAL WEST

It is commonly believed that it was rare to live to old age in the preindustrial west. This misconception arises from confusion between average life expectancy at birth and the actual life spans of those who survived the high mortality years of early life. For example, in England life expectancy at birth averaged around thirty-five years between the 1540s and 1800. But those who survived the hazardous first years of life had a good chance of living into their fifties and beyond. The proportion of the English population aged over sixty fluctuated between 6 and 8 percent through the seventeenth and eighteenth centuries. It fell to 6 percent in the nineteenth century, when high birth rates raised the percentage of the very young. Proportions of older people in all European countries varied from community to community, generally high in depressed rural areas, which younger people left in search of work, lower in expanding towns. France, by contrast, experienced falling birth rates in the nineteenth century. In the mid-eighteenth century, 7 to 8 percent of the population were aged sixty or above; by 1860 the proportion was 10 percent.

It is also sometimes asserted that it was rare for women to live to old age. But in England women were a clear majority among those age sixty and above from the time that vital statistics began to be officially and comprehensively recorded in 1837; in fact, women appear to have had a longer life expectancy, on average, for long before. Medieval commentators noted that women seemed to have the longer life expectancy, and they wondered how that could be when it seemed "natural" that men were stronger and should live longer. Physicians in eighteenth-century France were still puzzled by the consistency with which females "went against nature" and outlived men. It is sometimes thought that before the nineteenth century, female life expectancy must have been sharply reduced by death in childbirth. But though such deaths undoubtedly, and tragically, occurred more frequently than in the twentieth century, childbirth was not a mass killer of women. It was no more lethal than the ravages of work, war, and everyday violence on the lives of men of comparable age.

How was "old age" defined?

Was the boundary between middle and old age the same in all time periods? Generally historical demographers choose the ages sixty or sixty-five, the conventional age boundary of the later twentieth century, as the lower limit of "old age." It is essential to choose a fixed age threshold if statistical comparisons of age structure are to be made over time. But did people perhaps become "old" at earlier ages in previous centuries, when living standards were lower? Strikingly, the ages of sixty and seventy have been used to signify the onset of old age in formal institutions in Europe at least since medieval times. Sixty was long the age at which law or custom permitted withdrawal from public activities on grounds of old age. In medieval England men and women ceased at age sixty to be liable for compulsory service under the labor laws, to be prosecuted for vagrancy, or (in the case of men only) to perform military service. From the thirteenth century, seventy was set as the upper limit for jury service. Similar regulations held elsewhere in Europe. It can be argued that governments had an incentive to set such ages as high as possible, especially when they might exact taxation in lieu of service, but it is unlikely that they could have been set at levels far removed from popular perceptions of the threshold of old age. Furthermore, appointments were made to elite positions at advanced ages. In England the average age at death of the nine seventeenth-century archbishops of Canterbury (the leader of the Church of England) was seventy-three, and the average age of appointment was sixty.

On the other hand, it was long assumed that most manual workers could not remain fully active at their trades much past age fifty, especially when performance depended upon such physical attributes as eyesight. Literary evidence from the sixteenth century suggests that the fifties were regarded as the declining side of working maturity, the beginning of old age. This is still popularly assumed at the end of the twentieth century and again suggests that cultural definitions of old age have not changed greatly over time. For women old age was often thought to start earlier, in the late forties or around fifty, as menopause became visible, though the evidence on this is ambiguous and there are many signs of women in their fifties and beyond leading active and respected lives in their communities. For men the defining, and more visible, characteristic was capacity for full-time work.

For both men and women in preindustrial Europe old age was defined by appearance and capacities rather than by age-defined rules about pensions and retirement, hence people could be defined as "old" at variable ages. English poor relief records in the eighteenth century first describe some people as "old" in their fifties, others not until their seventies. Suppliants for public service pensions in eighteenth-century France ranged in age from fifty-four to eighty years.

This suggests that over many centuries old age has been defined in different ways, different contexts, and for different social groups. Three of the most common ways of framing old age are chronological, functional, and cultural. A fixed threshold of *chronological old age* has long been a bureaucratic convenience, suitable for establishing age limits to rights and duties, such as access to pensions or eligibility for public service. It has become more pervasive since industrialization. *Functional old age* is reached when an individual cannot perform the tasks expected of him or her, such as paid work. *Cultural old age* occurs when an individual "looks old" according to the norms of the community and behaves and is treated as old. Despite impressive continuities over long time periods in both official and popular definitions of the onset of old age, undoubtedly a high proportion of survivors in medieval and preindustrial societies felt and looked old at earlier ages than has become the norm since industrialization. In consequence, the numbers of people who appeared to be old in past communities might have been greater, and they would have been a more visible cultural presence, than is revealed simply by calculating the numbers past age sixty.

Also, it has long been recognized that there is immense variety in the experience of human aging, that people do not age at the same pace or in the same ways, and they continue to change even after the formal threshold of "old age" is passed. Since antiquity commentators have divided old age into stages. Some of these were elaborate, such as the medieval "ages of man" schema, which divided life into three, four, seven, or twelve ages. These stylized age divisions often had didactic or metaphorical rather than strictly descriptive purposes. More commonly, in everyday discourse, old age was divided into what in preindustrial England was called "green" old age, a time of fitness and activity, with perhaps some failing powers, and the later phase of decrepitude. The sad decline with which some, but not all, older lives end was never represented positively.

How did older people support themselves in the preindustrial west?

Some older people possessed property, often in substantial amounts, on which they could live until death, employing others to care for them, if necessary, either in institutions or in their own households. From the earliest times in most western countries aging individuals could legally assign property to relatives or nonrelatives in return for guaranteed support until death, and they could invoke the protection of the law if the agreement was not honored. Older people determinedly sought to control their own lives and to retain their independence throughout much of western culture through time. For the propertyless and impoverished there was, in most times, little choice but to work for pay for as long as possible, whereas the propertied could in all times retire from work when they chose. In Norwich, England, in 1570, three widows, ages seventy-four, seventy-nine, and eighty-two, were described only as "almost past work" and they were still earning small sums at spinning. Poor relief systems encouraged older men and women to work, supplementing but not replacing meager incomes. Most communities provided specified tasks for poor older people. Roadmending, caring for the churchyard, fetching, and tending horses on market days were tasks for old men. It was often easier for women to support themselves at later ages, by caring for children, providing casual domestic labor, such as cleaning or washing, taking in lodgers, or running small shops or alehouses.

Another important resource was family support. As far back in time as can be traced, it has not been the norm in all western societies for older people to share households with their married children. To do so was conventional in Mediterranean societies and in some north European peasant cultures, such as Ireland and parts of France, where land was the family's only asset and the heir shared land and household with the elders until their death. In much of northwestern Europe, however, elders retained control of their own households for as long as they were able, rarely sharing them with adult married children, though they might move to the home of a relative when they were no longer capable of independence, perhaps for a short time before death. North European folklore, even in medieval times, expressed few illusions about intergenerational support, but long conveyed warnings of the danger to older people of placing themselves and their possessions under the control of their children. Such stories achieved their most sublime expression in William Shakespeare's *King Lear*.

Most countries incorporated into law some obligation upon adult children and sometimes other close relatives to support their elders. How frequently such practices were implemented was variable, not least because the kin of the aged poor were often very poor themselves and could not realistically be expected to give support. The customs and practice of the Old World were transported to the New. Settler societies gave even greater salience to the independence and self-help that was necessary for survival, and such societies took time to build the communal, often religious-based, institutions which supplemented self- and family support in much of Europe.

But the fact that older people did not conventionally share a home with close relatives, and determinedly retained their independence for as long as they were able, does not mean that there were not close emotional ties and exchanges of support between the generations. Parents and adult offspring might not share a household, but they often lived in close proximity, even in the highly mobile society that England was for centuries before industrialization. Generally in western societies "kinship did not stop at the front door" (Jutte, p. 90). Sociologists Rosenmayr and Kockeis have described the north European family as characterized by "intimacy at a distance", the intimacy being as important as the distance. Old people could in general expect help from their children based on the sustenance and protection provided by parents during the childhood period. Family members at all social levels exchanged support and services from a mixture of material, calculative, and emotional motives. That it was often an exchange relationship should be emphasized. Older people in the past, as now, were rarely simply dependent upon others, unless they were in severe physical decline. They cared for grandchildren, for sick people, supported younger people financially when they could afford it, and performed myriad other services for others. Intergenerational exchange often took the form of services (a daughter performing housework or providing meals, a grandparent caring for grandchildren) or gifts in kind rather than of cash.

But not all older people had families to support them. High death rates meant that parents might outlive children. Up to one-third of women living to age sixty-five in England between the seventeenth and the nineteenth centuries had no surviving children. Geographical mobility was limited at a time when transport was slow, and many people who were illiterate might break contacts even between survivors.

Those who had no families could create them. Older men married younger women able to look after them; older women married younger men if the men were wealthier, or could care for children after a wife's death. Orphan children were adopted by older people, gaining a home in return for giving service. Unrelated poor people shared households for mutual support.

Charity and poor relief

When families were not able, willing, or available to help, many older people needed the support of charity or public welfare. Not all older people were poor, but in most preindustrial societies they were more likely than younger people to be very poor, especially if they were female. All European societies had some collectively funded system of provision for the aged and other poor people, and charitable funds, often religious in motivation and institutionalization. This system could provide payments in cash or kind (food, clothing, medical care) or shelter in a hospital or workhouse. Provision was of variable quality, within each country as well as over time, and it was guided by varied principles: supportive, rehabilitative, or punitive. Everywhere old people were numerous among recipients of relief, along with widows and children, but nowhere did reaching a defined age automatically qualify anyone for relief. The essential qualification was destitution.

Countries of the "new" world tended to reject publicly funded welfare systems because initially they lacked both an established, substantial wealthy class capable of funding them and the mass of miserable poor that required them. Also, nineteenth-century migrants were often fleeing from punitive relief systems in Europe and had no desire to replicate them. Ideologically, too, they placed a premium upon independence and

self-help. Australia and New Zealand never introduced publicly funded poor relief systems, relying instead upon voluntary charity, sometimes (and increasingly over time) subsidized from public funds. The picture was similar in nineteenth-century Canada. In parts of the United States the extent of unmet need necessitated the introduction of poor relief, but "welfare" early acquired and retained more stigmatizing associations than elsewhere in the west. Most nation-states, at least by the eighteenth century and commonly in the nineteenth, provided publicly funded pensions for public servants and for the disabled veterans of war and sometimes for their families.

Declining status of older people

It is sometimes argued that the dependence and marginalization of older people has increased, that they are less valued in industrial than in preindustrial societies. The belief that the status of older people is always declining has a very long history. It is discussed, and dismissed, even in the opening pages of Plato's *Republic* and in a long succession of texts through the centuries. The longevity of this narrative trope suggests that it expresses persistent cultural fears of aging and neglect, and real divergence in experience in most times and places, rather than representing transparent reality.

Early historical inquiry into old age tended to echo this narrative of decline. George Minois's history of old age in western culture from antiquity to the Renaissance acknowledged variations and complexities in experiences and perceptions of old age over this long time span, but he still concluded that "the general tendency however is towards degradation" (pp. 6–7). Studies of old age in the United States since the eighteenth century find the status of old people to be in decline over a variety of time scales: from the late eighteenth century to the early nineteenth, in the mid-nineteenth, and between the late nineteenth and twentieth centuries. These were mostly studies of white males in specific situations. The fact that some older men exerted power at a particular time does not necessarily suggest that all older people at that time and place were highly regarded. In all times in western culture, older people (female and male) who retained economic or any other form of power, along with their faculties, could command, or enforce, respect. In contrast, at all times powerless older people have been marginalized and denigrated, though not universally.

Attitudes toward and experiences of older age in all times and over time were varied and complex, following no simple trajectories, and historical texts must be read with care. It may be tempting, for example, to conclude that Shakespeare's famous climax to the "seven ages of man" described by Jaques in *As You Like It*—"second childishness and mere oblivion; sans teeth, sans eyes, sans taste, sans everything"—is representative of sixteenth century English perceptions of old age. If, that is, you fail to note that Jaques is a relatively young man, but is given the conventional literary attributes of an old man, such as melancholy; and that the dismal description of the "seventh age" is subverted by the immediate entrance on stage of an octogenarian, Adam, who has earlier been represented as "strong and lusty." The pervasiveness in English popular drama and literature (for example, in the work of Chaucer) of such dialogue between conflicting representations of old age, negative and positive, and its evident familiarity to pre-industrial audiences, suggests its deep roots in English culture and probably in that of other western societies.

PATRICIA M. THANE

See also AGE; AGE NORMS; GERONTOCRACY; LITERATURE AND AGING; STATUS OF OLDER PEOPLE: THE ANCIENT AND BIBLICAL WORLDS; STATUS OF OLDER PEOPLE: MODERNIZATION.

BIBLIOGRAPHY

ACHENBAUM, W. A. *Old Age in the New Land. The American Experience since 1978.* Baltimore: John Hopkins University Press, 1978.

BOTELHO, L., and THANE, P. *Women and Ageing in Britain Since 1500.* London: Routledge, 1999.

BURROW, J. A. *The Ages of Man: A Study in Medieval Writing and Thought.* Oxford, U.K.: Oxford University Press, 1986.

COLE, T. R. *The Journey of Life. A Cultural History of Aging in America.* Cambridge, U.K.: Cambridge University Press, 1992.

DICKEY, B. *No Charity There: A Short History of Social Welfare in Australia.* Melbourne: Thomas Nelson, 1980.

FISCHER, D. H. *Growing Old in America.* New York: Oxford University Press, 1978.

HABER, C. *Beyond Sixty-Five: The Dilemma of Old Age in America's Past.* New York: Cambridge University Press, 1983.

HABER, C., and GRATTON, B. *Old Age and the Search for Security. An American Social History.* Bloomington: Indiana University Press, 1994.

JOHNSON, P., and THANE, P., eds. *Old Age from Antiquity to Post-Modernity.* London: Routledge, 1998.

JUTTE, R. *Poverty and Deviance in Early Modern Europe.* Cambridge, U.K.: Cambridge University Press, 1994.

MINOIS, G. *History of Old Age. From Antiquity to the Renaissance.* Translated by S. Hanbury-Tenison. Oxford, U.K.: Polity, 1989.

MONTIGNY, E.-A. *Foisted upon the Government. State Responsibilities, Family Obligations, and the Care of the Dependent Aged in Late Nineteenth Century Ontario.* Montreal: McGill-Queens University Press, 1997.

PELLING, M., and SMITH R. M., eds. *Life, Death, and the Elderly: Historical Perspectives on Ageing.* London: Routledge, 1991.

ROSENMAYR, L., and KOCKEIS, E. "Proposition for a Sociological Theory of Aging and the Family." *International Social Science Journal* 3, (1963): 418–419.

ROSENTHAL, J. T. *Old Age in Late Medieval England.* Philadelphia: Temple University Press, 1996.

SCHOFIELD, R. S. "Did the Mothers Really Die? Three Centuries of Maternal Mortality in 'The World We Have Lost'." In *The World We Have Gained.* Edited by L. Bonfield et al. Oxford, U.K.: Blackwell, 1986. Pages 231–260.

SEARS, E. *The Ages of Man: Medieval Interpretations of the Life Cycle.* Princeton: Princeton University Press, 1986.

SHAHAR, S. *Growing Old in the Middle Ages.* London: Routledge, 1997.

THANE, P. *Old Age in English History: Past Experiences, Present Issues.* London: Oxford University Press, 2000.

TROYANSKY, D. G. *Old Age in the Old Regime: Image and Experience in Eighteenth Century France.* Ithaca, N.Y.: Cornell University Press, 1989.

WRIGLEY, E. A., and SCHOFIELD R. S *The Population History of England, 1541–1871:A Reconstruction.* London: Edward Arnold, 1981.

STATUS OF OLDER PEOPLE: TRIBAL SOCIETIES

To anthropologists, a tribal society is an uncentralized grouping of autonomous local communities linked by common cultural features and associations. These social entities are connected by kin-based organizations such as clan, or associations based on age grading or special activities such as ritual, which cross-cut kinship and territorial boundaries (Haviland). Households tend to be egalitarian, having relatively equal access to available material and social resources, although there can be significant differences based on gender and age. Community size tends to be small, ranging from one hundred to one thousand, but it varies over the annual cycle as the separate communities might come together to initiate a new age grouping or carry out some vital economic activity. Tribal communities typically have an economic base in horticulture or animal herding, although foraging and hunting in rich environments sometimes supports this kind of sociopolitical organization.

In such small scale, kin-focused societies, passage through the life span allows the accumulation of social debt and cultural knowledge that forms the basis of respect and support of older adults. In such cultural settings, the wide embrace of family frequently provides what Andrei Simic calls a *life-term arena*—a stable setting for the engagement of an entire life. The lack of economic specialization through a division of labor tends to enable people of all ages to link their changing abilities and knowledge to the varied tasks over the annual work cycle. There are two important effects from this that are common in tribal societies. First, work groups are often age heterogeneous, and second, these arrangements facilitate the learning of new work skills as one passes through the life cycle (Halperin).

There is now a large body of literature on the status of older people in tribal societies. Much of this material was written before the 1970s, and has had to be mined from disparate ethnographic reports, which in some cases gave tantalizingly short and often enigmic information about the situation of elders in tribal communities. The first major effort to make sense out of this literature was the seminal book by Leo Simmons, *The Role of the Aged in Primitive Society* (1945). His study examined the interrelation of 109 sociocultural traits, grouped under habitat and economy, political and social organization, and religious beliefs and ritual. Despite some serious methodological flaws, Simmons's book remains a vital resource of anthropological knowledge on the elderly in tribal societies.

It was not until the publication of *Aging and Modernization,* edited by George Cowgill and Lowell Holmes, in 1972, that knowledge from modern ethnographic studies was employed to test gerontological theory. Here, detailed studies of fourteen different societies were compared to examine the impact of industrialization, urbanization, and Westernization on the status of the aged. The theoretical propositions developed by Cowgill and Holmes in this and later works have served as a most controversial stimulus to subsequent work on aging done around the world. Access to this rapidly expanding literature can be found in several edited compilations and texts: *The Politics of Age and Gerontocracy in Africa* (Aguilar); *The Cultural Context of Aging,* 2nd edition (Sokolovsky); *Other Cultures, Elder Years,* 2nd edition (Holmes and Rhodes); *Old Age in Global Perspective* (Albert and Cattell); *The Aging Experience* (Keith and Associates); *Aging Around the World* (Cowgill); and *Aging and Its Transformations* (Counts and Counts); *Other Ways of Growing Old* (Amoss and Harrel). Information about new and ongoing ethnographic aging research and related publications can be followed through the Cultural Context of Aging Web site at www.stpt.usf.edu/~jsokolov.

Longevity

There is a lack of good longevity data from tribal societies, especially prior to the drastic dislocations of these societies during the nineteenth and twentieth centuries caused by the colonial expansion of European nations. What data exists indicates that only about 10 percent of those born will survive beyond age sixty, compared to well over 80 percent in the United States. Average life expectancy within tribal settings tends to be low, typically less than thirty years of age, primarily due to high levels of infant and child mortality. As a result, only about 3 percent of a village population contain persons over age sixty-five (Weiss). However, those who survive until their fifth and sixth decades of life are often exceptionally fit by Western standards. People in such societies do in fact sometimes survive the full human life span, into their ninth or tenth decades. It is also important to note that reports of extraordinary life spans of over 120 years reported during the 1970s for tribal peoples of the Korakoram mountains of Pakistan or among Abkhasian peasants in the Caucasus region of the former Soviet Union have been completely discredited (Cowgill). Such erroneous reports were based on systematic age exaggeration, confusing and fraudulent written documentation and small sample sizes.

The cultural construction of elders and older adulthood

The construct of a stage of elderhood or of later adulthood appears to exist in all tribal societies and is largely based on combining social and functional definitions of one's place in the life cycle. Often there is a distinction between elderhood as a marker of social maturity in relation to others in the community contrasted to boundaries of old age that can take some of the criteria of elderhood and combine them with how a person's physical being and behavior reflects the biological aging process. Elderhood on the one hand is a relative status marker, accomplished by passing through ritual transitions, and is not necessarily tied to extended chronological years. Persons who do not pass these ritual markers will not be considered elders no matter what their age. Among Australian aboriginal tribes as well as in Africa, persons could enter the beginning ranks of elderhood in their early thirties and proceed over time and through ritual passage into different elder statuses.

Older adulthood on the other hand links changes in the persons physical being (reduction of work capacity, beginning of menopause) with social changes (such as the birth of grandchildren) to create a culturally defined sense of oldness, which like elderhood, can have various gradations that can even extend beyond the point of death. Steve Albert and Maria Cattell make a helpful distinction between old age, ancients, and ancestors. The first notion of *old age* typically begins in tribal societies between the fourth and fifth decades of life, with a change in social/economic role being the most common beginning marker (Glascock and Feinman).

Factors such as invalid status and senility are quite rare as primary indicators of a general designation of old, since tribal culture begins using such labels before such changes are likely. However, many tribal societies also recognize those truly ancient adults who show sharp declines in functional skills as a different category of old, which may lead to a dramatic loss of status and even neglect and actions that hasten a person's death (Glascock).

Ancestorhood is another social category very common among tribal cultures. In such societies, whether in the Amazon or Sub-Saharan Africa, ancestral spirits remain part of the family system and have the ability to affect the lives of their descendants, both for good and evil. In some societies, such as the Tiriki of Kenya, ancestral spirits are perceived to be the mystical source of all human life and vitality (Sangree). Very old adults that are close to death are thought to have a special connection to ancestors and may ask them to intercede on behalf of their family, or even call upon them to curse a kinsperson who is acting badly.

Gender and age

Despite the strong male dominance in many tribal societies, some authors have begun to document a pattern of positive changes of role, power, and status by women as they pass into the middle and later adult years. These occur when women enter their postreproductive phase, and culminate when mastery of the domestic sphere is complete—as marked by control of the daughter-in-law and other adult female kin, influence over married sons and their children, greater authority over life-cycle ritual, and the gradual withdrawal of a woman's older spouse out of his public domain and into her hearth-centered life. As P. Silverman notes, "even in male dominated societies, like the Comanche in North America, the Mundurucu of South America and the Ewe of West Africa, women who have reached menopause fill important decision-roles otherwise restricted to men" (Silverman, 1987, p. 335). While some theorists have stressed the cultural turning points linked to procreative and family cycles, others have suggested that universal intrapsychic personality development best explains the frequent reversals observed among older adults (Gutmann). A classic description of this process is provided by Kaberry in an early anthropological study of Australian aboriginal women:

As the women become older they often assume more authority, become more assertive, tender their advice more frequently and interfere where the activities of any of their kindred are likely to run contrary to the tribal law. On the other hand, when anger mounts high and threatens the peace, even safety of others in the camp, they take the initiative in stemming the disputes and temporarily establishing order again. Amidst the shouting, the barking of dogs, the voice of an old woman will make itself heard above the uproar as she harangues men and women impartially (Kaberry, 1937, p. 181).

Old age in myth and folklore

Many tribal peoples use older adults in their mythology to teach morality and worn of dire consequences if ethical behavior is not followed. For example, the Murgin aboriginal peoples of Australia have an important myth of the "Old Woman and the Turtle Flipper." This story tells of a turtle hunt by men of the Gwiyula clan. After the hunt a good piece of meat is given to all local clan members except an older woman, who gets a flipper. This insulted woman asks, "How can anyone find fat on a flipper?" and states "You men are greedy." She then precedes, through magical powers, to produce pestilence that kills all individuals except for a man and a woman who eventually repopulate the world (Warner).

In another area of the Pacific, among the Asmat people of southwestern Irian Jaya (Indonesian New Guinea), a mythological personage called "the oldest man" and also "father of the people," was responsible for creating the ritual system and determining where and how people should live. There is also mythic belief in an old man named "famiripits" who carved wooden figures of humans, placed them in the men's ceremonial house and then proceeded to drum them to life. Peter Van Arsdale, who studied these people, asserts that such beliefs under precolonial conditions led to an equation of age with greater potential for knowledge, influence, and the ability to shape the direction of human development.

Age and generation as organization

In some tribal societies where age is used as the most powerful organizing principle, different spans along the life cycle are sharply set apart by highly managed images involving spectacular ritual, distinct dress, specialized tasks, modes of speech, comportment, and deferential gestures. Persons move through the life cycle collectively and form tightly bound groups, or age-sets, performing specific tasks. Societies where age plays such a powerful role in ordering social life have been found in Africa, among certain Native American groups and Australian aborigines, and in Papua, New Guinea (Bernardi). The most elaborate forms of such cultural systems are found among East African nomadic herders, such as the Samburu of Kenya (Spencer). Here, age-sets of males initiated together move through the life cycle collectively. Over time and through elaborate ritual, they progressively enter, as a group, age-bounded roles of herders, warriors, and, finally, three levels of elders who exert control over the lives of younger community members. The middle-level elders, in their

fifth and sixth decades, gain substantial power through maintaining large polygynous households, holding wealth in their numerous cattle and having a ritual link to their ancestors, whom they can call upon to curse younger persons who misbehave. As is the case for most such age-based societies, a Samburu woman's social maturation is accomplished through individual life-cycle rituals and her status is much more tied to the her place in family units (see Kertzer and Madison for a description of one of the rarer cases of women's age-sets). Societies such as the Samburu are said to be gerontocracies (from *gerontes,* old men), where authority and esteem cumulate in the eldest males. In reality, it is often the middle group of elders in their fifties and early sixties who typically hold the most power in such societies.

All too often such cultures have been held up as exemplars of places where a strong positive image of the elderly reaches its zenith. It is important to note that this is frequently accomplished at the expense of intense intergenerational conflict, of exploiting and repressing the young and preventing women from gaining an equitable place in the community. Among the Samburu, older women in fact do not share the very powerful image associated with old men. When they are widowed, women are not permitted to marry again and suffer both materially and socially.

Status of the aged

In tribal societies, older adults commonly function as a storehouse of knowledge about such things as family lineage, religious rituals, lore and myth that explain tribal origins and identity as well as in-depth knowledge about the environment and how to exploit it for survival. Among many African tribal peoples, older adults are the gatekeepers for the ritual management of life, from the naming of children to the planting songs chanted by West African village women to assure the younger female farmers that the harvest will be good.

Despite the respect that relative age often generates in tribal societies, many anthropologists find that chronological age itself is seldom the basis for respect or authority. Pamela Amoss and Steven Harrell have proposed that there are two key factors that determine how older adults fare in their particular cultural settings. The first is the relative balance between the contributions older persons make and the costs to society that they represent; the second is the control older persons have over resources that are important to younger members of the community. Amoss and Harrell sum this up succinctly by predicting that "the position of the aged in a given society can be expressed in terms of how much old people contribute to the resources of the group, balanced by the cost they exact, and compounded by the degree of control they have over valuable resources" (1981, p. 6).

While this formulation has not been cross-culturally tested through a large sampling of societies, the issue of control of resources has received a great deal of study in relation to status and treatment of older adults.

A series of global statistical studies have corroborated in many respects the association of status and deference with the control of informational and administrative roles, as well as with valued activities and extended family integration (Silverman). This research shows that, in terms of resource and information control, only certain types of control, particularly administration and consultation, correlate with beneficent treatment of the elderly. Some forms of supernatural information control, especially transformational powers are, in fact, a potential threat to the elderly. This fact is highly relevant to some historically known situations of massive societal change, such as in Europe during the thirteenth through the sixteenth centuries, where the majority of persons burned at the stake for their transformational knowledge (witchcraft) were middle-aged and older females (Bever).

Some worldwide statistical studies have dealt with the darker side of aging, including various types of nonsupportive, and even harsh, treatment directed toward the elderly. This work makes it clear that being old in a small-scale, traditional, face-to-face community does not necessarily prevent cultural variants of death hastening from occurring. Anthony Glascock found that killing of the aged was found in about one-fifth of his global sample, and that 84 percent of the societies exhibited various forms of nonsupportive treatment. However, few societies enforce a single treatment of their elderly, and it was commonly found that both supportive behavior and death-hastening behavior coexisted in the same social setting. Glascock's study demonstrates that cultural distinctions drawn between intact, fully functioning older adults and

decrepit individuals who find it difficult to carry out even the most basic tasks are critical. It is persons placed in this latter category toward which geronticide or death hastening is most frequently applied.

JAY SOKOLOVSKY

See also AGE; AGE NORMS; GERONTOCRACY; STATUS OF OLDER PEOPLE: PREINDUSTRIAL WEST.

BIBLIOGRAPHY

AGUILAR, M., ed. *The Politics of Age and Gerontocracy in Africa: Ethnographies of the Past and Memories of the Present.* Lawrenceville, N.J.: Africa World Press, 1998.

ALBERT, S., and CATTELL, M. *Old Age in Global Perspective: Cross-Cultural and Cross-National Views.* New York: G. K. Hall, 1994.

AMOSS, P., and HARRELL, S., eds. *Other Ways of Growing Old: Anthropological Perspectives.* Stanford: Stanford University Press, 1981.

BARKER, J. "Between Humans and Ghosts: The Decrepit Elderly in a Polynesian Society." In *The Cultural Context of Aging: World-Wide Perspectives*, 2d ed. Edited by J. Sokolovsky. Westport, Conn.: Bergin and Garvey, 1997. Pages 107–125.

BERNARDI, B. *Age Class Systems.* Cambridge: Cambridge University Press, 1985.

BEVER, E. "Witchcraft Fears and Psychosocial Factors in Disease." *Journal of Interdisciplinary History* 30 (2000): 573–590.

CATTELL, M. "African Widows, Culture and Social Change: Case Studies from Kenya." In *The Cultural Context of Aging: World-Wide Perspectives*, 2d ed. Edited by J. Sokolovsky. Westport, Conn.: Bergin and Garvey, 1997. Pages 71–98.

COUNTS, D., and COUNTS, D., eds. *Aging and Its Transformations: Moving Toward Death in Pacific Societies.* New York: University Press of America, 1985.

COWGILL, D. *Aging Around the World.* Belmont: Wadsworth, 1986.

COWGILL, D., and HOLMES, L. D., eds. *Aging and Modernization.* New York: Appleton-Century-Crofts, 1972.

GLASCOCK, A. "When Killing is Acceptable: The Moral Dilemma Surrounding Assisted Suicide in America and Other Societies." In *The Cultural Context of Aging: World-Wide Perspectives*, 2d ed. Edited by J. Sokolovsky. Westport, Conn.: Bergin and Garvey, 1997. Pages 56–70.

GLASCOCK, A., and FEINMAN, S. "Social Asset or Social Burden: Treatment of the Aged in Non-Industrial Societies." In *Dimensions: Aging, Culture and Health.* Edited by C. Fry. New York: Praeger, 1981.

GUTMANN, D. *Reclaimed Powers: Toward a New Psychology of Men and Women in Later Life.* New York: Basic Books, 1987.

HALPERIN, R. "Age in Cross-Cultural Perspective: An Evolutionary Approach." In *The Elderly as Modern Pioneers.* Edited by P. Silverman. Bloomington, Ind.: Indiana University Press, 1987. Pages 283–311.

HAVILAND, W. *Anthropology,* 9th ed., New York: Harcourt, 2000.

KABERRY, P. *Aboriginal Women.* New York: Gordon Press, 1939.

KEITH, J.; FRY, C.; et al. *The Aging Experience: Diversity and Commonality Across Cultures.* Thousand Oaks, Calif.: Sage, 1994.

KERNS, V., and BROWN, J., eds. *In Her Prime: New Views of Middle-Aged Women,* 2d ed. Urbana: University of Illinois Press, 1992.

KERTZER, D., and MADISON, O. B. B. "Women's Age-Set Systems in Africa: The Latuka of Southern Sudan." In *Dimensions: Aging, Culture and Health.* Edited by C. Fry. Brooklyn, N.Y.: J. F. Bergin, 1981. Pages 109–130.

PUTNAM-DICKERSON, J., and BROWN, J., eds. *Women Among Women: Anthropological Perspectives on Female Age Hierarchies.* Champaign, Ill.: University of Illinois Press, 1998.

RHOADS, E., and HOLMES, L. D. *Other Cultures, Elder Years,* 2d ed. Thousand Oaks, Calif.: Sage, 1995.

SANGREE, W. "The Childless Elderly in Tiriki, Keyna, and Iriqwe, Nigeria: A Comparative Analysis of the Relationship Between Beliefs about Childlessness and the Social Status of the Childless Elderly." *Journal of Cross-Cultural Gerontology* 2 (2001): 201–223.

SILVERMAN, P., ed. "Comparative Studies." In *The Elderly as Modern Pioneers.* Bloomington: Indiana University Press, 1987. Pages 312–344.

SIMIC, A. "Introduction: Aging and the Aged in Cultural Perspective." In *Life's Career Aging: Cultural Variations on Growing Old.* Edited by B. Myerhoff and A. Simic. Beverley Hills, Calif.: Sage, 1978. Pages 9–22.

SOKOLOVSKY, J., ed. *The Cultural Context of Aging: World-Wide Perspectives,* 2d ed. Westport, Conn.: Bergin and Garvey, 1997.

SPENCER, P. *The Samburu: A Study of Gerontocracy in a Nomadic Tribe.* Berkeley: University of California Press, 1965.

VAN ARSDALE, P. "The Elderly Asmat of New Guinea." In *Other Ways of Growing Old: Anthropological Perspectives.* In P. Amoss and S. Harrell. Stanford: Stanford University Press, 1981. Pages 111–123.

WARNER, L. *A Black Civilization: A Social Study of an Australian Tribe,* rev. ed. New York: Harper and Brothers, 1958.

WEISS, K. "Evolutionary Perspectives on Aging." In *Other Ways of Growing Old.* Edited by P. Amoss and S. Harrell. Stanford, Calif.: Stanford University Press, 1981. Pages 25–58.

STEREOTYPES

See AGEISM; IMAGES OF AGING; SOCIAL COGNITION

STRESS

The concept of stress as a change in the environment that results in an internal response in living organisms can be traced to the nineteenth-century ideas of the physiologist Claude Bernard (1813–1878). Initially, the stress response involves important adaptive changes throughout an organism that are necessary to restore *homeostasis,* a term coined by Walter Cannon (1871–1945) to describe the internal bodily balance in physiological systems. Living organisms make adjustments within their cells to internal and external sources of stress in order to adapt, maintain function, and survive challenges to homeostasis. In contrast to the adaptive role of the stress response, Hans Selye (1907–1982) discovered that stress-related diseases were often the result of chronic effects of stress. Thus, the stress response is a double-edged sword with both beneficial and detrimental effects for the whole organism. Failure to mount an adequate stress response, or to terminate the stress response, or unrelenting stress results in additional threats to homeostasis over and above the stress that elicited the response in the first place. This is especially true during aging, when it becomes more difficult to maintain homeostasis due to accumulated damage and inadequate repair of molecules and cells. In his 1992 book on stress and aging, Robert Sapolsky pointed out that theorizing by gerontologists about stress focuses on both the decreased ability of older organisms to respond to stress and an increased incidence of stress-related diseases during aging.

Different stressful conditions produce a similar stress response, which Selye named the *gener-*

al adaptation syndrome. The ability of organisms to adapt to stress is regulated by the integration of the nervous, immune, and endocrine systems; is mediated by hormones; and is ultimately played out at the level of cells and molecules. Hence, stress has a prominent role in cellular aging. Cells have to withstand and respond to major types of stress in their environment, including genotoxic, heat shock, and oxidative stress. Old cells are more vulnerable than young cells to stresses in their environment. Lower organisms with short life spans serve as experimental models to study the effects of stress on cellular responses in relation to aging. In 2001, a Swedish group using fruit flies to screen for bacterially induced genes found a new humoral factor, *Turandot A*, that is released systemically in response to many types of stress and also at advanced ages. Overexpression of *Turandot A* helps adult fruit flies to survive heat stress without inducing heat shock or immune genes or its own synthesis, and therefore may act through a separate pathway or at a point where many types of stress converge. Cellular defense mechanisms important in aging include DNA repair, detoxification of chemicals, production of antioxidants and heat shock proteins, and even cell suicide as a result of initiating a cell death program. The effects of the major types of stress on cellular aging will be taken up in succeeding sections, following a general discussion of the stress response in relation to development of disease and altered function during aging.

Stress response

The actions of counterregulatory hormones that are released as part of the stress response are important in restoring the balance in physiological systems. Stress increases the release of physiological mediators from the autonomic nervous system and adrenal glands, including fast-acting catecholamines and slow-acting steroids (mainly glucocorticoids), that participate in the adaptive response. The signal to release stress mediators into the blood is first transmitted from a physical (e.g., heat) or psychological (e.g., predator odor) stress through the nervous and immune systems to the brain. These signals are integrated in the brain, where they are converted into defensive behaviors (reflex withdrawal of a limb or running away from a predator) and hormonal responses that are important for survival. For example, glucocorticoids mobilize energy (glucose) stored in the liver for use by muscle, and they inhibit

processes (e.g., growth and reproduction) that are not necessary for adaptation. Glucocorticoids are essential for surviving severe stress, but their effects exerted throughout the body can be damaging if the stress is prolonged, and may eventually result in disease. There are controls in place to prevent excess secretion of glucocorticoids, called a *negative feedback loop*. After the stress-induced increase in glucocorticoids in the blood, these hormones turn down their own production by decreasing the synthesis of factors made in the hypothalamus of the brain and in the pituitary gland that promote their synthesis and secretion from the adrenal gland.

Age-related changes in the adrenal glands and nervous system contribute to a decreased ability of elderly individuals to adapt to stress. Since glucocorticoids regulate natural defense mechanisms (e.g., immunity and inflammation) with both permissive and suppressive actions to protect against stress, decreased sensitivity to glucocorticoids may increase vulnerability to stress. Excess production of glucocorticoids by the adrenal glands could also be a culprit, as proposed by Sapolsky in his *glucocorticoid cascade hypothesis*, since elevated levels of this steroid hormone do not always return to baseline as quickly in older individuals after stress. Therefore, catabolic effects of glucocorticoid excess may contribute to the development of conditions that are prevalent in elderly persons, including immune suppression and cancer, muscle atrophy, osteoporosis, diabetes, and memory decline. An association between reduced negative feedback regulation of the hypothalamic-pituitary-adrenal axis during aging, especially in the face of stress, disease, and other forms of challenge (exercise, driving test) supports this hypothesis. Based on studies supported by the John D. and Catherine T. MacArthur Foundation through its Research Networks on Successful Aging and on Socioeconomic Status and Health, the interplay of these same factors is also associated with cognitive decline (learning, memory, and language loss).

Since the findings of neuron loss by Philip Landfield in the late 1970s, much has been made of the harmful effects of glucocorticoids in the hippocampus, a part of the brain that is involved in learning and memory. Follow-on studies by Robert Sapolsky and Michael Meaney beginning in the middle 1980s, when they were doctoral students in Bruce McEwen's laboratory at the Rockefeller University, suggested that chronic stress and excess production of glucocorticoids resulted in the death of hippocampal neurons during aging, thus contributing to age-related memory loss. However, memory impairment in old rats correlates better with loss of connections between neurons than with the loss of principal neurons in the hippocampus. Studies performed by McEwen's group between 1995 and 2000 demonstrate that chronic stress induces synaptic loss and atrophy of the hippocampus similar to that which occurs during aging. The reversibility of these effects in rodents may help to explain how humans who are routinely treated with high doses of glucocorticoids for long periods do not seem to have extensive hippocampal damage and memory impairment. Beginning in 1987, researchers at McGill University in Canada conducted a longitudinal study sampling individuals over a three- to six-year period, and found that memory impairment occurred only in a subgroup of healthy elderly individuals with both a high and an increasing cortisol (glucocorticoid) level. The increasing inability of these individuals to decrease their hormone level over time is an indication of failure in the nervous and endocrine systems. Together with the MacArthur Foundation studies conducted by Teresa Seeman, this work highlights the importance of individual variability in response to stress. The good news is that some deleterious effects of stress may be reversible even in elderly persons. Since psychosocial factors are important in how an individual responds to stress, it may be possible, with effective stress management, to decrease excess glucocorticoid production in humans.

Glucocorticoid excess and chronic stress are unlikely to be the only factors that result in an inability to adapt to stress during aging. In a 1998 article published in the *New England Journal of Medicine,* McEwen suggests a revision in the approach to understanding the relationship between changes in the environment and biological responses to emphasize both beneficial and detrimental effects of stress mediators and, in particular, the costs of adaptation to stress. Short-term beneficial effects result in *allostasis,* which means the capacity to adapt or restore homeostasis through change, whereas long-term detrimental effects constitute an *allostatic load* (the cost of having to adapt to challenges and changes in the environment). By measuring allostatic load at earlier ages, it may be possible to identify risk factors (e.g., overactivity of the hypothalamic-pituitary-adrenal axis) that result in late onset diseases (e.g., Type II diabetes, dementia). Since cellular responses are of primary importance in adaptation to stress, it is necessary to determine how stress mediators regulate cellular responses to achieve allostasis during aging. Age-related changes in cellular constituents involved in these responses may result in an increased allostatic load, thus contributing to a reduced capacity of older organisms to adapt and restore homeostasis. Three major types of stress are discussed in the following sections in relation to cellular aging changes.

Genotoxic stress

The integrity of the genome and the faithful transmission of the genetic material it contains to the next generation are important for survival of species. Similarly, the integrity of genomic and mitochondrial DNA and the transmission of the information they contain are important for the survival of individuals. DNA damage in the form of mutations or genomic instability result from genotoxic stress caused by exposure to toxic agents, including the sun's ultraviolet rays, background ionizing radiation, chemicals in food and the environment, and highly reactive molecules produced within cells during metabolism. Similar types of DNA damage occur in response to various agents and include mutations, removal of bases and nucleotides, formation of dimers, strand breaks, cross-links, and chromosomal aberrations. Some of these types of damage accumulate in nuclear or mitochondrial DNA during aging (e.g., point mutations, single-strand breaks, DNA cross-links, additions/deletions, oxidative damage, and methylated bases). In a chapter in *Hormones and Aging* (1995), Suresh Rattan reviews DNA damage and repair and the evidence for genomic instability, loss of cell proliferation, production of altered proteins, and altered cellular responsiveness as a result of damage to DNA in cells and genes during aging. The ability to repair DNA damage may be related to length of the life span, since humans repair DNA faster than mice, but is not always related to maximum life span because premature aging is not always associated with a reduced capacity to repair DNA. Although there is little evidence to suggest an overall decline in the capacity of cells to repair DNA during aging, thus far only a few DNA repair pathways have been studied in any detail.

The sensitivity of cells to genotoxic stress increases during aging. Age-related deficits in protein synthesis and the responsiveness of cells to stress, decreased cell-cell communication, and inefficient signal transduction may render old cells less able to withstand stress. The ability to repair DNA may be compromised by other toxic agents, leading to loss of function in molecules and cells and shortening of life span. A decrease in the ability to repair genomic DNA may lead to increased incidence of cancer in elderly persons. Similarly, mitochondrial DNA damage and mutations increase with aging, as does susceptibility to age-related diseases such as diabetes, Parkinson's, and Alzheimer's disease. In 2000, Jay Robbins and colleagues at the National Cancer Institute and a European group independently established a link between faulty DNA repair caused by defects in nucleotide excision repair and neurodegeneration, a link that was proposed by Robbins twenty-five years previously. Some patients with xeroderma pigmentosum show, in addition to greatly exaggerated risks of skin cancer, premature neuron death and DNA lesions similar to those in Alzheimer's disease. Although cancer susceptibility and neuron death can both result from defects in DNA repair, the precise mechanisms may differ. Mouse models that are deficient in nucleotide excision repair also show increased incidence of tumors in response to genotoxic stress and a decreased life span, but they have reduced neurological deficits compared with human syndromes. These mice are being used to understand the involvement of DNA repair in genotoxic sensitivity and cancer susceptibility and in the process of aging.

Studies pioneered by Richard Setlow in the 1970s showed a correlation between DNA repair and species life span, but were largely based on crude measures of DNA repair. In 1998, using improved techniques that allowed specific genes to be assessed, Arlan Richardson's group in San Antonio, Texas, demonstrated that nucleotide excision repair of DNA in liver cells from old rats challenged with UV irradiation depended on whether the strand was actively transcribed or silent. The rate of repair of the transcribed strand of albumin DNA (transcription-coupled repair) was 40 percent less compared with young rats, but the extent of repair was not different at the end of the experiment. This was in contrast to the extent of repair of the silent strand, which was 40 percent less in old rats compared with young rats. Thus accumulation of DNA damage and mutations during aging may occur in nontranscribed regions of the genome. Richardson's

studies also showed that both age-related deficits in DNA repair could be reversed by caloric restriction, which retards aging by increasing life span and reducing or delaying many of the diseases associated with aging.

Beginning in the 1990s, modern approaches to screening for changes in the expression of genes and proteins have fueled searches for cellular responses to genotoxic stresses, which may hold clues for understanding the process of aging. Hundreds of genes are induced in mammalian cells, most of which represent general responses to cell injury (e.g., induction of the immediate early genes, c-fos and c-jun). Many DNA-damaging agents and their activated signaling pathways converge on the transcription factor p53, which functions as a sensor for DNA damage and regulates the transcription of hundreds of genes. However, changes in a few critical genes, such as those involved in DNA repair or information transfer, may underlie genomic instability during aging. Candidates are poly(-ADP-ribose polymerases, or PARPs, a family of nuclear enzymes, some of which bind nicked DNA and guard the genome by regulating DNA repair and cell death. The activity of PARPs in white blood cells from thirteen mammalian species correlates with life span, yet knockout of the PARP-1 gene confers resistance to stroke and diabetes. Other candidates are helicases (DNA unwinding enzymes) or their associated proteins. Helicases are involved in DNA repair and regulation of transcription, and are mutated in premature aging syndromes. Overlapping aging phenotypes in some helicase disorders and normal aging implicate common pathways, especially transcriptional regulation. Further studies of PARPs and helicase enzymes and their functions during aging could establish a stronger link with cellular or organismal aging. Mouse models that are deficient in nucleotide excision repair also show increased incidence of tumors in response to genotoxic stress and a decreased life span, although they have reduced neurological deficits compared with human syndromes. These mice are being used to understand the involvement of DNA repair in genotoxic sensitivity and cancer susceptibility, and in the process of aging.

Heat shock stress

Nonlethal heat stress induces a characteristic set of proteins in cells that are called heat shock proteins. This stress response is ancient and highly conserved throughout living organisms. Many types of stress in addition to mildly elevated temperature can induce heat shock proteins. Heat shock proteins act as molecular chaperones by helping cells to repair or remove damaged proteins and by participating in the intracellular transport of newly synthesized proteins. Therefore, they are important regulators of cellular adaptation to stress. An important function of heat shock proteins in relation to aging is their ability to confer resistance or tolerance to future insults. The mechanisms for protection against future stresses are poorly understood but may involve the ability of heat shock proteins to promote cell survival by interfering with a cell death program that leads to cell suicide. The synthesis of heat shock proteins is also linked to neuroendocrine responses to stress. For example, elevated glucocorticoid secretion can induce specific heat shock proteins in different cells as a beneficial effect of the stress response. Their role in protein degeneration and the stress response is highlighted by their accumulation in plaques and tangles, the brain deposits associated with Alzheimer's disease pathology.

In the 1990s, researchers in the field of aging, including Richardson, Nikki Holbrook, and Marcelle Morrison-Bogorad, thought that the decreased ability of aged individuals to maintain homeostasis in the face of insults could be due to inadequate cellular responses to stress like the heat shock protein response. They found that the induction of heat shock proteins in response to stress decreases with age. Richardson's group found that the induction of heat shock protein 70 by heat stress in liver cells cultured from old rats was reduced by 50 percent compared with young rats. Furthermore, the decrease in heat shock protein 70 induction occurred at the transcriptional level of regulation and was dependent on reduced binding of a transcription factor to the promoter of the heat shock protein 70 gene. Holbrook's group at the National Institute of Aging used transplantation studies to determine whether the deficit in heat shock protein 70 response in blood vessels was due to the age of the tissue or to the environment. Transplantation of old vessels to a young host restored their response, and transplantation of young vessels to an old host resulted in a reduced response. In the case of blood vessels, heat exposure produced less of an increase in blood pressure in old rats than in young rats, which resulted in less heat shock protein 70 induction. In other circumstances, hormonal or metabolic changes that occur during aging could result in aged cells receiving less of a stimulus to induce the response. Age-related changes could also reduce the effectiveness of the heat shock proteins. For example, genotoxic stress can damage heat shock proteins in the cells of aged individuals due to mutated DNA, errors in translation of mRNA into protein, or reduced repair, and also diminish their role in stress tolerance. Therefore, the environment is a factor that should be considered in interpreting age-related differences in the response of cells to stress.

Richardson and Holbrook proposed in a 1996 review that the widespread reduction in stress-induced heat shock protein 70 expression in aged organisms indicates the importance of this response in both cellular and organismal aging. Consistent with this hypothesis is the ability of caloric restriction to restore the stress-induced heat shock response during aging. Furthermore, mutants that increase life span in nematodes also overexpress heat shock proteins in response to stress, and overexpression of heat shock protein 70 sometimes results in increased life span in fruit flies. Basal levels of heat shock protein 70 are usually not different between young and old individuals, but other members of the heat shock protein family do increase during aging in mice, fruit flies, and nematodes. Age-related increases in basal heat shock protein expression may be a response to accumulated damage and oxidative stress. Therefore, as proposed by Gordon Lithgow and Tom Kirkwood in 1996, heat shock proteins that function as molecular chaperones may regulate organismal aging.

Oxidative stress

Oxidative stress occurs when highly reactive molecules called free radicals overwhelm the cell's natural defenses against their attack. It is a battle that is fought in cells every day. Each cell in the body produces billions of free radicals a day, and some of them are used in physiological relevant reactions; oxygen itself is a free radical. Free radicals derived from oxygen are formed in the course of aerobic life when chemical bonds are broken during the production of energy in the mitochondria. Usually free radical reactions are controlled by free radical scavenging molecules that remove excess free radical scavenging molecules and antioxidants that neutralize free radicals. Chemical reactions with free radicals occur in all living organisms and can amplify their effects in the cell. Under conditions of oxidative stress, free radicals attack other molecules and form molecules that are foreign to cellular machinery (e.g., cross-linking of proteins makes them resistant to proteases), so they fail to turn over, accumulate, and eventually impair function by slowing down physiological processes. Free radicals are also produced in response to genotoxic stress by exposure to ionizing radiation from ultraviolet rays of the sun, chemical pollutants, and smoking.

Denham Harman first proposed the role of oxygen-derived free radicals in the aging process in 1956. An introduction to the concepts of free radical production and oxidative stress during aging is presented in a 1992 *Scientific American* article titled "Why Do We Age?" A more in-depth review by Toren Finkel and Nikki Holbrook appeared in *Nature* in 2000 as part of a series titled "Ageing." During aging an imbalance occurs between production of free radicals and antioxidant defenses, resulting in an accumulation of free radicals and oxidative attack or damage to DNA, protein, lipids, membranes, and mitochondria. Although enzymes that repair proteins, lipids, and DNA are produced, the ability to repair cellular oxidative damage decreases with age, resulting in a reduced ability of old cells to withstand oxidative stress. The repair enzymes may be less efficient because they, too, are attacked or cross-linked and the whole system breaks down, resulting in impaired function and susceptibility to disease. Furthermore, free radicals build up over time and can damage the mitochondria, resulting in less energy production. The decrease in energy results in oxidative stress and a further increase in free radicals, which eventually damage other cellular components. Oxidative damage to organelles results in cellular injury and cell death. Free radical reactions with cellular components and cross-linking of proteins and DNA increase with aging. In addition, various types of stress, including injury and disease, amplify these reactions during aging. An effect of aging on oxidative damage to nuclear and mitochondrial DNA was first reported by Bruce Ames's laboratory. Richardson's group showed that the increase in DNA oxidative damage during aging was not due to inability to repair the damage but, rather, to increased sensitivity to oxidative stress. Richardson's group also showed that caloric restriction could reduce the levels of DNA oxidative damage in aged rats,

supporting the role of oxidative stress in the process of aging.

Evidence from mutants in fruit flies and nematodes, reviewed by Finkel and Holbrook, supports a role for molecules that are capable of scavenging free radicals or of decreasing the accumulation of free radicals and oxidative stress in extension of life span. Surprisingly, mutants with altered life span can have their normal life span restored by expression of the normal protein specifically in neurons, suggesting that neurons control how long an organism can live. Overexpression of *superoxide dismutase,* an enzyme that neutralizes the superoxide free radical, in motor neurons can extend life span by up to 48 percent in fruit flies that also exhibit resistance to oxidative stress, and partially rescues the normal life span of a short-lived superoxide dismutase null mutant in a dose-responsive manner. The long life span of *age-1* and *daf-2* mutants rescued with expression of these genes only in neurons is also associated with higher levels of free-radical scavenging enzymes and protection of neurons from oxidative damage. According to Gabrielle Bouliame, whose group performed the experiments on fruit fly motor neurons, it is possible that these neurons, through neuroendocrine signals, regulate the functional reserve or adaptive capacity of tissues in the organism, which in turn influences life span.

Theories of aging

The process of aging is characterized by imbalances that result in dysfunction manifested at different biological levels and culminate in death of the organism. Some of these changes are programmed and begin from within the cell, and others occur in response to the intrinsic or extrinsic environment. Stress is an important concept in many theories of aging, including systemic, cellular, and molecular theories, and especially in those which explain aging in terms of ability to maintain and restore homeostasis. However, the effects of prolonged stress on an individual may be due to the development of disease and not a result of normal aging process. Questions that remain are whether the effects on aging are due to stress or to stress-induced disease processes that overwhelm the defense or repair systems, and are then life-threatening in old individuals. With these caveats in mind, the stress response is important in the neuroendocrine theory of aging and oxidative stress is important in the free radical theory of aging.

New humoral or systemic factors are being described that differentially regulate the cellular stress response during aging. As shown by studies from Dan Hultmark's group in Sweden, a humoral factor that increases heat shock protein 70 prevents cell death and restores stress resistance in old cells. These factors implicate neural and endocrine signals in the control of aging. The neuroendocrine theory of aging proposes that the ability to respond to stress is an important factor in reduced ability to maintain homeostasis during aging. Furthermore, the control of homeostasis becomes disorganized during aging, resulting in loss of adaptive capacity, decreased resistance to stress, and increased allostatic load. Thus, aging is the price the organism has to pay for surviving stress. Convincing evidence supports the theory that free radicals and oxidative stress play an important role in the aging process, and indicates that oxidative damage to neurons may be related to life span and aging, as well as to neurodegeneration. This knowledge may be used to find ways of slowing aging and increasing average life span in humans.

Rate of Aging

Aging is a complex process and is unlikely to result from a single cause or a single gene. Conditions that slow or accelerate aging and genes that control the rate of aging provide clues about what causes aging. Although aging is not equal to life span, genes that regulate life span are often important in resistance to stress and may be able to slow aging: superoxide dismutase prevents the accumulation of free radicals, and nucleotide excision repair enzymes repair DNA. Furthermore, cell stress resistance is correlated with maximum life span across species. Based on the evolutionary theory of aging, Thomas Kirkwood and Steven Austad predict that key enzymes that regulate the rate of aging are those involved in maintenance and repair. A gene involved in maintenance and repair that can regulate the rate of aging is exemplified by stress-induced *p53*. Free radicals, oxidative stress, DNA-damaging agents, and environmental stresses (including heat) result in increased activation of *p53*. The activation of *p53* can lead to DNA repair, to cell cycle arrest in order to limit DNA replication (cellular replicative senescence), or to cell death, which is how it acts as a tumor suppressor to prevent cancer. In a study published in *Nature* in January 2002, transgenic mice that express mutant-activated *p53*, which augments wild-type *p53* activity, show a resistance to tumors and early signs of some aging phenotypes, including reduced life span, osteoporosis, and multiple organ atrophy. Importantly, these mice also display a reduced ability to tolerate stress, as shown by delayed wound healing and reduced recovery from stress in old mice. These data suggest a role for the stress-induced cellular *p53* response in organismal as well as cellular aging and in acceleration of some aging changes.

Caloric restriction not only retards aging but also reverses the effects of stress during aging by putting cells in a survival mode. It decreases free radical production and oxidative stress, reduces the load of damaged molecules, decreases sensitivity to genotoxic stress, and postpones declines in DNA repair. Caloric restriction also alters the expression of genes that regulate damage and stress-response pathways. Both heat shock stress and exposure to mild oxidative stress can result in *hormesis*, a beneficial effect that occurs in response to very low doses of agents that are toxic at higher doses. Minimal stress not only increases survival in fruit flies and nematodes but also increases life span. Caloric restriction also results in hormesis and may slow the aging process by inducing a mild stress response, including increases in heat shock protein 70 and glucocorticoids that afford protection against stress. In contrast, premature aging syndromes with shortened life spans result from single gene mutations that result in genomic instability, inability to repair DNA, and some of the phenotypes of aging.

The psychosocial environment determines how an individual perceives stress, and coping ability plays a role in age-associated functional decline. Few studies of stress focus on the oldest old (greater than eighty-five years), although they have frequent physical, emotional, and social changes that decrease their sense of control and require adaptation to stress. It is interesting that within this group are centenarians who have greater functional reserve and adaptive capacity, enabling them to overcome a disease or injury or to cope with stresses more effectively.

NANCY R. NICHOLS

See also NUTRITION: CALORIC RESTRICTION; THEORIES OF BIOLOGICAL AGING: DNA DAMAGE;

BIBLIOGRAPHY

BOULIANNE, G. L. "Neuronal Regulation of Lifespan: Clues from Flies and Worms." *Mechanisms of Ageing and Development* 122 (2001): 883–894.

BUNK, S. "DNA and Dementia." *The Scientist* 14 (2000): 26–28.

CHROUSOS, G. P. "Stressors, Stress, and Neuroendocrine Integration of the Adaptive Response. The 1997 Hans Selye Memorial Lecture." *Annals of the New York Academy of Sciences* 85 (1998): 311–335.

EKENGREN, S.; TRYSELIUS, Y.; DUSHAY, M. S.; LIU, G.; STEINER, H.; and HUTMARK, D. "A Humoral Stress Response in *Drosophila*." *Current Biology* 11 (2001): 714–718.

FINKEL, T., and HOLBROOK, N. J. "Oxidants, Oxidative Stress and the Biology of Ageing." *Nature* 408 (2000): 239–247.

GUO, Z. M.; HEYDARI, A.; and RICHARDSON, A. "Nucleotide Excision Repair of Actively Transcribed Versus Nontranscribed DNA in Rat Hepatocytes: Effect of Age and Dietary Restriction." *Experimental Cell Research* 245 (1998): 228–238.

HARMAN, D. "Aging: A Theory Based on Free Radical and Radiation Chemistry." *Journal of Gerontology* 11 (1956): 298–300.

HARMAN, D. "The Aging Process: Major Risk Factor for Disease and Health." *Proceedings of National Academy of Sciences USA* 88 (1991): 5360–5363.

HOLLIDAY, R. *Understanding Ageing.* New York: Cambridge University Press, 1995.

KIRKWOOD, T. B., and AUSTAD, S. N. "Why Do We Age?" *Nature* 408 (2000): 233–238.

KIRKWOOD, T. B.; KAPAHI, P.; and SHANLEY, D. P. "Evolution, Stress, and Longevity." *Journal of Anatomy* 197 (2000): 587–590.

LITHGOW, G. J., and KIRKWOOD, T. G. "Mechanisms and Evolution of Aging." *Science* 273 (1996): 80.

MCEWEN, B. S. "Protective and Damaging Effects of Stress Mediators." *New England Journal of Medicine* 338 (1998): 171–179.

NICHOLS, N. R.; ZIEBA, M.; and BYE, N. "Do Glucocorticoids Contribute to Brain Aging?" *Brain Research Reviews* 37 (2001): 273–286.

RATTAN, S. L. S. "Cellular and Molecular Basis of Aging." In *Hormones and Aging.* Edited by P. S. Timiras, W. B. Quay, and A. Vernadakis. Boca Raton, Fla.: CRC Press, 1995. Pages 267–290.

RICHARDSON, A., and HOLBROOK, N. J. "Aging and the Cellular Response to Stress: Reduction in the Heat Shock Response." In *Cellular Aging and Cell Death.* Edited by N. J. Holbrook,

G. R. Martin, and R. A. Lockshin. New York: Wiley-Liss, 1996. Pages 67–80.

RUSTING, R. L. "Why Do We Age?" *Scientific American,* December (1992): 86–95.

SAPOLSKY, R. M. *Stress, the Aging Brain and the Mechanisms of Neuron Death.* Cambridge, Mass.: MIT Press, 1992.

SAPOLSKY, R. M. *Why Zebras Don't Get Ulcers: An Updated Guide to Stress, Stress Related Diseases and Coping.* New York: W. H. Freeman, 1998.

SAPOLSKY, R. M.; ROMERO, L. M.; and MUNCK, A. U. "How Do Glucocorticoids Influence Stress Responses? Integrating Permissive, Suppressive, Stimulative and Preparative Actions." *Endocrine Reviews* 21 (2000): 55–89.

SEEMAN, T. E., and ROBBINS, R. J. "Aging and Hypothalamic-Pituitary-Adrenal Response to Challenge in Humans." *Endocrine Reviews* 15 (1994): 233–260.

SMITH, S. "The World According to PARP." *Trends in Biochemical Sciences* 26 (2001): 174–179.

TATAR, M. "Evolution of Senescence: Longevity and the Expression of Heat Shock Proteins." *American Zoology* 39 (1999): 920–927.

TIMIRAS, P. S.; QUAY, W. B.; and VERNADAKIS, A., eds. *Hormones and Aging.* Boca Raton, Fla.: CRC Press, 1995.

TYNER, S. D.; VENKATACHALAM, S.; CHOI, J.; JONES, S.; GHEBRANIOUS, N.; IGELMANN, H.; LU, X.; SORON, G.; COOPER, B.; BRAYTON, C.; PARK, S. H.; THOMPSON, T.; KARSENTY, G.; BRADLEY, A.; and DONEHOWER, L. A. "p53 Mutant Mice That Display Early Aging-Associated Phenotypes." *Nature* 415 (2002): 45–53.

VOLLOCH, V., and RITS, S. "A Natural Extracellular Factor That Induces Hsp72, Inhibits Apoptosis, and Restores Stress Resistance in Aged Human Cells." *Experimental Cell Research* 253 (1999): 483–492.

STRESS AND COPING

Stress and coping with stress have been among the most popular research topics in the social and behavioral sciences over the past twenty years. Despite a long history and a substantial amount of literature on stress and coping, less attention has been paid to stress and coping processes among older adults than in younger persons. This is unfortunate because research on stress and coping in later life can not only improve our understanding of human development and adaptation, but also serve as a basis for interventions and social policies to enhance well-being in later life.

Research suggests that exposure to high levels of stress leads to increased vulnerability to physical and psychological problems in older adults. Highly stressed individuals are more likely to have various health problems, including diminished immune functioning, greater risk of infectious illness, psychological distress such as depressive symptoms, and even increased mortality. However, stress does not produce universally negative outcomes; because of individual differences in coping, some individuals report minimal ill effects from stress or even demonstrate personal benefits from stress. Thus, the study of stress requires attention not only to environmental stressors, but also to factors that may increase vulnerability or provide protection against the ill effects of stress.

There are various models of stress and coping, and different types of stressors and coping resources have been found to affect well-being in older adults. Common and important sources of stress in late life include health problems, family caregiving, and bereavement. There are, however, methodological and conceptual controversies that are particularly important in the field.

The stress process paradigm

A widely cited definition of the term *stress* describes it as a "particular relationship between the person and the environment that is appraised by the person as taxing or exceeding his or her resources and endangering well-being" (Lazarus and Folkman, p. 19). Fundamental to this definition is the inclusion not only of stressors, or environmental demands, but also the individual's appraisals and coping resources. Thus stress is much more than objective negative events that buffet an individual; a person's reactions and subjective interpretations of potential stressors determine whether an environmental demand is even viewed as a stress, or leads to negative effects. Also of note in this definition is the idea that the stressfulness of a stimulus is related to levels of resources; individuals with strong coping skills, adaptive personality traits, strong social supports, and plentiful financial resources are likely to fare well when facing environmental demands. Although there are some variations in the specific content of stress process models, fundamental variables in the stress process can be generally summarized as stressors,

appraisals, internal and external resources, coping responses, and the manifestations or outcomes of stress.

Types of stressors

Stressors refer to hardships, challenges, threats, and other circumstances that have the potential to adversely affect well-being. Stressors are broadly categorized into two types: life events and chronic strains. Life events are discrete stressors that have a relatively clear onset, an example being the death of a spouse. In contrast, chronic strains are continuing and enduring problems or threats, such as chronic disease and disability, or caregiving for a disabled family member. These two types of stressors are viewed by researchers as important risk factors that can threaten physical and psychological well-being. Some researchers have focused on the stressfulness of daily hassles—relatively minor daily events such as arguments or inconveniences. While life events, chronic strains, and daily hassles are conceptually distinct, in reality their effects may be difficult to disentangle. For example, the death of a spouse may follow years of caregiving strain; it may coexist with a chronic health problem; and it may lead to a variety of daily hassles, such as managing financial matters or the complexities of Medicare reimbursement.

Contrary to the widespread belief that old age is a highly stressful period of life, it has been found that older persons generally have a reduction in many kinds of stressful experiences, including family conflict and job stress. However, older adults are more likely to encounter some stressful situations, including health deterioration, reduced income, and the death of friends or a spouse. Some theorists believe that even though older adults experience fewer negative life events, once they occur, their adverse impacts are greater because aging may lead to declines in some coping resources. However, it is important not to assume that older persons are highly vulnerable. Many studies have found that common stressors in old age (such as health problems and the death of a spouse) may be stressful but are expected and normative experiences in late life, and that these events have less of an impact in older adults because older people are psychologically prepared to cope with them. Presumed stressors such as retirement are often found to have no ill effects among healthy persons retiring voluntarily.

Studies assessing exposure to stressful life events using checklists of life events have been utilized with older adults with mixed success. While greater numbers of negative life events have been found in a number of studies to predict depression in older adults, results have not been consistent and the magnitude of the life events–depression relationship is generally small. Because these instruments generally require individuals to report on events that have occurred in the past (such as the previous six months or year), retrospective reporting biases can occur. In addition, life events scales can confound stressors with outcomes. For example, life events such as family problems may be a result and not a cause of depression, and health problems may be included both as stressors and dependent variables. Special concerns have been raised about the use of life-events questionnaires in studies of older adults. Scales initially designed for younger adults include inappropriate items and exclude common events faced by older persons. The Louisville Older Persons Events Scale (LOPES) is an exception in that it was specifically designed for older adults on the basis of extensive pretesting with older populations.

Another tactic in studying the impact of life events is to identify individuals who have faced a particular type of life event, such as retirement, natural disasters, or the death of a spouse, and then to assess the impact of this particular event on well-being. Cross-sectional studies may compare individuals who have experienced a life event (such as the death of a spouse), with controls who have not experienced the event. Prospective longitudinal projects have assessed large populations at an initial point in time (perhaps with a life-events checklist), and then identified individuals who subsequently experience onset of a major life event, allowing for a prospective study of the consequences of a stressor. This strategy avoids the problems faced when assessing life events via checklists, but requires large samples and longitudinal research projects. Research utilizing prospective methods has demonstrated that stressors, including the trauma of a major flood, and spousal bereavement, increase the risk of depression in older adults.

Compared to the voluminous literature on life events, chronic strains have been understudied. Chronic strains are the enduring problems, conflicts, and threats that people face in their daily lives. The extended duration of chronic strains may deplete an individual's resources and eventually have adverse physical and psychological effects. A number of different chronic strains have been identified that are both common in older adults and are risk factors for declining mental and/or physical health. These include chronic health problems, physical disability, and family caregiving for relatives with dementia. Chronic strains have been consistently shown to be risk factors for depression in older adults.

There has been considerable debate on whether life events or chronic strains are greater risks to well-being. However, studies have consistently shown that chronic strains have a greater negative impact than life events. Chronic strains are continuing and unresolved demands, and they therefore have more power to undermine equilibrium.

Regarding the interaction of life events and chronic strains, some researchers have suggested that chronic strains have the power to amplify the impact of life events. For example, individuals with chronic illness may be more susceptible to the effects of other stressful events. A combination of chronic strains and life events may therefore cause more adverse outcomes. In contrast, other researchers suggest that experience with chronic strains might actually mute the impact of minor stressful events, because those minor stressful events pale in comparison to the more chronic stressors. In sum, chronic strains and discrete life events may shade into one another and interact in a variety of ways, and both should be taken into consideration in models of the stress and coping process.

Individual differences in coping with stress

Both clinical experience and the results of research demonstrate that older adults vary considerably in the impact that stress has upon well-being. Stress-process models have identified a number of factors that may decrease the negative impacts of stressors, including appraisals, internal and external resources, and coping responses. These may be thought of as factors that can protect a person from the negative consequences of stress. From the perspective of a stress-process model, the experience of stress may be seen as a "balancing act" between stressors and resources. High levels of stressors, with few resources, will place individuals at high risk, while individuals with substantial psychological or social resources may be less vulnerable.

Depending on the mechanism through which variables affect the relationship between stressors and well-being, these responses and resources may have direct effects, or they may serve as either *mediators* or *moderators* of the relationship between stressors and well-being. In a direct effect, people with a high level of a resource (such as income) may be found to have higher well-being regardless of whether highly stressful circumstances occur. A moderator variable, on the other hand, may confer either risk or protection only on individuals facing a high level of stress. For example, research on the stress-buffering hypothesis suggests that under circumstances of high stress, individuals with strong social support may be at lower risk for depression than individuals with weaker social support, but that social support may matter little under conditions of low stress. In other words, the moderator model tests the significance of interactions among independent variables in predicting outcome. A mediator functions as an intermediate factor between stress and well-being; for example, research may find that a life event only affects depression if is subsequently appraised as a threat to well-being. Identification of these mechanisms of vulnerability and resistance to stress may be very useful in targeting interventions that may be helpful when a life event occurs.

Early writers who addressed coping in older persons tended to view older adults as unable to cope with stress, and they suggested that coping in late life was characterized by rigidity in coping mechanisms, and even regression. Contrary to these early speculations, older adults are often found to cope with stress as well as, if not more successfully than, younger individuals, due in part to the benefits of life experience. Older persons often face stressors that are expected, and they have either coped successfully with such stresses themselves or seen their peers cope with common late-life stressors.

Appraisals of stress. Appraisal is a subjective judgment about the nature of a stressor. It reflects individual variations in how people perceive and interpret their events or circumstances. One widely studied type of appraisal is *primary appraisal,* which is the perception of the degree of threat, harm, or challenge represented by potentially stressful life events. Research on family caregivers of patients with Alzheimer's disease has shown that, even after controlling for the objective stressors of caregiving, subjective primary appraisals are important factors predicting caregiver depression.

In addition to primary appraisals, appraisals of self-efficacy, or one's ability manage a stressor, can be important factors in successful coping. Other appraisals that have been studied include perceptions of the predictability or controllability of a stressor. A relatively recent innovation in stress-process research is the study of positive appraisals. Contrary to earlier research that focused only on the negative impacts of stress, it has been increasingly found that individuals undergoing stress may report benefits and positive experiences. For example, people may find meaning in adversity, or stress may provide a way to strengthen relationships or develop spiritual growth. The ability to appraise stress as being a challenge or growth experience, and to identify positive aspects of stress, may be a major asset in coping.

The consideration of appraisal as a variable has led researchers to go beyond the assumption that stressors can be quantified regarding their relative stressfulness, and to study individual differences in appraisal of stress. For example, the death of a spouse after a long and painful illness may be experienced quite differently than a sudden, unexpected death. A financial stress may be appraised as less threatening by an individual with substantial financial resources. Thus, assessment of the occurrence of life events may be less informative than the personal appraisal of such events in evaluating the potential impact on depression or life satisfaction. Despite important theoretical distinctions between occurrence and appraisals of life events, subjective appraisals of the impact of life events in older adults have received much less attention than studies viewing stressors as objective experiences.

In terms of age differences in the appraisal process, older adults are more likely to perceive their situations as unchangeable, but they are also more likely to face situations that are objectively difficult to change. As discussed below, an appraisal of the changeability of a stressor is an important predictor of the type of coping response utilized.

Internal resources. Individuals' psychological resources constitute an important domain of individual differences in the stress process. Psychological resources include the personality characteristics that people draw upon to respond to stress. Research has demonstrated that psychological resources have great effects on how individuals perceive stressors and how stressors manifest themselves. Some positive personality traits such as optimism, self-esteem, internal locus of control, and mastery—and more negative traits such as neuroticism—have been shown to affect appraisal and choice of coping responses. For example, neurotic individuals are likely to focus on negative aspects of stressors, while optimists are more likely to view stress as a challenge and to cope positively.

As of 2002, there has been increasing interest in the role of spiritual beliefs and religious participation as factors promoting successful coping, although few studies of this topic have been completed. Results suggest that religious or spiritual beliefs and religious participation may improve coping with a variety of stressors. Possible mechanisms for such effects include aiding people in finding meaning in the face of adversity, and allowing access to a social support network including clergy and others in the faith.

External resources. Besides internal sources of coping, such external factors as economic resources or social resources may be valuable aids in dealing with stress. Higher socioeconomic status and income are often found to be protective factors in studies of stress, because financial resources can be used to provide concrete assistance such as transportation, medical care, and optimal housing arrangements. Other important external resources include social networks and social supports. Social networks are comprised of individuals with whom an older person can interact, and they represent potential sources of assistance. Social support refers to the actual receipt of some emotional, tangible, or informational help from others, and the subjective perceptions of support. Numerous studies have confirmed that social resources play important roles in improving life satisfaction and well-being Studies indicate that individuals with strong social networks and social support are often in better physical and mental health.

Coping responses

Older adults vary in the extent of their coping resources, and thus in the types of coping that they bring to bear when under stress. Coping responses are behavioral responses, which refer to what people do in confronting stress. In one widely used definition, coping is defined as "constantly changing cognitive and behavioral efforts to manage specific external and/or internal demands that are appraised as taxing or exceeding the resources of the person" (Lazarus and Folkman, p. 141). Coping involves those things individuals do to prevent, avoid, or control emotional stress in order to maintain psychosocial adaptation during stressful situations and conditions; it encompasses direct actions to resolve the problems as well as cognitive responses to control emotional distress.

Coping behaviors are used to help alleviate a difficult situation, to reduce perceived threats, and to manage the symptoms of stress. One basic classification of coping strategies recognizes two types of coping: *problem-focused coping* and *emotion-focused coping*. Presented by Folkman and Lazarus (1980), this classification has been used as a guideline in coping research. Problem-focused coping includes active strategies to change stressful situations, whereas emotion-focused strategies are efforts to control one's emotional responses to modify the meaning of the stress. Coping is most effective when the strategy employed matches the characteristics of the individual, the individual's needs, and the nature of the stressors involved.

Some studies have shown that older individuals use fewer active problem-focused strategies and employ more emotion-focused strategies. However, such age differences between young and old may be due to functions of different types of stressors. Older persons facing relatively uncontrollable stressors (such as a chronic disease) may cope effectively via acceptance and other emotion-focused coping strategies. In fact, empirical studies have shown that after controlling for types of stressors, few age differences exist in either the number of coping strategies or in their effectiveness. Therefore, it is important to consider the types of stressors and their natures when trying to identify true age differences in coping. Also, older adults have gone through a variety of stressful experiences through life course transition. They may come to know what strategies are effective in particular situations, and to develop their own ways to cope from their experiences. Therefore, older adults may use fewer but more effective coping strategies.

Nolen-Hoeksema and Davis (1999) published a paper on bereavement illustrating the way that stressors, personality, coping, and social support interact. Individuals who suffered the loss of a loved one and who scored high in a personality dimension indicating a tendency to ruminate as a coping style were increasingly likely to seek out social support from others after bereavement. These high ruminators also tended to appraise themselves as having received low levels of social support, but showed increased benefit from social support, when compared with low ruminators. Thus the personality trait not only affected the use of social support as a coping technique, but also the subjective perception and effectiveness of support.

Outcomes of stress

Studies focusing on stress and coping in older adults find considerable evidence that stress places older adults at risk for problems in both mental and physical health. Reviews of literature on stressors such as chronic health problems, bereavement, and family caregiving conclude that these stressors are significantly associated with greater risk of negative outcomes such as mortality, lower psychological well-being, and higher incidence of mental disorders such as depressive symptoms. One study of caregiving stress deserves special attention. Schulz and Beach (1999) found evidence that caregivers who feel highly stressed in their roles showed a 63 percent increase in mortality over a four-year period compared with noncaregivers. This increase in risk of mortality was found only among caregivers who reported being highly stressed; caregivers who did not report the subjective experience of being stressed showed no elevation in mortality. Other studies of caregivers and health functioning have provided convincing evidence that caregivers can experience elevated blood pressure, altered lipid profiles, impaired immune functioning, and greater vulnerability to infectious illness due to caregiving stress. These projects find that negative effects of stress are not uniform and vary according to the types of coping strategies and psychological and social resources used to cope.

Future directions

Research on stress and coping has successfully identified a variety of stressful life events and chronic strains that are risk factors for depression and declining health in older adults. In addition, research has identified promising mediating and moderating factors that can be useful both for research and clinical purposes aimed at enhancing coping with stress. Intervention research has generally been promising, in that older adults can successfully be taught new coping skills that improve coping with such stressors as family caregiving, health problems, and bereavement.

However, several major concerns are apparent. Research on stress and coping in old age usually examines age differences using cross-sectional study designs. Few attempts have been made to explore developmental changes in stress and coping processes with advancing age. An important issue to explore is how stress appraisals and coping strategies change over time in the context of development.

Another concern is that the widespread use of checklists to assess stressful life events and coping strategies may have serious limitations in advancing our knowledge about stress. New research methods using self-monitoring have been developed to look at the coping of individuals with daily stressors across daily episodes of coping. Some of these studies have focused specifically on problems relevant to aging (such as coping with pain and alcohol use as a coping strategy) and may provide researchers with new methodologies to improve our understanding of this vital area of research.

Finally, a relatively unexplored area has been the study of racial and ethnic diversity as factors affecting stress and coping in late life. A small but compelling body of literature suggests that such stressors as caregiving may be coped with quite differently by subgroups such as African Americans and Mexican Americans. For example, African Americans have been found to perceive caregiving in late life as a relatively benign and expected responsibility, and to evidence lower levels of depression than white caregivers in several studies. As the older population in the United States is becoming increasingly diverse, studies of how cultural diversity affects stress and coping will be extremely important.

WILLIAM HALEY
YURI JANG

See also LIFE EVENTS; STRESS.

BIBLIOGRAPHY

ALDWIN, C. M. *Stress, Coping, and Development— An Intergrative Perspective.* New York: Guilford Press, 1994.
ANESHENSEL, C. S.; PEARLIN, L. I.; MULLAN, J. T.; ZARIT, S. H.; and WHITLATCH, C. J. *Profiles in*

Caregiving. San Diego, Calif.: Academic Press, 1995.

AVISON, W. R., and GOTLIB, I. H. *Stress and Mental Health—Contemporary Issues and Prospects for the Future.* New York: Plenum, 1994.

BISCONTI, T. L., and BERGEMAN, C. S. "Perceived Social Control as a Mediator of the Relationships among Social Support, Psychological Well-Being and Perceived Health." *The Gerontologist* 39 (1999): 94–103.

BODNAR, J. C., and KIECOLT-GLASER, J. K. "Caregiver Depression After Bereavement: Chronic Stress Isn't Over When It's Over." *Psychology and Aging* 9 (1994): 372–380.

COSTA, P. T., and McCRAE, R. R. "Psychological Stress and Coping in Old Age." In *Handbook of Stress: Theoretical and Clinical Aspects.* Edited by L. Goldberger and S. Breznitz. New York: Free Press, 1993. Pages 403–412.

FOLKMAN, S.; LAZARUS, R. S.; PIMLEY, S.; and NOVACEK, J. "Age Differences in Stress and Coping Processes." *Psychology and Aging* 2 (1987): 171–184.

GEORGE, L. K. "Social Factors and Illness." In *Handbook of Aging and the Social Sciences.* Edited by R. H. Binstock and L. K. George. San Diego: Academic Press, 1996. Pages 229–252.

GLASS, T. A.; KASL, S. V.; and BERKMAN, L. F. "Stressful Life Events and Depressive Symptoms among the Elderly." *Journal of Aging and Health* 9 (1997): 70–89.

GOODE, K. T.; HALEY, W. E.; ROTH, D. L.; and FORD, G. R. "Predicting Longitudinal Changes in Caregiver Physical and Mental Health: A Stress Process Model." *Health Psychology* 17 (1998): 190–198.

GOTTLIEB, B. H. *Coping with Chronic Stress.* New York: Plenum, 1997.

HALEY, W. E., and BAILEY, S. "Research on Family Caregiving in Alzheimer's Disease: Implications for Practice and Policy." In *Research and Practice in Alzheimer's Disease*, Vol. 2. Edited by B. Vellas and L. J. Fitten. Paris, France: Serdi Publisher, 1999. Pages 321–332.

HALEY, W. E.; ROTH, D. L.; COLETON, M. I.; FORD, G. R.; WEST, C. A. C.; COLLINS, R. P.; and ISOBE T. L. "Appraisal, Coping, and Social Support as Mediators of Well-Being in Black and White Family Caregivers of Patients with Alzheimer's Disease." *Journal of Consulting and Clinical Psychology* 64 (1996): 121–129.

KAPLAN, H. B. *Psychological Stress—Perspectives on Structure, Theory, Life-Course, and Methods.* San Diego, Calif.: Academic Press, 1996.

KIECOLT-GLASER, J. K.; DURA, J. R.; SPEICHER, C. E.; TRASK, O. J.; and GLASER, R. "Spousal Caregivers of Dementia Victims: Longitudinal Changes in Immunity and Health." *Psychosomatic Medicine* 53 (1991): 345–362.

LAZARUS, R. S. "The Role of Coping in the Emotions and How Coping Changes over the Life Course." In *Handbook of Emotion, Adult Development, and Aging.* Edited by C. Magai and S. H. McFadden. San Diego: Academic Press, 1996. Pages 289–306.

LAZARUS, R. S., and FOLKMAN, S. *Stress, Appraisal, and Coping.* New York: Springer Publishing Company, 1984.

McCRAE, R. R. "Age Differences and Changes in the Use of Coping Mechanisms." *Journal of Gerontology: Psychological Sciences* 44 (1989): P161–P169.

MURRELL, S. A.; NORRIS, F. H.; and HUTCHINS, G. L. "Distribution and Desirability of Life Events in Older Adults: Population and Policy Implications." *Journal of Community Psychology* 12 (1984): 301–311.

NEWSOM, J. T., and SCHULZ, R. "Social Support as a Mediator in the Relation Between Functional Status and Quality of Life in Older Adults." *Psychology and Aging* 11 (1996): 34–44.

NOLEN-HOEKSEMA, S., and DAVIS, C. G. "Thanks for Sharing That: Ruminators and Their Social Support Networks." *Journal of Personality and Social Psychology* 77 (1999): 801–804.

PARGAMENT, K. I., and BRANT, C. R. "Religion and Coping." In *Religion and Mental Health.* Edited by Harold G. Koenig. San Diego: Academic Press, 1998. Pages 111–128.

PEARLIN, L. I., and SKAFF, M. M. "Stressors and Adaptation in Later Life." In *Emerging Issues in Mental Health.* Edited by M. Gatz. Washington, D.C.: American Psychological Association, 1995. Pages 97–123.

ROBERT, B. L.; DUNKLE, R.; and HAUG, M. "Physical, Psychological, and Social Resources as Moderators of the Relationship of Stress to Mental Health of the Very Old." *Journal of Gerontology: Social Sciences* 49 (1994): S35–S43.

SCHULZ, R., and BEACH, S. R. "Caregiving as a Risk Factor for Mortality—The Caregiver Health Effects Study." *Journal of the American Medical Association* 282 (1999): 2215–2219.

SOMERFIELD, M. R., and McCRAE, R. R. "Stress and Coping Research—Methodological Challenges, Theoretical Advances, and Clinical Applications." *American Psychologist* 55 (2000): 620–625.

STALLINGS, M. C.; DUNHAM, C. C.; GATZ, M.; BAKER, L. A.; and BENGTSON, V. L. "Relationship among Life Events and Psychological Well-Being: More Evidence for A Two-Factor Theory of Well-Being." *Journal of Applied Gerontology* 16 (1997): 104–119.

ZAUTRA, A. J.; HOFFMAN, J. M.; and REICH, J. W. "The Role of Two Kinds of Efficacy Beliefs in Maintaining the Well-Being of Chronically Stressed Older Adults." In *Coping with Chronic Stress*. Edited by B. H. Gottlieb. New York: Plenum Press, 1997. Pages 269–290.

STROKE

A stroke is defined as a sudden loss of brain function due to a blocked or burst blood vessel. There are two classifications of stroke, ischemic and hemorrhagic. Ischemic strokes account for approximately 80 percent of all strokes and result from blockage of the blood supply to the brain. Hemorrhagic strokes account for the remaining 20 percent of all strokes and result from bleeding in the brain. When the bleeding is in the brain itself, it is an intracerebral hemorrhage; if the bleeding occurs between the brain and the skull, it is a subarachnoid hemorrhage.

The brain needs a continuous and fresh supply of oxygen and glucose to function. Oxygen and glucose are carried in the blood and reach the brain through four arteries arranged in two systems. The carotid arteries in the neck carry most of the blood to the brain. The vertebral arteries in the spine join at the base of the brain to form the basilar artery. They supply blood to the core of the brain, which deals with vital functions. Any interruption of blood supply to the brain interferes with the brain's ability to function.

Causes of ischemic stroke

Ischemic stroke occurs when the blood supply to the brain is blocked. The most common cause of blockage is blood clots. Blood clots can form almost anywhere in the body, dislodge, and travel through the arteries eventually lodging and diminishing or cutting off blood flow. They originate most commonly in the heart. Blood clots form in the heart for many reasons, including birth defects, malfunctioning or damaged heart valves, and an irregular heartbeat (atrial fibrillation).

Damaged arteries represent another leading cause of ischemic stroke. There are three main causes of damage to the arteries. Atherosclerosis can occur in any artery in the body but causes stroke most often when it is found in the neck arteries. As people age, small streaks of fat settle in the walls of the arteries. These streaks can grow into plaque that can trap cells in the blood platelets that start clotting. The fatty deposits build up and can eventually fester and crack, forming clots that either close off a neck artery or wash up into the brain, resulting in a stroke.

Accidental damage to the neck arteries can also cause stroke. An artery has three layers, and any sudden twist of the neck or direct trauma to the neck can cause the arterial layers to shear apart (dissection) and either close the vessel or create clots that will cause blockage that results in stroke.

In people who suffer from high blood pressure, their brain blood vessels can become thick, stiff, and brittle. Because there is less room for blood to flow and the vessels are not flexible enough to accommodate increased blood pressure, they can either close off completely or rupture. Diabetes can also weaken the small blood vessels of the brain.

Blood abnormalities can be a potential source of stroke. Abnormalities in the blood can cause clotting, bleeding, or both.

Blood supply is essential to the health and operation of the brain. The areas of the brain that do not receive enough blood or no blood at all will die, resulting in dead tissue (infarct) and loss of brain function.

Causes of hemorrhagic stroke

Hemorrhagic stroke occurs when there is bleeding within the brain. It is less common than ischemic stroke but is often more severe.

There are three main causes for bleeding in the brain (intracerebral hemorrhages). High blood pressure can weaken the arteries so that they eventually rupture and cause bleeding. Blood can become too thin as a result of blood thinning medication (anticoagulants). And as people age, they tend to have abnormal deposits of amyloid protein (amyloid angiopathy) in blood vessels, which can lead to bleeding in the brain.

Bleeding around the brain, known as subarachnoid hemorrhage, most often results from a burst aneurysm. An aneurysm develops on a weakened part of a blood vessel and resembles a pouch. A bursting aneurysm is usually signaled by a sudden, unusual, and severe headache. Some have suggested that it feels like being struck on the back of the head by a baseball bat.

Other symptoms associated with a burst aneurysm may include neck stiffness and double vision. Not all aneurysms are dangerous or require surgery, but if an aneurysm ruptures it is quite serious.

The second most common cause of subarachnoid hemorrhages is the rupture of a cluster of abnormal blood vessels in the brain, the arteriovenous malformation.

Areas of the brain and effects of damage

The brainstem is considered to be an extension of the spinal cord and is nestled below the larger part of the brain. It is responsible for critical automatic functions of the body, such as breathing, maintaining blood pressure and heart rate, swallowing, chewing, eye movements, and quick reflexes. It is also the site of major passageways to and from the upper brain and the rest of the body. A stroke that originates in the brainstem is usually fatal. Fortunately, many strokes involve only part of the brainstem. Double vision, imbalance, trouble swallowing, and weakness or numbness of the face or limbs may result, depending on the part of the brain stem that is affected.

At the back of the brainstem is the "little brain" or cerebellum. The cerebellum coordinates movements and balance, and stores the memory of habitual muscle movements, such as the pattern of the muscle movement used to swing a baseball bat. A stroke that hits the cerebellum can cause unsteadiness, lack of coordination, and awkwardness of the limbs.

Some consider the cerebrum to be the most important part of the brain. It is the most highly developed area of the brain and is what defines people as humans. The cerebrum receives information from all parts of the body, processes the information, and reacts almost instantaneously. A stroke in the cerebrum can affect so many aspects of day-to-day living. To better understand how a stroke survivor can be affected, one should look at all of the parts of the cerebrum.

The cerebrum is divided into two hemispheres, right and left, each controlling the side of the body opposite to it. Each hemisphere controls certain functions, but the two are connected by nerve fibers that allow them to work together or compensate for one another.

The right hemisphere recognizes shapes, angles, proportions, and visual patterns such as people's faces. The right hemisphere is responsible for emotions, musicality, creativity, and imagination. It also controls a person's spatial self-awareness. For example, some people who have had their right hemisphere damaged by a stroke no longer feel that their body is their own, and some who are paralyzed on the left side of their body may not recognize their own left hand.

The left hemisphere controls speech, logic, analytical thought, problem solving, language, and movements on the right side of the body. Stroke in the left hemisphere may result in paralysis of the right side of the body and difficulty with communicating and understanding.

The hemispheres are further divided into four lobes. The occipital lobe is the vision center, and a person can be left blind even if the eyes are not damaged when the stroke hits here.

The temporal lobe forms and stores memories, and unless both the right and left temporal lobes are affected, memory loss is not likely to be permanent. Hearing and understanding speech are other functions of the temporal lobe. Wernicke's area spreads from the temporal lobe into the neighboring parietal lobe, and a stroke here impairs ability to understand language but almost never affects hearing.

The parietal lobes influence the sense of space, perspective, and interpretation. They also contain a strip of sensory cortex that receives and interprets information from the body. The motor cortex is located in front of the sensory cortex, and if it is damaged, paralysis of the face, arm, or leg can occur.

Behavior, anticipation, emotion, thinking, motor function, planning, and speech expression are controlled in the most highly developed part of the brain, the frontal lobes. The frontal lobes influence much of what is considered to be an individual's personality, and as a result the ability to test the damage to frontal lobes and the degree of impairment is difficult. Stroke can change personality and thinking. A patient may appear to act out of character and the ability to determine what is socially appropriate and what is not may be impaired. Increased difficulty with completing tasks can also be seen. This can be a result of the patient's forgetting sequences of steps to finish something or inability to send the message to the appropriate muscles to complete a task.

The human brain is a very complicated organ, and stroke damage can be devastating.

However, the prognosis is not always so bleak. The brain's ability to have other parts of it assume lost function and its ability to adapt are just being discovered, bringing greater hopes of recovery for the future.

Warning symptoms

Typically, many think of stroke as a disease affecting only elderly persons, particularly men. This is not the case at all. Stoke can strike an individual of any age, race, or gender. As people age, the risk for stroke increases, but the warning signs of stroke are something that everyone should know.

A person who suddenly experiences one or more of the following symptoms may be having a stroke: (1) weakness or numbness of the face, arm, or leg; (2) loss or slurring of speech; (3) loss or blurring of vision; (4) a sensation of motion (vertigo); (5) difficulty with balance; (6) unusual or severe headache. The sudden onset of any one or more of these symptoms requires immediate action. Stroke is a medical emergency and must be treated accordingly. The sooner medical help is obtained the better the chances for surviving a stroke.

Symptoms of stroke usually occur within seconds. If the symptoms come on quickly and disappear just as quickly, a doctor should be contacted. If the symptoms still persist after fifteen minutes, the person should be taken to the emergency department of the nearest hospital where a specialist can assess the symptoms.

Symptoms of migraine headaches can sometimes be confused with symptoms of stroke. The key difference in the onset of symptoms lies in the timing. Migraine symptoms usually progress over minutes, whereas stroke symptoms occur in mere seconds. Timing is a critical factor in assessing stroke.

Transient ischemic attacks, more commonly known as TIAs, are a crucial warning sign of an impending stroke. The symptoms of a TIA are exactly the same as of a stroke; the only difference is that the symptoms usually disappear within fifteen minutes. Just because a symptom goes away does not mean that the person is not at risk. TIAs can indicate that the brain is having difficulty receiving the required amount of blood and the person is therefore more likely to have a stroke. Immediate diagnosis of symptoms can drastically reduce the chance of a stroke. Having a TIA does not mean a person will definitely have a stroke, but it is a key indicator that medical attention is needed.

Heart attack can be associated with stroke. The term "brain attack" was invented to advise people that the stroke is serious and that urgent medical attention is required. The most common cause of heart attack is also the most common cause of stroke. Hardening of the arteries (atherosclerosis) impedes blood flow and can create blood clots, leading to either heart attack or stroke. People who suffer a stroke may also suffer a heart attack, and vice versa. One reason for this may be that people who have either a stroke or a heart attack, have common risk factors for atherosclerosis, such as family history, high blood pressure, smoking, diabetes, high cholesterol, or homocystenemia.

There are three major differences between heart attack and stroke. First, there are many more causes of stroke than of heart attack. Second, heart attack is more easily diagnosed by either an electrocardiogram or a cardiac enzyme test, whereas images of the brain may not show any changes in the brain until hours after the onset of stroke symptoms. As a result, the diagnosis of stroke relies heavily on clinical judgment.

Last, chest pains (angina) are a clear indication of an impending heart attack. The greater the chest pain, the greater the problem. This is not the case with stroke. Whether a person has one TIA or several, the risk of stroke is the same. Preexisting conditions and risk factors contribute more to the chance of stroke than does how often TIAs occur.

Some other medical conditions can mimic stroke; for instance, the shearing of the artery within the skull or a brain tumor can create symptoms that may at first appear to be those of a stroke. Clinical diagnosis by a physician is the only way to determine if a person has had a stroke.

Diagnosis

As more knowledge is gained about the brain, the prognosis for stroke survivors becomes better. The clinical diagnosis of stroke is an essential part of the treatment process. When a patient arrives at the hospital, the first thing the doctor will do is assess his or her condition. A primary care doctor may be the first doctor one sees, but once a problem with the brain or nervous system is identified a specialist will be called. Neurologists are specialists who diagnose and treat conditions of the brain, but they do not perform surgery. Neurosurgeons perform surgery on the brain and other parts of the nervous system. Other medical specialists may be consulted if the problem involves their area of expertise.

After taking a verbal history, the physician conducts a physical exam. The physician may begin by evaluating muscle strength, reflexes, coordination, balance, capacity to hear, see, smell, and feel, and ability to speak. On the basis of physician's findings, other diagnostic tests may be ordered.

An image of the brain is important in diagnosing a stroke. The physician is looking to see if there is blood on the brain, and if so, where it is. The physician is also trying to see if there is dead tissue (infarct) in the brain, and, if there is, to confirm that this is the result of a stroke (and not something that mimics stroke). Two main ways to get an image of the brain are computerized tomography scan (CT scan) and magnetic resonance imaging (MRI). During the CT scan, a painless procedure, the patient's head is placed in a device that looks like a big salon hair dryer. The patient simply lies back and relaxes while X-rays are beamed to reveal the structure of the brain. The MRI may look more intimidating than the CT scan because the patient is put on a bed in a large machine, but it too, is a painless procedure. MRI uses radio frequencies to image the brain and the blood vessels in the head and in the neck. Because technology for the MRI is increasing at a rapid rate, and it is providing more information, it is becoming the diagnostic method of choice.

Ultrasonography has two uses: (1) to measure the speed of blood flow, which helps to determine where there are blockages in arteries; and (2) to produce an image of the blood vessel. The carotid Doppler test is done by moving a device up and down the neck to see if there is a narrowing of the arteries, and a transcranial Doppler test is an ultrasound technique that gives information about the blood flow in the main arteries of the brain.

Imaging of the brain can usually detect the presence of blood, but in some circumstances a spinal puncture, or spinal tap, will be performed to rule out the possibility. The procedure involves taking a small needle, inserting it between the vertebrae in the back, and taking a sample of cerebrospinal fluid to analyze.

Echocardiograms and electrocardiograms are the two types of tests used to detect any abnormalities in the heart that could have caused a stroke. In an echocardiogram, ultrasound creates an image of the heart from which the doctor can see if any blood clots are in pockets of the heart and if the valves of the heart are normal or abnormal. The electrocardiogram maps the heartbeat, making it possible to detect irregular heartbeats, insufficient blood supply, and damaged parts of the heart. Analyzing the heart is important because the heart can be a source for blood clots that break away and reach the brain.

Blood tests are generally done to identify problems that could complicate stroke. Depending on the patient's medical history, liver and kidney tests may also be done to detect damage. All of these tests and procedures play a part in the physician's diagnosis.

Treating acute stroke

Stroke patients can be treated in many different settings, but the ideal place for treatment is a stroke unit, where the doctors, nurses, and therapists work together as a specialized unit. When a stroke patient arrives at the hospital, overall medical treatment includes maintaining blood pressure, reducing elevated temperature, and normalizing blood glucose levels. Specific measures performed by the stroke team include attempting to reopen closed blood vessels, protecting the brain, and preventing complications.

Maintaining blood pressure of the patient is important because after stroke, the brain may be unable to control its own blood supply (autoregulation). Blood supply depends on blood pressure, and if the blood pressure is not high enough to pump blood to the damaged area, brain cells will die. To prevent further damage to the brain after stroke, the medical team makes sure that blood pressure is maintained by measuring and medicating if necessary.

Temperature is another factor when treating a stroke patient. An increase in body temperature of even one degree centigrade will double the risk of death or disability in a stroke patient. In addition, patients with a high level of blood glucose at the time of a stroke are less likely to recover; therefore, reducing blood glucose in the acute situation benefits the patient.

The most common cause of stroke is the closing off of a blood vessel to the brain. Some studies have shown that giving the patient a clot-busting (thrombolytic) drug may reopen the closed blood vessels to the head. Thrombolytic drugs are effective only if given early in the onset of stroke and also carry a great risk of causing more bleeding to the head, thus causing more damage and possibly death. The drug in this classification that has been receiving much attention is tissue plasminogen activator (t-PA). It has been used with success in the treatment of heart attacks and is currently being used in treating stroke. The side effect of bleeding to the head may result in death, so it is important that thrombolytic drugs be researched and tested in centers where there are experts in stroke and facilities to deal with the possible consequence of bleeding into the head. With time and caution, thrombolytic treatment may play a more important role in the treatment of acute stroke.

Another type of drug works to protect the brain after stroke. In laboratory studies these drugs have protected the brain when blood deprivation occurred. They are now being tested in clinical studies.

Brain cell repair is the future of recovery after stroke. More is being learned about how the brain repairs injury and the potential of injecting engineered cells to help healing. It may be the case that a combination of drugs that open the blood vessels to the brain protect the brain from breakdown, and speed up the repair of the brain will be the ideal treatment of the future.

Surgery is not used in the acute treatment phase unless a blood clot is pressing on one of the vital parts of the brain or if an aneurysm has ruptured and there is bleeding around the brain (subarachnoid hemorrhage). Timing is important when dealing with a ruptured aneurysm. There are two approaches considered by the neurosurgeon: (1) to operate before the brain vessels go into spasm (vasospasm), or (2) to wait a for the vasospasm to disappear and then operate. Operating early has a higher rate of complication, but waiting allows vasospasm to cause further damage. Thus, early surgery is often chosen despite the overall risk.

Aneurysms that have been found by diagnostic testing and have not bled, do not necessarily require surgery. If the aneurysm is less than 10 mm in diameter, the patient usually will be monitored. If the aneurysm measures greater than 10 mm in diameter, surgery or treatment with balloons or coils delivered through a tube (catheter) in the blood vessel may be considered.

Preventing complications is a main concern of the stroke team. When a patient is bedridden for a long period of time, blood becomes stagnant and tends to pool, which may make the patient more prone to developing blood clots, resulting in further damage and even death. Lying in the same position for a long time can also cause painful bedsores and the shortening of muscles (contractures). Initially, the stroke team will move an immobilized patient and perform range of motion exercises to keep muscles limber. As the patient gains ability, he or she can take over some of these exercises to help prevent complications. Stroke patients are also at higher risk for infection, and are carefully monitored by the doctor and nurses to ensure that they remain as healthy as possible.

In the first few hours after a stroke, it can become fairly clear what the prognosis for the patient will be. In some cases the result of stroke can be more grievous than death, and the family will be told what they can expect. At a time when emotions are so highly charged, it may be difficult to make a decision that is best for the patient, especially if the patient is unable to communicate his or wishes. Situations like this can be avoided by having a living will or an advance health care directive in place. This document is prepared beforehand for emergency situations and lets the doctors and family know what the patient would like done in certain situations if he or she is unable to communicate. For example, an incapacitated patient who goes into cardiac arrest may not wish to be revived. This is something that can be established legally before a catastrophic event. Advance health care directives may have different names and different regulations governing them in the states and provinces. Having an advance health care directive in place makes the person's wishes clear and removes the burden of not knowing what to do from the family.

Rehabilitation

Rehabilitation begins as soon as possible after stroke, and recovery involves several different health disciplines. Along with the stroke survivor and his or her family and friends, the recovery team can include the physician, nurses, physiotherapist, occupational therapist, speech therapist, dietitian, social worker, and psychologist.

Not knowing the effects of a stroke is one of the most frightening aspects when beginning rehabilitation. The stroke survivor is faced with the prospect of not only lasting physical disability, but also lasting mental disability. The extent of damage that the stroke survivor must overcome depends largely on the type of stroke experienced and where the stroke damaged the brain. The rehabilitation team is there to support the patient and the family in recovering lost ability and learning to accept what cannot be changed.

The rehabilitation team's first task begins as soon as the patient's health has stabilized. The main goals are to prevent a second stroke and avoid any complications that may delay recovery. Keeping the patient as mobile as possible helps to prevent blood clots from forming and any stiffening of the joints.

Common effects on muscles and movement of the patient include weakness, paralysis, spasticity, loss of sensation, and loss of bladder and bowel control. Most patients suffer from some sort of muscle weakness after stroke, either because the muscle has been directly affected or because the muscle is atrophying from lack of use. Paralysis is another common effect and tends to involve one side of the body. If the arm and the leg on the same side of the body are affected, it is referred to as hemiplegia. Rehabilitation concentrates on maximum recovery of use of the paralyzed limbs, but if recovery is limited or not possible, the rehabilitation team teaches the patient techniques to compensate.

Spasticity occurs when the brain loses control over the contraction of a muscle and the muscle contracts involuntarily. It is a common physical response to any injury to the brain. The muscle does not, and cannot, obey the brain's signals to relax, and remains stiff, taut, and painful. Spasticity sometimes is reduced but more often than not it remains. Physiotherapists help move the affected limbs through range of motion exercises to stretch the muscle, and casts, splints, or local anesthesia may be used as temporary measures. Any medication to treat spasticity must be used with caution, so as not to interfere with any medication being taken to control the stroke. Only in rare, severe cases is surgery performed.

Damage to one side of the brain can cause the patient to lose sensation in the opposite side of the body. For instance, some patients scalded themselves with water because they could not feel its temperature. The rehabilitation team can help set up the stroke survivor's home with basic safety features to avoid such mishaps.

Difficulty with bladder and bowel control happens to some stroke patients. The most common problem is frequency. The patients must empty their bladder more often and cannot avoid wetting accidents if a toilet cannot be found quickly. Bowel incontinence is not as common and both conditions can be helped by the use of medication and adult diapers.

Speech problems are common in stroke survivors. This can be one of the hardest aspects of stroke recovery because many people associate mental incompetence with speech disorders. Speech disorders are a result of the brain being unable to function properly rather than a reflection of mental competence.

There are two basic categories of speech disability: aphasia and dysarthria. Aphasia, a disorder of language, can be divided into two main categories: expressive, or Brace's aphasia (the most common form of aphasia) is the term used when a patient cannot express thoughts verbally or in writing. Frustration is common in patients with aphasia because they understand what people say to them and they know how they want to respond but are unable to find and say the proper words. Receptive, or Wernicke's aphasia, occurs when the patient cannot understand spoken or written language.

Dysarthria is a speech disorder that causes the patient to slur words or make the pronunciation hard to understand. Pitch of the voice and ability to control the volume of voice may also be affected. As soon as possible, a speech therapist will involve the patient in a series of exercises to try to recover any lost function of the brain. Over time, aphasia and dysarthria can sometimes be partially reversed.

Helping the patient to adapt is a key function of the rehabilitation team. They can teach the patient and the family new methods for coping and techniques that will make routine tasks easier. Practicing routines with the patient also plays a part, particularly when the patient is having difficulty thinking. It is common for the stroke survivor to suffer from a decreased attention span, lack of concentration, limited memory, or decreased ability to make a decision or solve a problem. The rehabilitation team can provide simple, step-by-step instructions and practice a routine with a patient who is having difficulty remembering how to start a task or difficulty processing the steps required to finish it. Accepting that it may take longer to think, make decisions, or complete tasks can help reduce the frustration that the patient feels.

Stroke often makes a formerly independent individual dependent on others for even the most basic tasks. This can leave the individual with feelings of anger, inadequacy, unworthiness, and discouragement. As a result, clinical depression is a very common aftereffect of stroke, not only for the stroke survivor but for the caregiver as well. Depression is a natural reaction to any loss, and the rehabilitation team can help the stroke survivor and the family come to terms with the loss by offering methods for coping, contact with support groups, and, in some cases, medication.

A patient who is depressed after a stroke also commonly suffers from emotional lability, the dramatic swing of emotions from tears to laughter and back. This swing is uncontrollable and may appear to happen for no reason at all. Fortunately these responses tend to occur less often over time.

When the brain is injured as a result of stroke, personality and behavior may change. A stroke survivor who previously was always cheerful and helpful, may now be surly and despondent. Emotional and behavioral responses to stroke are often interlinked. The stroke survivor may have damage in a part of the frontal lobe that is causing him or her to act in such a manner, and may also be reacting emotionally to a sudden and devastating situation. A physician's diagnosis and the rehabilitation team's support will help the patient and their family find ways to cope with all of the changes.

There is no set timeline for the recovery of stroke survivors; however, neurological recovery tends to peak within the first few months after a stroke and then lessen. The physical recovery tends to be slower than the neurological recovery but usually continues for a longer period of time. Ultimately, the earlier recovery begins the better the prognosis, though individual determination and a strong support system have proven to be big factors in the recovery of stroke survivors.

Risk factors

There are many factors to consider when assessing risk for stroke. Some risk factors are nontreatable and some are treatable, and there are other factors that protect against stroke. The first step is to have a medical assessment of risk. If risk factors are managed and protective, and factors are enhanced in accordance with medical advice, then chances of having a stroke will decrease.

Nontreatable risk factors include age, gender, family history, and ethnicity. In general, the greater the age the greater the risk for stroke; however, it is important to note that someone young or seemingly healthy may still be at risk for stroke. Stroke has been documented as early as when a child is still in the womb. Such cases are less common, but the important point is that it is never too soon to be aware of risk factors for stroke.

Traditionally stroke has been associated with men. This is not the case at all. From the ages forty-five to seventy-five, men tend to have more strokes than women, but from ages fifty-five to eighty-five, women assume similar risks to men. While initially the number of strokes for men may be slightly higher than for women, the effects on women tend to be more devastating. Many more men recover from stroke than do women. Heart attack and stroke account for more deaths in women than any other disease. The notion that stroke is gender-specific is a dangerous one. Both sexes need to be aware of risk factors for stroke.

Hypertension, diabetes, and a history of heart disease are three main factors considered when taking a family medical history. Hypertension and diabetes are often inherited, and are both risk factors; heart disease may suggest a tendency to have hardening of the arteries (atherosclerosis). While individuals cannot escape their family history, they can use it to their advantage by making their doctor aware of conditions in their family that put them at risk for stroke.

Similarly, ethnicity cannot be controlled. Studies have shown stroke to be an important concern for Asian and African-American populations, whose risk for stroke is slightly higher than for Caucasians.

With medical advice, the following treatable risk factors can be managed and the chance for stroke reduced.

High blood pressure makes the muscular wall of blood vessels thicker. When the walls cannot thicken any more to accommodate the increasing blood pressure, they become brittle. This can result in the blood vessel closing off or rupturing, thus causing bleeding in the brain.

Smoking is a risk factor for all types of stroke as well as for heart disease. It directly damages the lining of the arteries. Smoking breaks down the elastin that gives the blood vessels flexibility. For a person who smokes, the risk of sudden death from heart attack doubles.

Homocystenemia leads to hardening of the arteries and increased clotting of the blood. High levels of the natural chemical homocysteine in the blood can be treated with vitamin B-6, vitamin B-12, and folate.

High cholesterol builds up deposits in the lining of the blood vessels, making it more difficult for blood to flow through and increasing the chances of a blockage resulting in stroke.

Diabetes damages the lining of blood vessels, which can lead to stroke.

Weight is an indirect risk factor for stroke. In general, a healthy body weight improves overall health and reduces the potential risk for disorders, such as high blood pressure, high cholesterol, and diabetes that may lead to stroke.

Heart disease can lead to clots forming on damaged areas of the heart and then finding their way to the brain, resulting in stroke.

Prior strokes increase the risk for later strokes. The medical history may indicate that a continued risk for stroke, but with medical attention the risk may be reduced.

TIAs are the body's way of warning that a person is at risk for stroke. Those affected should seek medical attention immediately.

Chiropractic treatment involving vigorous twisting of the neck can shear the lining of the arteries in the brain, potentially leading to stroke. Individuals who are at risk for stroke may want to consider the type of treatment they receive.

Oral contraceptives used to contain a higher dose of estrogen, which could increase the chance of stroke. Low-estrogen contraceptives do not put women at risk for stroke unless they also smoke; in that case, the combination increases the chances for stroke.

Medications in rare cases, have been linked to heart valve damage, high blood pressure, seizures, heart attack, stroke, and death. Using medication only when necessary and following instructions, are important because misuse of a "safe" medication can increase the risk of stroke.

Substance abuse can cause stroke. Cocaine increases blood pressure dramatically and if the individual has weakened blood vessels, a major stroke will follow. Heroin inflames the blood vessels, thus increasing the risk for stroke. Contaminated needles are also a concern because they can cause an infection in the heart valves that will produce clots that go to the brain.

Migraine headaches do not necessarily warn of a stroke, but it has been documented that people who suffer from migraine with visual symptoms (classical migraine) are at a slightly higher risk for stroke. The combination of migraine headaches and either smoking or taking birth control pills can also increase the risk for stroke.

Stress is unavoidable for most people, but the degree of stress and how an individual handles stress are important factors in controlling the risk for stroke. Studies have indicated that stress and the way it is handled is an indirect factor for stroke based on elevated blood pressure and progression of atherosclerosis.

Enhancing protective factors can also reduce the risk for stroke. These factors include diet, exercise, estrogen, and aspirin. A doctor will be able to give more individualized information. Not every patient will benefit by taking aspirin as a preventive measure, nor will all women require estrogen replacement therapy.

A healthy diet, reducing alcohol consumption, and a moderate exercise plan are good ideas for prevention of many medical diseases, including stroke and heart disease. Again, it is a good idea to meet with a medical professional before making major changes so that the patient can be advised how to proceed and what to be aware of.

Prevention

The best way to prevent stroke or reduce the chances for stroke is to manage the risk factors listed above. In more serious cases, a physician may prescribe medication or recommend surgery.

The two main factors that lead to stroke are disease in the large and small arteries (atherosclerosis) and heart disease. In these conditions, clots can form and travel to the brain. Two main types of medication are prescribed for treatment: antiplatelet drugs and anticoagulant drugs. Antiplatelet drugs prevent clots by preventing the clumping of blood cells. These drugs include aspirin, ticlopidine, Clopidogrel, and dipyridamole. They prevent clots by thinning the blood, and include warfarin and coumadin.

Under the right circumstances, surgery can be used to considerably reduce the chance of stroke in an individual. The most common and most successful procedure is a carotid endarterectomy, first performed in the 1950s. If a patient has been found to have a narrowing in the carotid artery (the artery that takes blood to the brain), then surgery may be required to remove the narrowing. Surgery is not beneficial or even necessary in every case, so it is best to consult a specialist.

Perhaps the biggest part of prevention is knowledge, including learning the warning signs for stroke, having an annual check-up, and being aware of risk factors that can be controlled; educating oneself but not diagnosing oneself (instead consulting a professional) if unsure; and, making sure that information comes from a reliable source. It is best to rely on stroke information from national organizations because the main purpose of television is to entertain (e.g., certain information may be sensationalized), and information on the Internet can come from anyone.

VLADIMIR HACHINSKI
LARISSA HACHINSKI

See also CHOLESTEROL; DIABETES MELLITUS; EPILEPSY; HEART DISEASE; HIGH BLOOD PRESSURE; LANGUAGE DISORDERS; PRESSURE ULCERS; REHABILITATION; VASCULAR DEMENTIA.

BIBLIOGRAPHY

ADAIR E. S., and PFALZGRAF, B. Pathways: Moving beyond Stroke and Aphasia. Detroit, Mich: Wayne State University Press, 1990.

AHN, J., and FERGUSON, G. Recovering from Stroke. New York: HarperCollins, 1992.

American Heart Association. The American Heart Association Family Guide to Stroke Treatment, Recovery and Prevention. New York: Times Books, 1994.

ANCOWITZ, A. The Stroke Book. New York: William Morrow & Company, 1993.

BERGQUIST, W. H.; MCCLEAN, R.; and KOBYLINSKI, B. A. Stroke Survivors. San Francisco: Jossey-Bass, 1994.

DONAHUE, P. J. How to Prevent a Stroke: A Complete Risk-Reduction Program. Emmaus, Penn: Rodale Press, 1989.

FOLEY, C., and PIZER, H. F. The Stroke Fact Book. New York: Bantam Books, 1985.

GORDON, N. F. Stroke: Your Complete Exercise Guide. Champaign, Ill: Human Kinetics Publishers, 1993.

Heart and Stroke Foundation of Canada. The Canadian Family Guide to Stroke Prevention, Treatment and Recovery. Toronto, Ontario: Random House of Canada, 1996.

JOSEPHS, A. The Invaluable Guide to Life After Stroke: An Owner's Manual. Long Beach, Calif.: Amadeus Press, 1992.

KLEIN, B. S. Slow Dance, A Story of Stroke, Love and Disability. Toronto, Ontario: Knopf Canada, 1997.

LARKIN, M. When Someone You Love Has a Stroke. A National Stroke Association Book. New York: Dell Publishing, 1995.

MCCRUM, R. My Year Off. Toronto, Ontario: Knopf Canada, 1998.

National Stroke Association. Living at Home after Your Stroke. Englewood, Col.: National Stroke Association, 1994.

NEWBORN, B. Return to Ithaca. Rockport, Mass.: Element Books Limited, 1997.

SENELICK, R. C.; ROSSI, P. W.; and DOUGHERTY, K. Living with Stroke: A Guide for Families. Chicago, Ill: Contemporary Books, 1999.

SHINBERG, E. F. Strokes: What Families Should Know. Westminister, Mary.: Random House, 1990.

WEINER, F.; LEE, M.; and BELL, H. Recovering at Home after a Stroke: A Practical Guide for You and Your Family. New York: The Body Press/Perigee Books, 1994.

SUBJECTIVE WELL-BEING

"Do people get less happy as they get older?" This question has been addressed by researchers who focus on aging and subjective well-being (SWB). SWB is used to describe the subjective experience, as opposed to the objective conditions, of life (Okun and Stock). What matters most in this regard is how people perceive life rather than the actual circumstances of their lives. SWB has both an affective (emotional) and a cognitive (mental) component (Diener et al.).

The affective component of SWB involves people's moods and emotions that represent their feelings about their current experiences. If one were to inventory the amounts of positive affect and negative affect that a person experienced, one could arrive at an index of happiness by subtracting the amount of negative affect from the amount of positive affect. Happiness refers to the degree to which positive affect exceeds negative affect. The cognitive component of SWB is primarily an evaluation (or mental judgment) concerning how well one's life has turned out.

This older women seems to be experiencing subjective well-being during a pleasant phone conversation. (Photo copyright © Suzanne Khalil.)

This judgment reflects the degree to which people are satisfied with their lives (Okun and Stock).

How is SWB measured? Researchers tend to rely upon self-reports in response to questions or statements. A typical statement of life satisfaction is "If I could live my life over, I would change almost nothing." Typical questions used to assess positive and negative affect are respectively: "During the past few weeks did you ever feel pleased about having accomplished something?" and "During the past few weeks did you ever feel upset because someone criticized you?"

People generally agree that happiness for other people peaks in middle age. Why do many people judge the later years to be less happy for other people? What often comes to mind when considering old age is the loss of family, friends, money, career, health, activity, and competence. Simply put, the ratio of gains to losses appears to be less favorable as people age (Baltes and Baltes). However, contrary to the popular belief that "people get less happy as they get older," age is unrelated to SWB (Diener et al.). Most people maintain their SWB unless their income and health diminish below a critical threshold. That the losses associated with aging do not adversely affect the SWB of older adults has been labeled "the paradox of well-being" (Filipp). How is this paradox of well-being explained? One class of explanations is that older people maintain a relatively happy existence by employing self-protective strategies (Brandtstädter and Greve).

Self-protective strategies

Social downgrading is a self-protective strategy that involves the comparison of oneself with less fortunate individuals. Older adults believe that other people's problems are more serious than their own across several domains, such as children, fitness, and finances (Heckhausen and Brim). One type of comparison is a downward social comparison. For example, an older woman who uses a cane may compare herself with an older woman who is confined to a wheelchair. A second kind of comparison (a temporal comparison) involves evaluating one's present circumstances against past conditions. For example, an older man who is struggling financially might compare his current situation with the economic hardship that he endured in the Great Depression.

In addition to comparisons, older people may maintain their SWB by minimizing the gap between their ideal and actual selves. Older people perceive their actual and ideal selves to be much more closely aligned than younger people do. Finally, older people may protect themselves by shuffling their priorities. Flexible goal attainment—the willingness to adjust one's goals in order to accommodate changing circumstances—increases with age (Brandtstädter and Greve).

Personality and emotion regulation

A second class of explanations for the paradox of SWB focuses on personality dispositions and emotion regulation strategies. Extraversion and neuroticism are stable across the adult years, and happy people are low on neuroticism and high on extraversion. From the dispositional perspective, age is irrelevant; it is individual differences in personality that contribute to variation in SWB.

In contrast, Carstensen offers a developmental explanation for why older people maintain their SWB. She found that as people age, their goals related to the self shift from developing an identity to regulating emotions. Because of the focus on emotion regulation, older adults are posited to be more selective in choosing members of their social networks. They are less likely than younger adults to have negative social exchanges. Older adults appear to be better than younger adults at regulating their emotions (Carstensen). For example, older couples appear to be more adept than younger couples at preventing arguments from escalating. Having a positive spousal relationship can buffer the stressors that accompany aging.

Sense of control

A third class of explanations for the paradox of SWB focuses on one's sense of control. Having a sense of control over one's life circumstances is a strong predictor of SWB (DeNeve and Cooper). Older people can exert control over their world either by selectively investing their resources and time to pursue their goals (selective primary control) or by minimizing the negative effects of losses (compensatory secondary control) (Schulz and Heckhausen). Older adults can increase their SWB by engaging in activities that promote either selective primary control or compensatory secondary control. Selective primary control can be enhanced by engaging in age-appropriate developmental tasks (e.g., developing a leisure repertoire). An example of a compensatory secondary control strategy is to discount the importance of activities that must be forsaken.

To age "well," it is important for people to be happy and satisfied with their lives (Baltes and Baltes). Perhaps part of the reason why wisdom is related to SWB is that older people have learned that happiness often eludes those who strive to obtain it directly. Instead, happiness is best obtained as a by-product of striving to obtain other goals that are within reach, enjoyable, and supported by trustworthy others (McGregor and Little).

SUZANNE L. KHALIL
MORRIS A. OKUN

See also EMOTION; QUALITY OF LIFE; PHILOSOPHICAL AND ETHICAL DIMENSIONS.

BIBLIOGRAPHY

BALTES, P. B., and BALTES, M. M. "Successful Aging: A Psychological Model." In *Successful Aging: Perspectives from the Behavioral Sciences.* Edited by P. B. Baltes and M. M. Baltes. New York: Cambridge University Press, 1990. Pages 1–34.

BRANDTSTÄDTER, J., and GREVE, W. "The Aging Self: Stabilizing and Protective Processes." *Developmental Review* 14, no. 1 (1994): 52–80.

CARSTENSEN, L. L. "Motivation for Social Contact Across the Life-Span: A Theory of Socioemotional Selectivity." In *Nebraska Symposium on Motivation,* vol. 40. Edited by J. Jacobs. Lincoln: University of Nebraska Press, 1993. Pages 209–254.

DENEVE, K. M., and COOPER, H. "The Happy Personality: A Meta-analysis of 137 Personality Traits and Subjective Well-Being." *Psychological Bulletin* 124, no. 2 (1998): 197–229.

DIENER, E.; SUH, E. M.; LUCAS, R. E.; and SMITH, H. L. "Subjective Well-being: Three Decades of Progress." *Psychological Bulletin* 125, no. 2 (1999): 276–302.

FILIPP, S. H. "Motivation and Emotion." In *Handbook of the Psychology of Aging,* 4th ed. Edited by J. E. Birren and K. W. Schaie. San Diego: Academic Press, 1996. Pages 218–235.

HECKHAUSEN, J., and BRIM, O. G. "Perceived Problems for Self and Others: Self-Protection by Social Downgrading Throughout Adulthood." *Psychology and Aging* 12, no. 4 (1997): 610–619.

MCGREGOR, I., and LITTLE, B. R. "Personal Projects, Happiness, and Meaning: On Doing Well and Being Yourself." *Journal of Personality and Social Psychology* 74, no. 2 (1998): 494–512.

OKUN, M. A., and STOCK, W. A. "Correlates and Components of Subjective Well-being Among the Elderly." *Journal of Applied Gerontology* 6, no. 1 (1987): 95–112.

SCHULZ, R., and HECKHAUSEN, J. "A Life-Span Model of Successful Aging." *American Psychologist* 51, no. 7 (1996): 702–714.

SUB-SAHARAN AFRICA

In Africa south of the Sahara, many older persons (especially women) are illiterate and do not know their birthdate or chronological age. African cultural definitions of old age usually are functional: people are "old" when they lose their strength, and also, for women, when they no longer menstruate or give birth to children. The United Nations defines *older persons* as those age sixty and over (sixty-plus) though Africans themselves may use different criteria, and people much younger than sixty may consider themselves old.

In a world that is growing older, less-developed countries are aging more slowly than industrial nations, with Africa aging more slowly than any other region. In developed nations, including Europe, Japan, and the United States, the proportion of those age sixty-plus was in the range of 15 to 22 percent in the year 2000, and is expected to reach 25 percent or more in some countries by the year 2025. By contrast, the proportion of those age sixty-plus in most African nations was under 5 percent in the year 2000, and will reach a modest 6 percent by the year 2025. Sub-Saharan Africa's most populous nation, Nigeria, had a total population of 110 million in 1998, over 5 million (5.2 percent) of whom were age sixty-plus. In the region as a whole, in 2000, there were 32 million older Africans; by 2025 there will be 75 million.

In the year 2000, about two-thirds of older Africans lived in rural areas, where most older people will probably continue to live well into the twenty-first century. Rural areas have weak social services, poor infrastructure, few opportunities to generate income, and heavy out-migration of younger adults seeking employment. This out-migration has serious consequences for older individuals, including loss of male labor on family farms, increased workloads for women and elders, more female-headed households, economic interdependence of migrants and rural family members, disruptions in family relationships, families with households in both rural home-lands and urban workplaces, and difficulties of children in meeting filial obligations to aging parents. Nevertheless, most older Africans, in both rural and urban settings, live with family members, usually spouses, children and/or grandchildren, often in multigenerational households. Many of the 3 to 5 percent who live alone probably have kin nearby.

The economic situation of older Africans

Though poverty was not unknown in pre-colonial Africa, it seems to have been limited mainly to persons of low social status—slaves, persons of low caste, or, sometimes, widows. Older men controlled most strategic resources, including access to housing, land, and livestock. Older women controlled food, and elders of both genders controlled the labor and reproduction of younger persons and intangible assets such as utilitarian knowledge and ritual power. In this gerontocratic system, it seems likely that most

older persons in need were adequately cared for—though in fact this is an open question, as little research has addressed the issue.

In the nineteenth and twentieth centuries, Africans experienced conquest, colonial rule, incorporation of formerly self-sufficient economies into the world political economy, and the material impoverishment of Africa and Africans. Details of these transformations varied locally, but everywhere they have put pressures on African families and made the lives of many—young and old—precarious. In addition, Africans suffer from repressive dictatorships and military regimes, corruption, widespread conflict, violence, civil wars, recurrent droughts, livestock epidemics, famines, endemic malnutrition, infectious diseases, high unemployment, and very deep poverty. In 2000, Africa had about ten million refugees and internally displaced persons, including unknown numbers of older persons. By 2000, about 34 million Africans had been infected by HIV/AIDS—in that year, 2 million of them died. The economic and social impacts of the AIDS pandemic are many, including care by older persons of their dying adult children—followed by care of orphaned grandchildren—and elders left without family support. Perhaps the single worst condition affecting Africans is poverty, which affects the great majority of Africans of all ages (and African governments as well). Money would not end political repression or war, but it could alleviate many other problems.

Because of the slow pace of economic development in Africa, opportunities for formal employment are modest, with men favored in the formal economy. Men without wage employment, and most women, earn money in the informal economy, through petty trading, making and selling craft items, and various micro-enterprises. In rural areas, cash crops provide income, but scarce land and/or labor may reduce the production of subsistence crops. In sub-Saharan Africa, women do the major part of agricultural labor. Much other work is carried out almost entirely by women and children, including fetching wood and water, cooking, laundry, housecleaning, childcare, and caregiving of sick and elderly family members. All these activities are continued as long as possible, with elders thus making substantial social and economic contributions to their families.

Most older people live in rural areas and continue working as long as they are able, retiring only when forced by frailty. For those few in formal employment, mandatory retirement age is as low as fifty in some African countries. Pensions—usually inadequate and often in the form of a single lump sum—are available to very small proportions (under 10 percent) of workers, except in Namibia and South Africa, which have comprehensive, noncontributory old-age pensions. Many retirees return to their rural homes and become involved again in the rural subsistence economy.

Older Africans in urban areas, like their rural counterparts, are likely to be poor, to participate in income-generating and maintenance activities as long as they can, live with family members, and receive assistance from relatives. Their access to health care and other services is slightly better, though they are unlikely to grow food crops. Those who are foreign nationals, coming as labor migrants or refugees, may be cut off from their families. Some older persons, especially widows without land rights, may migrate to urban areas to live with children, and large cities may attract older beggars, especially widows, who have fallen through the family support network (though even some beggars receive family support).

The social situation of older Africans

Respect is a core cultural value in sub-Saharan Africa. Indigenous ideologies strongly affirm the respect due those older than oneself, especially elders nearing death and ancestorhood. Respect is shown through obedience, deferential behavior, and participation in reciprocal exchanges of goods and labor among kin. Parents should care for children properly, and children should reciprocate by providing support and care for parents—not just when parents became frail, but all their lives. Elders should be social guides for younger generations.

In Africa in the early twenty-first century, respect remains a strong cultural value, and families are deeply concerned for their older members. However, the ability of families to provide has diminished as a consequence of widespread poverty, labor migration, and having to make hard choices between the competing needs of children and aging parents. Furthermore, in the twentieth century, elders lost much control over strategic resources, as younger adults (especially men) pursued options in the new economic and political orders where wealth, prestige, and power did not depend on elders. The formal educational system and new technologies and information undermined the importance of elders' knowledge and diminished their roles as social guides. As the economic and cultural bases of elders' prestige and power declined, elders' status and influence declined in various ways, though not uniformly nor entirely. Many elders are still given respect, though it may sometimes be superficial: they may not be consulted for their advice nor receive family support—and even when received, support may be inadequate.

The central issues in African aging revolve around families, intergenerational relations, and whether modern African families provide adequate support and care to older members. Is the African family falling apart, disintegrating, or disappearing? Or is it changing and adapting to modern conditions? Much research indicates that many elderly Africans, perhaps even a majority, receive substantial assistance from their families, especially spouses, children, and grandchildren. Other research questions the universality of these findings. In any case, inadequate support is not surprising, given Africa's widespread poverty.

Vulnerable elders

African elders vary along many dimensions in their vulnerability to risk, including rural or urban residence; embeddedness in family; gender; health; access to resources; and local political and economic conditions. Underlying many problems is Africa's deep poverty—poverty exacerbated by natural disasters and human violence that affect everyone, especially children and older persons lacking the resilience and strength to cope. The resulting poverty of old age is worse for women, because lifelong discrimination in educational and employment opportunities, property rights, nutrition, and other aspects of life brings them to old age with thinner resources than men. Widows (the majority of older women) sometimes encounter further difficulties if their husband's family seizes their property and abandons them.

Since most older Africans depend on children for support and care, childless elders are especially at risk, with women a little more likely than men to be childless (polygamy gives men more chances to have children). With sons commonly responsible for older parents, sonless elders may be no better off than childless persons—though, increasingly, daughters support parents.

As with older people everywhere, physical frailty, disabilities, illness, and malnutrition have serious consequences in terms of self-support versus the need for physical care. Institutional solutions, including long-term care, scarcely exist in Africa, except for persons of European descent, so frail African elders must depend on their families. Care is more uncertain for women, who are themselves the caregivers. The great majority of older men are cared for by wives, but women must depend on daughters, daughters-in-law, and grandchildren, if they are available. As Africa's older population increases, there will be more frail elders, and fewer caregivers due to the combined effects of migration, AIDS, and rapidly declining birth rates.

Policy and practical implications

What can be done? Clearly, poverty must be alleviated, gender justice must be achieved, and solutions to African problems must take an indigenous approach. Family-oriented policies and community-based initiatives offer feasible alternatives to the prohibitive cost of state interventions and the infrastructural constraints of rural areas where most elders live. Action-oriented participatory research will empower older Africans as they express their needs and envision solutions based on African social and cultural strengths.

Families will no doubt remain the basic resource for elders (as is the case throughout the world). Hence, it makes sense to target families for services to older persons, for example, by strengthening the resources of women, the traditional caregivers. Programs supporting the productive activities of women and elders—such as literacy and vocational education, rural cooperatives, small-scale village industries, and small loans to fund microenterprises—would benefit all family members. Such interventions would expand the impact of existing self-help and mutual aid groups, such as rotating credit associations and work groups. More extensive rural development, including improved employment opportunities, technical support, and service infrastructure, could induce more younger people to remain in their rural homes and could also benefit older persons, both economically and by having their relatives near.

Limited resources for medically based health care in Africa have led to an emphasis on community-based primary health care. Locally trained community health workers could provide nutrition and preventive-care education for older persons, especially women, thus benefiting all family members, given the involvement of women in feeding and caring for family members. In addition, indigenous healing practices and medications need consideration, especially as many Africans consult local practitioners instead of, or in addition to, going to doctors and hospitals.

Finally, policies and laws (including African customary laws) aimed at achieving gender justice would break the cycles of discrimination against women in their rights to land, property, and their children—and in access to knowledge and legal advice. These cycles have made African women of all ages especially vulnerable to poverty and violence. As with other problems of African elders, solutions need to be aimed not solely at older people, but at improving the situation of women, families, and communities and achieving economic development for all. Such improvements will enable older people to continue their self-support and substantial contributions to their families, and will enable families to give their elders adequate support and care. The situation of Africa, and African elders, is grim but not hopeless. Africans are resilient, creative, hardworking people with many social and cultural resources to call upon in changing things for the better.

MARIA CATTELL

See also MIDDLE EASTERN COUNTRIES; POPULATION AGING; POVERTY.

BIBLIOGRAPHY

APT, N. A., and KATILA, S. "Gender and Intergenerational Support: The Case of Ghanaian Women." *Southern African Journal of Gerontology* 3, no. 2 (1994): 23–29.

CAMPBELL, C. "Intergenerational Conflict in Township Families: Transforming Notions of 'Respect' and Changing Power Relations." *Southern African Journal of Gerontology* 3, no. 2 (1994): 37–42.

CATTELL, M. G. "Caring for the Elderly in Sub-Saharan Africa." *Ageing International* XX, no. 2 (1993): 13–19.

CATTELL, M. G. "African Widows, Culture and Social Change: Case Studies from Kenya." In

The Cultural Context of Aging: Worldwide Perspectives, 2d ed. Edited by J. Sokolovsky. Westport, Conn.: Bergin & Garvey, 1997. Pages 71–98.

FERREIRA, M.; APT, N.; and KIRAMBI, A., compilers. Ageing in Changing Societies: Africa Preparing for the Next Millennium (AGES Workshop Report). Accra, Ghana: African Gerontological Society (AGES), 1999.

HAMPSON, J. "Marginalisation and Rural Elderly: A Shona Case Study." Journal of Social Development in Africa 5, no. 2 (1990): 5–23.

MØLLER, V., and SOTSHONGAYE, A. "'My Family Eat This Money Too': Pension Sharing and Self-Respect among Zulu Grandmothers." Southern African Journal of Gerontology 5, no. 2 (1996): 9–19.

MYSLIK, W. D.; FREEMAN, A.; and SLAWSKI, J. "Implications of AIDS for the South African Population Age Profile." Southern African Journal of Gerontology 6, no. 2 (1997): 3–8.

NYANGURU, A. C.; HAMPSON, J.; ADAMCHAK, D. J.; and WILSON, A. O. "Family Support for the Elderly in Zimbabwe." Southern African Journal of Gerontology 3, no. 1 (1994): 22–26.

OKOJIE, F. A. "Aging in Sub-Saharan Africa: Toward a Redefinition of Needs Research and Policy Directions." Journal of Cross-Cultural Gerontology 3 (1988): 3–19.

PEIL, M. "The Small Town as a Retirement Centre." In The Migration Experience in Africa. Edited by J. Baker and T. A. Aina. Sweden: Nordiska Afrikainstitutet, 1995. Pages 149–166.

PEIL, M.; BAMISAIYE, A.; and EKPENYONG, S. "Health and Physical Support for the Elderly in Nigeria." Journal of Cross-Cultural Gerontology 4 (1989): 89–106.

RWEZAURA, B. A. "Changing Community Obligations to the Elderly in Contemporary Africa." Journal of Social Development in Africa 4, no. 1 (1989): 5–24.

SAGNER, A. "Urbanization, Ageing, and Migration: Some Evidence from African Settlements in Cape Town." Southern African Journal of Gerontology 6, no. 2 (1997): 13–19.

TOGONU-BICKERSTETH, F.; AKINNAWO, E. O.; AKINYELE, O. S.; and AYENI, E. "Public Alms Solicitation among the Yoruba Elderly in Nigeria." Southern African Journal of Gerontology 6, no. 2 (1997): 26–31.

UDVARDY, M., and CATTELL, M. G., eds. "Gender, Aging and Power in Sub-Saharan Africa: Challenges and Puzzles." Journal of Cross-Cultural Gerontology 7, no. 4 (1992).

VAN DER GEEST, S. "Between Respect and Reciprocity: Managing Old Age in Rural Ghana." Southern African Journal of Gerontology 6, no. 2 (1997): 20–25.

SUCCESSFUL AGING

One might think that successful aging would be a noncontroversial topic, one that everyone would agree is a good goal to pursue. However, considerable controversy has arisen over its definition, causes, and consequences. This controversy has been fueled in part by the fact that as more and more people enter the *third age* (over age sixty), concern has begun to shift from medically prolonging life to ensuring that a prolonged life is worth living. The concept itself is rather paradoxical: it combines a positive term (successful) with one usually perceived as negative (aging). How can one be "successful" at a process which usually means decrement and disability? The answer lies in the definitions.

Definitions

The concept of successful aging, which appeared early in studies of aging, has sometimes been equated with life satisfaction or happiness, and, sometimes with good health or with longevity. A more comprehensive definition of successful aging would combine all three of these elements: longevity (without which successful aging is impossible), health (lack of disability), and happiness (life satisfaction).

M. Powell Lawton (1983) has defined "the good life" (in old age) as consisting of four independent dimensions:

1. Behavioral competence (health, perception, motor behavior, and cognition)
2. Psychological well-being (happiness, optimism, congruence between desired and attained goals)
3. Perceived quality of life (subjective assessment of family, friends, activities, work, income, and housing)
4. Objective environment (realities of housing, neighborhood, income, work, activities, etc.)

More recently, Rowe and Kahn have urged a distinction between *usual* and *successful* aging within the category of *normal*, or nonpathological, aging. They define *usual aging* as aging in which extrinsic factors heighten the effects of intrinsic aging processes (normal functional decrements); whereas *successful aging* refers to aging in which extrinsic factors counteract intrinsic aging, so that there is little or no functional loss. Successful aging thus includes three key characteristics:

1. Low risk of disease and disease-related disability
2. High mental and physical function
3. Active engagement with life

Causes

The longevity component of successful aging has been studied through research on causes of mortality and longevity. There have been numerous studies of factors associated with mortality, and a few studies of predictors of longevity. Predictors of longevity include being female; being physically active; not smoking; having good cognitive functioning; higher than average socioeconomic status; high levels of social activity; life satisfaction, and work satisfaction; a high happiness rating; and satisfying sexual activity. In general, the predictors of longevity also predict better health (less disability). This is contrary to the popular theory that greater longevity causes greater disability.

Other studies have focused on factors associated with life satisfaction. These factors include good health, higher than average socioeconomic status, being single or married (as opposed to widowed, divorced, or separated), and high levels of social activity (especially organizational activity). Lawton found that the factors most closely correlated with feelings of well-being were health and activity level.

Usually, there is little or no relationship between life satisfaction and age, race, sex, or employment—once controls are made for health and income. The lack of relationship to age is explained by Brandstädter and Greve as being due to three interdependent processes that older persons use to maintain their life satisfaction as they grow older: assimilation (instrumental coping to attain desired goals), accommodation (changing desired goals), and immunization (filtering out threatening information). A series of analyses of studies of the causes of happiness (e.g., Okun, Stock, Haring, and Witter) also found that health (especially self-rated health), was the most potent correlate of happiness. Achieved social status variables (such as income), as well as lifestyle variables (such as social activity and housing), were modestly related to happiness.

There have been few longitudinal studies of the predictors of happiness or life satisfaction. In the Second Duke Longitudinal Study, the strongest predictors of life satisfaction were health, social activity, and sexual enjoyment. There is considerable overlap between these two sets of predictors: both longevity and satisfaction were predicted by health, higher socioeconomic status, social activity, and sexual enjoyment.

An analysis of the predictors of successful aging in the Second Duke Longitudinal Study of Aging (Palmore) defined successful aging as survival to age seventy-five and being generally happy. Multiple regression analysis found that the significant independent predictors of successful aging were secondary group activity (organizational groups and reading), work satisfaction, physical activity, physical abilities, and happiness. These findings support the activity theory of aging, in that two of the strongest explanatory predictors of successful aging were group activity and physical activity. There is probably a reciprocal causal relationship between these variables: those who remain active are more likely to be healthy and happy, and vice versa.

Avoiding disease and disability

Rowe and Kahn assert that most older people, even the very old and weak, have the capacity to increase their muscle strength, balance, walking ability, and overall aerobic power. We now know that there are many things that can prevent or ameliorate the chronic diseases common in old age, including:

- Early detection (regular medical examinations and self-examinations, combined with X-rays and laboratory tests of blood and urine)
- Healthful nutrition (low fat, high fiber, multivitamin and mineral supplements)
- Vigorous exercise (aerobic, flexibility, balance, and strength building)
- Safe driving (seat belts, observing speed limits, not using cell phones while driving)
- Safe sex (protection against AIDS and venereal disease)
- Vaccinations (against the flu, pneumonia, and tetanus)
- Avoiding obesity, tobacco, alcohol abuse, and drug abuse
- Social support—according to David Myers, those who enjoy close relationships eat bet-

ter, exercise more, and smoke and drink less; he suggests that a supportive network helps people evaluate and overcome stressful events.

Maintaining mental function

The maintenance of mental function is usually considered an essential component of successful aging. A 1999 study (Gould et al.) found that adults continue to grow new brain cells throughout life. This has encouraged a shift from the old assumption that cognitive powers inevitably decline with age to new theories that older people can bolster their learning and memory abilities, and even stave off declines. Several studies have found that the major ways to maintain mental function include:

- Continuing education and mental challenges (reading, skill games, puzzles, learning new subjects, problem solving). Laurence Katz, a professor of neurobiology at Duke University, says that his *neurobic* exercises help the brain not only to maintain connections between nerve cells, but also aid in developing new connections.
- Maintaining cardiovascular fitness through daily aerobic exercise (which avoids the effects of stroke and other diseases on the brain)
- Engaging in useful, satisfying work or voluntary activities (especially complex, challenging, and self-directed work)
- Memory training (concentration, memory devices, learning techniques
- Maintaining appropriate social support (getting encouragement and help when needed)

Engagement with life

According to Rowe and Kahn, there are two main aspects of active engagement (which they define as a component of successful aging): social support and productive activity. Or, as Freud put it, "love and work."

Social support involves giving and receiving positive information, trust, care, love, esteem, network membership, and mutual obligation. Two kinds of support are important for successful aging: socioemotional support (e.g., affection, liking, love, esteem) and instrumental support (e.g., assistance or care when one is ill, help with household chores, transportation, loans, gifts).

However, it is best if the support is mutual: receiving support should be balanced by giving support, insofar as is possible.

The importance of productive activity was demonstrated in longitudinal studies of aging at Duke University (Palmore and Jeffers), which found that work satisfaction (defined broadly as any kind of useful activity) was one of the best predictors of longevity. Rowe and Kahn found three main factors that promote productive activity: health, social support, and self-efficacy. All three of these factors interact and reinforce each other. As was indicated previously, social support seems to help overcome stress and promote healthful lifestyles.

Heredity

In general, most studies agree that successful aging is, for the most part, not determined by genetics (as many believe), but by lifestyle choices in diet, exercise, mental challenges, self-efficacy, and involvement with others. There is a popular saying, "If you want to live long, choose long-lived parents." This saying, although humorous, oversimplifies the findings of studies of longevity among older persons. While it is true that genetics can cause inherited diseases such as sickle-cell anemia and hemophelia, these tend to take their toll early in life. If one survives to middle age, one probably has a healthy set of genes, and at that age the primary determinants of successful aging become the lifestyle, psychological, and social factors discussed above.

Criticisms

There are two main criticisms of the concept of successful aging: (1) it is a categorical concept rather than a continuum; and (2) it tends to blame those who do not measure up to high standards of aging. However, the view of successful aging as "categorical" fails to recognize that there are many shades of gray between the ideal of successful aging and failure (usual aging). No one can be perfectly successful on all dimensions of aging. Many people have some chronic illness or disability and still manage to function fairly well and remain involved. Many others are relatively healthy and functional despite having disengaged from most of life. Critics say that these people should be considered relatively successful, despite imperfections.

Regarding the second criticism, one must consider that many elders cannot measure up to the high standards of successful aging on some or all dimensions, through no fault of their own. There are accidents, genetic weaknesses, psychological blocks, ignorance, lack of resources, and other external factors that prevent successful aging in many elders. Critics say that they should not be blamed and made to feel guilty for their "failure." Nevertheless, successful aging is such a positive and useful concept that it has enjoyed widespread acceptance among both professional gerontologists and nonspecialists.

ERDMAN B. PALMORE

See also FUNCTIONAL ABILITY; HEALTH, SOCIAL FACTORS; LONGEVITY: SOCIAL ASPECTS; QUALITY OF LIFE, DEFINITION AND MEASUREMENT; SUBJECTIVE WELL-BEING.

BIBLIOGRAPHY

BALTES, P., and BALTES, M., eds. *Successful Aging.* New York: Cambridge University Press, 1990.

BRANDSTÄDTER, J., and GREVE, W. "The Aging Self." *Developmental Review* 14 (1994): 52–80.

GOULD, E.; REEVES, A.; GRAZIANO, M.; and GROSS, C. "New Brain Cells." *Science* 286 (1999): 548–552.

HAVIGHURST, R. "Successful Aging." *Gerontologist* 1 (1961): 4–7.

KATZ, L., and RUBIN, M. *Keep Your Brain Alive.* New York: Workman, 1999.

LARSON, R. "Thirty Years of Research on the Subjective Well-Being of Older Americans." *Journal of Gerontology* 33 (1978): 109–125.

LAWTON, M. "Environmental and Other Determinants of Well-Being in Older People." *Gerontologist* 23 (1983): 349–357.

MYERS, D. *The Pursuit of Happiness.* New York: Avon, 1993.

NOWLIN, J. "Successful Aging." In *Normal Aging III: Reports from the Duke Longitudinal Studies, 1975–1984.* Edited by E. Palmore. Durham, N.C.: Duke University Press, 1985.

OKUN, M.; STOCK, W.; HARING, M.; and WITTER, R. "Health and Subjective Well-Being." *International Journal of Aging and Human Development* 19 (1984): 111–132.

PALMORE, E., ed. *Normal Aging III.* Durham, N.C.: Duke University Press, 1985.

PALMORE, E., and JEFFERS, F., eds. *Predictors of Life Span.* Lexington, Mass.: D. C. Heath, 1971.

PALMORE, E., and KIVETT, V. "Change in Life Satisfaction." *Journal of Gerontology* 32 (1977): 311–316.

ROWE, J., and KAHN, R. *Successful Aging.* New York: Pantheon, 1998.

WILLIAMS, R., and WIRTH, C. *Lives Through the Years.* New York: Atherton Press, 1965.

SUICIDE

Among industrialized countries that provide statistics on suicide, nearly all report that suicide rates rise progressively with age, with the highest rates occurring for men age seventy-five and older. In the United States in 1997, older white males age eighty-five and older had a rate of 65.4 per 100,000. This latter rate is almost six times the rate of all ages combined. Reviewed here is the available research evidence on correlates and risk factors in later life suicidal behavior, and suggested opportunities for prevention.

Demographic correlates and methods of later life suicide

U.S. data on completed suicides by sex, age, race, marital status, and method are based on vital statistics information gathered by the Centers for Disease Control and Prevention's National Center for Health Statistics, with each state reporting from death certificates. From this data source we know that increased age among persons sixty-five and older is associated with higher rates of suicide. Also, older adults as a group are more likely to use a firearm as a suicide method compared to the total U.S. rate; 70 versus 60 percent. In terms of demographic correlates of suicide deaths, male sex, white race, older age, and unmarried status are associated with higher rates of suicide.

Older suicide victims are more likely to have lived alone than younger suicides. However, older adults are also likely to be those members of the population who live alone, so the potency of living arrangement as a risk factor for suicide is not clear. A correlate associated with living arrangement is marital status. The suicide rate for unmarried older adults is higher than the suicide rate for married older adults. For older men, the suicide rate for those who are divorced or widowed is much higher when compared with older females or with their married counterparts (Buda and Tsuang).

Psychological status and life events associated with later life suicide

In the absence of adequate prospective studies, the psychological autopsy (PA) method has been used to reconstruct a detailed picture of the victim's psychological state prior to death, including psychiatric symptomatology, behavior, and life circumstances during the weeks or months before death. This includes interviewing knowledgeable informants, reviewing available clinical records, and comprehensive case formulation by one or more mental health professionals with expertise in postmortem studies. The PA method has been used to provide an inclusive, well-defined sample of all persons who die by suicide within a defined catchment area, region, or population. One of the most striking and consistent findings of the PA method is that psychiatric disorder and/or substance use is present in about 90 percent of all suicides, with affective disorder as the most common psychopathology, followed by substance use and schizophrenia (Conwell and Brent).

When compared to younger suicide victims, older victims are more likely to have had a physical illness, and to have suffered from depression that is not comorbid with a substance disorder (Conwell and Brent). The type of depression found in the majority of later life suicides is usually a first episode of depression, uncomplicated by psychoses or other comorbid psychiatric disorders, and, ironically, is the most treatable type of late-life depression. Such age-related patterns have appeared in reports from a number of countries including the United States, Finland, and the United Kingdom.

Although substance use is less frequent among elderly suicides, there is some evidence that among the "young old," alcohol may be a correlate. For men with early onset alcoholism who have survived to their fifties and sixties, the combination of continued alcohol abuse and burn out among their social support network may be lethal. Murphy and his associates described that for older male alcoholics, loss of the last social support can be a pivotal event in suicide risk (Murphy, Wetzel, Robins, and McEvoy). How current, as well as past alcohol abuse, lowers the threshold for suicidal behavior in later life requires further systematic examination. Although it is often assumed that medication misuse (e.g., benzodiazepine dependence, psychotropic medication with alcohol abuse) is a risk for late life suicide, there is little published information on this topic.

Despite high rates of dementia and delirium in later life, few studies have found these diagnoses to be risk factors for suicide (Conwell and Brent). Controlled PA studies are needed to determine what other factors in combination with mental and physical disorders are related to risk for later life suicide.

The PA has been used to explore possible personality traits that may increase risk for later life suicide (Duberstein). Duberstein used an informant-based personality inventory measure to examine possible personality traits among older and younger suicides, relative to age- and sex-matched controls. The inventory measured five general personality traits: neuroticism, extroversion, openness to experience, agreeableness, and conscientiousness. Suicides were found to have higher neuroticism scores than normal controls, and older suicide victims had lower openness to experience scores than both younger suicides and normal controls.

Hopelessness, a set of beliefs related to lack of anticipated positive outcomes about the future, has also been examined in the context of later life suicide. A prospective investigation of a retirement community found a single item asking about hopelessness was related to later completed suicides (Ross, Bernstein, Trent, Henderson, and Paganini-Hill).

Suicide intent has also been examined in older adult suicide victims. Using the PA method, older adults were found to be more intent compared to younger suicide victims (Conwell, Duberstein, Cox, Herrmann, Forbes, and Caine). That is, older adults were more likely to have avoided intervention, taken precautions against discovery, and were less likely to communicate their intent to others. Moreover, older men, in particular, were less likely to have had a history of previous attempts.

The PA method has also been used to examine patterns of health services use among suicide victims. Health services for older adults who later suicided was typically available, and used. A number of reports indicate that approximately 70 percent of older suicide victims had seen a primary health care provider within a month (Conwell). In contrast, few older adult suicide victims have had a history of mental health care.

Neurobiological correlates of late life suicide

Postmortem brain tissue studies of suicide victims have found that the sertonergic systems (presynaptic and nontransporter nerve terminal binding sites) had reduced activity (Mann). Although there is optimism about new refinements and applications of neurobiological, brain imaging, and candidate gene markers to identify high risk individuals, there are currently no specific biological markers for suicidal behavior. With regard to older adults, it is conceivable that a "neurobiological vulnerability" to suicide might be modulated by age-related changes in neurobiological systems (Schneider). The consistency of increased suicide risk with age and male sex across nations also suggests a possible neurobiological process. Decreased brain concentrations of serotonin, dopamine, norepinephrine and their metabolites (HVA, 5-HIAA); increased brain MAO-B activity; increased hypothalamic-pituitary-adrenal (HPA) activity; and increased sympathetic nervous system activity are associated with both depression and normal aging (Schneider). Although several reviews have examined the evidence for neurobiologic abnormalities among older suicide victims relative to controls, there are too few studies that included sufficient "older" subjects (older than sixty years) to draw any conclusions (Conwell and Brent). This is particularly true of the subgroup of the older adults most at risk: those eighty-five and older.

Suicide attempts in later life

There are currently no national surveillance data of suicide attempts in the United States. Using data from the National Institute of Mental Health Epidemiologic Catchment Area study of five communities, Moscicki and her associates found a much lower prevalence of lifetime suicide attempts for older adults than younger populations. For persons age sixty-five and older, the lifetime prevalence for suicide attempts was 1.1 percent. By comparison, the rate was 4 percent for persons age twenty-five to forty-four. Other community-based studies have estimated lower attempt to completion ratios for older, compared to younger, adults (e.g., Nordentoft et al.). These findings support Conwell and colleagues's 1998 report that older adults are more intent in their efforts to commit suicide.

Other information about attempted suicide in late life comes from studying the characteristics of older persons recently admitted to a hospital due to the attempt. Draper reviewed twelve studies of later life suicide attempts published be-

tween 1985 and 1994. Despite variation in sampling contexts and approaches to measurement, and lack of adequate control groups, he reported several consistent factors associated with attempted suicide in late life: depression, social isolation, and being unmarried. The degree to which physical health was a risk factor was unclear. In some studies it appeared to play a major role, while in another only about one-third of the patients identified health as a salient factor.

The relationship between hopelessness and suicide attempts in later life was examined by studying the course of hopelessness in depressed patients (Rifai et al., 1994). Patients who had attempted suicide in the past had significantly higher hopelessness scores than nonattempters during both the acute and continuation phases of psychiatric treatment. Moreover, a high degree of hopelessness persisting after the remission of depression in older patients appeared to be associated with a history of suicidal behavior. This study by Rifai and her associates also suggested that a high degree of hopelessness may increase the likelihood of premature discontinuation of treatment and lead to future attempts or suicide. One prospective study of older depressed inpatients followed over a year found that 8.7 percent attempted suicide (Zweig and Hinrichsen). Patients who attempted suicide were more likely to have an incomplete remission of depression, history of suicide attempts, and familial interpersonal strain compared to those who did not attempt within the one year follow-up.

Prevention strategies

Prevention strategies should follow the most potent risk factor findings. Since the majority of older adults use firearms as a means of suicide, some have proposed that reduction in access to firearms may be an effective, preventive measure. However, others have argued that substitution in suicide methods may minimize the potency of this prevention approach (1990).

Research findings of increases in intent with age suggest that older persons who are at risk for suicide may be more difficult to identify as being at imminent risk than is the case for younger persons. Thus, clinical intervention strategies that target individuals who are at high risk for suicide, as indicated by a variety of demographic and psychiatric variables, may be more effective for preventing suicide than interventions that solely target individuals with suicide ideation or behavior. The fact that the majority of older adults are seen in primary care settings within the month of their deaths, coupled with the finding that most later life suicide victims have had a late onset, depressive episode, suggests that detecting and treating depression in primary care may be an efficient way to prevent later life suicides.

Although the identification and adequate treatment of depression is proposed as the most promising research avenue when considering preventive interventions in late life suicide, there are a number of factors that work against these prevention efforts. Ageism works against outreach efforts. Many health providers, family members, and older adults themselves believe that depression and suicidal ideation are part of the normal aging process. Prevention efforts will need to consider these issues in public education and provider training to advance efforts in increased detection and treatment of depression.

JANE L. PEARSON

See also DEPRESSION; EUTHANASIA AND SENICIDE; SUICIDE AND ASSISTED SUICIDE, ETHICAL ASPECTS.

BIBLIOGRAPHY

BUDA, M., and TSUANG, M. T. "The Epidemiology of Suicide: Implications for Clinical Practice." In *Suicide Over the Life Cycle: Risk Factors, Assessment, and Treatment of Suicidal Patients.* Edited by S. J. Blumenthal and D. J. Kupfer. Washington, D.C.: American Psychiatric Press, Inc., 1990. Pages 17–37.
CONWELL, Y. (1994). "Suicide in Elderly Patients." In *Diagnosis and Treatment of Depression in Late-Life.* Edited by L. S. Schneider, C. F. Reynolds, B. D. Lebowitz, and A. J. Friedhoff. Washington, D.C.: American Psychiatric Association, 1994. Pages 397–418.
CONWELL, Y., and BRENT, D. "Suicide and Aging I: Patterns of Psychiatric Diagnosis." *International Psychogeriatrics* 7 (1995): 149–181.
CONWELL, Y.; DUBERSTEIN, P. R.; COX, C.; HERRMANN, J. H.; FORBES, N. T.; and CAINE, E. D. "Age Differences in Behaviors Leading to Completed Suicide." *American Journal of Geriatric Psychiatry* 6 (1998): 122–126.
DRAPER, B. "Attempted Suicide in Old Age." *International Journal of Geriatric Psychiatry* 11 (1996): 577–587.
DUBERSTEIN, P. R. "Openness to Experience and Completed Suicide across the Second Half of Life." *International Psychogeriatrics* 7 (1995): 183–198.
MANN, J. J. "The Neurobiology of Suicide." *Nature Medicine* 4 (1998): 25–30.
MOSCICKI, E. K.; O'CARROLL, P.; RAE, D. S.; LOCKE, B. Z.; ROY, A.; and REGIER, D. A. "Suicide Attempts in the Epidemiologic Catchment Area Study." *Yale Journal of Biology and Medicine* 61 (1988) 259–268.
MURPHY, G. E.; WETZEL, R. D.; ROBINS, E.; and MCEVOY, L. "Multiple Risk Factors Predict Suicide in Alcoholism." *Archives of General Psychiatry* 49 (1992): 459–463.
NORDENTOFT, M.; BREUM, L.; MUNCK, L.; NORDESTGAARD, A. G.; HUNDING, A.; and BJÆLDAGER, P. A. L. "High Mortality by Natural and Unnatural Causes: A 10 Year Follow Up Study of Patients Admitted to a Poisoning Treatment Centre after Suicide Attempts." *British Medical Journal* 306 (1993): 1637-1641.
RIFAI, A. H.; GEORGE, C. J.; STACK, J. A.; MANN, J. J.; and REYNOLDS, C. F. "Hopelessness in Suicide Attempters After Acute Treatment of Major Depression in Late-Life." *American Journal of Psychiatry* 151 (1994): 1687–1690.
ROSS, R. K.; BERNSTEIN, L.; TRENT, L.; HENDERSON, B. E.; and PAGANINI-HILL, A. "A Prospective Study of Risk Factors for Traumatic Death in the Retirement Community." *Preventive Medicine* 19 (1990): 323–334.
SCHNEIDER, L. S. "Biological Commonalities among Aging, Depression, and Suicidal Behavior." In *Suicide and Depression in Late-Life: Critical Issues in Treatment, Research and Public Policy.* Edited by G. J. Kennedy. New York: John Wiley & Sons, Inc., 1996. Pages 39–50.
SZANTO, K.; REYNOLDS, C. F., 3D; CONWELL, Y.; BEGLEY, A. E.; and HOUCK, P. "High Levels of Hopelessness Persist in Geriatric Patients with Remitted Depression and a History of Attempted Suicide." *Journal of the American Geriatrics Society* 46 (1998): 1401–1406.
ZWEIG, R. A., and HINRICHSEN, G. A. "Factors Associated with Suicide Attempts by Depressed Older Adults: A Prospective Study." *American Journal of Psychiatry* 150 (1993): 1687–1692.

SUICIDE AND ASSISTED SUICIDE, ETHICAL ASPECTS

Contemporary exploration of the ethical issues concerning suicide and assisted suicide has focused almost exclusively on a single form of suicide: physician-assisted suicide in terminal illness. Ethical issues concerning suicide in old age, independent of illness, are rarely if ever openly

Controversial assisted suicide advocate Jack Kevorkian (right) speaks at a press conference held with his attorney Geoffrey Fieger. Kevorkian, a Michigan physician, claimed to have assisted in more than 130 suicides before he was convicted of second-degree murder for assisting with the suicide of Thomas Youk, 52, who suffered from Lou Gehrig's disease. (Archive Photos, Inc.)

discussed. This entry first examines the debate over physician-assisted suicide in the public arena as a preamble to its central task, and then explores the ethical issues concerning suicide and assisted suicide in old age.

The public debate over physician-assisted suicide

The 1970s, 1980s, and 1990s saw the emergence of what is known as the right-to-die movement, a civil-rights inspired, populist social movement dedicated to enhancing the autonomy and well-being of terminally ill patients. In the wake of Elizabeth Kübler-Ross's 1969 book *On Death and Dying,* this movement encouraged open discussion of dying, full disclosure of terminal prognoses, and greater attention to psychological and social aspects of fear, pain, suffering, loss, grieving, and hope in the context of dying. This movement secured legal changes, including the passage of "natural death," "living will," and "durable power of attorney" statutes intended to protect patients from unwanted treatment by giving them the right to stipulate treatment choices and to appoint surrogate decision-

makers before incompetence at the end of life sets in. This movement also lobbied for better funding of programs and facilities for the dying, including hospice; for better education of physicians in matters of dying, especially pain control; for regulations designed to require health care facilities to respect patients' (non)treatment choices; and for greater protections of patients' privacy and interests in specific terminal conditions, then including AIDS.

But as it pursued these issues, the right-to-die movement also raised the question of what role the physician might play in directly assisting the patient's dying and what role the dying person might play in shaping his or her own death. Public rhetoric quickly labelled the practice at issue "physician-assisted suicide," although less negatively freighted labels such as "physician aid-in-dying" or "physician-negotiated death" have also been advanced as more appropriate. The label physician-assisted *suicide* and its linkage with terms like self-*killing* ensured that the policy battles concerning both social acceptance and legalization would be fought on volatile ideological turf.

Physician-assisted suicide: The philosophical argument. Proponents of legalizing physician-assisted suicide have argued in its favor on two principal grounds: 1) autonomy, the right of a dying person to make his or her own choices about matters of deepest personal importance, including how to face dying, and 2) the right of a person to avoid pain and suffering that cannot be adequately controlled. Proponents have insisted on both principled and consequentialist grounds that physician-assisted suicide is ethically acceptable—it is in accord, they argue, with basic principles of liberty and self-determination, and by allowing a dying person to satisfy his or her own values without posing serious harms to others, it satisfies the requirements of consequentialist, utilitarian moral systems.

Opponents challenge both claims, that of autonomy and that of freedom from suffering, and offer instead two principal competing claims. They insist 1) that fundamental morality prohibits killing, including self-killing, and 2) that allowing even sympathetic cases of physician assistance in suicide would lead down the "slippery slope," as overworked doctors, burdened or resentful family members, and callous institutions eager to save money would manipulate or force vulnerable patients into choices of suicide that were not really their own. Pressures would be particularly severe for patients with disabilities, even those who were not terminally ill. The result, opponents insist, would be wide-scale abuse.

Compromise efforts and response to the philosophical argument. Evaluating the philosophical argument and the various components of it has been the project of many bioethicists, theologians, social policy theorists, and others; there is little resolution, however, of the competing claims of autonomist and social-consequences views both for and against. Compromise efforts, launched by figures on both sides, have focused primarily on improving pain control, including accelerated research, broader education of physicians, rejection of outdated concerns about addiction associated with opiate drugs, and recourse to terminal sedation or induced permanent unconsciousness if all else fails. These efforts typically assume that if pain in terminal illness can be alleviated, requests for assistance in suicide will no longer arise. Compromise views also hold that assistance in suicide should remain, if available at all, a last resort in only the most recalcitrant cases.

However, although proponents welcome advances in pain control, many reject this sort of compromise. It constricts the freedom of a dying person to face death in the way he or she wants, proponents say; apparent compromises like terminal sedation are both repugnant and can be abused, since full, informed consent may not actually be sought. Proponents also object on grounds of equity: it is deeply unfair, they insist, that patients dependent on life-support technology like dialysis or a respirator can achieve a comparatively easy death at a time of their own choosing by having these supports discontinued—an action fully legal—but patients not dependent on life-supports cannot die as they wish, but must wait until the inevitable end. Many opponents reject attempts at compromise as well, sometimes arguing on religious grounds that suffering is an aspect of dying that ought to be accepted, sometimes holding that patients' wishes for self-determination ought not override the scruples of the medical profession, and sometimes objecting to any resort at all to assisted dying, even in very rare, difficult cases. Like the social arguments over abortion, there is little current resolution of the issue of physician-assisted suicide at either the level of public ferment or at the deeper level of philosophical principle, although the raising of the issue itself has meant far greater attention to issues of terminal illness.

Suicide in old age: historical views. The currently vigorous public debate over physician-assisted suicide, however, may appear to overlap very little with concerns about suicide and assisted suicide associated with aging. The debate over physician-assisted suicide has focused virtually exclusively—at least in the United States, though not in the Netherlands—on patients who are terminally ill, usually understood as expected to die within six months. In contrast, death is not seen as imminent in the same way for older persons. All older persons eventually die, but issues about suicide in the elderly typically focus on the older person's debility and loss of function, not nearness to death, and the public debate has not directly addressed the issue of suicide in old age for reasons of age alone. Nor has it addressed the issue of suicide in a variety of other circumstances often discussed in the historical literature, including disgrace, poverty, altruistic self-sacrifice, martyrdom, symbolic protest, and the like. Yet however veiled at the moment, the issue of suicide in old age has a rich history, both in western and nonwestern cultures.

Suicide in old age: Western views. The Greek and Roman Stoics, particularly Seneca (4 B.C.–A.D. 65), Marcus Aurelius (A.D. 121–180), and Epictetus (c. A.D. 55–c. 135), praised suicide as the act of the "wise man" or ideal individual, a choice that could be fully voluntary, fully rational, and wholly responsible. Although, according to Stoic thought, one should seek to make oneself immune to the buffetings of fortune and the storms of the emotions (and so be less vulnerable to the kinds of reactive pathologies that can lead to suicide), one should not assign overly great importance to mere life itself. Rather, on the Stoic view, the wise man is one who achieves the disengagement and wisdom required to end his (or her) own life at the appropriate time and for the appropriate reasons. Suicide can represent a rational choice in preference to circumstances like slavery, disgrace, or a degrading and painful death; it is seen as the ultimate act of freedom.

To end one's life at the appropriate time and for the appropriate reasons could also mean avoiding the conditions of old age, though the Stoics did not hold that old age alone always provided reason for suicide. In his essay "On Old Age," Cicero (106–43 B.C.), drawing on Stoic influences, holds a generally optimistic view of old age, but says that "the old must not grasp greedily after those last few years of life, nor must they walk out on them without cause." The Stoics were particularly concerned to explore the rationality of choices about suicide and the false assumptions involved in various objections to suicide. Suicide need not cut a life short, insisted Seneca, in the same way that a journey may be cut short; the journey cut short is incomplete, but the life ended by suicide can nevertheless be complete, if it is lived well. For the Stoics, it is the quality, not the quantity of life that is important. Particularly characteristic is the Stoic sensitivity to the sense of a complete life that may be attained in old age, ended not in what they saw not as depression or withdrawal, but as actively brought to a natural conclusion. In "On Old Age," Cicero continues,

it seems to me that once we have had our fill of all the things that have engaged our interest, we have had our fill of life itself. There are interests that are proper to childhood: does a full-grown man regret their loss? There are interests that belong to early manhood: when we reach full maturity—what is called "middle age"—do we look back to them with longing? Middle age itself has its special concerns; even these have lost their attraction for the old. Finally, there are interests

peculiar to old age; these fall away, too, just as did those of the earlier years. When this has happened, a sense of the fullness of life tells us that it is time to die.

Christian thought utterly rejected such arguments. It saw life and death as within the power of God to bestow; it saw a personal afterlife that could reward suffering in this life, and it made faith, not simply reason, the center of its ethic. Since life was a gift from God, to commit suicide would be to reject it, to abandon one's duty, to give up hope, to reject God. This view was held to be constant with the acceptance—indeed, the ardent embrace—of voluntary martyrdom, which—even when it involved deliberate courting of death and the voluntary performance of actions certain to result in one's own death—was seen as an act done for the sake of God, not against God's will. Early Christian writers disagreed about whether a virgin might kill herself to avoid sexual violation—no, intimated Tertullian (c. 160–c. 220); yes, implied Ambrose (c. 339–397)—but by the fourth century A.D., Augustine (354–430) had articulated the position that would become universal in Christianity: suicide was a sin so severe that it could not atone for any other sin. Biblical suicides like Samson (who in pulling the temple down on the Philistines killed himself as well) and Saul (who fell on his sword to avoid capture by the enemy) were to be understood, according to Augustine, as acting under a special commission from God. There could be no justification for suicide to protect virginity, since sin did not occur when consent to sex had not been given: in the words of Augustine, "lust will not pollute, if it is another's lust." By the time of Thomas Aquinas (c. 1225–1274), the Christian opposition to suicide was universal and fundamental: to take one's one life was a sin more grievous even than to take the life of another, and Judas' suicide after the betrayal of Jesus could only compound his sin, not atone for it. In general, however, throughout early and medieval Christian argumentation over suicide, the issue of suicide in old age is virtually never raised. Suicide is not seen as an act justified by self-respecting reasons, and, on the Christian view, whatever sufferings old age might involve should be borne with faith.

Suicide in old age: nonwestern views. In a variety of nonwestern cultures, however, considerations of age have been central. A number of traditional, oral cultures have developed elderly suicide and senicide practices, reported with varying degrees of reliability by early explorers and ethnographers. The Eskimo, for instance, are reported to have practiced socially encouraged or enforced suicide in old age "not merely to be rid of a life that is no longer a pleasure, but also to relieve their nearest relations of the trouble they give them" (Rasmussen, p. 144). The early Japanese are said to have taken their elderly to a mountaintop to die, a practice typically involving consent. The Vikings took violent death to be preferable to dying in bed of illness or old age. While the Hindu practice of *sati* could also involve young women, wives who outlived their husbands were expected to throw themselves on his funeral pyre, an expectation that particularly affected older women. Various migratory American Indian tribes abandoned their infirm members by the side of the trail, and among the Natchez of the lower Mississippi, an act like *sati* was practiced: when an individual belonging to the ruling group died, the widow or widower and other chosen family members would allow themselves to be strangled. And in traditional Melanesian cultures, especially in Fiji, aged parents were said to have felt a sense of duty to have themselves killed. Many other nonwestern cultures have had practices that permitted, encouraged, or required suicide of aged persons.

Suicide: twentieth century and contemporary views. In the late nineteenth and early twentieth centuries, suicide came to be seen as a function of social organization—this was the sociologist Émile Durkheim's contribution—and of psychopathology, the contribution of Etienne Esquirol, Sigmund Freud, and many others. Suicide was increasingly seen as a socially controlled, typically reactive, pathological act, something always to be prevented if possible. Epidemiologists explored suicide rates; the law developed policies permitting involuntary hospitalization and treatment for those who were a "danger to themselves"; psychiatry and medicine explored discursive and pharmacological ways of reducing suicidality. Efforts have focused on explaining trends in rates of suicide, including differences in male and female rates of suicide, differences in rates of suicide in different countries and cultures, and differences in the incidence of suicide and attempted suicide associated with such factors as age, alcohol use, religiosity, flexibility of coping skills, willingness to seek professional help, social support systems, use of lethal means, and failure in primary adult roles like economic success and relationship-building. Demographic

findings became increasingly important, including such findings as male suicide rates increase with age; suicide rates are highest in men over seventy-five—higher than for women at any age, and higher than for male adolescents or middle-aged adult males. But although elder suicide rates are high, suicide-prevention efforts have tended to focus on the politically more appealing category of adolescents—a category that does not raise issues about the ethical acceptability of suicide. Elderly suicide is less frequently the focus of suicide-prevention efforts, and ethical issues surrounding suicide in old age, for reasons of old age, are rarely raised.

Suicide and old age: contemporary ethical issues. In general, in both historical argumentation and the very small amount of contemporary theorizing about suicide in old age, two distinct sets of reasons for suicide, are at issue, though in practice they are often intertwined:

1) *Reasons of self-interest*: suicide in order to avoid the sufferings, physical limitations, loss of social roles, and stigma of old age;
2) *Other-regarding reasons*: suicide in order to avoid becoming a burden to others, including family members, caretakers, immediate social networks, or society as a whole.

Contemporary thought, at least explicitly, entertains neither of these. With regard to self-interested reasons, modern gerontology maintains a resolutely upbeat and optimistic view of old age, insisting that it is possible to ameliorate many of the traditional burdens of old age—chronic illness, isolation, poverty, depression, and chronic pain—by providing better medical care, better family and caregiver education, and more comprehensive social programs. With regard to other-regarding reasons, including altruistic reasons, contemporary views consider it unconscionable—especially in the wealthy societies of the West—to regard elderly persons as burdens to families or to social units or to the society; nor is it thought ethical to allow or encourage elderly persons to see themselves this way. While the notion that the elderly are to be venerated is associated primarily with the traditional cultures of the East, especially China, western societies also insist (though often ineffectually in a youth-oriented culture), on respect for the aged and on enhancing long lives. Simply put, the currently prevalent assumption in the West is that there can be no good *reasons* for suicide in old age, even though suicide is frequent in men in old age and may be associated with many different biological, psychological, cognitive, and environmental risk factors and causes.

Some contemporary thinkers and public figures have raised issues that are closely related. For example, Daniel Callahan exposes contemporary medicine's relentless drive for indefinite extension of life, arguing that the elderly should forgo heroic life-prolonging care and refocus their attention instead on turning matters over to the next generation. Janet Adkins, who became the first suicide assisted by the pathologist Jack Kevorkian, in effect raised the issue of whether suicide might be acceptable to avoid conditions like Alzheimer's disease. Colorado Governor Richard Lamm's widely misquoted remark that the terminally ill elderly have a "duty to die" unleashed a small storm of academic and public discussion. And C. G. Prado has raised the issue of "preemptive" suicide in advanced age, exploring issues of declining competence and whether the mind that is beginning to deteriorate can choose to avoid further deterioration by suicide. Prado's is the most direct contemporary approach to issues of suicide in old age, though it is occupied more with epistemological than ethical issues; there is comparatively little other discussion. Direct focus on old age, independent of illness, as a reason for suicide has simply not become part of contemporary public thinking, despite its rich tradition in the Stoic roots of the west and in the practices of a variety of primitive nonwestern societies, and despite the vastly extended life expectancies of contemporary people in advanced industrial societies. On the contrary, public policy has in general supported not only health care and social services for the elderly, but renewed research and concern for suicide prevention, assuming that it is appropriate across the board, at all ages.

Hints of real social friction can be seen, however, over both self-interested and other-regarding and altruistic reasons for suicide in old age. Having fully legalized physician-assisted suicide and voluntary active euthanasia, the Netherlands is now considering whether to honor advance directives like living wills in which a now-competent person requests physician-aided death after the onset of Alzheimer's disease, a condition particularly frequent among the elderly. Double-exit suicides, often of married partners in advanced age, sometimes though only one is ill, raise issues about dominance and com-

parative submission within a domestic relationship, and joint suicides like the 2 January 2002 deaths of Admiral Chester Nimitz and his wife Joan, at 86 and 89 respectively, though clearly the choice of both, make it still more difficult to distinguish between suicide to avoid future ill health and suicide to avoid future old age in general. Disputes over generational equity in the face of rising health care costs question whether life prolongation means merely the extension of morbidity and whether health care ought to be preferentially allocated to the young rather than the old. The issue of whether a person may ethically and reasonably refuse medical treatment in order to spare health care costs to preserve an inheritance for his or her family is already beginning to be discussed; the same issue also raises the question of suicide. And issues about suicide in old age are posed by far-reaching changes in population structure, the "graying" of societies in Europe and the developed world: as birthrates fall and the proportion of retirees threatens to overwhelm the number of still-working younger people, could there be any obligation, as Euripides put it in *The Suppliants* nearly 2,500 years ago, to "leave, and die, and make way for youth"? No party now encourages suicide for the elderly, and indeed no party even raises the issue; but the issue of suicide as a response to self-interested avoidance of the conditions of old age and to other-interested questions about social burdens of old age cannot be very far away. Drawing as they might on both Stoic and Christian roots in the West and on nonwestern practices now coming to light, the ethical disputes over suicide in old age, independent of illness, are likely to be difficult: can suicide in old age represent, as one author puts it, the last rational act of autonomous elders, or does it represent the final defeated event in that series of little tragedies that old age often involves?

MARGARET P. BATTIN

See also AUTONOMY; EUTHANASIA AND SENICIDE; SUICIDE.

BIBLIOGRAPHY

BATTIN, M. P. *Ethical Issues in Suicide*. New York: Prentice-Hall, 1982, 1995.

BATTIN, M. P. *The Least Worst Death*. New York: Oxford University Press, 1994.

BINSTOCK, R. H.; POST, S. G.; and WHITEHOUSE, P. J., eds. *Dementia and Aging: Ethics, Values, and Policy Choices.* Baltimore and London: Johns Hopkins University Press, 1992.

CALLAHAN, D. *False Hopes: Why America's Quest for Perfect Health Is a Recipe for Failure.* New York: Simon & Schuster, 1998.

CICERO. *On Old Age.* Translated by Frank O. Copley. Ann Arbor: The University of Michigan Press, 1967.

DELEO, D., ed. *Suicide and Euthanasia in Older Adults: A Transcultural Journey.* Göttingen-Toronto-Bern: Huber/Hogrefe Publishers, forthcoming 2001.

FRANCIS, L. P. "Assisted Suicide: Are the Elderly a Special Case?" In *Physician Assisted Suicide: Expanding the Debate.* Edited by Margaret P. Battin, Rosamond Rhodes, and Anita Silvers. New York and London: Routledge, 1998. Pages 75–90.

HARDWIG, J. "Is There a Duty to Die." *Hastings Center Report* 27, no. 2 (March/April 1997): 34–42.

JECKER, N. S., ed. *Aging and Ethics. Philosophical Problems in Gerontology.* Clifton, N.J.: Humana Press, 1991.

PRADO, C. G. *The Last Choice: Preemptive Suicide in Advanced Age.* New York: Greenwood Press, 1990.

RASMUSSEN, K. *The Netsilik Eskimos: Social Life and Spiritual Culture (Report of the Fith Thule Expedition 1921–24).* Copenhagen: Gyldendalske Boghandel, Nordisk Forlag, 1931.

SENECA. *Ad Lucilium Epistulae Morales (Moral Letters to Lucilius),* Letters 70 ("On the Proper Time to Slip the Cable"), 77 ("On Taking One's Own Life"), 78 ("On the Healing Power of the Mind"). Translated by Richard M. Gummere. New York: G. P. Putnam's and Sons, 1920. Vol. 2, pp. 57–73, 169–199.

STILLION, J. M., and McDOWELL, E. E. *Suicide Across the Life Span: Premature Exits,* 2d ed. Washington D.C.: Taylor & Francis, 1996.

SUNDOWN SYNDROME

The term *sundown syndrome,* also known as *sundowning,* refers to an increase in agitation during the late afternoon and evening hours in individuals with Alzheimer's Disease and related dementias. Agitation is a class of behavior problems that include disruptive vocalization, physical aggression, and motor restlessness. This syndrome is said to affect between 10 and 37 percent of dementia patients. Although it is observed in both community and nursing-home settings, it appears to be more common in nursing homes.

Sundowning has entered the common parlance of dementia caregivers and many professionals; however, researchers have questioned whether sundowning is as common as assumed. Agitation does appear to be associated with various temporal factors in many dementia patients, including factors occurring in the late afternoon and evening. The few methodologically sound studies that have examined temporal patterns of agitation show that some nursing-home residents are predictably more likely to display agitation in the evening hours; other residents, however, show higher probabilities of occurrence in the morning, and still others show peaks of agitation during more than one time period in the day.

Further complicating the situation is the fact that the term *agitation* refers to a class of different behavior problems that range from simple pacing to physical aggression. Preliminary data suggest that some components of agitation (e.g., physical aggression) do occur more often during the late afternoon and evening hours, while repetitive requests for attention occur more often in the late morning and afternoon. Whether or not an individual demonstrates reliable temporal patterns of agitation depends on his or her sensitivity to physiological and environmental factors that can influence the occurrence of agitation during a twenty-four hour cycle.

One hypothetical cause of sundowning and other temporal patterns of agitation is a dysfunction of circadian rhythms. Neurological damage associated with dementia can, in itself, affect these rhythms, which have also been shown to be affected by the presence of light. Thus, factors such as the lack of exposure to natural light and an overexposure to artificial light during the evening can result in an increase in dementia patients' activity level and, perhaps, agitation during the evening and nighttime. Another hypothesized cause of sundowning is frequent nighttime awakenings, which are common with aging and even more common in dementia. In addition to biological causes of nighttime awakening, researchers have found that staff in nursing homes awaken nursing-home residents frequently to check for urinary incontinence or to take vital signs. When awakened, dementia patients are more likely to have problems distinguishing reality from a dream-state. Thus, agitation at nighttime can be related to these frequent awakenings and the resulting disorientation. It has also been reported that fractured nocturnal sleep can result in more frequent agitation during the day. In addition, temporal patterns of agitation might be affected by the dosing schedule of the tranquilizing drugs sometimes used for the control of agitation. For example, if the drug is administered once in the morning and once in the evening, peaks in agitation can occur before the next dosage of the drug has taken effect.

A host of environmental factors have been posited as possible determinants of temporal patterns of agitation. Essentially, any environmental event that has a reliable temporal pattern can influence patient disruptive behaviors and produce temporally patterned agitation. The pattern reported by researchers of increased agitation for some dementia patients during both morning and evening time periods might be related to morning and evening care routines (e.g., dressing and bathing) conducted by staff at those times. Several researchers have reported higher frequencies of agitation during the three to five P.M. time period, which coincides with change-of-shift for nursing-home staff. It is thought that the increase in staff activity and general confusion during this time might be responsible for an increase in agitation for susceptible patients.

In summary, although there are sufficient data to suggest that some dementia patients display sundowning, the data are not sufficient to suggest that sundowning is a prevalent syndrome. A more accurate description is that agitation does show reliable temporal patterns in an unknown but marked number of dementia patients, particularly in nursing-home settings. These patterns have been related to both physiological (e.g., disruption of circadian rhythms) and environmental events that display temporal patterns and can influence the expression of agitation.

Discovering a reliable temporal pattern in a dementia patient's display of agitation can be beneficial for treatment. For example, if agitation is linked with the dosing or scheduling of tranquilizing drugs, the dosage or scheduling can be changed so that agitation is less likely to occur. For residents who become particularly agitated during care routines, staff can be taught verbal and nonverbal communication skills that are less likely to affect a resident negatively, and consequently are less likely to result in agitation.

LOUIS D. BURGIO
RACHEL RODRIGUEZ

See also DEMENTIA.

BIBLIOGRAPHY

BLIWISE, D. L. "What is Sundowning?" *Journal of the American Geriatrics Society* 42, no. 9 (1994): 1009–1011.
EVANS, L. K. "Sundown Syndrome in Institutionalized Elderly." *Journal of the American Geriatrics Society* 35, no. 2 (1987): 101–108.
GALLAGHER-THOMPSON, D.; BROOKS, J. O. I.; BLIWISE, D.; LEADER, J.; and YESAVAGE, J. A. "The Relations among Caregiver Stress, "Sundowning" Symptoms, and Cognitive Decline in Alzheimer's Disease." *Journal of the American Geriatrics Society* 40, no. 8 (1992): 807–810.
TAYLOR, J. L.; FRIEDMAN, L.; SHEIKH, J.; and YESAVAGE, J. A. "Assessment and Management of 'Sundowning' Phenomena." *Seminars in Clinical Neuropsychiatry* 2, no. 2 (1997): 113–122.

SUPPLEMENTAL SECURITY INCOME

The Supplemental Security Income program (SSI) was established, in 1974, to provide assistance to poor aged, blind, and disabled people—including children. This entry describes why SSI was created, how the program works, and why it matters to millions of Americans.

SSI is a federal program, funded through the general revenues and supplemented by the states, that provides cash assistance to needy people—an eighty-year-old widow living alone and having no other income than her $125 Social Security benefit and her SSI check; a thirty-five-year-old man with a mental disability, unable to participate in the paid labor force and having no income other than his SSI check; a seven-year-old child with mental retardation living with a single mother whose marginal income leaves the family well below the poverty threshold. For these and millions of other vulnerable people with low or no income, SSI is the program that saves them from destitution.

Early assistance programs

The Social Security Act, legislated in 1935, created the basic programs known today as Old Age, Survivors, and Disabilities Insurance (OASDI) that provides a base of income security for workers and their families when their income stopped due to retirement, disability, or death of the breadwinner. Some, however, did not qualify for these benefits and others qualified only for benefits that were very low. To aid these people, state-administered, means-tested assistance programs for the aged (1935), blind (1935), and disabled (1950) were added to the original Social Security Act. These additions to the law provided only very broad guidelines to the states. There were no maximum or minimum requirements for benefit amounts; federal matching grants augmented whatever payments the states provided.

Within this system well over one thousand different state and local administrative units were created to operate the Old Age Assistance (OAA), Assistance for the Blind (AB), and Assistance to the Permanently and Totally Disabled (APTD) programs—each with different eligibility criteria, different payment systems, and differing benefit amounts. In 1972, for example, a maximum OAA benefit for a couple age sixty-five could be as low as $85 (in several South Carolina jurisdictions) and as high as $414 (in a California county).

Creation of SSI

Legislated in 1972 as title XVI of the Social Security Act (Public Law 92-603), the SSI program began in 1974 to better meet the needs of poor aged, blind, and disabled people by unifying the wide-ranging state and local programs. SSI established a uniform, federally provided, base benefit and gave the states the option to supplement that base.

In essence, SSI reversed the federal and state roles in providing assistance to needy aged, blind, and disabled people. Henceforth the federal government would be responsible for

- Funding a basic benefit for aged, blind, and disabled people
- Administering a uniform standard for eligibility and benefits based on "facts that can be objectively determined" (i.e., level and type of resources and degree of disability or blindness)
- Offering an efficient way of providing benefits
- Providing "very substantial" fiscal relief to the states and localities.

The state governments would be responsible only for supplementing the federal benefit as they saw fit to meet the needs of their populations.

Administration and funding

The Congress chose the Social Security Administration (SSA) to administer SSI. SSA had a long-standing reputation for dealing with the public in a fair and humane way, yet with scrupulous regard for the requirements of the law. In addition, SSI would be able to take advantage of SSA's nationwide network of offices and procedures for paying benefits to large numbers of people. Another advantage of using SSA as the administering agency was that recipients could go to a Social Security rather than a welfare office to apply for benefits. It was hoped that needy elderly who refused "welfare handouts" would see SSI as a supplement to their Social Security, not "welfare."

One disadvantage of SSA as administrator was that it created the ongoing misperception that SSI takes money away from the Social Security (Old Age, Survivors, and Disability Insurance) trust funds. This is not the case. Even though SSI is administered by SSA, federal SSI benefits are administratively and financially distinct from Social Security benefits. SSI is funded from the general revenues, and benefits are based on need. SSI state supplements are paid from state general revenues and are based on state-designed criteria. Social Security benefits, on the other hand, are paid from individuals' and employers' FICA taxes, and are based on workers' contributions and time in the workforce.

SSI federal benefits and poverty

SSI was described in a 1972 U.S. Senate Finance Committee Report as "designed to provide a positive assurance that the nation's aged, blind and disabled people would no longer have to subsist on below-poverty incomes." Yet at no time in its history has the federal SSI benefit alone brought recipients up to or above the poverty threshold. The designers of the program assumed that SSI recipients would also be eligible to receive benefits from other programs, such as food stamps, Social Security, and Medicaid. They also assumed that the states would provide supplements that, together with the federal SSI benefit, would bring the total benefit package up to the poverty threshold. In 1974 the federal benefit for an individual was approximately 71 percent of the poverty threshold. That proportion has increased only slightly over the years. According to Deputy Commissioner of Social Security John Dyer, "the SSI monthly benefit rate over the years has consistently represented just 74 percent of the Federal poverty guideline for an individual [and] 82 percent of the guideline for two persons."

Even though SSI benefits alone have never been sufficient to bring recipients above the poverty threshold, benefits maintain their real value (purchasing power) over time. SSI benefits are adjusted every January on the basis of the annual increase in the consumer price index (CPI). This annual cost-of-living adjustment (COLA) is extremely important because it means that federal SSI benefits, by keeping up with inflation, retain their purchasing power over time.

SSI federal benefit levels

The maximum monthly federal SSI benefit amount is the same in all states. In 2000 it was $512 per month for an individual and $769 per month for a couple. Not all beneficiaries receive exactly this amount because some individuals live in states that provide supplements to the federal benefit. In 1999, for example, an SSI recipient in Iowa who was blind and lived independently could receive a state supplement of $22 per month. In Rhode Island a couple receiving federal SSI benefits could also receive a monthly supplement of $120.50 from the state. (State supplements are discussed in a later section.)

Some individuals receive less than the maximum SSI benefit because they or their family members receive other income. SSI benefits are reduced dollar for dollar by the amount of a person's "countable income"—usually cash, checks, and other items that can be used directly, such as food, clothing and shelter.

The aged have consistently received the lowest average SSI benefit amount, followed by the blind. The disabled have consistently received the highest. In December 1999 the average benefit amounts were the following:

- $249.36 per month for a person over age sixty-five
- $350.72 per month for a person who is blind
- $364.24 per month for a person with a disability.

The lower average benefits for those age sixty-five and over can be partially explained by the fact that almost two out of three aged SSI recipients are also Social Security beneficiaries. In addition one in five has a small amount of additional income. These other income sources offset the federal SSI benefit.

Living arrangements can also affect SSI benefits. Federal benefits of persons who live in the home of another and receive support and maintenance in kind are reduced by two-thirds. Recipients in hospitals or medical institutions who have more than half their bill paid by Medicaid receive only a personal needs allowance of $30, which. is intended to take care of personal expenses in an institutional setting. In general, recipients who live in public institutions, such as prisons or halfway houses, are ineligible for SSI benefits. (There are exceptions, such as emergency shelters for the homeless.)

SSI categorical eligibility requirements

The standard requirements for the three basic categories of SSI recipients are clearly delineated.

- Aged. The person is at least sixty-five years old.
- Blind. The person is totally blind or has very poor eyesight that prevents substantial gainful activity (SGA) (defined in 2000 as earnings of at least $1,170 per month).
- Disabled. The person has a medically determinable physical or mental impairment that is expected to last twelve months or to result in death, and prevents the person (age eighteen or over) from doing SGA ($700 per month in 2000). Because children cannot be evaluated on the basis of their ability to do work, children under eighteen must have severe functional limitations.

SSI income and resource eligibility requirements

Actual need for assistance is determined using very strict income and asset rules (see Table 1). SSI takes into account all of an individual's income and resources. After benefits have been awarded, SSI recipients are reviewed from time to time, to be sure that they continue to meet the requirements.

Income. Income determines both eligibility for and level of benefits. As a recipient's "countable" income increases, benefits decrease, usually on a dollar-for-dollar basis. In most cases a person is not eligible when countable income is more than the federal base benefit.

Work incentives. A person does not have to be totally without income to receive SSI. Provisions in the law include special work incentives that encourage people who are receiving SSI to try to work while continuing to receive benefits. The first $65 of monthly earned income is excluded, as is half of remaining earnings. Expenses related to work are subtracted from income for blind recipients, and impairment-related work expenses are subtracted for recipients with disabilities. Resources or income set aside to achieve a work goal in a plan for achieving self-support, such as tuition, a computer, or start-up fees for a small business, are also excluded.

Section 1619 (a) of the Social Security Act gives special cash benefits to those who cease to be eligible for benefits because of earnings over the SGA limit, and section 1619 (b) allows working persons with a disability to continue to be eligible for Medicaid after earnings have made them ineligible for monthly cash payments.

Resources. An individual cannot own many things and qualify for SSI. Interestingly, while federal law does not allow countable resources of more than $2,000 for an individual and $3,000 for a couple, "countable" is not defined. Rather, the law provides a list of some things that are not countable resources. For example, an individual's home and the land it stands on are not counted, but the value of an individual's car over $4,500 is counted.

SSI state supplements

Approximately one-third of SSI recipients also receive state supplements. There are two types of state supplements: optional and mandatory. States have always had the option to supplement the federal benefit in order to meet the needs of their special populations. In addition, states are required by law to maintain the December 1973 income levels of people who were brought from the old state programs to the new SSI program in 1974. (Texas is an exception, because of its constitutional bar against mandatory supplementation.) Because most state benefits were very low and federal benefit amounts have increased steadily, only about eighteen hundred people continue to receive these benefit supplements.

The individual states determine whether they will provide optional supplements, to

Table 1
Basic Eligibility Requirements

Requirement	Definition	Exclusion
Aged	65 or older	
Blind	Individual is either totally blind or has very poor eyesight, and is unable to do "substantial" work.	In 2000 "substantial" work" was defined as a job that pays more than $1,170 per month.
Disabled	Individual has a physical or mental impairment that results in inability to do any "substantial" work and is expected to last 12 months or result in death.	In 2000 "substantial" work" was defined as a job that pays at least $700 per month. Income saved or used for a plan for achieving self-support is excluded.
Limited Income Aged, blind and disabled	Countable income in 2000 must be • Below $532 per month for single adult or child • Below $789 a month for couple	Some exclusions are • $20 per month of most income • $65 per month of wages and half of wages over $65 • food stamps • home energy and housing assistance
Limited Resources (property and other assets) Aged, blind and disabled	• $2,000 for single adult or child • $3,000 for couple	Some exclusions are • a person's home • a car, depending on its use or value • burial plots • burial funds up to $1,500 • life insurance with a face value of $1,500 or less

SOURCE: U.S. Social Security Administration

whom, and in what amount. Some states provide supplemental benefits to all SSI recipients, while others restrict their supplements to specific categories of people, such as residents of care facilities or those living in the home of another. In 2000 only seven states and one territory provided no supplement to the federal SSI basic benefit: Arkansas, Georgia, Kansas, Mississippi, Northern Mariana Islands, Tennessee, Texas, and West Virginia.

State supplement amounts vary widely. For example, in 2000 an individual living in a Medicaid facility in Arizona might receive a $10 monthly supplement, while an individual living alone in New York might receive $87. For those living in homes or residential care, the supplement is often higher. While federal SSI benefits are price-adjusted, no state increased supplements for aged individuals or couples as fast as inflation rose (U.S. Congress, House Committee on Ways and Means, 1998). In other words, over time SSI state supplements for those over age sixty-five have become worth less and less in terms of purchasing power.

Eligibility for other programs

SSI recipients are required to apply for all benefits for which they might be eligible.

Social Security. Social Security benefits are the single largest source of income for SSI recipients. However, Social Security benefits are considered countable income and so they offset SSI benefits dollar for dollar. For example, if an individual is eligible for a Social Security benefit of $200 per month, that person's $532 SSI benefit could be reduced to $322. The update to 2001 goes from $530 to $330.

Medicaid. The law allows SSI to enter into agreements with individual states to make all SSI recipients Medicaid eligible. Thirty two states and the District of Columbia cover their SSI recipients in this way. In seven states all SSI recipients are eligible for Medicaid, but a separate application is required for Medicaid. Eleven states have more restrictive criteria for Medicaid eligibility. These criteria include, for example, a more narrow definition of blindness or disability or more limited financial circumstances than SSI requires. (The law requires that individual state criteria be no more restrictive than the state's January 1972 medical assistance standards.)

Food stamps. The Food Stamp program was designed to end hunger and improve nutrition and health by assisting low-income households in buying the food they need for a nutritional diet. The program is overseen by the U.S. Department of Agriculture and operated by state and local welfare offices in 50 states, the District of Columbia, Guam, and the Virgin Islands. To be eligible for the program, a household must meet certain income and resource standards and work requirements. The amount of benefits an eligible household receives depends on the number of people in the household and the amount of income the household has. In all states except California, SSI recipients may be eligible for food stamps. Social Security offices notify both Social Security and SSI applicants and recipients of their potential food stamp eligibility and supply them with application forms. Social Security offices forward the applications to the local food stamp office, where the eligibility determination is made.

SSI Recipients

According to Social Security Administration data, the federal SSI recipient population had increased from almost four million in 1974 to over 6.5 million in 1999. In addition to an increase in size, the composition of the SSI population had changed significantly.

In 1974 aged beneficiaries comprised 58 percent of the recipients, and the blind and disabled made up the other 42 percent. Since then a notable reversal has taken place. In 1999 the number of aged recipients had dropped to only 19 percent of the total and, according to SSA estimates, was expected to continue to decline. In contrast, the number of blind and disabled recipients had risen to 81 percent of the total (see Figure 1). Included in the growing number of persons with disabilities was the category of disabled children. In 1974 children comprised only 1.8 percent of the total SSI population. By 1999 they represented 12.8 percent of SSI recipients.

Aged recipients. The decline in participation of the older population in SSI can be credited, at least in part, to the automatic cost-of-living adjustment applied annually to Social Security benefits since 1974. Keeping the value of Social Security benefits in line with the prices of goods and services helped reduce the number of older persons falling into poverty, which in turn reduced the number of older persons receiving SSI.

The significant drop in SSI participation rates, however, should not be construed as a signal that older people no longer need the program. More than two million individuals over age sixty-five are receiving SSI. Of these, 57 percent are age seventy-five or older, and 73 percent are women. Many, if not most, of these women are widowed. Only SSI stands between them and destitution.

Blind and disabled recipients. SSI recipients with disabilities are among the most vulnerable children and adults. SSA estimated that

Figure 1
Percentage of SSI Recipients (Aged, Blind, and Disabled) for 1974 and 1999

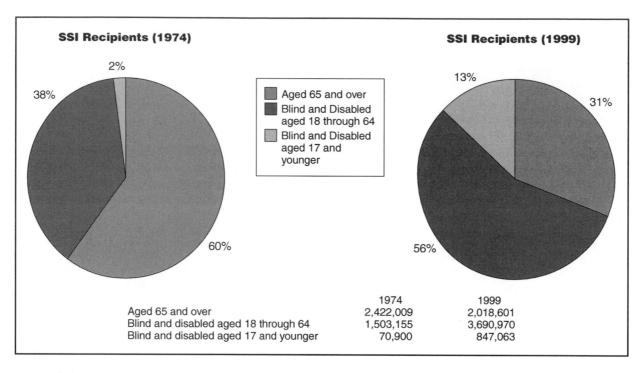

SOURCE: Author

there would be nearly 1.5 million SSI disability applications in 2000—a number projected to increase gradually up to the year 2025, in part because baby boomers (born between 1946 and 1964) are aging and becoming increasingly likely to experience disabilities.

This growth in the number of applications and recipients presents an enormous challenge to SSI: it must find effective ways to encourage and enable recipients with disabilities to work if they can, while ensuring that recipients who cannot work continue to receive the benefits to which they are entitled. To these ends, SSA is attempting to streamline its evaluation process, so that people who qualify can get SSI benefits as soon as possible, and continue to get them as long as they qualify. In 2000, in addition to the established incentives, SSI and SSA launched a series of new work incentives to promote and support return to work.

SSI growth and the economy

The SSI program has grown over its more than twenty years. Total SSI federal benefit pay-

ments in 1999 were more than seven times the amount of payments in the first year of the program—$3.8 billion in 1974 ($1.7 billion for the aged, and $2.1 billion for the blind and disabled) and $28.6 billion in 1999 ($3.6 billion for the aged, and $25 billion for the blind and disabled). However, it is important not to misinterpret the numbers. Putting SSI spending in the context of the growth of gross domestic product (GDP) provides a more accurate picture than looking at spending growth alone. When considering SSI as a proportion of GDP, a two-part question must be considered: Is the economy growing rapidly enough to absorb the rising cost of the SSI program? Or is SSI growing faster than overall economic output, thereby increasing the real burden of the program?

In 1974 SSI represented 0.26 percent of GDP. By 1999 that portion had increased to 0.32 percent. Thus, SSI represented a larger portion of the economy in 1999 than it did in 1974. However, the 1999 SSI annual report projects that by 2023 SSI costs as a percent of GDP will have dropped back to the original level of 0.26 percent.

LAUREL BEEDON

See also CONSUMER PRICE INDEX AND COLAS; ECONOMIC WELL-BEING; MEDICAID; POVERTY; SOCIAL SECURITY, ADMINISTRATION.

BIBLIOGRAPHY

BEEDON, L. E. *Supplemental Security Income (SSI): Yesterday, Today and Tomorrow.* Data Digest no. 43. Washington, D.C.: AARP Public Policy Institute, 2000.

FARRELL, W., et al. *Administration and Service Delivery in the Supplemental Security Income Program, 1974–83.* Washington, D.C.: U.S. Department of Health and Human Services, Social Security Administration, 1984.

Social Security Administration. *Annual Statistical Supplement to the Social Security Bulletin.* SSA. Publication no. 13-11700. Washington, D.C.: Social Security Administration, 1999. Pages 285–308.

Social Security Administration. *State Assistance Programs for SSI Recipients.* SSA Publication no. 13-11975. Baltimore: Social Security Administration, 1999.

U.S. Congress, House Committee on Ways and Means. *Social Security Amendments of 1971, Report of the House Committee on Ways and Means on H.R 1.* H. Rpt. 92-231, 92nd Cong., 1st sess. Washington, D.C.: U.S. Government Printing Office, 1971. P. 147.

U.S. Congress, House Committee on Ways and Means. *Green Book—Background Material and Data on Programs within the Jurisdiction of the Committee on Ways and Means.* Washington, D.C.: U.S. Government Printing Office, 1998. Pages 262–326.

U.S. Congress, Senate Committee on Finance. *Social Security Amendments of 1971, Report of the Committee on Finance to Accompany H.R.1.* S. Rpt. 92-1230, 92nd Cong., 2nd sess. Washington D.C.: U.S. Government Printing Office, 1972. Page 384.

U.S. General Accounting Office. *Supplemental Security Income Growth and Changes in Recipient Population: Call for Reexamining Program.* GAO/HEHS-95-137. Washington, D.C.: GAO, 1995.

WU, K.B. *Income, Poverty and Health Insurance in the United States in 1999.* Fact Sheet no 79. Washington, D.C.: AARP Public Policy Institute, 2000.

INTERNET RESOURCES

DYER, J. "Social Security Administration Communications to Congress, the House Committee on Ways and Means, Subcommittee on Human Resources on the SSI Fraud Prevention Act of 1999." Available on the World Wide Web at www.ssa.gov/policy

Social Security Administration. "Highlights of Supplemental Security Income Data, May 2000." Available on the World Wide Web at www.ssa.gov/policy

Social Security Administration. "SSI Annual Report [of the] Social Security Advisory Board." Available on the World Wide Web at www.ssa.gov

U.S. Department of Commerce, Census Bureau. "Poverty in the United States: 1998." P60–297. Available on the World Wide Web at www.census.gov

SURGERY IN ELDERLY PEOPLE

Surgery on elderly people was once uncommon, but as the population has aged it has become much more frequent. There has also been a change in who is thought of as *old*, and studies based on someone sixty-five years old provide incomplete insight into the issues surrounding appropriate therapies for the "new" geriatric patient.

The traditional view of risk for surgical procedures has focused more on chronological than biological age. Advanced age has generally been considered to carry a higher risk of illness and complications (morbidity), and of death (mortality). In consequence, life-saving procedures such as cardiac, vascular, or oncology procedures can be delayed or withheld. However, relying on age alone to determine a patient's response to surgery can be inappropriate.

Chronological age can, of course, serve as a marker for increased physiological frailty. Frail older adults (the "new" geriatric patient) frequently suffer from multisystem disease, several comorbidities, and polypharmaceutic regimens (an excessive number of medications). Frailty implies not just lower reserve capacity, but also an interaction of social and medical problems. In consequence, the decision to perform surgery should be multidisciplinary in nature, encompassing not only the suitability to withstand the stress of surgery, but also the rehabilitation and social supports required for hospital discharge.

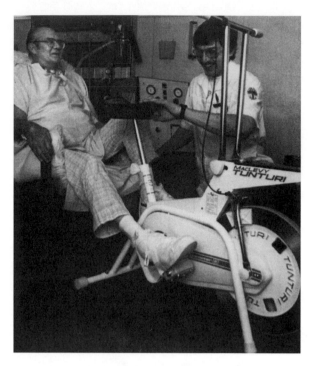

Dentist Dr. Barney Clark, 61, became the first man to receive an artificial heart when he had open heart surgery to implant the Jarvik-7 device at the University of Utah hospital in 1982. Clark, who is being monitored by therapist John Durkin while working out, lived for 112 days with the help of the mechanical device. (Photo by Corbis/Bettmann.)

Anesthetic considerations and operative issues

Complications seen in frail elderly people ore more often multifactorial than specific to any given process or organ system. Age-related anatomic changes (decreases in body surface area), physiologic changes (reduced cardiac function), and metabolic changes (e.g., reduced ability to metabolize and clear drugs) increase the risk of overdosing of any medication, including anesthetics. This leads to longer recovery from drugs, increased delirium (see below), poor mobility, and longer stays in an ICU or hospital setting.

It is uncertain whether regional anesthesia alters perioperative survival or reduces anesthetic-related complications. However, the use of anesthetic techniques that allow patients to remain conscious (such as spinal, epidural, or regional blockade) are increasingly being used in minor procedures, such as hernia repair, and major surgery, such as hip and arm procedures, carotid endarterectomy, and procedures in the lower abdomen and pelvis. Nevertheless, it is important to note that regional techniques can produce the same problems with blood pressure (hypotension) and stress to the heart as general anesthesia, and therefore are not without risk.

Less invasive surgery. Current trends in surgery are increasingly moving towards minimalization. "Keyhole" surgery using fiber-optic cameras, less radical tumor resections with utilization of adjuvant radiotherapy and chemotherapy, and cardiac procedures performed on a beating heart (off-pump surgery) are a few examples. The desired effect of this technological advancement is to reduce intraoperative risk, the trauma of the invasive procedure, postoperative pain, infective complications, and length of hospital stay.

Atypical symptoms and impaired inflammatory responses. Older adults frequently have a reduced capacity to mount the normal immune/inflammatory response when confronted with injury, infection, or disease (e.g., eroding peptic ulcer, pneumonia). This manifests as a fever or pain as the inner surface of the thoracic or abdominal cavity becomes inflamed. In consequence, disease presentation in older adults can be subtle. With reduced ability to generate an inflammatory response, older adults often present later in the disease process, and they may not demonstrate the normal progression of the disease process. For example, an elderly patient who initially presents with early diverticulitis (inflammation of outpouches in the colon) may not demonstrate progressive symptoms until the point where a diverticula becomes necrotic and perforates. Patients with low physiologic reserves typically decompensate rapidly, and subsequently face a higher risk of a surgical emergency. In consequence, careful vigilance by the nursing staff and physicians via serial physical examination and bloodwork has the potential to reduce a delayed surgery, and thus reduce morbidity and mortality. In addition, the mortality rate is lower when certain elective procedures (e.g., major vascular surgery) are performed after the appropriate cardiac workup.

In addition to reduced inflammatory responses, comorbidities such as diabetes and hypertension are more prevalent in elderly people. These disease processes can produce a dysautonomia (failing or remodeling of the autonomic nervous system) resulting in altered baroreflex, vasomotor, and cardiac function.

Perioperative pain management

Pain control in older adults carries its own set of challenges. Compared with younger people, older adults typically experience and report less subjective pain. Conversely, they are more sensitive to any side effects of analgesics and narcotics. Monitoring of pulse, blood pressure, respiratory rate, and mental status are therefore important when administrating opiates. Adequate pain management should utilize a multidisciplinary approach involving anesthesia, acute-pain team services, and nursing and pharmacy support.

Adequate pain control is important for many reasons. A decrease in ventilatory function, partly due to splinting (the inability to take a deep breath due to incision discomfort), is often experienced after thoracic or upper abdominal surgery and is exacerbated if there is poor pain management. Pain management helps prevent splinting and thereby enables patients to breath deeply and expectorate more efficiently. This avoids atelectasis (microcollapse of lung tissue involved in respiration) and assists in clearing mucous secretions, which in turn reduces the postoperative risk of pneumonia and hypoxia. Conversely, an overdose of narcotic agents can reduce respiratory drive and level of consciousness, increasing the risk of delirium, hypoxia, and aspiration.

Pain management reduces circulating catecholamines (e.g., epinephrine and norepinepherine) released during the stress of surgery. This lessens cardiovascular demand, which is of particular importance in elderly people with coronary artery disease, in whom it can exacerbate postoperative myocardial ischemia and infarction.

Proper postoperative pain management helps patients walk and rehabilitate early and reduces the length of stay in an acute care setting. However, the response is highly variable between patients, and careful drug administration and individualization is necessary.

Delirium and postoperative cognitive dysfunction

Delirium (an acute state of confusion) is a common complication of surgery in older adults and causes significant anxiety and stress for both patients and their families. Postoperative delirium is characterized by fluctuating levels of consciousness and cognition, often interspersed with episodes of transient lucidity. Characteristically, the sleep/wake cycle is altered through disruption, agitation, slowed locomotion, paranoia, and hallucinations. *Postoperative cognitive dysfunction*, as measured by psychometric tests, is frequently seen in the elderly perioperatively. The etiology of this impairment is unknown, though it is generally felt to be a transient phenomenon. In some cases, however, (e.g., following some cardiac surgery procedures) cognitive dysfunction can be permanent. Approximately 25 to 50 percent of elderly patients experience some degree of delirium following surgery. The incidence of perioperative delirium increases due to:

- Major cardiac, thoracic and vascular surgery.
- Anesthetic and narcotic overdosing—particularly certain anesthetics, opiods (e.g., meperidine, morphine), sedatives and tranquilizers (e.g., benzodiazepines), and anticholinegics.
- Pre-existing cognitive impairment, such as pre-existing dementia or alcohol abuse.
- Metabolic disturbances, including hypoxia, fluid and electrolyte disturbances, alterations in glycemic control, thyroid disturbances, or impaired renal or hepatic function.
- Prolonged ICU stay, causing *intensive care unit psychosis*: Noisy ventilator and monitor machinery, anesthetic and opiod use, sleep deprivation, frequent interruptions for nursing care, altered circadian rhythms, and an inability to keep track of time can all contribute to this type of confusion and disorientation.

Agitation is a frequent component of the symptomology of delirium. Patients may cause harm to themselves by removing intravenous catheters, surgical drains, and temporary pacemaker wires, or they may fall and injure themselves when getting out of bed. Other patients experience *silent* delirium. These frequently unrecognized patients comprise approximately one-third of patients suffering from delirium. They suffer the same disorientation and alteration in consciousness; but they do not display the agitation experienced by others.

The etiology of delirium is often multifactorial, and there is no specific treatment available other than supportive care. Correcting metabolic disturbances, safely minimizing narcotic usage, and reducing interruption in the normal sleep/wake cycle can minimize confusion and disorientation. Additionally, keeping patient rooms brightly lit, placing a calendar and clock in plain view, and having a family member by the bedside are also important components in reducing delirium.

Occasionally, a patient's agitation can become a great enough risk that extra precautions are necessary. Constant nighttime attendance (e.g., by a family member or special aide) is often used and is preferable to the use of physical or chemical restraints. Physical restraints have been shown to increase the risk of harm to elderly patients, and therefore should not be used unless absolutely necessary. If adjuvant sedation is required, the uses of antiagitation/antipsychotic drugs (e.g., haloperidol) with low anticholinergic properties are preferable to tranquilizers (e.g., diazepam or lorazepam). Additionally, minimizing exposure to noisy intensive care unit or recovery room environments is often helpful.

Other complications

Hypertension. How best to control blood pressure around the time of surgery is controversial. Patients with longstanding hypertension may be relatively hypotensive and have low organ perfusion pressures, which would otherwise be considered tolerable by younger patients without hypertension. Additionally, antihypertensive and antianginal drugs such as beta-blockers and calcium channel blockers may not allow a patient to respond appropriately to hypotension and hypovolemia (dehydration), putting them at greater risk of inadequate tissue/organ perfusion.

Common causes of perioperotive hypotension include:

- Hypovolemia. The most common causes of postoperative hypotension are inadequate replacement of intraoperative fluid loss, surgical hemorrhage, or third-space losses (i.e., peritoneal or pleural cavities).
- Sepsis. This complication may occur following abdominal surgery (e.g., intra-abdominal sepsis), burns, wound infection, pneumonia, or urinary tract infections.
- Low Cardiac Output. Many frail elderly patients have limited cardiac reserves and are extremely sensitive to small changes in intravascular volume status. Before surgery, congestive heart failure and myocardial ischemia should be ruled out in patients who

have unrevascularized coronary artery disease or known heart failure problems.
- Polypharmacy. Most older adults are on at least one drug preoperatively. Opiates. anticholinergics (e.g., antinausea medications) and sedation agents can depress myocardial function.

Renal dysfunction. Kidney function is reliably shown to decrease with age, increasing the risk of renal dysfunction (kidney failure) after surgery. This can be exacerbated by inappropriate fluid administration following a surgical procedure, by the toxic effect of medications used (e.g., NSAIDS, certain antibiotics) or by poor or incomplete bladder emptying due to an anatomical obstruction (e.g., large prostate, blocked urinary catheter tube), or autonomic failure. Drug administration must also account for a reduced clearance due to this reduced renal capacity, and dosages need to be adjusted accordingly.

Complications due to mobility and nutritional problems. Older adults whose mobility is compromised are more prone to complications seen with immobility at any age. They are more likely to suffer from lung microcollapse (atelectasis), which also predisposes them to pneumonia. Similarly, they are more likely to develop blood clots in the legs (deep vein thrombosis) that can break off and travel (embolize) to the lung. This potentially serious complication can aggravate hypoxia and myocardial stress, and can be fatal in some cases.

Nutritional deficiencies that either existed preoperatively or develop after surgery can significantly impact recovery by impairing wound healing, preventing adequate mobilization, and through pressure-sore development. Aggressive nutritional support should be implemented early in malnourished patients, in those with significant complications or infection (e.g., sepsis), and in those who have lost more than 10 percent of their pre-illness body weight.

Decreased mobility predisposes patients to develop pressure sores, in which the skin overlying bony surfaces breaks down and ulcerates. In some cases these can be quite extensive and require debridement and reconstructive repair. In the majority of cases these actions can be avoided through vigilant nursing care, adequate nutrition, and early mobilization and/or physical therapy.

Surgical intensive care

Another controversial and ethically challenging area of geriatric medicine involves patient care in an intensive care setting. Frail, debilitated patients who undergo major surgery typically require prolonged ventilation on a mechanical breathing machine.

Traditionally, age is associated with a greater incidence of negative outcomes and a poorer quality of life for surgery patients who have a prolonged postoperative ICU stay. An examination of this issue was performed by Udekwu et al., using perceived quality of life and activities of daily living survey scores as an indication of value of care, in surgical ICU survivors over seventy years of age. The investigators found that age, by itself, did not increase the level of death experienced in a surgical intensive care unit, and therefore age should not restrict access to critical care. The investigators concluded that while overall functional levels fell for these patients, perceived quality of life was high. Additionally, full dependency (e.g., full-time nursing care) rose only slightly from a baseline level. The status of the whole patient needs to be considered when evaluating the appropriateness of utilization of critical care resources by the older adult.

Rehabilitation

Early mobilization and comprehensive discharge planning are essential to return elderly patients back to a reasonable quality of life following a surgical procedure. Optimally, this should be a multidisciplinary approach consisting of people who can anticipate the sorts of complications to which older adults, especially those who are frail, are liable.

Directives for rehabilitation should ideally be initiated on admission to the hospital. Issues concerning an older patient's premorbid state (e.g., physical deconditioning, living alone) and the nature of the procedure are most efficiently dealt with through early involvement of the patient, nurses, allied health professionals (physical therapists, occupational therapists, speech therapists, social workers), psychologists, and family members.

Complications that arise from surgery (e.g., prolonged ventilation, delirium, and cognitive impairment) should not excessively delay early mobilization and rehabilitation. The appropriate use of an interdisciplinary team should be utilized early to help debilitated persons maintain or recover physical capacities.

Conclusion

In many ways, surgical management of elderly patients reflects procedures seen in other areas of clinical medicine. For example, special considerations are also necessary when dealing with the pediatric population or pregnant women. The appropriate study of surgical outcomes in the older adult has been incomplete, however, and care of this growing population has tended to be somewhat marginalized as a result. There is a growing body of knowledge that indicates that outcomes following surgery are not a product of age, but rather of the whole-body physiology of the individual. An increasing life expectancy among older adults mandates a reexamination of the rationalization of health care resources and considerations of quality of life following surgical intervention. To achieve these goals, an approach is required to ensure adequate quality of care and to expedite the return of patients to their baseline level of function and home environment.

RAKESH C. ARORA
KENNETH ROCKWOOD

See also ANESTHESIA; DECONDITIONING; DELIRIUM; FRAILTY; HIP FRACTURE; MULTIDISCIPLINARY TEAM; PAIN MANAGEMENT; REHABILITATION; REVASCULARIZATION, BYPASS SURGERY, AND ANGIOPLASTY.

BIBLIOGRAPHY

AUDISIO, R. A.; VERONESI, P.; FERRARIO, L.; CIPOLLA, C.; ANDREONI, B.; and AAPRO, M. "Elective Surgery for Gastrointestinal Tumours in the Elderly." *Annals of Oncology* 8, no. 4 (1997): 317–326.

BERGER, D. H., and ROSLYN, J. J. "Cancer Surgery in the Elderly." *Clinics in Geriatric Medicine* 13, no. 1 (1997): 119–141.

KARL, R. C.; SMITH, S. K.; and FABRI, P. J. "Validity of Major Cancer Operations in Elderly Patients." *Annals of Surgical Oncology* 2, no. 2 (1995): 107–113.

KEMENY, M. M.; BUSCH-DEVEREAUX, E.; MERRIAM, L. T.; and O'HEA, B. J. "Cancer Surgery in the Elderly." *Hematology and Oncology Clinics of North America* 14, no. 1 (2000): 169–192.

UDEKWU, P.; GURKIN, B.; OLLER, D.; LAPIO, L.; and BOURBINA, J. "Quality of Life and Functional Level in Elderly Patients Surviving Surgical Intensive Care." *Journal of the American College of Surgery* 193, no. 3 (2001): 245–249.

VENTURA, S. J.; PETERS, K. D.; MARTIN, J. A.; and MAURER, J. D. "Births and Deaths: United States, 1996." *Monthly Vital Statistics Reports* 46 (1997).

ZENILMAN, M. E. "Surgery in the Elderly." *Current Problems in Surgery* 35, no. 2 (1998): 99–179.

SURVEYS

Most surveys have several common characteristics (Fowler). Their purpose is to generate information that statistically summarizes issues of interest in the study population. This information is collected by asking people (respondents) questions, either in person or over the telephone. In most cases, a sampling strategy is used to select only a fraction of the population that is actually interviewed. Those interviews are highly structured and standardized such that each respondent is asked the same questions in the same way and is provided a predetermined set of response categories.

Explaining survey mechanics is beyond the scope of this entry. Instead, we suggest two survey methods books geared toward nonmethodologists. Aday approaches designing good surveys by building on a reporter's stock questions: who do you want to study, what do you want to know about them, where will the data be collected, when do you want to do the field work, why is this information needed, and how will the questions be asked. Fowler pragmatically focuses on enhancing the quality of collected data by identifying the best practices for question design, interviewing procedures and skills, and achieving high response rates. Two user-friendly electronic resources are also recommended. One is a methodology reference tool (Trochim), and the other is a statistics reference tool (Statsoft).

Using good survey design and best practices helps to minimize survey error. Survey errors are deviations of the observed findings from their "true" values (Groves), and come in two categories. Sampling errors result from the fact that when a sample is drawn, there is a chance that it may not be representative of the population from which it is taken. If probability-sampling methods are used, sampling errors can be calculated, and confidence intervals can be established. Confidence intervals are often expressed using statements like "these results have a margin of error of +/− 5 percent." The best way to reduce sampling error in a probability sample usually involves increasing sample size. When nonprobability sampling methods are used, such as convenience samples of people approached on street corners or in shopping malls, it is not possible to determine the accuracy of the findings, or to know what broader population the sample represents.

The second category of survey errors involves nonsampling errors. Three sources contribute to this problem: the interviewer, the questions, and the respondent (Aday). Good interviewers can increase response rates (the percent of people who participate), minimize the number of questions that are not answered (missing data), and increase the consistency of the measurement process (reliability). Well-designed and crafted questions are easy for interviewers to ask and for respondents to answer. Such questions are brief, use simple and familiar words that do not have multiple meanings, avoid technical jargon, use the active voice and good grammar, and do not involve compound sentences or double negatives.

When using survey methods with older adults, one wonders whether there will be more nonsampling errors than usual. Older adults are more likely to experience health and cognitive problems than younger adults, and these may prevent older adults from participating or diminish the quality of the information that they provide (Herzog and Rodgers). Although more research is needed, the literature has generally not identified disproportionately larger nonsampling errors among older adults. For the oldest old and the least healthy, however, there is some evidence that both willingness to participate and the quality of the information provided may be compromised (Herzog and Rodgers). Therefore, when designing surveys for those subgroups, special emphasis on minimizing respondent burden and providing greater flexibility is warranted.

Cross-sectional versus longitudinal surveys

An important distinction among surveys involves cross-sectional versus longitudinal studies. Cross-sectional surveys are exemplified by public opinion polls conducted during election campaigns. These polls typically use random digit dialing telephone surveys of a sample of the voting age population, and their purpose is to gauge voting preferences. The findings can be used to see whether voting preferences vary across age groups. For example, approval ratings can be examined within age decades, and one might find that the older the age group, the more likely that conservative candidates were preferred over liberal ones.

Such age-group comparisons represent inter-individual (or between individual) differences associated with age at a single point in time. They can not be interpreted as intra-individual (i.e., aging or within individual) effects such that as people grow older they become more likely to support conservative candidates. That would reflect the life course fallacy in which cross-sectional age differences are attributed solely to the aging process (Riley). In fact, age-group comparisons involve aging and cohort effects. Cohort effects reflect the fact that older individuals have not simply aged more than the younger individuals, they also went through their formative years, as well as other life course stages, during different historical periods. Consider the case where the number of years of formal education is compared across age groups. The results likely will show that each successively older age group has achieved less education. Surely this does not reflect the aging process, because that would mean we lose years of education as we age. Rather, such results reflect cohort succession, or the process by which educational aspirations and opportunities have steadily increased with each new generation.

Longitudinal studies are necessary to avoid the life course fallacy. In longitudinal studies the same sample is followed over time. Typically this involves interviewing the same respondents every year or so. Using these data one can examine intra-individual effects. Longitudinal data would likely show that the cross-sectional age-group differences in educational attainment reflected cohort succession rather than the aging process. That is, we would see that as birth cohorts age, their educational attainment levels remain largely unchanged. The drawback to longitudinal studies lies in their opportunity and tracking costs. These include identifying and obtaining baseline data on an appropriate birth cohort, and then continuing to track those individuals over time.

Even with longitudinal data there may be another problem. If the sample of persons is restricted to the members of a single birth cohort, then the results would be subject to the cohort centrism fallacy. The cohort centrism fallacy is that just because we observe changes of a certain type in one birth cohort over time does not mean that similar changes will occur in other birth cohorts (Riley). No two birth cohorts experience the same life course stages during the same historical periods. Thus, some birth cohorts have their lives shaped by a remarkably unique set of experiences, such as "the greatest generation" (Brokaw).

The best way to avoid both the life course and cohort centrism fallacies is to have comparable longitudinal data on several successive cohorts. This can be done two ways (Campbell). One involves designing longitudinal studies to include samples from several birth cohorts, and to follow those cohorts over a prolonged period. A more pragmatic approach involves using available data from several different birth-cohort-specific longitudinal studies that are now available courtesy of the Inter-university Consortium for Political and Social Research (ICPSR; for a complete listing see their website at www.icpsr.umich.edu).

Limitations of survey research and problems with interpretations

Surveys obtain information by asking people questions. Those questions are designed to measure some topic of interest. We want those measurements to be as reliable and valid as possible, in order to have confidence in the findings and in our ability to generalize beyond the current sample and setting (i.e., external validity). Reliability refers to the extent to which questions evoke reproducible or consistent answers from the respondent (i.e., random measurement error is minimized). Validity refers to the extent to which the questions are actually getting at what we want them to measure (i.e., nonrandom measurement error is minimized). The relationship between reliability and validity can be intuitively seen using the metaphor of a target containing a series of concentric rings extending from the "bulls eye" (Trochim). A reliable and valid measure would look like a tightly clustered group of shots all in the bulls-eye; a reliable but invalid measure would look like a tightly clustered group of shots at the target periphery; a valid but unreliable measure would look like a scattering of shots all over the target; and an unreliable and invalid measure would look like a scattering of shots across only one side of the target.

Table 1
Selected features of nine recent large-scale surveys

Surveys	Eligibility Rules	Birth Cohort	Observation Window	Interview Frequency	Sample Size	Main Topics	Administrative Record Linkages
General Social Survey (GSS)	National sample of noninstitutionalized persons age 18 years old or older	All adults	Annually since 1972 (except 1979, 1981, and 1982) and biennially since 1994	Single cross-sectional surveys	About 1,500 every year before 1994, and about 3,000 since then	The core includes socioeconomic status, social mobility, social control, the family, race relations, sex relations, civil liberties, and morality. Topical modules vary from year to year.	None
National Health And Nutrition Examination Survey (NHANES III)	National sample of noninstitutionalized persons age 2 months old or older	All birth cohorts	1988–1994	A single cross-sectional survey	33,994	Demographic and socioeconomic informaiton, blood pressure, cholesterol, obesity, smoking disease history, immunization status, and dietary intake obtained from survey data and medical examinations	None
Longitudinal Study on Aging I (LSOA I)	National sample of noninstitutionalized persons 70 years or older in 1984	1914 and earlier	1984–1990	Biennially	7,527	Demographics, social and economic factors, living arrangements, functional status, disability status, and use of health services	Medicare and death records
Longitudinal Study on Aging II (LSOA II)	National sample of noninstitutionalized persons 70 years old or older in 1994	1924 and earlier	1994–2000	Biennially	9,447	Demographics, social and economic factors, living arrangements, functional status, disability status, and use of health services	Medicare and death records
Australian Longitudinal Study on Aging	Noninstitutionalized persons 70 years old or older in 1992 in Adelaide, Australia	1922 and earlier	1992–1997	Annually	2,087	Demographic, social and economic factors, disease history, functional status, disability status, mental health, and use of health services from survey data, in home performance tests, and clinical assessments	None
Established Population for the Epidemiologic Study of the Elderly (EPESE)	Noninstitutionalized adults 65 years old or older in 1982 in Boston, (MA), New Haven (CN), two Iowa Counties in five counties in North Carolina (1986)	1917 and earlier	1981–1993	Annually	14,145	Demographics, social and economic factors, functional status, disability status, mental health, disease history, health habits, and the use of health services from survey data and in-home performance tests	Death records
Hispanic EPESE	Noninstitutionalized Hispanic adults 65 years old or older, residing in Arizona, California, Colorado, New Mexico and Texas	1928 and earlier	1993–1994	Single cross-sectional survey	3,050	Demographics, social and economic factors, functional status, disability status, mental health, disease history, health habits, and the use of health services from survey data and in-home performance tests	None

(continued)

SOURCE: Author

Table 1 (continued)
Selected features of nine recent large-scale surveys

Surveys	Eligibility Rules	Birth Cohort	Observation Window	Interview Frequency	Sample Size	Main Topics	Administrative Record Linkages
National Long-Term Care Survey (NLTCS)	Random sample of persons listed in the Medicare Beneficiary Enrollment Files who were 65 years old or older	1917 and earlier	1982–1994	1982, 1984, 1989, 1994	In 1982, 6,393 community living persons with at least 1 ADL or IADL disability, their 1,925 care-givers, and 1,992 residents of institutions. Aged-in samples added at each follow-up to maintain the ability to generate valid prevalence estimates	Demographics, social and economic factors, functional limitations, disability, avail-ability and use of informal caregivers, use of health services, institutionalization, and death	Medi-care and death records
Health and Retirement Study (HRS) and Survey on Assets and Health Dynamics of the Oldest-Old (AHEAD)	Now a nationally representative sample of non-institutionalized persons 50 years old or older	1947 and earlier	1992–present	Biennially	Originally created as separate studies of those 51-61 in 1992 (HRS) and 70 and in 1993 (AHEAD), the studies were combined in 1998 and new birth cohorts are periodically added to main-tain constant ability to be representative of those 50 years old or older	Demographics, health status, cognition, family structure, health care, functional status disability status, work and employment histories, income, assets, wealth, and insurance status	Medi-care and death records

At the root of these measurement issues is how the survey questions are asked. Careful crafting of survey questions is essential, and even slight variations in wording can produce rather different results. Consider one of the most commonly studied issues in aging: activities of daily living (ADLs). ADLs refer to the basic tasks of everyday life such as eating, dressing, bathing, and toileting. ADL questions are presented in a staged fashion asking first whether the respondent has any difficulties in performing the task by themselves and without the use of aids. If any difficulty is reported, the respondent is then asked how much difficulty he or she experiences, whether any help is provided by another person or by an assisting device, how much help is re-ceived or how often the assisting device is used, and who is that person and what is that device.

Surprisingly, prevalence estimates of the number of older adults who have ADL difficulties vary by as much as 60 percent from one national study to another. In addition to variations in sampling design, Wiener, Hanley, Clark, and Van Nostrand report that differences in the prevalence estimates result from the selection of which specific ADLs the respondents are asked about, how long the respondent had to have the ADL difficulty before it counts, how much diffi-culty the respondent had to have, and whether the respondent had to receive help to perform the ADL. Using results from a single study in which different versions of ADL questions were asked of the same respondents, Rodgers and Miller (1997) have shown that the prevalence rate can range from a low of 6 percent to a high of 28 percent. With those same data, Freedman has found that the prevalence of one or more ADL difficulties varies from 17 percent to nearly 30 percent depending on whether the approach reflects residual difficulty (i.e., even with help or the use of an assisting device) or underlying difficulty (i.e., without help or using an assisting device).

A related concern is the correspondence between self-reported ADL abilities and actual performance levels. Although there are obvious drawbacks to direct observation of ADLs (including privacy), performance-based assessments of lower and upper body physical abilities can be conducted in personal interviews. Examples for the upper body include assessing grip strength using hand-held dynamometers, the ability to hold a one gallon water jug at arms length, and to pick up and replace pegs in a pegboard, while examples for the lower body include measured and timed walks, standing balance tests, and repeated chair stands. Simonsick and colleagues have shown that carefully crafted questions eliciting self-reports of lower- and upper-body physical abilities are generally consistent with performance-based assessments on the same respondents.

Even when reliable and valid questions are asked, there can still be serious problems due to missing data. Missing data comes in three varieties: people who refuse to participate (the issue of response rates), questions that are left unanswered (the issue of item missing values), and (in longitudinal studies) respondents who are lost to follow-up (the issue of attrition). The problem is that missing data results in (1) biased findings if the people for whom data is missing are systematically different, (2) inefficient statistical estimates due to the loss of information, and (3) increased analytic complexity because most statistical procedures require that each case has complete data (Little and Schenker). Methods to deal with missing data include naive approaches like unconditional mean imputation (i.e., substituting the overall sample mean), and sophisticated methods like expectation-maximization algorithms or multiple imputation procedures. The utility of these methods depends on whether the data is missing completely at random, or if it

reflects a nonignorable pattern. The latter requires use of the more sophisticated approaches.

The most important limitation of surveys has to do with internal validity, or the establishment of causal relationships between an independent variable (the cause, denoted by X) and a dependent variable (the effect, denoted by Y). There are three fundamental criteria for demonstrating that X is a probabilistic cause of Y (Suppes): (1) the probability of Y given that X has occurred must be greater than the probability of Y in the absence of X; (2) X must precede Y in time; and, (3) the probability of X must be greater than zero. Implicit in the first criterion is the presence of a comparison group. Several threats to internal validity exist that constitute rival hypotheses for the explanation that X causes Y (Campbell and Stanley). When well designed and administered, the classic two-group experimental design eliminates these because the assignment to either the experimental or control group is randomly determined and both groups are measured before and after the experimental group is exposed to X. Therefore, the potential threats to internal validity are equivalent for both the experimental and control groups, leaving the difference between the before and after comparisons due solely to the experimental group's exposure to X. Thus, experimental designs meet the criteria for probabilistic causation.

In survey research, however, this is not the case because assignment to the experimental versus control group has not been randomized and the time sequence has not been manipulated. Therefore, the survey researcher must make the case that the causes are antecedent to the consequences, and that the groups being compared were otherwise equivalent. The former is often only addressable by logic, and the latter is only addressable by matching the groups being compared on known risk factors, or by statistically adjusting for known risk factors. In contrast, well-performed randomization creates equivalence on everything, whether it is known or not. That is why survey-based research traditionally includes numerous covariates in an attempt to resolve the problem of potential confounders. Basically, survey researchers must rule out all competing explanations of the observed relationship between X and Y in order to suggest (but not demonstrate) that a causal relationship exists.

Given the limitations of surveys that have been mentioned in this entry, one might ask why surveys are conducted at all. There are several important reasons. Surveys gather data about relationships between people, places, and things as they exist in the real world setting. Those relationships can not all be examined in laboratory experiments. Moreover, surveys allow the collection of data about what people think and feel, and facilitate the collection of information in great breadth and depth. Surveys are also very cost-efficient. Finally, surveys are an excellent precursor for planning and designing experimental studies. Thus, despite their limitations, surveys are and will continue to be a major source of high-quality information with which to explore the aging process.

Major recent surveys

We now briefly turn to recent, major surveys with which analyses of the aging process are conducted. Due to space constraints, we can neither identify all nor describe in detail any of these surveys. Therefore, we have simply selected nine recent and widely used large-scale surveys that are publicly available from or through the ICPSR. These surveys include the General Social Survey (GSS), the third National Health and Nutritional Examination Study (NHANES III), the Longitudinal Studies on Aging (LSOA I and II), the Australian (Adelaide) Longitudinal Study of Aging, the Established Populations for the Epidemiologic Study of the Elderly (EPESE), the Hispanic EPESE, the National Long-Term Care Survey (NLTCS), and the now combined Health and Retirement Survey (HRS) and Survey on Assets and Health Dynamics of the Oldest-Old (AHEAD). Table 1 provides a thumbnail sketch of each of these surveys in terms of their eligibility rules, birth cohorts, observation windows, interview frequency, sample size, major topical foci, and the availability of linked administrative records. Further details on these and nearly eight thousand other surveys can be found at the ICPSR Internet site.

FREDERIC D. WOLINSKY
DOUGLAS K. MILLER

See also COHORT CHANGE; PANEL STUDIES; QUALITATIVE RESEARCH.

BIBLIOGRAPHY

ADAY, L. A. *Designing and Conducting Health Surveys: A Comprehensive Guide,* 2d ed. San Francisco: Jossey-Bass, 1996.

BROKAW, T. *The Greatest Generation.* New York: Random House, 1998.

CAMPBELL, D. T., and STANLEY, J. C. *Experimental and Quasi-Experimental Designs for Research.* Chicago: Rand McNally, 1963.

CAMPBELL, R. T. "A Data-Based Revolution in the Social Sciences." *ICPSR Bulletin* 14, no. 3 (1994): 1–4.

FOWLER, F. J., JR. *Survey Research Methods,* 2d ed. Newbury Park, Calif.: Sage, 1993.

FREEDMAN, V. A. "Implications of Asking 'Ambiguous' Difficulty Questions: An Analysis of the Second Wave of the Assets and Health Dynamics of the Oldest Old Study." *Journal of Gerontology: Social Sciences* 55B (2000): S288–S297.

GROVES, R. M. *Survey Errors and Survey Costs.* New York: John Wiley, 1989.

HERZOG, A. R., and RODGERS, W. L. "The Use of Survey Methods in Research on Older Americans." In *The Epidemiologic Study of the Elderly.* Edited by R. B. Wallace and R. F. Woolson. New York: Oxford University Press, 1992. Pages 60–90.

LITTLE, R. J. A., and SCHENKER, N. "Missing Data." In *Handbook of Statistical Modeling for the Social and Behavorial Sciences.* Edited by G. Arminger, C. C. Clogg, and M. E. Sobel. New York: Plenum Press, 1995. Pages 39–75.

RILEY, M. W. "A Theoretical Basis for Research on Health." In *Population Health Research.* Edited by K. Dean. London, England: Sage Publications, 1993. Pages 37–53.

RODGERS, W., and MILLER, B. "A Comparative Analysis of ADL Questions in Surveys of Older People." *Journals of Gerontology* 52B (1997 Special Issue): 21–36.

SIMONSICK, E. M.; KASPER, J. D.; GURALNIK, J. M.; BANDEEN-ROCHE, K.; FERRUCCI, L.; HIRSCH, R.; LEVEILLE, S.; RANTANEN, T.; and FRIED, L. P. "Severity of Upper and Lower Extremity Functional Limitation: Scale Development and Validation with Self-Report and Performance-Based Measures of Physical Function." *Journal of Gerontology: Social Sciences* 56B (2001): S10–S19.

Statsoft, Inc. *The Electronic Statistics Textbook.* Tulsa, Okla.: Statsoft, 1999. Available on the World Wide Web at www.statsoft.com

SUPPES, P. *Models and Methods in the Philosophy of Science: Selected Essays.* Dordrecht, Netherlands: Kluwer Academic Publishers, 1993.

TROCHIM, W. M. *The Research Methods Knowledge Base,* 1st ed. 1999. Available on the World Wide Web at http://trochim.human.cornell.edu

WIENER, J. M.; HANLEY, R. J.; CLARK, R.; and VAN NOSTRAND, J. F. "Measuring the Activities of Daily Living: Comparisons Across National Surveys." *Journals of Gerontology* 45 (1990): S229–S237.

SWALLOWING

Swallowing allows people to eat and drink, thus providing nutrients for growth and maintenance of body tissue. Saliva is regularly swallowed while awake and during sleep. Though swallowing usually occurs automatically, it involves a complex sequence of nerve and muscle coordination managed by the brain.

Normally, food and drink are formed into a mass by the mouth and channeled by the tongue to the back of the mouth, where the swallow is triggered. The pharynx and larynx, which are situated at the top of the esophagus (foodpipe) and trachea (windpipe), contract and elevate to protect the trachea. This is essential to prevent choking and inhalation of foreign substances. The mass is rapidly pushed through the pharynx into the esophagus, and then by coordinated muscular contractions to the stomach. Any disruption to this sequence can result in swallowing difficulties (technically known as dysphagia).

In the healthy adult noticeable swallowing difficulties are rare. However, changes associated with aging can affect the efficiency of the muscles that facilitate swallowing. As a result of these normal variations, some elderly people may be predisposed to dysphagia when they are ill. The likelihood of some illnesses increases with age, and a number of medical conditions are associated with dysphagia.

A common example is stroke. In the early stages of stroke, approximately half of those affected may develop dysphagia. Prevention of choking and consequent chest infection is a high priority. Fortunately, only a few stroke patients have persistent problems and recovery is common, even at advanced age. Other diseases develop more gradually (e.g., Parkinson's disease and the various types of dementia). Eating and drinking can be slow and effortful procedures that deteriorate progressively. The consistencies of food and drink that can be swallowed easily and safely become more limited over time. Sometimes the first signs of a disease are difficulties with speech and swallowing (e.g., in amyotrophic lateral sclerosis or myasthenia gravis). Chronic illness affecting the breathing muscles can interrupt the fine coordination between breathing and swallowing, contributing to recurrent chest infections. Any severe illness can lead to generalized muscle weakness and consequent dysphagia, though this is usually a temporary effect.

Mechanical problems may also be a source of swallowing difficulty. Elderly people are more prone to osteophytes. These are bony growths from the spine and may push into the throat muscles causing coughing or discomfort when food or drink pass over the misshapen area. Another example is the development of a pouch (like a small pocket) in the pharynx or upper esophagus, impeding the smooth progression of the food or fluid mass to the stomach. Infections (such as thrush) can cause painful swallowing. Surgical procedures to any area related to the swallowing anatomy can also result in swallowing difficulties. A sensation of something sticking in the throat is often reported. This may be due to organic disease of the esophagus or stomach. If no physical cause is found, the reason may be psychological.

In many conditions the swallowing either improves spontaneously or strategies are used to make swallowing easier. If effective swallowing is impossible to achieve, then it may be necessary to consider feeding via a tube. This can be used temporarily or for a long period.

CATHERINE EXLEY

See also STROKE; TUBE FEEDING.

BIBLIOGRAPHY

GROHER, M. E. *Dysphagia: Diagnosis and Management,* 3d ed. Boston: Butterworth-Heinemann, 1997.

JONES, B., and DONNER, M. W. *Normal and Abnormal Swallowing, Imaging in Diagnosis and Therapy.* New York: Springer-Verlag, 1991.

LOGEMANN, J. *Evaluation and Treatment of Swallowing Disorders.* Austin, Tex: Pro-ed., 1983.

LOVE, R. J., and WEBB, W. G. *Neurology for the Speech-Language Pathologist,* 2d ed. Newton, Mass.: Butterworth-Heinemann, 1992.

SYNCOPE

See FAINTING

T

TASTE AND SMELL

The sense of taste influences food preferences and food choices. When people describe how food tastes, they are actually talking about food flavor, and not just the basic tastes of sweet, sour, salty and bitter. The range of flavor experiences also includes aroma, texture, and mouth "feel"—and, some would say, even the pleasantness of foods.

Much of food flavor is perceived through taste and smell. The four taste qualities are perceived through receptors located on the tongue and elsewhere in the oral cavity. Some scientists count the taste of monosodium glutamate (MSG) as a fifth basic taste quality known as *umami*. Mouths also detect the texture and temperature of foods, and the chemical burn of chili peppers and other irritants. Other components of flavor (such as the aroma of vanilla or orange) are airborne particles that come directly through the nasal passages, or enter the nose from the back of the mouth through what is known as retronasal transport.

Scientists have always assumed that taste and smell would undergo dramatic declines with age, much as vision and hearing do. However, it now appears that the chemical senses are much more robust in older people than are vision, hearing, and even touch. Generally, age-related deficits in the sense of smell are more dramatic than taste deficits. These losses do not occur suddenly at any given age. Instead, a progressive decline begins by thirty or forty years of age and continues gradually in later life. Because of the very slow progression of sensory losses, an older person may not even be aware that a decline in taste or smell acuity has occurred.

Aging and the olfactory system

Odors are detected through some fifty million olfactory receptor cells. These cells die and are replaced every sixty days. They are located in the mucus membrane located at the top of the nasal cavities, each of which occupies about 1 square inch. Sniffing concentrates the odors, since less than 10 percent of the air entering the nasal cavity reaches the olfactory epithelium. Odor molecules must dissolve into the mucus membrane surrounding the olfactory receptors, which lines a piece of porous bone called the cribiform plate. Olfactory receptors send axons though the cribiform plate to the olfactory bulb, which lies at the base of the brain. Studies of olfactory epithelium indicate that it becomes scarred and abnormal with age. The scar tissue may block the pores in the cribiform plate, thereby preventing the olfactory receptors from sending axons to the olfactory bulb.

Older people need a higher concentration of a given substance in the air to detect a smell than do younger people. This rise in threshold may reduce the ability to react to the presence of harmful chemicals in the environment and thus may pose a danger to older adults. A study comparing the ability to detect ethyl mercaptan, an ingredient in liquid petroleum gas, showed that adults age seventy-four required ten times more of the chemical to detect it than did twenty-year-olds. However, the ability to detect odors varied across older adults, with some performing as well as younger subjects.

Older people find concentrated odors less intense. A 1986 survey conducted by the National Geographic Society involved a scratch-and-sniff test using six different odors. Respondents rated their intensity on a five-point scale. Intensity ratings declined with age, more so for some odors than for others. Studies normally find a broad loss in olfactory ability for a wide range of smells from pleasant to unpleasant. A more comprehensive scratch-and-sniff test using forty different odors, showed that a person's ability to identify odors by name starts to decline around the age of sixty. Sometimes that may be due to cognitive impairments or memory loss. The ability to detect an odor—without being able to name it—may remain unchanged.

Losing the ability to smell may affect the flavor and the enjoyment of food. One study compared the ability of young and older subjects to detect the herb marjoram in carrot soup. Older adults performed less well than younger subjects, and some were unable to detect marjoram at all. The deficit was related to smell as opposed to taste. When tested using nose clips, young subjects also were unable to detect or identify marjoram in the soup. Middle-aged and older adults were also less able to detect a woody alcohol odor, and sometimes failed to recognize such common odors as baby powder, chocolate, cinnamon, coffee, and mothballs.

Smell and disease

Smell losses with age are most often linked to upper respiratory infections, and may represent accumulated damage over time. Head trauma can cause sudden loss of the ability to smell. This may occur in whiplash-like accidents that cause a tearing of olfactory filaments near the cribiform plate. More rarely, head trauma may damage nerves involved in taste perception.

Alzheimer's disease is associated with a reduced sense of smell. This may result from a loss of nerve cells in the olfactory bulb that is sometimes observed prior to the onset of clinical dementia. Smell losses may therefore help in the early diagnosis of Alzheimer's disease. Patients with Parkinson's disease are also less able to perceive and identify odors.

Reduced odor perception through the back of the mouth has been observed in older subjects, even though odor perception through the nose is normal. This may be due to dentures that cover the roof of the mouth. Dentures may block the retronasal transport of odors from the mouth to the olfactory receptors, producing a decrease in the perceived flavor of food.

Aging and taste

Older people lose the ability to detect very low concentrations of bitter and salty substances. In contrast, the perception of sweet and sour is robust even in extreme old age. Not all bitter compounds are affected equally, however.

Age-related taste deficits are most pronounced when testing is localized to specific areas on the tongue. Instead of whole mouth tasting, the stimulus is applied locally to spots on the tongue by using a special apparatus or by applying the tastant with a cotton swab. Scientists believe that whole mouth perception may compensate for some of the regional losses of taste function with age.

Regional losses in taste might be expected, given the anatomy of the taste system. Tastes are detected in the mouth by specialized receptor cells located in the upper part of taste buds and near the taste pore. Taste buds are located not only on the tongue but also in the throat and on the roof of the mouth (soft palate). Taste buds are made up of thirty to fifty individual cells, which are organized into an oblong sphere, much like the segments of an orange. The entire taste bud is regenerated every two weeks. Individual taste cells live for only ten to twelve days, and new cells below them evolve to replace them as they die.

Taste buds in the front of the tongue are located in tiny, mushroom-shaped pieces of tissue known as fungiform papillae. These appear as small, round, pink bumps on the tongue surface. In humans each fungiform papilla contains a number of taste buds, each one opening to the outside through a tiny taste pore. Some people may have twenty-five or more taste buds per papilla. There are also regional differences in taste bud density. Fungiform papillae on the tip of the tongue have more taste buds than do those in the middle region of the tongue. A branch of the facial nerve innervates the fungiform papillae, and carries information about taste on the front of the tongue to the brain.

Papillae in the rear of the tongue, known as circumvallate papillae, are arranged in an inverted V shape and are level with the surface of the tongue. Information about taste in the rear of the tongue is carried to the brain by the glossopharyngeal nerve.

More taste buds are located in tissue folds on the sides of the tongue, just in front of the circumvallate papillae. These foliate papillae are mostly innervated by the glossopharyngeal nerve, but some appear to be innervated by the same nerve as papillae at the front of the tongue. Taste buds in the soft palate are innervated by a branch of the facial nerve, and taste buds in the throat are innervated by the glossopharyngeal nerve and the vagus nerve.

Because taste buds are found all over the oral cavity, the perceived taste of food appears to come from the entire mouth and not from isolated patches on the tongue, throat, and roof of the mouth. It is the sense of touch that serves to localize taste perception, such that the taste is perceived to be coming from the area that is stimulated by touch. Smelling chocolate odor while chewing on tasteless gum is interpreted by the brain as eating chocolate.

Taste and disease

It has always been assumed that the number of taste buds declines with age but that does not appear to be the case. There is no evidence that taste cells are no longer regenerated or that the structure of taste buds changes in healthy older adults. However, both disease and medication use may affect this process. For example, drugs that interfere with cell division or growth, such as cancer chemotherapy agents, can disrupt both taste and smell.

Some, if not all, of the observed taste losses with age may be caused by a cumulative history of disease or by the chronic use of medications. Nerve damage during the extraction of wisdom teeth has been found to reduce taste pore density (and presumably taste bud density) in the front of the tongue. Surgery to repair the nerve increases taste pore density and partially restores taste function.

Ear infections can also cause nerve damage. A history of middle ear infections has been associated with taste abnormalities. Damage from bacterial or viral infection may result in an enhanced perception of bitter taste or in taste phantoms. Taste phantoms are a taste sensation in the absence of a stimulus. Scientists believe that taste nerves mutually inhibit each other. A lessening of nerve input from one area of the tongue may cause another area to take over and thus maintain the level of taste sensation. This may explain why older people often do not perceive a loss in taste, even when damage to taste nerves is readily apparent to a medical professional.

The burning mouth syndrome

Some age-related taste abnormalities lead to clinical complaints. Patients with burning mouth syndrome report a persistent burning sensation, usually localized to the front of the tongue, as well as distorted and persistent bad tastes. This condition occurs most commonly in postmenopausal women. Patients with burning mouth syndrome are less sensitive to threshold concentrations of sweet and sour, and tend to rate high concentrations of sugar and salt as less intense than do healthy controls. Burning mouth syndrome is one of the very few conditions that affect taste response to sweet. Both taste and pain pathways may contribute to burning mouth syndrome. One suggested cause has been dry mouth associated with hormonal changes at menopause.

Taste perception is dramatically influenced by salivary function. Taste cells require the presence of gustin, a compound in saliva, in order to develop normally. One component of gustin is zinc. Therefore low dietary levels of zinc, disruption of salivation, or drugs that bind zinc and prevent its use by the body may contribute to taste loss. Patients with disruption in zinc metabolism often experience loss of both taste and smell. Circumvallate papillae of such patients show a disruption of taste buds and taste pores, with obvious cell death. Both taste and smell have been restored in some patients by oral zinc supplementation.

Taste and medication use

Medications may cause a pronounced taste loss or taste distortion. Many drugs prescribed for older adults, such as angiotensin converting enzyme (ACE) inhibitors, used in the treatment of high blood pressure, can bind to zinc. An unpleasant taste in the mouth is one of the main factors limiting use of the ACE-inhibitor captopril. Penicillamine, sometimes used to treat rheumatoid arthritis, also binds metals and interferes with taste perception. Diuretics, which reduce blood pressure by increasing urine output, have occasionally been associated with a loss of taste. Among the known side effects of antiglaucoma agents are changes in taste. Nicotine patches may interfere with taste perception, perhaps because they reduce salivary flow. Radiation treatment for oral cancer frequently directly damages salivary glands and thus can reduce taste function.

Diet and nutrition

There is no dramatic decline in taste or smell function in healthy aging. Rather, a subtle and gradual decline in sensitivity begins around middle age and continues in later life. Smell losses hinder the ability to identify familiar odors and reduce the perceived intensity of flavors in food. Taste losses, if present, are often localized and whole mouth taste sensation is often not affected.

The impact of such losses on diet, nutrition, and health has not always been clear. Some researchers have argued that irreversible changes in taste and smell lead directly to altered food preferences, reduced food consumption, and poor nutrition. However, very few studies have controlled for the subjects' health status. As noted above, sensory deficits may result not from advanced age but from ill health. Moreover, very few studies have examined taste or smell function, dietary intakes, and nutritional status in the same persons.

For example, it is unclear whether reduced perception of saltiness leads to increased salt intakes among older adults. One study found that older subjects needed twice as much salt to detect its presence in tomato juice as did young subjects. More than half of middle-aged subjects and older subjects (age sixty-seven to eighty-nine) failed to detect the presence of salt in soup. However, there is no clear relationship between the detection of saltiness and preference for salt. Some studies on salt taste preferences reported that older subjects preferred saltier mashed potatoes and chicken broth than did young people, while others found no age-related increase in preference for salt in soup or in tomato juice. These studies did not speak to the key question of whether changes in salt taste perception affect intake of saltier foods on a regular basis.

Findings that older subjects sometimes prefer higher concentrations of sugar and salt in both water and other beverages were interpreted to mean that they would select sweeter and saltier foods. However, food consumption was not actually measured. Very few studies measured salt taste perception, salt taste preference and actual salt consumption among the same respondents. In one such study, young and older adults did not differ in their saltiness intensity ratings for chicken broth. Moreover, older adults generally preferred *lower* salt concentrations in chicken broth. The hedonic response to salt in soup was not related to daily sodium intakes as assessed by fifteen days of diet records. Sodium intakes (expressed as mg per 1,000 kcal) did not increase with age.

The ability to perceive bitter taste also declines with age. Age was also the strongest predictor of food preferences. Older women expressed increased liking (or reduced dislike) for cruciferous vegetables and bitter salad greens. The reduced response to bitter may increase the acceptance of some bitter foods by women.

The age-associated decline in the sense of smell is also thought to have nutritional consequences. Some scientists believe that olfactory deficits reduce the pleasantness of foods and are the direct cause of reduced food intake and malnutrition in the elderly. A study of smell in eighty older women (sixty-five to ninety-three years of age) showed that half had severe olfactory dysfunction. The dysfunction did not affect appetite, and was unrelated to total energy intake, body weight, or the body mass index (BMI). Body mass index, weight divided by the square of height (1kg/m2), is a measure of body mass. However, women with smell losses reported a lower interest in food-related activities (e.g., enjoying cooking, eating a wide variety of foods); lower preference for foods with sour/bitter taste, such as citrus fruits; higher intake of sweets; and higher intake of fats. Smell losses may lead people to select foods that are sweet or rich in fat, such that the taste and texture will contribute to sensory appeal.

Amplifying foods with noncaloric flavors is thought to be a promising approach in promoting energy intake by older persons and reversing age-related anorexia. In one such study, 75 percent of elderly subjects preferred foods that had been amplified or enhanced with added flavor. In some cases, carrots were amplified with carrot flavor; in other cases, peas were enhanced with bacon flavor or cauliflower with a cheese flavor. The results showed that flavor enhancement, as opposed to a simple flavor amplification, was the more effective method. The most effective enhancers of food intake among older persons were synthetic meat flavors: bacon, roast beef, and ham.

Data from nutritional surveys suggest that dietary variety, defined as the number of different foods consumed each day, often declines with age. This effect was not observed among healthy older people of means, but is reported to be common among institutionalized persons. Researchers believe that the mechanism of sensory-specific satiety encourages the consumption of a varied diet. Sensory specific satiety reduces preference for the just-consumed foods and foods much like them. In contrast, preferences for new foods are maintained at higher levels. In laboratory studies, sensory-specific satiety diminished with age and was lowest in persons over sixty-five. Though the reason for this reduction was unclear, it was unlikely to be caused by any deficits in sensory function.

Consumer studies show that food choices are very largely determined by how foods taste. However, economic factors and health concerns also play a role. Demographic and psychosocial factors have a major impact on the quality of the diet of older adults. When it comes to food choices, deficits in taste and smell, if present, can be compensated for by prior learning and experience.

ADAM DREWNOWSKI
SUSAN E. COLDWELL
BARBARA J. ROLLS

See also HEARING; MALNUTRITION; VISION.

BIBLIOGRAPHY

DOTY, R. L.; SHAMAN, P.; APPLEBAUM, S. L.; GIBERSON, R.; SIKSORSKI, L.; and ROSENBERG, L. "Smell Identification Ability: Changes with Age." *Science* 226 (1984): 1441–1443.

DREWNOWSKI, A.; HENDERSON, S. A.; DRISCOLL, A.; and ROLLS, B. J. "Salt Taste Perceptions and Preferences are Unrelated to Sodium Consumption in Healthy Older Adults." *Journal of the American Dietetic Association* 96 (1996): 471–474.

DREWNOWSKI, A.; HENDERSON, S. A.; DRISCOLL, A.; and ROLLS, B. J. "The Dietary Variety Score: Assessing Diet Quality in Healthy Young and Older Adults." *Journal of the American Dietetic Association* 97 (1997): 266–271.

DREWNOWSKI, A., and WARREN-MEARS, V. "Chemical Senses and Food Choices in Aging." In *Handbook of Nutrition in the Aged.* Edited by R. R. Watson. Boca Raton, Fla.: CRC Press, 2000. Pages 237–250.

DUFFY, V. B.; BACKSTRAND, J. R.; and FERRIS, A. M. "Olfactory Dysfunction and Related Nutritional Risk in Free-Living, Elderly Women." *Journal of the American Dietetic Association* 95 (1995): 879–884.

ROLLS, B. J. "Appetite, Hunger and Satiety in the Elderly." *Critical Reviews in Food Science and Nutrition* 33 (1993): 39–44.

ROLLS, B. J. "Do Chemosensory Changes Influence Food Intake in the Elderly?" *Physiology and Behavior* 66 (1999): 193–197.

ROLLS, B. J., and DREWNOWSKI, A. "Diet and Nutrition." In *Encyclopedia of Gerontology.* Edited by J. E. Birren. San Diego: Academic Press, Inc. 1996. Pages 429–440.

SCHIFFMAN, S. S., and WARWICK, Z. S. "Effect of Flavor Enhancement of Foods for the Elderly on Nutritional Status: Food Intake, Biochemical Indices, and Anthropometric Measures." *Physiology and Behavior* 53 (1993): 395–402.

TAXATION

Elderly persons are treated very well by the U.S. federal tax system and by the tax systems of many states and localities. They get an extra federal standard deduction, Social Security benefits are taxed lightly or not at all, pensions get special relief, and state and local property tax burdens are often offset by income tax relief. It is not, however, easy to provide a simple, widely accepted philosophical justification for taxing an elderly person at a lower rate than a younger person with the same income.

These tax concessions may simply reflect the political power of elderly voters. People sixty-five and over constituted 16.5 percent of the voting age population in the 1996 election, but provided over 20 percent of the votes. Their political importance will grow considerably when an increasing number of baby boomers reach age sixty-five in the years following 2010.

Despite the political power of older voters, it is hard to believe that significant tax breaks would be possible without the tacit support of the younger population. Older people are popular. Many are peoples' grandparents, and young people certainly hope to survive to an age at which they too can enjoy the tax concessions granted older adults.

However, it must be noted that the benefits conveyed to older Americans have a considerable cost—a cost that will rise as the population ages. The related revenue loss must be added to the much larger benefits appearing on the spending side of the budget. Social Security is now the largest single federal program and Medicare spending will soon exceed defense spending. Those over sixty-five absorb about 50 percent of the civilian, noninterest expenditures of the federal government. Although the tax preferences given to older Americans are quite small relative to the benefits received on the spending side of the budget, they do add up. They also imply that younger workers are forced to pay higher taxes than they would otherwise. Given American hostility to higher taxes, it is probable that the benefits conveyed to older adults on both the spending and tax side of federal, state, and local budgets tend to crowd out other government activities in areas such as defense, child welfare, and highways.

Federal tax law

The most important federal tax break involves the taxation of Social Security. Benefits are completely excluded from taxable income for lower-income elderly taxpayers. Single taxpayers with $25,000 to $34,000 in income, and couples between $32,000 and $44,000, receive 50 percent or more of their benefits tax-free, while singles with incomes above $34,000 and couples above $44,000 must pay taxes on up to 85 percent of benefits. A complex formula is used to phase in the taxation of benefits, and it has the peculiar result that over certain ranges of income the marginal tax rate on an extra dollar of non-Social Security income is higher than on an extra dollar of benefits. During the phase-in ranges, Social Security recipients are also subjected to very high marginal tax rates on extra earnings or on extra income from investments, because every extra dollar of such income has a double impact on a person's tax bill. It is subject to taxation itself, and it adds to the portion of Social Security benefits that will be taxed. This could create disincentives to work and to save. The exclusion of Social Security benefits from ordinary taxable income cost the federal government $17.1 billion in lost revenue in fiscal year 1999.

It has been proposed that it would be proper to include 85 percent of Social Security benefits in taxable income for everyone. The other 15 percent reflects the estimated return of principal invested out of after-tax dollars in a typical private pension plan that enjoys no tax advantages. However, the creation of IRAs, Keoghs, 401(k) plans, and the like has made tax law much more favorable to private retirement savings. Contributions to such plans are deducted from taxable income and withdrawals are fully taxed. Only contributions in excess of the limits imposed for such plans are deprived of tax advantages and contributions of this type are uncommon.

If Social Security is seen as a typical tax-advantaged retirement plan and treated like most other retirement saving plans, it would be appropriate to subject 50 percent of benefits to taxation while allowing 50 percent to be tax free. That is because the 50 percent of the payroll tax that is paid by employers is deducted from their taxable income, while the 50 percent that is paid by employees is financed out of after-tax income.

On the other hand, it might not be appropriate to regard Social Security as a typical retirement plan, because the level of benefits is only loosely related to the payment of payroll taxes. People with lower lifetime earnings receive a higher rate of return than those with higher earnings, dependent spouses receive an extra benefit equal to 50 percent of that of the principal earner, and the return on one's payroll tax contribution can depend on when income was earned. Consequently, it may be more accurate to regard Social Security as a transfer program that distributes money from high to low earners rather than as a pension program. But there is no consistent rule governing the taxation of transfer payments. For example, unemployment insurance benefits are included in taxable income, while welfare payments are not.

The taxation of benefits obviously reduces their net value, particularly for those affluent taxpayers who are in the highest tax brackets. Thus, the taxation of benefits can be seen as an indirect approach to means-testing Social Security since the tax imposes the largest burden on the most affluent beneficiaries. Given the rapidly rising economic burden that will be imposed by Social Security once baby boomers start to retire, there may be a strong argument for subjecting 100 percent of benefits to taxation as a way of strengthening means-testing.

It should be noted that the taxation of Social Security benefits is a relatively recent phenomenon. Before 1983, benefits were not taxed at all. After that time, a maximum of 50 percent of the benefit was brought into taxable income. The proportion brought into taxable income was not raised to 85 percent for more affluent taxpayers until 1993.

A less important federal tax concession provides an extra standard deduction to each individual age sixty-five and older. In 1999, this equaled $1,000 for single taxpayers and $800 each for married taxpayers. The associated revenue loss was $1.8 billion in fiscal 1999. There is also a nonrefundable tax credit for low-income retirees whose retirement income is mostly taxable, but this credit is rarely used.

Because the use of the standard deduction declines as income rises, the extra standard deduction is most valuable, on average, to lower-income elderly taxpayers. Only about 10 percent of elderly couples with incomes between $20,000 and $30,000 itemize deductions while itemized deductions are used by a substantial majority of those with incomes above $80,000. However, only 15 percent of elderly couples had incomes that high in 1998.

The elderly receive Medicare and Medicaid benefits tax-free, as well as an untaxed subsidy for the purchase of insurance for physician services. Although it would be practically possible to tax such items, it would be extremely unpopular politically. It should be noted that employer-provided health insurance is also tax-free, as are Medicaid benefits.

As noted earlier, private saving for retirement is now highly favored by the federal tax system. Employers' contributions to defined benefit plans are not, for the most part, considered to be taxable income to the employee. Employer and employee contributions to defined contribution plans are deductible up to specified limits that differ from plan to plan. The tax saving associated with the deduction for contributions into a retirement account is sufficient to pay the tax on future withdrawals if the tax saving is invested at the same rate of return as the rest of the account—and if withdrawals are taxed at the same tax rate as was applicable when the contribution was made. Put another way, it is equivalent, under these very special assumptions, to eliminating the entire tax on income saved for retirement. If the retiree is in a lower tax bracket when funds are withdrawn than when funds were contributed, he or she receives a tax subsidy for retirement saving. That is to say, the after-tax return on the retirement account becomes greater than the before-tax rate of return.

The law provides for a confusing array of defined benefit and defined contribution accounts that have different deduction limits and are subjected to different tax rules. The regulation of such accounts, especially defined benefit plans, is also extremely complicated. The system badly needs simplification.

Whether tax-favored, private retirement accounts improve the income of retirees depends on the extent to which the tax incentives actually increased the retirement savings of people while they were working. There is profound disagreement among economists on this point. Some believe that the tax concessions induce a sizeable increase in retirement saving. Others argue that the savings deducted from taxable income largely represents either transfers from other accounts or saving that would have occurred even in the absence of tax concessions. The naysayers believe that the increase in private saving is less than the associated revenue loss to the federal treasury.

State income taxation

Tax burdens on older adults vary greatly from state to state. Many replicate federal law in allowing an extra standard deduction, and some do not tax Social Security benefits at all. Many also exclude a large portion of other types of retirement income. This creates a severe inequity between people whose income flow is in the form of pensions and people who get exactly the same income from interest and dividends that are fully taxed. Table 1 describes selected tax provisions that especially affected elderly taxpayers in different states in 1998. It does not include provisions related to property taxes.

The combination of federal and state income tax burdens

The total income-tax relief given older adults can be very important. The precise amount of the relief, however, depends on how income is received. In *Tax Benefits for the Elderly* (2000) Rudolph Penner presents a number of examples, loosely based on data from the Statistics of Income (U.S. Treasury, Internal Revenue Service). One example involves a retired couple age sixty-five or older with $67,372 in income (in 1998) who get 24 percent of their income from Social Security, 40 percent from pensions and annuities, 30 percent from interest and dividends, and 5 percent from earnings. In Hawaii, such a couple would pay about $5,500 less in taxes than a younger couple receiving the same total income from wages. The tax liability of the older couple is thus reduced by 36 percent, or by 8.1 percent of income. In South Carolina, the elderly couple would receive a tax cut of about $4,000, or 6.0 percent of income. In Georgia, the benefit is about $2,100, or 3.2 percent of income. None of the above figures count property tax concessions.

Table 1

Selected Characteristics of State Income Tax Systems (Tax Year 1998)

State	Income Basis	Additional Exemption/ Deduction for the Elderly (joint filers)	Additional Credit for the Elderly (joint filers)	Private Pension/ Retirement Exclusion (joint filers)	Social Security Benefits Exemption	Number of Tax Brackets	Low Rate	High Rate
Arizona	AGI	$4,200			Yes	5	2.870%	5.040%
California	AGI		$140		Yes	6	1.000%	9.300%
Colorado	TI			$20,000-$40,000[1]	Yes	1	5.000%	5.000%
Connecticut	AGI				No	2	3.000%	4.500%
Delaware	AGI	$2000 (+$4,000)[2]	$200	$3,000 maximum	Yes	7	2.600%	6.400%
District of Columbia	AGI	$2,740			Yes	3	6.000%	9.500%
Georgia	AGI	$2,600		$12,000 maximum	Yes	6	1.000%	6.000%
Hawaii	AGI	$2,080		All pension/annuity	Yes	8	1.600%	8.750%
Idaho	AGI	$1,700			Yes	8	2.000%	8.200%
Illinois	AGI	$2,000		All pension/annuity	Yes	1	3.000%	3.000%
Indiana	AGI	$2,000	$80 - $140[3]		Yes	1	3.400%	3.400%
Iowa	AGI		$40	$10,000 maximum	No	9	3.600%	8.980%
Kansas	AGI	$1,400			No	3	4.100%	6.450%
Kentucky	AGI		$40	$35,000 maximum	Yes	5	2.000%	6.000%
Louisiana	AGI		$40	$12,000 maximum	Yes	3	2.000%	6.000%
Maine	AGI	$4,800			Yes	4	2.000%	8.500%
Maryland	AGI	$2,000		$15,900 maximum[4]	Yes	4	2.000%	4.850%
Michigan	AGI	$1,800		$67,620 maximum	Yes	1	4.400%	4.400%
Minnesota	TI	$12,000 maximum[5]			No	3	6.000%	8.500%
Missouri	AGI	$8,800			No	10	1.500%	6.000%
Montana	AGI	$3,160		$3,600 maximum[6]	Yes	10	2.000%	11.000%
Nebraska	AGI	$1,700			No	4	2.620%	6.990%
New Mexico	AGI	$8,000 maximum[7]			No	7	1.700%	8.200%
New York	AGI			$40,000 maximum*	Yes	5	4.000%	6.850%
North Carolina	TI	$1,200		$4,000 maximum*	Yes	3	6.000%	7.750%
North Dakota	TI				No	8	2.670%	1.200%
Ohio	AGI	$40	$50	$25 - $200 credit	Yes	9	6.730%	6.799%
Oklahoma	TI	$2,000		$4,400 maximum[8]	Yes	8	5.000%	5.750%
Oregon	TI	$2,400		9% maximum credit[9]	Yes	3	5.000%	9.000%
Rhode Island	FL	$1,700*			No	(25.6 % of federal liability)		
South Carolina	TI	$23,000		$10,000	Yes	6	2.500%	7.000%
Utah	TI	$1,700		$15,000[10]	No	6	2.300%	7.000%
Vermont	FL				No	(25% of federal liability)		
Virginia	AGI	$25,600[11]			Yes	4	2.000%	5.750%
West Virginia	AGI	$16,000			No	5	3.000%	6.500%
Wisconsin	AGI		$50[12]		No	3	4.770%	6.770%

AGI = Federal Adjusted Gross Income; TI = Federal Taxable Income; FL = Federal Income Tax Liability.

Notes: States using TI as a starting point implicitly recognized additional $1,700 at federal level.

[1] Colorado: Based on allocation of income between spouses. Social Security benefits are included on prorated basis in income calculation for the exclusion.

[2] Delaware: $4,000 exemption for those with AGI (minus pension and Social Security income) under $20,000 and earned income under $5,000.

[3] Indiana: Limit less than $10,000 income.

[4] Maryland: Based on Social Security benefits.

[5] Minnesota: Limit $42,000 AGI and $12,000 in nontaxable Social Security income plus Railroad Retirement income plus Schedule R income.

[6] Montana: Phased out between $30,000 and $31,800 income.

[7] New Mexico: Phased out between $30,000 and $51,000 income.

[8] Oklahoma: Limit less than $25,000 income.

[9] Oregon: Limit less than $45,000 income (minus Social Security benefits) or $15,000 in Social Security benefits.

[10] Utah: phased out above $32,000.

[11] Virginia: Includes $24,000 deduction and additional $1,600 exemption.

[12] Wisconsin: Phased out for AGI above $40,000.

SOURCE: Author

In all cases, the tax cut for older couples would be much lower if almost all income came from wages and interest and dividends.

For lower incomes, the percentage cut in the tax liability is usually higher, although the absolute value of the cut declines. Assuming $28,323 of income, with 37 percent derived from Social Security, 33 percent from pensions and annuities, 15 percent from interest and dividends, and 15 percent from earnings, the percentage tax cuts in Hawaii, Georgia, and South Carolina are 12.1 percent, 9.8 percent, and 9.2 percent, respectively. Because the percentage cut tends to grow at lower income levels, it can be said that the tax concessions given to elderly persons tend to be progressive. However, it must be re-emphasized that they also tend to be erratic. A person who decides to work after the normal retirement age and who does not benefit from a tax-free pension will, in many states, receive much less of a tax break than a retired person with exactly the same income from Social Security and private pensions. Because people tend to retire earlier if they have a more generous pension, the tax concessions provided for retirement income undoubtedly encourage some to retire earlier than they would without the tax concession.

Property tax relief

Many states provide income tax relief related to property taxes paid at the state and local level. Often, the relief is restricted to elderly persons. In some states, such as Washington, people as young as sixty-one can qualify. The disabled often also qualify.

There are two types of relief. The first is often referred to as a *circuit breaker* and is confined to low-income taxpayers. For example, Connecticut, Nebraska, New Jersey, Ohio, and Washington all have special provisions of this type focused on the elderly, but in all cases, the relief phases out at relatively low income levels. The second type of relief provides a property tax exemption that does not depend on income. Alabama, Kentucky, Mississippi, South Carolina, and West Virginia have provisions of this type targeted at the elderly. For example, an exemption of assessed value up to $20,000 is provided in West Virginia. The average residential property-tax rate in the state is about 1.2 percent, so that the amount of relief for average property owners is $240. Generally, property-tax relief consists of relatively small concessions compared to the income-tax relief described earlier.

Death taxes

Estate and inheritance taxes are imposed at the time of death and are extremely important to affluent elderly persons. The federal estate tax exempts $675,000 of lifetime taxable transfers of wealth, and this amount is now scheduled to rise in steps described in a tax law passed in May of 2001. The first increase is to $1,000,000 in 2002 and 2003, and ultimately the exemption is increased to $3.5 million in 2009. With a modicum of estate planning, couples can double the basic exemption although the new law will impose limits on this privilege in future years. After the exemption is exhausted, a tax rate of 37 percent is currently applied—a rate that gradually rises to 55 percent on taxable estates greater than $3 million, but these rates are to be lowered in the future. The federal estate tax is supposed to disappear altogether in 2010 and then to be reimposed in 2011, but that, as well as scheduled exemptions and rate reductions, could be changed many times before then.

Because of the large exemption, only 2 percent of estates pay the federal estate tax, but that figure greatly understates its effects. Only one member of a couple actually pays the tax, but it is of concern to both. Moreover, many avoid paying only because of judicious planning. Perhaps more important politically, many aspire to be rich enough to be affected, although few will attain the requisite amount of wealth.

For whatever reason, the tax is extremely unpopular and many who have no hope of paying it still regard it as being extremely unfair. Many consider it to be a tax on those who are frugal, hard working, and altruistic toward their descendants. Although special provisions ease the burden of the tax on those wishing to convey farms and small businesses to family members, many do not think that the special provisions are lenient enough and complain that the need to pay the tax forces sales of property. However, such sales are actually extremely rare.

Proponents of the tax praise its progressivity and see it as a tool for extracting taxes from those who have been skilled at avoiding income taxes through their lifetime, either legally or illegally. It is also seen as a device for preventing great concentrations of wealth.

The federal estate tax law now allows a 100 percent credit up to a certain limit against the federal estate tax for estate taxes levied by states. The limit on the credit is related to the taxable value of the estate. Because a state estate tax levied up to the limit does not impose any extra cost on taxpayers, all states impose so-called pick-up taxes that exploit the entire federal limit. The new law gradually reduces these credits and repeals them entirely in 2005.

Thirteen states and Puerto Rico levy inheritance taxes in addition to pick-up taxes, while four states have additional estate taxes. An inheritance tax depends on the size of the bequest left to an individual heir, whereas an estate tax depends on the total value of the estate left by the decedent, regardless of how it is spread among heirs. Estate and inheritance tax rates and basic exemptions vary greatly from state to state and often depend on the relationship between the beneficiary and the decedent, with close relatives being favored.

A strong trend has developed at the state level toward reducing or eliminating estate and inheritance taxes because they are so unpopular politically. In 1989, eighteen states levied inheritance taxes and eight levied estate taxes in addition to pick-up taxes. In January 1999, only fourteen states had inheritance taxes and four still had estate taxes. New York has been reducing its very heavy estate tax by raising exemptions and cutting rates.

Effects of state and local tax policy on location decisions

States have an additional reason to lower their estate and inheritance taxes. They do not want to pressure affluent elderly taxpayers into moving to states that have only pick-up taxes or very-low estate and inheritance taxes.

More generally, states and localities tend to use tax policy to compete for older Americans. They are considered to be attractive residents, especially those who are more affluent, because they are law abiding, often attract other forms of economic activity, and do not impose costs on local school systems.

Duncombe, Robbins, and Wolf (2000) have investigated the effect of state and local fiscal policy on the migration of retirees. They have found that inheritance, income, and property tax policies have more effect on location decisions than expenditures on social services and law enforcement. However, it takes very large tax cuts to

provoke even tiny amounts of in-migration. The authors conclude the revenue losses are likely to far outweigh any economic and fiscal benefits derived from attracting older adults. In a much older study, Voss, Gunderson, and Manchin (1988) also concluded that tax factors are significant, but not overwhelmingly important. Both studies suggest that amenities offered by a state, such as climate, are much more important in affecting the migration patterns of older adults. Both studies also do statistical analyses that result in the perverse conclusion that high estate taxes seem to attract certain types of older migrants. This obviously fallacious result would seem to provide a further indication that tax burdens are a relatively unimportant determinant of where older people choose to live.

Conclusions

Federal, state, and local tax systems tend to treat elderly taxpayers very generously. The costs of this generosity will rise rapidly after 2010 when the number of elderly persons will grow at an extremely rapid rate and the number of workers will stagnate because of the continuation of low birth rates that began in the 1960s.

The devices used to provide tax relief to older adults often have erratic and inequitable effects. People with the same income can face quite different tax bills depending on how the income is received. If it is deemed desirable to provide tax relief to older individuals, it would be more equitable to do it with an extra exemption, a tax credit, or lower tax rates for all those over a certain age, say sixty-five, rather than concentrating relief on specific types of income likely to be received by old people, such as Social Security or pensions. Whether one chooses a credit, an extra deduction, or a lower tax rate would depend on how one believes that the tax relief should be shared by different income groups. Superficially, it appears somewhat odd to provide any tax relief at all to very affluent older taxpayers. However, the current tax and transfer system, along with private policies such as means tests for college financial assistance, already contain numerous disincentives for accumulating wealth. It is necessary therefore, to be cautious as to how far we should go in continually making the system more progressive.

RUDOLPH G. PENNER

See also ESTATE PLANNING; PENSIONS; RETIREMENT PLANNING; SAVINGS; SOCIAL SECURITY.

BIBLIOGRAPHY

DUNCOMBE, W.; ROBBINS, M.; and WOLF, D. "Chasing the Elderly: Can State and Local Governments Attract Recent Retirees?" *Aging Studies Program*. Paper 22. Syracuse, N.Y.: Center for Policy Research, 2000.

ENGEN, E. M.; GALE, W. G.; and SCHOLZ, J. K. "The Illusory Effects of Savings Incentives on Saving." *The Journal of Economic Perspectives* 10, no. 4 (1996): 113–138.

GALE, W. G., and SLEMROD, J. B. "Ancestor Worship." *The Milken Institute Review* 2, no. 3 (2000): 36–49.

HUBBARD, R. G., and SKINNER, J. S. "Assessing the Effectiveness of Savings Incentives." *The Journal of Economic Perspectives* 10, no. 4 (1996): 73–90.

NALEBUFF, B., and ZECKHAUSER, R. J. "Pensions and the Retirement Decision." In *Pensions, Labor, and Individual Choice*. Edited by David A. Wise. Chicago: University of Chicago Press, 1985. Pages 283–316.

National Conference of State Legislatures. *Fiscal Affairs: State Death Taxes*. Available on the World Wide Web at www.ncsl.org

PENNER, R. "Tax Benefits for the Elderly." *The Retirement Project Occasional Paper No. 5* Washington, D.C.: The Urban Institute, 2000.

POTERBA, J. M.; VENTI, S. F.; and WISE, D. A. "How Retirement Savings Programs Increase Saving." *The Journal of Economic Perspectives* 10, no. 4 (1996): 91–112.

U.S. Office of Management and Budget. "Tax Expenditures." *Analytic Perspectives: The Budget of the United States Government, Fiscal Year 2001*. Washington, D.C.: U.S. Government Printing Office, 2000.

U.S. Treasury, Internal Revenue Service. *Individual Income Tax Returns 1998*. Washington, D.C.: IRS, 2001.

VOSS, P.; GUNDERSON, R.; and MANCHIN, R. "Death Taxes and Elderly Interstate Migration." *Research on Aging* 10 (1988): 420–450.

TECHNOLOGY AND AGING

The term "technology" embodies a broad variety of concepts. In *The New Industrial State*, John Kenneth Galbraith described technology as the "systematic application of scientific or other organized knowledge to practical tasks." Within this broad definition technology may intersect with the lives of older persons in a variety of ways. Technology may include new knowledge gained through basic research on the biology of cellular aging or the development of new vaccines, as well as advances in communications between patients and physicians that enhance the goal of increased mobility and functioning. Technology also encompasses such processual developments as the emergence of new social institutions and complex organizational structures to accommodate changing health care needs of the older population. This includes not only changes in the clinical application of geriatric medicine and reform of the formal health care system, but also the ways in which kin structures evolve and adapt to the changing needs of their members (Litwak and Kulis).

The most familiar forms of technology for most people, however, are those referred to as "hard technology." In this form technology comprises any product or device designed to enhance the well-being of the individual. Of greatest importance to the older population are innovations in three forms of technology: medical technology (including diagnostic and therapeutic devices such as CAT scans, or MRIs); ecological technologies (including environmental modifications and assistive devices); and information technology (comprising communications technology, computers, and the Internet).

Medical technologies

One of the most striking changes in the nature of medical care that has resulted from recent technological innovations has been the movement of medical treatment from predominantly hospital settings to physicians' offices, freestanding specialty clinics, urgent care centers, and even the home. This transformation has resulted from the advent of minimally invasive surgery, new pharmaceutical treatments to replace surgery, and the development of increasingly sophisticated diagnostic and monitoring equipment for people to use in the home (Wilson; Stoeckle and Lorch). This movement might be even more pervasive but for the fact that many medical technologies are not designed for use by patients, but require trained professionals to operate them (Charness and Holley). As an increasing number of technologies are adapted for home use, the sophistication of community-based medical care should increase.

Another important innovation has been the development and use of biomaterials in medical treatment from gene therapy to prostheses to transplantation. Recent innovations in the use of biomaterials include the use of bioadhesive material to deliver drugs through the skin; the use of donor cornea cells as cornea replacements; and the application of bioengineered materials as bone grafts in hip replacement procedures or arterial replacements.

Now that technology has made it possible to map the human genome (or almost all of it), the understanding of the genetic, behavioral, and environmental origins of later life diseases is opening up rapidly. The potential of gene therapy to change the future of medicine has only begun to be perceived. Gene therapies are largely experimental, and testing and development of further therapies are presently complicated by scientific, legal, and ethical hurdles.

Advances in information technology are also helping to improve medical care for older persons in the community and in institutions. In general the use of computers and other communication equipment to connect patients and health care providers is referred to as telemedicine. There is relatively little evidence as yet to show whether telemedicine either improves or worsens health (Heathfield et al.), but the number of pilot programs is rapidly increasing. The use of telemedicine is generally thought to be effective for one-time emergency evaluations, follow-up contacts, medication checks, and primary care in isolated areas, but its usefulness for more extensive diagnostic applications or for long-term chronic disease management is not yet known. Telemedicine can improve patient access to physicians, improve communication among health care providers, reduce transportation costs, and eliminate some of the environmental barriers deterring patients from seeking care. In addition, access to computers and the Internet may make it possible for older persons to view their own medical records, may provide reminders for medication and other home treatments, and may distribute medical information that is individually tailored to the patient's comorbidities and medications (Deatrick).

The adoption of new medical technologies by physicians, hospitals, and patients varies by patient and provider characteristics and across geographic regions. There is often a perception that older patients do not desire to receive aggressive or high-technology treatments for serious illnesses, but there is substantial evidence that the opposite is true (Mead et al., 1997). High-tech interventions also can be high-cost interventions, and thus will likely drive an increasing concentration of such interventions into a limited number of large medical institutions. Similarly, increasingly complex surgical procedures require investment in the training of physicians and other staff, and consequently are often concentrated in particular locations (Wilson). To some extent the problems engendered by the increasing localization of treatment options could be lessened by the growing use of telemedicine, leading eventually to savings. However, the acceptance of telemedicine faces hurdles related to patient privacy and confidentiality, liability, and licensure issues.

Ecological and assistive technology for the disabled

Assistive technologies may be defined as "any item . . . that is used to increase, maintain, or improve the functional capabilities of an individual with a disability" (Brandt and Pope). According to this definition, assistive technology may include assistive devices, environmental modifications, prosthetics, personal response systems, and other "smart house" technology. About two-thirds of disabled older Americans use some form of assistive technology to assist then with limitations in the activities of daily living; the most common items are simple devices that assist with mobility, such as canes and walkers (Agree and Freedman), and this number has been growing (Manton et al.).

The use of assistive technology is highly task-specific, and the successful adoption and retention of assistive devices has been shown to depend largely upon three main factors: the nature of the disability and its severity, the design of the device, and appropriate training of the user (Sanford et al.; Kohn et al.). Environmental barriers also may impede use of equipment, particularly for older persons in aging and/or substandard housing. Though the perceived stigma of using a device also may be a significant factor (Gitlin; Covington), it may depend upon the availability of alternative forms of coping, and not enough is known about these informal adaptations.

Whereas assistive technology is used to enhance the capabilities of the user, environmental modifications serve to reduce the disabling effects of the physical environment, eliminating barriers and increasing the ability of assistive devices to work properly. Recent developments in adaptation of the physical environment have focused on universal and transgenerational design. Universal design is intended to make products useful by persons of all abilities, without expensive or hard-to-find special features (Story). Transgenerational design is a form of universal design specifically developed "as a strategy for eliminating design discrimination against older members of the population" (Pirkl). It is intended to address the needs of ordinary individuals as they age and to create products that are useful across generations and over time.

The growth in assistive technology use and the increase in barrier-free environments in public spaces may be directly linked to political developments since 1960. The growth of advocacy groups for the disabled during the 1960s and 1970s in the United States contributed to major changes in the understanding and treatment of disabled persons. The return of disabled veterans from Vietnam, as well as a general political climate focused on civil rights, generated the independent living movement. This political movement promoted a new paradigm by which disabled individuals have been elevated from a status as deviants who are either tolerated or hidden away, to members of a disadvantaged minority group to whom the state owes a responsibility for full participation as citizens (Albrecht). The ultimate result of this shift in attitudes was the passage of the Americans with Disabilities Act in 1990. This legislation may have been mainly the result of activism by younger persons with lifelong disabilities, for whom incapacity has a very different meaning than that experienced by older persons, but both groups have benefited from greater access to public spaces and protection from discrimination as a result.

Information technology and older adults

One of the most exciting areas of development in new technologies is information technology, specifically the role of the Internet. Computer use among the older population has grown dramatically but still lags behind that of other age groups. In 1984 only 1 percent of Americans age sixty-five or older used a computer anywhere; by 1997 use was up to 10 percent and as of August 2000, 28 percent of Americans over age sixty-five owned a computer (author's tabulations from Current Population Survey).

Nevertheless, the gap between older and younger adults in use of both home computers and network services widened between 1993 and 1997.

About two-thirds of persons age sixty-five and over have no computer in their household, and many of these persons say that they do not want to become "connected" (Russell). According to a study by the Pew Internet and American Life Project, 74 percent of those over fifty who do not presently have Internet access have no plans to get online, and the majority of them feel they are not missing out on anything (Lenhart).

A good proportion of this age gap may be a cohort effect, and as younger, more computer-literate cohorts age, the gap in technological use will likely shrink dramatically in the near future. About 64 percent of those age fifty to fifty-four in 2000 use a computer, compared with 28 percent of those sixty-five and over (tabulations from August 2000 CPS), and the older age group is the most rapidly growing segment of the computer-using population (Bucur et al.).

Design issues also contribute to age differences in computer use. Poorly designed computer and Internet interfaces can be particularly difficult for older persons to use (Bucur and Kwon). Across many studies older persons report more difficulties in mastering computer technologies, and these problems are not corrected merely by improvements in training. System design must also be taken into account to increase the usefulness of computers for the older population (Mead et al., 1999).

The Internet offers a tremendous potential for older persons. Although only a small proportion of persons over sixty-five currently use the Internet for anything other than E-mail (Bucur et al.), it can be an important source of health and investment information, as well as a resource for purchase and delivery of goods such as prescriptions and groceries, and can facilitate the location and purchase of specialized assistive technologies for the disabled. Post-retirement careers can be launched, and cognitive capacity can be maintained, through online educational programs—more and more colleges and universities are offering courses and degrees via distance education over the Internet (Morrell et al.). It is also an important virtual community that can provide support to caregivers or persons whose mobility is impaired. In addition, conquering the brave new world of computing can increase feelings of efficacy and mastery (McConatha). Sherer, and McConatha et al., have shown that the use of personal computers by nursing home residents is associated with both mental and emotional benefits.

Conclusion

The future of technology is vast and largely unforeseeable. Many of the innovations described in this entry were unimagined in the 1980s or 1990s, and undoubtedly future developments will be equally surprising. Some features will certainly become a more important part of the technological solutions applied to everyday aspects of aging. The increasing use of "intelligent" systems, and eventually of robotics, seems assured. Even now, technologies such as specially designed global positioning systems, to reduce wandering among Alzheimer's patients, and intelligent wheelchairs are being tested. Further research is needed to understand the limitations of technology. For example, an increased dependence upon assistive technology should not replace rehabilitation therapy, and no number of "smart" devices can assure complete independence for an older person with advanced dementia. In addition, the broader use of computers for day-to-day tasks, such as shopping and banking, has yet to resolve problems related to the reliability of information on the Internet, privacy concerns, access to technology for low-income persons, and the needs of the disabled elderly.

EMILY M. AGREE

See also AMERICANS WITH DISABILITIES ACT; HOME ADAPTATION AND EQUIPMENT; HUMAN FACTORS.

BIBLIOGRAPHY

AGREE, E. M., and FREEDMAN, V. A. "Incorporating Assistive Devices into Community-Based Long-Term Care: An Analysis of the Potential for Substitution and Supplementation." *Journal of Aging and Health* 12, no. 3(2000): 426–450.

BRANDT, E. N., and POPE, A. M., eds. *Enabling America: Assessing the Role of Rehabilitation Science and Engineering.* Washington D.C.: National Academy Press, 1997.

BUCUR, A., and KWON, S. "Computer Hardware and Software Interfaces: Why the Elderly Are Underrepresented as Computer Users." *Cyber Psychology and Behavior* 2, no. 6 (1999): 535–543.

BUCUR, A.; RENOLD, C.; and HENKE, M. "How Do Older Netcitizens Compare with Their Younger Counterparts?" *Cyber Psychology and Behavior* 2, no. 6 (1999): 505–513.

CHARNESS, N., and HOLLEY, P. "Computer Interface Issues for Health Self-care: Cognitive and Perceptual Constraints." In *Human Factors Interventions for the Health Care of Older Adults.* Edited by W. A. Rogers and A. D. Fisk. Mahwah, N.J.: Lawrence Erlbaum 2001.

COVINGTON, G. A. "Cultural and Environmental Barriers to Assistive Technology: Why Assistive Devices Don't Always Assist." In *Designing and Using Assistive Technology: The Human Perspective.* Edited by D. B. Gray, et al. Baltimore: P. H. Brookes, 1998.

DEATRICK, D. "Senior-Med: Creating a Network to help Manage Medications." *Generations* (Fall 1997): 59–60.

GITLIN, L. N. "Why Older People Accept or Reject Assistive Technology." *Generations* 19, no. 1 (1995).

LENHART, A. *Who's Not Online.* Washington, D.C.: Pew Internet and American Life Project, 2000.

MCCONATHA, D. "Aging Online: Toward a Theory of E-Quality" In *The Older Adult and the World Wide Web.* Edited by Roger Morrell. Mahwah, N.J.: Lawrence Erlbaum, in press.

MCCONATHA, D.; MCCONATHA, J. T.; and DERMIGNY, J. "The Use of Interactive Computer Service to Enhance the Quality of Life for Long-term Care Residents." *The Gerontologist* 34, no. 4 (1994): 553–556.

MEAD, G. E.; PENDLETON, N.; PENDLETON, D. E.; HORAN, M. A.; and NUALA, BENT. "High Technology Medical Interventions: What do Older People Want?" *Journal of the American Geriatric Society* 45, no. 11 (1997): 1409–1411.

MEAD, S. E.; BATSAKES, P.; FISK, A. D.; and MYKITYSHYN, A. "Application of Cognitive Theory to Training and Design Solutions for Age Related Computer Use." *International Journal of Behavioral Development* 23, no. 3 (1999): 553–573.

MORRELL, R. W.; MAYHORN, C. B.; and BENNETT, J. "Older Adults Online in the Internet Century." In *Older Adults, Health Information, and the World Wide Web.* Edited by R. W. Morrell. Mahwah, N.J.: Lawrence Erlbaum, 2002.

PIRKL, J. J. *Transgenerational Design: Products for an Aging Population.* Florence, Ky. : Van Nostrand Reinhold, 1994.

RUSSELL, C. "The Haves and the Want-Nots." *American Demographics* 20 (April 1998): 10–12.

SHERER, M. "The Impact of Personal Computers on the Lives of Nursing Home Residents." *Physical and Occupation Therapy in Geriatrics* 14 (1996): 13–31.

STOECKLE, J. D., and LORCH, S. "Why Go to See the Doctor? Care Goes from Office to Home as Technology Divorces Function from Geography." *International Journal of Technology Assessment in Health Care* 13, no. 4 (1998): 537–546.

STORY, M. F. "Maximizing Usability: The Principles of Universal Design." *Assistive Technology* 10, no. 1 (1998): 4–12.

WILSON, C. B. "The Impact of Medical Technologies on the Future of Hospitals." *British Medical Journal* 319 (1999): 1–3.

THANATOLOGY

See DEATH AND DYING; DEATH ANXIETY; FUNERAL AND MEMORIAL PRACTICES

THEORIES OF BIOLOGICAL AGING

The complexity of the aging process diminishes the probability that any one theory would satisfactorily explain aging. The concept that some age-related changes may be programmed, whereas others are stochastic and unpredictable, is now generally accepted. However, some theories include both kinds of changes and are impossible to classify as one or the other. In fact, experts probably would not even agree on a common list of aging theories, so the following list should not be regarded as definitive or exhaustive. A further complication is the need to distinguish between the aging process itself and the effects due to phenomena such as diseases. A detailed discussion of various theories can be found in *Modern Biological Theories of Aging* (Warner et al., eds.).

Random damage theories

The most prominent random damage theory of aging was proposed by Denham Harman in 1955. This theory postulates that free radical reactions, primarily oxygen-free radicals, cause slowly accumulating damage to nucleic acids, proteins, and lipids that eventually leads to loss of their specific functions in the cell. This damage is caused primarily by the production of oxygen-free radicals as a by-product of normal metabolism in the mitochondria.

Thus, while this damage may be slow, it is continuous, and the well-accepted assumption is that the individual cells are unable to neutralize all of the free radicals generated by the mitochondria or to completely repair the damage that occurs. A small amount of free radicals may also be generated in nonmitochondrial biochemical reactions, and by external insults such as radiation. This general phenomenon is also referred to as oxidative stress, and the theory predicts either that the generation of free radicals increases with age, or that antioxidant defense systems decrease with age, or both.

Many scientific reports have attempted to prove this theory of aging. They document increased levels of oxidative damage with increasing age in a variety of animal model systems, but rarely has it been possible to implicate this increased damage as a cause of aging. Nevertheless, there is strong evidence that oxidative stress is a major factor in the damage occurring following a stroke or heart attack, two major age-related events leading to loss of organ function or death. It is also thought that oxidative stress is a factor in the age-related loss of neurons that accompanies a variety of neurodegenerative pathologies. Thus, any comprehensive theory of aging must include oxidative stress as a likely factor in the loss of biological function through human aging.

The free radical, or oxidative stress, theory of aging is a prototype for other, similar theories that suggest random damage occurs and that much, but not all, of it can be repaired. Complete repair is thought to be impossible, so damage slowly accumulates and eventually leads to dysfunction and overt pathology. These related theories include error catastrophe theory and DNA damage theory. The *glycation theory* of aging proposes that the nonenzymatic condensation of glucose with amino groups in proteins leads to dysfunction of those proteins, a process that is accelerated in diabetics because of their increased level of circulating glucose. This is well documented in hemoglobin, and for proteins in the eye lens, leading to premature cataract formation. Glycation also leads to protein cross-linking, which not only alters both the structure and function of these proteins, but also prevents their normal degradation. The *rate of living theory* proposes that aging rate is proportional to the rate of the organism's metabolism, so that small mammals with high metabolic rates, like mice, will have much shorter life spans than large mammals, such as humans. This may generally be true for mammalian species, but birds live much longer than might be predicted by their high metabolic rates and high circulating glucose levels. The *wear and tear theory* of aging is a similar version of this class of theories.

Programmed aging theories

The other major group of theories postulates that genetically programmed changes that occur with increasing age are responsible for the deleterious changes that accompany aging. It is well known that development is genetically programmed, so logic dictates that aging changes might also be programmed. The principal systems implicated in this group of theories are the endocrine and immune systems. It has been easy to demonstrate that the immune system changes with age. The major function of the immune system is to recognize foreign biological entities (antigens) and destroy or inactivate them either by tagging them with very specific antibodies or by directly killing them. To do this, mammals produce circulating cells called lymphocytes in either the thymus (T-lymphocytes) or the bone marrow (B-lymphocytes). However, the thymus gradually disappears and is essentially gone by young adulthood. Thus, further production of T-lymphocytes depends upon cell proliferation and expansion of the existing pool of T-lymphocytes. The lymphocyte pool always consists of naive T-lymphocytes, which are not yet responsive to a specific antigen, and memory T-lymphocytes, which are programmed to respond to a particular antigen. As age increases, memory T-lymphocytes comprise an increasing percent of the T-lymphocyte pool, and the remaining T-lymphocytes are less able to respond to an immunologic challenge such as a bacterial infection.

The immune system is also able to distinguish between foreign antigens and nonforeign antigens. The immune system's response to nonforeign antigens is called autoimmunity, and the frequency of autoimmune interactions increases with age. In fact, a number of age-related diseases are thought to be due to these inappropriate autoimmune responses; thus these apparently programmed changes could be important factors in aging.

It is also known that the levels of circulating hormones may change with age. This is particularly true for growth hormones, dehydroepiandrosterone (DHEA), and melatonin. It is not known whether the decreases observed are developmentally programmed to benefit the organism in some way, or whether they are simply another example of dysregulation with increasing age. A much clearer example is provided by estrogen. Estrogen declines rapidly after menopause in women, and menopause is programmed to occur at about age fifty. Besides the loss of reproductive capability, this decline in estrogen production greatly increases the risk of age-related diseases such as osteoporosis and cardiovascular disease. Thus, late-life programmed changes may produce a variety of effects, many of which are not beneficial.

System/organ failure

It is clear that humans die for a variety of reasons. Usually one or more organ or system is more compromised than the others, so failure of that system is identified as the cause of death. Two examples are heart failure and stroke. Whereas the immediate cause of death in both cases is a blood clot that obstructs blood supply to critical cells (heart muscle cells or neurons, respectively), the aging-related cause is the gradual obstruction of arteries by protein and lipid deposits. Both genetic and environmental factors may contribute to this deposition, but it can hardly be considered programmed. A continuing controversy is whether there is such a thing as aging without such disease, or whether aging is simply the accumulated effects of wear and tear from disease and the various other life stresses.

Are there genes for aging?

While it is clear that longevity is genetically determined, it is widely believed that specific age-related changes cannot have evolved by natural selection, because most aspects of aging manifest themselves well after reproduction has ceased in humans. This does not mean that aging cannot be altered by genetic intervention. Work begun in the 1980s, and continued with great success in the 1990s, demonstrated clearly that life span in diverse invertebrate organisms can be dramatically extended by mutations in, or overexpression of, specific genes (e.g., antioxidant enzyme genes), often referred to as longevity assurance genes. These genes also code for a wide variety of proteins involved in processes such as signal transduction, hormone production, protein synthesis, and metabolic regulation. It has also been possible to isolate a long-lived strain of fruit flies by selecting for female flies that reproduce late in life, suggesting that certain gene combinations may be particularly beneficial in slowing aging. However, although it is clear that genes do control longevity and the rate of aging, this does not mean that aging is precisely genetically programmed in most organisms.

HUBER R. WARNER

See also ACCELERATED AGING: ANIMAL MODELS; CELLULAR DAMAGE AND REPAIR; GENETICS; LIFE SPAN EXTENSION; THEORIES OF BIOLOGICAL AGING: DISPOSABLE SOMA; THEORIES OF BIOLOGICAL AGING: DNA DAMAGE; THEORIES OF BIOLOGICAL AGING: ERROR CATASTROPHE; THEORIES OF BIOLOGICAL AGING: PROGRAMMED AGING.

BIBLIOGRAPHY

Warner, H. R., et al., eds. *Modern Biological Theories of Aging*. New York: Raven Press, 1987.

THEORIES OF BIOLOGICAL AGING: DISPOSABLE SOMA

Senescence and ageing are processes that affect all organisms and have been described as the diminishing probability of survival accompanied by a reduction of fecundity with increasing age (Partridge, 2001). The disposable soma theory was proposed in an attempt to ascribe an evolutionary framework to understand the existence of, and variations in, the universal process of ageing (Kirkwood, 1977; Kirkwood and Rose, 1991). It proposes that individuals should invest in the maintenance and repair of their soma in relation to their expected life history objectives. However, an individual's expectation of future survival prospects, and the likelihood of reproduction, are not constant. Distinct species, and sometimes distinct individuals within a species, therefore need to sustain their somas for different lengths of time. The disposable soma theory of aging predicts that species and cohorts in a population expecting, on average, to have high survival and low reproductive rates should invest more heavily in protecting their somas than species and populations that expect a short lifespan and to reproduce rapidly. When animals are released from natural selection, differences in somatic repair and maintenance manifest themselves in interspecific and interpopulation differences in aging rate and lifespan.

Support for the idea that the predation rate on a given population affects that population's life-history strategy, including the evolution of altered life span, comes from studies of wild guppies. Such evolution in early life-history stategy occurs very quickly in response to mortality rate changes (Reznick, Buckwalter, et al.). Guppy populations that suffer high predation rates are smaller, grow faster, produce young at an earlier age, and allocate more resources to reproduction than those found in low-predation environments (Reznick, Buckwalter, et al.; Reznick, Butler, et al.). In has also been suggested that one reason why birds and bats live longer than ground-dwelling animals of similar size is that, through flight, they have been released from much of the predation pressure experienced by ground animals. (Austad and Fischer; Ricklefs). One study that tested some of the ideas behind the disposable soma theory was carried out on two distinct U.S. populations of Virginia opossums (Austad). One population was found on Sapelo Island, Georgia, and had no mammalian predators; the other population, found on the Georgia mainland, was predated by pumas, foxes, and bobcats. When life-history parameters were measured for both groups, it was found that the island population produced fewer pups per litter than the mainland group and generally survived to a second reproductive season, when they bred again. The island group had, on average, a 25 percent greater average life span and a 50 percent longer maximum life span than the mainland group.

It is important to note that because the disposable soma theory is an evolutionary theory, the linkage between survival, reproduction, and aging is ultimate rather than proximate. Hence, if an individual animal forgoes breeding, it is not expected to achieve immortality, because it has been selected only to protect its soma for the duration that the average individual within that species is expected to survive. However, forgoing reproduction may have a positive impact on aging and longevity (Hamilton and Mestler; Westendorp and Kirkwood). This is not because of the ultimate evolutionary connection between survival expectancy, reproduction, somatic protection, and longevity anticipated by the disposable soma theory, but rather because of an immediate, proximate trade-off between somatic protection and reproduction, possibly mediated via energy allocation strategies. The disposable soma theory suggests that there are two ultimate reasons why individuals might vary in the extent of soma protection. The first is that increases in adult expectation of mortality should lead to decreased protection. If the animal does not expect to live as long, it has less need to protect itself. The second is that increases in the expected rate of reproduction should lead to decreases in somatic protection, as individuals anticipate the trade-off in energy allocation.

The disposable soma theory does not postulate a particular mechanism underpinning somatic defense and therefore is compatible with various mechanistic theories, such as the free radical theory of aging (Harman). In particular, species that have the lowest levels of extrinsic mortality and low reproduction also have the highest rates of resistance to oxidative stress (Ku and Sohal; Barja, Cadenas,. . .Perez-Campo, 1994; Barja, Cadenas,. . .Lopez-Torres, 1994). Further support for this association comes from the opossums mentioned above, where the Sapelo Island population exhibited a reduced rate of age-associated damage in its collagenous tissues compared with the mainland opossums (Austad). DNA repair is lower in rodents than in primates (Cortopassi and Wang), and the somatic cells of mice are far more susceptible to oxidative stress induced by chemical stressors such as paraquat and hydrogen peroxide than are longer-lived mammals (Kapahi et al.). The renal epithelial cells of relatively long-lived birds also are more resistant to both chemical and radioactive insult than those of mice (Ogburn et al.).

Overall, the disposable soma theory provides a useful evolutionary framework for understanding the aging process. There is a considerable body of correlative evidence supporting the theory but strong experimental tests are still lacking.

COLIN SELMAN
JOHN R. SPEAKMAN

BIBLIOGRAPHY

AUSTAD, S. N., and FISCHER, K. E. "Mammalian Ageing, Metabolism, and Ecology: Evidence from the Bats and Marsupials." *Journal of Gerontology* 46 (1991): 47–53.

AUSTAD, S. N. "Retarded Senescence in an Insular Population of Virginia Opossums (*Didelphis virginiana*)." *Journal of Zoology* 229 (1993): 695–708.

AUSTAD, S. N. *Why We Age.* New York: John Wiley and Sons, 1997.

BARJA, G.; CADENAS, S.; ROJAS, C.; LOPEZ-TORRES, M.; and PEREZ-CAMPO, R. "A Decrease of Free Radical Production Near Critical Targets as a Cause of Maximum Longevity in Animals." *Comparative Biochemistry and Physiology* 108B (1994): 501–512.

BARJA, G.; CADENAS, S.; ROJAS, C.; PEREZ-CAMPO, R.; and LOPEZ-TORRES, M. "Low Mitochondrial Free Radical Production Per Unit O_2 Consumption Can Explain the Simultaneous Presence of High Longevity and High Aerobic Metabolic Rate in Birds." *Free Radical Research* 21 (1994b): 317–328.

CORTOPASSI, G. A., and WANG, E. "There is Substantial Agreement among Interspecies Stimates of DNA Repair Activity." *Mechanisms of Ageing and Development* 91 (1996): 211–218.

HAMILTON, J. B., and MESTLER, G. B. "Mortality and Survival: Comparison of Eunuches with Intact Men and Woman in a Mentally Retarded Population." *Journal of Gerontology* 24 (1969): 395–411.

HARMAN, D. "Aging: A Theory Based on Free Radical and Radiation Chemistry." *Journal of Gerontology* 11 (1956): 298–300.

KAPAHI, P.; BOULTON, M. E.; and KIRKWOOD, T. B. L. "Positive Correlations between Mammalian Lifespans and Cellular Resistance to Stress." *Free Radical Biology and Medicine* 26 (1999): 495–500.

KIRKWOOD, T. B. L. "Evolution of Aging." *Nature* 270 (1977): 301–304.

KIRKWOOD, T. B. L. *Time of our Lives: The Science of Human Ageing.* London: Weidenfeld and Nicolson, 1999.

KIRKWOOD, T. B. L., and ROSE, M. R. "Evolution of Senescence: Late Survival Sacrificed for Reproduction." *Philosophical Transactions of the Royal Society of London* B332 (1991): 15–24.

KU, H. H., and SOHAL, R. S. "Comparison of Mitochondrial Pro-oxidant Generation and Antioxidant Defenses between Rat and Pigeon: Possible Basis of Variation in Longevity and Metabolic Potential." *Mechanisms of Aging and Development* 72 (1993): 67–76.

OGBURN, C. E.; AUSTAD, S. N.; HOLMES, D. J.; KIKLEVICH, J. V.; GOLLAHON, K.; RABINOVITCH, P. S.; and MARTIN, G. M. "Cultured Renal Epithelial Cells from Birds and Mice: Enhanced Resistance of Avian Cells to Oxidative Stress and DNA Damage." *Journal of Gerontology* 53 (1998): B287–B292.

PARTRIDGE, L. "Evolutionary Theories of Ageing Applied to Long-lived Organisms." *Experimental Gerontology* 36 (2001): 641–650.

REZNICK, D.; BUCKWALTER, G.; GROFF, J.; and ELDER, D. "The Evolution of Senescence in Natural Populations of Guppies (*Poecilia reticulata*): A Comparative Approach." *Experimental Gerontology* 36 (2001): 791–812.

REZNICK, D.; BUTLER, M. J.; and RODD, H. "Life-History Evolution in Guppies. VII. The Comparative Ecology of High- and Low-Predation Environments." *American Naturalist* 157 (2001): 126–140.

RICKLEFS, R. E. "Intrinsic Aging-Related Mortality in Birds." *Journal of Avian Biology* 31 (2000): 103–111.

WESTENDORP, R. G. J., and KIRKWOOD, T. B. L. "Human Longevity at the Cost of Reproductive Success." *Nature* 396 (1998): 743–746.

THEORIES OF BIOLOGICAL AGING: DNA DAMAGE

The idea that DNA damage may be a major factor in aging has been popular since 1974, when Ronald Hart and Richard Setlow demonstrated a direct correlation between life span and capacity for DNA repair. The idea is still largely unproven, although much data supporting it have been obtained. DNA damage includes altered bases, mismatched base pairs, strand cross-linking, and both single- and double-strand breaks. The three main repair pathways are nucleotide excision repair, base excision repair, and direct reversal of damage. As the molecular mechanisms of DNA repair pathways became clearer during the 1980s and 1990s, it became possible to study this question with greater sophistication, but the importance of DNA damage and repair in aging remains unclear.

The possible role of DNA damage in an error-catastrophe scenario is discussed in the next essay, Theories of Biological Aging: Error Catastrophe. As pointed out there, studies to document age-related changes in the fidelity of DNA polymerases have not provided convincing support for either theory, even though DNA polymerase β, the main polymerase involved in DNA repair, is relatively error-prone. The major DNA polymerase in mammalian cells, DNA polymerase α, copies DNA with very high fidelity, and early reports of decreasing fidelity of this enzyme with increasing age have not held up.

Early work on DNA repair focused mainly on the repair of pyrimidine dimers in DNA. Pyrimidine dimers are produced by the cross-linking of two adjacent pyrimidine bases (thymine or cytosine) when DNA is exposed to ultraviolet light. In the 1980s it became clear that such dimers may not be the most abundant DNA lesion *in vivo*, as few cells are actually exposed to ultraviolet light.

It is now recognized that altered bases due to oxidative stress occur much more frequently than dimers, and it has been estimated that as many as 100,000 oxidized bases may be generated in DNA per cell, per day. Such damage is repaired by a pathway known as base excision repair, which begins by removal of the damaged base, followed by DNA breakage at the site of the missing base, removal of the remaining damage, and replacement of the missing nucleotide(s) by DNA polymerase β. This enzyme is absolutely essential for mammalian viability, although cells lacking it can be grown in culture. This suggests that a certain amount of DNA damage can be tolerated in single cells grown in culture, but that the combined effect of many damaged cells in one or more critical tissues is not tolerable.

Much of the early—and generally inconclusive—work on this theory focused on looking for changes in the levels of DNA repair enzymes as a function of age. Work in the late 1990s used transgenic mice and focused on looking at the level and nature of spontaneous mutations as a function of age. The general results from these experiments include: (1) mutation frequency does increase with age, (2) mutations tend to be greater in proliferating tissues than in nonproliferating tissues, and (3) the nature of the mutations varies with age and tissue examined. Both point mutations (single base-pair change) and chromosomal rearrangements accumulate with age in most examined tissues, and it is assumed that the latter has more serious implications for the aging individual. It is certainly clear that DNA rearrangements are closely associated with cancer induction.

The belief that DNA damage may contribute to aging is bolstered by the discovery that the protein coded for by the gene for Werner's syndrome (which simulates accelerated human aging), possesses two enzyme activities known to be involved in DNA metabolism. Both of these activities could play an essential role in DNA repair, with the obvious inference that a DNA repair deficiency may be a cause of premature aging. Cells from Werner's syndrome patients do show an increase in mutations and chromosome alterations, although these two enzyme activities could also be required for DNA replication, transcription, or recombination.

Finally, mutations in mitochondrial DNA also increase with age, particularly in the form of deletions. The level of these deletions increases exponentially with age in human tissues, but it is not clear what role this plays in aging, as most human cells have hundreds of mitochondria and the level of any given deletion rarely reaches more than a few percent of all mitochondrial genomes. The deletion frequencies are highest in mitochondria from postmitotic tissues such as muscle, heart, and brain, but different brain regions may exhibit widely varying deletion frequencies.

It is generally assumed that both nuclear and mitochondrial mutations are largely the result of oxidative stress, and that this stress is greater in the mitochondria than in the nucleus. What is still generally lacking are results that unequivocally relate oxidative stress, mutation induction, and aging.

HUBER R. WARNER

See also ACCELARATED AGING: ANIMAL MODELS; ACCELERATED AGING: HUMAN PROGEROID SYNDROMES; CELLULAR AGING; GENETICS; LIFE SPAN EXPANSION; MUTATION; THEORIES OF BIOLOGICAL AGING: ERROR CATASTROPHE.

BIBLIOGRAPHY

OSHIMA, J. "The Werner Syndrome Protein: An Update." *Bioessays* 22 (2000): 894–901.

VIJG, J., and KNOOK, D. L. "DNA Repair in Relation to the Aging Process." *Journal of the American Geriatrics Society* 35 (1987): 532–541.

WARNER, H. R., and JOHNSON, T. E. "Parsing Age, Mutations and Time." *Nature Genetics* 17 (1997): 368–370.

THEORIES OF BIOLOGICAL AGING: ERROR CATASTROPHE

The error catastrophe theory of aging was proposed by Leslie Orgel in 1963 and it was originally a very popular theory because it made a great deal of sense. Although the theory per se has by now been largely discarded due to a lack of experimental supporting evidence, elements of the theory are still being investigated as possible factors in aging.

The genetic blueprint for each biological species occurs in the deoxyribonucleic acid (DNA) in the nucleus of each cell. When the cell divides, an enzyme known as DNA polymerase makes a new copy of the DNA by combining the appropriate building blocks known as deoxyribonucleotides in the correct sequence in a process known as DNA replication. The genetic sequences in the DNA are then transcribed by another kind of copying enzyme, known as RNA polymerase, into a ribonucleic acid (RNA) molecule called messenger RNA. Specific messenger RNAs contain the instructions for synthesizing individual proteins of the correct amino acid sequence, corresponding to the original blueprint in the DNA. This final protein synthesizing process is called translation.

The original theory posited that low levels of mistakes in the form of misincorporation of amino acids into proteins occur during protein synthesis, although this misincorporation may actually be due to copying mistakes made during DNA replication or messenger RNA synthesis. Although these mistakes can occur in any protein made by the cell, when these mistakes occur in the enzymes and other proteins responsible for synthesizing DNA and RNA, or in the protein synthesizing machinery itself, this could lead to an increasing cascade of errors, referred to as an error catastrophe. This escalating process could turn what is initially a very low error rate in young individuals into a significant rate of accumulation of errors in older individuals, and one would predict that the rate of error accumulation might continue to increase exponentially throughout the life of the individual.

The importance of maintaining high fidelity in biological replicating systems has long been recognized. This is particularly true during DNA replication, as many DNA polymerases possess the ability to recognize mismatched bases, then back up and correct their own mistakes. In addition, very robust DNA repair systems are present to correct mistakes made during synthesis, or afterward by chemicals able to damage DNA. Thus, the error frequency in DNA replication is usually extremely low, perhaps less than one in a million bases. Studies to demonstrate age-related changes in the copying fidelity of polymerases or DNA repair capacity have not provided convincing support for the error catastrophe theory.

In general, RNA polymerases also combine ribonucleotide building blocks to make RNA with high sequence fidelity, but lower than that exhibited by DNA polymerases. However, the overall instability and turnover of messenger

RNA tends to attenuate the impact of any mistakes made during messenger RNA synthesis. Protein synthesis is also generally carried out with high fidelity, and there is little evidence to suggest that this changes with age.

Research trying to prove the error catastrophe theory has focused primarily on identifying differences in either amino acid sequence or the 3-dimensional structure of specific proteins. Attempts to detect errors in sequence as a function of aging have generally failed, but it is thought that sequencing procedures are only sensitive enough to pick up fairly gross sequence errors. However, it has been possible to demonstrate significant changes in physical properties of proteins, suggesting that the 3-dimension structure of old proteins differs from that of young proteins due to differences in protein folding. These differences have mainly been indirectly identified through studies of heat sensitivity of proteins, although very sophisticated biophysical methodologies were employed beginning in the 1990s. The general conclusion has been that aging of proteins is due to changes in the way proteins fold up to form 3-dimensional structures, rather than accumulation of proteins with an incorrect sequence of amino acids. Both kinds of altered proteins tend to aggregate and/or become better substrates for protein-degrading enzymes, thereby, removing the altered protein from the cell. Thus, the rate of accumulation of altered proteins in a cell is a balance between rates of generation and degradation of altered proteins, so the actual rate of generation of altered proteins is difficult to determine with great accuracy.

A related question is whether modification of existing proteins plays a role in aging. Several lines of evidence indicate that proteins do become randomly altered after they are synthesized; a variety of such processes is collectively referred to as post-translational modification because it occurs after synthesis of the protein using the messenger RNA as a template has been completed. Although distinct from the damage hypothesized in the original error catastrophe theory, post-translational modification of proteins could functionally resemble an error catastrophe. These modifications include oxidation of amino acid sidechains, racemization of certain amino acids, and condensation of the lysine side chain amino group with aldehyde groups such as those found in glucose. This latter process is known as non-enzymatic glycation. Biochemical

mechanisms exist to repair the damage caused during some of these processes, suggesting they could have biological significance with implications for aging. However, there is a dearth of evidence unequivocally indicating that damage-inducing processes, damage accumulation, or repair processes are casually related to aging in mammalian species.

In summary, although altered proteins do accumulate with increasing age in mammals, the error catastrophe theory itself is no longer regarded as a viable theory. Nevertheless, there remains a healthy research interest in determining what roles damaged proteins, and the processes that either destroy the damaged protein or repair the damage, might play as casual factors in aging.

HUBER WARNER

See also ACCELERATED AGING; CELLURAL AGING; DNA DAMAGE AND REPAIR; GENETICS; LIFE SPAN EXTENSION; THEORIES OF BIOLOGICAL AGING; THEORIES OF BIOLOGICAL AGING: DNA REPAIR.

BIBLIOGRAPHY

ORCEL, L. E. "The Maintenance of the Accuracy of Protein Synthesis and Its Relevance to Aging." *Proceedings of the National Academy Sciences, USA* 49, April (1963): 517–521.

ROTHSTEIN, M. "Evidence For and Against the Error Catastrophe Hypothesis." In *Modern Biological Theories of Aging*. Edited by Huber R. Warner et al. New York: Raven Press, 1987. Pages 139–154.

THEORIES OF BIOLOGICAL AGING: PROGRAMMED AGING

In the past, many investigators tried to develop a unified theory of biological aging. Evidence that environmental factors can induce mutations and damage cells, and that repair processes are a normal part of cell function, led to development of error and damage theories of aging. According to these theories, accumulation of damage eventually outstrips the ability of the cells to repair themselves, leading to cell senescence and death. Other investigators felt that these theories focus attention on essentially random events, such as DNA damage induced by radiation, and do not provide a convincing explanation for vastly different longevity of different cell types within the same individual, or individuals from different species living in the same environment. Therefore they proposed a theory that aging is programmed (i.e., predetermined). The proposed mechanisms of programmed senescence included the existence of a life-span-determining clock or perhaps a system of tissue- or organ-specific clocks controlled by a master clock. A master clock would presumably control systems responsible for integration of various functions of the organism, such as the endocrine or the central nervous system.

Further refinement of the programmed senescence theory was developed by Bernard Strehler, who proposed that as cells differentiate to perform specific functions within the organism, they lose some of the ability to translate their genetic information, and that this eventually will lead to senescence. Although the specific mechanisms invoked by this and other theories of programmed aging are now of little more than historical interest, they served to establish some important concepts. The importance of the genetic endowment of an individual in aging and life expectancy has been proved beyond any doubt. Therefore, aging can be viewed as being genetically programmed. Furthermore, the concept that senescence is a price paid for development and differentiation is consistent with the life histories of different species. Early maturation and intensive, early reproductive effort are characteristic of short-lived species, whereas late puberty and low reproductive rate tend to be associated with delayed aging.

Recent research in gerontology focuses on the suspected mechanisms of aging. Theories of aging have been classified as organ, physiological, and genetic. Organ theories focus on the importance of age-related changes in the function of organ systems (e.g., neuroendocrine regulation or immune defenses). The physiological theories focus on a particular mechanism of aging, for example, the role of reactive oxygen species in damaging various components of the cell, as proposed by Denham Harman in his oxidative theory of aging. The genetic theory emphasizes the importance of somatic and mitochondrial mutations and the concept of programmed aging. The various aging theories are no longer viewed as mutually exclusive; instead, the multiplicity of mechanisms involved in senescence and regulation of longevity is appreciated. It is now understood that specific genes determine the ability of cells to deal with oxidative stress, and that oxidative damage to cells can lead to organ failure, senescence, and death. Thus, the program theory, physiological theory, and organ theory blend into one comprehensive picture.

Appreciation of the genetic control of aging can be viewed as a modern version of the program theory of aging. Convincing evidence for genetic programming of aging and life span was derived from the study of the effects of specific genes on longevity. Most of the available information on the genetics of aging came from the studies of three species widely used in biological experimentation: a microscopic worm, *Caenorhabditis elegans*; a fruit fly, *Drosophila melanogaster*; and a mouse, *Mus musculus*. In worms and flies, the life span can be greatly extended by experimental manipulation of the expression of specific genes. Overexpression of some of these genes by transgenic technology and the elimination or silencing others by targeted disruption (the so-called gene knockout) can delay aging and prolong life. The mechanisms involved in these effects remain to be fully elucidated but certainly include increased activity of enzymes which control oxidative damage by reducing the levels of reactive oxygen species. Other suspected mechanisms include alterations in energy metabolism, growth, and reproduction.

Results obtained in mice prove that genetic control of aging also applies to mammals. In hereditary dwarf mice, mutation of a single gene produces numerous alterations. These include changes in endocrine function, reduced growth and the characteristic dwarf phenotype, delayed aging, and extension of life span by approximately fifty percent (i.e., from two years to three years). In terms of human life, this would correspond to changing life expectancy from 80 to 120 years. The mechanisms responsible for this impressive extension of life span appear to include a long list of primary and secondary consequences of mutation of these particular genes. The list includes improved antioxidant defenses, increased responsiveness to insulin, reduced blood sugar levels, reduced adult body size, delayed sexual maturation, reduced body temperature, and altered level of expression of numerous genes. Most of these effects can readily be traced to the primary effects of the mutations involved (i.e., deficiency of three pituitary hormones: growth hormone, thyrotropin, and prolactin). The importance of reduced growth hormone action is strongly supported by recent evidence from mice with knockout of the growth hormone receptor gene. These mice are very small and live longer than normal mice. The concept that inhibition of growth and maturation, combined with hypothermia, hypoglycemia, and chronic alterations in blood hormone levels can program an individual for long life may seem surprising. However, these findings are entirely consistent with the overwhelming evidence that reducing food intake (caloric restriction), which causes similar alterations in growth, body temperature, and so on, can greatly prolong life in mice, rats, and apparently monkeys. There is also considerable but somewhat controversial evidence that shorter people live, on the average, longer than taller individuals.

Ongoing studies on humans, including studies of twins as well as exceptionally long-lived people and their relatives, should soon reveal to what extent human aging and life span are genetically programmed.

ANDRZEJ BARTKE

See also ACCELERATED AGING: ANIMAL MODELS; CELLULAR AGING; CELLULAR AGING: BASIC PHENOMENA; ENDOCRINE SYSTEMS; GENETICS; LONGEVITY ASSURANCE; GROWTH HORMONE; LIFE SPAN EXTENSION.

BIBLIOGRAPHY

COMFORT, A. *The Biology of Senescence,* 3d ed. New York: Elsevier North Holland, 1979.
HAYFLICK, L. "Theories of Biological Aging." *Experimental Gerontology* 20 (1985): 145–159.
HEKIMI, S., ed. *The Molecular Genetics of Aging.* Results and Problems in Cell Differentiation, 29 Berlin and Heidelberg: Springer-Verlag, 2000.
LAMB, M. J. *Biology of Aging.* New York: John Wiley and Sons, 1977.
MOBBS, C. V., and HOF, P. R., eds. *Functional Endocrinology of Aging.* New York: Karger, 1998.

THEORIES, SOCIAL

A *theory* is defined, minimally, as a statement (or more typically a set of interrelated statements) that explain or account for a phenomenon of interest. In formal terms, such statements generally have two elements. The *explanandum* refers to the phenomenon or event of interest—the outcome to be explained. The *explanans* is the statement that provides the postulated explanation (Hempel, 2001). Often, the term *theory* is used quite informally to refer to broad and general paradigms of explanation (e.g., the *big bang theory, behaviorism*). Such paradigms are sometimes described in terms of paired opposition such as "nature/nurture" or "activity/disengagement."

The object of the preposition in the phrase *theory of x* defines the explanandum, while an adjective modifying the word *theory* indicates the nature of the explanans—the general explanatory principle being proffered (Hempel, 2001). In the case of *social theories of aging,* both explanans and explanandum warrant further discussion.

Theories of aging is a deceptively expansive phrase, because the range of phenomena encompassed by the word *aging* is so broad, even if the scope is limited to human aging, as it is in this discussion. Although aging is generally assumed to be a property of individuals, some important age-related phenomena are essentially and irreducibly collective features of populations (such as mortality rates); and others are irreducibly social-structural (such as the usage of *age* as a legal criterion)—as in, "being old enough drive"—or as a basis for social norms—"she's too old to be dating him." Confusion can arise because, while age can thus be a feature of populations or of legal, normative, or other symbolic aspects of social systems, it is still ultimately anchored in the measurement and perception of individual age. The focus here will be on theories of age as a feature of individuals, populations, and structures.

Social theories of aging individuals

Whether at the level of microinteraction or macroinstitutions, a social theory's claim, by definition, is that some socially organized aspect of experience or activity, or some set of cultural practices, plays a role in influencing or accounting for some significant aspect of aging. The general idea that how a person lives affects health, length of life, and how that person ages has long been familiar in both popular culture and science. However, not all theories of aging espoused by social scientists could properly be considered "social" theories.

Indeed, one of the most famous and centrally influential theories of aging—*disengagement theory*—is not a social theory of aging at all. It is more properly understood as an organically based theory of society. This is because it considers the disengagement of the aged to reflect an "inevitable" human process operating "in all societies" (Cumming and Henry, pp. 14–15), yet anchored in the fact of chronological age. Such a theory cannot permit much scope to the social realm because it defines aging as a universal, biologically based process inherent to the human species. Because it posits disengagement as a mutual process of withdrawal of others (and hence of social connectedness and social resources) from the aging individual, as well as the reverse, it is an organismic theory not only of individual aging, but of society. It envisions a social order in which the removal of aged individuals from the mainstream of social life is both normal and desirable. The extent to which this theory was initially accepted by social scientists is indicated by the fact that the pre-eminent U.S. sociologist, Talcott Parsons, wrote a foreword for *Growing Old: The Process of Disengagement*, which was the initial monograph setting forth disengagement theory (1961). The positive reception of this work by many sociologists may be taken as an example of how scientists—even social scientists—are limited in their perspectives by assumptions about the society and culture in which their own existence is located. This condition is endemic to the scientific enterprise, and it requires a strong measure of self-critical reflexivity on the part of those who practice science to avoid such pitfalls.

The evidence for the initial formulation of disengagement theory was drawn primarily from the fabled Kansas City studies of aging, spearheaded by Bernice Neugarten in the 1950s. Interestingly, the same data were simultaneously used by others to argue precisely the opposite—that continued activity was both possible and desirable among those with advancing age. This is the premise of *activity theory*. Each of these perspectives was energized by the claims of its competitor, and the result was a crystallization of the classic debate between the two. This debate has framed the parameters and terms of much subsequent theorizing, some of which has turned out to be useful in illuminating and resolving this debate.

The debate is partly resolvable by distinguishing the actual from the possible. Theorists located in the activity tradition cannot dispute the fact that disengagement has been an accurate description of the experiences of many older people in the "late modern" societies of the middle and late twentieth century. At the same time,

within and beyond these societies, there are individuals, subcultures, and even entire societies that challenge this generalization. These challenges fuel the contention that disengagement is not a universal or inevitable pattern, but one that is encouraged, and even naturalized (made to seem natural and taken-for-granted), by the structure of modern societies.

Such a resolution is only made credible, and perhaps only possible, thanks to the subsequent elaboration of several distinct approaches of social theories of aging, each of which has provided illuminating concepts and evidence. These approaches can be divided into two general subgroups that can, at the risk of some oversimplification, be called *micro* and *macro* approaches. For present purposes, *micro* approaches can be considered those that locate explanation at the level of individual, interpersonal, or small-group social dynamics; *macro* approaches locate explanation in the more encompassing dimensions of social organization that form the broader context of experience, including microinteraction. The discussion that follows focuses on how various theories treat the explanatory forces that each nominates as important in explaining aging.

The discussion does not systematically distinguish types of age-related outcomes, since many of these approaches consider their respective explanatory principles to be applicable to a wide range of age-related social, psychological, and physiological outcomes. There is widespread adherence to the view that, even though a given study may focus only on one or two factors—such as stress, psychological adjustment, or economic status—these factors are themselves interrelated, so that, for example, stress affects mood, mood can affect immune functioning, immune functioning affects health, and health affects functional status. This sequence is overly simplistic, as multiple complex interactions occur at each of these nodes at the same time that other processes are having simultaneous impacts. Rather than specifying the exact relations among such largely psychological and organismic processes, the discussion that follows focuses on the difference in how social theories conceptualize the dimensions of the social.

Microlevel approaches. Most microlevel approaches generally involve direct attention to the experiences and social-interaction processes that occur in everyday life. One established tradition to note here is the *symbolic interaction* (SI) approach, which has deep classical roots in both European and North American traditions of social theory. More than its name implies, the SI approach stakes a foundational claim for social interaction. The general model can be thought of in terms of a cyclical process involving: (1) interaction as essential to the development and experience of human beings and (2) human activity as constitutive of interaction. SI thus begins by recognizing that the transformation of raw organisms into human beings does not occur without sustained participation in a somewhat stable set of relationships with other people, and that these relationships, constituted through human interaction, form part of the social context within which individuals develop and age. SI researchers focus on interactive processes such as negotiating and making alliances. While the SI perspective is widely recognized as capturing an important general dynamic that can be applied to the domain of aging, critics charge that symbolic interactionists omit any clear concept of social structure, leaving the impression that social life consists of a somewhat creative and indeterminate process in which concepts like negotiation permit a high degree of uncertainty and an unrealistic amount of efficacy is credited to the actions of individuals.

Such charges have merit. However, some concepts that derive from SI, such as *labeling*, recognize how elements of structure, such as normative expectations, shape the direction and outcomes of interaction, even as the interaction that results reconstitutes those structural elements. Thus, *labeling theory* analyzes how the subjective processes of interpretation and appraisal that are integral to interaction lead to characterizations of others, which sometimes are unwarranted. Applied to old age, Vern Bengtson and associates have proposed a *social breakdown* model, which traces how, for example, stereotypic expectations are used to interpret small and perhaps random episodes of "functional lapse" or "misbehavior" as signaling serious problems, so that the "deviating" individual is declared unfit: when he or she responds with disputation or anger, it is taken as confirmation that a problem exists—thus generating a deviance-amplifying "vicious cycle" interpretation that can be quite destructive for individuals. *Social breakdown theory* is thus predicated on a view of action as, in substantial part, a self-amplifying system, and a self-fulfilling prophecy. Thus, it can be

considered a more sophisticated and systematic elaboration of the SI perspective. Properly understood, this model carries the important implication that the social effects on aging are not limited only to such matters as *meaning* or *status*, but also go to the core of self-identity, and that they can affect organismic aspects of aging, such as health and functional abilities. This point draws on a range of related interpretive traditions (illustrated by the classic work of Peter Berger and associates), as well as empirical social-psychological studies demonstrating how experience systematically affects values and intellectual functioning (as in the classic studies conducted by Melvin Kohn and associates) and health (as studied by Michael Marmot and associates).

Other insights in the study of microinteraction have come from ethnomethodology, a related tradition that focuses on the processes of how people make sense of their everyday lives. For example, Jaber Gubrium and colleagues have analyzed interaction sequences and probed the thinking of study participants to excavate the operating assumptions of a wide variety of actors—from elementary school teachers to nursing home staffers to clinicians diagnosing Alzheimer's disease—engaged in "constructing age." Their work also shows how the structure of pre-existing assumptions creates a "reality of aging" that is specific to the culture that carries those assumptions.

Some efforts at microlevel theorizing derive from a tradition fundamentally different from interactionism. The general approach of *exchange theory* is to make predictions about behavior, taking the values and perceived self-interests of actors as a starting point, without attempting to probe the subtleties of meaning and interpretation that are part of appraisal processes; meaning is taken as a "given," a starting point for analysis. James Dowd attempted to apply exchange theory to explain the behavior of individuals of different ages. He proposed that if old people have fewer resources than younger individuals, this could account for their withdrawal because younger individuals would find it "more costly" to interact with them. For the old, there could also be stress and other psychic costs attending the loss of status.

One of the best-known approaches to explaining and interpreting age-related outcomes, the *life-course approach*, can be seen as something of a bridge between the micro and macro levels. It is here classified as *micro* because its key explanatory strategy focuses on how earlier life events and circumstances shape individuals in ways that are decisive for later-life outcomes—thus meeting the above-referenced criterion that explanation is located at the individual level. At the same time, the life-course approach also has a macro-level explanatory component, since it focuses on the role of major historical events and watershed circumstances of social change in producing the effects. In a well-known classic study, for example, Glen Elder (1982) showed that the long-term effects of encountering the Great Depression as a child were important, but also that they were different for different people, depending on age, on social class, and on the degree of deprivation experienced. Subsequent work in this tradition has continued the theme that such effects have enduring consequences. For example, Elder and colleagues found that mothers in middle-class families who experienced the deprivation of breadwinner job loss were in better "emotional health" by the time they were seventy years old than were middle-class mothers who did not experience deprivation or working-class mothers, regardless of whether or not they experienced deprivation (Elder and Liker). Such an interaction effect, Elder and colleagues suggest, is predicted by theories that focus on the character-building effects of difficult experiences. Analyses such as these have generated great interest, although they have been criticized for omitting important information about the contingencies and events impacting such women. Until recently, few sources of data existed to use for such analyses (which require following the same individuals over many decades).

Macro approaches. Macro approaches look to more encompassing dimensions of social organization or to the features of entire populations for explanatory principles. One of the earliest and best-known of such theories is *modernization theory*. First advanced by Donald Cowgill and Lowell Holmes in the 1960s, this theory offered a direct challenge to disengagement theory by mobilizing the evidence contained in earlier anthropological work, some of which had already been analyzed by Leo Simmons and others. Modernization theory focused on the position of the elderly in societies with different types of value systems. A value system that encompasses "individualistic achievement places the older person at a disadvantage as compared with a value sys-

tem which submerges the individual in the group" (Cowgill, p. 12). Subsequent work consistent with the general thesis of modernization theory has provided considerable specification of the dynamics involved. The value differences described in modernization theory have been linked to important technological, demographic, and economic dimensions of a social order. For example, historical scholars such as Andrew Achenbaum have specified aspects of the general thesis, using historical data from the United States and Europe to suggest that factors such as the lack of authoritative, scientific knowledge in matters of health and the rarity of surviving elders combined to give older adults high status; others focused on the control of wealth by elders (though not all were wealthy).

Theories in the modernization tradition have thus become more than efforts to account for the status or behavior of individual elderly people as they age. They have also offered an explanation of age as a cultural ideal. That is, they suggest that the symbolic meaning and nature of aging also changed when elders were no longer seen as the gatekeepers of knowledge, wealth, and opportunity. The more general model underlying modernization theory, seldom articulated explicitly, is simply that the basic principles on which a society is organized to perform its essential functions will dictate the meaning, significance, and location of different age groups.

At about the same time that Cowgill and Holmes were writing about modernization, Matilda Riley introduced the *age stratification perspective*. This perspective shared the general view that macrosocial forces must be understood in order for aging itself to be understood, and introduced a more systematic approach to understanding the relationship between aging and social change, but it differed in several important respects. It offered a broader view of the features of society that could potentially impact individual aging—rather than focusing mainly on questions of status and values. It also offered a broader view of the explananda, envisioning a broad range of individual age-related characteristics likely to be altered by features of social structure.

The age stratification perspective (recently renamed by Riley as the "aging and society perspective") made explicit the potential effects, not only of social change, but also of enduring and stable aspects of social structures upon aging. Thus, it also contributed a more explicit conceptualization of the importance of social structure as having a causal force upon aging. By making explicit the systems-analysis distinction between people as actors and roles as components of a social system, this framework sharpened questions of the "fit between persons and roles," and even proposed that "fit" could itself be a factor in explaining age-related outcomes. For example, the phenomenon of disengagement was, from this vantage point, interpreted as a result of a dearth of meaningful roles for older people and consequent social exclusion, leading to possible adverse psychological and health consequences. The question of the fit between persons and roles also invited analysis of age-related features of the population at any given point in time. For example, Joan Waring (1976) and Richard Easterlin (1980) argued that the size of a birth cohort would have fateful consequences for the patterns of aging of its members: their movement through the age-graded structures of society would be influenced by the availability of age-graded roles. Specifically, both argued that being in a large cohort (such as the baby-boom cohorts born from 1946 to 1965 in many Western societies) would increase the competition for resources typically allocated on an age-graded basis, and that members of such large cohorts would not fare as well as those of smaller ones.

In such theorizing, age is recognized not merely as a feature of individuals, but as a component of culture. The socially constructed aspects of aging are claimed to affect physical aspects of aging, as well as its psychosocial and status dimensions. Because of these socially specific aspects, such theorizing implies that what seems to be natural aging is only loosely related to the presumed biological imperatives of aging. For example, in contemporary Western societies, age is associated with physical changes such as increases in blood pressure. Evidence from some traditional societies suggests that such physiological changes do not occur in their populations, and detailed analysis demonstrates that they do not occur for everyone in late modern societies. While the exact cause of such variations are not well understood, such findings invite social hypotheses, social factors such as diet, activity patterns, and experience-based stress have been proposed as playing a role in accounting for such outcomes.

The general notion of roles as components of social systems has been given new specificity and timeliness through the explicit analysis of the life course as a social institution. Martin Kohli was a leader in articulating the "institutionalization of the life course." This notion referred to the expansion of a set of social institutions based on age-specific characteristics (from daycare centers to nursing homes) designed to process individuals from birth to death. Such a notion makes explicit that the life course (with its putative age-graded needs and characteristics) is itself a social institution that defines the character of "normal aging," but, again, in a historically specific and rather arbitrary way. There is nothing "natural" about having teenagers' activities structured by school curricula any more than it was "natural" for Native American teenagers of three centuries ago to hunt buffalo on the northern plains of North America. Despite this historical and social myopia, which Matilda Riley has called "cohort-centrism," the force of such institutions define what is normal and natural with regard to age; thus, they also can operate as self-fulfilling prophecies in shaping the patterns of aging of the individuals who are processed through them.

Social theories of population patterns

Some outcomes studied by demographers, political economists, and others cannot be conceptualized at the individual level. By focusing on the intersection of social change and age-related population patterns, and on "cohort flow" (Riley and Foner)—the movement of entire cohorts through the age-graded institutions of a social system over time—it is possible to discover features of population aging that may be reflected in, yet are not reducible to, the level of individual experience. Such analyses take the entire cohort as the unit of analysis. One well-known example of such work focuses on aspects of cohort transition behavior, and more specifically on the phenomenon of compression (see Hagestad and Neugarten, 1976), leading to more strongly and clearly defined life-course transitions within and between individuals. For example, during the twentieth century, the span of time in which the discrete life events that mark the transition to adulthood (e.g, leaving school, entering the workforce, marrying) occurred was reduced dramatically, and succeeding cohorts underwent these transitions at an increasingly similar chronological age (see Hogan). Thus, cohorts seemed to be moving through major transitions in increasingly lockstep fashion.

Both personological and social explanations have been advanced for such trends. Personological explanation locates the effective casual force at the individual level, in the characteristics or agency of individual actors. (Dannefer and Uhlenberg). One noted personological explanation assumes that, as prosperity increased in the United States during the twentieth century, members of each succeeding cohort were increasingly able to implement a life plan of their own choosing, and the increasingly standardized behavior thus reflects the existence of similar underlying preferences. For example, greater economic resources permit more years of education and earlier age of marriage for more people. The sociological explanation focuses on social-policy-based incentives and normative pressures leading to the same outcome. As age-graded institutions designed to standardize the life course expanded their scope to broader and broader segments of the population through policies (e.g., compulsory education and retirement) and a through a growing normative sense of "age-appropriateness," the transition behavior of individuals became more and more regimented to respond to the resulting structures of opportunity and status. Given the dynamic quality of human decision-making, it is difficult to disprove definitively either of these proposed explanations—even though the idea of choice leading to greater conformity seems, at best, paradoxical. A current apparent reversal in these demographic trends has been interpreted as a "deinstitutionalization" of the life course—resulting from or reflecting late modern economic, technological, and policy changes.

As its name implies, the *political economy approach* has focused on the distribution of resources among age strata or cohorts. In the United States and in Europe, many such analyses examine the role of policy in altering or reinforcing the distribution of resources. Another cohort characteristic that has received growing attention over the past decade is the distribution of resources within birth cohorts. This question has been of particular interest since it has been shown that inequality among age peers appears greater among older adults than among other age groups, and it appears to increase systematically as members of a cohort age. Again, both personological and social explanations have been advanced, but in both cases the nature of the explanation is different than in the transition case. The personological explanation is based on an assumption of fixed individual differences in, for example, personality or health that become ac-

centuated over time and that may have an impact on work preferences or earning power, so that differences that were present early become even more pronounced. The social explanation, by contrast, is based on institutional and other social-interactional processes that tend to encourage cumulation of advantage, and also cumulation of disadvantage. Quoting the Gospel of Matthew (and misstating the intent of Jesus' words), Robert Merton called this general process the *Matthew effect*: "To him that hath, more shall be given, but to him that hath not, that shall be taken away, even that he hath." Within the political economy or other Marxist traditions, such a process might be better termed *capital accumulation*. Adjudication of the competing explanations is difficult in this case as well. However, the close tracking of changes in resource distributions with policy changes provide at least some support for a structural explanation for changes in income inequality. The general structural argument here also links such a macroanalysis back to micro-level approaches, which also describe a cyclical, cumulative process, such as labelling theory.

Age as a cultural construct and the study of age as a cultural practice

At several points, the above discussion has alluded to value differences in the meaning of age, or in the degree of age awareness. Social scientists who study culture recognize such differences as problems to be explained. But, in this case, age is a characteristic of neither a person nor a collectivity, but of culture, of the symbolic apparatus of a social order. Thus, modernization theory provides an example of a tradition of work in which societies are distinguished based on the relative status of various age groups within them; age is thus seen as a property of a status system that can be explained by broader aspects of the prevailing value system. Subsequent work debated the relative contributions of values, technology, economics, and demography in producing the observed differences—and the debate continues.

In his important book on age norms, *How Old Are You?: Age Consciousness in American Culture* (1989), Howard Chudacoff proposed that societies not only differ in how they value age, but in how much awareness they have of age. He traces the rise of what he calls *age consciousness* in the United States over the past century, explaining it on the basis of a combination of changes in education, work policies, and institutions, and a growing emphasis on both age and age-appropriateness in public depictions of age—depictions that were disseminated by an increasingly centralized and influential set of media institutions.

Taking seriously the implications of either the historical relativization of Chudacoff and Achenbaum or the cultural relativization of Cowgill and Holmes requires theorists of age to confront the circumstance that no aspect of age can be understood and studied apart from concepts that have been constructed, however rigorously, by scholars who are themselves actors located in social and historical space—with their own sets of taken-for-granted assumptions. This recognition requires that an adequate theorizing of age cannot avoid a mobilization of the sociology and anthropology of knowledge. From this vantage point, one can readily understand the youth-glorifying and socially uncritical acceptance of the "mutual withdrawal" of society and its older members that was presented in disengagement theory: such a view has an "elective affinity" with the pervasiveness of those same characteristics throughout North American culture in the 1950s and 1960s. But many of its effects are more subtle. One example is the longstanding neglect of questions concerning systematic changes in inequality, which were suppressed by the underlying assumptions of organismic theories rooted in an evolutionary model, and which themselves were argued to resonate with an age-graded bureaucratic order. Such theories tend to assume that aging can be best characterized by describing the modal or normative aspects of a population and treating variation as random, rather than as an opportunity to study the constitutive interaction between aging and other factors. Since such analyses suggest that participation in a wider society and culture frames the theorizing of virtually every scholar, it particularly behooves scholars of aging to engage regularly in the practice of self-critical reflexivity as an effort to understand how their operating assumptions reflect their own biographical experience.

Summary

In sum, then, age is a characteristic of individuals, but it can also be treated as a characteristic of both populations and of social and cultural systems. While these are analytically distinct phenomena, they are related. Consequently, the explanations of age-related outcomes have some commonality across these different types of outcomes. While few dispute that social forces play a significant role in producing age-related outcomes, the precise magnitude of that role and the mechanisms through which social effects occur are difficult to specify with precision. Thus, whatever the specific phenomenon being studied, debates involving the potency of these social theories of aging are likely to continue for some time to come.

DALE DANNEFER

See also AGE; AGE NORMS; DISENGAGEMENT; LIFE COURSE; STATUS OF OLDER PEOPLE: MODERNIZATION.

BIBLIOGRAPHY

BAUMAN, Z. *Liquid Modernity.* Malden, Mass.: Blackwell, 2000.

CHUDACOFF, H. *How Old Are You?: Age Consciousness in American Culture.* Princeton, N.J.: Princeton University Press, 1989.

COWGILL, D. O., and HOLMES, L. D. *Aging and Modernization.* New York: Meredith Corporation, 1972.

CUMMING, E., and HENRY, W. E. *Growing Old.* New York: Basic Books, 1961.

DANNEFER, D. "Aging As Intracohort Differentiation: Accentuation, the Matthew Effect, and the Life Course." *Sociological Forum* 2 (1987): 211–235.

DANNEFER, D. "Differential Gerontology and the Stratified Life Course: Conceptual and Methodological Issues." In *Annual Review of Gerontology and Geriatrics,* Vol. 8. Edited by G. L. Maddox and M. P. Lawton. New York: Springer. 1988. Pages 3–36.

DANNEFER, D., and UHLENBERG, P. "Paths of the Life Course: A Typology." In *Handbook of Theories of Aging.* Edited by V. L. Bengston and K. W. Schale. New York: Springer, 1999.

EASTERLIN, R. *Birth and Fortune.* New York: Basic Books, 1980.

ELDER, G. H., JR. *Children of the Great Depression.* Boulder, Colo.: Westview Press, 1998.

ELDER, G. H., JR., and LIKER, J. "Hard Times in Women's Lives: Historical Differences across 40 Years." *American Journal of Sociology* 58 (1982): 241–269.

HOGAN, D. *Transitions and Social Change: The Early Lives of American Men.* New York: Academic Press, 1981.

KATZ, S. *Disciplining Old Age: The Formation of Gerontological Knowledge.* Charlottesville, Va.: University of Virginia Press, 1996.

KUYPERS, J., and BENGTSON, V. L. "Perspectives On The Older Family." In *Independent Aging: Family and Social Systems Perspectives.* Edited by W. H. Quinn and C. A. Houghston. Rockville, Md.: Aspen Systems, 1984.

MORSS, J. R. *The Biologising of Childhood: Developmental Psychology and the Darwinian Myth.* East Sussex, U.K.: Lawrence Erlbaum, 1990.

NEUGARTEN, B. L., and HAGESTAD, G. O. "Age and the Life Course." In *Handbook of Aging and the Social Sciences.* Edited by R. H. Binstock and E. Shanas. New York: Van Nostrand Reinhold, 1976. Pages 35–55.

RILEY, M. W.; JOHNSON, M. E.; and FONER, A. *Aging and Society*, Vol. III: *A Sociology of Age Stratification.* New York: Russell Sage, 1972.

RILEY, M. W.; KAHN, R. L.; and FONER, A. *Age and Structural Lag: Society's Failure to Provide Meaningful Opportunities for Work, Family and Leisure.* New York: Wiley-Interscience, 1972.

WARING, J. "Social Replenishment and Social Change." *American Behavioral Scientist* 19 (1975): 237–256.

TIP-OF-THE-TONGUE PHENOMENON

See MEMORY

TOUCH, SENSE OF

Sensations of touch arise by the activation of sensory receptors located in the skin that are responsive to mechanical stimuli. *Proprioception,* the perception of the position and movement of the limbs of the body, arises as a result of neural activity in sensory receptors located in and around the muscles underneath the skin. Advancing age is associated with diminished functioning of sensory systems, and the cutaneous and proprioceptive senses are no exception. For example, the ability to detect mechanical disturbances on the skin, such as those produced by a vibrating probe, and the ability to discriminate changes in the spatial patterns of stimulation of the skin, such as those produced by introducing a spatial gap between two objects pressed against the skin, tend to decline with age. An elderly person who has difficulty with the perception of the position and movement of limbs, or who has problems in moving quickly and accurately, may be experiencing an age-related decline in proprioception. The effects of aging on tactile sensitivity and proprioception can best be understood in light of what is known about the anatomy and physiology of receptors and how they conduct neural information about tactile and proprioceptive stimuli to the brain.

The sensory receptors for touch and proprioception are complex in structure, but the basic organization is that of a neuron that has an ending, endings responsible for mechano-electric transduction. Once the mechanical stimulus is transduced into an electrical impulse, the neuron transmits this information very quickly to the spinal cord and then to the brain. Information arising from the mechanoreceptors of the body and face goes to specific regions within the brain that interpret the signals in terms of tactile perceptions. The cortical regions devoted to this function have many independent representations of the body surface.

Many types of mechanical stimuli are used to understand how the tactile and proprioceptive systems work. For example, mechanical stimuli produced by pins or probes applied perpendicularly or tangentially to the skin have been used to determine the basic properties of the transduction of mechanical stimuli to electrochemical neural responses, as well as the subsequent transmission of these neural responses to the central nervous system. These stimuli indent the skin and can be either of a vibratory nature or of the ramp-and-hold variety. Vibratory stimuli are delivered by a probe that moves the skin at a particular amplitude and frequency of oscillation. Ramp-and-hold stimuli consist of an initial dynamic (ramp) indentation of the skin by the probe, followed by static (hold) indentation of the probe until it is withdrawn. The rate and depth of the initial ramp indentation and the duration of the hold state can be varied widely, as can the rate of withdrawal. Other types of stimuli that have been used to understand taction include periodic and aperiodic gratings moved across the skin surface, airpuffs, embossed letters, and everyday items such as sandpaper, cloth, and steel wool.

The classification of mechanoreceptors both in the periphery and in the central nervous system is based on the receptor's responses to ramp-and-hold-like stimuli. Mechanoreceptors have been found to be either fast adapting (FA) or slowly adapting (SA). Here, adaptation refers to the rate of decline in neural activity with time in response to ramp-and-hold-like stimuli. There are two subclasses of FA and SA mechanoreceptors: FA I and FA II, and SA I and SA II. It has been fairly well established that the FA Is are the Meissner corpuscles and the hair receptors, the FA IIs are the Pacinian corpuscles, the SA Is are the Merkel cell-neurite complexes and the touch pads and the SA IIs are the Ruffini endings. They are defined historically. One could use the phrasiology-corpuscles first discovered by Meisser, corpuscles described by Pacini and the cell-neurite complexes as shown by Merkel. Ruffini was the first to show the existence of another tactile ending.

In psychophysical tasks involving the detection of vibration on the skin, it is possible, by carefully choosing the frequency of vibration, the size of the stimulus, and the site of stimulation, to examine the effects of aging on each of four information processing channels designated as the P, NP I, NP II, and NP III channels. Each of these channels has, as its input stage, one of the four receptor types described above. Experiments on the effects of aging have revealed that the sensitivity of each channel declines with age, especially for the P channel, a finding that can be explained by understanding the functional and structural characteristics of the channels.

At the level of the peripheral nervous system, the inputs to the P channel are FA II nerve fibers of Pacinian corpuscles. This channel is extremely sensitive at the optimal frequency of vibration of 250 Hz, with psychophysical thresholds in young adults being as low as 0.1 micrometers in the amplitude of vibration required to be detected. The exquisite sensitivity of the P channel is attributed partially to the capacity of this channel for spatial summation, which is the improvement in sensitivity that results as the size of the stimulus is increased, activating an increasing number of sensory receptors. The other three information-processing channels, NP I, NP II, and NP III, with their inputs from FAI, SA II, and SA I peripheral nerve fibers, respectively, are less sensitive than the P channel, mainly due to their inability to exhibit spatial summation. The fact that the deleterious effects of aging are substantially greater in the P channel than in any of the three NP channels is due, in part, to this unique capacity for spatial summation. Specifically, as people age, mechanoreceptors die, resulting in a progressive reduction in receptor density that becomes profound by about sixty-five or seventy years of age. Because one mechanism of spatial summation in the P channel is the integration of neural activity over a large number of receptors, the reduction in the density of Pacinian corpuscles has a particularly severe effect on sensitivity. Reduced neural input to the central nervous system from receptors—resulting from a reduction in the number of Pacinian corpuscles—results in elevated detection thresholds in older individuals. The smaller loss of sensitivity with aging found in the NP channels is thought to be due to the fact that the sensitivities of these channels, which are not dependent on spatial summation, are less affected by the reduction of receptor density.

Other factors associated with aging known to affect tactile sensitivity include changes in the physical properties of skin (such as reduced skin compliance) and changes in the peripheral and central nervous systems, resulting in some cases from a reduced blood supply to neurons, which can be due to a variety of vascular problems, including atherosclerosis. At a practical level, a decreased touch sensitivity in elderly individuals can cause a wide range of problems, including the inability to recognize objects by touch and an impaired ability to detect an object that has come into contact with the skin.

Proprioception is mediated by proprioceptors that are located in muscles and joints. The proprioceptive endings are: (1) the muscle spindles located in the muscles themselves, (2) Golgi tendon organs, which attach the muscles to bone, and (3) joint capsules that contain a group of endings similar in structure to the tactile receptors. The decline in proprioception in older individuals is often manifested in dramatic effects on motor performance, including very long reaction times and inaccurate and highly variable motor responses, such as those involved in walking, picking up objects, and driving a car. Of course, a decline in motor performance may result from factors other than, or in addition to, the loss of sensory feedback provided to the brain by proprioceptors. For example, motor performance may decline as a result of impairment of the brain areas associated with movement, cognition, and balance.

GEORGE A. GESCHEIDER
STANLEY J. BOLANOWSKI

See also BALANCE, SENSE OF; MOTOR PERFORMANCE; SKIN.

BIBLIOGRAPHY

BOLANOWSKI, S. J.; GESCHEIDER, G. A.; VERRILLO, R. T.; and CHECKOSKY, C. M. "Four Channels Mediate the Mechanical Aspects of Touch." *Journal of the Acoustical Society of America* 84 (1988): 1680–1694.

CAUNA, N. "The Effects of Aging on the Receptor Organs of the Human Dermis." In *Advances in Biology of the Skin,* Vol. 6 *Aging.* Edited by W. Montagna. Elmsford, N.Y.: Pergamon Press, 1965. Pages 63–96.

GESCHEIDER, G. A.; BOLANOWSKI, S. J.; HALL, K. L.; HOFFMAN, K.; and VERRILLO, R. T. "The Effects of Aging on Information Processing Channels in the Sense of Touch: Absolute Sensitivity." *Somatosensory and Motor Research* 11 (1994): 345–357.

STEVENS, J. C., and PATTERSON, M. Q. "Dimensions of Spatial Acuity in the Touch Sense: Changes over the Life Span." *Somatosensory and Motor Research* 12 (1995): 29–47.

VERRILLO, R. T., and VIOLET, V. "Sensory and Perceptual Performance." In *Aging and Human Performance.* Edited by N. Charness. Chichester, U.K.: Wiley, 1985. Pages 1–46.

TREMOR

Tremors are involuntary, purposeless movements of a body part around a fixed plane in space. A tremor can be classified on the basis of whether it occurs with a certain posture, at rest, or during movement. It can be localized to the affected body part and characterized by what makes the tremor better or worse.

A physiological tremor is a variation of what is normal while a pathological tremor is not. The two most common types of pathological tremors are essential tremors and tremors associated with Parkinson's disease. In addition, disease in the cerebellum of the brain may also cause a tremor of intention (i.e., with movement). Other less common causes of tremor include alcohol withdrawal or diseases of the peripheral nerves.

An essential tremor is also known as a benign tremor. It is about ten to twenty times more common than the tremor of Parkinson's disease. It is most noticeable when a person holds their hands outstretched or makes fine movements. By contrast with the tremor of Parkinson's disease, essential tremor tends to disappear when the hands and arms are relaxed. Sixty percent of essential tremors are inherited and are known as familial tremors.

Parkinson's disease occurs in about 1 percent of people aged sixty-five years or older, increases to 2.5 percent of persons over eighty years of age. The hallmark of Parkinson's disease is an asymmetrical tremor that occurs at rest. A relatively low frequency and medium amplitude characterize the tremor. Classically, it is described as a pill rolling tremor of the hands (a term of distant origin, referring to the days when pharmacists made pills on site) yet it can also affect the chin. Typically, this tremor only rarely affects the neck or voice. This tremor diminishes with purposeful movements and therefore it usually does not cause motor disability. Parkinson's disease does not evolve from essential tremors.

Cerebellar tremors tend to be related to movement and increase in severity as the extremity approaches its target, often resulting in the extremity moving part of its object (so-called pist points) and having to rely on visual input ultimately to find the target. They are associated with other signs of cerebellar malfunction such as abnormalities of gait, speech, and eye movements. A postural tremor may also be associated with damage to the cerebellum. Causes of cerebellar postural tremor are diseases like multiple sclerosis, tumors, stroke or nonspecific neurodegenerative disease of the brain.

Drugs used for treatment of essential tremor include beta-adrenergic blockers, benzodiazepines, or anticonvulsants. Small doses of alcohol have been found to provide temporary relief of essential tremors although excess alcohol intake is strongly discouraged and can make them worse, especially as the blood level is reduced.. Replacement of dopamine is used for treatment of Parkinson's disease and therapy can be augmented with anticholinergic agents or dopamine agonists. Thalamotomy (or the surgical disruption of a deep brain structure known as the thalamus) is a surgical procedure used to treat patients with severe, drug resistant essential tremor or patients with Parkinson's disease who have severe, disabling, predominantly unilateral tremor. Pallidotomy (surgical destruction of the globus pallidus) is an alternative to thalamotomy in the treatment of parkinsonian tremor. Implantation of an electrode in the thalamus can suppress some tremors. All surgical therapies should only be considered for patients who have debilitating symptoms that persist despite adequate medical therapy.

Tremor is an important sign in aging, which can occur in the absence of disease. Although, sometimes embarassing, essential tremor on its own is neither disabling nor a sign of impending brain disease.

PHILIP E. LEE
B. LYNN BEATTIE

See also PARKINSONISM.

BIBLIOGRAPHY

ADAMS, R. D.; VICTOR, M.; and ROPPER, A. H. "Tremor, Myoclonus, Focal Dystonias and Tics." *Principles of Neurology*, 6th ed. New York: McGraw-Hill, 1997. Pages 94–113.

ALPERS, B. J., and MANCALL, E. L. "Interpretation of Neurological Symptoms and Signs." *Essentials of the Neurological Examination*. Philadelphia, Pa.: F. A. Davis Co., 1971. Pages 68–69.

ANOUTI, A., and KOLLER, W. C. "Tremor Disorders: Diagnosis and Management." *Western Journal of Medicine* 162, no. 6 (June 1995): 510–513.

CHARLES, P. D.; ESPER, G. J.; DAVIS, T. L.; MACIUNAS, R. J.; and ROBERTSON, D. "Classification of Tremor and Update on Treatment." *American Family Physician* 59, no. 6 (15 March 1999): 1565–1572.

FAUCI, A. S., et al. *Harrison's Principles of Internal Medicine*, 14th ed. New York: McGraw-Hill, 1998. Pages 2356, 2359.

HALLETT, M. "Classification and Treatment of Tremor." *Journal of the American Medical Association* 266, no. 8 (1991): 1115–1117.

LAITINEN, L. V. "Pallidotomy for Parkinson's Disease." *Neurosurgery Clinics of North America* 6 (1995): 105–112.

LOUIS E. D.; OTTMAN R.; and HAUSER W. A. "How Common Is the Most Common Adult Movement Disorder? Estimates of Essential Tremor Throughout the World." *Movement Disorder* 13 (1998): 5–10.

UITTI, R. J. "Tremor: How To Determine if the Patient Has Parkinson's Disease." *Geriatrics* (May 1998): 30–36.

YAHR, M. D., and PANG, S. W. H. "Movement Disorders" (Chapter 84). In *The Merck Manual of Geriatrics*. Edited by William B. Abrams and Robert Berkow. Whitehouse Station, N.J.: Merck and Co. Inc., 1990. Pages 981–982.

TUBE FEEDING

Tube feeding is an optional medical treatment to deliver nutrition when a patient lacks the ability to eat or swallow independently. The most common device used for long-term tube feeding in the institutionalized older population is the percutaneous endoscopic gastrostomy (PEG) tube. A PEG tube is placed directly into the stomach through a small hole in the skin during a simple procedure requiring only mild sedation and local anesthetic. A jejunostomy tube (J-tube) is similar to a PEG tube but is used less often. A J-tube delivers food into the first part of the small intestine rather than the stomach. If it is anticipated that tube feeding will be needed for less than two weeks, a temporary tube may be placed through the nose into the stomach (nasogastric tube), but this route is usually inappropriate for long-term use. Once a feeding tube is placed, commercially prepared liquid food, designed to provide a balanced diet, is delivered to the patient through the tube.

The most common reasons that tube feeding is used in U.S. nursing homes are advanced dementia (52 percent), stroke (24 percent), Parkinson's disease (9 percent), and malignancy (7 percent) (Kaw and Sekas). In situations where the underlying condition causing the swallowing problem is potentially reversible, such as an acute stroke, the feeding tube may be indicated for only a short time. For chronic conditions where the underlying condition is unlikely to improve (e.g., dementia or Parkinson's disease), tube feeding is a long-term intervention.

The insertion of a feeding tube is relatively safe. Although local bleeding, infection, dislodgment, or bowel perforation can occur, these complications are unusual and rarely life-threatening. More common adverse effects of tube feeding among older persons include electrolyte disturbances, diarrhea, and agitation leading to the use of restraints or administration of psychotropic medications.

Although dementia is the leading diagnostic condition for use of a feeding tube among older patients, there is limited evidence to support its use in this setting (Finucane et al.; Gillick). Eating problems generally occur at the very end stages of dementia, and the decision to initiate tube feeding rather than adopt a palliative approach can be difficult. Unfortunately, there are no randomized controlled trials of tube feeding to guide this decision. However, a review of the best available evidence failed to find an association between tube feeding and survival in the nursing home population (Mitchell and Tetroe). Data from nonrandomized studies also indicate that the placement of a feeding tube in older patients will not prevent aspiration (Finacare and Bynum). Tube feeding has not been shown to improve nutritional status, nutritional markers, or the clinical consequences of malnutrition, such as pressure ulcers in demented patients with eating problems. Finally, tube feeding has not been found to improve the comfort, functional status, or quality of life in this population.

Due to the lack of proven benefits of tube feeding, experts advocate the judicious use of hand-feeding in older patients with dementia whenever possible. For less debilitated older patients with eating problems, ethical decision-making requires weighing the potential risks and benefits of tube feeding in the specific situation with the values and preferences of the patient.

SUSAN L. MITCHELL

See also ALZHEIMER'S DISEASE; DEMENTIA; ETHICAL ISSUES; LONG-TERM CARE ETHICS; SWALLOWING.

BIBLIOGRAPHY

FINUCANE, T. E., and BYNUM, J. P. W. "Use of Feeding Tubes to Prevent Aspiration Pneumonia." *The Lancet* 348 (1996): 1421–1424.

FINUCANE, T. E.; CHRISTMAS, C.; and TRAVIS, K. "Tube Feeding in Patients with Advanced Dementia: A Review of the Evidence." *Journal of the American Medical Association* 282 (1999): 1365–1370.

GILLICK, M. R. "Rethinking the Role of the Tube Feeding in Patients with Advanced Dementia." *New England Journal of Medicine* 342 (2000): 206–210.

KAW, M., and SEKAS, G. "Long-Term Follow-up of Consequences of Percutaneous Endoscopic Gastrostomy (PEG) Tubes in Nursing Home Patients." *Digestive Diseases and Sciences* 39 (1994): 738–743.

MITCHELL, S. L., and TETROE, J. M. "Survival After Percutaneous Endoscopic Gastrostomy Placement." *Journal of Gerontology: Medical Sciences* 55A (2000): M735–M739.

TWITCHES

Twitches are brief, sudden, and fine contractions caused by electrical impulses that stimulate muscle fiber activity. Some twitches are under voluntary control, but most are involuntary. Twitches have been called muscle jerks, spasms, and fasciculations, and these terms are often used interchangeably.

Fibrillation is a contraction of a single muscle fiber. It occurs when the muscle fiber loses electrical stimulation from the nervous system. A fibrillation is not visible through the skin. This spontaneous activity often goes unnoticed and it is usually harmless. In rare instances it can be associated with inflammatory diseases of the muscle, such as polymyositis.

Fasciculation, a contraction of a group of muscle fibers that makes up a motor unit, is caused by nerve irritability. Fasciculation is seen in many older adults and most often involves the muscles of the thighs, calves, or hands. It can be chronic, lasting for days, weeks, or even years without any progression or evidence of underlying disease. When fasciculation is associated with muscle weakness or wasting, the likelihood of an underlying problem with the neuromuscular system—such as amyotrophic lateral sclerosis—increases.

Myoclonus is a rapid, brief contraction of either a proximal or a distal muscle in a nonrhythmic manner that results in movement of a body part. The most common type of myoclonus occurs in people as they are drifting off to sleep. The presence of this type of myoclonus does not imply disease. Myoclonus can be inherited in families or occur spontaneously in otherwise healthy subjects. More generalized myoclonus can occur in patients with diseases such as epilepsy or certain rare neurodegenerative disorders such as Creutzfeldt-Jakob disease. Myoclonic jerking can accompany any severe metabolic disturbance due to respiratory disease, chronic kidney failure, liver failure, or electrolyte disturbances. It can be seen in alcohol and drug withdrawal, or follow severe brain damage due to lack of oxygen to the brain. Myoclonus can be very resistant to treatment, although it may respond to treatment with certain anticonvulsant drugs like valproic acid or to a tranquilizer like clonazepam.

Restless leg syndrome is characterized by numbness and tingling of the calves. This sensation is difficult to describe, but it often causes the irresistible urge to move the legs. The symptom occurs most frequently in the evening, and it can cause significant sleep disturbance when severe. It seems to be aggravated by sleep deprivation or stress. Restless leg syndrome overlaps with a disorder known as periodic leg movements or nocturnal myoclonus. Periodic leg movements can involve the whole leg or smaller portions. The person is usually unaware of these movements, and often sleeps through them. There is an association between both disorders and increasing age, although the exact mechanism is not well understood. Medical treatments that have been tried include medications used for Parkinson's disease, opiates, and tranquilizers.

PHILIP E. LEE
B. LYNN BEATTIE

See also DECONDITIONING; SARCOPENIA.

BIBLIOGRAPHY

ALPERS, B. J., and MANCALL, E. L. *Essentials of the Neurological Examination.* Philadelphia, PA: F. A. Davis, 1971. Pages 68–69.

BLIWISE, D. L. "Sleep Disorders." In *Oxford Textbook of Geriatric Medicine,* 2d ed. New York: Oxford Medical Publications, 2000. Pages 754–756.

BROWN, D. D., and DEGOWN, R. L. *Diagnostic Examination.* Edited by Richard L. Degowin. Toronto, Canada: Collier Macmillan Canada, 1981. Pages 794–795.

EISEN, A. "Motor Neurone Disease (Amyotrophic Lateral Sclerosis)." In *Oxford Textbook of Geriatric Medicine,* 2d ed. New York: Oxford Medical Publications, 2000. Pages 791–792.

FAUCI A. S., et al. *Harrison's Principles of Internal Medicine.* 14th ed. New York: McGraw-Hill, 1998. Pages 114–2279.

Periodic Paralysis Association. "The PPA Online." www.periodicparalysis.org

U

URINARY INCONTINENCE

Urinary incontinence may affect as many as two hundred million people around the world. Urinary incontinence is not well understood by those affected, or by health care workers. It is not a dangerous condition, but it has a huge influence on the sufferer's quality of life. The International Continence Society, established in 1970, defines urinary incontinence as a condition where involuntary loss of urine is a social or hygienic problem and is objectively demonstrated

Prevalence

Reports of the prevalence of urinary incontinence in women vary because of differences in the definition of urinary incontinence, the study samples, and underreporting due to variation in the methodology of surveys. The condition is more common in women. Systematic reviews conclude that there is a community prevalence of 20 to 30 percent in young adults, 30 to 40 percent in middle-aged women and 30 to 50 percent in elderly women. In long-term care institutions, the prevalence is higher. If incontinence severity is considered, however, the prevalence of bothersome or significant incontinence (i.e., that which is severe enough to have a significant impact on a person's quality of life) is between 5 and 10 percent of the community. Initial data suggests that the prevalence is higher in caucasian women; though prevalence in noncaucasian women worldwide requires further study.

There is little information on the proportions of types of urinary incontinence. There are very few incidence studies, and remission may occur either naturally or with treatment. Urinary incontinence is more prevalent during pregnancy and following childbirth, menopause, and hysterectomy. Obesity, lower urinary tract symptoms (e.g., blood in the urine, urine cloudiness, and foul smelling urine or urinary burning), and problems with mobility (functional impairment) or thinking (cognitive impairment) are associated with urinary incontinence. The prevalence of urinary incontinence in men is half that of women and rises more gradually with age. In the United States alone, the economic impact of this condition has been estimated at 18 billion dollars per year, including costs for nursing hours, surgery investigations, pads, and devices for containing incontinence.

Neurological control

The urinary bladder, and the urethral sphincter (a muscular band around the urethra that prevents urine flow) are the two lower urinary tract structures, that together with the supporting muscular pelvic floor, are important for control of urination. Their functions are regulated by coordinated peripheral, autonomic (involuntary), and central (voluntary) nervous system control. The two phases of lower urinary tract function—urine storage and voiding (emptying)—are controlled by urine storage and voiding reflexes. In an infant, during urine storage, the bladder relaxes with filling and the sphincter, under autonomic nervous system control, remains closed. At a certain level of filling, a primitive spinal reflex causes sphincter relaxation and simultaneous bladder (detrusor) contraction, resulting in voiding of urine through the urethra. With maturation of the central nervous system pathways, continence is learned, with inhibition of the primitive spinal reflexes by voluntary control through the frontal cerebral cortex.

Causes of incontinence

The compression of pelvic nerves and the stretching of the pelvic floor during vaginal delivery can result in neuromuscular damage. The function of the urethral sphincter may thus be compromised, contributing to the higher prevalence of stress urinary incontinence (SUI; loss of urine with stress maneuvers such as coughing, laughing, or sneezing) in women who have had many children, compared with women who have had none. Aging and/or diseases that affect the peripheral, autonomic, or central nervous system control of continence, can also result in urinary incontinence. Some older men and women lose cerebral cortical control for unclear reasons, resulting in an unstable, "overactive" bladder (so called idiopathic detrusor instability). This condition is manifested by urinary urgency (e.g., the sudden need to void) and urgency incontinence.

Diseases affecting the cerebral cortex, such as strokes and multiple sclerosis, may result in bladder overactivity (detrusor hyperreflexia) because of central nervous system involvement. Diseases that affect the midbrain or spinal cord, such as multiple sclerosis and spinal cord injury, interfere with the coordination of sphincter relaxation during voiding. This loss of synchronization of sphincter relaxation with bladder contraction is termed *detrusor-urethral dyssynergia*, and results in voiding that is uncoordinated and incomplete.

Interference of bladder sensory nerves due to long-standing diabetes or physical injury to the pelvic motor nerves may result in loss of bladder sensation or contractility of the detrusor muscle. This causes the bladder to contract poorly, resulting in incomplete emptying of the bladder and urine retention. Obstruction to the flow of urine from the bladder commonly occurs in elderly men due to prostatic gland enlargement. Narrowing of the urethra (*urethral stricture*) in men or women can also cause physical obstruction to urine flow, resulting in urinary retention and overflow incontinence. In older men, radical surgery for prostate cancer can interfere with sphincteric urinary control. However, urgency urinary incontinence is the most common type of incontinence in men, with lower urinary tract symptoms, functional and cognitive impairment, prostatectomy and urological conditions as recognized risk factors. This condition can be a symptom of an enlarged prostate.

In developing countries where health care resources are scarce, maternal birth injury due to obstructed labor is not uncommon. Injury to the urethra, bladder, and vagina can result in the formation of fistula, which are abnormal tracts that connect the bladder or urethra directly with the vagina, resulting in constant uncontrolled urine loss. For women affected, this is a devastating complication.

Post-menopausal estrogen decline may cause changes in the urogenital tract, especially shrinkage (atrophy) of supporting tissue. With age, pelvic muscle function is reduced and pelvic tissues lose elasticity. Obesity in older women increases abdominal pressure and may be a contributing factor to SUI.

Assessment

A detailed continence history, bladder diary, physical examination, and measurement of residual urine in the bladder after voiding are components of a continence assessment. Commonly questions are asked about congenital abnormalities, attainment of continence, previous urinary tract infections, obstetric history, neurologic diseases, and previous gynecologic surgery. Some medications have an adverse influence on lower urinary tract function and may promote incontinence. Questions about the quality, type, and timing of fluid intake over a twenty-four hour period; and about smoking, bowel pattern of function, sexual function, and quality of life, can identify reversible lifestyle factors. A one-week bladder diary captures frequency of voiding and wet (incontinent) events. A bladder diary can be repeated after treatment to show objective improvement. If continence pads are used, the number and type are noted. In some instances, measurement of the voided volume is helpful. The loss of urine with stress maneuvers such as coughing, sneezing, or exercise, or loss of urine with urgency may suggest the underlying mechanism of incontinence. Sometimes these symptoms occur together.

In women, the physical examination includes vaginal inspection for signs of post-menopausal estrogen deficiency, pelvic organ prolapse, urogenital fistula, and assessment of voluntary contraction of the muscular pelvic floor. In men, digital rectal examination assesses the size, symmetry, and consistency of the prostate gland, and the examination helps rule out prostate cancer.

Neurologic examination rules out diseases such as stroke, multiple sclerosis, and Parkinson's disease, and also assesses the nerve and muscular function of the anal sphincter and sacral sensation. Mental state and mobility are also assessed in the elderly. The former will rule out dementia and assess the person's ability to learn behavioral interventions.

Any urine remaining in the bladder after voiding is usually abnormal and can be measured by passing a catheter in and out through the urethra. Noninvasive assessment can be done by ultrasound examination of the bladder. Further in-depth assessment of the bladder and urethral structure may be indicated using a cystoscope inserted into the bladder through the urethra. The coordinated function of the bladder and urethra may be evaluated by further sophisticated urodynamic tests. These tests are indicated if there is no improvement with conservative behavioral interventions and drug therapy, or if surgery is contemplated.

Management

Attention to lifestyle issues is an essential part of management. A fluid intake of approximately 1,500 mls in twenty-four hours is usually an adequate amount, except in very warm environmental conditions. Excessive caffeine and alcohol intake will promote urine production and may increase urinary frequency. Fluid intake in the evening or at night may contribute to night-time voiding and incontinence. Smoking promotes coughing and is also associated with SUI. Attention to regular bowel function and avoidance of constipation is important.

Behavioral interventions may be effective in reducing or resolving urinary incontinence. These include timed voiding (bladder retraining) and pelvic muscle exercises. Pelvic muscle exercises can strengthen and improve the responsiveness of the pelvic floor and external sphincter. If the pelvic muscles are contracted rapidly during episodes of urinary urgency, the urgency may be suppressed. Biofeedback and electrostimulation are other modalities that have been tried for various types of incontinence with varying success.

Medications that relax or reduce bladder-muscle overactivity are often effective in reduc-

ing urinary urgency and urge incontinence. Side effects such as dry mouth or urinary retention may limit their use in some people, however. For overflow incontinence, medications that reduce the sphincter tone may improve bladder emptying. Intermittent catheterization two to three times per day or, rarely, an indwelling catheter, are appropriate options. Surgery in men to relieve prostatic obstruction that doesn't respond to medication is often indicated. In women, estrogen replacement for symptoms of estrogen deficiency may reduce urinary urgency or frequency. For urogenital prolapse, vaginal support devices (pessaries) can resolve the prolapse, but not necessarily the associated SUI.

Stress urinary incontinence that doesn't respond to behavioral interventions responds to a variety of injectable bulking agents, such as collagen, or surgical procedures in up to 90 percent of women. Five-year follow-up studies of these procedures show some return of incontinence. For bladder-vaginal fistula, surgery is successful in 50 to 100 percent of women. Containment of incontinence may be improved with specially designed absorbent pads or external catheter devices in men.

Prevention

The First International Conference for the Prevention of Incontinence, held in England in 1997, made a number of recommendations, including providing information to the public on healthy bladder habits, on when and how to seek help on supportive toilet training practices and attitudes by parents (and their effect on successful attainment of continence), as well as simply providing information that incontinence can be treated. Relatives of people with existing incontinence are likely a receptive group to target with information on treatment. For example, by age seven, 10 to 16 percent of boys and 5 to 15 percent of girls have bedtime incontinence (nocturnal enuresis). By age twelve, this prevalence is 5 percent in boys and 2 percent in girls. This benign delay in maturation will usually respond to appropriate advice on eating, drinking, regular daytime voiding, and reducing fluid intake later in the day.

For prenatal women, regular pelvic muscle exercises can improve the strength and function of the pelvic floor and may reduce the likelihood of postpartum stress urinary incontinence. Regulation of bowel function with diet, avoidance of constipation or straining during voiding also reduces the likelihood of stress incontinence or the falling down (prolapse) of the bladder or rectum into the vagina. Factors that contribute to maternal birth injury, such as childbearing in adolescent females (when pelvic growth is incomplete) and a lack of obstetrical services that can provide prompt Cesarean section, are potentially preventable.

In summary, urinary incontinence is a complex symptom that results from a variety of causes, requiring careful assessment of the type of incontinence and of contributing factors. Urinary incontinence will respond to a variety of measures. Generally, lifestyle and behavioral interventions, which are noninvasive, should be tried first. A positive message for those with incontinence who have never received assessment or treatment is that incontinence may be resolved, improved, or better contained in all sufferers.

MICHAEL J. BORRIE

See also CONSTIPATION; MENOPAUSE; PROSTATE; SEXUALITY.

BIBLIOGRAPHY

ABRAMS, P.; KHOURY, S.; and WEIN, A. *Incontinence: Proceedings of 1st International Consultation on Incontinence, June 28–July 1, 1998, Monaco.* Plymouth, U.K.: Health Publications Ltd., 1999.

Agency for Health Care Policy and Research. *Urinary Incontinence in Adults: Acute and Chronic Management.* Clinical Practice Guidelines No. 2, 1996 update, AHCPR publication No. 96-0682. Washington D.C.: U.S. Department of Health and Human Services, Agency for Health Care Policy and Research, 1996.

Canadian Continence Foundation. "Clinical Practice Guidelines for Adults." Available on the World Wide Web at www.continence-fdn.ca

URINARY TRACT INFECTION

Infections of the urinary tract are the most frequent bacterial infections identified in older adults. The variation in illnesses that these infections produce is quite wide, and can range from bacteria present in the urine without symptoms (asymptomatic bacteriuria) to infections producing chiefly bladder symptoms (symptomatic urinary tract infections, or UTIs) that spread to the blood (sepsis) and can give rise to complications such as shock and even death. The prevalence of both bacteriuria and symptomatic UTI increases with age (Sobel and Kaye). Bacteriuria is present in 20 percent of older women and 10 percent of older men living in the community (Sobel and Kaye). This prevalence increases to 20–25 percent in both sexes residing in long-term care facilities and to 30–50 percent in hospitalized older adults (Baldassare and Kaye). Although most studies have failed to identify an association between bacteriuria or symptomatic UTI and increased overall mortality in older adults, these infections frequently lead to significant morbidity (Baldassare and Kaye; Nicolle, 1992). Urosepsis (infection in the blood stemming from urinary tract) accounts for up to 56 percent of sepsis in older adults, and mortality can be as high as 25 percent (Richardson; Leibovici et al.). Difficulty in distinguishing between asymptomatic bacteriuria and symptomatic UTI in institutionalized older adults often leads to the unnecessary use of antibiotics and diagnostic testing, with the attendant risks.

Pathogenesis of bacteriuria

Many factors predispose older adults to bacteriuria and symptomatic UTI. In older women, loss of estrogen's protective effect on the genitourinary mucosa results in increased colonization of the vagina with uropathogens (Baldassare and Kaye; Nicolle, 1992). Relaxation of pelvic muscles and the presence of such genitourinary abnormalities as prolapse of the bladder or rectum into the vagina and bladder diverticula outpouching lead to inefficient bladder emptying and allow multiplication of bacteria in the residual urine (Sobel and Kaye; Baldassare and Kaye; Nicolle, 1992). Prostatic hypertrophy in older men leads to outlet obstruction, resulting in increased residual urine volume. Increased prostate size also leads to turbulent flow within the urethra, which facilitates entry of bacteria into the urethra and bladder. The presence of chronic bacterial prostatitis often makes sustained eradication of pathogens from the urine difficult and contributes to the high relapse rate of bacteriuria in treated men (Baldassare and Kay; Marrie et al.). The increased burden of comorbid illness in institutionalized older adults is commonly associated with functional impairment. Immobility and urinary and fecal incontinence contribute to the higher prevalence of bacteriuria and UTI observed in this population (Nicolle, 1993). In addition, the use of indwelling urinary catheters is a significant risk factor for bacteriuria in this population. Even with meticulous catheter care and a closed drainage system, all patients with chronic indwelling catheters eventually become bacteriuric (Nicolle, 1993). Condom catheters are a potential predisposing factor for UTIs in older men and may also lead to soft-tissue infection of the penis (Warren).

Diagnosis and management of UTI

Asymptomatic bacteriuria. Asymptomatic bacteriuria is defined as $\geq 10^5$ bacteria/ml in midstream urine on two confirmatory urine cultures in the absence of urinary tract symptoms (Sobel and Kaye). Clinically the distinction between symptomatic UTI and asymptomatic bacteriuria is often difficult. Asymptomatic bacteriuria in older adults is almost always associated with white cells (pus) in the urine (pyuria), making finding the pyuria nonspecific (i.e., it does not distinguish bacteriuria from infection) (Nicolle, 1992). The high frequency of chronic genitourinary symptoms, such as incontinence, and frequency and urgency of urination, experienced by institutionalized older adults makes the interpretation of a positive urine culture difficult. In other words, it is difficult to know whether the symptoms are those of infection or whether they relate to other diseases of the urinary tract, or even are simply changes associated with aging.

The significance of asymptomatic bacteriuria, and therefore its management, is controversial. Studies performed in both community-dwelling and institutionalized older men and women have failed to demonstrate benefit from identification and treatment of asymptomatic bacteriuria (Sobel and Kaye). In several studies, treatment failed to reduce subsequent symptomatic infections, antimicrobial therapy was associated with adverse side effects, and prolonged eradication of bacteriuria was usually not observed. No differences in mortality have been observed between treated and untreated patients (Baldassare and Kaye; Nicolle, 1992). The use of frequent courses of antibiotics in this population, in an attempt to maintain sterile urine, provokes the emergence of resistant organisms and leads to early recurrence (Nicolle, 1993). For these reasons it is currently recommended that asymptomatic bacteriuria not be treated routinely.

However, the incidence of post-procedure bacteremia (bacteria in the blood) following procedures involving trauma to the urogenital mucosa is very high in the presence of infected urine (Cafferkey et al.). Therefore, the need for an invasive genitourinary procedure is a clear indication for eradication of asymptomatic bacteriuria in both community-dwelling and institutionalized older adults.

Symptomatic UTIs. The presentation of UTI in ambulatory older adults without indwelling catheters is generally similar to that described for younger adults. In patients with cystitis, irritative lower urinary tract symptoms including pain with urination, frequent and urgent urination, and suprapubic discomfort usually predominate. The presentation of UTI typically includes flank pain and tenderness, and fever. However, frail older adults unable to communicate their symptoms may present with confusion, falls, immobility, deterioration of urinary continence, mental status changes, or reduced appetite. These individuals may lack the ability to mount a febrile response and may even be hypothermic (Baldassare and Kaye). Moreover, not all patients with pyelonephritis report either lower or upper urinary tract symptoms and often may be mistakenly diagnosed with intestinal obstruction, pneumonia, diverticulitis, or ureteral stones. In spite of the potential for atypical presentation of UTI in older adults, UTI rarely causes nonspecific deterioration without fever or localizing genitourinary symptoms (Nicolle, 1992). Individuals with long-term indwelling urinary catheters and UTI may present with suprapubic pain, discomfort or catheter obstruction (Brier).

Symptomatic UTI in older adults should be treated. The choice of antimicrobial agent should be based upon efficacy, adverse drug effects, cost, and emergence of resistance. Initial therapy should be directed by endemic institutional pathogens and anticipated susceptibilities. Trimethoprim-sulfamethoxazole, nitrofurantoin, norfloxacin, and amoxicillin-clavulanate are suitable initial choices with prompt adjustment of therapy based on culture results.

Duration of therapy is not well studied. Many older women with lower UTI will be cured with a three-day course of antibiotics (Baldassare and Kaye; Nicolle, 1992). However, many authorities recommend a seven-day course of therapy for presumed lower UTI in older women (Baldassare and Kaye; Brier). There is no role for short-course therapy of UTI in men. Men presenting with lower UTI symptoms should receive an initial fourteen-day course of therapy (Baldassare and Kaye; Brier). Recurrent UTI in older men frequently represents prostatic infection and should be treated with six to twelve weeks of therapy (Baldassare and Kaye; Blair).

Both men and women presenting with fever and upper urinary tract symptoms should receive a fourteen-day course of therapy (Baldassare and Kaye). Older adults with acute pyelonephritis who appear to be seriously ill or who have structural abnormalities such as stones should be hospitalized for aggressive treatment. Debilitated older patients with UTI are more likely to have bacteria in the blood. Initial antibiotic therapy traditionally includes intravenous ampicillin and gentamicin, but reasonable single-agent alternatives include amoxicillin-sulbactam, ciprofloxacin, and aztreonam. Because elderly patients are more prone to ototoxicity and nephrotoxicity from aminoglycosides, if this agent is used, appropriate alternative agents should be initiated when culture and sensitivity data becomes available, in order to minimize toxicity. A switch to oral antibiotics to complete the fourteen-day course can be made in three to five days when the patient is fever free and improving clinically. Follow-up cultures should be done.

Catheter-associated infections. Older adults remain at high risk of infection as long as they are catheterized. Treating asymptomatic bacteriuria in catheterized individuals is generally not recommended. Symptomatic bacteriuria as manifested by fever and suprapubic pain or discomfort should be treated with systemic antimicrobial agents, which should be selected on the basis of documented prior efficacy, susceptibility, and patient tolerance. Recommended oral agents include trimethoprim-sulfamethoxazole and quinolones. If the patient requires intravenous (injection) therapy, ampicillin with an aminoglycoside antibiotic is generally recommended. In order to limit the emergence of resistant organisms and yeast, the duration of therapy is limited to five to seven days. The benefit of routine catheter replacement with initiation of therapy for UTI has not been studied and is currently not recommended (Nicolle, 1994).

Long-term suppressive therapy. Long-term suppressive therapy may be considered in older women with recurrent urinary tract infections (Nicolle, 1992). The antibiotic chosen should be well absorbed, excreted in urine, and inexpensive. It should not alter intestinal flora, should have few side effects, and should have a low incidence of development of resistance. Once-daily trimethoprim-sulfamethoxazole, nitrofurantoin, or norfloxacin are potential options. In older women with recurrent UTI, low-dose oral or intravaginal estrogen has been shown to reduce the frequency of symptomatic infection by restoring intravaginal pH and normal vaginal flora (Nicolle, 1992). Estrogen therapy may be of benefit as an adjunct to antimicrobial therapy in this population. Daily ingestion of cranberry juice has been shown to decrease the occurrence of bacteriuria and pyuria in older women, possibly by decreasing adherence of *E Coli* to uroepithelium, and may also be a useful adjunct to antibiotics in women with recurrent UTI (Avorn et al.).

SHELLY A. MCNEIL
LONA MODY

See also DISEASE PRESENTATION; MENOPAUSE; NURSING HOMES; PROSTRATE.

BIBLIOGRAPHY

AVORN, J.; MONANE, M.; GURWITZ, J. H.; GLYNN, R. J.; CHOODNOVSKIY, I.; and LIPSITZ, L. A. "Reduction of Bacteriuria and Pyuria After Ingestion of Cranberry Juice." *Journal of the American Medical Association* 271 (1974): 751–754.

BALDASSARE, J. S., and KAYE, DONALD. "Special Problems of Urinary Tract Infection in the Elderly." *Medical Clinics of North America* 75, no. 2 (1991): 375–390.

BRIER, M. T. "Management of Urinary Tract Infections in the Nursing Home Elderly: A Proposed Algorithmic Approach." *International Journal of Antimicrobial Agents* 11 (1999): 275–284.

CAFFERKEY, M. T.; FALKINEN, F. R.; GILLESPIE, W. A.; and MURPHY, D. M. "Antibiotics for Prevention of Septicemia in Urology." *Journal of the Antimicrobial Chemotherapy* 9 (1982): 471–477.

MARRIE, T. J.; SWANTREE, C. A.; and HARTLEN, M. "Aerobic and An-aerobic Urethral Flora of Healthy Females in Various Physiologic Age Groups and of Females with Urinary Tract Infections." *Journal of Clinical Microbiology* 11 (1980): 654–659.

NICOLLE, L. E. "Urinary Tract Infection in the Elderly. How to Treat and When?" *Infection* 20, no. 1 (1992): S261–S265.

NICOLLE, L. E. "Urinary Tract Infections in Long-term Care Facilities." *Infection Control and Hospital Epidemiology* 14 (1993): 220–223.

NICOLLE, L. E. "Prevention and Treatment of Urinary Catheter-Related Infections in Older Patients." *Drugs and Aging* 4, no. 5 (1994): 379–391.

NICOLLE, L. E.; BENTLEY, D.; GARIBALDI, R.; NEUHAUS, E.; SMITH, P.; SHEA Long-term Care Committee. "Antimicrobial Use in Long-term Care." *Infection Control and Hospital Epidemiology* 17 (1996): 119–128.

RICHARDSON, J. P. "Bacteremia in the Elderly." *Journal of General Internal Medicine* 8 (1993): 89–92.

SOBEL, J. D., and KAYE, D. "Urinary Tract Infections." In *Principles and Practice of Infectious Diseases,* 5th ed. Edited by G. L. Mandell, R. G. Douglas, Jr., and J. E. Bennett. New York: Churchill Livingstone, 2000. Pages 773–800.

WARREN, J. W. "Catheter-Associated Bacteriuria in Long-term Care Facilities." *Infection Control and Hospital Epidemiology* 15 (1994): 557–562.

VARICOSE VEINS

See VASCULAR DISEASE

VASCULAR DEMENTIA

Introduction

Vascular dementias (VaDs) are the second most common causes of dementia, but much still needs to be done to sort out some basic ideas about how to describe the area. In the first instance, vascular dementias (the plural is used because unlike, say, Alzheimer's disease, there is clearly more than one type) are related to cerebrovascular disease. Cerebrovascular disease, however, is also related to Alzheimer's disease (AD) so that vascular factors are cognitive impairment world-wide (Hachinski).

Historic and conceptual context

As early as 1896 "arteriosclerotic dementia" (referring to VaD) was separated from "senile dementia" (referring to AD). Nevertheless, until the 1960s and 1970s cerebral atherosclerosis by chronically impairing blood supply to the brain was thought to be the commonest cause of dementia, and AD was regarded as a rare cause affecting only younger patients. Tomlinson et al. (Tomlinson, Blessed, and Roth) rediscovered AD as the more frequent cause of dementia than that of arteriosclerotic dementia. In 1974 Hachinski and colleagues used the term multi-infarct dementia (MID) to describe the mechanism by which they considered VaD was produced (Hachinski, Lassen, and Marshall). As the pendu-

lum swung in the direction of AD, vascular forms of dementia became relegated to a position of relative obscurity.

Until the 1990s, the concept of VaD has been dominated by MID, i.e., a dementia caused by small or large brain infarcts. VaD has come full circle to be understood as cognitive impairment caused by chronic ischemic with or without stroke.

Epidemiology

With the varying conceptions of vascular dementia, one understanding of epidemiology has been affected by variations in the definition of the disorders, the clinical criteria used, and the clinical methods applied.

Prevalence. VaD is the second most common single cause of dementia, accounting for 10 to 50 percent of the cases, depending on the geographic location, patient population and clinical methods used (Hebert, Brayne; Lobo et al.). The prevalence of VaD seems to be higher in China and Japan than in Europe and North America. In a recent European collaborative study using population-based studies of persons aged sixty-five years and older conducted in 1990s the age-standardized prevalence of dementia was 6.4 percent (all causes), 4.4 percent for AD and 1.6 percent for VaD (Lobo et al.). In this study 15.8 percent of the cases had VaD and 53.7 percent AD. As expected, a large variation in VaD prevalence was seen across studies. The prevalence ranged from 0.0 percent to 0.8 percent at age sixty-five to sixty-nine years, and from 2 percent to 8.3 percent at age ninety years and over in different studies. There was a difference in preva-

Figure 1

Complex interactions between vascular etiologies, brain changes, host factors, and cognition.

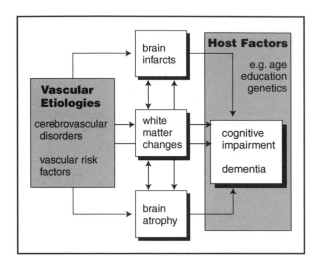

SOURCE: Author

lence between men and women; under eighty-five years of age the prevalence of VaD was higher in men compared to women and thereafter the prevalence was higher in women.

Incidence. The incidence of VaD has varied between six to twelve cases per year in one thousand persons aged seventy years and older (Hebert and Brayne). The incidence of VaD increases with increasing age, without any substantial difference between men and women.

Prognosis. The mean duration of any VaD is around five years (Hebert and Brayne), and their survival is less than for the general population or AD. Post-stroke dementia is an independent predictor of mortality.

Post-stroke dementia

Recent studies from around the world have shown that CVD increases the risk of dementia. The risk is higher than those associated with any other known risk factor for dementia.

Etiology and pathophsyiology

VaD as a clinical syndrome relates to different vascular mechanisms and changes in the brain, and has different causes and clinical manifestations. As noted, VaD is not only the traditional dementia of multiple strokes (Erkinjuntti

Table 1

Etiologies of vascular dementia

Cerebrovascular Disorders

Large artery disease
    Artery-to-artery embolism
    Occlusion of an extra- or intracranial artery
Cardiac embolic events
Small vessel disease
    Lacunar infarcts
    Ischemic white matter lesions
Hemodynamic mechanisms
Specific arteriopathies
Hemorrhages
    Intracranial hemorrhage
    Subarachnoidal hemorrhage
Hematological factors
Venous diseases
Hereditary entities

Risk Factors

Arterial hypertension
    Atrial fibrillation
    Cardiac abnormalities
        Myocardial infarction
        Coronary heart disease
    Diabetes
    Generalized atherosclerosis
    Lipid abnormalities
    Smoking
High age
Low education

SOURCE: Author

and Hachinski, 1993; Chui). The pathophsyiology of VaD incorporates interactions between vascular etiologies (CVD and vascular risk-factors), changes in the brain (in strokes, white matter lesions and atrophy), host factors (age, education) and cognition (see Figure 1).

Etiologies of VaD include both CVDs and risk factors (see Table 1). The main CVDs include large artery disease, cardiac embolic events, small vessel and hemodynamic mechanisms.

Risk factors for VaDs (see Table 1) include risk factors for CVD, stroke, white matter lesions, but, at the same time, also those of any cognitive decline and AD (Skoog).

Many changes in the brain are associated with VaD including several types of strokes, white matter lesions, and incomplete ischemic injury (occurring when brain cells are injured by chronic low blood flow to the brain.

Heterogeneity of vascular dementias

As reviewed, VaD is not a distinct disease, but a group of more or less heterogeneous syn-

Table 2
Vascular mechanisms and changes in the brain in main subtypes of vascular dementia.

Vascular Mechanisms	Changes in the Brain
Cortical Vascular Dementia or Multi-infarct Dementia	
Large vessel disease	Arterial territorial infarct
Cardiac embolic events	Distal field (watershed)
Hypoperfusion	infarct
Strategic Infarct Dementia	
Large vessel disease	Arterial territorial infarct
Cardiac embolic events	Distal field (watershed)
Small vessel disease	infarct
Hypoperfusion	Lacunar infarct
	Focal and diffuse white matter lesions
Subcortical Vascular Dementia or Small Vessel Dementia	
Small vessel disease	Lacunar infarct
Hypoperfusion	Focal and diffuse white
Incomplete ischemic injury	matter lesions

SOURCE: Author

dromes. One way to clarify this heterogeneity is to study possible clinical subtypes. Subtypes of VaD included in current classifications are cortical VaD (or MID), the subcortical VaD (small vessel dementia) and hypoperfusion dementia. Further subtypes suggested include hemorrhagic dementia, hereditary vascular dementia, and combined or mixed dementia (AD with CVD).

Main subtypes of vascular dementia

Cortical VaD (MID) is seen in connection with large vessel disease, cardiac embolic events and also hypoperfusion (see Table 2). It shows predominantly cortical and cortico-subcortical arterial territorial and distal field (watershed) infarcts. Typical clinical features are changes in strength or sensation on one side of the body, with facial problems such as language impairment, comprehension, and abrupt onset of cognitive impairment.

Strategic infarct dementia. Focal, often small, ischemic lesions involving specific sites critical for higher cortical functions are usually classified separately from other types of VaD. A stroke in one specific area, known as angular gyrus can give a syndrome almost indistinguishable from Alzheimer's disease, except that it has

a sudden onset. Subcortical infarcts can also give rise to dementia. Depending on the strategic location in question, the time-course and clinical features vary greatly.

Subcortical VaD. This type of VaD incorporates two entities "the lacunar state" and "Binswanger disease." It relates to small vessel disease and is characterized by lacunar infarcts, focal and diffuse ischemic white matter lesions, and incomplete ischemic injury.

Ischaemic lesions in substantial VaD affect not only the subcortical areas, but also their link to prefrontal cortex. Indeed, the so called "subcortical syndrome" is its primary clinical manifestation. This syndrome includes several factors, such as weakness without sensory changes, motor difficulties with speech and swallowing, a gait disorder, depression and emotional liability, and, especially, deficits in executive functioning. Patients with subcortical VaD often have multiple lacunes and extensive white matter lesions on neuroimaging often do not give a clinical history characteristic to stroke.

Mixed dementia

The so-called "mixed dementia syndrome" (which usually refers to the combination of Alzheimer's disease and VaD) may have been underrepresented in our estimation of dementia subtypes. VaD and AD seem to be more closely linked than might be explained on the basis of coincidence. Several vascular risk factors related to VaD have been shown also to be risk factors of clinical AD. In addition, infarcts and WMLs relate to an earlier clinical manifestation of AD. Further VaD and AD also share common pathogenic mechanisms such as delayed neuronal death and apoptosis. Overlap of these two mechanisms relate especially to the late-onset AD.

Clinical recognition of patients with mixed dementia or AD with CVD can be a problem. These patients can give a clinical history and signs of CVD, in this respect being clinically closer to VaD. On the other hand, many patients with AD are only found to have ischemic features in the neurophosis. In search of the therapeutic approaches however, we may have to choose a new focus. Instead of being prisons of old diagnostic dichotomies (pure AD vs. pure VaD), we should change the focus on etiopathogenetic factors, measure both the vascular burden of the brain, as well as the Alzheimer burden of the brain, and their consequences.

Clinical features of subcortical and cortical VaD

The early cognitive syndrome of subcortical VaD is characterized by (1) dysexecutive syndrome including slowed information processing, (2) memory deficit (may be mild), and (3) behavioral and psychological symptoms. The dysexecutive syndrome in subcortical VaD includes impairment in goal formulation, initiation, planning, organising, sequencing, executing, setsifting and set-maintenance, as well as in abstracting. The memory deficit in subcortical VaD is often mild. Sometimes it is manifested by impaired recall but relatively intact recognition. In consequence, patients often benefit from cues. Mild disorders are also commonly seen in subcortical VaD as is incontinence.

Clinical neurological findings especially early in the course of subcortical VaD include mild upper motor neuron signs, gait disorder, imbalance and falls. Often, however, these focal neurological signs are subtle or even transient.

By contrast, patients with cortical VaD, more commonly exhibit the neurological signs classically associated with stroke.

Onset and course. In subcortical VaD, the onset is variable, whereas in cortical VaD, it is typically sudden, with a step-wise deterioration following.

Diagnostic criteria

Several sets of clinical criteria for VaD have been used. The two cardinal components of all clinical criteria for VaD are the definition of dementia, and the definition of a vascular cause.

Each of the sets of clinical criteria are consensus by symptom experts, compared with criteria based on experimental studies. Each is based on the MID model of VaD.

Differential diagnosis

The differential diagnosis of VaDs include a number of conditions (see Table 3), but chiefly AD.

In consequence, the focus in a clinical diagnosis of AD has been on early episodic memory impairment, followed by often cognitive features, with a progressive course, with progressive dependence in function. This picture is distinct from early classical VaD.

Table 3
Differential diagnosis of vascular dementia

Alzheimer's disease
AD and CVD (mixed dementia)
Normal pressure hydrocephalus
White matter lesions and dementia
Frontal lobe tumor
Intracranial mass
Lewy body dementia
Frontotemporal dementia
Parkinsons's disease and dementia
Progressive supranuclear palsy
Multisystem atrophy

SOURCE: Author

In its classical conceptual form, probable VaD is characterized by an abrupt onset, a fluctuating and stepwise course, signs of cerebrovascular disease and ischemic lesions on brain imaging. By contrast, AD is characterized by an insidious onset, progressive course, without clinical signs of CVD and without signs of CVD in brain imaging.

AD and CVD (Mixed dementia). The issue of mixed dementia is a challenge. Increasing evidence shows that different vascular factors are related to AD, and frequently CVD coexists with AD. This overlap is increasingly important in older populations. Clinical recognition of patients with mixed dementia or AD with CVD, however, is a problem. As detailed in the neuropathological series of Moroney et al., these patients have a clinical history and signs of CVD, being clinically closer to VaD. In fact, in this series, fluctuating course (OR 0.2) and history of strokes (OR 0.1) were the only items differentiating AD from the mixed cases.

Problematic clinical examples include stroke unmasking AD in patients with post-stroke dementia, insidious onset and/or slow progressive course in VaD patients, and cases where difficulty exists in assessing the role of less extensive WMLs or of distinct infarcts on neuroimaging. This clinical challenge may be solved when a sensitive and specific ante-mortal marker for AD is available, and the distinction between AD and VaD could be supported by more detailed knowledge on which site, type and extent of ischemic brain changes are critical for VaD and

Table 4
Differential diagnosis between vascular dementia and Alzheimer's disease.

VASCULAR DEMENTIA	ALZHEIMER'S DISEASE
EARLY COGNITIVE SYNDROME	
Dysexecutive Syndrome Impaired planning, sequencing, speed of processing	**Impaired Episodic Memory** Ineffective learning, increased forgetting, impaired recognition, poor response to cues, intrusion errors Ineffective learning, less forgetting
Memory Impairment (often mild) Preserved recognition, good response cues, perseveration	
Cortical Symptom(s) (variable) Aphasia, apraxia, agnosia, visuospatial and constructive difficulty	**Anomia (mild)** **Visuospatial impairment (mild)**
EARLY CLINICAL FEATURES	
Mild UMN signs (motor deficit, decreased coordination, brisk tendon reflexes, Babinski's sign) Gait disorder, imbalance Urine frequency Dysarthria Mood changes, depression	Absence of focal neurological signs Dysthymia, mild depression
ONSET	
Variable: Relatively abrupt insidious	Insidious
CLINICAL COURSE	
Variable: Fluctuating, stepwise, progressive, stable	Progressive May have plateaus

SOURCE: Author

which extent and type of medial temporal lobe atrophy specifies AD.

Prevention and treatment of vascular dementia

Primary prevention aims to reduce the incidence of a disease by eliminating its causes or main risk factors. In VaD dementia the targets are CVD, including arterial hypertension, atrial fibrillation, myocardial infarction, coronary heart disease, diabetes, generalized atherosclerosis, lipid abnormalities and smoking. In addition, the use of estrogen, anti-inflammatory agents and antioxidants appear to reduce the risk of VaD.

Secondary prevention aims to prevent established disease from progressing. It emphasizes early detection and treatment. Treatment is aimed at treating the underlying cause, such as large artery disease (e.g., aspirin, dipyridamole, clopidragril, carotid endarterectomy), cardiac embolic events (e.g. anticoagulation, spirin), small-vessel disease (e.g. antiplatelet therapy as in large vessel disease), and hemodynamic mechanisms (e.g. control of hypotension and cardiac arrythmias).

How well all this works still is unclear. While a considerable degree of progress in our understanding of vascular dementia has been made, it is clear that much needs to be done before we will have effective treatment of this common and disabling problem.

TIMO ERKINJUNTTI
KENNETH ROCKWOOD

BIBLIOGRAPHY

CHUI, H. C. "Rethinking Vascular Dementia: Moving from Myth to Mechanism." In *The Dementias*. Edited by J. H. Growdon and M. N. Rossor. Boston: Butterworth-Heinemann, 1998. Pages 377–401.

Erkinjuntti, T., and Hachinski, V. C. "Rethinking Vascular Dementia." *Cerebrovascular Diseases* 3 (1993): 3–23.

ERKINJUNTTI, T.; BOWLER, J. V.; DECARLI, C.; et al. "Imaging of Static Brain Lesions in Vascular Dementia: Implications for Clinical Trials." *Alzheimer's Dis Assoc Disord* 13 (1999): S81–90.

ERKINJUNTTI, T.; OSTBYE, T.; STEENHUIS, R.; and HACHINSKI, V. "The Effect of Different Diagnostic Criteria on the Prevalence of Dementia." *New England Journal of Medicine* 337 (1997): 1667–1674.

FRATIGLIONI, L.; LAUNER, L. J.; ANDERSEN, K.; et al. "Incidence of Dementia and Major Subtypes in Europe: A Collaborative Study of Population-Based Cohorts." *Neurology* 54 (2000): S10–S15.

Hachinski, V. "Preventable Senility: A Call for Action Against the Vascular Dementias" [see comments]. [Review]. *Journal of the American Geriatrics Society* 340 (1992): 645–648.

Hachinski, V. C.; Lassen, N. A.; and Marshall, J. "Multi-infarct Dementia. A Cause of Mental Deterioration in the Elderly." *Journal of the American Geriatrics Society* ii (1974): 207–210.

HEBERT, R., and BRAYNE, C. "Epidemiology of Vascular Dementia." *Neuroepidemiology* 14 (1995): 240–257.

KONNO, S.; MEYER, J. S.; TERAYAMA, Y.; MARGISHVILI, G. M.; and MORTEL, K. F. "Classification, Diagnosis, and Treatment of Vascular Dementia." *Drugs & Aging* 11 (1997): 361–373.

LOBO, A.; LAUNER, L. J.; FRATIGLIONI L.; et al. "Prevalence of Dementia and Major Subtypes in Europe: A Collaborative Study of Population-Based Cohorts." *Neurology* 54 (2000): S4–S9.

Moroney, J. T.; Bagiella, E.; and Desmond, D. W., et al. "Meta-analysis of the Hachinski Ischemic Score in Pathologically Verified Dementias." *Neurology* 49 (1997): 1096–1105.

ROCKWOOD, K.; BOWLER, J.; ERKINJUNTI, T.; HACHINSKI, V.; and WALLIN, A. "Subtypes of Vascular Dementia." *Alzheimer Dis Assoc Disord* 13 (1999): S59–S64.

Skoog, I. "Status of Risk Factors for Vascular Dementia." [Review]. *Neuroepidemiology* 17 (1998): 2–9.

Tomlinson, B. E.; Blessed, G.; and Roth, M. "Observations on the Brains of Demented Old People." *Journal of the Neurological Sciences* 11 (1970): 205–242.

VASCULAR DISEASE

With the increase in life expectancy that has occurred since the early twentieth century, greater numbers of older adults are suffering from atherosclerosis and vascular-related diseases.

Atherosclerosis

Atherosclerosis is a generalized disorder of the arterial tree, manifested by *plaque* formation along the inner surface of arteries. The formation of plaque involves a dynamic process of biologically active endothelial cells (cells lining the inner surface of arteries) interacting with various hemodynamic, mechanical, metabolic, and chemical forces and substances. Normally, endothelial cells serve to maintain the integrity of the arterial wall, adapting to stress and injury by increasing wall thickness or altering the diameter to the lumen (channel cavity) of the vessel, increasing (vasodilatation) or decreasing (vasoconstriction) its size.

In atherosclerosis, the usual endothelial response to stress and injury becomes maladaptive. Dead cells, tissue debris, cholesterol, calcium, and other products are deposited beneath a layer of over-exuberant healing (hyperproliferative) endothelial cells to form a plaque. As the plaque continues to mature, its core becomes necrotic and a fibrous cap forms over the surface. Over several years, this narrowing ultimately reduces blood flow to the heart and the extremities to the point where it becomes insufficient to meet its aerobic and metabolic demands. In some cases, the fibrous cap that forms on top of the plaque can rupture, thus exposing the previously contained debris to the coagulation factors of the bloodstream, leading to an acute thrombosis (blood clot) that may completely occlude the vessel lumen, often with catastrophic consequences.

Large-vessel atherosclerosis. *Large-vessel* atherosclerosis refers to disease in the aorta and its major branches above the level of the chest. Some arterial thickening and changes in the size of arterial walls appear to be, in part, due to the aging process. While there does not appear to be any one single identifiable etiologic cause, several risk factors have been associated with the genesis of atherosclerosis. Nonmodifiable factors include gender, age, and genetics. Males are more prone than females. Incidence increases with age, reaching approximately 10 percent in adults over the age of seventy. There also appears to be an increased incidence of significant atherosclerosis in those having a first degree relative who has experienced atherosclerosis. Additionally, people with a family history of atherosclerosis, high blood pressure, or heart disease are at greater risk than the rest of the population.

Modifiable risk factors include smoking, hyperlipidemia, hypertension, and diabetes. The disease appears to be exacerbated in those who have a sedentary lifestyle, who are obese, and who have high levels of emotional stress. Elderly persons carry the additional complication of being prone to multi-system disease (disease that affects more than one organ).

The lower legs and feet, being farthest "down the pipe" of the arterial circulation, are often the first areas of the body to show the effects of this disease. Alternatively, other patients may manifest their initial symptoms as a transient ischemic attack (TIA, or mini-stroke) or significant permanent stroke from plaque formation in the carotid arteries in the neck. This arterial disease can occur anywhere along the vascular tree, but occurs more commonly at branch points, where blood vessels bifurcate.

Symptoms vary, depending on the degree of restriction of blood flow caused by the atherosclerotic stenosis (narrowing of the vessel lumen). Initially, patients may experience *intermittent claudication* which is an exercise-induced, crampy, heavy feeling in the muscles of the calf, and thigh, or disease in the arterial tree. With disease progression, ischemic symptomology is elicited with less and less activity, eventually occurring at rest. Patients may also experience cyanosis (a blue or pale discoloration) and decreased sensation or parathesias (a *pins and needles* feeling) in toes or feet. Additionally, patients with this disease may experience decreased hair growth; nail bed changes (onycogryphosis, or the thickening of the toenails); persistent, nonhealing ulcers or infections, and gangrenous (dead tissue) changes in the lower extremities. This is referred to as critical ischemia and occurs in about twenty percent of patients with large-vessel atherosclerosis.

Diagnosis. Diagnosis of chronic occlusion atheromatous disease consists of a thorough clinical exam, including both noninvasive and invasive testing. A Doppler ultrasound is used to determine flow patterns in the legs and ascertain the level and severity of disease. The information gathered will establish the appropriate course of treatment. If the findings indicate that surgery is required, a catheter-based dye test (angiogram) is performed to develop a "road-map" of the diseased arteries and determine the appropriate operative strategy.

Treatment. The initial treatment for limb ischemia should be conservative, consisting of a daily walking and biking regimen in an attempt to stimulate collateral vessel growth (vessels that naturally "bypass" the blockage in the artery). Often, in a diligent patient, this may be the only treatment necessary. Other medical therapy consists of agents that dilate vessels or decrease blood viscosity. However, both of these approaches may not be suitable for elderly patients due to concurrent comorbidities (i.e., osteoarthritis) and possible polypharmaceutical interactions.

The goal of surgical treatment is to reestablish flow to (revascularize) the ischemic tissue. This can be done percutaneously with angioplasty and stenting, or (more invasively) by using an alternate conduit to bypass the blockages in the diseased artery. For the a peripheral artery bypass a vein graft synthetic material (e.g., Gortex) is used, depending on the location of the stenosis. Both of these interventional concepts are also the current standard treatment of coronary arteriosclerosis. If these treatments are unsuccessful or the patient is deemed to be unsuitable for them, amputation of nonviable portions of the foot or leg is the only remaining surgical recourse. Approximately 2 to 10 percent of patients with critical ischemia will require amputation of the affected limb.

Deciding on a surgical treatment for large-vessel atherosclerosis involves an analysis of the risk/benefit ratio for each patient. In other words, is the risk of morbidity and mortality greater than the probable benefit of the surgery for the patient? The methodology of determining this ratio involves looking at epidemiological surgical outcomes and application of the data to the individual patient. It has traditionally been felt that elderly patients carry a greater risk than benefit for vascular reconstruction, and amputation has thus principally been the procedure of choice for these patients. However, many studies looking at this population have been incomplete and/or flawed, leaving the question open to debate.

Amputation carries high rates of mortality (13 to 23 percent) in elderly patients. Reasons for this high mortality is multifactorial, and contributing factors include a multi-system disease, associated comorbidity, and inadequate nutrition. Additionally, it has been shown that up to two-thirds of elderly amputees (depending on the level of amputation) are unable to be adequately rehabilitated, resulting in further functional disabilities. Anesthetic techniques that avoid a general anesthetic and increased use of invasive and noninvasive surgical techniques have substantially decreased morbidity and mortality in elderly patients following vascular procedures. Additionally, octogenarians with critical ischemia have an average life expectancy of four years. For these reasons, utilization of more aggressive interventions appear warranted.

Arterial aneurysms

The incidence of abdominal aortic aneurysm (AAA) tripled in the United States between 1970 and 2000, accounting for more than 15,000 deaths per year in 2000. A ruptured AAA is the tenth leading cause of death among those over fifty-five. The incidence of AAA in men over the age of eighty is 6.0 percent, and in women over the age of ninety it is 4.5 percent.

An aneurysm is a dilatation of the arterial vessel to between one-and-a-half and two times its normal diameter. These abnormal vessels can be subsequently divided into two broad categories: true and false aneurysms. A *true* aneurysm is one that involves a weakness of all three layers of the vessel wall (the intima, media, and adventitia). These are likely to be congenital malformations (e.g., Marfan's syndrome or some other connective tissue abnormality) or, more commonly, an acquired weakness (e.g., atherosclerosis) of the blood vessel. Conversely, a *false* aneurysm is one that involves only part of the arterial wall. Examples of these are usually seen following a traumatic injury to the vessel, at sites of previous vascular surgery, anastomosis (surgical opening between blood vessels), and arterial puncture sites for diagnostic catheterization.

Aneurysms, like atherosclerosis, can occur anywhere in the arterial tree, but they most commonly involve the aorta. The aorta is the large artery that conducts the oxygenated blood from the heart to the rest of the body. The normal diameter of the abdominal aorta is between 1.8 and 2.5 centimeters (cm). When the aorta becomes larger, 3.5 or 4 cm, it is deemed aneurysmal.

The principle factor for acquired aneurysm formation appears to be atherosclerosis. It is not clear what causes the arterial wall to become weakened in some people, while others develop occlusive disease. There has been some suggestion that people who develop aneurysms may have a less elastic media (the middle layer of the artery), and subsequently weaker blood vessel walls. The risk factors for aneurysm development are the same as for large-vessel atherosclerosis (see above). Additionally, sites of aneurysm formation mirror sites of aortic occlusive disease—below the level of the kidneys and major branch sites.

Complication of aneurysms include the following:

- Pain. Most AAAs are asymptomatic. A patient with an inflammatory aneurysm may have complaints of chronic back or flank pain, while a ruptured AAA usually presents as a sudden onset of severe, deep, abdominal, flank, or back pain.
- Thrombosis/embolization. The dilated portion of the vessel displays turbulent blood flow patterns that predispose these areas to blood-clot formation. Portions of the blood clot may break off and migrate (embolize) and occlude an artery downstream, or the blood clot may block off the entire lumen of the aorta, producing an acute arterial occlusion.
- Compression. As the aneurysm enlarges, it may encroach on other structures, such as the esophagus or ureters from the kidneys.
- Fistual Formation. An aneurysm can also erode into other structures and form an abnormal connection. An example is an aorto-enteric fistula, in which the aorta erodes into the duodenum or some other portion of the small bowel. These patients present with catastrophic upper gastro-intestinal tract bleeding.
- Rupture. The most worrisome and devastating complication (see below).

Eighty percent of all aneurysms grow in diameter as time progresses. On average, an AAA grows about 0.2 cm in diameter per year. As the aneurysm gets larger, more tension is placed on the vessel wall and there is a greater risk of rupture. Other risk factors for rupture are: greater than 0.5 cm increase in diameter per year; an inflammatory AAA (a special type of aneurysm that involves an aggressive inflammatory process of the retro-peritoneum), elevated diastolic blood pressure, chronic obstructive pulmonary disease, and larger initial size. Aneurysms smaller than 4 cm rarely rupture. Risk of rupture for aneurysms measuring 5 to 6 cm in diameter is 10 to 12 percent per year, giving cumulative risk of 60 percent over five years. An 8 cm aneurysm has a risk of rupture of nearly 80 percent over two years.

Fifty to ninety percent of patients with a ruptured AAA do not survive the trip to the hospital. Of those that do make it to the hospital in time for an urgent procedure, only 50 percent survive to be discharged. The most common complications following repair of a ruptured AAA are cardiac complications, respiratory failure, and renal failure.

Diagnosis. A physical examination is relatively unreliable, unless the patient is thin and the aneurysm is quite large. Most commonly, the AAA is found incidentally on an abdominal ultrasound done for other reasons. Abdominal ultrasound is accurate in diagnosing and determining the size of AAA, is relatively quick and painless, and does not expose the patient to X-ray radiation. Additionally, it can be used for serial examination to monitor changes in size. Computerized tomography (CT scan) with intra-arterial contrast is still the "gold-standard," however with diagnosis sensitivity of nearly 100 percent. A CT scan has an advantage over ultrasound in assessing an AAA rupture or leak. The disadvantages of a CT scan are that it is relatively time-consuming and requires exposure to contrast material and X-ray radiation.

Treatment. The goal of treatment is to prevent rupture and other complications, and to restore arterial continuity. Medical therapy has been largely unsuccessful in preventing progressive AAA dilatation. As such, surgery has been the mainstay of therapy. As with large-vessel atheromatous disease, the decision to treat an aneurysm must weigh the risks of surgery against the risk of complication of the disease process itself. The mortality and morbidity of an open, elective AAA repair is 4 to 10 percent, depending on size, characteristics, and comorbidities of the individual patient. Complications of surgery include myocardial infarction (in a nonrevascularized patient), renal failure, and colonic ischemia. These complications are greater in high-risk patients and elderly patients, again secondary to comorbidities.

For an abdominal aortic aneurysm less than 4 cm the risk of rupture is nearly zero. In general, the accepted sized of an AAA that necessitates surgery is 5 cm or greater. Various surgical and epidemiological studies have determined thus that the risk/benefit ratio favors operative treatment at this size. The traditional open repair of an AAA involves a large incision in the abdomen to gain direct access to the aorta. The aneurysmal segment is then replaced by a synthetic graft (usually Gortex or Dacron) to re-establish continuity to the "normal" artery above and below the weakened segment (in actuality, the artery above and below is rarely entirely normal; however, the goal is to achieve continuity to a normal caliber segment). More recently, a less invasive technique of endovascular stenting is being used.

An endovascular stenting procedure is usually done in concert with both a radiologist and a vascular surgeon. Instead of the large abdominal incision, a smaller incision is made in the groin to get access to the femoral artery (the main blood vessel in the leg). A catheter is then fed in a retrograde fashion into the abdominal aorta to deploy a synthetic graft/stent in the aneurysmal area. This procedure, in essence, achieves the same goal as the open procedure by excluding the weakened dilated arterial wall and establishing arterial continuity with two relatively normal segments. Most studies on patients who have undergone this procedure report a mortality rate of less than 1.2 percent for elective procedures.

Medical treatment for a rupture has a success rate of zero percent. The only hope of survival is operative treatment. However, as stated above, the thirty-day perioperative mortality rate is extraordinarily high (nearly 50 percent).

AAA repair in elderly patients. Like large vessel atheromatous disease of the aorta, older adults with an AAA have traditionally been deemed to be high-risk patients. As such, they have often gone untreated, and thus have a great risk of rupture. As previously discussed, the survival rate in this setting is dismal. It has now been shown that elective, direct AAA resection/repair carries equivalent mortality in octogenarians as in younger counterparts. With regards to the endovascular technique in suitable patients age seventy and older, the operative mortality rate is 1 percent. This outcome is far preferred to those found in the setting of a rupture repair.

Surgical decision-making for the octogenarian with a ruptured AAA is perhaps less clear. Johnston et al. have examined the preoperative, intraoperative, and postoperative risk factors associated with poor outcomes following ruptured AAA repair. In their analysis of 117 patients, they were unable to find a combination of preoperative risk factors or comorbidities that provided little or no chance of survival. Specifically, a ruptured AAA in a patient age seventy-five or older carries a survival rate of approximately 10 percent at six years post-repair. While this rate of death is still extraordinarily high (as compared to the elective group) it is still greater than zero. As such, the decision to treat the elderly with a ruptured AAA should be made on an individual basis, with the appropriate discussion held with the patient and his or her family.

Varicose veins

Veins (vessels that carry de-oxygenated blood) from most areas of the body contain one-way flap valves that are designed to assist in the unidirectional flow of blood towards the heart. When one or more of these valves becomes incompetent ("leaky"), some blood is able to flow retrograde (away from the heart) and tends to overfill and distend branches of superficial veins under the skin. Over a period of time, this additional pressure causes the veins to stretch and bulge. These often unsightly blue and twisted vessel are called *varicose veins.* They can cause the skin to itch (pruritis); the legs to swell; and the feet to be uncomfortable with a throbbing, heavy sensation. Approximately 10 to 20 percent of adults suffer from varicose veins, with a preponderance of women affected (nearly 70 percent of all patients with varicosities).

Varicose veins are most commonly experienced in the back of the calf or on the inside of the leg between the groin and the ankle, but they may occur in almost any part of the body. Varices can cause enlargement of veins around the anus (hemorrhoids), the esophagus (esophageal varices) and the testicle (varicocele).

The legs consist of two systems of veins. The first are the deep veins, which carry about 90 percent of the blood. The others are surface veins that are visible just underneath the skin and are less well supported. At all of these sites there is a major junction at which superficial veins (those subject to varicose veins) flow into the important deep veins of the leg, with a one-way valve to control flow at the junction.

Normally, blood is pumped upwards through the leg into the abdomen and back to the heart, and the valves in the veins prevent the blood from flowing back down the leg. Sometimes, however, these valves become defective, resulting in the pooling of blood and the backflow of blood down the leg and causing the formation of superficial veins that become swollen and distorted.

Causes: nonmodifiable. Causes and risk factors for varicose veins include:

- Age. Incidence increases with age, and may approach 50 percent of people older than fifty years of age.
- Sex. Women are affected more often than men, and the increased weight of the uterus during pregnancy may compress the iliac veins and cause an increased backpressure in the veins leading to varicosity.
- Heredity. There is a strong familial predisposition, and this may be the most important risk of all.
- Surgery. Any surgery performed near the hips can make vein problems more likely.
- Congestive heart failure. CHF and thrombus obstruction can also promote the development of varicose veins.

- Arterial-venous fistula. This is an abnormal connection between the arterial and venous system.

Modifiable causes and risk factors include:

- Posture. Standing erect can increase the pressure in the veins several-fold (compared to lying down). It is unlikely that standing actually causes varicose veins, however, people who spend a great deal of time on their feet are certainly more likely to notice, and experience discomfort from, their veins.
- Obesity. Being overweight can increase intra-abdominal pressure, impeding blood flow in the veins or decreasing the support of the veins themselves.
- Pregnancy. The extra weight of the fetus/ uterus can increase intra-abdominal pressure, impeding the return of blood flow from the leg. Additionally, hormonal changes that occur during pregnancy may contribute to weakened support of the superficial venous system.
- Thrombophlebitis. Past history of inflammation of a vein before a blood clot forms can damage or destroy the valves in the venous system, rendering them incompetent.

Diagnosis. For successful operative treatment, a detailed understanding of the abnormal varicose veins is required. For most primary (previously unoperated) cases, a clinical examination by an experienced surgeon will establish the cause (and therefore the treatment) of the varicose veins. Most surgeons would supplement the clinical examination by using a handheld ultrasound probe or an outpatient duplex scan, both of which provide a rapid and extremely useful method of identifying sites of faulty venous valves.

A duplex scan is a more elaborate ultrasound scanner, capable of producing both the visual image and information on the direction of blood flow within the venous system. This scan produces a more detailed "roadmap" of superficial and deep veins in the leg and aids in the planning of more complex varicose vein surgery. A venogram (an X-ray of the vein) has traditionally been used in the diagnosis of venous system abnormalities. This test requires the injection of a radio-opaque contrast into the venous system of the leg, with subsequent images captured using standard X-ray technology. While this test can provide detailed pictures of anatomy, the dye used can be harmful to veins in and of itself, and as such is reserved for only select cases that can't be imaged adequately with a Duplex scan. As stated above, it is paramount to have a complete understanding of the anatomy to ensure a successful operation.

Treatment. Varicose veins, particularly minor ones, may not require any treatment. However, it does appear that varicose veins are a progressive disease, and there are some surgeons who advocate for early intervention. As with all surgical procedures, it is important to understand the rationale for invasive treatments and to balance the expected benefits against the obvious disadvantages of having a surgical operation (e.g., inconvenience, post-operative pain, time off work, potential anesthetic and surgical complications).

Surgical treatment of varicose veins may be appropriate for a number of reasons including *symptoms* such as aching, throbbing or tenderness of the veins; *medical complications* such as eczema around the ankle (with or without actual skin ulceration) and thrombophlebitis (clotting and acute tender inflammation of the varicose veins); and also for *cosmetic* reasons—they become "unsightly" for the patient.

Properly fitted elastic stockings may be a useful short- or long-term method of alleviating the majority of symptoms or avoiding complications if either patient or surgeon is keen to avoid surgery. Varicose veins operations take the following forms:

- Sclerotherapy. This involves the injection of a chemical that intentionally causes the affected vein to thrombose and scar, thereby obliterating the lumen of the vessel. This therapy generally produces the best results for smaller varicosities.
- Multiple ligation and local excision. The veins are identified preoperatively with a handheld ultrasound or Duplex scan, and the overlying skin is marked with ink. Using these landmarks, the abnormal veins are removed through several small *stab* incisions. The operation is often largely cosmetic due to the size of veins that can be avulsed (pulled out) through these tiny incisions.
- Vein stripping. This technique is utilized for the long, straight segments of varicose, superficial veins. This stripping is usually car-

ried out in conjunction with an exploration through a 3 to 4 cm incision in the groin and/ or behind the knee. This results in a more satisfactory result when removal of superficial veins in the thigh can ensure more thorough disconnection of varicose veins lower in the calf and reduce the risk of future recurrence. Additionally, the underlying vein and its connection with the deep veins of the leg are identified. All associated superficial branches are carefully cut and tied, and the superficial vein itself is tied and divided at its junction with the deep vein. This part of the operation is essential, as it corrects the principle underlying pathology of the varicose veins.

A frequent concern is the potential side effects of tying and removing veins from the leg. Varicose vein surgery is limited to the superficial venous systems, collecting blood principally from the skin, and, as such, contributes little overall drainage from the leg. Approximately 90 percent of venous blood in the leg is contained in the deep veins within the leg. Additionally, there is a complex interconnected network of both superficial and deep veins with inherent redundancy, so that blood can travel via alternate routes out of the leg after varicose veins are tied or removed.

Complications of the operation. While the majority of operations carried out for varicose veins are routine, and serious complications are uncommon, no surgical procedure is completely free of risk. Additionally, the concurrence of increased comorbidities in elderly patients increases the possibility of complications. This should be borne in mind when considering the pros and cons of surgical treatment for varicose veins. Complications include the following:

- Anesthetic complications. Varicose vein surgery is increasingly performed with the usage of local or regional anesthetic, obviating the need for a general anesthetic. However, cardiac and respiratory complications can still occur, and are certainly more common in the elderly and in those with pre-existing problems. Abnormal reactions or allergies to anesthetic drugs are uncommon and largely unpredictable.
- Bleeding. This is one of the more common complications encountered, since the operation deals directly with blood vessels. Signifi-

cant hemorrhage requiring a blood transfusion is uncommon, but can occur if a major vein is injured or if the patient is on anticoagulant medications (i.e., blood thinners or an antiplatelet agent).

- Wound infection. Infection can occur following any surgical procedure, but is more common after long procedures, in obese patients, in the presence of contaminated ulcers, or in patients with a depressed immune system.

- Damage to surrounding anatomical structures. While this is uncommon, there is small risk of damage to the main arteries, veins, and even major nerves of the leg in explorations at the groin and behind the knee. Injury to small, sensory nerve branches in the skin is extremely common and largely unavoidable when veins are stripped or avulsed. This can result in small patches of numbness, burning, or altered skin sensation close to surgical scars or where varicose veins have been avulsed in the calf.

- Deep vein thrombosis (DVT). Blood clot formation (a DVT) is also an uncommon but serious complication or varicose vein surgery. Clinically significant DVTs occur in the deep venous system, which may be injured or inflamed during varicose vein surgery. A potentially lethal consequence is detachment of a blood clot that then migrates (embolizes) to the heart and lungs (pulmonary embolus). A major pulmonary embolus can result in sudden cardiac arrest and death.

RAKESH ARORA

See also CHOLESTEROL; HEART DISEASE; HIGH BLOOD PRESSURE; REVASCULARIZATION, BYPASS SURGERY, AND ANGIOPLASTY; SMOKING; SURGERY IN ELDERLY PEOPLE.

BIBLIOGRAPHY

BAGUNEID, M. S.; FULFORD, P. E.; and WALKER, M. G. "Cardiovascular Surgery in the Elderly." *Journal of the Royal College of Surgery Edinburgh* 44 (1999): 216–221.

BEEBE, H. G., and KRITPACHA, B. "Screening and Preoperative Imaging of Candidates for Conventional Repair of Abdominal Aortic Aneurysm." *Seminars in Vascular Surgery* 12, no. 4 (1999): 300–330.

BERGAN, J. J. "The Current Management of Varicose and Telangiectatic Veins." *Surgery Annual* 25, no. 1 (1993): 141–156.

CAMMER, PARIS B. E., and CASSEL, C. "Aortic Aneurysm in Elderly Patients." *Annals of Internal Medicine* 129, no. 2 (1998): 166.

CHANT, A. D. "Recurrent Varicose Veins." *Lancet* 348 (1996): 684–685.

CRIADO, E.; RAMADAN, F.; KEAGY, B. A.; and JOHNSON, G. J. "Intermittent Claudication." *Surgery, Obstetrics, and Gynecology* 173 (1991): 163–170.

DEAN, R. H.; WOODY, J. D.; ENARSON, C. E.; HANSEN, K. J.; and PLONK, G. W., JR. "Operative Treatment of Abdominal Aortic Aneurysms in Octogenarians. When is Too Much Too Late?" *Annals of Surgery* 217 (1993): 721–728.

DEAN, R. H.; WOODY, J. D.; ENARSON, C. E.; HANSEN, K. J.; and PLONK, G. W., JR. "Operative Treatment of Abdominal Aortic Aneurysms in Octogenarians. When is Too Much Too Late?" *Annals of Surgery* 217, no. 6 (1993): 721–728.

"Does Surgery Ease Varicose Vein Discomfort?" *Health News* 5, no. 4 (1999): 6.

EMERICH, J., and FIESSINGER, J. N. "Abdominal Aortic Aneurysm." *Lancet* 7, no. 349 (1997): 1699.

FINLAYSON, S. R.; BIRKMEYER, J. D.; FILLINGER, M. F.; and CRONENWETT, J. L. "Should Endovascular Surgery Lower the Threshold for Repair of Abdominal Aortic Aneurysms?" *Journal of Vascular Surgery* 29, no. 6 (1998): 973–985.

GORTON, M. E. "Current Trends in Peripheral Vascular Surgery. When is Surgical Intervention the Best Option?" *Postgraduate Medicine* 106, no. 3 (1999): 87–94.

HARRIS, K. A.; VAN SCHIE, L.; CARROLL, S. E.; DEATHE, A.; MARYNIAK, O.; MEADS, G. E.; and SWEENEY, J. P. "Rehabilitation Potential of Elderly Patients With Major Amputations." *Cardiovascular Surgery (Turin)* 32, no. 4 (1991): 463–467.

JOHNSON, M. T. "Treatment and Prevention of Varicose Veins." *Journal of Vascular Nursing* 15, no. 3 (1997): 97–103.

LONDON, N. J., and NASH, R. "ABC of Arterial and Venous Disease." *British Medical Journal* 320 (1000): 1392–1394.

O'HARA, P. J.; HERTZER, N. R.; KRAJEWSKI, L. P.; TAN, M.; XIONG, X.; and BEVEN, E. G. "Ten Year Experience With Abdominal Aortic Aneurysm Repair in Octogenarians: Early Results and Late Outcome." *Journal of Vascular Surgery* 21, no. 5 (1995): 830–837.

PATY, P. S.; LLOYD, W. E.; CHANG, B. B.; DARLING, R. C.; LEATHER, R. P.; and SHAH, D. M. "Aortic Replacement for Abdominal Aortic

Aneurysm in Elderly Patients." *American Journal of Surgery* 166, no. 2 (1993): 191–193.

PELL, J., and STONEBRIDGE, P. "Association Between Age and Survival Following Major Amputation. The Scottish Vascular Audit Group." *European Journal of Vascular and Endovascular Surgery* 17 (1999): 166–169.

PERLER, B. A. "Vascular Disease in the Elderly Patient." *Surgical Clinics of North America* 74, no. 1 (1994): 199–216.

PLECHA, F. R.; PLECHA, E. J.; AVELLONE, J. C.; FARRELL, C. J.; HERTZER, N. R.; and RHODES, R. S. "THE EARLY RESULTS OF VASCULAR SURGERY IN PATIENTS 75 YEARS OF AGE AND OLDER: AN ANALYSIS OF 3259 CASES." *JOURNAL OF VASCULAR SURGERY* 2, NO. 6 (1985): 769–774.

RUBIN, J. R., and GOLDSTONE, J. "Peripheral Vascular Disease: Treatment and Referral of the Elderly." *Geriatrics* 40, no. 6 (1985): 34–39.

SCHER, L. A.; VEITH, F. J.; ASCER, E.; WHITE, R. A.; SAMSON, R. H.; SPRAYREGEN, S.; and GUPTA, S. K. "Limb Salvage in Octogenarians and Nonagenarians." *Surgery* 99, no. 2 (1986): 160–165.

SEELIG, M. H.; ODENBURG, W. A.; HAKAIM, A. G.; HALLETT, J. W.; CHOWLA, A.; ANDREWS, J. C.; and CHERRY, K. J. "Endovascular Repair of Abdominal Aortic Aneurysms: Where Do We Stand?" *Mayo Clinic Proceedings* 74, no. 10 (1999):999–1010.

THOMPSON, M. M., and BELL, P. R. "ABC of Arterial and Venous Disease. Arterial Aneurysms." *British Medical Journal* 29 (2000): 1193–1196.

VAN DAMME, H.; SAKALIHASAN, N.; VAZQUEZ, C.; DESIRON, Q.; and LIMET, R. "Abdominal Aortic Aneurysms in Octogenarians." *Acta Chirgin's Belgium* 98, no. 2 (1998): 76–84.

WALSTON, J., and FINUCANE, T. "Abdominal Aortic Aneurysm." *New England Journal of Medicine* 329, no. 17 (1993): 1276.

WILMINK, A. B., and QUICK, C. R. "Epidemiology and Potential for Prevention of Abdominal Aortic Aneurysm." *British Journal of Surgery* 85 (1998): 155–162.

WONG, D. T.; BALARD, J. L.; and KILLEEN, J. D. "Carotid Endarterectomy and Abdominal Aortic Aneurysm Repair: Are these Reasonable Treatments for Patients Over 80?" *American Surgeon* 64, no. 10 (1998): 998–1001.

VETERANS CARE

Since the 1970s, the U. S. Department of Veterans Affairs (VA) has responded to a vital demographic trend: Although the total number of veterans is declining, the proportion of older veterans is increasing dramatically. In addition, the proportion of older persons in the veteran population far exceeds the proportion of older persons in the U.S. population in general. Anticipating the needs of a rapidly aging veteran population, VA initiated a comprehensive, three-pronged plan encompassing clinical services, research, and education and training. In meeting the challenge of this aging imperative, VA has become recognized as a national leader in the development and implementation of innovative health care services for older persons (Cooley, Goodwin-Beck, and Salerno). This entry summarizes VA's mission and health care service delivery structure; demographic trends in the veteran population; VA's aging-related clinical programs, research, and health care provider education and training; and examples of emerging VA initiatives in aging.

Mission and service delivery structure

VA's mission is to serve America's veterans (individuals who have been honorably discharged from U. S. military service) in three major areas: health care, which is coordinated by the Veterans Health Administration (VHA); socioeconomic support and assistance, coordinated by the Veterans Benefits Administration; and burial services, coordinated by the National Cemetery Administration.

VHA operates the largest health care system in the nation, encompassing 172 hospitals, 132 nursing home care units, 40 domiciliaries, and over 600 outpatient clinics. VHA also contracts for care in non-VA hospitals and in community nursing homes, provides fee-for-service visits by non-VA physicians and dentists for outpatient treatment, and supports care in one hundred state veterans homes in forty-seven states.

Since 1995, VHA has undergone a major reorganization. There are twenty-two regional Veterans Integrated Service Networks (VISNs), each comprised of from five to eleven facilities. The VISN, rather than the individual medical center, is the basic planning and budgetary unit of health care delivery in the new VHA structure. VISNs are responsible for providing a coordinated continuum of care for veterans treated in each network of facilities and for supporting research and health profession education activities. Key domains of health care value in which VISN performance is measured include access to care, quality of care, patient satisfaction, patient functional status, and cost-effectiveness.

In addition, VHA has shifted from an inpatient, hospital bed-based system to outpatient, primary, and ambulatory care. There is increased emphasis on noninstitutional settings such as outpatient clinics, home-based services, and other ambulatory and community-based venues.

Demographic trends

In 2000, the median age of veterans was fifty-seven years (U. S. Department of Veterans Affairs), compared to only thirty-six years for the general U. S. population (Administration on Aging). Over 37 percent of the veteran population (9.5 million of the total 25.5 million veterans) was age sixty-five or older, compared to 13 percent of the general population. By 2020, nearly half of the entire veteran population (7.6 million, or 45 percent, of the total 16.9 million veterans) will be age sixty-five or older. Although most veterans are male, the number of female veterans is growing. In 2000, over 5 percent (1.4 million) of all veterans and 3 percent (325,000) of veterans age sixty-five or older were female. By 2020, over 9 percent (1.6 million) of all veterans and 4 percent (316,000) of veterans age sixty-five or older will be female. Among female veterans, the proportion age sixty-five or older was 23 percent in 2000 and is projected to be 20 percent in 2020. As in the general U.S. population, the "old-old" are the fastest-growing segment of the veteran population. By 2020, 6 percent of all veterans and 13 percent of veterans age sixty-five or older will be age eighty-five or older (1.1 million). Thus, VA will continue to encounter a very large group of potentially frail, older veterans in the next twenty years.

Clinical programs in aging

Typically, older persons have higher use of health care services, including increased number of physician visits, short-term hospital stays, number of days in the hospital, and greater need for long-term care services. Anticipating these needs, VA has developed a broad continuum of geriatrics and extended care services that are provided in a wide variety of settings, including home and the community, outpatient clinics, hospitals, and nursing homes. Together these programs provide preventive, acute, rehabilitative, and extended care on an outpatient and inpatient basis. Home- and community-based programs are emphasized, with coordinated use of hospital and nursing home programs. The shared purpose of these programs is to prevent or lessen the burden of disability on older, frail, chronically ill patients and their families, and to maximize each veteran's functional independence.

Several innovative home- and community-based services are offered. These include Home-Based Primary Care (HBPC), which provides in-home primary medical care to veterans with chronic illnesses. A home-based, interdisciplinary treatment team prescribes medical, nursing, social, rehabilitation, and dietetic regimens and provides training in supportive care to the patient and family caregivers. In addition, VA's homemaker/home health aide program enables selected patients who meet criteria for nursing home placement to remain at home through the provision of personal care services purchased by VA from public and private agencies in the community, with case management provided directly by VA staff. VA also offers Adult Day Health Care, which provides health maintenance and rehabilitation services to veterans in a congregate, outpatient setting during daytime hours. This program uses a medical model of services, which in some circumstances may be a substitute for nursing home care. Another community-based program is Community Residential Care/ Assisted Living, in which private homes provide room, board, personal care, and general health-care supervision, at the veteran's expense. Veterans in this program do not require hospital or nursing home care, but because of health conditions, they are not able to live independently and have no suitable support system to provide needed care. All residential care homes are regularly inspected by a multidisciplinary team of VA staff, and veterans in this program receive monthly visits from VA health care professionals who monitor the care provided in the home.

VA Domiciliaries are residential rehabilitation and health maintenance centers for veterans who do not require hospital or nursing home care but are unable to live independently because of medical or psychiatric disabilities. Veterans receive medical and psychiatric care, rehabilitative assistance, and other therapeutic interventions on an outpatient basis from the host hospital, while residing in the structured, therapeutic, homelike environment of the domiciliary. There are specialized, interdisciplinary treatment programs for rehabilitation of head trauma, stroke, mental illness, chronic alcoholism, heart disease, and a wide range of other disabling conditions. For some veterans, domiciliary care can help prepare for return to independent or semi-independent community living.

In the area of geriatric assessment, VA pioneered the concept of the Geriatric Evaluation and Management (GEM) program, which includes inpatient units, outpatient clinics, and consultation services. An interdisciplinary health care team provides comprehensive, multidimensional evaluations for a targeted group of older patients with multiple acute and chronic diseases, functional impairments, and psychosocial problems.

For veterans in need of skilled nursing care and related medical services, there are VA hospital–based nursing home care units. These units employ an interdisciplinary care approach to meet the multiple physical, social, psychological, and spiritual needs of patients. Many also provide sub-acute and post-acute care.

All VA facilities have a hospice consultation team, which coordinates a hospice and palliative care program of pain management, symptom control, and other medical services to terminally ill veterans, as well as bereavement counseling to their families. In addition, VA provides respite care to relieve spouses or other caregivers from the burden of caring for a chronically disabled veteran at home. Respite is provided for planned, brief periods of care in a variety of settings, including the veteran's home, community nursing home, or VA hospital or nursing home.

Veterans with Alzheimer's disease or other dementias participate in the full range of VA services, including in-home, community-based, and institutional-based acute and extended care services. In addition, some VA facilities have developed specialized inpatient or outpatient dementia services for diagnosis; management of comorbid medical, emotional, and behavioral problems; or palliative care. Programs for family caregivers of persons with dementia include support groups and caregiver education.

Research in aging

VHA is one of the nation's largest research organizations, with a research appropriation from Congress of $316 million in 1999.

A cornerstone of VA's response to its "aging imperative" is the Geriatric Research, Education and Clinical Center (GRECC) program, which began in 1975. As centers of excellence in geriatrics, GRECCs' mission is to improve the health and care of older veterans through research, training and education, and the development and evaluation of innovative models of care. GRECCs are widely recognized as having provided leadership in geriatrics and gerontology, both within VA and throughout the nation (Goodwin and Morley). In 2000, there were twenty GRECCs across the VA system, each with a specific programmatic focus (e.g., osteoarthritis and osteoporosis; stroke rehabilitation, neurobiology and management of dementia; prostate disease; falls and instability; exercise in frail elderly; end of life care).

VA also funds a wide range of aging-related research, including basic biomedical, applied clinical, rehabilitation, and health services topics, as well as cooperative studies involving multiple VA sites. Aging is one of nine designated research areas used to prioritize VA research funding. In addition to individual investigator awards, VA supports aging research at Health Services Research and Development Centers of Excellence and at Rehabilitation Research and Development Centers. In 1999, VA provided $19.9 million for 150 aging-related research projects. VA investigators received another $33.8 million from non-VA sources to support another 339 aging-related research projects.

Education and training in aging

VA conducts the nation's largest coordinated education and training effort for health care professionals, with over 100,000 health profession students receiving clinical training in VA facilities annually, including the GRECCs and other geriatrics and extended care settings described above. VA's creation of a physician fellowship program in geriatric medicine in the 1970s played a significant role in the later recognition of geriatric medicine as a specialty in the United States (Goodwin and Morley). In addition, VA has developed a wide range of other fellowships and specialty training in geriatrics for psychiatrists, dentists, nurses, psychologists, and other associated health professions. VA also pioneered the concept and practice of interdisciplinary team training in geriatrics. In addition to student training, VA also provides aging-related continuing education for professional staff from VA and the community on a regular basis.

New initiatives in aging

In 2000, an area of intense focus within VA was the integration of primary care, geriatrics, and mental health. One initiative is the Unified Psychogeriatric Biopsychosocial Evaluation and Treatment (UPBEAT) project, in which elderly patients with symptoms of depression, anxiety, and substance abuse in VA medical and surgical hospital settings are evaluated by an interdisciplinary psychogeriatric team and followed by care coordinators on an outpatient basis. Preliminary results indicate cost savings from fewer hospital days for patients managed in this way. A second initiative is the Primary Care Research in Substance Abuse and Mental Health for the Elderly (PRISMe) project, a four year controlled study cosponsored by VA and the U. S. Department of Health and Human Services. Eleven sites, including five VA-funded sites, will compare two models for delivering mental health and substance abuse services to older adults in primary care settings: One model uses an integrated team of primary care and mental health/substance abuse professionals, and the other uses referrals to specialty mental health/substance abuse care. A key question to be examined is under what conditions are integrated or referral models most effective in terms of access, treatment adherence, patient outcomes, and cost. A third initiative in this area is the VA's Primary Care Multidisciplinary Education Committee (PCMEC). In 2000, PCMEC identified over twenty-five innovative and promising models of integrated primary care, mental health, and geriatrics at VA facilities. A variety of educational activities will be developed to evaluate and disseminate best practices from these model programs.

Other innovative projects are underway in the area of dementia care. One is the Chronic Care Networks for Alzheimer's Disease (CCN/AD) project, co-sponsored by the National Chronic Care Consortium and the Alzheimer's Association. VA's Upstate New York Healthcare Network (VISN 2) is among seven partnerships of health care organizations and Alzheimer's Association chapters that are testing new, integrated approaches to serving persons with dementia and their families through networks of primary, acute, and long-term care. A set of clinical tools has been developed to facilitate dementia diagnosis and care management in the CCN/AD study sites. A second dementia project is Advances in Home-Based Primary Care for End of Life in Advancing Dementia (AHEAD). Begun in 2000, this project will involve approximately fifteen VA HBPC teams using a rapid cycle change process to improve end of life care at home for individuals with dementia.

In 2000, other significant initiatives were underway as part of the implementation of Public Law 106–117, the Veterans Millennium Healthcare and Benefits Act, which was passed by Congress in November 1999. This major legislation includes numerous provisions related to VA long-term care services, such as inclusion of certain noninstitutional extended care services in the medical benefits package and specification of priority groups for nursing home care.

Conclusion

As VA enters the new millennium, health care needs of older veterans remain a high priority. Through its early and continued response to a demographic aging imperative, VA has demonstrated leadership in geriatric research, clinical program development, and professional education. VA's health care network structure presents great opportunities for comprehensive, coordinated care and evaluation of innovative service delivery models. Lessons learned from VA's past and future aging initiatives will benefit veterans and their families as well as all older Americans.

SUSAN G. COOLEY
JUDITH A. SALERNO

See also GERIATRIC MEDICINE; LONG-TERM CARE.

BIBLIOGRAPHY

Administration on Aging. "Resident Population of the United States: Estimates by Age." 2000. Based on 1990 U. S. Census. Available on the World Wide Web at www.aoa.gov

COOLEY, S. G.; GOODWIN-BECK, M. E.; and SALERNO, J. A. "United States Department of Veterans Affairs Health Care for Aging Veterans." In *Geriatric Programs and Departments Around the World.* Edited by B. Vellas, J. P. Michel, and L. Z. Rubenstein. New York: Springer Publishing Co., 1998. Pages 183–198.

GOODWIN, M., and MORLEY, J. E. "Geriatric Research, Education and Clinical Centers: Their Impact in the Development of American Geriatrics." *Journal of the American Geriatrics Society* 42 (1994): 1012–1019.

KIZER, K. W. "Geriatrics in the VA: Providing Experience for the Nation." *Journal of Ameri-*

can *Medical Association* 275, no. 17 (1996): 1303.

U.S. Department of Veterans Affairs. *Vet Pop 2000*. (version 2.07, 30 September 2000) [Data file]. Available on the World Wide Web at www.va.gov

VISION AND PERCEPTION

Perceiving is a constructive act. Using the data supplied by the senses and his knowledge of the world, the perceiver constructs his reality of the moment. Since the sensory systems have a limited capability for acquiring information, the constructed reality will reflect not only the present data but the person's interpretation of the information and its context. The perceiver does not simply record the actions of the physical world but reconstructs that world moment by moment. There are two factors constraining the construction of the percept: data and resource limitations. Data refers to the amount of information that may be acquired by a perceiver. This places the first restriction on the final construction of what is perceived. The influence of past experiences and knowledge on the creation of the percept is what is referred to as resource limitations. This entry will focus on the restrictions on the quality of the percept as influenced by data limitations associated with aging.

The descriptions are based on the average performance of adults as they age. As a presentation of normative information, it is not a prescription for what happens to each person. There is as much heterogeneity in the performance of elderly adults as there is in younger persons. This point is made because it is inappropriate to create a stereotype of an aging person as one who is affected by all of the changes described below. Instead, it is better to view this information as a guide to the potential changes that may occur to varying extents in the population.

In examining changes in vision and perception, it is important to consider the scope of the visual system. The eye is a complex structure whose optical properties, governed by the lens, and the shapes of the cornea and eyeball, as well as the neural structure and function of the retina dictate the quantity and quality of the sensory data that is acquired. These centers extract different types of information from the signal pattern, such as color and shape. Alterations in structure or function in one or more areas may underlie the age associated effects discussed in this entry.

Visual pathology

There are several vision disorders that are more common as one ages. These pathological changes alter the structure and function of the eye and can severely limit vision if not treated. The most common disorder is *cataracts*. A cataract is a pathological increase in lens opacity that severely limits visual acuity. While there is a reduction in lens clarity for nearly all elderly individuals, cataracts affect only one in twenty persons over the age of sixty-five. It is the leading cause of functional blindness in older adults but it can be successfully treated by simply removing the affected lens and replacing it with a prosthetic lens.

Glaucoma. is the second leading cause of blindness in the United States. Although the pressure within the eye remains essentially constant until the later decades of life, a pathological increase sometimes occurs. Glaucoma is characterized by both increased intraocular pressure and the resulting atrophy of the nerve fibers at the optic disk. The behavioral symptom of the disorder is a reduction in the perceiver's visual field. That is, a person loses sensitivity in the periphery of his vision. Unfortunately, this alteration in vision often goes unnoticed until the damage is quite advanced. Regular screening for glaucoma by measuring intraocular pressure would permit the detection of the disease at a point when medical intervention could be effective in limiting damage to vision.

Macular degeneration is a deterioration of the retina in the area of central vision that is critical for the perception of fine detail and color. The afflicted person has difficulty with all visual tasks that are ordinarily dependent on central vision, such as reading, face identification, and television viewing. Strong magnification can be used to improve reading ability. Since the peripheral fields are not affected, the person does not have difficulty in walking and moving through his environment.

Visual processing

While diseases of the eye offer clear limitations to the acquisition of information and the accurate perception of the world, they only affect a minority of older adults. There are other changes which occur in vision that are considered normative, that is, they occur to most people. These alterations in structure and function can be shown to have a marked effect on the visual experiences of older persons. An appreciation of these factors can help us to understand the perceptions of elderly adults and to create behavioral interventions to compensate for their effect.

Light sensitivity. Perhaps the most important limit on data acquisition is the reduction in light sensitivity that occurs in adulthood. It is a common experience for a child to be chided by a parent or grandparent to turn on more lights while they read. "You'll ruin your eyes trying to read in that light!" the parent may exclaim. This event illustrates the difference in light sensitivity between the child and older person. While the child has sufficient sensitivity to light to be able to read easily, the parent would require more light to perform the same task.

Our maximum sensitivity to light starts to decline in the third decade of our lives. Indeed, starting with age twenty, the intensity of illumination must be doubled for every increase of thirteen years for a light to be just seen.

One reason for the reduction in sensitivity is that less light actually reaches the retina, the receptive surface of the eye, as we age. It has been estimated that the retinal illuminance of a sixty year old is only one-third that of a twenty year old. The reduction in retinal illuminance can be attributed to several factors including the marked reduction in pupil diameter known as senile miosis. That is, in older adults the pupil simply does not open as wide to capture light. The gradual opacification, or cloudiness, of the lens and the reduction of transparency in the vitreous body also contribute to the reduction in retinal illuminance. Finally, there is evidence of the loss of photoreceptor cells that would reduce light sensitivity.

A simple intervention to compensate for the reduction in light sensitivity is to increase the level of illumination for older adults. However, care must be taken to avoid *glare* effects, which are more common in elderly adults. Excessively bright light or light which is scattered by opacities in the lens can reduce visual performance by dazzling a person or reducing the contrast of an object. One can compensate for glare effects in reading by using high contrast or large size material. In driving, however, glare is an issue for nighttime drivers who are exposed to the headlights of oncoming cars. A concern is that it takes a substantially longer time for persons to recover from glare, as they grow older. The temporarily impaired driver is at greater risk for an accident.

Acuity is the capability to resolve fine detail. It is ordinarily assessed by asking the patient to read letters or symbols that are printed in high contrast. The smallest element, which can be resolved accurately, is the acuity limit of the observer. We have all noticed as we grew older that optical corrections became common among our peers. Acuity improves from childhood into adolescence and then starts to show a steady decline in early adulthood. Indeed, even when adults are fit with their best optical correction, a gradual decline with age in peak acuity is noted starting late in the third decade of life. Thus, older adults with corrective lenses can be expected to have more difficulty than their younger counterparts in resolving fine detail.

To focus light on the macula, which is the portion of the retina capable of resolving fine detail, the lens must accommodate or change shape. The flexibility or accommodative power of the lens diminishes with increasing age. At about the mid-forties this loss of accommodative power becomes serious enough to affect the ability to focus on near objects. This loss of accommodative power for near vision is known as *presbyopia*.

Contrast sensitivity. The measurement of acuity assesses the ability to resolve small details at a high level of contrast. It is also important to determine the ability of a person to resolve objects under lower levels of contrast. In the assessment of contrast sensitivity the minimum contrast required to detect difference between light and dark regions is determined. A common definition of contrast is (Lmax − Lmin) / (Lmax + Lmin) where Lmax is the maximum luminance in a stimulus display and Lmin is the minimum level of luminance present.

One method in the clinical assessment of contrast sensitivity is achieved by having the patient read letters of fixed size that vary in contrast. At the top of the chart the letters are very dark against a light background. The contrast or darkness of the letters is successively reduced in each line of the chart. The lowest contrast at which the person can read the letters accurately marks their contrast sensitivity. A person who can read very light letters has a better contrast sensitivity than one who is successful only with dark letters.

Stimuli composed of gratings or stripes in which the contrast is sinusoidally modulated are also used in assessment. At high contrast levels, the grating appears to be composed of fuzzy stripes against a light background. The lighter stripe or the lower level of the contrast at which a person can detect the grating, the better their contrast sensitivity. The width of the stripes is also varied to permit the determination of contrast sensitivity for different size stimuli. The variation of stimulus size is described in terms of spatial frequency where the number of stripes per unit area on the retina is a measure of the spatial frequency of the stimulus.

Contrast sensitivity peaks in adolescence and starts to decline in early adulthood. As would be expected from the acuity data, older adults require very high contrast to resolve small objects, or high spatial frequencies, at even higher levels of illumination. This difficulty also extends to low and intermediate spatial frequencies under lower levels of illumination. Measures of spatial contrast sensitivity have been shown to be superior to acuity measures in predicting performance on a wide variety of tasks. Since the accurate processing of lower spatial frequencies are important for reading, face and object recognition, and road sign identification, the reduction of contrast sensitivity to these spatial frequencies places the older perceiver at a disadvantage for quick and accurate responding.

Color perception.   The ability to discriminate among colors peaks in the early twenties and declines steadily with advancing age. The discrimination of shorter wavelength colors, blues and greens, is particularly challenging for older observers. This reduction in color discrimination may be attributed to at least two sources. First of all, the lens yellows with adult aging causing a selective absorption of shorter wavelengths and consequently less light from that region to strike the retina. Secondly, there is evidence that there is a selective loss of sensitivity of the photoreceptors that are responsive to short wavelengths.

A consequence of the loss of sensitivity to shorter wavelengths is that white light, which is composed of all wavelengths, may appear faintly yellow. Also, blue objects may appear particularly dark and blues and dark greens may be indistinguishable. Such changes in color perception may affect the sartorial choices of older adults.

Depth perception.   People live in a three-dimensional world. But we must infer the structure of that world from the two-dimensional array of light on our retinas. The construction of the third dimension is accomplished by using a number of cues, such as interposition, shading, and relative height. Only stereopsis sensitivity has been studied among different adult age groups. *Stereopsis* is the depth cue derived from the different images projected on the retinas by an object. Objects that are less than twenty feet from the observer will fall at slightly different positions on each retina. The disparity of these images is a cue for depth. The greater the disparity, the closer the object to the perceiver. As with the other vision characteristics that we have reviewed, stereopsis peaks in early adulthood with notable decreases in sensitivity after the fourth decade of life. Reductions in stereopsis sensitivity may affect the ability of a person to perform a number of important tasks such as hitting a curve ball, judging the distance from an object while parking a car, and walking. In the latter case, objects, such as sidewalk cracks and stair treads, whose depth is not appropriately discriminated, may become tripping hazards. More work is needed to fully appreciate the depth perception capabilities of older adults.

Motion perception.   Objects in motion create a changing pattern of light on our retinas. Our ability to detect and discriminate these shifts of light stimulation is critical for our ability to determine not only the movement of objects but also our body motion and stability. While it is a subject that has generated a lot of interest, few studies of the impact of aging on motion perception have been reported. In one study of individuals from twenty-five to eighty years of age, the investigators reported that there was a linear decline of motion sensitivity with age. As with the decline in light sensitivity, such a pattern of change is suggestive of an age-related neurodegeneration in the visual system. However, several studies comparing the motion sensitivity of young and elderly adults have reported that the deficit in motion sensitivity was restricted to elderly women. That is, these studies reported that only elderly women and not men had poorer motion perception. A reason for such gender effects has not been suggested.

Beyond the detection of motion it is important to be able to judge the speed of an object. Accurate speed judgments permit drivers to merge onto highways and ballplayers to hit a baseball. In general, young adults are quite accurate in their speed judgments. One area where there is a critical failure in speed estimates that affects all ages is in the perception of large objects. A large plane appears to be floating very slowly on to the runway as it lands yet it is travelling at nearly two hundred miles per hour. A train approaching an intersection appears to be moving slowly enough for a driver to avoid a collision yet the seventy-mile-per-hour locomotive slams into the car. It is a strong illusion that large objects appear to move more slowly than their actual speed.

There has been limited work on the ability of older adults to judge the speed of automobiles. The evidence suggests that older people overestimate the speed of slowly moving cars while underestimating the speed of cars travelling at highway speeds. Such an effect may account for the hesitancy of older drivers to cross an active intersection or to merge on a highway. The importance of motion perception in general and speed judgments specifically demands that more work is required to understand the impact of aging on these abilities.

Stimulus persistence. The experience of a visual event does not end when the stimulus is removed. There is a phenomenal persistence of the event not to be confused with an afterimage. The latter occurs because of the fatigue and recovery of receptors while persistence is a continuation of information transmission. The duration of the persistence is inversely related to the luminance, contrast, and duration of the stimulus. That is, stronger visual events lead to shorter periods of visible persistence. It may be that weak stimuli persist longer to permit the perceiver to continue to extract needed information from the stimulus event. The cost of prolonged persistence is that separate stimulus events may blend together yielding indistinct perceptual events. An example of such blending is the fusion of light pulses in a fluorescent light. There are distinct pulses of light and dark intervals emitted by the fluorescent tube. Each light pulse results in a residual persistence of the light in our visual system. Because the rate of flicker is so fast, the persistence of the light is long enough to fill the dark interval leaving the viewer with the experience of continuous light. The pulse rate of light and dark intervals at which a person perceives the light as continuous is termed the *critical flicker fusion* (CFF) threshold.

Given the reduced light and contrast sensitivity of elderly adults and the inverse relationship between stimulus strength and persistence, it is to be expected that older perceivers will experience longer persistence. Indeed, the CFF threshold is lower for older observers. This means that an older adult presented with a relatively slowly flickering light will report that it is continuous while a young person will note the flicker. The fact that a stimulus event has weaker temporal integrity for elderly adults suggests that there may be significant misperceptions of sequentially occurring events. Indeed, it has been argued that prolonged stimulus persistence may be at the root of a number of perceptual deficits reported for elderly observers.

Perceptual span. We have noted a number of factors that limit the data available to older perceivers. A direct measure of the impact of these limitations on the construction of a percept may be made by noting the amount of information that a person can acquire in a brief glance. Such a measure is the perceptual span, which is also known as iconic memory. The visual information is available for only a brief period of time, such as a quarter of a second. The span is affected by the strength of the stimulus. Following the theme, which has been developed here, young adults are capable of capturing a large amount of data while older adults have a more limited capacity. The limit on the span of the older observers may be related to their reduced light and contrast sensitivities that result in relatively weak stimuli. This point was supported by a study that compensated for the reduced sensitivity of the elderly participants and found that under this special condition age differences in span were eliminated.

The limit on the perceptual span may be linked to what has been identified as the *useful field of view* (UFOV). The UFOV is the spatial extent within which highly accurate stimulus detection and identification can be performed. Measurement of the UFOV emphasizes the capability to acquire information in peripheral fields of vision where elderly adults have reduced light sensitivity. The UFOV of elderly participants is three times more restricted than young adults, meaning that they can examine only relatively small areas of the visual field. This restriction in the UFOV has been shown to be related to the incidence of automobile accidents at road intersections.

Conclusion

It has been shown that there are multiple factors that limit visual data acquisition by older perceivers. It also has been demonstrated that in some tasks the sensory limitations may be compensated by using stronger visual stimuli. An appreciation of the nature of the variables that influence our construction of reality will help us to understand the differences in perceptual experience as we age.

GROVER C. GILMORE

See also EYE, AGING-RELATED DISEASES; HEARING; HOME ADAPTATION AND EQUIPMENT; MEMORY.

BIBLIOGRAPHY

BOTWINICK, J. *Aging and Behavior: A Comprehensive Integration of Research Findings,* 2d ed. New York: Springer Publishing Co., 1978.

CORSO, J. F. *Aging Sensory Systems and Perception.* New York: Praeger, 1981.

CORSO, J. F. "Sensory-Perceptual Processes and Aging." In *Annual Review of Gerontology and Geriatrics,* vol. 7. Edited by K. Warner Schaie and Carl Eisdorfer. New York: Springer Publishing Co., 1987.

GILMORE, G. C.; WENK, H.; NAYLOR, L.; and STUVE, T. "Motion Perception and Aging." *Psychology and Aging* 7 (1992): 654–660.

KLINE, D. W., and SCHIEBER, F. "Vision and Aging." In *Handbook of the Psychology of Aging,* 2d ed. Edited by James E. Birren and K. Warner Schaie. New York: Van Nostrand Reinhold Company, 1985.

OWSLEY, C., and SLOANE, M. E. "Contrast Sensitivity, Acuity, and the Perception of 'Real World' Targets." *British Journal of Ophthalmology* 71 (1987): 791–796.

OWSLEY, C.; BALL, K.; McGWIN, G., JR.; SLOANE, M. E.; ROENKER, D. L.; WHITE, M.; and OVERLEY, T. "Visual Processing Impairment and Risk of Motor Vehicle Crash Among Older Adults." *Journal of the American Medical Association* 279 (1998): 1083–1088.

SCHIEBER, F. "Aging and the Senses." In *Handbook of Mental Health and Aging,* 2d ed. Edited by James E. Birren, R. Bruce Sloane, Gene D. Cohen, Nancy R. Hooyman, Barry D. Lebowitz, May H. Wykle, and Donna E. Deutchman. San Diego: Academic Press, 1992.

SCIALFA, C. T.; GUZY, L. T.; LEIBOWITZ, H. W.; GARVEY, P. M.; and TYRELL, R. A. "Age Differences in Estimating Vehicle Velocity." *Psychology and Aging* 6 (1991): 60–66.

TRICK, G. L., and SILVERMAN, S. E. "Visual Sensitivity to Motion: Age Related Changes and Deficits in Senile Dementia of the Alzheimer Type." *Neurology* 41 (1991): 1437–1440.

VISUAL ARTS AND AGING

Older adults have been represented surprisingly often in the visual arts. Over half of Rembrandt's works represent an elderly person. This includes fifty-five drawings, etchings, and paintings taken from the single biblical story of the elderly blind man Tobit and his wife Anna. Rembrandt's other important images of aging persons include the famous series of self-portraits recording his own aging process, *Old Woman Reading* (Rijksmuseum, Amsterdam), *Portrait of an Old Woman* (Hermitage, Leningrad), and many others. Important images of elderly people by other painters include Ghirlandaio's *An Old Man and His Grandson* (Louvre, Paris); Albrecht Dürer's *Saint Jerome* (Albertina, Vienna); Peter Paul Rubens's *Philemon and Baucis* (Art History Museum, Vienna); Velázquez's *The Old Water Seller of Seville* (Wellington Museum, London); Georges de Tour's *Saint Joseph, Carpenter* (Louvre, Paris); and Leonardo's *Self Portrait* (Turin, Royal Library), to mention only a few works from the history of European painting. In the twentieth century, major artistic statements about aging include Pablo Picasso's *The Old Guitarist* (The Art Institute of Chicago), Kathe Kollwitz's *Self Portrait* (National Gallery, Berlin), and Henry Tanner's *The Banjo Lesson* (Hampton University Museum of Art). But here again, there are many others that could be mentioned. In China, the classic mountain landscape painting almost always includes an elderly person traveling up a mountain stream or pathway. Indeed, one might argue that the genre is as much about old age as about landscape. Major masterpieces in this tradition include *Walking With a Staff* by Shen Chou (Ming Dynasty, National Palace Museum, Taipei), *Recluse in A Mountain Abode* by Kuo Hsi (Sung Dynasty, National Palace Museum, Taipei), and *Looking at the Waterfall* by Ma Lin (Sung Dynasty, The Palace Museum, Beijing). Numerous representations of elderly people are found in Islamic miniatures, such as the thirteenth-century anonymous work *Men Assembling Wood* (Metropolitan Museum of Art, New York), and Aqa Mirak's *Scene in a Mosque,* an illustration in the Falnameh or *Book of Divination* (Musee d'art et d' historie, Geneva). In nineteenth-century Japan, Katsushika Hokusai thought as seriously as Rembrandt had about the visual representation of aging. His *A Self Portrait at the Age of Eighty Three* and *Head of an Old Man* (both at National Museum of Ethology, Leiden) and *A Peasant Crossing a Bridge* (Honolulu Academy of the Arts)

The painting The Banjo Lesson *by Henry Ossawa Tanner* (Photo provided by the Hampton University Museum of Art, Virginia. Reproduced with permission.)

are typical expressions of his interest in representing elderly people.

Older adults have also been represented in sculpture throughout history. Notable examples are *Old Woman Going to Market*, an anonymous Roman sculpture of the second or third century (Metropolitan Museum of Art, New York), Donatello's *Penitent Magdalen* (Museo dell' Opera, Florence), Michelangelo's figure *Twilight* for the tomb of Julius II (Lorenzo, Florence), several figures in Rodin's ensemble *Burghers of Calais*, and his numerous studies of Honoré de Balzac, Victor Hugo, Georges Clemenceau, and others.

Besides painting and sculpture, film has been a major source of visual representations of aging in art. The aging Walter Houston won the Academy Award for best actor for his portrayal of the crusty old prospector Howard in the 1948 film *The Treasure of the Sierra Madre*, and Geraldine Page won the academy award for best actress in the 1985 film *The Trip to Bountiful*, for her portrayal of the elderly widow Carrie Watts. Ingmar Bergman's *Wild Strawberries* has attracted extensive comment for its insightful portrayal of the elderly character Dr. Borg.

Finally, the art of photography has produced some unforgettable images of the aging face, and some of these have become virtual icons of twentieth-century culture. Examples are Yousuf Karsh's photographic portraits of Winston Churchill and Albert Einstein, Irving Penn's *Colette*, and Dorothea Lange's *White Angel Bread Line*.

Portrayals

To understand how frequently elderly people are depicted in art, it is a good exercise to study the almost innumerable images of St. Jerome as wise elder that have been produced in the history of European painting, and the vast range and variety of perspectives on the aged person that have been presented through the use of that theme. Visual images of this popular fifth-century saint in his old age are standard fixtures in hotels, restaurants, hospitals, government buildings, and other public places over most of Europe. In much of Asia, representations of the elderly Chinese sage in a remote mountain retreat, referred to above, are similarly common. Another good way to discover how frequently artists create images of elderly people is this: go to any museum of art, and, excluding galleries devoted solely to twentieth-century abstract work, try to find a room or gallery that does not contain at least one representation of an elderly person. It is enlightening to discover how infrequently one is able to do so. In the same vein, try to name a film in which no elderly character appears in at least a significant supporting role. It can be done, but not often.

Visual artists have been careful and astute observers of elderly people, often seeing beyond conventional false stereotypes. A conventional negative stereotype of age in the West is that the physical appearance of old age is without beauty. But most visual artists have insisted that the characteristic look of the aging face and typical gestures of the aging body are of great beauty and aesthetic value. The testimony of artists in support of this view can be seen in the frequency and care with which they have created exquisitely beautiful images of older persons. In China, this division between the conventional view of aging and the observations of artists does not exist, because Chinese popular culture, like China's visual artists, attributes great physical beauty in the aging face and body. Artists have also created numerous images that combat the stereotype of older adults as frail or without physical vigor or energy. Against this, elderly people are regularly depicted in the visual arts as being physically robust and vigorous. See, for example, La Tour's *Saint Joseph, Carpenter* (cited above) and Rembrandt's *Old Woman Cutting Her Nails* (Metropolitan Museum of Art, New York).

Another consistent motif in art showing careful observation of older adults is the representation of a special relationship between elderly people and children. This was a favorite theme of Velázquez, which he explored repeatedly. Examples are his *The Old Water Seller of Seville* (cited above) and *Old Woman Cooking* (National Galleries of Scotland, Edinburgh). Tanner's *Banjo Lesson* (cited above) is a strong statement of the same theme. In images like these the artist expresses ideas and attitudes about the passing of culture from generation to generation, a fundamental process of civilization.

One way to gauge the soundness of what artists say in their representations of aging is to compare it with findings in the modern social science of gerontology. For example, a central observation of the modern psychology of aging is that many people, as they grow into their later years, tend to "disengage" or to withdraw from the activities and interests that motivated them in youth and middle age, and increase the time spent in inner reflection. Many representations of elderly people in the history of art record and explore this change of orientation. Representative examples include the paintings by Dürer and Rembrandt cited above, the many representations of Saint Jerome in the desert found in European painting, the motif of withdrawal to a mountain retreat or hermitage in the Chinese landscape, and representations of the elder as aesthetic wanderer in Hindu art.

Another discovery of modern psychology of aging is that people tend to reminisce more often, and apparently with greater interest, as they advance into late adulthood. Many paintings of elderly people in the history of art evoke an unmistakable mood of reminiscence, showing the artist's awareness of this phenomenon of late life. In the Chinese landscape, for example, the elderly person is often shown high in a mountain promontory, looking back over the path ascending from the valley below—an unmistakable met-

The painting Saint Jerome *by Albrecht Durer, circa 1521* (Historical Picture Archive/Corbis)

aphor for "looking back" over one's life. Early in the film *The Treasure of the Sierra Madre*, the old miner Howard engages in a deeply felt account of his past life, and the film *The Trip to Bountiful* actually centers on the theme of Carrie Watts's irrepressible need to revisit the past. Finally, much of modern scientific study of human aging concerns the possibility of achieving special insights, or wisdom, in old age. Here again, early artists have anticipated twentieth-century thought. The story of Tobit, so often represented in Rembrandt's works, is a story of illumination and understanding achieved in old age. Indeed, Rembrandt's life-long persistence in representing that theme in his painting would seem to indicate an interest in the possibility of old age wisdom, for the story's central event is the old blind man (Tobit) recovering his sight. A much repeated image of a wise elder who understands much is that of the father in the biblical story of the prodigal son. Powerful interpretations of that theme have been produced by many leading European and Islamic artists. Innumerable other paintings depict elderly people as either wise elders, or as pilgrims in search of wisdom. In the Western tradition, images of elders often show them with books, the illumination of candles, or keys, all symbols of the quest for and achievement of special insight. More often than not, Chinese paintings that depict the elderly at all show them as "sages," that is, as older adults who have achieved wisdom. A repeated theme in Chinese art shows the elderly sage thoughtfully watching or listening to a waterfall. There is a reason for this. In Chinese thought the waterfall is said to contain opposites, because the waterfall is forever moving and changing, and yet also forever staying in the same place. So the elderly sages' contemplation of it symbolizes the ultimate wisdom; namely understanding the underlying unity of all opposites.

Symbolism

As this example of the Chinese sages and the waterfall makes clear, it is difficult to understand what painters and sculptors have wanted to say about the experience of human aging without knowing something about symbols. These artists do not communicate what they wish to say about aging in words, as writers might do, so they often use instead the language of symbols. For example, bridges, doorways, windows and gates often appear in paintings of older adults to symbolize the aging person's transition to a new stage of life, old age. Many of the works cited above feature this symbolism. In many of his representations of the story of Tobit, for example, Rembrandt shows the old blind man waiting by or walking toward a doorway or window. Similarly, the elderly gentleman in Shen Chou's *Walking With a Staff* is shown approaching a bridge that crosses over a turbulent stream. Another common symbol in visual representations of older adults is the musical instrument, usually a string instrument such as the guitar or the violin. Such an image shows an older person creating harmony from separate sounds that individually have no meaning. But this in turn is a symbol of the aging person's ability to integrate disparate aspects of life into one understandable whole, which is a kind of wisdom. Often the symbolic old musician is shown as blind, recalling Plato's dictum that as outer vision weakens with age, inner vision (wisdom) grows. Of course many symbols of time and its passage are used in images of elderly people, including clocks, hourglasses, and used-up candles. The abstract form of the circle is sometimes used to symbolically express a feeling of life having come to completeness or to full closure. A striking example is the composition of Rembrandt's *Artist's Mother* (Art History Museum, Vienna), but the symbolism is

The painting Rembrandt's Mother Seated at a Table *by Rembrandt Harmensz van Rijn* (Historical Picture Archive/Corbis).

widely used. To understand representations of aging by artists outside one's own culture, it is useful to know something of the special symbolism of that culture. For example, the elderly people who appear so frequently in Chinese paintings are often shown with cranes, peaches, or pine trees, all familiar symbols in Chinese culture of late adulthood. Finally, the most potent symbol in an art work depicting an elderly person is often the image of the elderly person itself. For the elderly face, body and gestures are themselves "mythic" for us, in the sense that they powerfully convey important meanings such as endurance, courage, inner strength, and vulnerability.

For purposes of discerning what an artist is saying specifically about aging in a particular work, it is useful to distinguish between the story being illustrated (Isaac blessing Jacob, or Saint Jerome's retreat to a desert hermitage) and the artist's specific manner of representing the elderly person who appears in the work. To appreciate how distinct these things are, a good exercise is to study the difference of treatment of the same elderly person in the same story. One might compare, for example, Raemerswael's *Saint Je-*

rome in His Study (Musee des Beaux Artes, Antwerp), and Massy's *Saint Jerome* (Art History Museum, Vienna). Both artists are offering creative images of the same events in the life of the same aging man, yet the meanings they see in these things are very different.

Assessing the image

An important question to consider when viewing a representation of old age is whether the artist is representing it in a positive or negative light. This will sometimes be quite evident at first sight. Leonardo's caricatures of age (Royal Collection, Windsor Castle) and Ivan Albright's *Fleeting Time Thou Has Made Me Old* (Metropolitan Museum of Art, New York) are obviously and uncompromisingly negative. Many art works give positive interpretations of aging that are equally evident. But many express perspectives on aging with various degrees of ambivalence or mixed nuances, which makes it more challenging to interpret the artist's specific message about aging. In all cases, when forming a judgment about what an artist is saying about aging in a particular work, it is useful to consider the following questions. Is the overall feeling the artist seems to create about aging primarily negative or positive? Does the artist present aging exclusively as a matter of physical change, or are other, nonphysical, dimensions of aging also represented, such as social relationships, psychological growth or decline, increased knowledge, wisdom or emotional fulfillment? If nonphysical dimensions of aging are suggested, are they shown in a positive or negative light? Are aging persons shown as having any importance for others in society, and if so, what difference are they shown as making to the lives of others? Is the elderly person shown as engaged in a process of spiritual growth, and if so, how? Does the artist use line or color to express ideas, feelings, or attitudes about aging, such as color harmonies or disharmonies, or lines that are either disturbingly tense or reassuringly peaceful? What symbols does the artist use to convey attitudes or ideas about aging?

Formal resources that artists use to communicate about the aging face and body include lines, used to represent and interpret the facial wrinkles of the aging face. Line used in this way can eloquently express many characteristics naturally associated with the aged person, such as burdensome memories and depth of thought (see Dürer's *Saint Jerome*, and Leonardo da Vinci's *Self Portrait*, both cited above, as examples of this use of line). A parallel use of facial lines to express emotions related to age can be seen in the scarification of many African masks. In typical Chinese masterpieces, line was skillfully used to show the distinctive gestures and postures of the aging human body, whose forms can be poignantly expressive. Color is another formal element artists use to express feelings and attitudes about age. The shiny, cadaverish greys used in Albright's images of aging express a revulsion toward it, while in Rubens' portrait of Saint Jerome, the strongly dominant red expresses an upbeat optimism and sense of vitality. Selection of harmonious or disharmonious color schemes can also communicate a lot about an artist's outlook on age. The sculptor has, in addition, a third dimension created by a plastic medium, which presents the opportunity to go beyond line and organization of areas to raised surfaces and volumes. These, in turn, are used to create the ruggedly textured quality of the aging face, expressing the depth of experience and character associated with age. Rodin's representations of elderly persons illustrates this approach especially well.

Many images of elderly people are simply portraits, in which recording a particular person's appearance, and capturing something of that individual's essential personality, is the goal. But many representations of the elderly occur in the larger context of a story or genre scene. Sometimes the elder pictured in such a scene is the main protagonist, as in the images of Tobit and Anna in paintings depicting that biblical story. But even more often one or more elderly persons appear in an image, but in only a secondary, supportive role. Examples are the old woman who looks on from the sidelines in Rubens's *Samson and Delilah,* or the elderly violinist who plays in the background of many of Edgar Degas's ballerina paintings. Such "secondary" images of aging should not be overlooked or dismissed, for the statement they make about aging is sometimes of great interest and important to the overall meaning of the work. Degas's old musician, for example, symbolizes the need for old age wisdom, which enables the younger generation to carry on its own life or "dance."

A topic of debate among art scholars is whether artists adopt a different style—often referred to as "late style"—as they age. Late style is said to be characterized by greater economy or simplicity of means, whereby a powerful statement is made with relatively little differentiation of detail. Michelangelo is said to have followed such a path of development because his late sculptures are strikingly less complex, yet no less powerful, than his earlier works. The point at issue can be observed by comparing two of his works on the same theme, the pieta, one early (*Pieta,* c. 1499, Saint Peter's, Rome) the other late (*Pieta,* c. 1564, Castillo Sforzesco, Milan). The same evolution of style has been said to characterize Kathe Kollwitz's artistic development, and can be seen by comparing her early and late self-portraits.

PATRICK L. MCKEE

See also AGEISM; LITERATURE AND AGING.

BIBLIOGRAPHY

AMHEIM, R. "On the Late Style of Life and Art." *Michigan Quarterly Review.* Edited by Kathleen Woodward and David Van Tassel. (spring 1978): 149–156.

CLARK, K. *The Artist Grows Old.* Cambridge, U.K.: Cambridge University Press, 1962.

CLARK, K. "Rembrandt's Self Portraits." *Proceedings of the Royal Institute os Great Britain* 39 (1962): 145–171.

ERIKSON, E. "Reflections of Dr. Borg's Life Cycle." In *Aging, Death, and the Completion of Being.* Edited by D. Van Tassel. Philadelphia: University of Pennsylvania Press, 1979. Pages 29–68.

HELD, J. *Rembrandt and the Book of Tobit.* Princeton, N.J.: The Gehenna Press, 1964.

MCKEE, P. L. "Old Age in the Chinese Mountain Landscape." *The Journal of Aesthetic Education* 24 (1990): 59–73.

MCKEE, P. L., and KAUPPINEN, H. *The Art of Aging: A Celebration of Old Age in Western Art.* New York: Human Sciences Press, 1987.

SPICKER, S., et al. *Aging and the Elderly: Humanistic Perspectives on Gerontology.* Atlantic Highlands, N.J.: Humanities Press, 1978.

WANG, S.-C. *Introduction to Three Hundred Masterpieces of Chinese Painting in the National Palace Museum.* Taipei: National Palace Museum, 1959.

WINKLER, M. G. "Walking to the Stars." *Handbook of the Humanities and Aging.* Edited by Thomas R. Cole, David D. Van Tassel and Robert Kastenbaum. New York: Springer Publishing, 1992. Pages 258–284.

VITAMINS

A vitamin is defined as a chemical (organic compound) present in variable small quantities in natural foodstuffs and essential for the normal processes of growth and maintenance of the body. Vitamins do not furnish energy, but are essential for the transfer of energy and regulation of metabolism (chemical processes) involved in the normal growth and maintenance of the body (Parker).

The word *vitamin* was coined in 1912 by the Polish-born American biochemist Casimir Funk (1884–1967) to describe a "vital amine" from rice husks that cured beriberi, a disease that affects brain and nervous function (Thadani; Horton). Indeed, thiamine or vitamin B^1, contains an amine (nitrogen) group. However, the term is a misnomer because not all vitamins contain nitrogen. For example, vitamins A, D, E, and K are not amines and do not contain nitrogen.

What are some common vitamin deficiencies seen with age?

Vitamin deficiencies in older adults may be caused by decreased food intake, changes in taste, smell, hearing and vision, loss of teeth, ongoing illness or medications. For example:

1. Loss of teeth can result in decreased food intake and a diet favoring a limited number of pre-prepared pureed foods. In these cases, it is important to identify foods that need to be modified in consistency and those that can be eaten as is (for example, fresh bananas) to prevent vitamin deficiencies.
2. In older adults a diet lacking zinc can contribute to a loss of taste. This can be remedied with a zinc supplement.
3. Acid production in the stomach slows with age decreasing the amount of iron and vitamin B^{12} absorbed. This may lead to *anemia.* Illnesses like ulcer, hemorrhoids, and colon cancer can also cause blood loss leading to anemia. Regular use of aspirin as an anti-inflammatory at higher doses can also cause blood loss in the stomach and contribute to anemia.

A nutritionally balanced diet and routine physical checkups help to prevent disease and maintain health during a lifetime.

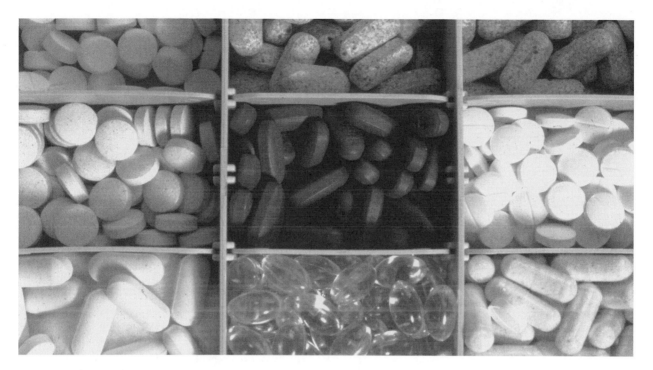

Many people use vitamins like these to supplement their daily diet. Vitamins come in all shapes, sizes, and colors. (Archive Photos Inc.)

What are antioxidants?

Vitamins A, C, and E are often described as *antioxidants*. They are substances that prevent a chemical reaction called oxidation. Oxidation can produce chemicals that are very reactive and sometimes harmful to the cells in the body. Natural antioxidants such as vitamins A, C, and E work together to prevent oxidation and therefore have a protecting effect for body cells. The potential role of antioxidants in reducing the risk of heart disease, cancers, and cataracts is currently being studied.

Can vitamins be used to treat medical conditions?

Some vitamins can have a therapeutic use also. For example, in 1955 it was found that niacin in very large doses (1.5 to 3 g per day) could decrease serum cholesterol. While it can be used for this purpose, it is important to know that side effects such as flushing of the skin, itching, nausea, and liver damage limit its use (Gillis). A physician should supervise any large-dose vitamin therapy.

Conclusion

A plan for health promotion and disease prevention includes a diet that incorporates a variety of foods, adequate fluid consumption, moderate fat intake, regular physical activity, limiting alcohol intake, and avoiding smoking. The use of supplements should be considered together with diet and exercise to meet individual nutritional needs.

MEERA B. THADANI

See also DEMENTIA; HEART DISEASE; HERBAL THERAPY; MALNUTRITION; NUTRITION.

BIBLIOGRAPHY

GILLIS, M. C., ed. *Compendium of Pharmaceuticals and Specialties.* Ottawa: Canadian Pharmacists Association, 2000.

HORTON, H. R. *Principles of Biochemistry.* Englewood Cliffs, N.J.: Neil Patterson Publishers, 1993.

PARKER, S. P., ed. *McGraw-Hill Dictionary of Scientific and Technical Terms,* 5th ed. New York, McGraw-Hill Inc., 1994.

THADANI, M. *Medicinal and Pharmaceutical Uses of Natural Products.* Winnipeg: Cantext Publications, 1996.

VOLUNTEER ACTIVITIES AND PROGRAMS

Volunteering may be defined as unpaid work that is willingly performed. In the academic and professional literature, the term is usually restricted to describe unpaid work that is done for formal organizations. In some cases, the term *volunteering* is used more broadly to include informal assistance to neighbors and strangers or discretionary tasks performed on behalf of relatives. This discussion is concerned solely with volunteering that is done on behalf of formal organizations. In some instances the distinction between paid and unpaid work for organizations is blurred because "volunteers" receive some financial compensation in the form of a stipend, living allowance, or reimbursement for expenses. Some analysts resolve this issue of definition by counting all who are compensated with less than the minimum wage as volunteers; other analysts use the term "stipended volunteer" to identify a hybrid role that incorporates some aspects of a volunteer and some of a paid employee.

In the United States and many other countries, nonprofit organizations that rely extensively on volunteers are of great importance to community life. Churches, schools, hospitals, political campaigns, environmental organizations, community recreation, and arts organizations are prominent examples of formal organizations that make extensive use of volunteers. In some instances like contemporary hospitals and schools, volunteers supplement paid employees. In other settings such as certain churches, political campaigns, and arts organizations, volunteers outnumber paid workers. Some of these efforts are viable only because of the efforts of volunteers (Ellis and Campbell).

In the United States, volunteering is widespread. On the basis of a review of many studies of the extent of volunteering in the United States, Fischer and Schaffer concluded that, among adults, between 18 and 55 percent volunteer. (Estimates of the extent of volunteering vary greatly because of differences in the definitions of volunteering that were employed in various studies.) Typically, the time that volunteers contribute is modest—usually no more than a few hours a week.

Elders are of particularly great importance to nonprofit organizations as volunteer resources because of the major changes that have taken place in recent decades in employment patterns and longevity. The young and middle-aged married women who once spearheaded community-service volunteering are much less available as volunteers because most are now involved in extensive gainful employment. On the other hand, older people tend to be permanently out of the workforce at relatively young ages with the expectation of living in good health for many years. The young elders who are retired or working part-time have the potential to replace married middle-class women as the major volunteer resource for many nonprofit organizations (Morris and Caro).

Elders do not volunteer more than other adults. Recent surveys indicate that young elders are similar to middle-aged adults in their rates of volunteering. Rates of volunteering tend to fall off among those over seventy-five years of age. Several background characteristics have consistently been found to predict volunteering among elders. Those with higher incomes, higher levels of formal education, who are religiously active and in good health are more likely than other elders to volunteer. Those who have consistently volunteered throughout their adult lives are likely to continue volunteering. Despite the large numbers who have retired early and are in good health, there is no evidence that rates of volunteering increase after retirement. However, there is evidence that among volunteers, the number of hours per week devoted to volunteering tends to increase modestly after retirement (Fischer and Schaffer).

Altruism is a major reason for volunteering among elders. Helping others and contributing to their community are often given by elders as reasons for volunteering. Ideology or the importance of the cause are also common reasons for volunteering among elders. Volunteering that supports a religious cause is particularly common among elders. Social factors are also important; many elders volunteer to make friends and to sustain friendships. Elders are less likely than other adults to volunteer in order to develop new skills, to gain experience, or to make useful professional contacts (Fischer and Schaffer).

The circumstances that surround assignments also affect willingness to volunteer. Elders are more likely to agree to volunteer when they are asked personally to take on the assignment, when the assignment is of short duration, and when there is flexibility in scheduling. Elders also respond positively to cash or in-kind incentives. Free meals, free parking, and reimbursement for out-of-pocket expenses are positive factors in recruiting and retaining elder volunteers.

Sound administration is also vital to successful deployment of elders as volunteers. Assignments must be clearly defined; responsibilities must be appropriate for the skills of potential volunteers; appropriate training and support must be provided; the volunteer effort should be recognized even if only through symbolic expressions of appreciation.

Volunteering is believed to be a potentially beneficial activity for elders (Fischer and Schaffer). Statistical evidence is available that links activity generally and volunteering specifically with health among elders (Musick, Herzog, and House). Active elders tend to enjoy greater health. While good health makes activity easier for elders, the stimulation provided by activities like volunteering may also promote good health. The intellectually stimulating aspects of volunteer assignments may be helpful in sustaining and even improving the intellectual functioning of elders. To the extent that volunteer assignments have attractive social aspects, they may be helpful to otherwise socially isolated elders in combating loneliness. The opportunity to contribute to an important cause as a volunteer may also help to give some elders reason for taking constructive steps to stay healthy.

Substantial critical concerns surround volunteering. That only a minority of elders are intensively engaged in volunteer work reflects structural issues in volunteering. Both the displacement of nonprofit organizations by for-profit organizations and the tendency in nonprofit organizations for paid employees to displace volunteers have tended to marginalize volunteers (Ellis and Campbell). Many community service organizations that began as volunteer efforts are now staffed entirely by paid employees. Typically, in community service organizations, when paid professionals have gained dominance, volunteers have come to be seen as "amateurs" whose skills and reliability are suspect. When volunteering is seen to be of marginal importance within an organization, little is invested in developing assignments for volunteers or in recruiting, placing, and supervising volunteers. In many organizations only nonessential tasks are left for volunteers. Frequently, these tasks are of a highly routine nature. A pattern is established in which little is asked of volunteers, and in turn, little is given by volunteers.

In some settings, volunteers have been seen as an economic threat to paid workers. In some of these cases, labor unions have raised formal objections to volunteers. Some of those with an interest in volunteering also do not want to take work away from the paid staff. Organizations address these concerns by providing assurances that volunteer assignments do not duplicate any assignments that are carried out by paid personnel. From the perspective of volunteers, the risk in measures that protect paid personnel is that assignments left for volunteers are tedious and of minor importance to the organization (Brudney).

Volunteers have fared better in community service organizations that can afford few if any paid employees. Under the best of circumstances, these organizations have sufficient resources to hire enough paid personnel to provide strong administrative support to the volunteers who carry out the service mission of the organization. Some school mentoring, youth recreation, adult literacy, friendly visiting, and information and referral programs work effectively on this basis.

Particularly at risk are organizations that face multiple diverse demands with such limited staffing that the organization relies heavily on volunteers, but volunteer administration receives insufficient attention. Among the highly vulnerable are organizations with a single paid employee whose multiple responsibilities include volunteer management.

Volunteer opportunities. Most volunteer opportunities are strictly of a local nature. Religious congregations, day care centers, elementary schools, after school programs, recreational programs for children and youth, hospitals, hospices, nursing homes, home delivered meal programs, soup kitchens, shelters, political campaigns, libraries, museums, environmental protection organizations, senior citizens centers, and small town governments are prominent among the settings in which there is demand for volunteers.

The roles that elder volunteers perform are also highly varied. Many assignments involve one-to-one service to individuals. Examples include visiting the homebound, escorting frail elders to health care appointments, tutoring children, providing information to the public about offerings of service organizations, and providing guidance to individuals on tasks ranging from tax preparation to applications for public entitlement programs. Other assignments involve assistance to groups such as coaching and umpiring in youth recreation programs, interpreting museum exhibits to visitors, and reading to young children in libraries. Assignments that take place behind the scenes include food preparation, shopping for the homebound, writing and editing of newsletters, preparation of mailings, and physical labor on behalf of civic beautification efforts.

Some volunteer opportunities are part of national initiatives. Outlined below are illustrations of these volunteer assignments. Some are explicitly for older people; others are open to people of all ages.

The Retired Senior Volunteer Program (RSVP) is one of three volunteering programs for seniors administered by the Corporation for National Service. RSVP provides varied volunteer opportunities for retirees who are fifty-five years of age and older. The specific volunteer opportunities that are available vary depending on local initiatives. Most common assignments involve assistance within multipurpose senior centers, congregate and home-delivered meal programs, hospitals, and nursing homes. Typically, RSVP volunteers contribute only a few hours a week. RSVP volunteers do not receive stipends. In 1997, the program enlisted the efforts of 450,000 volunteers at over 70,000 stations. Additional information on the RSVP program can be obtained by visiting the following Web site: www.seniorcorps.org/index.html

The Senior Companion Program is a federal program administered by the Corporation for National Service that combines supported employment with volunteering. Eligibility is limited to low income people sixty years of age and older. Senior Companions usually work twenty hours a week for which they receive a living allowance. They provide assistance to frail, community-residing individuals. Typically, a senior companion serves between two and four people each week. Senior Companions develop friendships with their clients, run errands for them, and provide transportation and escort for them to medical appointments. Most of those served are older people. In 1997, almost 14,000 people were active as Senior Companions; they served close to 50,000 clients. For additional information on the Senior Companion Program and for a listing of program sites in your state, visit the Senior Companion Program Web site at: www.cns.gov

The Foster Grandparents Program is the third federal volunteer program explicitly for seniors and is administered by the Corporation for National Service. Like the Senior Companion program, the Foster Grandparent program offers living allowances to low-income people who are at least sixty years of age and commit themselves to serving twenty hours a week. Foster Grandparents serve children and youth with special needs. The settings in which they work include schools, hospitals, Head Start Programs, and youth centers. In 1997, 25,000 elders were active as Foster Grandparents in 8,400 settings. For additional information on the Foster Grandparents Program and for a listing of program sites in your state, visit the Foster Grandparents Program Web site at: www.cns.gov

Service Corps of Retired Executives (SCORE) provides counseling to small businesses in the United States. Both retired and working executives provide free counseling and low-cost workshops. SCORE is administered through 389 chapters. In a typical year, SCORE enlists the efforts of over 12,000 volunteers. In 1998, more than 350,000 businesses were assisted by SCORE. Though SCORE is a nonprofit, private association, it enjoys a partnership relationship with the federal government's Small Business Administration. Additional information can be obtained by visiting the SCORE Web site at: www.score.org

International Executive Service Corp (IESC) is a nonprofit organization that provides assistance to small and medium-sized businesses in many countries. Volunteers help clients in such matters as preparation of business plans, development of marketing strategies, and achievement of production efficiencies. Some of the projects are designed to help the public sector in host countries further democratic governance. Both retirees and employed executives serve as volunteers. Most IESC projects take one to three months to complete. Each year IESC takes on approximately one thousand projects. Additional information can be obtained by visiting the IESC Web site at: www.iesc.org

The American Association of Retired Persons (AARP) relies on volunteers to provide staffing for a variety of programs that it has developed to help elders. Volunteers are needed, for example, to operate AARP's Consumer Housing Information Service for Seniors, which provides information on housing options; the Medicare/Medicaid Assistance Program (MMAP), which helps older people file claims; the Supplemental Security Income Outreach Project, which helps low-income people apply for the program; the Tax Aide program, which helps people file their income taxes; and the 55 Alive/Mature Driving, which provides classes to improve the skills of older drivers. AARP has a computerized referral service that links those interested in volunteering with various programs. Registration forms can be obtained by writing: AARP Volunteer Talent Bank, Dept. NB, 601 E Street, Washington, D.C. 20049. Additional information can be obtained by visiting the AARP Web site on the Volunteer Opportunities for Senior Citizens: www.aarp. org/volunteerguide

OASIS is a private program for those fifty-five years and older that combines education with volunteering. OASIS is sponsored jointly by a department store chain and a health system. Active in twenty-six cities in the United States, the program serves 350,000 members. Volunteer opportunities are available for members in three broad categories: tutoring children, teaching in the educational program, and management of the OASIS program. Additional information can be obtained by visiting the OASIS Web site at: www.oasisnet.org

The National Retired Volunteer Coalition (NRVC) is a network of corporate retiree programs that has merged with Volunteers of America, a spiritually based national, nonprofit organization that provides diverse social services to the elderly, to families, to children and youth, to the homeless, and to those in correctional facilities. Over one hundred corporations have been a part of the coalition. Historically, each participating corporation developed its own projects, which have ranged from the development of assistive technology for those with disabilities, to mentoring school children, to serving meals to the homeless, and to raising vegetables for a local food bank. Additional information can be obtained by visiting the NRVC Web site at: www.nrvc.org

Shepherd's Centers of America (SCA) is a faith-based national umbrella organization that coordinates nearly one hundred centers throughout the United States that are designed to meet varied needs of older people. The movement began in 1972 as a collaboration of Catholic, Jewish, and Protestant congregations. Shepherd's Centers offer varied programs and activities that include home services, classes for intellectual stimulation, and health education classes. Participants are encouraged to engage in community service. They may serve as volunteers in the home services offered by their center such as home-delivered meals, home maintenance, and telephone reassurance. Alternately, participants can volunteer to teach in an educational program offered by their center. Additional information can be obtained by visiting the SCA Web site at: www.shepherdcenters.org

Although primarily a program that combines learning experiences with travel for mature adults, ELDERHOSTEL Service Programs now offers experiences for mature adults that combine travel and education with service. Participants travel at their own expense to a setting for a limited period of time (usually less than a week) where they engage in service activities such as assisting on an archaeological dig, protecting sand dunes on a seashore, tutoring students from an Indian Reservation, restoring natural landscapes, and identifying and counting migrating birds. Additional information can be obtained by visiting the Elderhostel Web site at: www. elderhostel.org

Literacy Volunteers of America (LVA) is an important example of a specific purpose volunteer network that serves adults of all ages and draws upon volunteers of all ages. LVA is a network of 350 locally based programs that teach both basic literacy and English for speakers of other languages. LVA provides professional training to its volunteers on teaching methods. Volunteer tutors are expected to make a one-year commitment. During that year, they typically meet with their students for 90 to 120 minutes per week. Additional information can be obtained by visiting the LVA Web site at: www.literacyvolunteers.org

The Long-Term Care Ombudsman Program is an advocacy program for residents of nursing homes, board and care homes, and assisted living facilities that relies primarily on certified volunteer ombudsmen. Ombudsmen identify, investigate, and resolve complaints that involve residents of long-term care programs. Ombudsmen also provide information to residents and the general public about long-term care services. In 1998, the program was active in 587 localities in the United States. In that year, 7,000 individuals served as volunteer ombudsmen. The program investigated 200,000 complaints and provided information on long-term care to 200,000 people. Information about how to serve as an ombudsman can be obtained from state units on aging. Or visit the Administration on Aging Web site at www.aoa.dhhs.gov for a directory of state long-term care ombudsman programs.

Obtaining information about volunteer opportunities

Information about volunteer opportunities can be obtained in various ways. Many Councils on Aging or senior centers provide information to elders about various local volunteer opportunities. Volunteer coordinators in senior centers can be particularly helpful as matchmakers when they are personally acquainted with both the would-be volunteer and potential assignments. Retirees from corporations that participate in the National Retiree Volunteer Coalition are able to obtain information about retiree volunteer programs developed through their former employers. Some newspapers regularly carry listings of volunteer opportunities. In some cases, volunteer opportunities for elders are listed separately. Nationally, the Points of Light Foundation identifies organizations throughout the country that serve as volunteer clearinghouses. These local agencies keep listings of volunteer opportunities and provide placement services for potential volunteers. A listing of local volunteer centers is available through the Points of Light Web site at: www.pointsoflight.org

FRANCIS G. CARO

See also EDUCATION; LEISURE; PRODUCTIVE AGING.

BIBLIOGRAPHY

BRUDNEY, J. L. *Fostering Volunteer Programs in the Public Sector: Planning, Initiating, and Managing Voluntary Activities.* San Francisco: Jossey-Bass, 1990.

CHAMBRE, S. M. *Good Deeds in Old Age: Volunteering by the New Leisure Class.* Lexington, Mass.: Lexington Books, 1987.

ELLIS, S. J., and CAMPBELL, K. N. *By the People: A History of Americans as Volunteers.* San Francisco: Jossey Bass, 1990.

FISCHER, L. R., and SCHAFFER, K. B. *Older Volunteers: A Guide to Research and Practice.* Newbury Park, Calif,: Sage, 1993.

MORRIS, R., and CARO, F. "The Young-old, Productive Aging, and Public Policy." *Generations* 19, no. 3 (1995): 32–37.

MUSICK, M. A.; HERZOG, A. R.; and HOUSE, J. S. "Volunteering and Mortality among Older Adults: Findings from a National Sample." *Journals of Gerontology: Psychological and Social Sciences* 54B, no. 3, (1999): S173–S180.

WALKING AIDS

As people get older, they become more likely to have difficulty walking independently, and the risk of falls increases. The appropriate use of walking aids can help provide stability and safety in some elderly people with mobility problems. Mobility aids include canes, crutches, and walkers.

Canes

Using a cane correctly will help to improve balance by widening the base of support and by providing additional sensory input. The usual base of support is the area under and between the two feet. This area of support is enlarged with the use of a cane. A cane can also reduce the amount of weight that must be borne by the legs, which can be important in people with arthritis or weakness of the legs. There is good evidence to support the use of a cane in elderly people with decreased vision, peripheral nerve problems, previous stroke, as well as those who have had surgery for a hip fracture. Some patients may be reluctant to start using a cane, as they fear it makes them look frail. Consistent encouragement and emphasizing that using the cane will allow them to walk farther and more safely can usually overcome this hurdle.

Single point wooden canes, while relatively inexpensive, must be carefully fitted to the correct size relative to the patient's height and arm length. Lighter weight aluminum canes can easily be adjusted for proper height. The length of the cane should ideally result in between twenty and thirty degrees of elbow flexion. This can be achieved by measuring from the floor to the wrist crease, with the arm hanging loosely at the patient's side. The cane should be held in the hand opposite to the impaired (weak or painful) leg, and moved forward with the impaired leg. By doing this, the amount of weight bearing experienced by that leg is reduced proportionate to the amount of weight put through the cane.

Canes should always be fitted with rubber tips, to prevent slipping. The standard cane has a smooth, curved handle. A built-up molded handle is used in people with impaired hand function, for example in severe arthritis. Multiple point canes, such as quadruped canes (commonly called quad canes), provide a greater base of support and thus even greater stability, and can stand by themselves. They are often prescribed in stroke patients. However, they are cumbersome and difficult to use on uneven surfaces or by people who move relatively quickly, as all four feet must be on the ground at the same time else the increased base of support is lost and the extra feet may get entangled in furniture. A straight cane has the advantage of being maneuverable in tight quarters.

Crutches

Bilateral crutches are infrequently used in older adults to eliminate weight bearing on one leg. Crutches are made of either aluminum or wood, and are adjustable in height at the base and hand piece. The top bar should be two inches below the armpit, and the hand pieces should allow a fifteen-degree angle at the elbow. Crutches require considerable balance, strength, and coordination (for proper sequencing of crutches and legs) to use safely, and have been associated

Canes are a common walking aid used by the elderly, as demonstrated by this older couple walking through a temporary camp set up to aid earthquake victims in Leggiana, Italy, in October 1997. (AP photo by Angelo Scipoioni.)

with injury to the axillary artery. As crutches are often too difficult for older persons to use, walkers are generally preferred when weight bearing is only permitted on one leg.

Walkers

A walker provides a movable stable platform that increases the base of support anteriorly and laterally, greater than that provided by a cane. Walkers are indicated for poor balance in general, as well as for bilateral leg problems (where one would otherwise have difficulty deciding in which hand to carry a cane), to achieve non-weight bearing status for one leg, for those afflicted with Parkinson's disease, and to transmit weight through the arms rather than through a painful spine. Walkers are made of aluminum and are adjustable in height. Many can be easily folded up when not in use. There are three main types of walkers: standard, front-wheeled, and four-wheeled. Patients whose grip is impaired from weakness or arthritis, can lean on a forearm-support walker with their forearms.

Standard walkers. A standard or pick-up walker is a metal, four-legged frame with rubber tips, which must be lifted and moved forward with each step or two. This type of walker is used when maximum assistance with balance is required or when restrictions on weight bearing are present. While easier to use than a cane, this style of walker does require some degree of upper body strength and cognitive ability to use safely, and results in a fairly abnormal gait.

Front-wheeled walkers. For people who have weak arms or a tendency to fall backward, a walker with wheels on the front two posts can be used. This type of walker promotes a forward displacement of the center of gravity and allows a more normal gait, as the person can continue walking without stopping to lift the walker. The front-wheeled walker is particularly useful in patients with Parkinson's disease, as it reduces the risk of falling backwards. In addition, it is less likely to allow the patient to pick up speed as he goes along, relative to the four-wheeled walker.

Four-wheeled walkers. The most normal gait is seen when using a four-wheeled walker. While easiest to use of the three types, they also provide the least stability. Wheeled walkers for use in the community can be equipped with hand brakes, baskets for shopping, and a seat that allows the person to stop and rest. However, the user must be capable of learning to apply the brakes in order to use them safely.

Unlike canes, which must be moved in correct sequence relative to the legs, walkers generally require less instruction to use effectively, and can be ideal in older adults with mild to moderate cognitive impairment and balance or strength problems. Some instruction is necessary so that the walker is not used in an attempt to get up out of a chair. Advanced cognitive impairment can make the proper use of a walker impossible, and may be best managed by human assistance for ambulation. Disadvantages of walkers are that they require more space in which to maneuver than a cane, they may not roll well on carpeting, they make crossing thresholds difficult, and they can not be used on stairs. The use of any walking aid, in particular walkers, results in a slower gait speed and requires considerably more energy and cardiovascular fitness than walking unassisted.

SUSAN FRETER

See also ARTHRITIS; BALANCE AND MOBILITY; HOME ADAPTATION AND EQUIPMENT; REHABILITATION.

BIBLIOGRAPHY

AXTEL, L. A., and YASUDA, Y. L. "Assistive Devices and Home Modifications in Geriatric Rehabilitation." In *Clinics in Geriatric Medicine: Geriatric Rehabilitation*, vol. 9, no. 4. Edited by K. Brummel-Smith. Philadelphia: W.B. Saunders, 1993. Pages 803–821.

BOHANNON, R. W. "Gait Performance with Wheeled and Standard Walkers." *Perceptual and Motor Skills* 85 (1997): 1185–1186.

FISHBURN, M. J., and DE LATEUR, B. J. "Rehabilitation." In *Geriatrics Review Syllabus*, 3d ed. Edited by D. B. Reuben, T. T. Yoshikawa, and R. W. Besdine. Dubuque, Iowa: Kendall/Hunt Pub. Co., 1996. Pages 93–103.

KUMAR, R.; ROE, M. C.; and SCREMIN, O. U. "Methods for Estimating the Proper Length of a Cane." *Archives of Physical Medicine and Rehabilitation* 76, no. 12 (1995): 1173–1175.

MULLEY, G. "Walking Frames." *Biomedical Journal* 300 (1990): 925–927.

RUSH, K. L., and OUELLET, L. L. "Mobility Aids and the Elderly Client." *Journal of Gerontological Nursing* 23, no. 1 (1997): 7–15.

WELFARE STATE

The term *welfare state* originated in the wartime Britain of the 1940s. The term initially contrasted the ideals of the British "welfare state" with those of Nazi Germany's "Warfare State." First used by William Temple, Archbishop of York, it signified a commitment to ensuring basic social protections for all citizens, rather than a commitment to waging war. The most basic definition of the welfare state refers to government responsibility for tending to its people's welfare.

It is not an accident that, in all postwar capitalist democracies, the government has instituted some type of welfare-state programs. Gøsta Esping-Anderson suggests that capitalist economies create pressure for the development of the welfare state. In a capitalist economy, commodities such as food, clothing, and shelter are bought and sold on the market. Individuals and families cannot survive without purchasing these commodities. In order to obtain money to purchase goods and services, they must sell their labor power to an employer. If they cannot find an employer, they cannot purchase the commodities to satisfy their wants. The capitalist economy, making it impossible for most individuals and families to survive without employment, puts people at the mercy of economic misfortune. The resulting human misery creates pressure for public policies that cushion the negative effects of unemployment. Welfare-state policies can help to fill this gap, allowing people to maintain an acceptable standard of living outside the market. For instance, public pension programs and means-tested welfare programs both allow individuals to survive without selling their labor.

However, some analysts, particularly those working within the Marxist tradition, argue that these programs allow the state to deflect demands for the more fundamental (radical) changes they believe are needed. In *Regulating the Poor*, Francis Fox Piven and Richard Cloward contend that welfare-state programs expand in times of high unemployment, controlling the widespread discontent that threatens the established capitalist order.

The term *welfare state* is broad and encompasses many government programs designed to meet needs with respect to housing, education, transportation, nutrition, and social services; but the reference is most typically to programs designed to meet needs with respect to social insurance, social assistance (welfare), and health care.

Social insurance programs, such as Social Security, are considered middle-class programs. They protect primarily working- and middle-class workers from the loss of income due to such contingencies as old age, unemployment, and disability. These programs are often associated with *entitlements* that are awarded independent of any proof of economic need. In contrast, welfare programs, such as Supplementary Security Income, provide benefits that are means-tested, that is, awarded after proof of economic need. Typically, these benefits are restricted to those with very low income and asset levels.

Welfare states differ widely in the scope of their means-tested and entitlement programs and their mix of private and public provision. Esping-Anderson (1990) differentiates between three types of welfare states. The first, found in France, Germany, and several other Western European nations, is designed to preserve pre-retirement status differences. Germany has, since the inception of its old-age pension program in 1889, relied heavily upon public pension benefits that were closely linked to payroll contributions over the years. The second type of welfare state, illustrated by Norway, puts greater emphasis on the principle of the universal rights of citizenship. In addition to its earnings-related pension, Norway provides a generous universal flat-rate old-age pension. The third type of welfare state generally found in Anglo-Saxon nations tend to be more residual in nature, being means tested, as with the old-age pension in Australia. Similarly, approximately one-third of British pensioners rely on means-tested benefits for at least part of their income.

Although most advanced welfare states have come to include a variety of different programs designed to meet the needs of different segments of society, including different age groups, programs for the older population have often played an important role during the early stages of welfare-state development. The early welfare-state programs in prewar Europe generally focused on social insurance benefits. Although pension programs were among the first of these programs, during the prewar years most nations provided relatively meager benefits intended primarily to protect workers against destitution in old age. During the decades following World War II most industrial nations enacted pension reforms calling for much more generous benefits; in many cases these pensions eventually came to replace a substantial fraction of the worker's pre-retirement standard of living.

American exceptionalism

Although in most Western capitalist democracies the lion's share of welfare-state expenditures goes to older adults, this age group has played a particularly important role in the development of the welfare state in the United States. Today no other welfare state is so heavily focused on programs for older adults. It is the only industrial nation that restricts national health insurance coverage to the older population (and the poor). In contrast to the European nations, the United States never developed a family allowance program (monthly cash benefits based on the number of children in the household). The large expenditures that go to programs for older persons have prompted sociologist John Myles to refer to the American welfare state as a "welfare state for the aged." A large proportion of federal expenditures goes to age-based policies such as Social Security and Medicare, programs that use age as a criterion in awarding benefits.

Jill Quadagno notes that the United States was late to develop a welfare state for several reasons. The enduring split between North and South assured that the working class would not be strong enough to push for welfare-state programs. Because of the inability of the working class to push for reform, programs for older adults took center stage in the development of the American welfare state. Before the 1930s, the primary welfare-state programs in the United States were pensions. For instance, some states provided public pensions for which very few people were eligible. In addition, the Civil War pension system, introduced in 1862, provided benefits to former Union soldiers and their dependents, regardless of race. By 1910, over one-quarter of all American men age sixty-five or older were receiving Civil War benefits. Because these pensions provided benefits to many well into the twentieth century, they ended up delaying the introduction of social insurance–based old age pensions.

After the Civil War generation and their dependents died out, several voluntary organizations campaigned for old age pensions including the Fraternal Order of Eagles, Upton Sinclair's pension movement, the Ham and Eggs movement, and the Abraham Epstein's American Association for Social Security. The most successful of such organizations was the Townsend movement; it eventually attracted over one million supporters. Francis Townsend proposed that all Americans over age sixty-five receive a pension of two hundred dollars per month. The Great Depression hit older adults hard, producing higher rates of unemployment and poverty among older workers. President Franklin D. Roosevelt's push for the adoption of the Social Security Act of 1935 was intended in part to respond to (or, more precisely, to undercut the demands from) such groups. By increasing the purchasing power of and discouraging labor force participation among older adults (and thus opening up jobs for younger workers), the act was intended to help stabilize the economy. The adoption of this legislation instituted a mandatory, contributory pension system for the United States.

In addition to the relatively late development of a national pension system, the United States is the only industrialized nation never to have developed a system of universal health insurance. The health insurance system is predominantly private, with two primary forms of public insurance: Medicare and Medicaid. Medicare insures the population eligible for Social Security, typically covering only acute care and rehabilitation costs. Medicaid is a means-tested program limited primarily to persons who receive Temporary Assistance for Needy Families (TANF) or Supplemental Security Income (SSI). Of these, Medicare is the most explicitly age-based. Enactment of Medicare in 1965 during the Johnson administration was preceded by several legislative failures during the Truman and Kennedy administrations. The bill was backed by a labor-senior coalition including the American Federation of Labor, the American Association of Retired Workers, and the National Council of Senior Citizens. Simultaneously, the original opponents of Medicare put forward a more modest alternative proposal called the Eldercare bill, which promised to provide more extensive benefits to a limited population of elderly persons. A health-industry coalition, including the American Medical Association, the American Hospital Association, the National Association of Manufacturers, and the Chamber of Commerce backed the Eldercare bill. In general, these organizations opposed government intervention into health insurance.

Welfare-state contraction begins

Between the mid-1960s and the mid-1970s the number and size of welfare-state programs expanded rapidly, but beginning in the mid-1970s, a combination of economic, social, and political factors led to a reversal of the trend. Stagflation (the combination of high rates of unemployment and high rates of inflation) and recession led many Americans to question America's economic future. As workers faced stagnating wages and reductions in their standard of living, resentment toward welfare-state programs increased, particularly with respect to programs targeted at the poor, such as Aid to Families with Dependent Children (AFDC). The Watergate crisis provided evidence of corruption at the highest level of government and contributed to widespread cynicism. The economic downturn of the 1970s and evidence suggesting that many of the nation's costly antipoverty programs were not producing the desired results in the "war against poverty" contributed to a political shift toward the right. This shift was reflected in successful tax revolts in several states, including Proposition 13 in California and Proposition 2 in Massachusetts. Ronald Reagan's election as president in 1980 was in part a reflection of discontent with existing welfare policies. His campaign openly advocated dismantling or severely cutting back many social welfare programs aimed at the low-income population.

During the late 1970s and again during the early 1980s Social Security faced a short-term funding problem and a number of changes had to be made, including an increase in the payroll taxes and some modest benefit cuts. Some political commentators on the right argued that Social Security faced a "crisis" that necessitated a reduction in promised future Social Security benefits to "save" the program. While the program remained very popular with the general public, for the first time a substantial segment of the population came to fear that their Social Security benefits might not be there when they retired.

During this same period, criticisms of Medicare centered on the growing costs of medical treatment, often referred to as "medical inflation." The Health Care Financing Administration, created in 1977 to administer Medicare and Medicaid, failed to control the rapid increase in federal spending. The Reagan administration succeeded in pinning much of the blame for medical inflation on the Medicare program, which was viewed as encouraging older adults to overutilize health care, requesting and getting treatments and services that they otherwise would not have asked for.

The generational equity debate

During the mid-1980s one form that the debate over welfare spending took was attention to the relative amount of federal spending on different age groups. It became clear that the federal government was spending much more on elderly persons than it was spending on children. Those on the political right used this to frame what came to be called the "generational equity" debate (Williamson and Watts-Roy). Their argument was that the nation was spending too much on Social Security, health care, and other programs for the elderly, thereby leaving too little for other age groups, particularly children. Another part of the argument was that each generation should be expected to pay for its own retirement. Opponents of this framing of the debate over welfare spending argued that it was not reasonable to expect each generation to pay the full costs of its own retirement as special events such as war or depression can handicap certain generations. These opponents of the generational equity framing also argued that the emphasis on generational equity was being used as an excuse to ignore other important equity issues, such as those linked to race, class, and gender.

The generational equity debate came to include the issue of health care rationing. Daniel Callahan, in *Setting Limits,* made the controversial argument that, as the population continued to age, Americans would need to limit the share of health care resources that older persons received. Callahan's critics claimed that he was scapegoating older adults, unfairly blaming them for the poor management of health care financing in the United States. They pointed to the evidence that many other nations are able to provide health care for the entire population while spending a much smaller share of the gross national product to provide that care.

Even the opponents of the generational equity framing of the debate over the future of the welfare state recognize that the nation will need to make some adjustments to help pay for the retirement of the baby boomer generation. The costs of providing Social Security pensions and health care as well as spending on housing and social service programs aimed primarily at the older population are likely to increase when the boomers retire. Both conservatives and liberals recognize that some cuts in projected spending will need to be made to compensate for the increased number of beneficiaries.

The trend toward privatization

In recent years the debate over the future of the welfare state in the United States has come to focus on the decision whether or not to partially privatize Social Security. The publication of the 1997 report of the Advisory Council on Social Security, with its proposals to partially privatize Social Security, marked a major shift in thinking about the future of the welfare state. Proposals to partially privatize the core of the welfare state, which had long been advocated by the political right, had moved to the political mainstream. Whereas Social Security had traditionally been a defined benefit program involving substantial redistribution from high-income to low-income workers, partial privatization would reduce the extent of redistribution. This in turn would contribute to greater income inequality among elderly persons and to an increase in the proportion of elderly persons falling below the poverty line.

Whereas the emphasis in the American welfare state has to this point been on social insurance with its emphasis on shared risk and protecting old-age pensions against the effects of inflation and dramatic shifts in financial markets, the privatization alternative calls for shifting the risks (and costs) from the government to the individual and his or her family. Even a partial privatization of Social Security would represent a major shift in the direction of the American welfare state. It would represent a decision to reduce the role of the government in providing social welfare benefits, particularly its role in providing benefits to the working class and the middle class. It would represent a step in the direction of reducing the size of the American welfare state and targeting welfare-state spending on the poor.

The welfare-state contraction evident in the United States in recent years is part of a broader trend that includes most other industrial nations as well, even nations such as Sweden that have much more comprehensive welfare-state programs. Recent cutbacks in state programs for the older population in Germany, the introduction of individual accounts and the partial privatization of pensions in Sweden, and the trend toward greater emphasis on privatization in Britain all reflect the contraction of welfare-state programs that is taking place throughout the world. In most explanations of the welfare-state reform in Western states, changing economic and demographic conditions have received much attention. One fear is that population aging will lead to unacceptably high future pension and health care spending unless changes are made.

The nations of east central Europe and Latin America are developing alternative models of social provision that put greater emphasis on privatized individual accounts and reflect a trend away from traditional social insurance provision. East Asian nations have developed relatively modest welfare-state programs that implicitly assume the emphasis should be on individual and family as opposed to public provision in meeting social welfare needs.

Future prospects

During the era when welfare-state programs were expanding, the emphasis was on the politics of "credit taking." However, as we look to the future the focus is likely to be on further welfare-state retrenchment, which will in large measure be an exercise in "blame avoidance." To this end we should expect legislation that phases in further benefit cuts and tax increases gradually. It is likely that the trend to make benefits, particularly pension benefits, correspond more closely to actual payroll contributions made is likely to continue and with it a corresponding weakening of provisions calling for redistribution.

Current trends suggest that the goal of a highly developed cradle to grave welfare state may be an idea whose time has passed. The era of generous and ever-increasing public commitment to social welfare programs aimed at the working class, the middle class, and the poor may be ebbing. The current trend is clearly toward individual provision and the privatization of what had for many years been government funded welfare-state programs. However, the tide may change yet again when we next experience a prolonged period of economic contraction. At that point the limits of individual provision and privatization may become more evident; we may see a swing back in the direction of public provision and possibly a renewed interest in welfare-state programs and the philosophy that undergirds such programs.

TAY K. McNAMARA
JOHN B. WILLIAMSON

See also AGE-BASED RATIONING OF HEALTH CARE; CANADA, INCOME AND HEALTH PROTECTION OF RETIREES; GENERATIONAL EQUITY; MEDICAID; MEDICARE; POLITICAL BEHAVIOR; SOCIAL SECURITY, ADMINISTRATION; SOCIAL SECURITY, AND THE U.S. FEDERAL BUDGET; SOCIAL SECURITY, HISTORY AND OPERATIONS; SOCIAL SECURITY, LONG-TERM FINANCING AND REFORM; SUPPLEMENTAL SECURITY INCOME.

BIBLIOGRAPHY

BERKOWITZ, E. D. "The Historical Development of Social Security in the United States." In *Social Security in the 21st Century.* Edited by E. R. Kingston and J. H. Schulz. Oxford, U.K.: Oxford University Press, 1997. Pages 22–38.

BINSTOCK, R. H. "Framing the Generational Equity Debate." In *The Generational Equity Debate.* Edited J. B. Williamson, D. M. Watts-Roy, and E. R. Kingston. New York: Columbia University Press, 1999. Pages 157–184.

CALLAHAN, D. *Setting Limits: Medical Goals in an Aging Society.* New York: Simon and Schuster, 1987.

ESPING-ANDERSEN, G. *The Three Worlds of Welfare Capitalism.* Princeton, N.J.: Princeton University Press, 1990.

ESPING-ANDERSEN, G. "After the Golden Age? Welfare State Dilemmas in a Global Economy." In *Welfare States in Transition: National Adaptations in Global Economies.* Edited by G. Esping-Andersen. London: Sage Publications, 1996. Pages 1–31.

ESTES, C. L. "The Reagan Legacy: Privatization, the Welfare State, and Aging in the 1990s." In *States, Labor Markets, and the Future of Old-Age Policy.* Edited by J. Myles and J. Quadagon. Philadelphia, Pa.: Temple University Press, 1991. Pages 59–83.

HICKS, A. *Social Democracy and Welfare Capitalism: A Century of Income Security Politics.* Ithaca, N.Y.: Cornell University Press, 1999.

HUDSON, R. B. "The History and Place of Age-Based Public Policy." In *The Future of Age Based Policy.* Edited by R. B. Hudson. Baltimore, Md.: Johns Hopkins University Press, 1997. Pages 1–22.

KANE, R. L., and KANE, R. A. "Health Care for Older People: Organizational and Policy Issues." In *Handbook of Aging and the Social Sciences,* 3d ed. Edited by R. Binstock and L. K. George. San Diego: Academic Press, 1990. Pages 415–437.

MARMOR, T. R. *The Politics of Medicare,* 2d ed. New York: Aldine de Gruyter, 2000.

MYLES, J. *Old Age in the Welfare State: The Political Economy of Public Pensions,* rev. ed. Lawrence: University of Kansas Press, 1989.

PIERSON, P., and SMITH, M. "Shifting Fortunes of the Elderly: The Comparative Politics of Retrenchment." In *Economic Security and Intergenerational Justice: A Look at North America.* Edited by T. R. Marmor, T. M. Smeeding, and V. L. Greene. Washington, D.C.: Urban Institute Press, 1994. Pages 21–60.

PIVEN, F. F., and CLOWARD, R. A. *Regulating the Poor: The Functions of Public Welfare.* New York: Vintage Books, 1971.

POWELL, L. A.; BRANCO, K. J.; and WILLIAMSON, J. B. *The Senior Rights Movement: Framing the Policy Debate in America.* New York: Twayne Publishers, 1996.

QUADAGNO, J. *The Transformation of Old Age Security: Class and Politics in the American Welfare State.* Chicago: University of Chicago Press, 1988.

SKOCPOL, T. *Protecting Soldiers and Mothers: The Political Origins of Social Policy in the United States.* Cambridge, Mass.: Belnap Press of Harvard University Press, 1992.

WILENSKY, H. L. *The Welfare State and Equality: Structural and Ideological Roots of Public Expenditures.* Berkeley: University of California Press, 1975.

WILLIAMSON, J. B., and PAMPEL, F. C. *Old Age Security in Comparative Perspective.* New York: Oxford University Press, 1993.

WILLIAMSON, J. B., and WATTS-ROY, D. M. "Framing the Generational Equity Debate." In *The Generational Equity Debate.* Edited by J. B. Williamson, D. M. Watts-Roy, and E. R. Kingson. New York: Columbia University Press, 1999. Pages 3–38.

WERNER SYNDROME

See ACCELERATED AGING: HUMAN PROGEROID SYNDROMES

WEST EUROPE

The population of western Europe—presently most of the countries of western Europe are part of the European Union (EU)—grew strongly during the twentieth century, with the last major growth period occurring during the post war era and lasting into the 1960s. Following these years, fertility declined while life expectancy continued to rise. As elsewhere, the aging population of western Europe is the result of these two factors: a declining fertility and rising life expectancy. In fact, during the last decades of the twentieth century the fertility in western Europe declined to the lowest level on earth: 1.5 children per woman. Nevertheless, differences exist between these countries. In 1998, northern countries such as Iceland and Norway, with their high levels of female representation in the labor market and well-established provision for childcare, had higher levels of fertility (around 2.0) than southern countries like Spain and Italy (around 1.2).

By 2000 life expectancy became more equalized in western Europe than it had been in 1970. Especially in the countries of southern Europe, life expectancy for women had been much lower than in the northern countries. Between 1950 and 1993 more than fourteen years were added to the life expectancy of Portugese men, whereas in Sweden male life expectancy increased by little more than four years. In most western European countries life expectancy for women averages around eighty years, with the highest in France (81.5) and Spain (81), and the lowest in Denmark and Portugal (77.8). For men the average life expectancy at birth is around 74 years, with the highest found in Sweden and Greece (75.5 years), and the lowest in Portugal (70.6). But even within countries there are regional variations. For instance, in areas where older types of industrial production has prevailed for a long time, such as central England, northern France, and the Ruhr region of Germany, greater unemployment, poverty, environmental pollution, and unhealthy lifestyles have resulted in higher levels of morbidity, especially among men.

In most scenarios the proportion of older Europeans will grow considerably. In 2000, for every one hundred people between the ages of twenty and sixty there were anywhere from thirty to forty people age sixty or older, although that number is expected to rise to sixty or more persons over age sixty in the coming years, especially in the southern countries. However, the ratio of younger to older populations may be impacted by greater participation among older adults in the labor force, as a consequence of better health. Moreover, the results of immigration (immigration from outside Europe by relatively young people who participate in the labor force), which gained momentum in the last decades of the twentieth century, may have influenced the

An elderly farm couple stands along a rural road in Normandy in France. (Corbis photo by Peter Turnley.)

overall picture. While changes in dependency rates are statistically important, such information is often overly simplified, adding alarm to the complex debate about population aging.

One important phenomenon is the so-called feminization of old age in western Europe. On average, the category of oldest old (those age ninety-five or older) includes three women for every man; in some countries (France, Austria, Finland, Denmark, and the United Kingdom) there are five women for every man in this group. This phenomenon has important consequences for the financial security of European women in old age.

Living arrangements

As the population of western Europe ages, more older people tend to live alone. As women generally live longer, surviving alone in old age will be the rule. In Europe's southern countries, the percentage of older people living alone is much lower than in northern countries. However, in the southern countries there are clear differences between urban and rural regions; in the latter, family solidarity is stronger but also threatened by urbanization. According to the Eurobarometer Survey, most older people generally remain well integrated with their families and neighbors (Walker). Older people in need are provided with high levels of family care, especially from daughters and spouses. Older Europeans also care for the young: many grandparents care for their grandchildren and assist their own children. However, there is evidence that family ties will erode or become less clearly defined in the future, particularly since a greater number of older adults are childless.

Although living alone is not necessarily synonymous with social isolation, there is a greater vulnerability to problem situations. Many countries have developed initiatives designed to prevent social isolation, such as open day centers for older adults. In most western European countries, older adults remain active and maintain social contact with others through involvement in voluntary organizations.

Generally, there is a striking difference between high levels of social integration of the aged within informal relations (family, neighbors), on the one hand, and a strong social exclusion from the economic system, on the other. The economic realm of older Europeans appears to be largely limited to the consumer sector, with few opportunities for those who want or need to find employment.

Employment and retirement

In recent years, the fate of western Europe's older workers has been determined not by age but by the dynamics of the labor market. Sharp declines in participation in the labor force among workers age fifty-five to sixty-four occurred during the 1970s and 1980s, with the sharpest reductions found in the Netherlands (to 45 percent) and France (to 43 percent). Interestingly, the exit of older workers from the labor market was more a result of an economic recession that led to a downsizing of the older working population than of changes in pension systems. Sometimes there were attempts to manipulate the welfare systems in order to find creative ways to downsize older employees—for example, by designating disabilities when none existed. Consequently, one observes a sharp and sudden increase in disability status during this period.

In many countries of western Europe the retirement systems have been changed from fixed-age retirement to flexible retirement. However, this supposed flexibility did not translate into greater worker control over retirement, but simply mandated earlier retirement ages. Consequently, in western Europe today, outside the more informally organized agricultural sector, work is largely unavailable for men and women after the age of sixty-five. In 1999, the highest employment rates for men age sixty-five to sixty-nine were found in Portugal (32.2 percent) and Ireland (23.7 percent), and for women age sixty-five to sixty-nine the highest employment rates were also in Portugal (18.9 percent). Most of the other countries show much lower employment rates: the lowest rate for men and women in the same age category was found in France (3 percent and 1.3 percent, respectively) (Eurostat Labour Force Survey).

Economic status

In industrial countries worldwide the financial position of unemployed older people depends on three factors: a basic pension and other social security income provided by the state; a supplementary occupational pension; and personal savings. The economic status of elderly people is the outcome of an interaction between the economic status they achieved during their working lives and the particular pension systems they depend on during retirement. Initially, most pension systems were based on the implicit model of the male head of the family, as a wage earner who would be working for forty or fifty years in the same job until retirement, thereafter enjoying old age with the same wife he married when he was young. As a result of this, people who deviate from this implicit cultural pattern often encounter severe problems. Such problems may arise for men who have changed employers and unknowingly built up only a fragmented pension, but typically the negative effects of the pension system fall on women, who traditionally engaged in activities of the domestic sphere, such as raising and educating children. Women often work in paid jobs for a relatively small part of their lives or have only part-time jobs. Consequently, many older women have not built a sufficient pension. Paradoxically, a system that was constructed to prevent poverty in old age has produced specific categories of poor older people. This gender-based inequality is widespread in western Europe. According to the Eurobarometer Survey only the Scandinavian countries, especially Denmark, have successfully evaded this feminization of poverty in old age through universal flat-rate pensions that are regarded as a right of citizenship regardless of one's employment record.

The European Observatory on Ageing and Older People has indicated that there are four main trends in the living standards and pension policies of European Union (EU) countries (see Walker and Maltby):

1. Living standards of older people have generally been rising in recent years.
2. There are wide variations between the different countries of the EU concerning the level of protection that pension schemes provide to retired people.
3. Within the older population, the gap in living standards is widening between recently retired, predominantly male members of higher social classes, with a long record of secure employment, on the one hand, and a considerably (at least five times) larger group, many of whom are likely to be women and older than the affluent group, on the other hand. There is an extreme polarization in pensioners' living standards, especially in the United Kingdom.
4. There is a continuing problem of poverty among older people, with considerable differences between the relative sizes of these minorities compared to the total population.

Although a clear definition of poverty is difficult and relevant statistics on poverty and the aged are limited, the European Observatory has distinguished three groups of countries in the EU with low, median, and high poverty rates among their elderly population. Countries with low poverty rates (less than 10 percent) include Denmark, Germany (the former Federal Republic of Germany), Ireland, and Luxembourg. Median poverty rates (10–29 percent) were measured in Belgium, France, the northern part of Italy, and the Netherlands. High poverty rates (30 percent and more) were measured in Greece, Portugal, Spain, southern Italy, and the UK.

Health care, long-term care

As noted earlier, one of the causes of the aging population of western Europe is increased longevity: more people than ever before are experiencing a long and often healthy life. To place the sometimes alarming discussions about the financial consequences of population aging in perspective, it should be emphasized that many elderly people do not need more care than other adults. Although there is some variation among countries, relatively low percentages (around 5 percent) of people aged sixty to sixty-nine regard themselves as needing considerable care. Several inconclusive reports suggest, however, that over one-third of people age eighty and over will suffer from a longstanding illness or disability, but this means that the majority of these people do not regard themselves as disabled to any major extent. In this sense, aging in western Europe is not a grim prospect.

Nevertheless, for those responsible for policy decisions regarding care, the numbers remain daunting. The main problem appears to be that many of the existing ways to organize and supply care are not adequate to provide for the very different needs of aging people. Costs of care may be unnecessarily high because there is a lack of residential long-term care, efficient rehabilitation programs, or differentiated care in the community. A major problem of health care and long-term care for the aging population is limited flexibility; the solution to this problem is in the restructuring and recoordination of the relevant services.

The process of population aging in western Europe occurs alongside important changes in lifestyle, primary relationships, and employment. This change, often referred to as "late mo-

dernity" or "postmodernity," has profound consequences for the supply of informal care for the aged because it affects the situation of female family members who have long served as the primary informal caregivers. Long-term caregiving remains the domain of women, although this is more true in the southern countries than in those of northern Europe. According to the Eurobarometer Survey, in the EU as a whole adult children (mainly daughters) were responsible for caring for older people in 40 percent of all cases. The ways in which this takes place differs considerably: in the southern countries more than one-third of these children were living in the same house as those for whom they provided care, whereas this occurred only seldomly in the Netherlands (2 percent) or in Denmark (4 percent).

The consequences of a postmodern aging society are manifold. As women leave the traditional patterns of family life, they are less available for caregiving or related tasks. These tasks will therefore be redistributed and renegotiated, and it remains an open question whether men will be able and willing to provide the same level of care to the elderly population. Moreover, as mobility increases, family members may live too far apart to provide such care. Finally, the changes in primary relations that have been going on for some decades will also affect the social situation of the aged population of the future. More older adults will live alone, will not have children, or may have a less intimate relationship with their children because of divorce, relocation, and so on.

Consequently, public and private forms of care will need to be restructured and developed in such a way that addresses such changes.

JAN BAARS

See also EAST EUROPE AND FORMER USSR; POPULATION AGING.

BIBLIOGRAPHY

Eurostat Labour Force Survey. Luxembourg: Eurostat, 1994.
KOHLI, M.; REIN, M.; GUILLEMARD, A.-M.; and GUNSTEREN, H. V. *Time for Retirement. Comparative Studies of Early Exit in the Labor Force.* Cambridge, U.K.: Cambridge University Press, 1991.
WALKER, A. *Age and Attitudes—Main Results from a Eurobarometer Survey.* Brussels: CEC, 1993.

WALKER, A., and MALTBY, T. *Ageing Europe.* Buckingham, U.K.: Open University Press, 1997.

WHEELCHAIRS

The wheelchair is made from many components ideally chosen to meet the needs of the person using the chair. The reasons to choose a wheelchair and the options available are as varied at the people who will use them. The most important thing before purchasing or renting a wheelchair is to make sure it will best fit the needs of the individual who will be using it. The best way to do this is to work with a wheelchair specialist (e.g., occupational therapist or physician) who can advise on many issues.

Cost

One point to remember is that the most economical chair is not always the cheapest chair. An inexpensive chair can be costly not only in the monetary sense (i.e., repairs and replacement), but to the individual's health, comfort, and safety. Getting advice from and experienced practitioner will allow you to choose the most appropriate and economical chair for yourself or your loved one.

Frames

Frames can be solid or folding. Folding frames make for easy transport and storage. The folding mechanism is flexible and gives the chair a smooth ride when negotiating uneven surfaces by allowing all four wheels to stay in contact with the ground more of the time. Rigid frames are strong and light. They usually require little maintenance, which can reduce long-term costs. They have a more responsive feel and allow for more precise alignment of the wheels. This latter feature is often desirable to the young or very active user. When choosing a frame it is important to consider the vehicle that will be used to transport the chair and where the chair will be kept (i.e., in the trunk versus the back seat). How the components break down or fold for transport will be important.

Seats

The seat supports the upper legs and the buttock region. The seat base can be of a sling or rigid type. The hammock or sling type base (Fig. 2) is the least expensive and folds easily with the chair. This is appropriate if a person is only using the chair on an occasional basis. If an individual is spending a great proportion of the day in a wheelchair a firmer base is needed. On the seat base a cushion will be placed. Every wheelchair should be fitted with a removable cushion for pressure distribution, shock absorption, and positioning. The types of cushions are innumerable but are most often foam, gel, air, or combination cushions. A proper cushion helps to decrease pressure by distributing it over as great an area of the person's legs and gluteal region as possible. For example, if the seat depth is too short it will decrease the weight that can be carried under the thighs and could cause dangerous increases in pressure in the gluteal areas leading to skin breakdown. It is generally recommended that users have one to two inches of space between the cushion edge and the back of the knees. On the other hand, if a cushion is too long it can create pressure behind the knees and interfere with the legs when used to assist in propelling the wheelchair. Sometimes cutouts or contours are made to the cushion so that a person can use the legs to assist in propelling.

The seat height can be lowered for people who can use their feet to move their wheelchair. Foam cushions can be contoured. For example, in a person with thigh spasms, a central hump or pummel can help keep the legs properly positioned. People with poor sensation are at even higher risk for pressure damage to the skin. Air or gel cushions may be recommended in such people to further reduce pressure. The cushion cover is important too. It should be removable for laundering, and if incontinence is a problem waterproof or water-resistant covers may be desirable. The dimensions of the compressed cushion will affect many of the wheelchair dimensions, such as backrest and arm rest heights, and thus the decision on the type of cushion should be made early.

Backrest

The backrest supports the spine and can extend to include support of the head if needed. The height will depend on the person's needs, but a proper back should support normal posture, prevent pain and fatigue, and allow maximal mobility. The hammock or sling back, like the sling seat, folds easily with the chair but does

Figure 2

Wheelchair: 1. Arm pad; 2. Desk-style removable arm rest; 3. Clothes guard; 4. Sling seat; 5. Down tube; 6. Foot rest; 7. Bottom rail; 8. Cross-brace; 9. Caster; 10. Caster fork; 11. Footplate; 12. Tipping lever; 13. Axle; 14. Seat rail; 15. Arm rest bracket; 16. Arm rest bracket; 17. Handrim; 18. Wheel; 19. Wheel lock; 20. Back post; 21. Sling back; 22. Push handle

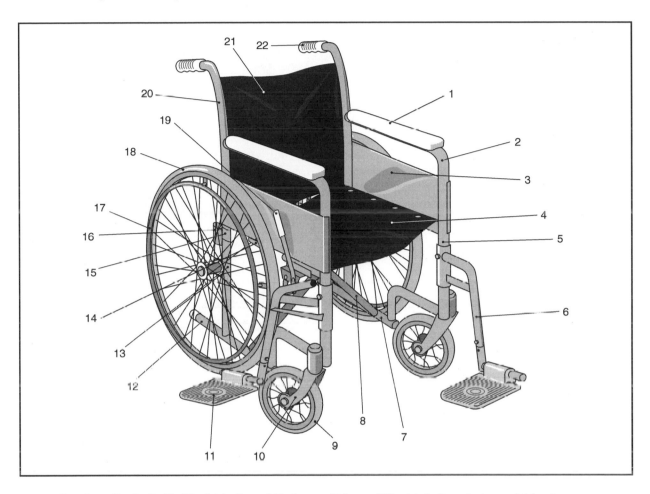

SOURCE: Based on: Currie, D. M.; Hardwick, K.; and Merburger, Rebecca. "Wheelchair Prescription and Adaptive Seating." In *Rehabilitation Medicine: Principles and Practice,* 3d ed. Edited by Joel A. DeLisa and Bruce M. Gans. Philadelphia: Lippincott-Raven Publishers, 1998. Page 764.

not provide a great deal of back support. More rigid backs provide increased support and there is a wide range of shapes and styles depending on what is needed. Those who are able to propel their own chairs using their arms benefit most from a backrest that ideally should not extend higher than about two inches below the lower angle of the shoulder blade. This allows easy propulsion and avoids rubbing or irritation of the arms during wheeling. A higher back rest may be needed for proper support by someone who does not propel themselves, has weaker trunk support, or uses a power wheelchair negating the need to propel themselves. A high backrest or

headrest may be needed if a tilting or reclining feature is being used on the chair. These features are often used in the more physically impaired person for repositioning and pressure relief to protect the skin.

Push handles can be part of the frame or the back rest and are generally added if the individual will need someone to assist them in propelling the chair all or part of the time.

Arm rests

The armrests support the arms and shoulders in comfortable positions and are often used to push off of for transferring from sitting to standing or held on to for balance. Desk-length armrests are shorter than standard length rests and are often chosen so that a person can pull up to a desk or table for easier access. The shorter length of these armrests is undesirable if the wheelchair user needs to use them to assist pushing into a standing position. In this case a full-length armrest would be preferred. Greater support may be needed if an arm is significantly impaired, as in the case of a person with an arm paralyzed from stroke or a person with a high-level spinal cord injury. The armrests in this situation may be padded and may be a trough-like configuration to assure proper support and protection of the limb. Armrests should always be removable to assist in sideways transfers. Wrap around armrests attach to the back of the frame instead of the side and can be used to help keep the width of the chair to a minimum. This can be helpful for easier mobility through doorways or other tight spaces.

Clothing guards

Clothing guards protect clothing from the wheels. They are optional and can be part of the armrest itself or a separate removable part.

Footrests

The footrest and legrest support protect the lower leg and feet. If they are too high they decrease the weight carried through the back of the thighs and can cause increased pressure over the buttock region. If they are two low they can cause pressure over the posterior thighs and cause problems with clearing barriers in the environment such as incline transitions. The suggested height of the footrest from the floor is two inches. Removable footrests are helpful for transferring users in and out of the chair. One may wish to remove one or both of the footrests at different times. A good example for such a need is when assisting a person who has had a stroke. They may want to leave a footrest on to support a weak or paralyzed leg and keep the other footrest off so that the strong leg can assist in propelling the chair. A person with an amputation or a person who chooses to use both feet to propel a chair may also wish to remove the footrests. It is important to remember in these situations that the footrest does help provide balance to the wheel chair and can act as a safety guard against forward tipping. Elevating footrests can be useful for controlling swelling or to temporarily support an injured limb. With the footrest in this position the chair becomes longer and therefore can be harder to maneuver. The elevated footrest can also create balance problems and an increased risk of tipping accidents and therefore should be used with caution.

Wheels

In the manual chair the usual size of the rear wheel ranges from twenty to twenty-six inches in diameter. A larger wheel increases the height of the seat off the ground and decreases the rolling resistance, thus easing the effort of pushing. The rear wheels can be solid or pneumatic. Solid wheels have a low rolling resistance and are very easy to maintain. They are ideal for use in institutional settings or for indoor use in noncarpeted areas. Pneumatic wheels have better grip on carpeted surfaces and are better if there is going to be significant outdoor use, but they run the risk of flats and require higher maintenance. The flat tire problem can be circumvented by the use of a foam insert that can prevent leaks. Wire spokes are lighter in weight but higher in maintenance. Most older persons will select large plastic spokes referred to as mag wheels. The wheels can be offset posteriorly to decrease the risk of tipping backwards.

Hand rims are used to propel the chair. The materials used in hand rims vary from steel to aluminum, and the rims are often coated with rubber or plastic materials to assist grip and protect hands. Modifications to hand rims such as lugs (knobs) can be added to assist the person with a weak grip in pushing the wheelchair. Most wheelchairs are meant to be propelled with two hands, however, one-arm drive mechanisms are available. The front wheels are called the casters. These are usually eight inches in diameter, but like the rear wheels vary in size. These allow turning of the wheelchair. One needs to assure that the casters and footrests are properly positioned so as not to interfere with each other.

Safety

Safety is a paramount concern. This starts with assuring that a wheelchair user works with the proper individuals, not only in purchasing a chair, but also in assuring that the caregivers and/or the wheelchair user knows how to operate the chair properly. There are 51.3 wheelchair deaths and 36,559 nonfatal wheelchair accidents per year reported in Umat and Kirby's 1995 article on wheelchair related injuries. Being safe in the chair includes having a chair that fits the user properly to avoid pressure and other injuries. It also includes knowing how to transfer, reach, balance, and propel safely so that the wheelchair becomes an aid to independence and not a threat to health and well-being. The best way to assure safety and prevent injury is to make sure a trained individual teaches the wheelchair user and any involved caregivers how to properly and safely use the wheelchair.

Safety components may include brakes, anti-tippers, grade aids, and belts.

There are numerous brake systems available. The most common form is the push handle style (Fig. 2); the lever on this style can be lengthened to assist someone who is weak or who does not have the strength or reach to apply the conventional style. It is essential that the caregiver and wheelchair user are able to apply and disengage them properly.

Anti-tippers are another safety feature. These prevent backward tips in situations such as when wheeling up a grade. As mentioned earlier the footrest can act as a forward anti-tipper. Grade aids decrease the work of propelling up hill. They also prevent the individual from rolling backwards in such a situation. Belts at the chest or waist level can help a person to safely maintain position in their chair. However, at the same time a user must be careful because they decrease the ability to shift position and if not placed or applied properly can run the risk of slipping or choking. In addition to the components, safe use of a wheelchair lies in the proper set up of a chair for a person to maximize balance and minimize tipping.

Power mobility

When an individual is not physically capable of propelling a manual chair or if endurance is a problem, then power mobility is an option. The individual can use power mobility, if they have the cognitive ability and some form of motor control—whether through head, hand, or mouth—that can be used to operate the chair. If the individual does not have the cognition to operate a power chair independently, power mechanisms can be used to assist the caregiver in pushing or positioning the individual. Power chairs can be

an expensive option and a user or caregiver should avoid entering a purchase agreement without consultation with a wheelchair specialist.

Wheelchairs have become an increasingly important intervention in the older adult. The options are endless and when combined properly can help maximize a person's independence, health, and well-being.

CHRISTINE SHORT

See also ARTHRITIS; HOME ADAPTATION AND EQUIPMENT; REHABILITATION; WALKING AIDS.

BIBLIOGRAPHY

BUSCHBACHER, R.; ADKINS, J.; LAY, B.; and BRADDOM, R. "Prescription of Wheelchairs and Seating Systems." In *Physical Medicine and Rehabilitation.* Edited by Randall L. Braddom and W. B. Saunders Co., 1996. Pages 381–400.

CURRIE, D. M.; HARDWICK, K.; and MERBURGER, R. "Wheelchair Prescription and Adaptive Seating." In *Rehabilitation Medicine: Principles and Practice,* 3d ed. Edited by Joel A. DeLisa and Bruce M. Gans. Philadelphia: Lippincott-Raven Publishers, 1998. Pages 763–788.

KIRBY, R. L. "Principles of Wheelchair Design and Prescription." In *Neurologic Rehabilitation.* Edited by Richard B. Lazar. New York: McGraw-Hill Health Professions Division, 1998. Pages 465–481.

KIRBY, R. L. "Manual Wheelchairs." In *PM and R Secrets.* Edited by Mark A. Young and Steven A. Steins. Philadelphia: Hanley and Belfus, Inc., 1996. Pages 117–120.

UMMAT, S., and KIRBY, R. L. "Nonfatal Wheelchair-related Accidents Reported to the National Electronic Injury Surveillance System." *American Journal of Physical Medicine and Rehabilitation* 73, no. 3 (1994): 163–167.

WIDOWHOOD

Widowhood is a very common experience in the United States today, as it is and has been in other times and places. Marriages can end in only two ways: divorce and widowhood. While divorce has become much more frequent in our society in the past several decades, widowhood is still the most likely way for marriages to end among older persons, and the most common marital status among the very old. To understand the lives of older persons, an understanding of widowhood and its implications is essential.

The demography of widowhood

In the United States in 1998, there were nearly 13,600,000 widowed persons (U.S. Bureau of the Census web site). Widows and widowers represent almost seven percent of the American population aged 18 and older (although approximately 5,000 widowed persons are under age 18). But widowhood is highly age-linked, of course; virtually one-third (actually 32.5 percent) of the population age sixty-five and older consists of widowed persons. And this estimate is at a single point in time, meaning that a relatively small number of widowed persons who have remarried, and a much larger number of persons who are currently married but will be widowed in the future, are not counted as widowed. Widowhood is a very common experience in the life cycle of contemporary Americans, as it is in other societies as well.

Widowhood is strongly connected to gender. In 1998, the latest year for which data are currently available, 2.7 percent of all men aged 18 and older, and 14.9 percent of all men age sixty-five and older and were widowed. For women, 10.8 percent of those 18 and over and 45.2 percent of those sixty-five and over were widowed. The percentage widowed rises dramatically with age for both sexes, but there is a remarkable sex difference even among the oldest: 42.0 percent of men 85 and over, and 77.4 percent of women in that age category, were widowed as of 1998 (U.S. Bureau of the Census web site).

Women are more likely than men to be widowed for two reasons. First, women live longer than men. As of 1997, life expectancies at birth were 73.6 years for men and 79.4 years for women. At age 65, men could expect another 15.9 years of life on the average, while women lived an average of 19.2 more years (Anderson, 1999). In addition, women tend to marry older men, although this gap has been narrowing. In 1998 median ages at first marriage were 26.7 years for men and 25.0 for women, for an average difference of 1.7 years. But fifty years ago, at a time when many of today's widowed persons were marrying, median ages at marriage were much lower and the sex difference was greater. In 1950 men married at an average (median) age of 22.8, and women at 20.3, reflecting an average

difference of 2.5 years. Because women live longer and marry older men, their odds of being widowed are much greater than men's.

The sex difference in the probability of widowhood is the primary factor driving the difference in the number of older men and women who are unmarried. In 1998 there were 3,363,000 unmarried men age sixty-five and older; at the same time there were 10,581,000 unmarried older women (U.S. Bureau of the Census web site). This greatly influences the probability of remarriage for widowed persons. While rates of remarriage are much lower among the widowed than the divorced, remarriage rates are much higher among older widowers (about 14 per 1000 per year) than widows (approximately 2 per 1000 per year)(U.S. Bureau of the Census, 1996). Remarriage rates are lower for women in large part because there are so few available men in the appropriate age ranges. This is exacerbated by the fact that older widowed men who remarry frequently marry younger women, while marriages of older women to younger men are much less common. Nonetheless, remarriage is uncommon among widowed persons, particularly when they are widowed late in life.

For several decades the proportion of our elderly population living alone has been increasing, especially among the oldest old (U.S. Bureau of the Census, 1996). This change has been driven largely by widowed persons. In 1998 about 17 percent of older men and 41 percent of older women lived alone. This sex difference, however, is due almost entirely to the sex difference in the probability of widowhood; most older men (72.6 percent) are married and living with their spouses, while only 40.7 percent of older women are similarly situated. Among the widowed, men and women are almost equally likely to live with other family members (25.6 percent and 28.1 percent respectively) or alone (66.6 percent and 70.1 percent, respectively)(U.S. Bureau of the Census web site). Men are more likely than women to live with nonrelatives.

The probability of widowhood varies substantially by many factors other than sex. Widowhood is considerably more common among blacks than whites in the contemporary United States. As of 1998, 14.1 percent of white males and 44.5 percent of white females age sixty-five or older were widowed. For blacks the comparable percentages were 24.7 percent and 54.4 percent for men and women, respectively. This is true in spite of the fact that blacks are also more likely than whites to be both never-married and divorced. In consequence, many fewer elderly blacks than whites are married. Less than one-quarter (24.3 percent) of elderly black women are married, compared to 44.5 percent of elderly white women.

While widowhood is a common, and indeed statistically "normal," experience for older persons and especially older women, a slightly smaller proportion of our elderly population is widowed today than was the case several decades ago. As noted above, in 1998 14.9 percent of all men and 45.2 percent of all women age sixty-five and over were widows. In 1960 the comparable percentages were 18.8 percent for men and 52.9 percent for women. The decrease in the proportion of the elderly population that is widowed is attributable to two factors: (1) increasing life expectancies, meaning that more people enter old age with their marriages still intact; and (2) the increasing prevalence of divorce. Since 1960 the percentages of older people who are divorced have increased from 1.6 percent for men and 1.5 percent for women to 6.3 percent for men and 6.7 percent for women (U.S. Bureau of the Census, 1996). The Census Bureau predicts that the proportion of the elderly population that is widowed will continue to decrease for these reasons, reaching 13.4 percent for men and 36.9 percent for women by 2050.

The consequences of widowhood

Many of the critical issues surrounding widowhood have to do with its consequences, particularly in regard to health and mortality, psychological well-being, and social relations.

Most studies find that widowhood elevates the risk of mortality. Widowed persons also report more physical health problems than do comparable married persons. Prigerson and colleagues (2000) found that the number of chronic conditions, nursing-home days, physician visits, and health care costs increased more among widowed persons than among married persons.

Not surprisingly, widowed persons have been found to score lower on measures of psychological well-being—and higher on measures of depression, loneliness, and anxiety—than married persons. However, many of these studies have found the adverse effects of widow-

hood on psychological well-being to be relatively small. This contradicts the common assumption that widowhood tends to be quite devastating psychologically.

Widowhood appears to be a crisis to which most people eventually adjust, and the negative effects on psychological well-being generally diminish with time. Some studies (e.g., Mendes de Leon et al., 1994) report that levels of depression, for example, return to prewidowhood levels in as little as a year after bereavement. But other studies (e.g., Lee et al., 1998; Wortman and Silver, 1990), primarily cross-sectional studies (that is, those that compare widowed people with married people at a single point in time), find widowed persons to be more depressed than married persons many years after widowhood.

Some of this discrepancy between studies may be due to the nature and timing of their comparisons. Lichtenstein and associates (1996) studied a sample of twins from Sweden. In each pair of twins, one had been widowed and the other was still married. The sample was followed over a nine-year period. Individuals who were widowed during the course of the study showed elevated levels of depression prior to widowhood, perhaps in response to their spouses' illness and the disruption in their lives caused by the illness. So a return to the pre-widowhood level of depression meant that widowed persons were still more depressed than their married twins. Although depression scores improved with time among the widowed, the researchers found that even those who had been widowed for extended periods of time (prior to the inception of the study) were more depressed (and more lonely and less satisfied with their lives) than their married twins on average.

The consensus that seems to be emerging is that, while widowhood is quite devastating psychologically in the short run for most people, over time most people adjust reasonably well. In some cases widowhood offers relief from caring for an ill or disabled spouse and allows the widower or widow to reorganize his or her life around other activities.

There has been considerable controversy as to whether widowhood is a more difficult experience psychologically for men or for women. Widowhood is generally a greater problem financially for women than men, and economic difficulties can lead to lower psychological well-being. Several studies (e.g., Schuster and Butler,

1989; Thompson, et al., 1989) have indeed found that widowhood has a greater adverse impact on the psychological well-being of women. Other studies, however (e.g., Lee, et al., 1998, 2001; Umberson et al., 1992) have reported stronger effects on men. The weight of the evidence at this point seems to favor the argument that widowhood is more difficult for men.

In cross-sectional studies such as those noted above, some of the apparent advantage in psychological well-being that widowed women have over widowed men is illusory. Men are more likely to remarry than women, which probably removes the least depressed men from the population of widowed persons, thereby decreasing the average of those remaining. In addition, because of their higher mortality rate (as well as their higher remarriage rates) widowed men are generally widowed for shorter periods of time than women, giving them less time to adjust.

On the other hand, widowhood has a stronger negative effect on the health of men than that of women, and poor health impacts psychological well-being. In addition, there is some evidence (e.g., Lee et al., 2001; Umberson et al., 1992) that widowed men find housework to be more daunting. Their dislike of housework, combined with the necessity of doing it, is associated with greater depression.

But widowhood is also more depressing for men because married men are the least depressed of any sex/marital status group. Some studies (e.g., Lee et al., 1998, 2001) indicate that men are more advantaged by marriage than women in terms of psychological well-being, making marriage a greater barrier against depression for men than for women. The end of a marriage, therefore, has greater negative psychological consequences for men than for women. Lee et al. (2001) found that widowed men were no more depressed than widowed women, but, because married men were less depressed than married women, the difference between married and widowed men was larger than the difference between married and widowed women.

Somewhat paradoxically, men may be disadvantaged in the process of adjusting to widowhood because it is relatively uncommon among them. As noted above, most widowed persons are women because wives are much more likely to outlive their husbands than to predecease them. The larger number of widowed women than wid-

owed men allows men a greater opportunity for remarriage, and they take advantage of this to some extent. However, this also means that they have fewer opportunities to form friendships with men in similar positions, and there are fewer male role models for successful adaptation to widowhood. It is also likely that few men expect to outlive their wives and when they do they have not prepared for it psychologically or socially.

Many studies (e.g., Bradsher, 1997) show that a strong and active support network of family and friends is important in helping widowed persons adjust to their situation. It is frequently the case that widowed parents move in with children, particularly if their own health is failing. Among persons in their seventies and above, widowed people are much more likely than married couples to live with children, although most widowed persons do live alone. Roan and Raley (1996) showed, based on a longitudinal study that followed people for five years, that adults whose mothers were widowed increased their frequency of visits, telephone calls, and letters to their mothers. However, it is possible that increased contacts by children with widowed parents occur primarily in the first few years after widowhood; comparisons of the long-term widowed with married people show few differences in this area.

Another very important issue for widowed persons is the question of who provides care when they become ill or infirm. The evidence is clear that children are the primary source of care for older persons without spouses. Daughters are much more likely to provide care to widowed parents than are sons, but this is largely due to the fact that most widowed parents in need of care are mothers. Widowed mothers are cared for overwhelmingly by daughters while widowed fathers who require care receive it about equally from sons and daughters. Those without children may receive care from friends, neighbors, or relatives, but are also more likely to be institutionalized.

Widowhood is, and has been, a statistically normal part of the life cycle, particularly for women. It is not a happy event, and there are many adverse consequences in terms of both physical and psychological health, including an elevated risk of mortality (especially for men). However, most widows and widowers appear to adjust successfully in the long run.

Gary R. Lee

See also BEREAVEMENT; KIN; MARITAL RELATIONSHIPS; MARRIAGE AND REMARRIAGE; WIDOWHOOD: ECONOMIC ISSUES.

BIBLIOGRAPHY

BRADSHER, J. E. "Older Women and Widowhood." In *Handbook on Women and Aging*. Edited by Jean M. Coyle. Westport, Conn.: Greenwood Press, 1997. Pages 418–429.

LEE, G. R.; DEMARIS, A.; BAVIN, S.; and SULLIVAN, R. "Gender Differences in the Depressive Effect of Widowhood in Later Life." *Journal of Gerontology: Social Sciences* 56B (2001): 556–561.

LEE, G. R., and DWYER, J. W. "Aging Parent-Adult Child Coresidence: Further Evidence on the Role of Parental Characteristics." *Journal of Family Issues* 17 (1996): 46–59.

LEE, G. R.; DWYER, J. W.; and COWARD, R. T. "Gender Differences in Parent Care: Demographic Factors and Same-Gender Preferences." *Journal of Gerontology: Social Sciences* 48 (1993): S9 S16.

LEE, G. R.; WILLETTS, M.; and SECCOMBE, K. "Widowhood and Depression: Gender Differences." *Research on Aging* 20 (1998): 611–629.

LICHTENSTEIN, P.; GATZ, M.; PEDERSEN, N. L.; BERG, S.; and MCLEARN, G. E. "A Co-twin Control Study of Response to Widowhood." *Journal of Gerontology: Psychological Sciences* 51B (1996): P279–P289.

LIEBERMAN, M. *Doors Close, Doors Open: Widows, Grieving and Growing*. New York: Grosset/Putnam, 1996.

LOPATA, H. Z. *Current Widowhood: Myths and Realities*. Thousand Oaks, Calif.: Sage, 1996.

MASTEKAASA, A. "The Subjective Well-Being of the Previously Married: The Importance of Unmarried Cohabitation and Time Since Widowhood or Divorce." *Social Forces* 73 (1994): 665–692.

MENDES D. L., CARLOS F.; KASL, S. V.; and JACOBS, S. "A Prospective Study of Widowhood and Changes in Symptoms of Depression in a Community Sample of the Elderly." *Psychological Medicine* 24 (1994): 613–624.

PETERS, A., and LIEFBROER, A. C. "Beyond Marital Status: Partner History and Well-Being in Old Age." *Journal of Marriage and the Family* 59 (1997): 687–699.

PRIGERSON, H. G.; MACIEJEWSKI, P. K.; and ROSENHECK, R. A. "Preliminary Explorations of the Harmful Interactive Effects of Widowhood and Marital Harmony on Health, Health Service Use, and Health Care Costs." *The Gerontologist* 40 (2000): 349–357.

ROAN, C. L., and RALEY, R. K. "Intergenerational Coresidence and Contact: A Longitudinal Analysis of Adult Children's Response to Their Mother's Widowhood." *Journal of Marriage and the Family* 58 (1996): 708–717.

SCHAEFER, C.; QUESENBERRY, C. P. J.; and WI, S. "Mortality Following Conjugal Bereavement and the Effects of a Shared Environment." *American Journal of Epidemiology* 141 (1995): 1142–1152.

SCHUSTER, T. L., and BUTLER, E. W. "Bereavement, Social Networks, Social Support, and Mental Health." In *Older Bereaved Spouses: Research with Practical Applications*. Edited by Dale A. Lund. New York: Hemisphere, 1989. Pages 55–68.

THOMPSON, L. W.; GALLAGHER, D.; COVER, H.; GALEWSKI, M.; and PETERSON, J. "Effects of Bereavement on Symptoms of Psychopathology in Older Men and Women." *Older Bereaved Spouses: Research with Practical Applications*. Edited by Dale A. Lund. New York: Hemisphere, 1989. Pages 17–24.

UMBERSON, D.; WORTMAN, C. B.; and KESSLER, R. C. "Widowhood and Depression: Explaining Long-Term Gender Differences in Vulnerability." *Journal of Health and Social Behavior* 33 (1992): 10–24.

U.S. Bureau of the Census. "65+ in the United States." *Current Population Reports, Special Studies*. Series P23, no. 190. Washington, D.C.: U.S. Government Printing Office, 1996.

WORTMAN, C. B., and SILVER, R. C. "Successful Mastery of Bereavement and Widowhood: A Life-course Perspective." In *Successful Aging: Perspectives from the Behavioral Sciences*. Edited by Paul B. Baltes and Margaret M. Baltes. New York: Cambridge University Press, 1990. Pages 225–264.

WIDOWHOOD: ECONOMIC ISSUES

Widowhood is defined as the status of an individual who was legally married to someone who subsequently died. Economically, the death of a spouse will result in loss of income and property that the deceased spouse received or owned, unless provision for their continuation and inheritance is made explicit in income program rules, laws of inheritance, or through the deceased spouse's will. For this reason, it is important to understand how marriage and inheritance rights to income and assets are defined in law and by programs that provide income to elderly persons.

Economic effects of widowhood

Widowed older women, on average, report lower incomes and are more likely to be poor than are other groups of elderly persons. This is true in the United States and in other countries as well, though the difference in the United States is greater overall than in other developed countries. In the United States, over 48 percent of the poor elderly are widows, even though widowed women account for only 26 percent of all persons age sixty-five and older. Compared to the slightly more than 4 percent of couples age sixty-five and older who are poor, about 20 percent of widowed women are poor. This poverty rate is considerably lower than the 50 percent of widows who were poor in 1970, reflecting gains in earnings for both men and women, as well as improvements in pension and Social Security benefits. Nevertheless, on average, married women in the United States experience a decline in income when their husbands die. Although widowers (men whose wives have died) are somewhat more likely to be poor than are married couples, data that follow couples over time do not show a decline in average economic well-being for men when wives die.

The decline in economic well-being upon widowhood is somewhat of a puzzle. There exists a well-functioning life insurance market that sells products that insure against the loss of income upon widowhood. In addition, legislation has increased the rights of spouses to spouses pension benefits. While the timing of death is uncertain for a given individual, death probabilities can be predicted with considerable accuracy, permitting the estimation of probabilities and length of widowhood. Information that is readily available on Social Security benefits, and requirements that pensions provide annual reports on workers' accrued benefits, would seem to provide the information necessary for couples to protect against any loss of income upon one spouse's death.

One explanation for the difference between the economic status of married couples and widows is the association between death probabilities and economic status. Poorer men are more likely to die than higher income men. This is partly because individuals with chronic health problems generally have lower lifetime earnings (and lower retirement income) and die at younger ages than healthier individuals. For these individuals, low wages and early death are both due to long-term health problems. On the other hand, individuals who work in lower-paying jobs may be engaged in more hazardous tasks, have no employer-provided health insurance, and be less able to pay out-of-pocket for health care. Their low earnings are a cause of poorer health and consequent higher mortality. Whatever the reason for the association between lower earnings and poorer health, the lower income of widows can be attributed in part to widows being drawn from couples who were economically worse off when married than were women of the same age whose husbands are alive. This, however, is only a partial explanation. Husbands in higher-income couples do die and, on average, a decline in economic status is measured for their widows as well.

For some couples the out-of-pocket costs of health care associated with a spouse's terminal illness or nursing home stay can diminish resources. However, there is little evidence that uncovered health care expenditures are a major contributor to higher poverty rates among widows. The concern that some spouses were left impoverished by payments to long-term care facilities for the care of the other spouse led to the 1988 amendments to the Social Security Act, which permits a community spouse to retain assets and incomes above the limit that previously had been allowed for nursing home reimbursement under the Medicaid program. Currently, the institutionalized spouse's eligibility for Medicaid reimbursement of long-term care costs is assessed after a specified share of the couple's income and assets (approximately half, up to a maximum amount) is allocated to the community spouse. The remaining share is allocated to the institutionalized spouse, and it is only this share that must be spent-down in order for the institutionalized spouse to be deemed Medicaid-eligible. While these provisions are important to some couples, their influence on widows' well-being is limited. Married men have a low probability of nursing home entry. That a similar decline in economic resources is not observed for married men when wives die suggests that the expenses of a terminal illness *per se* are not a major contributor to the lower economic status of widows.

There is stronger evidence that widows, in contrast to widowers, are more likely to suffer income declines due to the loss of the deceased spouse's Social Security and pension benefits. Why this happens, despite the availability of survivor benefits from Social Security and employer-provided pensions, is described below. While couples could insure against the loss of this income through the purchase of life insurance, research shows that many elderly couples are underinsured against probable income loss, and that life insurance is most likely to be purchased by relatively wealthy and healthy couples. The limited evidence available on asset change upon widowhood suggests that some decline in assets occurs upon widowhood. While it is expected that the growth in financial resources owned by women will reduce the financial consequences of widowhood, the persistent association between health, low income, and low assets means that the wives in couples with low lifetime earnings may remain vulnerable to economic insecurity as widows.

A final source of measured income differences between married and widowed women deserves mention. In surveys, some individuals identified as widows may not, in fact, have experienced the death of a marriage partner. This occurs for two reasons. First, it is known that divorced women whose former husbands die often describe themselves as widowed, an identification encouraged in part by the availability of divorced survivor benefits from Social Security. Second, it is also likely that women long separated from their husbands or in common-law marriages may term themselves widows after those partners die. The lower incomes and assets of these individuals may be due to their ineligibility for the benefits provided to widows by laws and programs. Their classification as widows not only exaggerates economic differences between widows and married couples, but also obscures the reasons these women are worse off. This situation may deter policy aimed at improving the economic position of divorced, separated, and never-married elderly women.

Survivor benefits: the U.S. social security program

The 1939 amendments to the Social Security Act provided benefits to wives and widows of retired and deceased workers. These benefits were initially paid to wives and widows age sixty-five or older. In 1950, widowers were made eligible for benefits, provided financial dependency on their wives prior to death could be established. In 1956, spouse and widow benefits were made available to women sixty-two to sixty-four years of age, and in 1961 to widowers in this age group. The age of eligibility for survivor benefits was reduced to sixty for widows in 1965 and for widowers in 1972, the same year that the dependency requirement for widowers was eliminated, making all Social Security survivor benefit provisions gender-neutral. Survivor benefits are payable to divorced spouses if the marriage lasted at least ten years. If each meets all eligibility rules, both a surviving spouse and divorced surviving spouse may receive benefits based on the deceased spouse's earnings record.

Survivor benefits are equal to 100 percent of the deceased worker's primary insurance amount, but may be reduced if the deceased worker had received retired-worker benefits prior to age of full benefit eligibility; if the survivor receives benefits early; if the survivor is eligible for other social security benefits (the *dual entitlement* provision described below); if a pension from noncovered work is received; or if the survivor reports other earnings (but only prior to the age of full benefit eligibility when the earnings limit is lifted). Some of these are described here, but program details are available at the Social Security Web site (www.ssa.gov).

Survivor benefits are payable at age sixty or, for disabled survivors, at age fifty-five. However, receipt before the age of full benefit eligibility reduces the amount received. As that age rises from age sixty-five to age sixty-seven (for those turning age sixty-two in 2022 or later) the monthly reduction will be adjusted such that 71.5 percent of the full survivor benefit is always payable at age sixty. A maximum and minimum payable amount applies to some survivor beneficiaries. For survivors who first receive survivor benefits no earlier than the age of full benefit eligibility (currently sixty-five, but increasing to sixty-seven) the survivor benefit can be no more than what was, or would have been, paid to the deceased worker. This means that a survivor of a retired worker who received benefits that were reduced for early retirement can receive no more than that amount, even if the survivor was older than age sixty-five (or, in the future, age sixty-seven) when survivor benefits were first received. Concern that the cap on benefits for widows of workers who received benefits early contributes to the lower income of widows and may lead to a lifting of the cap. The *Social Security Handbook* provides greater detail on specific program provisions.

Survivor benefits for which an individual is otherwise eligible may be reduced by the dual

Table 1

	Spouse 1's Benefit	Spouse 2's Benefit		Survivor Benefit
	Retired-worker	Retired-worker	Spouse	
	i	ii	iii	iv
Couple A	$1,600.00		$800.00	$1,600.00
Couple B	$ 800.00	$800.00	$400.00	$ 800.00

Note: Spouses in couples are both assumed to be age 65

SOURCE: Author

entitlement provision that, in effect, leads to the payment of the higher benefit for which an individual is eligible. The consequence is that survivors of one- and two-earner couples with identical retired-worker benefits may be paid quite different amounts, with the latter experiencing a larger decline in Social Security income than the former. Table 1, which shows the monthly benefits paid to two hypothetical couples, illustrates this (the higher hypothetical amount approximates the primary insurance amount of males awarded retired-worker benefits in 2000). Couple A is a single earner couple, while spouses in Couple B have identical covered work histories and benefits. The retired-worker benefit of the single earner couple ($1,200) is equal to the combined retired-worker benefits of the two-earner couple. Each spouse is also eligible for a spouse benefit equal to one-half of the other spouse's retired-worker benefit. The non-working spouse in Couple A will be paid an $800 spouse benefit, but, because only the higher of any two benefits is paid, neither spouse in couple B will receive an incremental benefit (the $300 spouse benefit would be less than each spouse's $600 retired-worker's benefit). Thus, when one spouse in each couple dies, the survivors are paid very different amounts. The survivor benefit is larger for couple A and equal to two-thirds of the pre-widowhood amount, compared to only one-half, for survivor B.

Differences in benefits paid to couples with identical earnings histories have motivated proposals for changes in Social Security survivor benefits. Most reform proposals call for the payment of a given percentage of a couple's combined benefits. This would increase the survivor benefits of Couple B, and for all couples that share earnings responsibility. Some proposals include the reduction or elimination of spouse benefits, a change that would equalize predeath benefits paid to couples such as A and B, but leave the survivor benefit differences intact. However, savings from their elimination would help finance the higher cost of uniform survivor benefits for all couples.

Survivor protection: employer-provided pensions and individual accounts

Widows may also experience a decline in income when their spouse receives a single life annuity, a benefit that ceases upon the death of the annuitant. The 1974 Employee Retirement Income Security Act (ERISA) was passed in part to increase the chances that a survivor would receive a benefit from a deceased worker's pension. ERISA requires both that private-sector, employer-provided pensions offer a *joint-and-survivor* benefit (i.e., one that pays some share of the retired-worker's benefit to the designated survivor) and that the default payment to a married worker be at least a *joint-and-one-half survivor* annuity, unless the worker chooses otherwise. The 1984 Retirement Equity Act amended the ERISA survivorship provision to require a spouse's notarized signature when the default joint-and-survivor option is rejected or another beneficiary designated.

Unlike Social Security, which does not reduce retired-worker benefits for a married worker with probable survivors, employer-provided pension plans (and other annuities) will reduce the amount paid to a worker when a joint-and-survivor benefit is chosen. This is because the pension is expected to be paid out over the longer period of time that includes the years when the survivor alone is alive. A survivor annuity is a specified percentage of the reduced benefit paid to the worker. Thus, a joint-and-one-half survivor benefit will pay an amount to the pensioner that is less than the single life annuity, and pay a benefit to the survivor, should the pensioner die, that is equal to 50 percent of this reduced amount. Unlike Social Security, which may pay survivor benefits to more than one surviving (or divorced, surviving) spouse, pensions are obligated only to consider one survivor.

Public employer-provided plans are not covered by ERISA, including its survivorship provisions. Although the majority of public plans offer joint-and-survivor benefits, they are not always the default, and they less frequently require notarized approval by the other spouse if a single life pension is selected. Further, the survivor provisions need not be met by retirement savings plans that are not employer-provided benefits.

About two-thirds of married male pensioners select some type of survivor benefit. For some women the loss of a husband's pension income (because they chose a smaller survivor percentage or no survivor benefit) is a major cause of a decline in resources. Men with smaller pensions, men with other sources of income to share with their potential widow, and men whose wives had their own pensions are more likely to choose a single life pension. This last finding suggests that the increase in retirement security for women due to their own pension coverage may be offset by reductions in the probability of husbands selecting survivor benefits.

State law and widowhood status

State law can influence resources of surviving spouses in two important ways: (1) by defining marriage, and, (2) by specifying property ownership and property inheritance rights. Generally, the Social Security program recognizes an individual as a survivor for purposes of receipt of survivor benefits if the courts of the state in which the deceased spouse was living at the time of death would recognize the union as a valid marriage or would recognize the survivor as having the same status as a widow for purposes of sharing in the distribution of personal property when the deceased left no will. Uncertainty under state law about the legal status of a marriage may arise if the relevant state does not recognize the marriage—even if performed legally elsewhere—if a prior divorce was not completed or filed, or if common-law marriage is not recognized in that state. Because Social Security does not obtain or maintain records on marital status prior to benefit application, the documentation of marriage, divorce, and death of a spouse is an important part of establishing eligibility for survivor benefits.

State property and inheritance laws are important in determining the assets inherited by survivors. In so-called community property states, assets and income acquired during marriage are considered equally owned by each spouse, and a surviving spouse has ownership rights to half of all property acquired during marriage, even if the deceased spouse had willed more than their share of property to another person. In so-called common-law property states, assets and income are considered to be owned and controlled by the income-earning spouse, although a spouse may still be able to claim a share of a deceased spouse's assets under the principle that a working spouse has an obligation to provide for the economic well-being of the other spouse.

Other national examples

Income in the later years of life, including during the period when only one spouse survives, is a result of life-long earnings and savings. In most developed countries, widowed women report lower incomes and are more likely to be poor than are other groups of elderly persons. In part, this is because they are drawn from poorer couples. But the larger explanation lies in the way in which public and private income and assets are, or continue to be, paid to surviving spouses. National social security systems can and do smooth out the consequences of earnings differences. While most developed countries provide survivor benefits (although Sweden has eliminated them), variations in rules about the share of inherited benefits, offsets for other income, minimum age of benefit receipt, minimum guarantees in public programs, and the role of the private sector in retirement income are all thought to contribute to differences in the well-being of widows. Clearly, the generosity and security of the underlying benefits paid to married retired workers provides the first layer of economic protection to surviving spouses. Survivor benefits build on this relative generosity.

The survivor benefits payable in Germany would seem less generous than in the United States, but they build on a more generous retirement base. During the first three months of widowhood, women receive 100 percent of the insured's pension. Thereafter, 60 percent of the pension is paid if the widow is age forty-five or older, if she is disabled, or if she is caring for at least one child. Otherwise, only 25 percent of the insured's pension amount is paid. These benefits are generally not taxed but they may be offset by other income. When the additional income exceeds a limit (equal to about one-third of the maximum benefit), benefits are reduced by 40 percent of the excess amount.

In contrast, the British national insurance system allows for inheritance of benefits with few offsets. Widows age forty-five and over without children get an age-graded share of the Basic Benefit, and at fifty-five they receive the full grant. While widows are eligible only for the higher of their own or their husbands' Basic Pension benefit, they may inherit their husbands' State Earnings Related Pension Scheme without offsets for other income or earnings. For widows of men who would have reached pensionable age before October 2002 (age sixty-five) the percentage inherited is 100 percent of the benefit, although it is scheduled to decline gradually to a maximum of 50 percent by October 2010.

In Canada, surviving spouses are eligible for a benefit consisting of two parts: a flat-rate benefit and an earnings-related benefit that is equal to a percentage of the benefit for which the deceased spouse would be entitled were he or she age sixty-five. After age sixty-five, this percentage is 60 percent, regardless of the age at which benefits were first received. Survivors may receive both the survivor benefit and their own benefits, subject to limits which may reduce their total below the combined benefits. Information on the Canadian plan can be found at www.hrdc-drhc.gc.ca/isp

KAREN C. A. HOLDEN
MEERYOUNG KIM

see also ECONOMIC WELL-BEING; EMPLOYEE RETIREMENT INCOME SECURITY ACT; MEDICAID; POVERTY; SOCIAL SECURITY, HISTORY AND OPERATIONS; WIDOWHOOD.

BIBLIOGRAPHY

AUERBACH, A. J., and KOTLIKOFF, L. J. "Life Insurance of the Elderly: Its Adequacy and Determinations." In *Work, Health, and Income Among the Elderly*. Edited by Gary Burtless. Washington, D.C.: Brookings Institution, 1987. Pages 229–267.

BURKHAUSER, R. B., and SMEEDING, T. *Social Security Reform: A Budget Neutral Approach to Reducing Older Women's Disproportionate Risk of Poverty*. Policy Brief. Syracuse, N.Y.: Syracuse University Center for Policy Research, 1994.

SMEEDING, T. M.; ESTES, C. L.; and GLASSE, L. "Social Security Reform and Older Women: Improving the System." Income Security Policy Paper Series no. 22. Syracuse, N.Y.: Syracuse University Center for Policy Research, 1999.

Social Security Administration. *Social Security Handbook*. Available on the World Wide Web at www.ssa.gov

WEIR, D. R., and WILLIS, R. J. "Prospects for Widow Poverty." In *Forecasting Retirement Needs and Retirement Wealth*. Edited by Olivia S. Mitchell, P. Brett Hammond, and Anna M. Rappaport. Philadelphia: Pension Research Council.

ZICK, C., and HOLDEN, K. C. "An Assessment of the Wealth Holdings of Recent Widows." *Journal of Gerontology: Social Sciences: Social Science* 55, no. 2 (2000): S90–S97.

WISDOM

Historical background

Throughout recorded history, wisdom has been viewed as the ideal endpoint of human development. Of course, the psychological study of wisdom is still rather young compared to its philosophical treatment, for the very definition of philosophy is "love or pursuit of wisdom." Historically, wisdom has been conceptualized in terms of a state of idealized being, as a process of perfect knowing and judgment (as in King Solomon's judgments), or as an oral or written product, such as wisdom-related proverbs or the so-called wisdom literature. It is important to recognize that the identification of wisdom with individuals, such as wise persons (the predominant approach in psychology), is but one of the ways by which wisdom is instantiated.

Historically, the interest in the topic of wisdom has waxed and waned, (Baltes and Staudinger, 2000). In general, two main lines of argument have been in the center of the historical evolution of the concept of wisdom: (1) the distinction between philosophical and practical wisdom, and (2) the question of whether wisdom is divine or human. Recently, interest in the concept of wisdom has been revived (Welsch, in press). Archeological and cultural work dealing with the origins of religious and secular bodies of wisdom-related texts in China, India, Egypt, and Old Mesopotamia has revealed invariance with regard to core features of the definition of wisdom across cultures and historical time. This relative invariance gives rise to the assumption that concepts such as wisdom, with its related body of knowledge and skills, have been culturally selected because of their adaptive value for humankind.

Psychological approaches to the definition of wisdom

Among one the major reasons for the emergence of the psychological study of wisdom in the late 1970s and early 1980s was the search for positive aspects of aging. An early approach to defining wisdom from a psychological perspective can be seen in its treatment in dictionaries. The Oxford English Dictionary defines wisdom as, "Good judgment and advice in difficult and uncertain matters of life."

In a next step, psychologists further specified the content and formal properties of wisdom-related phenomena. In 1922, Stanley Hall associated wisdom with the emergence of a meditative attitude, philosophic calmness, impartiality, and the desire to draw moral lessons, all of which tend to emerge in later adulthood. Furthermore, writers emphasized that wisdom involves the search for the moderate course between extremes, a dynamic between knowledge and doubt, a sufficient detachment from the problem at hand, and a well-balanced coordination of emotion, motivation, and thought (see Kramer, 2000).

Implicit (subjective) theories about wisdom

Most empirical research on wisdom in the field of psychology has focused on further elaboration of the definition of wisdom. Moving beyond the dictionary definitions, research explored the nature of everyday beliefs, folk conceptions, or implicit (subjective) theories of wisdom (see Sternberg, 1990).

These studies, in principle, build on research initiated by Vivian Clayton in 1976. Clayton found that three characters are typical of wise people: (1) affective characteristics such as empathy and compassion, (2) reflective processes such as intuition and introspection, and (3) cognitive capacities such as experience and intelligence.

A study conducted in 1986 by Robert J. Sternberg focused on the relationship of wisdom with characteristics such as creativity and intelligence. Wisdom was found to be defined by six aspects: reasoning ability, sagacity, learning from ideas and the environment, judgment, expeditious use of information, and perspicacity. A large overlap was found between intelligence and wisdom, though sagacity was found to be specific to wisdom. In later theoretical work,

Sternberg defined wisdom as balancing intrapersonal, interpersonal, and extrapersonal interests to achieve a common good (Sternberg, 1998).

Another major study on subjective theories of wisdom was conducted by Stephen Holliday and Michael Chandler, also in 1986. A factor analysis of the attributes judged to be "most prototypical" of a wise person revealed two factors: (1) "exceptional understanding of ordinary experience," and (2) "judgment and communication skills."

In 1999, Fritz Oser provided initial evidence on the implicit theories about wise acts, which seem to be characterized by seven features. Wise acts tend to be: (1) paradoxical and unexpected; (2) highly moral and (3) selfless; and they involve (4) overcoming internal and external dictates; (5) a striving towards equilibrium; (6) an implied risk; and (7) a striving towards improving the human condition.

Explicit theories and assessment of wisdom

Another recent line of empirical psychological inquiry on wisdom addresses the question of how to measure behavioral expressions of wisdom. Within this tradition, three lines of work can be identified: (1) assessment of wisdom as a personality characteristic, (2) assessment of wisdom in the Neopiagetian tradition of adult thought, and (3) assessment of wisdom as an expertise with regard to difficult problems involving the interpretation, conduct, and management of life (see Baltes and Staudinger, 2000).

Within personality theories, wisdom is usually conceptualized as an advanced stage, if not the final stage, of personality development. Wisdom, in this context, is comparable to "optimal maturity." Ryff and Whitbourne, for example, have undertaken an effort to develop self-report questionnaires based on the Eriksonian notions of personality development and focused on integrity or wisdom.

Central to Neopiagetian theories of adult thought is the transcendence of the universal truth criterion that characterizes formal logic. This transcendence is common to conceptions such as dialectical, complementary, and relativistic thinking. Such tolerance of multiple truths (ambiguity), has also been mentioned as a crucial feature of wisdom. Empirical studies in this tradition by Gisela Labouvie-Vief or Deirdre Kramer found that, at least up to middle adulthood, performance increases on such measures of adult thought are observed.

Besides these measures of wisdom as a personality characteristic or as a feature of mature thought, there is also work that attempts to assess wisdom as an expertise concerning the interpretation, conduct, and management of life. This approach is based on lifespan theory, the developmental study of the aging mind and aging personality, research on expert systems, and cultural-historical definitions of wisdom (see Baltes and Staudinger, 2000). By integrating these perspectives, wisdom is defined as a system of expert knowledge in the fundamental pragmatics of life. Such knowledge allows for exceptional insight, judgment, and advice involving complex and uncertain matters of the human condition.

The body of knowledge and skills associated with such wisdom entails insights into the quintessential aspects of the human condition, including its biological finitude and cultural conditioning. Wisdom involves a fine-tuned coordination of cognition, motivation, and emotion. More specifically, wisdom-related knowledge and skills can be characterized by a family of five criteria: (1) rich factual knowledge about life, (2) rich procedural knowledge about life, (3) *lifespan contextualism,* the ability to view issues in a lifespan perception, (4) *value relativism,* and (5) awareness and management of uncertainty (see Baltes, Smith and Staudinger 1992).

To elicit and measure wisdom-related knowledge and skills in this approach, research participants are presented with difficult life dilemmas such as the following: "Imagine that someone receives a phone call from a good friend who says that she/he can't go on anymore and has decided to commit suicide. What should one do and consider in such a situation?" Participants are then asked to "think aloud" about such dilemmas. The five wisdom-related criteria are used to evaluate these protocols. The obtained scores are reliable and provide an approximation of the quantity and quality of wisdom-related knowledge and skills of a given person (see Baltes and Staudinger, 2000). When using this wisdom paradigm to study people who were nominated as wise according to subjective beliefs about wisdom, it was found that wisdom nominees received higher wisdom scores than comparable control samples of various ages and professional backgrounds.

Part of this paradigm also is a general framework outlining the conditions for the development of wisdom as it is reflected in the thoughts and actions of individuals. The empirical work based on this model has produced outcomes consistent with expectations (see Staudinger 1999). Specifically, it seems that wisdom-related knowledge and judgment emerge between the age of fourteen and twenty-five. During adulthood, however, growing older is not enough to become wise. When age is combined with wisdom-related experience, such as professional specializations that involve training and experience in matters of life, higher levels of wisdom-related performance were observed. Besides experience, it was found that during adulthood wisdom-related performance was best predicted by openness to experience and measures drawing on both cognition and personality, such as a judicious cognitive style, creativity, and moral reasoning.

Is there wisdom-related potential?

Given the fact that wisdom-related performance had been successfully operationalized, a question has arisen as to whether it is possible to increase wisdom-related knowledge and judgment. At least three studies have been conducted to test this idea (see Baltes and Staudinger, 2000). In a 1993 study conducted within the Neopiagetian tradition, Kitchener and colleagues demonstrated that the level of reflective judgment in adolescence could be raised by presenting examples of higher-level responses.

Within the wisdom paradigm just described, two different approaches have been successful in activating wisdom-related potential (see Staudinger, 1999). The first study found that dyads who know each other quite well—having had a chance to discuss the wisdom problem before they individually responded (real dialogue)—demonstrated performance levels (significantly standard deviation) higher than observed in the standard setting. In line with notions of symbolic interactionism, increases in wisdom-related performance were also identified when participants thought about what other people might say while thinking about the problem (virtual dialogue). A second study focused on one of the five wisdom-related criteria—value relativism—and adopted a successful memory training technique (known as the *method of loci*). With this method participants trained to think about life problems as if they were taking place in different regions of the world. This process creates links between geographic locations and life problems in order to make it easier to remember the life problem. Participants trained in this knowledge-activating strategy significantly outperformed the control group (by more than half a standard deviation).

The concept of wisdom represents a fruitful topic for psychological research in that it emphasizes the search for continued optimization and the further evolution of the human condition, and because it allows for the study of collaboration among cognitive, emotional, and motivational processes. It is expected that future research on wisdom will be expanded in at least three ways: (1) toward the further identification of social and personality factors, as well as life processes, relevant for the ontogeny of wisdom, (2) exploration of wisdom as a meta-heuristic, and (3) it will examine how wisdom research can contribute to building a psychological art of life.

URSULA STAUDINGER

See also INTELLIGENCE; PROBLEM SOLVING.

BIBLIOGRAPHY

BALTES, P. B.; SMITH, J.; and STAUDINGER, U. M. "Wisdom and Successful Aging." *Nebraska Symposium on Motivation* 39 (1992): 123–167.

BALTES, P. B., and STAUDINGER, U. M. "Wisdom: The Orchestration of Mind and Virtue towards Human Excellence." *American Psychologist* 55 (2000): 122–136.

KRAMER, D. A. "Wisdom As a Classical Source of Human Strength: Conceptualization and Empirical Inquiry." *Journal of Social and Clinical Psychology* 19 (2000): 83–101.

STAUDINGER, U. M. "Older and Wiser? Integrating Results from a Psychological Approach to the Study of Wisdom." *International Journal of Behavioral Development* 23 (1999): 641–664.

STERNBERG, R. J., ed. *Wisdom: Its Nature, Origins, and Development.* Cambridge: Cambridge University Press, 1990.

STERNBERG, R. J. "A Balance Theory of Wisdom." *Review of General Psychology* 2 (1998): 347–365.

WELSCH, W. "Wisdom, Philosophical Aspects." In *International Encyclopedia of the Social and Behavioral Sciences.* Edited by N. Smelser and P. B. Baltes. London: Elsevier, in press.

WORKFORCE ISSUES IN LONG-TERM CARE

The concept of a long-term care workforce is of relatively recent origin. Throughout much of the history of the United States, only a small proportion of the population was old and infirm, and dependent aged persons were almost always cared for by family members. Institutional care was virtually unknown, with the exception of almshouses for the truly isolated and destitute. The professional provision of long-term care as it is known today began with the passage of the Social Security Act in 1935 and solidified with the advent of Medicare and Medicaid in 1965 (Olson).

Since that time, the enormous growth in the number of nursing homes, as well as in home care and community-based services, has produced a large number of individuals who care for older persons who are chronically ill and disabled. The care recipients require assistance for months or years and are very unlikely to return to totally independent living. Although long-term care workers have become essential to society, developments since the 1990s have made work in such settings increasingly challenging. There is now considerable concern, both at the public and at the personal level, about the supply and the caring capacity of long-term care workers.

National challenges

At the beginning of the twenty-first century, recruitment and retention of a committed long-term care workforce has become a serious challenge, and one that is likely to persist for several decades. There are a number of reasons for increasing difficulties in this area.

First, the explosive growth in the elderly population has created an enormous need for long-term care workers. The population age sixty-five and older will expand by eighteen million persons by 2010, from 35.7 million to 53.9 million. The number of elderly persons with functional disabilities will increase in that time by 1.6 million, from 8.8 million to 10.4 million (Congressional Budget Office). The growth in the latter group is particularly critical, because it constitutes the demand for long-term care. Much of the anticipated need for additional frontline workers is due to this increase.

Second, the long-term care population is becoming more disabled and more complex to care for. The emphasis throughout the 1990s on transferring elderly people from acute to long-term care settings has had a major impact on nursing homes in particular. This trend toward earlier discharge means that more residents have acute illnesses from which they have not completely recovered at the time they are transferred to long-term care facilities. One of the results of this trend is that nursing homes are now using technologies that previously were used only in hospitals. The burden of care for this increasingly impaired population falls on long-term care workers.

Third, the labor force as a whole is growing at a slower rate than the elderly population that needs care. When one examines the pool of persons most likely to become long-term care workers, there are good reasons to expect a continuing shortfall in the caregiving workforce. Women are the dominant providers in health care, representing 78 percent of health care positions in the United States in 2000. Most critical, 93 percent of paraprofessionals and 95 percent of nurses are women (Franks and Dawson). Therefore, a meaningful statistic is the relationship between the size of the elderly population (who are likely to need care) and the number of "traditional" caregivers—that is, working-age women. Nationally, this "caregiver ratio" shows a striking trend. In 2001, census data indicate that the caregiver ratio is fifty-eight elderly persons to every one hundred females age twenty-five to fifty-four. In 2025, the ratio will be slightly over ninety-nine elderly persons to one hundred females age twenty-five to fifty-four. This is very likely to lead to increased shortages of long-term care workers (U.S. Bureau of the Census).

Fourth, restrictive immigration policies reduce the labor pool. New immigrants are relied upon heavily in urban areas to fill frontline long-term care positions. However, employment-based legal immigration is largely limited to skilled workers; unskilled workers can wait years for work permits. Coupled with the shortage of younger workers, restricted immigration will result in a limited supply of new workers.

Makeup of the long-term care workforce

There are five major job categories in long-term care.

Certified nursing assistant (CNA). CNAs work under the supervision of the nursing staff, and provide 60 percent or more of the direct care to nursing home residents. CNAs assist residents with activities of daily living, such as eating, bathing, dressing, and transferring from bed to chair. They may provide skin care, take vital signs, and answer residents' call lights, and are expected to monitor residents' well-being and report significant changes to nurses.

Home health aides (HHA). HHAs carry out a number of tasks that are similar to those done by CNAs, but do so in an impaired individual's home, under the supervision of a nurse.

Personal care aides (PCA). PCAs, who are not certified, provide patients with assistance in activities of daily living in their homes. Major tasks include feeding, dressing, and bathing.

Licensed practical (or vocational) nurses (LPN). LPNs must be supervised by a registered nurse, and primarily provide direct care after a training program of between twelve and eighteen months. LPNs often have some supervisory responsibility for CNAs in long-term care.

Registered nurses (RN). RNs can take several types of educational programs that may last different periods of time, but all graduates take the same licensing examination. Some RNs focus on direct care of residents, but most have supervisory responsibilities in the long-term care setting.

Because the major actor in the nursing home setting is the CNA, and because workforce problems center around this job category, this entry focuses most heavily on CNAs.

Characteristics of the long-term care workforce

The National Center for Health Statistics estimated that in 1998, approximately 1,434,000 full-time-equivalent employees (FTEs) worked in nursing homes. Of this number, around 950,000 FTEs were nursing staff: RNs, LPNs, and CNAs. CNAs make up nearly two-thirds of staff who provide nursing services, while RNs account for just 15 percent. This is illustrated as well by the staff-to-bed ratio in nursing homes. CNAs have a staff-to-bed ration of 33.9 per 100 beds, followed by LPNs (10.6) and RNs (7.8). Thus, the world of nursing home care is heavily dominated by paraprofessionals. In home health care, there are approximately 368,000 HHAs.

The need for additional paraprofessional workers in long-term care will increase dramatically by 2010. Among nursing assistants, a 23.8 percent increase is anticipated by 2008, and for home health aides, the growth is expected to be fully 74.5 percent (Bureau of Labor Statistics, "Health Services").

Work as a CNA or HHA at the entry level usually does not require a high school education. CNAs must undergo at least seventy-five hours of training (some states have a higher minimum). The training program typically covers basics of geriatric care, such as nutrition, infection control, and body mechanics, as well as the techniques of personal care. Within four months of employment, the nursing assistant must pass a certification examination. Training for HHAs varies from state to state. For those who work in agencies that receive Medicare funding, a competency test is mandated that covers various areas of resident care. Federal law also suggests a seventy-five-hour training program for HHAs.

Motivation for long-term care work

Studies indicate that long-term care workers frequently derive important satisfaction from their jobs. For example, in a survey of approximately six hundred nursing assistants, respondents were asked why they chose nursing home work (Pillemer). They rated twelve possible reasons that have been found to be important to people in selecting jobs. The most frequently chosen reasons were those that related to the intrinsic worth of the job, and the sense that it was socially valuable and personally fulfilling. Three reasons were selected as important by the highest proportions of respondents: provides opportunity to help others (96 percent), makes respondent feel meaningful (93 percent), and the job is useful to society (84 percent). In addition to these "other-centered" reasons, the next most frequent reasons for working as a CNA had to do with rewarding aspects of the job itself: it offers a lot of contact with others (81 percent), is an interesting job (73 percent), and it gives the chance to do responsible tasks (72 percent).

In addition, frontline jobs in the long-term care field do not require extensive education and training, and are typically available to young people, displaced homemakers, new immigrants, people transitioning from welfare, and other persons with limited work histories. The jobs offer more varied and meaningful work than many positions in the hospitality, construction, and manufacturing industries (which also com-

pete for these employees). Further, especially in home care, the jobs offer a greater level of autonomy than other comparable professions.

Problems in long-term care work

Although many long-term care workers are highly committed to their work and derive satisfaction from it, research has extensively documented the many difficulties of the job. These factors have been found to be related to high rates of perceived job stress and burnout, and lower levels of job satisfaction. In the contemporary tight labor market, these problems lead to high rates of turnover in all positions.

Estimates of turnover of nursing home staff are quite high, with annual CNA turnover at 97 percent, RN turnover at 52.5 percent, and overall staff turnover at 69 percent (Harrington et al.). Although estimates differ, turnover is also a problem in home care. For this reason, understanding and reducing employee turnover in long-term care settings has become a major undertaking for both researchers and practitioners. As in other health care settings, turnover and short staffing have been found to have many negative consequences, including reduced employee efficiency and lower morale among employees who stay on the job (Cohen-Mansfield). More important, such staffing problems lead to decreased quality of care for residents (Wunderlich et al.; Harrington et al.).

The following are some major causes of stress, burnout, dissatisfaction, and turnover among long-term care workers.

Excessive work pressure. In surveys, many nursing assistants say that they routinely do not have enough time to complete their basic tasks. This sense of time pressure takes the enjoyment out of their work. Nursing assistants report that when time is short, they are not able to do more personal, satisfying tasks, such walking with residents, talking to them, helping with grooming, and so forth. As caregiving work is reduced to the most difficult and least gratifying tasks, and staff feel that they do not have time to complete even these tasks, job stress and burnout increase.

Understaffing. Work pressure is exacerbated by chronic understaffing in many long-term care facilities. The pressure caused by staff shortages is very severe, and leads to stress and burnout. Conversely, adequate staffing has been found to be the major factor leading to high staff morale. Wilner (1994) found that a major source of dissatisfaction and stress was working with too few other nursing assistants, or with new staff who were not adequately trained. Nursing assistants were especially anxious about injury to themselves, to the new staff member, and to the residents in these situations.

Problems in supervision.   Studies show that problems with supervisors are a major cause of job stress and burnout. Conflicts with supervisors are very stressful to frontline long-term care workers. Helmer and colleagues showed the extent of such dissatisfaction. Their survey of nursing assistants found that 71 percent wished administrators and nurses would show them more respect; only 37 percent felt they received sufficient recognition and appreciation for their work. Further, only 36 percent felt that management made them feel "in on things."

Lack of appropriate training.   Despite the view that frontline long-term care work is "unskilled labor," the job is in fact both technically and interpersonally complex. As noted earlier, the training given to nursing assistants and home health aides is very limited. Further, it focuses almost exclusively on the technical aspects of care, although there is evidence that difficulties in dealing with the psychosocial aspects of nursing home work are causes of stress and burnout.

Wages.   Funding for nursing assistants comes primarily from Medicaid and Medicare. In many cases, the wages offered keep some workers near the poverty level. In 1998, the mean hourly wage of CNAs was $8.32, and for HHAs it was $8.17. For the purposes of comparison, in the same year telemarketers earned an average of $9.40 per hour, and elevator operators an average of $14.77 (Bureau of Labor Statistics, 1998). Thus, wages for long-term care workers remain comparatively low, considering the difficult nature of the job. Further, some long-term care providers still do not provide CNAs with health benefits. When such benefits are offered, the premiums the CNAs must pay are often prohibitively high for them to participate.

Injury.   It is acknowledged that CNAs are at high risk of injury. Indeed, rates of injury in nursing and personal care homes exceed that of private industry in total by a significant amount. CNAs are particularly prone to injury from heavy lifting (Wunderlich et al.).

Relations with family members

An area of significant research interest is the way in which family members of care recipients relate to long-term care workers. Clearly, cooperation is essential to optimal resident care. However, research indicates that structural barriers to cooperation between the two groups exist. In the most influential theoretical approach to this problem, Eugene Litwak noted fundamental differences between large-scale formal organizations and primary groups, such as families. In nursing homes, the potential for family conflict with staff is heightened because long-term care facilities represent the classic case of a formal institution seeking to take over primary group tasks, and to fit the performance of such tasks into a bureaucratic, routinized, organizational framework.

Consistent with Litwak's view, one line of research has pointed to discrepancies between staff and family perceptions of appropriate tasks for each group Although studies vary in their estimates of the extent of such differences, it is clear that ambiguity regarding the division of labor between staff and relatives exists, particularly in the performance of nontechnical tasks, and can lead to conflict (Duncan and Morgan).

Even when families relinquish the technical aspects of care to the staff, they nevertheless feel compelled to monitor the quality of service delivery. Stephens and colleagues found that over one-third of relatives reported feeling that they had to remind staff to do things for their resident, and that they needed to tell the staff how to care for the resident.

Research has also identified poor communication between staff and families as an important problem. Many residents, especially those with cognitive impairments, are unable to give accurate, factual information about their experience in the facility. There is often little sharing of detailed information about residents, and families frequently feel that there is no one to whom they can bring their concerns. Further, relatives are sometimes hesitant about offering suggestions and criticism, out of fear that such comments might negatively affect the care provided to the resident. Additional barriers to communication include the fact that staff work under intense time pressure, which limits their availability for conversations with families. In addition, nursing home staff—and nursing assistants in particular—receive little or no training in communication skills (Pillemer et al.).

As a result of these problems, studies have found that both staff and family members were frequently annoyed, and sometimes very angry, during and after interactions with each other. Studies of nursing home staff have shown that problems relating to family members are a major source of stress.

Future directions

To upgrade the quality of the long-term care workforce, and to solve the problems of recruiting and retaining enough qualified workers, several options have been proposed.

Increasing minimum staffing requirements. One solution to staffing problems is to increase the number of caregivers in nursing homes. There is considerable consensus among researchers that higher staffing levels are positively associated with better outcomes for nursing home residents. This is particularly the case with RN staffing, but is also applicable to CNAs. Increasing staffing in nursing homes is likely not only to improve the quality of care but also to benefit staff morale, satisfaction, and retention by reducing the stress of providing care (Harrington et al.).

Increase and upgrade training. Although a body of rigorous evaluation research is lacking, there is evidence that training programs of various kinds improve the performance of CNAs and thus leads to improved outcomes for residents (Beck et al.).

Improve salaries and benefits. Many nursing homes and home health agencies have very devoted, long-term employees. However, some individuals do not consider long-term care work, or leave it after trying it, because the salaries are inadequate. Raising the salaries of workers and improving benefits is now a goal in many states.

Expand the range of roles. A number of experts suggest reexamining the official role of the frontline worker, and expanding what is now a monolithic job category into a career ladder of increasing responsibilities. In particular, new job categories can be developed in the nursing home, ranging from an entry-level resident attendant position, to several categories of CNAs. Workers can then can advance to positions of greater responsibility within the facility.

KARL PILLEMER
MARK S. LACHS

See also GERONTOLOGICAL NURSING; HOME CARE AND HOME SERVICES; LONG-TERM CARE; NURSING HOMES.

BIBLIOGRAPHY

BECK, C.; ORTIGARA, A.; MERCER, S.; and SHUE, V. "Enabling and Empowering Certified Nursing Assistants for Quality Dementia Care." *International Journal of Geriatric Psychiatry* 14 (1999): 191–212.

Bureau of Labor Statistics. "Health Services." In *Occupational Outlook Handbook, 2000–01 Edition.* Bulletin 2520. Washington, D.C.: U.S. Government Printing Office, 2000.

Bureau of Labor Statistics. *1998 National Occupational Employment and Wage Estimate.* http://stats.bls.gov

COHEN-MANSFIELD, J. "Stress in Nursing Home Staff: A Review and a Theoretical Model." *Journal of Applied Gerontology* 14 (1995): 444–466.

Congressional Budget Office. *Projections of Expenditures for Long-Term Care Services for the Elderly.* Washington, D.C.: U.S. Government Printing Office, 1999.

DUNCAN, M. T., and MORGAN, D. L. "Sharing the Caring: Family Caregivers' Views of Their Relationships with Nursing Home Staff." *The Gerontologist* 34 (1994): 235–244.

FRANK, B. W., and DAWSON, S. L. *Health Care Workforce Issues in Massachusetts.* Boston: Paraprofessional Health Care Institute, 2000.

GABREL, C. S. *An Overview of Nursing Home Facilities: Data from the 1997 National Nursing Home Survey.* Division of Health Care Statistics, Advance Data no. 311. Washington, D.C.: National Center for Health Statistics, 2000.

HARRINGTON, C.; KOVNER, C.; MERZEY, M.; KAYSER-JONES, J.; BURGER, S.; MOHLER, M.; BURKE, R.; and ZIMMERMAN, D. "Experts Recommend Minimum Nurse Staffing Standards for Nursing Facilities in the United States." *The Gerontologist* 40 (2000): 5–16.

HELMER, F. T.; OLSON, S. F.; and HEIM, R. I. "Strategies for Nurse Aide Job Satisfaction." *Journal of Long-Term Care Administration* 21 (1993): 10–14.

LITWAK, E. *Helping the Elderly: The Complementary Roles of Informal Networks and Informal Systems.* New York: Guilford, 1985.

OLSON, L. K. "Public Policy and Privatization: Long-Term Care in the United States." In *The Graying of the World: Who Will Care for the Elderly?* Edited by L. K. Olson. New York: Haworth Press, 1994. Pages 25–58.

PILLEMER, K. *Solving the Frontline Crisis in Long-Term Care.* Cambridge, Mass.: Frontline Publishing, 1996.

PILLEMER, K.; HEGEMAN, C. R.; ALBRIGHT, B.; and HENDERSON, C. "Building Bridges Between Families and Nursing Home Staff: The Partners in Caregiving Program." *The Gerontologist* 38 (1998): 499–503.

STEPHENS, M. A. P.; OGROCKI, P. K.; and KINNEY, J. K. "Sources of Stress for Family Caregivers of Institutionalized Dementia Patients." *Journal of Applied Gerontology* 10 (1991): 328–342.

U.S. Bureau of the Census, Population Division, Population Projections Branch. *National Households and Families Projections.* 2000. www.census.gov

WILNER, M. A. "Working It Out: Support Groups for Nursing Assistants." *Generations* 23 (1994): 39–40.

WUNDERLICH, G.; SLOAN, F. A.; and DAVIS, C. K., eds. *Nursing Staff in Hospitals and Nursing Homes: Is It Adequate?* Washington, D.C.: National Academy Press, 1996.

Y

YEAST

The yeast *Saccharomyces cerevisiae*, known popularly as bakers' or brewers' yeast, has been used extensively in aging research. Since 1990, it has emerged as an important model organism for the dissection of the biological aging process at the genetic and molecular levels. Its distant cousin, *Schizosaccharomyces pombe*, or fission yeast, was shown in 2000 to undergo a very similar aging process. This entry describes the research with *S. cerevisiae*, hereinafter called yeast, exclusively.

Yeast is a unicellular organism whose DNA is packaged into chromosomes that are localized in a subcellular structure called the nucleus. In addition to this organelle, yeast also possesses mitochondria, which are the power plants of the cell that generate the energy needed for cellular function. The mitochondrion also possesses its own DNA, but it is dependent on the nuclear genes for most of its biochemical functions. The yeast cell is very similar in structure and function to typical cells from higher organisms, including humans. It has been used widely to elucidate a variety of basic biological processes, because of the ease of experimentation. About 25 percent of human genes have yeast counterparts, and these human genes have frequently been shown to functionally replace the corresponding gene in the yeast cell.

Aging is not typically measured by time in yeast, but rather by the number of divisions an individual cell completes before it dies. An individual cell is easy to follow from birth to death because yeast divides asymmetrically by budding off new daughters. Unlike their mothers, the daughters start from scratch, having the potential for a full life span. Thus, individual cells are mortal, while the yeast population is immortal. The probability that a cell will continue dividing decreases exponentially as a function of the number of completed divisions. Thus, mortality rate increases exponentially with age. However, it plateaus at older ages in similarity to what has been observed in other species. Yeasts undergo a variety of changes as they age, and some of these are clearly detrimental. In view of this, it is reasonable to speak of an aging process. In practical terms, yeast life span is measured by observing individual cells periodically under a microscope and removing buds with a micromanipulator.

As of 2000, twenty genes that determine yeast life span had been identified. This has been achieved in three ways. First, genes whose activity changes during the life span were isolated, followed by an examination of their causal role in yeast aging. Second, genes were tested for their function in longevity on the basis of hypotheses formulated regarding the aging process. Third, yeast mutants were selected on the basis of a phenotype (property) frequently associated with aging. The characterization of the isolated genes has provided a rich description of the aging process at the physiological level. The powerful tools of yeast genetics and cell biology have extended this description. Further analysis of the pathways and processes that were revealed by these genes has in some cases been refined to the biochemical and molecular levels. Methods for the preparation of age-synchronized yeast cells have facilitated biochemical and molecular studies.

There are many advantages to the study of aging in the yeast model system:

1. The yeast cell is at the same time the yeast organism. Therefore, the study of yeast is pertinent to both cellular and organismal aging.

2. Because yeast are microbes they divide very rapidly, in a short time generating much material for physiological, biochemical, and molecular analysis.

3. Yeast mutants can be created and selected rapidly, again because it is a microbe producing many generations of progeny in a short time.

4. Yeast life spans are short, and last as little as a few days.

5. Methodologies for life span determination are in place. Several procedures for the bulk preparation of age-synchronized yeast cells are available.

6. The basic phenomenology of yeast aging is well established.

7. The yeast genome was the first to be completely sequenced. This has revolutionized yeast genetics. The priority of yeast in this field has resulted in rapid advances in the study of function at the whole genome level, providing a wide range of materials, tools, and concepts that are being applied to other organisms as well.

8. Several yeast genetic databases are accessible online, which facilitates functional genome analyses. In addition, cross-referencing databases are online, allowing comparative genomic analyses.

9. A large community of yeast researchers exists, and, consequently, there is a wealth of biological information and expertise that can be tapped.

Yeast also possesses certain disadvantages for aging research: (1) The role of cell-cell interactions and systemic mechanisms, such as endocrine function, in aging lies beyond the scope of yeast aging research; (2) the extent to which the results of studies in yeast can be extrapolated to an understanding of aging in humans has not as yet been demonstrated; and (3) the determination of yeast life spans and the preparation of age-synchronized yeast cells is tedious. The quantities of old yeast that can be obtained are relatively small.

Studies of yeast longevity have revealed the operation of four, broad physiological processes in yeast aging: metabolic control, stress resistance, gene dysregulation, and genetic stability. Interestingly, these processes appear to be important in the aging of other species as well. Two distinct metabolic control mechanisms play a role in yeast aging. One of them (*retrograde response*) appears to compensate for accumulating mitochondrial dysfunction. The other (*caloric restriction*) may help prevent dysfunction. Repeated bouts of stress reduce yeast life span. This can be overcome by enhancing the activity of certain longevity genes. An exposure to mild heat stress, on the other hand, appears to condition the yeast such that an extension of longevity occurs. Changes in the structure of the chromatin into which the DNA is packaged result in alterations in the normal activity of genes. This process intensifies with age. It can be prevented by manipulating certain genes, with an attendant increase in life span. Nuclear DNA can undergo rearrangements. Rearrangements that are not normally favored seem to occur with higher frequency as yeasts get older, constituting one of the causes of aging.

S. MICHAL JAZWINSKI

See also GENETICS; GENETICS: GENE EXPRESSION; GENETICS: GENE-ENVIRONMENT INTERACTION; GENETICS: LONGEVITY ASSURANCE; LONGEVITY: SELECTION.

BIBLIOGRAPHY

IMAI, S.-I.; ARMSTRONG, C. M.; KAEBERLEIN, M.; and GUARENTE, L. "Transcriptional Silencing and Longevity Protein Sir2 Is an NAD-dependent Histone Deacetylase." *Nature* 403 (2000): 795–800.

JAZWINSKI, S. M. "Molecular Mechanisms of Yeast Longevity." *Trends in Microbiology* 7 (1999): 247–252.

JIANG, J. C.; JARUGA, E.; REPNEVSKAYA, M. V.; and JAZWINSKI, S. M. "An Intervention Resembling Caloric Restriction Prolongs Life Span and Retards Aging in Yeast." *The FASEB Journal* 14 (2000): 2135–2137.

KIM, S.; BENGURIA, A.; LAI, C.-Y.; and JAZWINSKI, S. M. "Modulation of Life-span by Histone Deacetylase Genes in *Saccharomyces cerevisiae*." *Molecular Biology of the Cell* 10 (1999): 3125–3136.

KIRCHMAN, P. A.; KIM, S.; LAI, C.-Y.; and JAZWINSKI, S. M. "Interorganelle Signaling Is a Determinant of Longevity in *Saccharomyces cerevisiae*." *Genetics* 152 (1999): 179–190.

MORTIMER, R. K., and JOHNSTON, J. R. "Life Span of Individual Yeast Cells." *Nature* 183 (1959): 1751–1752.

MÜLLER, I.; ZIMMERMANN, M.; BECKER, D.; and FLÖMER, M. "Calendar Life Span Versus Bud-

ding Life Span of *Saccharomyces cerevisiae*."
Mechanisms of Ageing and Development 12
(1980): 47–52.

SINCLAIR, D. A., and GUARENTE, L. "Molecular
Mechanisms of Aging." *Trends in Biochemical
Sciences* 23 (1998): 131–134.

INDEX

Page references to entire articles are in **boldface.** Persons are indexed only when there is a substantial reference to them or a substantial quotation by them. Photos are indicated by a page number in italics, figures are indicated by a page number followed by the letter *f* in italics, and tables are indicated by a page number followed by the letter *t* in italics.

negative linguistic ageism,
758–761
social segregation as, 31
See also Age-based rationing of
health care; Ageism; Age
integration and
segregation; Job
performance
Age Discrimination in
Employment Act (ADEA)
administered by Equal
Employment Opportunity
Commission, 28, 487
amended by Older Workers
Benefit Protection Act of
1990, 430
court decisions defining scope
of, 29
job categories excluded from,
29
legal procedures for filing
charges under, 29
mandatory retirement age,
1059
progress against ageism related
to, 38
provisions of, 28–29
Age grades, 22
Age integration and segregation,
32–35
advantages and disadvantages
of, 34–35
age classed life course and,
22–23
age discrimination and, 31
continuing care retirement
communities, 279–280
definitions of, 32
future trends in, 35
historical changes in, 32–33
intergenerational skills
exchanges and, 34
social problems caused by, 33
work place changes and, 33–34
See also Age-segregated housing
Ageism, **36–39**
in advertising, 682–683
definition of, 36
evolution of, 38–39
existence in American culture,
37–38
media's role in supporting, 38
origin of term, 757
stereotypes about age and
elders, 36–37
ways for reducing, 39

See also Age discrimination;
Criminal victimization of
elderly; Elder abuse and
neglect; Images of aging;
Language about aging
Ageist language, 758–759, 760*tt*,
761
Agencies on aging, federal. *See*
Federal agencies on aging
Age norms, **40–42**
behavior and, 41–42
consequences of being off-time,
42
continuing controversies, 42
definition of, 40
formal and informal, 40
variation in, 41
age1 gene, 550*t*, 551, 1240
Age-period-cohort model, **43–45**
age effect in, 43
cohort succession and, 43–44
goal of, 43
period effects in, 43
social change theories and, 43
social movements with lasting
effects, 43, 44
See also Aging; Cohort change
Age-related disease
molecular therapy for, 945–948,
946*t*
See also Chronic disease; Illness
Age-segregated housing, **662–665**
activity level of elders in, 663
attitude of elders toward aging
and, 663
controversies about, 662–664
example of congregate housing
as, 663
future trends in, 665
types of, 664–665
See also Age integration and
segregation; Long-term
care; Retirement
communities
Age stratification perspective, in
social theory, 1430–1431
Aggregate savings, life-cycle
hypothesis, 872
AGHExchange, 1136
Aging, **45–48**
biology of, 130–133
cellular aging of fibroblasts,
1087–1090
coldness and dryness as symbol
for, in ancient world,
1330–1331
deconditioning vs., 320
developmental tasks, 342
equalizing effect of, 45
exercise for retarding, 468–469

fear of death and, 37
free-radical theory of, 371,
696–697, 939
genetics and, 798–799
geologic deep time and, 45–46
gerontological perspectives on,
565–566
heart aging, 1092, 1094–1097,
1096*f*
immunologic aspects, 692
language about, 757–761
life course perspective on, 776
life-span development, 792–795
literature and, 803–808
lung function and, 861–862
measuring human aging, 46–47
medicalization of, 883–886
memory and, 917, 989
metaphors of, 47–48
mitochondria and, 930–931,
943
molecular biology of, 942–943
neotenic, postnatal development
of humans and, 46
neurobiology and, 146–147,
977–979
neuroendocrine system and,
985–986
neuroendocrine theory of, 985
neuropsychological changes,
992–993
oldest old, 1030–1031
organized political action,
1110–1112
plasticity and, 1105
primary aging, 792
productive aging, 1130–1132
professional organizations,
1133–1138
prostate, changes in, 1143–1145
psychotherapy, 1151–1154
rates of, 45–46, 1352
reduction of resources and,
1257
secondary aging, 792–793
skeletal muscle and, 1099
social aging, 46–47
structure of life course and, 47
successful aging, 1087,
1374–1377
tempo of living vs. life span, 46,
133
usual vs. successful, 1374
See also Biomarkers of aging;
Cellular aging; Successful
aging; Theories of
biological aging

Balance training
  benefits of, 473–474
  examples of, 467
  intensity of, 467, 473
Baldness, 585, 586*f*–587*f*
Ballpark Estimate, retirement
    planning tool, 1215
Baltes, Paul, 340, 717
Bangladesh. *See* South Asia
Barthel Index, 1084
Basal cell carcinoma, 1276
Basal ganglia
  anatomy of, 145
  movement control, 148
Base excision repair (BER)
  identification of BER enzymes
    in mitochondria, 374
  mechanisms of, 371, 372
Base modifications, in DNA
    damage, 369–370, 370*f*
Basilar artery, stroke related to,
    1360
Battelle Memorial Institute, 671
Battered old persons syndrome,
    405
  See also Elder abuse and neglect
Baucus amendments, 897
Bayley, John, 808
B cells. *See* B lymphocytes
BCL2 gene
  cell death inhibited by, 207
  proto-oncogene expression and,
    174
BCR-ABL fusion protein, 174
Bear, Mark, 987
Bedsores, 1122–1123, 1123*t*,
    1124*t*
  See also Pressure ulcers
Bedtime for Frances (Hoban), 804
Behavior
  age norms and, 41–42
  modulation by central nervous
    system, 148
Behavioral Risk Factors
    Surveillance System, 1159
Behavior management, **115–117**
  antecedent strategies in,
    116–117
  categories of, 116
  consequent strategies in, 117
  definition of, 115–116
  dementia, 116
  sleep disorders, 1279–1280
  social learning theory and, 116
  urinary incontinence, 1443
Belgium
  pension system in, 1057
  retirement age in, 1059
Beliefs
  social cognition and, 1283

See also Religion
Belize, demographics of aging,
    768, 769*t*
Benign prostatic hyperplasia. *See*
    Prostatic enlargement,
    benign
Benzodiazepines
  aging and, 385
  sleep disorder therapy, 1280
Bequests and inheritance,
    118–123
  average amount of bequests,
    119, 119*t*
  behavioral effects of taxes on,
    122–123
  charitable, 120–121
  distribution of estates, 118–119,
    118*t*–119*t*
  estate taxes on, 121–122, 121*t*
  exchange-motivated, 120
  intergenerational altruism as
    reason for, 119–120
  reasons for leaving bequests,
    119–121
  test of bequest motive, 93–94
  See also Assets and wealth;
    Estate planning; Social
    Security
Bereavement, **123–124,** *124*
  anxiety disorders after, 126
  comorbidity in, 127
  components of normal grief,
    124–125
  demographic factors, 127–128
  depressive symptoms in, 125,
    336
  literary portrayal, 807–808
  major depression in, 126
  nature of death and, 128
  nature of relationship and, 128
  pathological grief in, 125–127
  post-traumatic stress disorder
    after, 126
  psychological disturbances
    related to, 124
  risk factors for pathological
    grief, 127–128
  separation anxiety and,
    124–125
  social support for, 128
  traumatic distress as, 125
  traumatic grief in, 126–127,
    127*t*
  treatment for traumatic grief,
    128–129
Berg Balance Scale, 1084
Berlin Aging Study, 908
Beta-adrenergic blockers
  arrhythmias, 614
  congestive heart failure, 612

hypertension, 623
  ischemic heart disease, 1225
  therapeutic use of, 615
  tremors, 1436
Beta-amyloid proteins, in
    Alzheimer's disease, 911
Beta-carotene, function of, 866
Bible, longevity in, 1329
Biblical world. *See* Ancient and
    biblical worlds
Bile acid–binding resins, for
    cholesterol reduction, 229
Binding, Karl, 454
Biodemography of aging and
    longevity, 459
Biogerontology, 130–131
Biography. *See* Life review;
    Narrative
Biological clocks, 24, 802
Biological death vs. social death,
    316
Biology of aging, **130–133**
  biogerontology as, 130–131
  cell senescence and, 131–132
  central effects of biological
    aging (CEBA), 147
  central effects of peripheral
    pathology (CEPP), 147–148
  genetic analyses, 131
  hormonal changes and, 132
  life span alteration and, 132
  model systems, 131
  neural aging, 132
  normal aging concept in, 130
  nutrition and, 132
  research approaches, 131
  See also Theories of biological
    aging
Biomarkers of aging, **133–135**
  cellular aging, *in vitro* and *in
    vivo*, 201–202
  criteria for, 134
  definition of, 133
  DHEA as, 343
  reliability of, 134
  validity of, 134
Biomaterials, in medical
    technology, 1415–1416
Biomedicalization, 884, 885
Biotransformation of drugs, 384
Bipolar disorders, life events and,
    786
Birth cohorts, 44, 241, 308, 777,
    1431
Birthday card, caricature of older
    adults, 759
Birth rate. *See* Fertility rate
Birth weight, low, diseases
    associated with, 554

VOL. 1: PP. 1–387; VOL. 2: PP. 389–755

I

K

Kaplan's Quality of Well-Being/
General Health Policy
Model, 1159
Kaufman, Sharon R., 973
Kazakhstan, 391, 391f
Kennedy's syndrome, 984
Keogh plans, 1055–1056, 1213
Kevorkian, Jack, *1381,* 1385
Kidney, **749–750**
age-related changes of, 749–750
drug metabolism in, 384–385,
749–750
filtration functions of, 749
hormonal functions, 750
postoperative function, 1396
regulation of fluid balance,
502–503
Kidney failure, 750
complication of coronary artery
bypass grafting, 1229
Kin, **750–754**
bilateral system, in North
America, 751
caregiving role, 185–186
children and grandchildren,
753
cultural differences and, 754
demographic changes affecting
supply of, 751–752
fictive, for gay and lesbian
families, 526, 751, 754
gender, and maintenance of kin
ties, 752
geographic proximity of, 753
importance of maintaining ties
with, 751
marital status, and maintenance
of kin ties, 752–753
matrilineal bias in, 751
older adults with weak kinship
ties, 754
siblings as, 753–754
South Asia, 1319–1320
women as kin-keepers, 725,
726, 751
See also Family; Friendship;
Grandparenthood;
Intergenerational
exchanges; Parent-child
relationship; Tribal
societies
Kinematic analysis, motor
performance, 956–957
King Lear (Shakespeare), 806
Klemperer, Victor, 808
Knock-out and knock-in mice,
1239

Kollwitz, Kathe *(Self Portrait),*
1469, 1474
Konorski, Jerzy, 987
Korea, health care expenditures,
594t–597t
Krapp's Last Tape (Beckett), 759
Krebs cycle, 939
mitochondria and, 939
Krout, John A., 1262–1266
Kuru, 293
Kuwait
population aging, 931t
See also Middle Eastern
countries

L

Labeling theory, in social theory,
1429
Labor Department, U.S., 428
Lamm, Richard, 24, 31, 1385
Lamotragine, for epilepsy, 445
Language about aging, **757–761**
designations for older adults,
757–759, 760t
disparaging language, 758
metaphoric language, 759
metonymy, 759
names and forms of address,
760–761
proverbial language, 760
slogans, 760
Language comprehension,
762–763
elderspeak, 763
inhibitory deficits and, 762
reading strategies and, 763
working memory and, 762, 763
Language, definition of, 764
Language disorders, **764–767**
anomia, 765
aphasia, 512–513, 764–765,
766, 1365
diagnosis of, 766–767
language of generalized
intellectual impairment,
765–766
progressive aphasia, 766
right hemisphere language
disorders, 765
See also Speech disorders
Language of generalized
intellectual impairment,
765–766
Larynx, speech production, 1323
Laslett, Peter, 1334, 1335
The Last Resort (Lurie), 807
Late-life marriages, 874–875
Late onset muscle soreness, 1099

Latin America, **767–770,** *768*
aging of population in,
767–769, 769t
demographics of, 767–768
disability rates in, 768
economic activity among older
men, 770
life expectancy in, 767, 768
literacy in, 768–769, 769t
living arrangements in, 769–770
pension system in, 770, 1056
retirement in, 770
sex ratio in, 528, 529f
Latinos. *See* Hispanics
La Tour, George de *(Saint Joseph,
Carpenter),* 1469, 1471
Lawton Brody scale, 1084
Laxatives
bulk, 258
docusate sodium, 258
osmotic, 258
stimulant or irritant, 258
LDL cholesterol, 228, 230
Learning, **771–772**
lifelong learning, *100–101,*
403–404
See also Education
Lebanon
population aging, 931t
retirement age in, 1059
See also Middle Eastern
countries
Legal assistance, Area Agencies
on Aging services, 81, 1309
Leg disorders
periodic limb movement
disorder, 1278
restless leg syndrome, 1278,
1438–1439
See also Foot; Peripheral
vascular disease
Leisure, **773–775**
active or passive pursuits, 775
economic impact of, 774–775
occupational therapy, 1024
psychological benefits of, 775
"time budgets," study of, 774
types of activities, 774
work as converse of, 773
See also Retirement
Leisure-oriented retirement
communities, 1186–1187
Lentigo maligna (Hutchinson's
freckle), 1275
Leptin, obesity and, 1020
Lesbians. *See* Gays and lesbians
Letter of last instructions, 447
Leukemia
acute, 137–138
chronic lymphocytic (CLL), 138

Mobility
brain aging and, 148
comprehensive geriatric
assessment of, 89
human factors engineering, 676
successful aging and, 1375
See also Balance and mobility;
Immobility
Mobility devices. See Walking
aids; Wheelchairs
Modeling Income in the Near
Term (MINT) model, 1195
Modernization theory,
1332–1336
conceptual framework, 1333
criticism of, 1334–1336
decline of status of elderly due
to, 1334
social gerontology and, 1336
social theories and, 1430
study of aging and, 1333–1334
transformation of Western
nations after World War II,
1333
See also Status of older people;
Theories, social
Molecular biology of aging,
942–943
Molecular therapy, **943–948**
age-related disease, 945–948,
946t
ex vivo gene therapy, 943, 947
life span and, 944–945
telomerized cells, 947
vectors for, 945–947
Money market accounts,
retirement planning and,
1211
Monkeys, caloric restriction and,
1015
Monoamine oxidase inhibitors
(MAOIs), 73, 337–338
reversible, 73
Monoclonal paraprotein, in
myeloma, 139
Monocyte-derived cells (MDCs),
692
Mood, male aging changes and,
60
Moral standing, persons with
dementia, 327
Morbidity
compression of, 248–249, 249f
hip fracture and, 630
Morocco, population aging, 931t
Morphemes, definition of, 764
Morphology, definition of, 764
Mortality, **948–953**
African American mortality
patterns, 308–309

body fat and, 1020, 1021f
causes of death, 823
coronary artery bypass grafts,
1227, 1229
delirium and short-term
mortality, 323
factors related to, 824–825
Gompertz equation, 221, 221f,
950–951
hip fracture, 630
hypertension correlated with,
622
myocardial infarction, 1225
rectangularization of, 822–823,
823t
social integration and,
1314–1315
South Asia, 1318, 1319t
survival curves, 821–822, 822f,
949–950, 951f
twentieth and twenty-first
century, 796, 952–953
weight loss and, 867
See also Death and dying
Mortality rate
calculation of, 949
from pneumonia, 1106
Mortensen, Christian, 221
Motion perception, in visual
processing, 1467–1468
Motivation, **953–955**
arousal theory, 953, 954–955
control-related issues, 954
developmental perspectives,
954–955
pets and, 1081
self-esteem and, 955
social motivation, 955
time-related issues, 954
Motor control, 959, 960
Motor performance, **956–960**
Fitt's law, 956, 957f
force production, 959
kinematic analysis, 956–957
movement subparsing, 957,
958f, 959, 960
movement time, 956
movement variability and
coordination, 959
visual monitoring, 959–960
Motor units, 1098
Mourning. See Bereavement
Mouth rinses, 334
Mouth, speech production, 1323
Movement optimization model,
957
Movement subparsing, 957, 958f,
959, 960
Movement time, 956

Multidisciplinary team, **961–962,**
992
adult day care, 11
delivery of health/long-term
care, 590
geriatric assessment in
emergency room, 415
Geriatric Assessment Unit
(GAU), 557
gerontology, 565–566
hospice care, 652–653
rehabilitation team, 1174
Multiple-jeopardy hypotheses of
inequality, 706–707
Multiple myeloma, 138–139
Multiple sclerosis, life events and,
786
Multiple system atrophy,
962–964
ataxia, 963
autonomic dysfunction, 964
clinical features, 963
cognitive function in, 964
natural history of, 964
treatment of, 964
Multiskilled team, 962
Murdoch, Iris, 808
Muscles, skeletal. See Skeletal
muscles
Muscle strength, assessment of,
1084
Musculoskeletal system
balance related to, 112–113
deconditioning of, 320
stroke effects, 1365
successful aging and, 1375
See also Skeletal muscles
Mutation, **965–968**
aging associated with, 211
cancer biology, 173, 176
cancer-causing, 174–175
causes of, 538
common deletions, 940
definition of, 538
DNA damage and, 1423
future research, 968
gain of function, 174
genomic instability and, 967
germ-line, 173
gross chromosomal alterations,
965
increased, with age, 176
neurodegenerative diseases,
972, 981–982
obesity, 1020–1021
selectable marker genes,
965–966
single-gene mutations, life span
extension due to, 465–466
spontaneous, 173

VOL. 1: PP. 1–387; VOL. 2: PP. 389–755

Nerve growth factors
environmental enrichment and, 149
maintenance of neurons, 149
Nervous system. *See* Brain; Central nervous system; Entries beginning with "Neuro-"
Nestor, king of Pylos, 1329
Netherlands
euthanasia in, 455
health care expenditures, 594t–597t
inpatient care, 598–599
late-life poverty in, 1120
long-term care in, 842
pension system in, 1057
physician-assisted suicide and, 455, 1385
public health insurance plans, 593
retirement age in, 1059
See also West Europe
Network events, 787
Net worth, 781
Neuraminidase inhibitors, for influenza, 713
Neurobiology, **977–979**
Neurochemistry, **979–981**
synaptic transmission, 980
See also Neuroplasticity; Neurotransmitters
Neurodegenerative diseases, **981–984**
mutations and, 981–982
Purkinje cell degeneration, 982
trinucleotide repeat disorders, 983
See also Alzheimer's disease; Dementia; Parkinson's disease
Neuroendocrine system, **985–986**
age-related changes in, 985–986
composition of, 985
theories of aging and, 985, 1352
Neurofibrillary tangles (NFTs), in Alzheimer's disease, 982–983
Neuroimaging
epilepsy, 444
frontotemporal dementia, 512
stroke, 1363
Neuroleptics
for delirium, 324
sensitivity syndrome, in dementia with Lewy bodies, 331
Neuromuscular system, balance related to, 113, 114f

Neurons
aging and, 146–147
blood supply requirements, 146
complexity of, 143, 144f
dendritic branches and spines of, 146
life span related to, 1351, 1352
neurotrophic factors, 149
nucleus of, 146
organization and anatomy of, 143–146, 144f
plasticity of, 148–149
toxic effects on, 146
transplantation of, 149
Neurons, loss of
regeneration and, 146
stress response as cause of, 1347–1348
Neuron theory of brain function, 993
Neuroplasticity, **987–989**
See also Neurochemistry; Plasticity
Neuroprotective agents, in Alzheimer's disease, 912–913
Neuropsychological testing, 991, 992–993, 1151
Neuropsychology, **990–993**
age-related changes, 992–993
clinical neuropsychology, 991
dementia diagnosis, 992–993
experimental neuropsychology, 990–991
Neurotransmitters, **993–995**
acetylcholine, 911, 912, 994–995
age-related changes in, 994
aging of, drug effects of, 385
Alzheimer's disease, 911
dopamine, 385, 983, 995, 1051, 1436
function of, 143, 979–980, 985
GABA, 995, 1051
glutamate, 146, 995
neurobiological correlates of suicide, 1379
receptors for, 143
See also Neurochemistry; Neuroplasticity
New Jersey
cashing out Medicaid waiver benefits, 850
long-term care in, 848
New York City Visiting Nurses Association, 660
New York, personal care Medicaid option, 1074
New Zealand
baby boom in, 103, 105f

long-term care in, 838, 840
pension system in, 1057
retirement age in, 1059
Nezu, A. M., 1129
Niacin, dietary reference intake (DRI), 866t
Nicaragua, demographics of aging, 769t
Nicotine replacement
smoking cessation therapy, 610
taste disorders associated with, 1407
Nicotinic acid, for cholesterol reduction, 229, 230, 1475
Nifedipine
aortic valve disease, 613
hypertension, incidence of dementia reduced by, 622
Nimitz, Chester and Joan, 1385
NIPA (National Income and Product Accounts), 1252–1253
Nitrofurantoin, suppression of urinary tract infections, 1446
Nitroglycerin
ischemic heart disease, 1225
therapeutic use of, 615
Viagra contraindicated with, 614
NMDA receptors, in Alzheimer's disease, 912–913
No Geographic Adjustment (NGA) poverty measure, 1119
Nonegocentric events, 787
Non-rapid eye movement (NREM) sleep, 1277
Nonsteroidal anti-inflammatory drugs (NSAIDs)
Alzheimer's disease and, 912
arthritis therapy, 86
contraindications to, in congestive heart failure, 612
protective effect against Alzheimer's disease, 54–55, 55t
Norfloxacin, suppression of urinary tract infections, 1446
Normal aging. *See* Aging; Physiological changes
Normalized jerk, 959
Nortriptyline, as antidepressant, 73
Norway, retirement age in, 1059
Nose, taste transport via, 1405
Note writing, for persons with cognitive impairment, 635

Pensions (cont'd)
Middle Eastern countries,
930–932
plan types and policy
approaches, 1060–1065
preservation of benefits, 1063
private pension plans,
1060–1061, 1068
profit-sharing and stock bonus
plans, 430, 1213
public pensions, 1065–1069
registered pension plans,
Canada, 168
regulation by ERISA, 428–432,
1062–1063, 1066
regulation of, 1054–1055, 1062,
1066–1067
retirement decision making
and, 1192
retirement planning and,
1207–1208, 1212–1213
salary reduction plans, 1213
self-employed workers, 1262
South Asia, 1321
special window plans, 1199
Sub-Saharan Africa, 1372
tax incentives, 1253–1254, 1411
termination benefits, 1063
thrift plans, 1213
total number of plans, 428
types of plans covered by
ERISA, 430
United States, 1057–1058
voluntary nature of, 428
West Europe, 1490–1491
See also Annuities; Assets and
wealth; Canada, income
protection for retirees;
Estate planning; Income;
Income support for
nonworkers; Retirement
planning; Social Security
Perceived control, **280–284,** 800
Perceived health, **1069–1070**
Perceptual span, in visual
processing, 1468
Perceptual speed, 907–908
Percutaneous endoscopic
gastrostomy (PEG) tube,
1437
Percutaneous transluminal
coronary angioplasty
(PTCA), 1229–1231, 1230*f*
Perimenopause, 450, 919
Periodic health examination,
1071–1073
cancer screening tests,
1072–1073
counseling, 1071–1072
elements of, 1071–1072, 1072*t*

inoculations, 1072
risk factors for cardiovascular
disease, 1072
Periodic limb movement
disorder, 1278
Peripheral nervous system, 145
Peripheral vascular disease
atherosclerosis as cause of, 1454
foot problems related to, 506
intermittent claudication in,
1455
molecular therapy for, 946*t*
Permanent income hypothesis
consumer spending and, 272
savings and consumption, 780
Personal care, **1074–1076**
consumer-directed, 259
Personal care aides (PCAs), 1508
Personal care units, continuing
care retirement
communities, 278
Personality, **1076–1080**
emotional expression and, 417,
420–421
measurement of, 1077
midlife crisis, 933–934
personality stability and change,
1077–1079
stroke-related changes, 1366
subjective well-being and,
1369–1370
suicide related to, 1378
trajectory model, 1079–1080
wisdom related to, 1505
See also Emotion; Psychological
assessment; Psychotherapy
Personality assessment, 1150
Personal names
diminutive form of first name,
761
inappropriate use of with older
adults, 760–761
Personal theft victimization,
299–300, 300*t*–301*t,* 302*f*
Perspectives on Aging, 1137
Peru
demographics of aging, 769*t*
pension system in, 770, 1056
See also Latin America
Pets, **1081–1083**
benefits of, 1081–1082
costs of, 1082–1083
Pharmaceuticals. *See* Drugs
Pharmacodynamics, 385
Pharmacokinetics, 383–385
Pharmacologic profile, 380
Pharmacology, definition of, 379
Phenotype
quantitative of continuously
distributed, 541

rodents, 1239
stress effects on, 543
Phenytoin, for epilepsy, 444–445
Philip, Claire, 808
Phobias, 77–78
Phones, 633
Phonology, definition of, 764
Phosphorus, dietary reference
intake (DRI), 866*t*
Photography, portrayal of aging
in, 1470
Physical activity
as leisure activity, 774
See also Exercise
Physical therapists, in home care
service, 638
Physical therapy, **1084–1085**
See also Occupational therapy
Physician assistant (PA), history
of, 996
Physician-assisted suicide. *See*
Suicide, physician-assisted
Physicians
age discrimination by, 30–31,
38
competency determination, 245,
248
home visits provided by, 639
informal health care rationing
by, 25
life and death decisions, 315
payment of, in national health
insurance programs, 597
restrictions on practice, in
national health insurance
programs, 596–597
Physiological changes, **1085–1103**
driving ability and, 376–377
fibroblast cells, 1087–1090
skeletal muscle, 1098–1099
stem cells, 1100–1103
Piaget, Jean, 716
Neopiagetian theories of
wisdom and, 1505–1506
Pick bodies, 512
Pick cells, 512
Pick complex, 513
Pick's disease. *See*
Frontotemporal dementia
Pickup (estate) tax, 449
Pickwickian syndrome, 1020
Pioglitazone, for diabetes
mellitus, 346–347
Placebo-controlled clinical trials,
381
Planned ignoring, in behavior
management, 117
Plasticity, **1104–1105**
aging and, 1105
definition of, 1104

ISBN 0-02-865471-4

90000